Tanzania

THE BRADT TRAVEL GUIDE

Third Edition

Philip Briggs

Bradt Publications, UK
The Globe Pequot Press Inc, USA

First published in 1993 by Bradt Publications,
This third edition published in 1999 by Bradt Publications
41 Nortoft Road, Chalfont St Peter, Bucks SL9 0LA, England
Published in the USA by The Globe Pequot Press Inc, 6 Business Park Road,
PO Box 833, Old Saybrook, Connecticut 06475-0833

ISBN 1 898323 86 0

British Library Cataloguing in Publication Data
A catalogue record for this book is available from the British Library

Library of Congress Cataloging-in-Publication Data
Briggs, Philip.
    Tanzania : the Bradt travel guide / Philip Briggs. — 3rd ed.
    p. cm.
    Includes index.
    ISBN 1-898323-86-0
    1. Tanzania Guidebook. I. Title.
DT437.7.B75 1999   IN PROCESS
916.7804'2—dc21   99-24571
                                              CIP

Maps Steve Munns
Photographs
Front cover Giraffe at sunset (Ariadne Van Zandbergen)
Text Nick Garbutt (NG), Catherine Harlow (CH), Ariadne Van Zandbergen (AZ)
Illustrations Sarah Elder, Annabel Milne

Typeset from the author's disc by Wakewing
Printed and bound in Italy by LEGO, Vicenza

Author and Contributors

Philip Briggs is a travel writer and tour leader specialising in equatorial and southern Africa. Born in Britain and raised in South Africa, he started travelling in East Africa in 1986 and has since spent the equivalent of five years exploring the highways and back roads of the continent. His first book *Guide to South Africa*, now in its third edition, was published by Bradt in 1991. Since then, Philip has written Bradt guides to Tanzania, Uganda, Ethiopia, Malawi, Mozambique and Ghana, as well as *East and Southern Africa: The Backpacker's Manual* and Southern Books' *Visitors' Guide to Kenya and East Africa*. He contributes regularly to a number of leading South African and British travel and wildlife magazines.

Ariadne Van Zandbergen, who took most of the photographs for this book and contributed greatly to the research, is a freelance photographer and tour leader. Born and raised in Belgium, she travelled through Africa from Morocco to South Africa in 1994/5 and is now resident in Johannesburg. She has visited more than 20 African countries, and her photographs have appeared in numerous books, magazines, newspapers, maps and pamphlets.

David Else, a seasoned travel writer specialising in Africa, is the author of several African travel guides, including the Bradt *Guide to Zanzibar*, which provided the foundation for the Zanzibar chapter in this guide.

Dr Jane Wilson-Howarth, who wrote the health chapter for this guide, is the author of two books about travel health, and contributes a regular column about travel health to the travel magazine *Wanderlust*.

Australian-born **Christine Osborne** who wrote the chapter on Mafia Island is no stranger either to Africa or the Indian Ocean islands. Since writing her first travel article – on Djibouti – in 1965 she has visited more than 17 countries on the African continent.

Contents

LIST OF MAPS

LONDON TELEPHONE NUMBERS

New London telephone numbers are to be phased in from June 1999. London 0171 codes will change to 0207, and 0181 codes to 0208. Both old and new codes will be acceptable until April 2000.

Acknowledgements

My greatest debt, as ever, is to my wife, travel companion and photographic collaborator Ariadne Van Zandbergen, whose support and dedication have kept me going, both at home and on the road.

We would both like to extend our gratitude and best wishes to Peter, Steven and Carrie of Hoopoe Adventure Tours for their unstinting support over three editions of this guide, and to Paul Chizi of Air Tanzania for getting us up there. For helping to enable us to expand and vastly improve the pivotal chapter on the northern safari circuit, many thanks to Leopold Kabendera of TAHI, Wanja Ngugi of Serena, Nicky Fitzgerald (and many others) of the Conservation Corporation Africa, and the management of Sopa. We'd also like to thank Terri Rice for company and assistance in Arusha; Teri Mclean for last-minute South Pare update info; Glyn Lewis of Sengo for clarification on the Natron situation; the management of Momella Lodge and Bushbuck Safaris; Fenella, Hartley and Max of the East African Safari and Touring Company; the eminently hospitable Emerson Skeens and Tom Green in Zanzibar; Khami Omar Khami for his patience while guiding us around the stone town; and John Addison of Wild Frontiers for his help in updating details of the southern safari circuit.

Many thanks to David Else, whose Bradt *Guide to Zanzibar* provided a peerless foundation for the relevant chapter in this guide; to Jane Wilson-Howarth for her ongoing efforts to produce the model health chapter; to Christine Osborne for the detailed coverage of Mafia Island; and to everybody at Bradt Publications for their support over the years. On the production side, I'm especially grateful to Sally Brock, typesetter and project manager of this third edition, for tolerating a merciless barrage of 'last minute' rewrites and changes as new information came to light.

My immense gratitude goes out to all the readers of earlier editions who wrote in with update information: Martin Hall, Rachel Avery, Richard Corcoran, Olly Stainer, Andrew Parker, Kevin Harvey, Peter White, Sarah Varneg, David Pritchard, Andy Philip, Liz Pickering, Katie Holmes, Birte Melchers, David and Vicky Fraser, Julia Rebstein, Kathryn Tinsley, Leo and Els Roubecks, Stephen Taylor, Andy Hunt, Gerhard Buttner, Nicola Keate, Iain Jackson, Dr Peter Stephenson, James Tice, Christopher Jerram, Peter Moore, Siobhan Blaschek, Peter Ede, Nicholas McWilliam, Geert Clauwaert, Steve and Helen Winchester, Simon Marriot, Peter Gubbins, Dr Bernard Leeman, Brian Currie, John Tyson, Nicola Comforth, Joe Williamson and Mike Wilks.

Finally, my ongoing gratitude to those whose efforts were acknowledged in earlier editions of this guide.

Introduction

It would be easy to reduce an introduction to Tanzania to a list of facts and figures. This vast East African country really is a statistician's dream: within its borders lie Africa's highest and fifth-highest mountains, the world's largest intact volcanic caldera, Africa's most famous national park and the world's largest game reserve, as well as portions of the three most expansive lakes on the continent, one of which is the second-largest freshwater body in the world, another the second-deepest.

When it comes to wildlife, Tanzania is practically without peer. An unprecedented 25% of the country is protected in national parks and other conservation areas, Together, these conservation areas support an estimated 20% of Africa's large mammal population, and one of them plays host to the singular spectacle of an annual migration of some two million wildebeest, zebra and gazelle. Furthermore, Tanzania is poised to overtake Kenya as boasting Africa's second-longest bird checklist (after the Democratic Republic of Congo), with significantly more than 1,000 bird species recorded, and new endemics being discovered all the time. And as if that were not enough, the three great lakes that lie along Tanzania's borders vie with each other for the honour of harbouring the world's greatest diversity of fish species.

The map of Tanzania may have statisticians salivating, but it will also touch the heart of any poet. It is a virtual litany of Africa's most evocate place names – Zanzibar, Kilimanjaro, Serengeti, Selous, Ngorongoro Crater, Olduvai Gorge, Gombe Stream, Dar es Salaam, Kilwa, Lake Victoria, Lake Tanganyika, Lake Malawi, the Rift Valley, the Maasai Steppe… In short, Tanzania is the Africa you have always dreamed about: vast plains teeming with wild animals; rainforests alive with cackling birds and monkeys; Kilimanjaro's snow-capped peak rising dramatically above the flat scrubland; colourful Maasai herding their cattle alongside herds of grazing wildebeest; perfect palm-lined beaches lapped by the clear warm waters of the Indian Ocean stretching as far as the eye can see.

You might expect a country that can be described in such superlative terms to be crawling with tourists. Yet, oddly enough, until recently Tanzania attracted a fraction of the tourism of countries such as Kenya, South Africa and Zimbabwe. When I first visited the country in 1986, it appeared to be in irreversible economic decline, and tourist arrivals were practically restricted to those backpackers who were crossing between Kenya and southern Africa and had no option but to pass through Tanzania. This dearth of tourism had several causes: an underfunded and underdeveloped tourist infrastructure, a reputation for corruption and bureaucracy, persistent food and fuel shortages, poor roads and grossly inefficient and uncomfortable public transport. Critically, too, Tanzania lacked international exposure – not because people hadn't heard of places such as Ngorongoro, Serengeti and Kilimanjaro, but because they tended to associate these archetypal East African reserves with Kenya.

Today, all this has changed. Modern Tanzania has an excellent tourist infrastructure, and the public transport along the main roads compares favourably with that of most African countries. What started off in the late 1980s as a trickle of tourism, lured across the Kenyan border to visit such big name attractions as the Serengeti, Ngorongoro Crater and Zanzibar, is threatening to become a veritable flood. However, practically all visitors to Tanzania follow the same well-defined tourist circuit, which combines some of Africa's finest game viewing with the historical old town and superb beaches of Zanzibar Island, and those who have two weeks or less in the country rarely stray much beyond it. This is not a criticism – I've visited most corners of Tanzania over the six-plus months I've spent travelling there between 1986 and 1998, and I have to confess that were my time in the country limited to a couple of weeks, then my first priorities would undoubtedly be the Serengeti, Ngorongoro and Zanzibar. They are very special places.

The important implication of this is that the parts of Tanzania most frequently visited by tourists are also the most atypical in terms of tourist development. It is not improbable that the number of tourists who descend daily into the Ngorongoro Crater would be greater than the combined monthly total of visitors to *all* the reserves of southern and western Tanzania; just as probable that there are restaurants on Zanzibar whose average daily custom exceeds the number of tourists who make it to the splendid medieval ruins on Kilwa Kisiwani in any given year. In other words, while a few select spots in Tanzania are heavily touristed and well equipped to cater for this, Tanzania as a whole remains a surprisingly low-key tourist destination.

This is of interest to two classes of visitor, ironically lying at the extreme ends of the spectrum. For those seeking exclusivity at a price, the southern and western tourist circuit, which includes Mafia Island, Selous Game Reserve, and Udzungwa, Ruaha, Mikumi, Mahale, Gombe Stream, Katavi and Rubondo Island National Parks, has generally retained a real wilderness atmosphere, offering quality lodge accommodation and (mostly) fly-in safari packages at a price comparable to an upmarket lodge safari on the more popular northern safari circuit. And make no mistake, these are *wonderful* reserves, forming a safari circuit that many African countries would kill for. Their relative obscurity is largely due to the fact that they lie in the same country as the renowned Serengeti ecosystem.

With the exception of Udzungwa National Park, the southern and western reserves are rather inaccessible to those on a tight budget, but adventurous travellers who are willing to learn a smattering of Swahili and prepared to put up with basic accommodation and slow transport will find Tanzania to be one of the most challenging, rewarding and fascinating countries in Africa. Virtually anywhere south of the Dar es Salaam-Mwanza railway line (the part of the country covered in Chapter 13 onwards) is miles from any beaten tourist track, and even in the more 'touristy' northeast there are plenty of attractive spots that see little tourism (check out Chapters 9 and 10).

Travel isn't simply about ticking off the sights. When you spend a long time in a country, your feelings towards it are determined as much as anything by the people who live there. I have no hesitation in saying that, on this level, my affection for Tanzania is greater than for any other African country I have visited. It is an oasis of peace and egalitarian values in a continent stoked up with political and tribal tensions, and its social mood embodies all that I respect in African culture. As a generalisation, I've always found Tanzanians to be polite and courteous, yet also warm and sincere, both amongst themselves and in their dealings with foreigners.

The one thing I can say with near certainty is that you will enjoy Tanzania. Whether you decide to stick to the conventional tourist circuit, opt to carry a dusty backpack around the southern highlands, or charter a plane to go chimp-tracking in the rainforests of Mahale, Tanzania is a wonderful country.

NOTES
Swahili names

In KiSwahili, a member of a tribal group is given an m- prefix, the tribe itself gets a wa- prefix and the language gets a ki- prefix (for example, an Mgogo person is a member of the Wagogo who speak kigogo). The wa- prefix is commonly but erratically used in English books; the m- and ki- prefixes are rarely used, except in the case of KiSwahili. There are no apparent standards; in many books the Swahili are referred to as just the Swahili while non-Swahili tribes get the wa- prefix. I have decided to drop all these prefixes: it seems as illogical to refer to non-Swahili people by their KiSwahili name when you are writing in English as it would be to refer to the French by their English name in a German book. I have, however, referred to the Swahili language as KiSwahili on occasion.

Lake Nyasa/Malawi

Many readers may not realise that Lake Nyasa and Lake Malawi are one and the same. Nyasa was the colonial name for the lake, just as Nyasaland was the colonial name for what is now the country of Malawi. For historical reasons, the name Nyasa has been retained in Tanzania and is used both officially and casually; if you ask a Tanzanian about Lake Malawi they will either look at you blankly or tell you to go to Malawi. Despite the initial confusion it may cause, for the purposes of this guide I have referred to the lake as Lake Nyasa.

Some words you might wonder about...

There are a few terms that crop up occasionally in the text which you might not know. Some are explained elsewhere, but this is as good a place as any to put them all together. *Koppie* (or *kopje*) is an Afrikaans word which in East Africa is used to refer to a small free-standing hill such as those which dot the Serengeti Plains. A *hoteli* is a local restaurant. *Miombo* and *acacia* are types of woodland; the first dominated by broad-leaved trees belonging to a variety of families, the second dominated by thorny, thin-leaved trees of the acacia family. The *cichlids* are a family of colourful fish found in the Rift Valley lakes. A *banda* is a hut; a *boma* is a homestead.

Part One

General Information

HOOPOE ADVENTURE TOURS TANZANIA LTD

Hoopoe Adventure Tours will take you anywhere you want to go in Tanzania, Kenya and Ethiopia at a price you can afford. Travel with us and our experienced Driver Guides by 4WD Landrover on an unforgettable safari in the wilds of East Africa. Enjoy the panoramic views, comfort and excellent food at our luxurious Kirurumu Tented Lodge, overlooking the spectacular Rift Valley scenery of Lake Manyara National Park. We arrange mountain climbs, walking safaris and Zanzibar trips, and cater for special interests with tailor-made, professionally led safaris both lodging and camping. Safari camps are mobile and can be very simple but comfortable, or more traditional and deluxe.

Enjoy East Africa to the full with HOOPOE ADVENTURE TOURS. For quotations and further information contact one of our offices.

"A traveller without knowledge is like a bird without wings"
(Mushariff-Ud-Din 1854–1291)

U.K.	TANZANIA
Suite F1, Kebbell House	India Street
Carpenders Park	PO Box 2047
Watford WD1 5BE	Arusha
Tel: 0181 428 8221	Tel: 057 7011/7541
Fax: 0181 421 1396	Fax: 057 8226
email: Hoopoeuk@aol.com	Hoopoe@form-net.com

Background and History

FACTS AND FIGURES
Location
The United Republic of Tanzania was formed in 1964 when Tanganyika on the African mainland united with the offshore island state of Zanzibar.

Tanzania lies on the east African coast between 1° and 11°45' south, and 29°20' and 40°35' east. It is bordered by Kenya and Uganda to the north; Rwanda, Burundi and Congo to the west, and Zambia, Malawi and Mozambique to the south.

Size
Tanzania covers an area of 945,166km^2 (364,929 square miles). It is one of the largest countries in sub-Saharan Africa, larger than Kenya and Uganda combined. To put it in a European context, Tanzania is about 4^1/$_2$ times the size of Britain; in an American context, it's about 1^1/$_2$ times the size of Texas.

Capital
Dodoma is now the official capital of Tanzania, displacing Dar es Salaam, which remains the most important and largest city in the country.

Population
The total population of Tanzania is about 30 million, of which roughly 600,000 live on Zanzibar. Apart from the towns, the most densely populated areas tend to be the highlands, especially those around Lake Nyasa and Kilimanjaro.

There are estimated to be 120 linguistic groups in Tanzania. None exceeds 10% of the country's total population. The most numerically significant groups are the Sukuma of Lake Victoria, the Wahaya of northwestern Tanzania, the Chagga of the Kilimanjaro region, the Nyamwezi of Tabora, the Makonde of the Mozambique border areas, the Hehe of Iringa and the Gogo of Dodoma.

Government
The ruling party of Tanzania since independence has been Chama Cha Mapinduzi (CCM). Up until 1995, Tanzania was a one-party state, under the presidency of Julius Nyerere and, after his retirement in 1985, Ali Hassan Mwinyi. Tanzania held its first multi-party election in late 1995, when the CCM under Benjamin Mkapa was returned to power with an overwhelming majority.

Major towns
Dar es Salaam is far and away the largest town in Tanzania, with a population of around 1.5 million. Other important towns, in rough order of size, are Mwanza, Tanga, Arusha, Mbeya, Dodoma, Zanzibar Town, Mtwara, Moshi, Tabora, Kigoma, Songea, Lindi and Iringa.

Economy

After independence Tanzania became one of the most staunchly socialist countries in Africa, but since the mid-1980s there has been a swing to free market systems. Tanzania is considered to be one of the five poorest countries in the world, with a per capita GNP of US$150 (1990). Less than 10% of the workforce is in formal employment; most Tanzanians have a subsistence lifestyle. The country's major exports are coffee, cotton, cashew nuts, sisal, tobacco, tea and diamonds. Zanzibar and Pemba are important clove producers. Gold, tin and coal are also mined.

Languages

KiSwahili and English are the official languages. Very little English is spoken outside of the larger towns, but KiSwahili is spoken by most Tanzanians.

Currency

The unit of currency is the Tanzanian Shilling (pronounced *Shillingi*), which is divided into 100 cents. The rate of exchange in early 1999 was around US$1.00 = Tsh 670.

Climate

Most of Tanzania has a tropical climate, but there are large regional variations. The coastal belt and the Lake Nyasa and Tanganyika areas are hot and humid, with little relief at night. The rest of the interior is hot and dry, cooling down significantly at night. Highlands such as Kilimanjaro, Ngorongoro and the various mountain ranges of eastern Tanzania are generally warm during the day and cold at night.

Tanzania is too near the Equator to experience a recognisable summer and winter. The months between October and April are marginally hotter than May to September. In Dar es Salaam, for instance, the hottest month is March (average maximum 32°C; average minimum 23°C), and the coolest month is July (28°C; 18°C).

Virtually all of Tanzania's rain falls between November and May. The division of this period into short rains (November to December) and long rains (March to May) only applies to coastal areas and the extreme north around Arusha and Lake Victoria, where there is relatively little rainfall in January and February. Available figures suggest that rain falls fairly consistently between mid-November and mid-April in other parts of the country.

Geography

The bulk of East Africa is made up of a vast, flat plateau rising from a narrow coastal belt to an average height of about 1,500m. This plateau is broken dramatically by the 20-million-year-old Great Rift Valley, which cuts a trough up to 2,000m deep through the African continent from the Dead Sea to Mozambique.

The main branch of the Rift Valley bisects Tanzania. A western branch of the Rift Valley forms the Tanzania–Congo border. Lakes Natron, Manyara, Eyasi and Nyasa/Malawi are all in the main rift, Lake Tanganyika lies in the western branch, and Lake Victoria lies on an elevated plateau between them.

East Africa's highest mountains are volcanic in origin, created by the same forces which caused the Rift Valley. Kilimanjaro is the most recent of these: it started to form about one million years ago, and was still growing as recently as 100,000 years ago. Mount Meru is older. Ngorongoro Crater is the collapsed caldera of a volcano that would once have been as high as Kilimanjaro is today. The only active volcano in Tanzania, Ol Doinyo Lengai, lies a short way north of Ngorongoro.

HISTORY

Tanzania's rich and fascinating history is also highly elusive. For a non-historian such as myself, unravelling it is a frustrating process. Specialist works often contradict each other to such an extent it is difficult to tell where fact ends and speculation begins, while broader or more popular accounts are riddled with obvious inaccuracies. This is partly because there are huge gaps in the known facts; partly because much of the available information is scattered in out-of-print or difficult-to-find books; partly because once an inaccuracy gets into print it becomes true, and spreads like a virus. For whatever reason, there is not, so far as I am aware, one concise and reliable account of Tanzanian history that is readily available to the layman.

I have tried to make the following account as comprehensive as possible while still keeping it readable. It is, to the best of my knowledge, as accurate as the known facts will allow, but at times I have had to decide for myself the most probable truth amongst a mass of contradictions, and I have speculated freely where speculation seems to be the order of the day. My goals are to stimulate the visitor's interest in Tanzanian history, and to give easy access to information that would have enhanced our trip greatly.

Pre-history of the interior

It is widely agreed that the evolution and early history of humanity were played out on the savannahs of East and southern Africa. The hominid (proto-human) evolutionary chain split from that of the pongoid apes (whose modern representatives include chimpanzee and gorilla) about 20 million years ago. Two hominid genera are recognised: *australopithecus* and *homo*. *Australopithecus* is unlikely to have been a direct ancestor of modern man; it lived contemporaneously with *homo* until about one million years ago.

A 1.75-million-year-old skull found by Mary Leakey at Olduvai Gorge in Tanzania in 1957 was the first to confirm man's great antiquity and Africa as the probable site of human evolution. Since then further skulls have been found at a number of sites in East Africa. The oldest known hominid skull, found in Namibia in 1991, is about 12 million years old.

The immediate ancestor of modern man, *homo erectus,* first appeared about 1.5 million years ago. *Homo erectus* was the first hominid to surmount the barrier of the Sahara and spread into Europe and Asia, and is credited with the discovery of fire and the first use of stone tools and recognisable speech.

Although modern man, *homo sapiens*, has been around for at least half a million years, only in the last 10,000 years have the African races recognised today more or less taken their modern form. Up until about 1,000BC, East Africa was exclusively populated by hunter-gatherers, similar in physiology, culture and language to the Khoisan (or bushmen) of southern Africa. Rock art accredited to the Khoisan is found throughout East Africa, most notably in the Kondoa-Iranga region of Tanzania near Lake Eyasi, home of the Hadza, the only remaining Tanzanian hunter-gatherers.

The pastoralist and agriculturalist lifestyles which emerged on the Nile Delta in about 5,000BC had spread to various parts of sub-Saharan Africa by 2,000BC, most notably to the Cushitic-speaking people of the Ethiopian Highlands and the Bantu-speakers of West Africa. Cushitic-speakers first drifted into Tanzania in about 1,000BC, closely followed by Bantu-speakers. Familiar with iron-age technology, these migrants would have soon dominated the local hunter-gatherers. By AD1,000, most of Tanzania was populated by Bantu-speakers, with Cushitic-speaking pockets in areas such as the Ngorongoro Highlands.

There is no detailed information about the Tanzanian interior prior to 1500, and even after that details are sketchy. Except for the Lake Victoria region, which by then supported large authoritarian kingdoms similar to those in Uganda, much of the Tanzanian interior is too dry to support large concentrations of people. In most of Tanzania, an informal system of *ntemi* chiefs emerged. The *ntemi* system, though structured, seems to have been flexible and benevolent. The chiefs were served by a council and performed a role that was as much advisory as it was authoritarian. By the 19th century there are estimated to have been more than 200 *ntemi* chiefs in western and central Tanzania, each with about 1,000 subjects.

The *ntemi* system was shattered when southern Tanzania was invaded by Ngoni exiles from what is now the province of Kwazulu-Natal in South Africa. In Kwazulu-Natal, the leader of the small Zulu clan, Chaka, had melded a giant kingdom from the surrounding clans using revolutionary military tactics based on horseshoe formations and a short-stabbing spear. By 1830, his marauding troops had either killed, incorporated or driven away most of the other tribes in the region. The exiled tribes swept northwards, taking with them Chaka's methods, and they in turn wreaked havoc over much of southern Africa, slaughtering existing tribes in order to take their land.

The Ngoni entered southern Tanzania in about 1840. They attacked resident tribes, destroying communities and leaving survivors no option but to turn to banditry. Their tactics were observed and adopted by the more astute *ntemi* chiefs, who needed to protect themselves, but had to forge larger kingdoms to do so. The situation was exacerbated by the growing presence of Arab slave traders. Tribes controlling the areas that caravan routes went through were able to extract taxes from the slavers and to find work with them as porters or organising slave raids. This situation was exploited by several chiefs, most notably Mirambo, who dominated the interior between about 1840 and 1880.

The coast to 1800

There have been links between the Tanzanian coast and the rest of the world for millennia, but only the barest sketch is possible of events before AD1,000.

The ancient Egyptians believed their ancestors came from a southerly land called Punt. In about 2,500BC an explorer called Sahare sailed there. He returned laden with ivory, ebony, and myrrh, which suggests he landed somewhere on the East African coast. There is no suggestion that Egypt traded regularly with Punt, but they did visit it again. Interestingly, an engraving of the Queen of Punt, made after an expedition in 1493BC, shows her to have distinctly Khoisan features.

The Phoenicians first explored the coast in about 600BC. According to the 1st-century *Periplus of the Ancient Sea* they traded with a town called Rhapta. This is thought to have been on the Tanzanian coast, at a major estuary such as that of the Pangani or Rufiji.

Bantu-speakers arrived at the coast about 2,000 years ago. It seems likely they had trade links with the Roman Empire: Rhapta gets a name check in Ptolemy's 4th-century *Geography* and a few 4th-century Roman coins have been found at the coast. The fact that the Romans knew of Kilimanjaro and the great lakes raises some interesting questions. One suggestion is that the coastal Bantu-speakers were running trade routes into the interior and that these collapsed at the same time as the Roman Empire, presumably because there was no longer anyone with whom they could trade. The idea is attractive and plausible, but the evidence seems rather flimsy. The Romans could simply have gleaned the information from Bantu-speakers who had arrived at the coast recently enough to have some knowledge of the interior.

Historians have a clearer picture of events on the coast from about AD1,000 onwards. By this time, trade between the coast and the Persian Gulf was well established. The earliest known Islamic buildings on the coast, on Manda Island off Kenya, have been dated to the 9th century AD. Items sold to Arab ships included ivory, ebony and various spices, while a variety of Oriental and Arabic goods were imported for the use of wealthy traders.

The coastal trade was dominated by gold, almost certainly mined in the Great Zimbabwe region. It arrived at the coast at Sofala, in modern-day Mozambique, probably via the Zambezi Valley, and was then transported by local traders to Mogadishu, where it was sold to the Arabs. The common assumption that Swahili language and culture was a direct result of Arab traders mixing with local Bantu-speakers is probably inaccurate. KiSwahili is a Bantu language. It spread along the coast in the 11th century; most of the Arab words which have entered it did so *after* this. The driving force behind a common coastal language and culture was almost certainly internal trade between Sofala and Mogadishu.

More than 30 Swahili city-states were operating between the 13th and 15th centuries, a large number of which were in modern-day Tanzania. This period is known as the Shirazi Era after the sultans who ruled these city-states, most of whom claimed descent from the Shiraz region of Persia. Each city-state had its own sultan; they rarely interfered in each other's business. The Islamic faith was widespread during this period, and many Arabic influences crept into coastal architecture. Cities were centred around a great mosque, normally constructed in rock and coral.

Many Arabs settled on the coast before and during the Shirazi Era. For a long time it has been assumed they controlled the trade, but this has been questioned in recent years. Contemporary descriptions of the city-states suggest they were predominantly populated by Africans. It is possible that African traders claimed Shirazi descent in order to boost their standing, both locally and with Shirazi ships.

In the mid-13th century, probably due to improvements in Arab navigation and ship construction, the centre of the gold trade moved from Mogadishu to the small island of Kilwa. Kilwa represented the peak of the Shirazi period. It had a population of 10,000 and operated its own mint, the first in sub-Saharan Africa. The multi-domed mosque on Kilwa was the largest and most splendid on all the coast, while another building, now known as Husuni Kubwa, was a gargantuan palace, complete with audience courts, several ornate balconies, and even a swimming pool. Kilwa is discussed more fully in Chapter 18.

Although Kilwa had been superseded in importance by Mombasa by the end of the 15th century, coastal trade was still booming. It came to an abrupt halt in 1505 when Mombasa was captured by the Portuguese and several other coastal towns, Kilwa included, were ransacked. Under Portuguese control the gold trade collapsed and the coast stagnated. In 1698, Fort Jesus, the Portuguese centre in Mombasa, was overthrown by Arabs from Oman. Rivalries between the Omani and the old Shirazi dynasties soon surfaced. In 1728, a group of Shirazi sultans went so far as to conspire with their old oppressors, the Portuguese, to overthrow Fort Jesus, but the Omani re-captured it a year later. For the next 100 years an uneasy peace gripped the coast, nominally under Omani rule but dominated in economic terms by the Shirazi Sultan of Mombasa.

Slavery and exploration in the 19th century

The 19th century was a period of rapid change in Tanzania, with stronger links established between the coast and the interior as well as between East Africa and Europe.

The decisive figure in the first half of the century was Seyyid Said, the Sultan of Muscat from 1804 to 1854. Britain had signed a treaty with Said's father, and in the wake of the Napoleonic Wars did not want to see the coast fall into French hands. In 1827, Said's small but efficient navy captured Mombasa and effectively took control of the coast. It is debatable whether this would have happened without British support.

Said chose Zanzibar as his East African base because of its proximity to Bagamoyo, which had been the terminus of a caravan route to Lake Tanganyika since 1823. Said's commercial involvement with Zanzibar began in 1827 when he set up clove plantations with scant regard for the land claims of local inhabitants. By 1840, when he moved his capital from Muscat to Zanzibar, commerce on the island was dominated by Said and his fellow Arabs.

The extent of the East African slave trade prior to 1827 is unclear. It certainly existed, but was never as important as the gold or ivory trade. The traditional centre of slave trading was West Africa, but trade there had recently been stopped by the British, leaving the way open for Said and his cronies. By 1839, over 40,000 slaves were being sold from Zanzibar annually. These came from two sources: the central caravan route between Bagamoyo and the Lake Tanganyika region, and a southern route between Kilwa Kivinje and Lake Nyasa.

The effects of the slave trade on the interior were numerous. The Nyamwezi of the Tabora region and the Yua of Nyasa became very powerful by serving as porters along the caravan routes and organising slave raids and ivory hunts. Weaker tribes were devastated. Villages were ransacked; the able-bodied men and women were taken away while the young and old were left to die. Hundreds of thousands of slaves were sold in the mid-19th century, and no-one knows how many more died of disease or exhaustion between being captured and reaching the coast.

The slave trade was the driving force behind the second great expansion of KiSwahili. This became the *lingua franca* along caravan routes.

Europeans knew little about the African interior in 1850. The first Europeans to see Kilimanjaro (Rebmann, 1848) and Mount Kenya (Krapf, 1849) were ridiculed for their reports of snow on the Equator. Arab traders must have had an intimate knowledge of parts of the interior, but no-one seems to have thought to ask them. In 1855, a German missionary, James Erhardt, produced a map of Africa based on third-hand Arab accounts. This showed a large slug-shaped lake in the heart of the continent. Known as the slug map, it fanned interest in a mystery that had tickled geographers since Roman times: the source of the Nile.

The men most responsible for opening up the East African interior to Europeans were Richard Burton, John Speke and David Livingstone, and later Henry Stanley. In 1858, on a quest for the source of the Nile funded by the Royal Geographical Society, Burton and Speke were the first Europeans to see Lake Tanganyika. Later that year, while Burton recovered from fever in Tabora, Speke was the first European to set eyes on Lake Victoria. Speke returned to the northern shore of Victoria in 1863 and concluded that Ripon Falls (near to modern-day Jinja in Uganda) was the Nile's source. Burton, perhaps the most forceful and intelligent of all the 19th-century explorers, ridiculed this conclusion. In 1864, on the eve of a public debate on the subject between the two men, Speke died of a self-inflicted gunshot wound. His death was described by the coroner as a shooting accident, but it seems likely he killed himself deliberately.

David Livingstone came from a poor Scots background. He left school at the age of ten, but educated himself to become a missionary. He arrived in the Cape in 1841 to work in the Kuruman Mission, but, overcome by the enormity of the task of converting Africa to Christianity, he decided he would be of greater service opening up the continent so that other missionaries could follow. Livingstone was the first European to cross the Kalahari Desert, the first to cross Africa from west to east and the first to see Victoria Falls. In the same year that Speke and Burton saw Lakes Tanganyika and Victoria, Livingstone stumbled across Africa's third great lake, Nyasa.

Like most explorers of his time, Livingstone was obsessed by the Nile issue. Nevertheless, he had ample opportunity to witness the slave caravans at first hand. Sickened by what he saw – the human bondage, the destruction of entire villages, and the corpses abandoned by the traders – he became an outspoken critic of the trade. He believed the only way to curb it was to open up Africa to the three Cs: Christianity, Commerce and Civilisation. Though not an imperialist by nature, Livingstone had seen enough of the famine and misery caused by the slavers and the Ngoni in the Nyasa area to believe the only solution was for Britain to colonise East Africa.

In 1867, Livingstone set off from Mikindani to spend the last six years of his life wandering between the great lakes, making notes on the slave trade and trying to settle the Nile debate. He believed the source of the Nile to be Lake Bengweulu (in northern Zambia), from which the mighty Lualaba River flowed. In 1872, he was found at Ujiji by Henry Stanley, an American journalist and explorer. Stanley's alleged greeting, 'Dr Livingstone, I presume', comprises probably the most famous words spoken in Africa. Livingstone died near Lake Bengweulu in 1873. His heart was removed and buried by his porters, who then carried his cured body over 1,500km to Bagamoyo.

Livingstone's quest to end the slave trade met with little success during his lifetime, but his death and highly emotional funeral at Westminster Abbey seem to have acted as a catalyst. Missions were built in his name all over the Nyasa region, while industrialists such as William Mackinnon and the Muir brothers invested in schemes to open Africa to commerce (which Livingstone had always believed was the key to putting the slavers out of business).

In the year Livingstone died, John Kirk was made the British Consul in Zanzibar. Kirk had travelled with Livingstone on his 1856-62 trip to Nyasa. Deeply affected by what he saw, he had since spent years on Zanzibar hoping to find a way to end the slave trade. In 1873, the British navy blockaded the island and Kirk offered Sultan Barghash full protection against foreign powers if he banned the slave trade. Barghash agreed. The slave market was closed and an Anglican church built over it. The trade continued on the mainland for some years – 12,000 slaves were sold at Kilwa in 1875 – but that too was stopped.

The slave trade continued on a small scale well into the 20th century and was only fully eradicated in 1918, four years after the British took control of Tanganyika. Within ten years of Livingstone's death, however, the volume was a fraction of what it had been in the 1860s. Caravans reverted to ivory as their principal trade, while many of the coastal traders started up rubber and sugar plantations, which turned out to be just as lucrative as their former trade.

In 1875, Henry Stanley resolved the Nile issue. Lake Bengweulu was the source of a large river all right, but it was the Congo. Speke had been right all along.

The partitioning of East Africa

The so-called scramble for Africa was entered into with mixed motives, erratic enthusiasm and an almost total lack of premeditation by the powers involved. Britain already enjoyed a degree of influence on Zanzibar which amounted to informal colonialism and it was quite happy to maintain this mutually agreeable relationship. The government of the time, led by Lord Salisbury, was opposed to the taking of African colonies.

The scramble was initiated by two events. The first, the decision of King Leopold of Belgium to colonise the Congo Basin, had little direct bearing on events in Tanzania. The partitioning of East Africa was a direct result of an about-face by the German Premier, Bismarck, who had previously shown no enthusiasm for acquiring colonies. Germany probably only developed an interest in Africa in the hope of acquiring pawns to use in negotiations with Britain and France.

In 1884, a young German metaphysician called Carl Peters arrived inauspiciously in Zanzibar, then made his way to the mainland to sign a series of treaties with local chiefs. The authenticity of these treaties is questionable, but when Bismarck announced claims to a large area between the Pangani and Rufiji Rivers, it was enough to set the British government into a mild panic. Britain had plans to expand the Sultanate of Zanzibar, its informal colony, to include the fertile lands around Kilimanjaro. Worse, large parts of the area claimed by Germany were already part of the Sultanate. Not only was Britain morally bound to protect these, it also did not want to surrender control of Zanzibar's annual import/export turnover of two million pounds.

Despite pressure put on the British government by John Kirk, angry that his promises to Barghash would not be honoured, there was little option but to negotiate with Germany. A partition was agreed in 1886, identical to the modern border between Kenya and Tanzania. You may read that Kilimanjaro was part of the British territory before Queen Victoria gave it to her cousin, the Kaiser, as a birthday present. This amusing story was possibly dreamed up by a Victorian satirist to reflect the arbitrariness of the scramble. It is a complete fabrication.

In April 1888, the Sultan of Zanzibar unwillingly agreed to lease Germany the coastal strip south of the Umba River. Germany mandated this area to Carl Peters' German East Africa Company (GEAC), which placed agents at most coastal settlements north of Dar es Salaam. These agents demanded heavy taxes from traders and were encouraged to behave high-handedly in their dealings with locals.

The GEAC's honeymoon was short. Emil Zalewski, the Pangani agent, ordered the Sultan's representative, the Wali, to report to him. When the Wali refused, Zalewski had him arrested and sent away on a German war boat. In September 1888, an uprising against the GEAC was led by a sugar plantation owner called Abushiri Ibn Salim. Except at Dar es Salaam and Bagamoyo, both protected by German war boats, GEAC agents were either killed or driven away. A horde of 20,000 men gathered on the coast, including 6,000 Shambaa who refused to relinquish their right to claim tax from caravans passing the Usambara. In November, the mission at Dar es Salaam was attacked. Three priests were killed and the rest captured. The coast was in chaos until April 1889 when the Kaiser's troops invaded Abushiri's camp and forced him to surrender. The German government hanged Abushiri in Pangani; they withdrew the GEAC's mandate and banned Peters from ever setting foot in the area.

The 1886 agreement only created the single line of partition north of Kilimanjaro. By 1890, Germany had claimed an area north of Witu, including Lamu, and there was concern in Britain that they might try to claim the rich agricultural land around Lake Victoria, thereby surrounding Britain's territory. Undeterred by the debacle at Pangani (and with a nod and a wink from Bismarck), Carl Peters decided to force the issue. He slipped through Lamu and in May 1890, after a murderous jaunt across British territory, he signed a treaty with the King of Buganda entitling Germany to most of what is now southern Uganda. This time, however, Peters' plans were frustrated. Bismarck had resigned in March of the same year and his replacement,

Von Kaprivi, wanted to maintain good relations with Salisbury's government. In any case, Henry Stanley had signed a similar treaty with the Buganda when he passed through the area in 1888 on his way from rescuing the Emin Pasha in Equatoria.

Germany had its eye on Heligoland, a small but strategic North Sea island that had been seized by Britain from Denmark in 1807. To some extent, German interest in Africa had always been related to the bargaining power it would give them in Europe. In 1890, Salisbury and Von Kaprivi knocked out an agreement which created the borders of Tanzania as they are today (with the exception of modern-day Burundi and Rwanda, German territory until after World War I). In exchange for an island less than 1km^2 in area, Salisbury was guaranteed protectorateship over Zanzibar and handed the German block north of Witu, and Germany relinquished any claims it might have had to what are today Uganda and Malawi.

German East Africa

The period of German rule was not a happy one. In 1891, Carl Peters was appointed governor. Peters had already proved himself an unsavoury and unsympathetic character: he boasted freely of enjoying killing Africans and, under the guise of the GEAC, his lack of diplomacy had already instigated one uprising.

The 1890s were plagued by a series of natural disasters. A rinderpest epidemic at the start of the decade was followed by an outbreak of smallpox and a destructive plague of locusts. A series of droughts brought famine and disease in their wake. Many previously settled areas reverted to bush, causing the spread of tsetse fly and sleeping sickness. The population of Tanganyika is thought to have decreased significantly between 1890 and 1914.

It took Peters a decade to gain full control of the colony. The main area of conflict was in the vast central plateau where, led by Mkwawa, the Hehe had become the dominant tribe. In 1891, the Hehe ambushed a German battalion led by Emil Zalewski. They killed or wounded more than half Zalewski's men, and made off with his armoury. Mkwawa fortified his capital near Iringa, but it was razed by the Germans in 1894. Mkwawa was forced to resort to guerrilla tactics, which he used with some success. In 1898, Mkwawa shot himself rather than face capture.

Germany was determined to make the colony self-sufficient. Sugar and rubber were well established on parts of the coast; coffee was planted in the Kilimanjaro region, a major base for settlers; and cotton grew well around Lake Victoria. The colony's leading crop export, sisal, was grown throughout the rest of the country. In 1902, Peters decided that the southeast should be given over to cotton plantations. This was an ill-considered move: the soils were not right for the crop and the scheme was bound to cause great hardship.

The people of the southeast had suffered throughout the 19th century and distrusted outsiders. They had been terrorised by the notoriously cruel Kilwa slavers and suffered regular raids by the Ngoni; the cotton scheme, which created backbreaking work for little financial return, was the final straw. In 1905, a prophet called Kinjikitile discovered a spring which spouted out magic water. He claimed that bullets fired at anyone who had been sprinkled with this water would have no effect. His messengers carried the water to people throughout the region; by August 1905 the entire southeast was ready to rise against the Germans.

The Maji-Maji (water-water) Rebellion began in Kinjikitile's village in the Mutumbi Hills near Kilwa. The house of the German agent in Kibatu was burnt down, as was a nearby Asian trading centre. Troops from the regional headquarters at Kilwa captured and hanged Kinjikitile, but the news of his magic water had already spread. A group of missionaries led by the bishop of Dar es Salaam was speared to death when they passed through the region, several trading posts were burnt along with their occupants, and the entire staff of the Ifakara garrison was killed.

The rebellion's first setback came when 1,000 warriors attacked the Mahenge garrison. The commander had been warned of the attack and a bank of machine guns awaited its arrival. Although many warriors were killed, the garrison was pinned down until troops from Iringa forced the rest to retreat. The Iringa troops then continued to the Ngoni capital of Songea. The Ngoni were extremely dubious about the water's power; when a few Ngoni were shot, the rest fled.

News of the water's ineffectiveness spread; the rebellion had lost much of its momentum by mid-October when Count Gotzen and 200 German troops arrived in the area. Gotzen decided the only way to flush out the ringleaders was to create a famine. Crops were burnt indiscriminately. Within months most of the leaders had been hanged. The ensuing famine virtually depopulated the area: over 250,000 people died of disease or starvation and the densely populated Mutumbi and Ungindo hills were reclaimed by *miombo* woodland and wild animals. They now form part of the Selous Game Reserve.

The Maji-Maji rebellion was the most important and tragic event during German rule, but it did leave some good effects in its wake. It was the first time a group of disparate tribes had dropped their own disputes and united against European invaders. Many Tanzanians feel the rebellion paved the way for the non-tribal attitude of modern Tanzania and it certainly affected the strategies used against colonial powers throughout Africa. More immediately, the public outcry it caused forced Germany to rethink its approach to its colonies.

Carl Peters was fired from the colonial service in 1906. He believed his African mistress had slept with his manservant, so he had flogged her close to death then hanged them both. His successor introduced a series of laws protecting Africans from mistreatment. To the disgust of the settler community, he created an incentive-based scheme for African farmers. This made it worth their while to grow cash crops and allowed the colony's exports to triple in the period leading up to World War I.

When World War I broke out in Europe, East Africa rapidly became involved. In the early stages of the war, German troops entered southern Kenya to cut off the Uganda Railway. Britain responded with an abortive attempt to capture Tanga. The balance of power was roughly even until Jan Smuts led the Allied forces into German territory in 1916. By January 1918, the Allies had captured most of German East Africa and the German commander, Von Lettow, retreated into Mozambique.

The war disrupted food production, and a serious famine ensued. This was particularly devastating in the Dodoma region. The country was taken over by the League of Nations. Ruanda-Urundi, now Rwanda and Burundi, was mandated to Belgium. The rest of the country was re-named Tanganyika and mandated to Britain.

Tanganyika

The period of British rule between the wars was largely uneventful. Tanganyika was never heavily settled by Europeans so the indigenous populace had more opportunity for self-reliance than it did in many colonies. Nevertheless, settlers were favoured in the agricultural field, as were Asians in commerce. The Land Ordinance Act of 1923 secured some land rights for Africans; otherwise they were repeatedly forced into grand but misconceived agricultural schemes. The most notorious of these, the Groundnut Scheme of 1947, was an attempt to convert the southeast of the country into a large-scale mechanised groundnut producer. The scheme failed through a complete lack of understanding of local conditions; it caused a great deal of hardship locally and cost British taxpayers millions of pounds.

On a political level, a system of indirect rule based around local government encouraged African leaders to focus on local rivalries rather than national issues. A low-key national movement called the TAA was formed in 1929, but it was as much a cultural as a political organisation.

Although it was not directly involved in World War II, Tanganyika was profoundly affected by it. The country benefited economically. It saw no combat so food production continued as normal, while international food prices rocketed. Tanganyika's trade revenue increased sixfold between 1939 and 1949. World War II was a major force in the rise of African Nationalism. Almost 100,000 Tanganyikans fought for the Allies. The exposure to other countries and cultures made it difficult for them to return home as second-class citizens. They had fought for non-racism and democracy in Europe, yet were victims of racist and non-democratic policies in their own country.

The dominant figure in post-war Tanganyikan/Tanzanian politics is Julius Nyerere. Schooled at a mission near Lake Victoria, he went on to university in Uganda and gained a master's degree in Edinburgh. After returning to Tanzania in 1952, Nyerere became involved in the TAA. This evolved into the more political and nationalist TANU in 1954. Nyerere became the president of TANU at the age of 32. By supporting rural Africans on grass roots issues and advocating self-government as the answer to their grievances, TANU gained a strong national following.

By the mid-1950s, Britain and the UN were looking at a way of moving Tanganyika towards greater self-government, though over a far longer timescale than TANU envisaged. The British governor, Sir Edward Twining, favoured a system of multi-racialism, which would give equal representation to whites, blacks and Asians. TANU agreed to an election along these lines, albeit with major reservations. Twining created his own 'African' party, the UTC.

In the 1958 election, there were three seats per constituency, one for each racial group. Electors could vote for all three seats, so in addition to putting forward candidates for the black seats, TANU indicated their preferred candidates in the white and Asian seats. Candidates backed by TANU won 67% of the vote; the UTC did not win a single seat. Twining's successor, Sir Richard Turnball, rewarded TANU by scrapping multi-racialism. In the democratic election of 1960, TANU won all but one seat. In May 1961, Tanganyika attained self government and Nyerere was made Prime Minister. Tanganyika attained full independence on December 9 1961. Not one life had been taken in the process.

Britain granted Zanzibar full independence in December 1963. A month later the Arab government was toppled and in April 1964 the two countries combined to form Tanzania.

Tanzania

At the very core of Tanzania's post-independence achievements and failures lies the figure of Julius Nyerere, who ruled Tanzania until his retirement in 1985. In his own country, where he remains highly respected, Nyerere is called *Mwalimu* – the teacher. In the West, he is a controversial figure, often portrayed as a dangerous socialist who irreparably damaged his country. This image of Nyerere doesn't bear scrutiny. He made mistakes and was intolerant of criticism – at one point Tanzania is said to have had more political prisoners than South Africa – but he is also one of the few statesmen to have emerged from Africa, and has been a force for positive change both in his own country and in a wider African context.

In 1962, TANU came into power with little policy other than their attained goal of independence. Tanganyika was the poorest and least economically developed country in East Africa, and one of the poorest in the world. Nyerere's first concerns were to better the lot of rural Africans and to prevent the creation of a money-grabbing elite. The country was made a one-party state, but had an election system which, by African standards, was relatively democratic. Tanzania pursued a policy of non-alignment, but the government's socialist policies and Nyerere's outspoken views alienated most Western leaders. Close bonds were formed with socialist powers, most significantly China, who built the Tanzam Railway (completed in 1975).

Relations with Britain soured in 1965. Nyerere condemned the British government's tacit acceptance of the Unilateral Declaration of Independence (UDI) in Rhodesia. In return, Britain cut off all aid to Tanzania. Nyerere also gave considerable vocal support to disenfranchised Africans in South Africa, Mozambique and Angola. The ANC and Frelimo both operated from Tanzania in the 1960s.

Nyerere's international concerns were not confined to white-supremacism. In 1975, Tanzania pulled out of an Organisation of African Unity (OAU) conference in Idi Amin's Uganda saying: 'The refusal to protest against African crimes against Africans is bad enough…but…by meeting in Kampala…the OAU are giving respectability to one of the most murderous regimes in Africa'. Tanzania gave refuge to several Ugandans, including the former president Milton Obote and the current president Yoweri Museveni. Amin occupied part of northwestern Tanzania in October 1978, and bombed Bukoba and Musoma. In 1979, Tanzania retaliated by invading Uganda and toppling Amin. This action was condemned by other African leaders, despite Amin having been the initial aggressor. Ousting Amin drained Tanzania's financial resources, but it received no financial compensation, neither from the West nor from any other African country.

At the time of independence, most rural Tanzanians lived in scattered communities. This made it difficult for the government to provide such amenities as clinics and schools and to organise a productive agricultural scheme. In 1967, Nyerere embarked on a policy he called villagisation. Rural people were encouraged to form *Ujamaa* (familyhood) villages and collective farms. The scheme met with some small-scale success in the mid-70s, so in 1975 Nyerere decided to forcibly re-settle people who had not yet formed villages. By the end of the year 65% of rural Tanzanians lived in *Ujamaa* villages. In many areas, however, water supplies were inadequate to support a village. The resultant mess, exacerbated by one of Tanzania's regular droughts, ended further villagisation. *Ujamaa* is often considered to have been an unmitigated disaster. It did not achieve what it was meant to, but it did help the government improve education and health care. Most reliable sources claim it did little long-term damage to agricultural productivity.

By the late 1970s Tanzania's economy was a mess. There were several contributory factors: drought, *Ujamaa*, rising fuel prices, the border closure with Kenya, lack of foreign aid, bureaucracy and corruption in state-run institutions, and the cost of the Uganda episode. After his re-election in 1980 Nyerere announced he would retire at the end of that five-year term. In 1985 he was succeeded by Ali Hassan Mwinyi. Nyerere remained chairman of the CCM, the party formed when TANU merged with the Zanzibari ASP in 1975, until 1990.

Under President Mwinyi Tanzania has moved away from socialism. In June 1986, in alliance with the IMF, he implemented a three-year Economic Recovery Plan. This included freeing up the exchange rate and encouraging private enterprise. Since then Tanzania has achieved an annual growth rate of around 4% (in real terms). Many locals complain the only result they have seen is greater inflation. In 1990 attempts were made to rout corruption from the civil service, with surprisingly positive results. The first multi-party election took place in October 1995, with the CCM being returned to power with a majority of around 75%, under the leadership of Benjamin Mpaka. As with independence, this transition caused no bloodshed.

Into its fourth decade of independence, most of Africa still suffers from the tribal problems it had at the outset. Nyerere's great achievement is the tremendous sense of national unity he created by making KiSwahili the national language, by banning tribal leaders, by forcing government officials to work away from the area in which they grew up, and by his own example.

Things look better for Tanzania now than they have at any time since independence. It remains one of the world's 25 least-developed countries, but most sources agree that the economic situation of the average Tanzanian has improved since independence, as have adult literacy rates and health care. Tanzania's remarkable political stability and its increasingly pragmatic economic policies are a positive base for future growth.

Tourism could play a big part in this. Until the closure of the Kenya border in the late 1970s, most of Tanzania's tourism came via Kenya, which profited from it more than Tanzania did. Tourism ground to a standstill during the early 1980s, but Tanzania is now developing a tourist infrastructure independently of an increasingly wobbly-looking Kenya.

When I first visited Tanzania in 1986, it looked to be beyond redemption. Ten years hence it could well be a beacon of hope, stability and relative prosperity in an increasingly turbulent continent.

uganda airlines
Boeing you to . . .

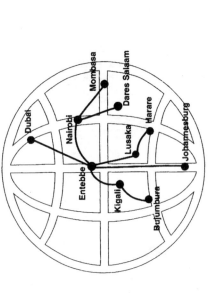

Uganda Airlines GSA British Airways, Travel Shops
200 Buckingham Palace Rd, London SW1W 9TA
Tel: 0171 730 2922, 0171 821 4058
Fax: 0171 821 4165
SITA: LONBXBA

Uganda Airlines Corporation
Ssebugwawo Drive
P.O. Box 187 Entebbe
Tel: 256-42 20456, 20546, 21058, 20329
Fax: 256-42 20355

Uganda Airlines Sales & Reservations
P.O. Box 5740 Kampala
Tel: 256-41 232990-7
Fax: 256-41 257279

Uganda Airlines Corporation
P.O. Box 59732 Nairobi Kenya
Tel: 221354, 228668, 215140
Tlx: 22923 UGAIR KE
Fax: 214744
Jomo Kenyata International Airport
Tel: 822430

Uganda Airlines
Ernest Openheimer Drive
P.O. Box 11298 Johannesburg 2000
Tel: (011) 6164672, 6166651, 6166724
Fax: (011) 6164620

Uganda Airlines Corporation
Air Masters Travel Rwanda s.a.r.l.
12 A Kigali
Tel: 74931, 73852
Fax: 73853
B.P. 10

Uganda Airlines
Jason Moyo Avenue
P.O. Box CY 470 Harare Zimbabwe
Tel: 795912, 795915
Fax: 263 4 733770

Uganda Airlines
Nasser Air Travel & Shipping Agencies
P.O. Box 1520, Dubai (UAE)
Tel: 04 238052 (D.L.) 04 214455
Fax: 04 211016

Uganda Airlines
Holiday Africa Tours and Safaris
P.O. Box 22636 Dar es Salaam
Tanzania
Tel: 22013/15, 21880/1
Fax: 255 51 46261

Uganda Airlines Corporation
P.O. Box 86546 Mombasa Kenya
Tel: 226407, 223780
Fax: 313347
Commercial Officer Tel: 223807

Uganda Airlines GSA Open Sky Ltd
32 Ben-Yehuda St
Tel Aviv 63805
Israel
Tel: 03 5253445
Tlx: 371251

Natural History

There are plenty of good reasons to visit Tanzania – its beautiful coastline, fascinating history and magnificent scenery – but for most tourists one attraction overwhelms all others. Tanzania is Africa's prime game-viewing country. Its national parks and game reserves, which include the famous Serengeti and Ngorongoro Crater, cover almost 25% of the country and protect an estimated 20% of Africa's large mammals.

All the national parks receive detailed coverage in the main part of the guide, as do any other conservation areas which are reasonably accessible. This chapter provides an overview of Tanzania's conservation areas and natural history, as well as descriptions of the more common large mammals.

CONSERVATION AREAS

There are 12 national parks in Tanzania, and numerous other conservation areas. The most important of these fit broadly into three groups: the northern, southern and western reserves.

Northern reserves

The northern reserves are the focus of Tanzania's safari industry, which is based in the town of Arusha. The traditional northern safari includes visits to Serengeti National Park, the Ngorongoro Conservation Area and Lake Manyara National Park. With luck, a visit to all three will yield sightings of all the so-called big five (lion, leopard, elephant, buffalo and rhino) and most other large African plains mammals.

The Serengeti is notable for its large migratory herds of wildebeest and zebra. It also harbours large numbers of predators; it is not unusual to see lion, leopard and cheetah in the same day. Although heavily touristed, the Serengeti is vast enough to handle it comfortably.

The centrepiece of the Ngorongoro Conservation Area is the magnificent 600m-deep crater after which it is named, the largest intact caldera in the world. Ngorongoro Crater supports large herds of ungulates and is said to have the world's densest lion population. It is the last place in East Africa where black rhinoceros are reasonably common. Ngorongoro is heavily touristed, and because it is open and its area is limited, this does detract from many people's visit.

Lake Manyara National Park is the least compelling of this triad of reserves. Its once famous elephant population has suffered badly at the hands of poachers, and its main claim to fame now is the tree-climbing lions which nobody ever seems to see. It is very scenic, however, and there is plenty of other game to be seen.

Many visitors incorporate visits to either Tarangire or Arusha National Park in a northern safari. Tarangire preserves a classic piece of African woodland, studded with plentiful baobabs. It is particularly rich in bird life. A number of localised species such as fringe-eared oryx and gerenuk are present, and elephant are abundant. Arusha National Park is the most low-key of the northern reserves, and

AFRICAN CONSERVATION

The plight of the rhinoceros and elephant has made African conservation a household concern in the West. Despite this, few Westerners have any grasp of the issues. What follows is certainly opinionated, and probably simplistic, but does attempt to clarify the root problem as I see it. You may well disagree...

We all romanticise Africa. An incredible amount of drivel was written about it during the colonial era, and this dominates our perception of the continent. The macho blustering of Hemingway and exaggerated accounts of the Great White Hunters vie in our heads with the nostalgic meandering of *Out of Africa*. For the West, Africa represents wildness and space, vast horizons and shimmering red sunsets; powerful images we do not want shattered by the realities of the late 20th century.

It was, of course, European settlers who destroyed the Africa they mythologised. The vast herds which had existed alongside people for millennia were decimated during the colonial era. By the early 1960s, when most of Africa became independent, these herds were by and large restricted to conservation areas that had been set aside by the colonial governments to preserve something of the Africa they loved. Their vision of unspoilt Africa did not include people: when an area was declared a national park, the people who lived there were moved to the fringes. Local people had both hunted and conserved the animals for centuries; now hunting was forbidden and they needed new sources of food.

Areas suitable for national parks are not normally densely populated; they tend to be relatively infertile. Even if someone succeeded in growing crops, their efforts could be wiped out by one hungry or angry elephant. This created a circle of poverty around many game reserves, a scenario which worked in the interests of ivory and rhino horn traders. People living on the verges of reserves would happily kill elephant or rhinoceros for what was a fraction of the market price, but a fortune in local terms.

As you are no doubt aware, rhinoceros are close to extinction in most Africa countries. In Tanzania, there are 20 left in the Ngorongoro Conservation Area and at best a couple of hundred in the Selous. Africa's elephant population is now thought to number about half a million. Tanzania is home to a significant number of these. There are an estimated 30,000 animals in the Selous alone, and at least as many scattered in other reserves.

In the late 1980s the elephant situation seemed hopeless. In some reserves, herds had been poached to within 20% of their size ten years previously. In the Selous, up to 20,000 were killed in a two year period. Most African governments lacked the finance to arrest this process; in some cases they also lacked the will, with strong rumours of corruption and the involvement of government officials. Anti-poaching units armed with old-fashioned rifles were fighting bands of poachers armed with AK47s, and losing. In 1988, I was driven through a part of Kenya's Tsavo East National Park, one of the worst hit reserves, with less than a quarter of its 1972 population of 17,000 animals left. We saw more elephant corpses than we did live animals; those elephant we did see ran off in terror at the approach of a vehicle.

A moratorium on the world ivory trade was implemented in 1989. There is a wide consensus this ban has worked: elephant numbers are on the increase and, without a market, poaching has virtually stopped. Southern African countries want this moratorium to be lifted. Herds in South Africa, Botswana and Zimbabwe are stable and growing, and as elephant are extremely destructive when overpopulated, excess animals are culled. This issue has been greatly misrepresented in Britain at least, where emotive and irresponsible newspaper columns and television programmes have equated culling with murder. Obviously culling is not the ideal solution, but it is difficult to see a practical alternative. (The suggestion most often put forward is that the animals could be moved. To the Cotswolds? Or somewhere else where African crops can be trampled?)

It has become evident to many conservationists that a complete change of approach is the only chance for the long-term survival of Africa's large animals. Local people must be included in the process. If they benefit from the reserves, they will side with conservationists; if they do not they will side with the poachers. Attempts must be made to ensure that locals benefit from money raised by the reserves, that they are given meat from culled animals, and that, wherever possible, work is found for them within the reserve. In an increasingly densely populated continent, reserves can only justify their existence if they create local wealth.

Zimbabwe is at the forefront of this more integrated approach to conservation. It is, by Western standards, a poor country, and could use the revenue raised by selling elephant tusks which are at present gathering dust. Zimbabwean conservationists argue that they have the right to sell these on a legitimate market; that Western countries would not be so keen to impose a moratorium if their commercial interests were at stake; that, ultimately, the West is yet again imposing its will on Africa.

Southern African countries suggest a cartel is created which sells only ivory from countries with stable elephant populations. Countries like Tanzania fear that such a cartel would be difficult to control, and may well lead to renewed poaching in their reserves. There is no simple solution to this conflict of interests. I believe it to be in the interests of most African countries that the moratorium stands for the meantime, but ultimately it should be lifted. Efforts should be made now to rethink conservation policies, so that when it is lifted the same old problems do not recur.

Africa does not belong to the West. I see no reason why Africans should conserve their wildlife for the sake of Western aesthetics, unless they perceive it to be in their interest to do so. If some gun-happy soul with a Hemingway fixation is idiot enough to pay enough money to support a village for a year in order that he can hunt an elephant, good. If the meat from an elephant can feed a village for a week, and the money from the sale of the ivory be put back into conservation, good. If we Westerners can drop the idealism and allow Africans to both conserve their wildlife and feed their bellies, only then is there a chance that our grandchildren will be able to see the Africa we want them to.

For further insight into the issues raised above, a recommended read is *At the Hand of Man: Peril and Hope for Africa's Wildlife* by Raymond Bonner (Alfred A Knopf, 1993).

considering its proximity to Arusha, it is surprisingly little visited. Despite this, it has a number of attractive features, including Africa's fifth-highest mountain, Meru, and its own mini-Ngorongoro, Ngurdoto Crater.

Kilimanjaro National Park encompasses the peaks and higher slopes of Africa's highest mountain. Thousands of tourists climb it every year. Mount Meru in Arusha National Park is also popular with hikers.

Southern reserves

Tanzania's southern reserves are less spectacular than those in the north, but they have more of a wilderness atmosphere. The most important reserve in southern Tanzania is the Selous Game Reserve, the largest reserve in Africa. It is bordered by two national parks: Mikumi and the recently proclaimed Udzungwa Mountains. A third national park, Ruaha, lies west of the Tanzam Highway.

With the exception of Udzungwa Mountains, the southern reserves are only really accessible if you go with an organised safari. These are generally more expensive than safaris to the northern reserves. You can, however, see something of Mikumi from the Tanzam Highway, and slow trains between Dar es Salaam and Mbeya pass through the Selous in daylight hours. The Udzungwa can be reached on public transport and once it is developed will be orientated towards hikers.

Western reserves

The western reserves are very different in character to those in the south and north of the country. They are low-key, have basic accommodation facilities only, and are time-consuming to visit. If you can afford the time, however, all are relatively easy to reach on public transport.

There are four national parks in western Tanzania: Gombe Stream, Mahale Mountains, Rubondo Island and Katavi. The first three are densely forested, noted for their chimpanzees, and can only be reached by boat. Katavi protects a similar habitat to the southern reserves, but is more remote.

HABITATS AND VEGETATION

The bulk of Tanzania is covered in open grassland, savannah (lightly wooded grassland) and woodland. Most typical African species are at home in all these habitats, but there are exceptions.

The Serengeti Plains are an archetypal African savannah: grassland interspersed with trees of the acacia family. Most acacia are quite short, lightly leaved and thorny. Many have a flat-topped appearance. An atypical acacia, the yellow fever tree, is one of Africa's most striking trees. It is relatively large, has yellow bark, and is often associated with water. Combretum is another family of trees typical of savannah.

Much of central Tanzania is dry savannah; during the dry season this area is so barren it resembles semi-desert.

Woodland differs from forest in lacking an interlocking canopy. The most extensive woodland in Tanzania is in the *miombo* belt which stretches from southern and western Tanzania to Zimbabwe. *Miombo* woodland typically grows on infertile soil, and is dominated by broadleaved *brachystegia* trees. You may come across the term mixed woodland: this refers to woodland with a mix of *brachystegia*, acacia and other species. Many woodlands are characterised by an abundance of baobab trees.

True forests cover less than 1% of Tanzania's surface area, but are its most botanically diverse habitat. The forests of the Usambara, for instance, contain more than 2,000 plant species. Most of the forest in Tanzania is montane. Montane forest is characteristic of a group of mountain ranges known as the Eastern Arc Mountains. These form a broken line from north to south, between 50km and

200km inland, and include the Pare, Usambara, Uluguru, Udzungwa and Poroto ranges. The forests of the Eastern Arc mountains, characterised by a high level of endemics (species found nowhere else), form one of Tanzania's most ecologically precious habitats. The most accessible montane forest is on the slopes of Kilimanjaro, Meru, the Udzungwa and the Usambara.

The lowland forests found in the extreme west of the country have strong affinities with the rainforests of Congo. Three national parks contain extensive lowland forests: Gombe Stream, Rubondo Island and Mahale Mountains.

Other interesting but localised vegetation types are mangrove swamps (common along the coast, particularly around Kilwa) and the heath and moorland found on the higher slopes of Kilimanjaro and Meru.

ANIMALS
Mammals

Over 80 large mammal species live in Tanzania. On an organised safari your guide will normally be able to identify all the mammals you see. For serious identification purposes or a better understanding of an animal's lifestyle and habits, it is worth investing in a decent field guide or a book on animal behaviour, but these sorts of books are too generalised to give much detail on distribution in any one country, so that the section that follows is best seen as a Tanzania-specific supplement to a field guide. A number of field guides are available (see *Further Reading*) and are best bought before you get to Tanzania.

In the listings below, an animal's scientific name is given in parenthesis after its English name, followed by the Swahili (Sw) name. The Swahili for animal is *mnyama* (plural *wanyama*); to find out what animal you are seeing, ask '*mnyama gani?*'

Cats, dogs and hyenas

Lion (*Panthera leo*) Sw: *simba*. Shoulder height: 100–120cm; weight: 150–220kg. Africa's largest predator, the lion is the animal that everybody hopes to see on safari. It is a sociable creature, living in prides of five to ten animals and defending a territory of between 20 and 200km². Lions hunt at night, and their favoured prey is large or medium antelope such as wildebeest and impala. Most of the hunting is done by females, but dominant males normally feed first after a kill. Rivalry between males is intense and takeover battles are frequently fought to the death, so two or more males often form a coalition. Young males are forced out of their home pride at three years of age, and male cubs are usually killed after a successful takeover. When not feeding or fighting, lions are remarkably indolent – they spend up to 23 hours of any given day at rest – so the anticipation of a lion sighting is often more exciting than the real thing. Lions naturally occur in any habitat but desert and rainforest, and once ranged across much of the Old World, but these days they are all but restricted to the larger conservation areas in sub-Saharan Africa (one remnant population exists in India). They are reasonably common in most savannah and woodland reserves in Tanzania, and the Serengeti and Ngorongoro Crater are arguably the best places in Africa for regular sightings.

Leopard (*Panthera pardus*) Sw: *chui*. Shoulder height: 70cm; weight: 60–80kg. The powerful leopard is the most solitary and secretive of Africa's large cat species. It hunts using stealth and power, often getting to within 5m of its intended prey before pouncing, and it habitually stores its kill in a tree to keep it from hyenas and lions. The leopard can be distinguished from the superficially similar cheetah by its rosette-like spots, lack of black 'tear marks' and more compact, powerful build. Leopards occur in all habitats, favouring areas with plenty of cover such as riverine

woodland and rocky slopes. There are many records of individuals living for years undetected in close proximity to humans. The leopard is the most common of Africa's large felines, found throughout Tanzania, yet a good sighting must be considered a stroke of extreme fortune. Relatively reliable spots for leopard sightings are the Seronera Valley in the Serengeti and the riverine bush in Ruaha National Park. An endemic race of leopard occurs on Zanzibar, though recent research suggests that it is probably extinct on the island, and that the handful of local reports of leopard sighting were probably the result of confusion with the African civet and introduced Javan civet.

Cheetah (*Acynonix jubatus*) Sw: *duma*. Shoulder height: 70–80cm; weight: 50–60kg. This remarkable spotted cat has a greyhound-like build, and is capable of running at 70km/hr in bursts, making it the world's fastest land animal. It is often seen pacing the plains restlessly, either on its own or in a small family group comprised of a mother and her offspring. A diurnal hunter, favouring the cooler hours of the day, the cheetah's habits have been adversely affected in areas where there are high tourist concentrations and off-road driving is permitted. Males are territorial, and generally solitary, though in the Serengeti they commonly defend their territory in pairs or trios. Despite superficial similarities, you can easily tell a cheetah from a leopard by the former's simple spots, disproportionately small head, streamlined build, diagnostic black tear marks, and preference for relatively open habitats. Widespread, but thinly distributed and increasingly rare outside of conservation areas, the cheetah is most likely to be seen in savannah and arid habitats such as the Serengeti Plains (where sightings are regular on

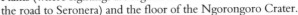

the road to Seronera) and the floor of the Ngorongoro Crater.

Similar species: The **serval** (*Felis serval*) is smaller than a cheetah (shoulder height: 55cm) but has a similar build and black-on-gold spots giving way to streaking near the head. Seldom seen, it is widespread and quite common in moist grassland, reed beds and riverine habitats.

Caracal (*Felis caracal*) Sw: *simbamangu*. Shoulder height: 40cm; weight: 15–20kg. This caracal resembles the European lynx with its uniform tan coat and tufted ears. It is a solitary hunter, feeding on birds, small antelope and livestock, and ranges throughout the country favouring relatively arid savannah habitats. It is nocturnal and rarely seen.

Similar species: The smaller **African wild cat** (*Felis sylvestris*) ranges from the Mediterranean to the Cape of Good Hope, and is similar in appearance to the domestic tabby cat. Like the caracal, it is common, but nocturnal, and infrequently seen.

African hunting dog (*Lycaon pictus*) Sw: *mbwa mwitu*. Shoulder height: 70cm; weight: 25kg. Also known as the wild or painted dog, the hunting dog is distinguished from other African dogs by its large size and cryptic black, brown and cream coat. Highly sociable, living in packs of up to 20 animals, the hunting dog is a ferocious hunter that literally tears apart its prey on the run. Threatened with extinction as a result of its susceptibility to diseases spread by domestic dogs, it is extinct in several areas where it was formerly abundant, for instance in the Serengeti and most other reserves in northern Tanzania. The global population of less than 3,000 hunting dogs is concentrated in southern Africa, though viable populations still occur in the Selous Game Reserve and Mikumi and Ruaha National Parks. The only place in northern Tanzania where hunting dogs can be seen is the Mkomazi Game Reserve, where a recently re-introduced population is reportedly thriving.

Black-backed jackal (*Canis mesomelas*) Sw: *mbweha*. Shoulder height: 35-45cm; weight: 8-12kg. The black-backed jackal is an opportunistic feeder capable of adapting to most habitats. Most often seen singly or in pairs at dusk or dawn, it is ochre in colour with a prominent black saddle flecked by a varying amount of white or gold. It is probably the most frequently observed small predator in Africa south of the Zambezi, and its eerie call is a characteristic sound of the bush at night. It is the commonest jackal in most Tanzanian reserves.

Similar species The similar **side-striped jackal** (*Canis adustus*) is more cryptic in colour, and has an indistinct pale vertical stripe on each flank and a white-tipped tail. Nowhere very common, it is distributed throughout Tanzania, and most likely to be seen in the southern reserves. The **common jackal** (*Canis aureus*), also known as the Eurasian or golden jackal, is a cryptically coloured North African jackal, relatively pale and with a black tail tip. Its range extends as far south as the Serengeti and Ngorongoro Crater, and it is probably more readily seen than the black-backed jackal on the crater floor, since it is more diurnal in its habits.

Bat-eared fox (*Otocyon megalotis*) Shoulder height: 30-35cm; weight: 35kg. This small, silver-grey insectivore, unmistakable with its huge ears and black eye-mask, is most often seen in pairs or small family groups during the cooler hours of the day. Associated with dry open country, the bat-eared fox is quite common in the Serengeti and likely to be encountered at least once in the course of a few days' safari.

Spotted hyena (*Crocuta crocuta*) Sw: *fisi*. Shoulder height: 85cm; weight: 70kg. Hyenas are characterised by their bulky build, sloping back, brownish coat, powerful jaws and doglike expression. Despite looking superficially canine, they are more closely related to mongooses and bears than to cats or dogs. Contrary to popular myth, hyenas are not exclusively scavengers: the spotted hyena in particular is an adept hunter capable of killing an animal as large as a wildebeest. Nor are they hermaphroditic, an ancient belief that stems from the false scrotum and penis covering the female hyena's vagina. Sociable animals, and fascinating to observe, hyenas live in loosely structured clans of about ten animals, led by females who are stronger and larger than males. The spotted hyena is the largest hyena, distinguished by its blotchily spotted coat, and it is probably the most common large predator in East and southern Africa. It is most frequently seen at dusk and dawn in the vicinity of game reserve lodges, campsites and refuse dumps, and is likely to be encountered on a daily basis in the Serengeti and Ngorongoro Crater.

Similar species The North African **striped hyena** (*Hyaena hyaena*) is pale brown with several dark vertical streaks and a blackish mane. It occurs alongside the spotted hyena in dry parts of Tanzania, but is scarce and secretive. The equally secretive **aardwolf** (*Proteles cristatus*) is an insectivorous striped hyena, not much bigger than a jackal, which occurs in low numbers in northern Tanzania.

African civet (*Civettictus civetta*) Sw: *fungo*. Shoulder height: 40cm; weight: 10–15kg. This bulky, longhaired, rather feline creature of the African night is primarily carnivorous, feeding on small animals and carrion, but will also eat fruit. It has a similarly coloured coat to a leopard or cheetah, and this is densely blotched with large black spots becoming stripes towards the head. Civets are widespread and common in many habitats, but very rarely seen.

Similar species The smaller, more slender **tree civet** (*Nandinia binotata*) is an arboreal forest animal with a dark-brown coat marked with black spots. The **small-spotted genet** (*Genetta genetta*) and **large-spotted genet** (*Genetta tigrina*) are the most widespread members of a group of similar small predators, all of which are very slender and rather feline in appearance, with a grey to golden brown coat marked with black spots and an exceptionally long ringed tail. Most likely to be seen on nocturnal game drives or scavenging around game reserve lodges, the large-spotted genet is golden brown with very large spots and a black-tipped tail, whereas the small-spotted genet is greyer with rather small spots and a pale tip to the tail.

Banded mongoose (*Mungos mungo*) Shoulder height: 20cm; weight: around 1kg. The banded mongoose is probably the most commonly observed member of a group of small, slender, terrestrial carnivores. Uniform dark brown except for a dozen black stripes across its back, it is a diurnal mongoose occurring in family groups in most wooded habitats and savannah.

Similar species Several other mongoose species occur in Tanzania, though several are too scarce and nocturnal to be seen by casual visitors. The **marsh mongoose** (*Atilax paludinosus*) is large, normally solitary and has a very scruffy brown coat. It's widespread in the eastern side of Africa where it is often seen in the vicinity of water. The **white-tailed ichneumon** (*Ichneumia albicauda*) is another widespread, solitary, large brown mongoose, easily identified by its bushy white tail. The **slender mongoose** (*Galerella sanguinea*) is as widespread and also solitary, but it is very much smaller (shoulder height: 10cm) and has a uniform brown coat and blackish tail tip. The **dwarf mongoose** (*Helogate parvula*) is a diminutive (shoulder height: 7cm), highly sociable, light-brown mongoose often seen in the vicinity of the termite mounds where it nests.

Ratel (*Mellivora capensis*) Sw: *nyegere*. Shoulder height: 30cm; weight: 12kg. Also known as the honey badger, the ratel is black with a puppyish face and grey-to-white back. It is an opportunistic feeder best known for its symbiotic relationship with a bird called the honeyguide which leads it to a bee hive, waits for it to tear the nest open, then feeds on the scraps. The ratel is among the most widespread of African carnivores, but it is thinly distributed and rarely seen.

Similar species Several other mustelids occur in the region, including the **striped polecat** (*Ictonyx striatus*), a common but rarely seen nocturnal creature with black underparts and bushy white back, and the similar but much more scarce **striped weasel** (*Poecilogale albincha*). The **Cape clawless otter** (Aonyx capensis) is a brown freshwater mustelid with a white collar, while the smaller **spotted-necked otter** (*Lutra maculicollis*) is darker with white spots on its throat.

Primates

Chimpanzee (*Pan troglodytes*) Sw: *sokwe-mtu*. Standing height: 100cm; weight: up to 55kg. This distinctive black-coated ape, along with the bonobo (*Pan paniscus*) of the southern Congo, is more closely related to man than to any other living creature. The chimpanzee lives in large troops based around a core of related males dominated by an alpha male. Females aren't firmly bonded to their core group, so emigration between communities is normal. Primarily frugivorous (fruit-eating), chimpanzees eat meat on occasion, and though most kills are opportunistic, stalking of prey is not unusual. The first recorded instance of a chimp using a tool was at Gombe Stream in Tanzania, where modified sticks were used to 'fish' in termite mounds. In West Africa, chimps have been observed cracking open nuts with a stone and anvil. In the USA, captive chimps have successfully been taught Sign Language and have created compound words such as 'rock-berry' to describe a nut. A widespread and common rainforest resident, the chimpanzee is thought to number 200,000 in the wild. In East Africa, chimps occur in western Uganda and on the Tanzanian shore of Lake Tanganyika, where they can be seen at the research centre founded by primatologist Jane Goodall in Tanzania's Gombe Stream, as well as at Mahale Mountains and on Rubondo Island.

Common baboon (*Papio cynocaphalus*) Sw: *nyani*. Shoulder height: 50–75cm; weight: 25–45kg. This powerful terrestrial primate, distinguished from any other monkey by its much larger size, inverted U-shaped tail and distinctive doglike

head, is fascinating to watch from a behavioural perspective. It lives in large troops which boast a complex, rigid social structure characterised by matriarchal lineages and plenty of inter-troop movement by males seeking social dominance. Omnivorous and at home in almost any habitat, the baboon is the most widespread primate in Africa, frequently seen in most Tanzanian game reserves.

There are several races of baboon in Africa, and these are regarded by some authorities to be full species. In Tanzania, the yellow baboon (*P. c. cynocephalus*) is the yellow-brown race occurring in the south and east of the country, while the olive or anubis baboon (*P. c. anubis*) is the hairy green-brown baboon found in the northern reserves.

Vervet monkey (*Cercopithecus aethiops*) Sw: *tumbili*. Length (excluding tail): 40–55cm; weight: 4–6kg. Also known as the green or grivet monkey, the vervet is probably the world's most numerous monkey and certainly the most common and widespread representative of the *Cercopithecus* guenons, a taxonomically controversial genus associated with African forests. An atypical guenon in that it inhabits savannah and woodland rather than true forest, the vervet spends a high proportion of its time on the ground and in most of its range could be confused only with the much larger and heavier baboon. However, the vervet's light-grey coat, black face and white forehead band should be diagnostic – as should the male's garish blue genitals. The vervet is abundant in Tanzania, and might be seen just about anywhere, not only in reserves.

Similar species The terrestrial **patas monkey** (*Erythrocebus patas*), larger and more spindly than the vervet, has an orange-tinged coat and black forehead stripe. Essentially a monkey of the dry northwestern savannah, the patas occurs in low numbers in the northern Serengeti.

Blue monkey (*Cercopithecus mitis*) Sw: *kima*. Length (excluding tail): 50–60cm; weight: 5–8kg. Also known as the samango, golden or Syke's monkey, or the diademed or white-throated guenon, this most variable monkey is divided by some

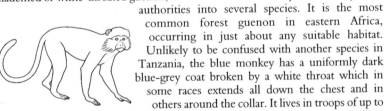

authorities into several species. It is the most common forest guenon in eastern Africa, occurring in just about any suitable habitat. Unlikely to be confused with another species in Tanzania, the blue monkey has a uniformly dark blue-grey coat broken by a white throat which in some races extends all down the chest and in others around the collar. It lives in troops of up to ten animals and associates with other primates where their ranges overlap. It is common in Arusha National Park, and in many forest reserves.

Similar species The **red-tailed monkey** (*Cercopithecus ascanius*) is a small brown guenon with white whiskers, a red tail and distinctive white heart on its nose. In Tanzania, it is restricted to forested parts of the Lake Tanganyika shore, such as

Mahale Mountains and Gombe Stream. The **crested mangabey** (*Cercocebus galeritus*) is a yellowish West African monkey, two isolated populations of which occur in East Africa, one in Tanzania's Udzungwa Mountains and another along Kenya's Tana River.

Black-and-white colobus (*Colobus guereza*) Sw: *mbega mweupe*. Length (excluding tail): 65cm; weight: 12kg. This beautiful jet-black monkey has bold white facial markings, a long white tail and in some races white sides and shoulders. Almost exclusively arboreal, it is capable of jumping up to 30m, a spectacular sight with white tail streaming behind. Several races have been described, and most authorities recognise more than one species. The black-and-white colobus is a common resident of forests in Tanzania, often seen in the forest zone of Kilimanjaro and in Arusha National Park.

Red colobus (*Procolobus badius*) Length (excluding tail): 60cm; weight: 10kg. The status of this variable monkey is debatable, with between one and ten species recognised. Most populations have black on the upper back, red on the lower back, a pale tufted crown and a long-limbed appearance unlike that of any guenon or mangabey. Four populations are known in East Africa, of which two live in isolated pockets in Tanzania, and are regarded by some authorities to be full species. The first of these is Kirk's red colobus *P. kirkii*, which is restricted to Zanzibar Island. Only 1,500 of these animals remain in the wild, but they are easily seen in the Jozani Forest on eastern Zanzibar. The Uhehe red colobus *P.gordonorum* is a fairly common and conspicuous resident of the Udzungwa Mountains in southern Tanzania.

Lesser bushbaby (*Galago senegalensis*) Sw: *komba*. Length (without tail): 17cm; weight: 150g. The lesser bushbaby is the most widespread and common member of a group of small and generally indistinguishable nocturnal primates, distantly related to the lemurs of Madagascar. More often heard than seen, the lesser bushbaby can sometimes be picked out by tracing a cry to a tree and shining a torch into its eyes.

Similar species The most easily identified bushbaby due to its size, the **greater bushbaby** (*Galago crassicaudatus*) occurs throughout the eastern side of Africa as far south as East London. It produces a terrifying scream which you'd think was emitted by a chimpanzee or gorilla.

Large antelope
Roan antelope (*Hippotragus equinus*) Sw: *korongo*. Shoulder height: 120–150cm; weight: 250–300kg. This handsome horselike antelope is uniform fawn-grey with a pale belly, short decurved horns and a light mane. It could be mistaken for the female sable antelope, but this has a well-defined white belly, and lacks the roan's distinctive black-and-white facial markings. The roan is widespread but thinly distributed in most reserves in southern Tanzania, and it is very rare in the Serengeti.

Sable antelope (*Hippotragus niger*) Sw: *pala hala*. Shoulder height: 135cm; weight: 230kg. The striking male sable is jet black with a distinct white face, underbelly and rump, and long decurved horns. The female is chestnut brown and has shorter horns. The main stronghold for Africa's sable population is the miombo woodland of southern Tanzania, where a population of 30,000 is concentrated in Ruaha National Park and Selous Game Reserve. The sable is absent from most reserves in northern Tanzania.

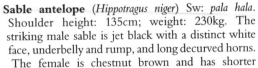

Oryx (*Oryx gazella*) Sw: *choroa*. Shoulder height: 120cm; weight: 230kg. This regal, dry-country antelope is unmistakable with its ash-grey coat, bold black facial marks and flank strip, and unique long, straight horns. The fringe-eared oryx is the only race found in Tanzania, where it is most common in Tarangire National Park, though present in small numbers in the northern Serengeti and Mkomazi Game Reserve.

Waterbuck (*Kobus ellipsiprymnus*) Sw: *kuro*. Shoulder height: 130cm; weight: 250–270kg. The waterbuck is easily recognised by its shaggy brown coat and the male's large lyre-shaped horns. The Defassa race of the Rift Valley and areas further west has a full white rump, while the eastern race has a white U on its rump. The waterbuck is frequently seen in small family groups grazing near water in all but the most arid of game reserves in Tanzania.

Blue wildebeest (*Connochaetes taurinus*) Sw: *nyumbu*. Shoulder height: 130–150cm; weight: 180–250kg. This ungainly antelope, also called the brindled gnu, is easily identified by its dark coat and bovine appearance. The superficially similar buffalo is far more heavily built. Immense herds of blue wildebeest occur on the Serengeti Plains, where the annual migration of more than a million heading into Kenya's Maasai Mara forms one of Africa's great natural spectacles. There are also significant wildebeest populations in the Ngorongoro Crater, Tarangire and in most reserves in southern Tanzania.

Hartebeest (*Alcelaphus buselaphus*) Shoulder height: 125cm; weight: 120–150kg. Hartebeests are ungainly antelopes, readily identified by the combination of large shoulders, a sloping back, red-brown or yellow-brown coat and smallish horns in both sexes. Numerous races are recognised, all of which are generally seen in small family groups in reasonably open country. The race found in northern Tanzania, Coke's hartebeest or kongoni, is common in open parts of the Serengeti and Ngorongoro. In southern Tanzania, it is replaced by Liechtenstein's hartebeest, regarded by some authorities to be a full species.

Similar species The **topi** or **tsessebe** (*Damaliscus lunatus*) is basically a darker version of the hartebeest with striking yellow lower legs. Widespread but thinly and patchily distributed, the topi occurs alongside the much yellower kongoni in the Serengeti National Park, where it is common.

Common eland (*Taurotragus oryx*) Sw: *pofu*. Shoulder height: 150–175cm; weight: 450–900kg. Africa's largest antelope, the common eland is light brown in colour, sometimes with a few faint white vertical stripes, and its somewhat bovine appearance is accentuated by relatively short horns and a large dewlap. It is widely distributed in East and southern Africa, and small herds may be seen almost anywhere in grassland or light woodland. The eland is fairly common in the Serengeti, but difficult to approach closely

Greater kudu (*Tragelaphus strepsericos*) Sw: *tandala*. Shoulder height: 140–155cm; weight: 180–250kg. In many parts of Africa, the greater kudu is the most readily observed member of the genus *tragelaphus*, a group of medium to large antelopes characterised by the male's large spiralling horns and a dark coat generally marked with several vertical white stripes. The greater kudu is very large, with a grey-brown coat and up to ten stripes on each side, and the male has magnificent double spiralled horns. A widespread animal occurring in most wooded habitats except for true forest, the greater kudu is rare in northern Tanzania, but common in the southern reserves, where it is most often seen in mixed- or single-sex herds of up to ten animals.

Similar species The thinly distributed and skittish **lesser kudu** (*Tragelaphus imberbis*) is an East African species largely restricted to arid woodland. In Tanzania, it often occurs alongside the greater kudu, from which it can be distinguished by its smaller size (shoulder height: 100cm), two white throat patches and greater number of stripes (at least eleven). Nowhere common, it is most likely to be encountered in Tarangire and Ruaha National Parks. The semiaquatic **sitatunga** (*Tragelaphus spekei*) is a widespread but infrequently observed inhabitant of west and central African swamps from the Okovango in Botswana to the Sudd in Sudan. In Tanzania, it is most likely to be seen on Rubondo Island. The male, with a shoulder height of up to 125cm and a shaggy fawn coat, is unmistakable in its habitat. The smaller female might be mistaken for a bushbuck (see below) but it has far more defined stripes.

Medium and small antelope
Bushbuck (*Tragelaphus scriptus*) Sw: *pongo*. Shoulder height: 70–80cm; weight: 30–45kg. This attractive antelope, a member of the same genus as the kudus, shows

great regional variation in colouring. The male is dark brown, chestnut or in parts of Ethiopia black, while the much smaller female is generally pale reddy-brown. The male has relatively small, straight horns for a *tragelaphus* antelope. Both sexes have similar throat patches to the lesser kudu, and are marked with white spots and sometimes stripes, though the last are never as clear as the vertical white stripes on the otherwise similar female nyala or sitatunga. One of the most widespread antelope species in Africa, the bushbuck occurs in forest and riverine woodland throughout Tanzania, where it is normally seen singly or in pairs. The bushbuck tends to be secretive and skittish except where it is used to people, so it is not as easily seen as you might expect of a common antelope.

Thomson's gazelle (*Gazella thomsoni*) Shoulder height: 60cm; weight: 20–25kg. Gazelles are graceful, relatively small antelopes which generally occur in large herds in open country and have fawn-brown upper parts and a white belly. Thomson's gazelle is characteristic of the East African plains, where it is the only gazelle to have a black horizontal stripe. It is common to abundant in the Serengeti and surrounds.

Similar species Occurring alongside Thomson's gazelle in many parts of East Africa, the larger **Grant's gazelle** (*Gazella granti*) lacks a black side stripe and has comparatively large horns. An uncharacteristic gazelle, the **gerenuk** (*Litocranius walleri*) is a solitary, arid country species of Ethiopia, Kenya and northern Tanzania, similar in general colour to an impala but readily identified by its very long neck and singular habit of feeding from trees standing on its hind legs. Good places to see it include Mkomazi, Tarangire and the Loliondio area.

Impala (*Aepeceros melampus*) Sw: *swala pala*. Shoulder height: 90cm; weight: 45kg. This slender, handsome antelope is superficially similar to some gazelles, but in fact belongs to a separate family. Chestnut in colour, the impala has diagnostic black and white stripes running down its rump and tail, and the male has large lyre-shaped horns. One of the most widespread antelope species in subequatorial Africa, the impala is normally seen in large herds in wooded savannah habitats, and it is one of the most common antelope in many Tanzanian reserves.

Reedbucks (*Redunca spp*) sw: *tohe*. Shoulder height: 65-90cm; weight: 30–65kg. The three species of reedbuck are all rather nondescript fawn-grey antelopes generally seen in open grassland near water. The mountain reedbuck (*Redunca fulvorufula*) is the smallest and most distinctive, with a clear white belly, tiny horns, and an overall grey appearance. It has a broken distribution, occurring in mountainous parts of eastern South Africa, northern Tanzania, Kenya and southern Ethiopia. The Bohor reedbuck is found in northern Tanzania, whereas the southern reedbuck occurs in southern Tanzania.

Similar species The golden brown **puku** (*Kobus vardoni*), similar in appearance to the kob of Uganda, lives in marsh and moist grassland from Lake Rukwa in Tanzania to the Okovango in Botswana.

Klipspringer (*Oreotragus oreotragus*) Sw: *mbuze mawe*. Shoulder height: 60cm; weight: 13kg. The klipspringer is a goat-like antelope, normally seen in pairs, and easily identified by its dark, bristly grey-yellow coat, slightly speckled appearance and unique habitat preference. Klipspringer means 'rockjumper' in Afrikaans and it is an apt name for an antelope which occurs exclusively in mountainous areas and rocky outcrops throughout Tanzania.

Steenbok (*Raphicerus cempestris*) Sw: *tondoro*. Shoulder height: 50cm; weight: 11kg. This rather nondescript small antelope has red-brown upper parts and clear white underparts, and the male has short straight horns. It is probably the most commonly observed small antelope in Africa, though it has a broken range, and is absent from southern Tanzania despite being common in the north of the country and in areas further south. Like most other antelopes of its size, the steenbok is normally encountered singly or in pairs and tends to 'freeze' when disturbed.

Similar species The **oribi** (*Ourebia ourebi*) is a widespread but uncommon grassland antelope which looks much like a steenbok but stands about 10cm higher at the shoulder and has an altogether more upright bearing. **Kirk's dik-dik** (*Madoqua kirki*), smaller than the steenbok and easily identified by its large white eye circle, is restricted primarily to Tanzania and Kenya, and it is particularly common in Arusha National Park.

Red duiker (*Cephalophus natalensis*) Sw: *pofu*. Shoulder height: 45cm; weight: 14kg. This is the most likely of Africa's 12 to 20 'forest duikers' to be seen by tourists. It is deep chestnut in colour with a white tail and, in the case of the East African race *C. n. harveyi* (sometimes considered to be a separate species) a black face. The red duiker occurs in most substantial forest patches along the eastern side of Africa, though it is less often seen than it is heard crashing through the undergrowth.

Similar species The **blue duiker** (*Cephalophus monticola*) is widespread in Africa and the only other forest duiker to occur in countries south of Tanzania, and it can easily be told from the red duiker by its greyer colouring and much smaller size (it is the smallest forest duiker, about the same size as a suni). **Abbott's duiker** (*Cephalophus spadix*) is a large duiker, as tall as a klipspringer, restricted to a handful of montane forests in Tanzania, including those on Kilimanjaro and the Usambara,

Udzungwa and Poroto Mountains. The endangered **Ader's duiker** (*Cephalophus adersi*) is presumably restricted to forested habitats on Zanzibar Island, where as few as 1,000 animals may survive, most of them in the Jozani Forest. Recent reports suggest that this duiker is extinct in the only other locality where it has been recorded, the Sokoke Forest in Kenya.

Common duiker (*Sylvicapra grimmia*) Sw: *nysa*. Shoulder height: 50cm; weight: 20kg. This anomalous duiker holds itself more like a steenbok and is the only member of its family to occur outside of forests. Generally grey in colour, the common duiker can most easily be separated from other small antelopes by the black tuft of hair that sticks up between its horns. It occurs throughout Tanzania, and tolerates most habitats except for true forest and very open country.

Other large herbivores

African elephant (*Loxodonta africana*) Sw: *tembe*. Shoulder height: 2.3–3.4m; weight: up to 6,000kg. The world's largest land animal, the African elephant is intelligent, social and often very entertaining to watch. Female elephants live in closely knit clans in which the eldest female plays matriarch over her sisters, daughters and granddaughters. Mother-daughter bonds are strong and may last for up to 50 years. Males generally leave the family group at around 12 years to roam singly or form bachelor herds. Under normal circumstances, elephants range widely in search of food and water, but when concentrated populations are forced to live in conservation areas, their habit of uprooting trees can cause serious environmental damage. Elephants are widespread and common in habitats ranging from desert to rainforest and, despite heavy poaching, they are likely to be seen on a daily basis in most of the country's larger national parks, the exception being the Serengeti where they are common only in the Lobo region.

Black rhinoceros (*Diceros bicornis*) Sw: *faru*. Shoulder height: 160cm; weight: 1,000kg. This is the more widespread of Africa's two rhino species, an imposing, sometimes rather aggressive creature that has been poached to extinction in most of its former range. It occurs in many southern African reserves, but is now very localised in East Africa, where it is most likely to be seen in Tanzania's Ngorongoro Crater.

Hippopotamus (*Hippopotamus amphibius*) Sw: *kiboko*. Shoulder height: 150cm; weight: 2,000kg. Characteristic of Africa's large rivers and lakes, this large, lumbering animal spends most of the day submerged, but emerges at night to graze. Strongly territorial, herds of ten or more animals are presided over by a dominant male who will readily defend his patriarchy to the death. Hippos are abundant in most protected rivers and water bodies, and they are still quite common outside of reserves, where they kill more people than any other African mammal.

African buffalo (*Syncerus caffer*) Sw: *nyati*. Shoulder height: 140cm; weight: 700kg. Frequently and erroneously referred to as a water buffalo (an Asian species), the African buffalo is a distinctive ox-like animal that lives in large herds on the savannah and occurs in smaller herds in forested areas. Common and widespread in sub-Saharan Africa, herds of buffalo are likely to be encountered in most Tanzanian reserves and national parks. The best place to see large buffalo herds is on the Ngorongoro Crater floor.

Giraffe (*Giraffa camelopardis*) Sw: *twiga*. Shoulder height: 250–350cm; weight: 1,000–1,400kg. The world's tallest and longest-necked land animal, a fully grown giraffe can measure up to 5.5m high. Quite unmistakable, the giraffe lives in loosely structured herds of up to 15, though herd members often disperse and are seen singly or in smaller groups. Formerly distributed throughout East and southern Africa, the giraffe is now more or less restricted to conservation areas, where it is generally common and easily seen. Two places in Tanzania where there are no giraffe are the part of the Selous south of the Rufiji and the Ngorongoro Crater floor.

Common zebra (*Equus burchelli*) Sw. *punda milia*. Shoulder height: 130cm: weight: 300–340kg. This attractive striped horse is common and widespread throughout most of East and southern Africa, where it is often seen in large herds alongside wildebeest. The common zebra is the only wild equine to occur in Tanzania, and is common in most conservation areas, especially the Serengeti.

Warthog (*Phacochoreus africanus*) Sw: *ngiri*. Shoulder height: 60–70cm; weight: up to 100kg. This widespread and often conspicuously abundant resident of the African savannah is grey in colour with a thin covering of hairs, wartlike bumps on its face, and rather large upward curving tusks. Africa's only diurnal swine, the warthog is often seen in family groups, trotting off briskly with its tail raised stiffly (a diagnostic trait) and a determinedly nonchalant air.

Similar species Bulkier, hairier and browner, the **bushpig** (*Potomochoerus larvatus*) is as widespread as the warthog, but infrequently seen due to its nocturnal habits and preference for dense vegetation. Larger still, weighing up to 250kg, the **giant forest hog** (*Hylochoerus meinertzhageni*) is primarily a species of the West African rainforest, though is does occur in certain highland forests in northern Tanzania, where the chance of a sighting practically non-existent.

Small mammals
Aardvark (*Orycteropus afer*) Shoulder height: 60cm; weight: up to 70kg. This singularly bizarre nocturnal insectivore is unmistakable with its long snout and huge ears. It occurs practically throughout the region, but sightings are extremely rare.

Similar species Not so much similar as equally dissimilar to anything else, **pangolins** are rare nocturnal insectivores with distinctive armour plating and a tendency to roll up in a ball when disturbed. Most likely to be seen in Tanzania is Temminck's pangolin (*Manis temmincki*). Also nocturnal, but spiky rather than armoured, several **hedgehog** and **porcupine** species occur in the region, the former generally no larger than a guinea pig, the latter generally 60–100cm long.

DANGEROUS ANIMALS

The dangers associated with African wild animals have frequently been overstated in the past by the so-called Great White Hunters and others trying to glamorise their chosen way of life. Contrary to the fanciful notions conjured up by images of rampaging elephants, man-eating lions and psychotic snakes, most wild animals fear us more than we fear them, and their normal response to human contact is to flee. That said, many travel guides have responded to the exaggerated ideas of the dangers associated with wild animals by being overly reassuring. The likelihood of a tourist being attacked by an animal is indeed very low, but it can happen, and there have been a number of fatalities caused by such incidents in recent years, particularly in southern Africa.

The need for caution is greatest near water, particularly around dusk and dawn, when **hippos** are out grazing. Hippos are responsible for more human fatalities than any other large mammal, not because they are aggressive but because they tend to panic when something comes between them and the safety of the water. If you happen to be that something, then you're unlikely to live to tell the tale. Never consciously walk between a hippo and water, and never walk along river banks or through reed banks, especially in overcast weather or at dusk or dawn, unless you are certain that no hippos are present. Watch out, too, for **crocodiles**. Only a very large croc is likely to attack a person, and then only in the water or right on the shore. Near towns and other settlements, you can be fairly sure that any very large crocodile will have been disposed of by its potential prey, so the risk is greatest away from human habitation. It is also near water that you are most likely to unwittingly corner a normally placid terrestrial animal – the waterbuck. The population on Crescent Island in Kenya's Lake Naivasha has acquired a nasty reputation for attacking on close approach, and the riverine-forest dwelling bushbuck has a reputation as the most dangerous African antelope when cornered.

There are areas where hikers might still stumble across an **elephant** or a **buffalo**, the most dangerous of Africa's terrestrial herbivores. Elephants almost invariably mock charge and indulge in some hair-raising trumpeting before they attack in earnest. Provided that you back off at the first sign of unease, they are most unlikely to take further notice of you. If you see them before they see you, give them a wide berth, bearing in mind they are most likely to attack if surprised at close proximity. If an animal charges you, the safest course of action is to head for the nearest tree and climb it. Black rhinos are prone to charging without apparent provocation, but they're too rare in Tanzania to be a cause for concern. Elephants are the only animals to pose a potential danger in a vehicle, and much the same advice applies – if an elephant evidently doesn't want you to pass, then back off and wait until it has crossed the road or moved further away before you try again. In general, it's a good idea to leave your engine running when you are close to an elephant, and you should avoid letting yourself be boxed in between an elephant and another vehicle.

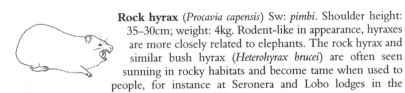

Rock hyrax (*Procavia capensis*) Sw: *pimbi*. Shoulder height: 35–30cm; weight: 4kg. Rodent-like in appearance, hyraxes are more closely related to elephants. The rock hyrax and similar bush hyrax (*Heterohyrax brucei*) are often seen sunning in rocky habitats and become tame when used to people, for instance at Seronera and Lobo lodges in the

There are campsites in Tanzania where **vervet monkeys** and **baboons** have become a pest. Feeding these animals is highly irresponsible, since it encourages them to scavenge and may eventually lead to them being shot. Vervet monkeys are too small to progress much beyond being a nuisance, but baboons are very dangerous and have often killed children and maimed adults with their vicious teeth. Do not tease or underestimate them. If primates are hanging around a campsite, and you wander off leaving fruit in your tent, don't expect the tent to be standing when you return. Chimpanzees are also potentially dangerous, but unlikely to be encountered except on a guided forest walk, when there is little risk provided that you obey your guide's instructions at all times.

The dangers associated with large **predators** are often exaggerated. Most predators stay clear of humans and are only likely to kill accidentally or in self-defence. Lions are arguably the exception, but it is unusual for a lion to attack a human without cause. Should you encounter one on foot, the important thing is not to run, since this is likely to trigger the instinct to give chase. Of the other cats, cheetahs represent no threat and leopards generally attack only when they are cornered. Hyenas are often associated with human settlements, and potentially are very dangerous, but in practise they aren't aggressive towards people and are most likely to slink off into the shadows when disturbed. A slight but real danger when sleeping in the bush without a tent is that a passing hyena or lion might investigate a hairy object sticking out of a sleeping bag, and you might be decapitated through predatorial curiosity. In areas where large predators are still reasonably common, sleeping in a sealed tent practically guarantees your safety – but don't sleep with your head sticking out and don't at any point put meat in the tent.

All manner of venomous **snakes** occurs in Tanzania, but they are unlikely to be encountered since they generally slither away when they sense the seismic vibrations made by a walking person. You should be most alert to snakes on rocky slopes and cliffs, particularly where you risk putting your hand on a ledge that you can't see. Rocky areas are the favoured habitat of the puff adder, which is not an especially venomous snake, but is potentially lethal and unusual in that it won't always move off in response to human foot treads. Wearing good boots when walking in the bush will protect against the 50% of snake bites that occur below the ankle, and long trousers will help deflect bites higher up on the leg, reducing the quantity of venom injected. Lethal snake bites are a rarity (in South Africa, which boasts almost as many venomous snakes as Tanzania, more people are killed by lightning than by snake bites) but some discussion of treatment is included in the chapter on health, page 88.

When all is said and done, the most dangerous animal in Africa, exponentially a greater threat than everything mentioned above, is the anopheles mosquito, which carries the malaria parasite.

Serengeti. The less common tree hyrax (*Dendrohyrax arboreus*) is a nocturnal forest creature which often announces its presence with an unforgettable shrieking call.

Similar species The **elephant shrews** (Sw: *sange*) are rodents that look like miniature kangaroos with absurdly elongated noses. A number of species are recognised, but they are mostly secretive and nocturnal, so rarely seen. I've only ever encountered elephant shrews at Amani in the Usambara Mountains, and in the Selous Game Reserve.

Scrub hare (*Lepus saxatilis*) This is the largest and commonest African hare or rabbit. In some areas a short walk at dusk or after nightfall might reveal three or four scrub hares. They tend to freeze when disturbed.

Unstriped ground squirrel (*Xerus rutilus*) An endearing terrestrial animal of arid savannah, the unstriped ground squirrel is grey to grey-brown with a prominent white eye ring and silvery black tail. It spends much time on its hind legs, and has the characteristic squirrel mannerism of holding food in its forepaws. In Tanzania, it is most likely to be seen in the Serengeti.

Bush squirrel (*Paraxerus cepapi*) This is the typical squirrel of the eastern and southern savannah, rusty brown in colour with a silvery black back and white eye rings. A great many other arboreal or semi-arboreal squirrels occur in the region, but most are difficult to tell apart in the field.

Birds

Tanzania is a birdwatcher's dream, with over 1,000 species recorded. Casual visitors will be stunned at the abundance of bird life: the brilliantly coloured lilac-breasted rollers and superb starlings, the numerous birds of prey, the giant ostrich, the faintly comic hornbills, the magnificent crowned crane – the list could go on forever.

For serious birders, virtually anywhere in Tanzania offers good birding; in many areas a reasonably competent observer could hope to see between 50 and 100 species in a day. Any of the northern reserves are recommended: Arusha and Lake Manyara National Park are both good for forest and water birds; the Serengeti and Tarangire are good for raptors and acacia and grassland species.

Forest is an especially important birding habitat. The forests of the Eastern Arc Mountains hold numerous endemics. Amani and the Udzungwa National Park are the most accessible places for seeing some of these. *Miombo*-associated species can be seen in the southern reserves: the Selous, with the advantage of the many birds which live along the Rufiji River, is particularly recommended. Western reserves such as Gombe Stream and Rubondo Island offer a combination of water and forest habitats, with the possibility of glimpsing one or two West African specials. If you visit Mwanza, don't bypass Saa Nane Island – in an hour there I saw five species I've not seen elsewhere in Tanzania.

Of special interest to birders visiting Tanzania are the 20-odd species thought to be endemic to the country. Details of these birds and where they are most likely to be seen follow.

The **Udzungwa partridge** (*Xenoperdix udzungwensis*) is the sort of bird that gets twitchers frothing: it was discovered in 1991 in Udzungwa National Park, and has been placed in its own genus. It is presumably restricted to forest interiors in the Udzungwa Range. The **rufous-winged sunbird** (*Nectarinia rufipennis*) is another Udzungwa special, a bird of forest undergrowth which was only discovered in 1981. **Lagden's bush shrike** (*Molaconotus lagdeni*) and the **Iringa akalat** (*Sheppardia lowei*) are both restricted to montane forests in the Udzungwa area.

The **Pemba green pigeon** (*Treron pembaensis*) is an attractive species, closely related to the green pigeon found on the mainland, but restricted to Pemba Island. Also unique to this island are the **Pemba white-eye** (*Zosterops vaughni*), **Pemba** sunbird (*Necterinia pembae*) and **Pemba scops owl** (*Otus pembaensis*). Oddly, perhaps, no birds are endemic to Zanzibar Island.

The stunningly beautiful **Fischer's lovebird** (*Agopornis fischeri*) is common in the Serengeti. Arguably, it is no longer a true endemic, as a feral population is found in Naivasha, Kenya, where it regularly interbreeds with the **yellow-collared lovebird** (*Agopornis personata*), another Tanzanian endemic that has gone feral in Kenya. Within its natural range, the yellow-collared lovebird is commonly seen in Tarangire National Park.

Also common in the Serengeti are the **grey-breasted spurfowl** (*Francolinus afer*), a game bird that lives in grassland scattered with trees, and the **rufoustailed weaver** (*Histurgops ruficauda*), an atypical member of the weaver family, which looks and behaves much like a babbler. The rufoustailed weaver is also common in Tarangire National Park, where you can be certain of seeing the **ashy starling** (*Cosmopsarus unicolor*), a rather drab member of this normally colourful group of birds.

Several species are restricted to the montane forests of northeastern Tanzania, among them three varieties of sunbird. The **banded green sunbird** (*Anthreptes longuemarei*) is a bird of forest fringes, while **Loveridge's sunbird** (*Nectarinia loveredgei*) is generally observed in forest undergrowth and **Moreau's sunbird** (*Nectarinia moreaui*) in forest interiors. Birds with a similar habitat preference and distribution are **Nicoll's weaver** (*Ploceus nicolli*) and **Mrs Moreau's warbler** (*Bathmoceros winifredae*).

The final four Tanzania endemics are the **Kungwe apalis** (*Apalis argentea*), found in forest and bamboo east of Lake Tanganyika; the **Uhehe fiscal** (*Lanius marwitzi*) a bird of open country in the Iringa area; the **Tanzanian masked weaver** (*Ploceus reichardi*), which lives in swampy areas in southwestern Tanzania; and the **Kilombera weaver** (*Ploceus burnieri*), which inhabits riverside swamp in the Mahenge region of southeastern Tanzania, along with two recently discovered and still undescribed species of the genus *cisticola*.

Field guides are discussed under *Further Reading*.

Reptiles

The world's largest reptile, the Nile crocodile (Sw: *mamba*), is common in most large rivers and lakes, except where it has been hunted out. On the Rufiji River, in Selous Game Reserve, we saw some of the largest crocodiles we have seen anywhere in Africa. Crocodile feed on a variety of fish and mammals; the latter they drag into the water, submerge till drowned, then store underwater for a period of time until suitably decomposed.

Hundreds of different snakes and lizards are found in Tanzania. Perhaps fortunately, snakes are generally shy and are very seldom seen. You can expect to see lizards everywhere, even in hotel rooms. Saa Nane Island near Mwanza is a prime spot for reptile enthusiasts, with colourful rock agama in abundance, a healthy population of water monitor (Africa's largest lizard which grows up to about 2m long), and a chance of seeing crocodile. Several species of chameleon are found in Tanzania, but though they are common, even in towns, they are difficult to find unless you know where to look. You're most likely to see a chameleon by luck; when you are on safari you could ask your guide to try to find one for you. Don't expect your chameleon to change its skin colour to match its background. This is a myth. Colour change is triggered by emotion.

Cichlids

Lakes Nyasa, Tanganyika and Victoria vie with each other for the distinction of harbouring the most fish species of any lake in the world (though, since the introduction of the Nile perch, many of Lake Victoria's endemics have become extinct; see *Chapter 9*). The majority of these fish are cichlids, a group of colourful fish well known to anyone who keeps a tropical aquarium (particularly the *mbuna* cichlids of Lake Nyasa). Many cichlid species are mouth brooders: the eggs are fertilised and left to hatch in the female's mouth, after which the young are released into secluded rocky crevices where they are safe from predators. If you have a mask and snorkel, the best place to look for cichlids is near rocky stretches of shore on Lakes Nyasa and Tanganyika (see *Matema Beach, Chapter 10*). You should be aware of the fact that areas favoured by cichlids may also attract crocodiles.

HIKING

In the 1980s, the only recognised hiking areas in Tanzania were Mount Kilimanjaro and more recently Mount Meru. Travellers who attempted to hike off the beaten track frequently met with suspicion, and if they did not have a permit they risked being arrested. This is no longer the case, and while few travellers explore the hiking possibilities in Tanzania, there are few obstacles preventing them from doing so.

When you hike through remote villages, it would be polite to exchange greetings with the village chairman. You are also less likely to arouse suspicion if you do this. Be discreet with your camera. Never photograph villagers without asking first and don't photograph anything in the vicinity of bridges, railway lines, radio masts or any other government property. It is forbidden to hike in national parks without a ranger or without paying the entrance fee. If you do the latter you could be arrested.

New hiking areas

It is not only Kilimanjaro and Arusha National Park (Mount Meru) that allow walking. In the west of the country, Rubondo Island and Mahale Mountains can only be explored by foot, while the newer and more accessible Udzungwa Mountains National Park boasts a number of good hiking trails. It is possible to hike in the Ngorongoro Conservation Area with the permission of the Conservation Authority in Arusha. Hiking in national parks is relatively expensive as an entrance fee of US$15–25 per 24 hours is charged along with a camping fee of US$20 per night. You may only hike if you are accompanied by an armed ranger, which costs US$10 per day.

Outside of the national parks, the most accessible areas for hiking are the Usambara and Pare Mountains in the northeast, Mount Hanang near Babati, the Uluguru Mountains near Morogoro, and the Mbeya Range and Poroto Mountains in the far south. As yet, only the Usambara is explored by travellers with any frequency, but all of these areas are beginning to open up and it is relatively easy to get up-to-date information about them.

Maps and equipment

In the national parks you may only walk when accompanied by a guide, so maps are probably not necessary. In the Poroto, Usambara and Mbeya Mountains there are day-hiking possibilities which would not require you to have detailed maps or specialist equipment. If you plan to undertake other hikes in these areas or to explore elsewhere, you will need good maps and equipment, and should ideally have some previous experience of wilderness hiking.

Essential equipment includes a compass, a tent, a sleeping bag and mat, warm clothing for areas at altitudes above about 1,500m, a stove and food, water bottles and, if you are hiking in the wet season, waterproof clothing. Unless you have a fair grip on the language already, a KiSwahili dictionary or phrase book will be more than useful.

You should be able to buy 1:50,000 survey maps of the area you plan to visit from the Department of Lands and Surveys in Dar es Salaam. This is a straightforward procedure and maps cost no more than $2 apiece. You must decide where you want to hike before you leave Dar es Salaam. You will not be able to get hold of maps elsewhere in the country.

Planning Your Trip

TOURIST INFORMATION

The Tanzania Tourist Board (TTB) has improved greatly over recent years, and their offices in London, New York, Stockholm, Milan and Frankfurt may be able to supply you with an information pack and leaflets about the country.

Head office PO Box 2485, Dar es Salaam; tel: 051 111244; fax: 051 116420; email: md@ttb.ud.or.tz
UK Tanzania Tourist Office, 78-80 Borough High St, London SE1; tel: 0171 407 0566
US Tanzania Tourist Office, 210 E 42 Street, New York, NY 10017; tel: 212 986 7124

WHEN TO VISIT

You can visit Tanzania at any time of year. Each season has different advantages, and unless you have strong reasons to travel in a certain season, I would tend to let the timing of your visit be dictated by your schedule at home rather than seasons in Tanzania. For those with the option, there is much to be said for trying to avoid peak tourist seasons, as the parks and other main tourist attractions will be less crowded, and you can often negotiate camping safaris at prices that wouldn't be offered in season. Broadly speaking, tourism arrivals are highest during the northern hemisphere winter, while the low season runs from the end of the Easter weekend until the end of September, though this is distorted by a surge of tourism over June and July, when the wildebeest migration is on in the Serengeti.

The rainy season between November and April is a good time to visit the Serengeti; it is when the countryside is greenest, and it offers the best bird-watching, with resident species supplemented by a number of Palaearctic and intra-African migrants. The rainy season is hotter than the period May to October, but in most parts of the country this will only be by a matter of a couple of degrees. The seasonal difference in temperature is most noticeable along the humid coast, which can be rather uncomfortable in the hotter months. The wettest months are March and April, when parts of the country may experience storms virtually on a daily basis.

The dry season, in particular March and September, offers the best trekking conditions on Mount Kilimanjaro and Meru. The dry season is the best time for hiking generally, and for travelling in parts of the country with poor roads. Temperatures at the coast tend to be more bearable during the dry season, which is also considerably safer than the wet season in terms of malaria and other mosquito-borne diseases.

RED TAPE

Check well in advance that you have a valid **passport**, and one that won't expire within six months of the date on which you intend leaving Tanzania. Should your passport be lost or stolen, it will generally be easier to get a replacement if you have a photocopy of the important pages.

If there is any possibility you'll want to drive or hire a vehicle while you're in the country, do organise an **international driving licence** (any AA office in a country in which you're licensed to drive will do this for a nominal fee), which you may be asked to produce together with your original license. You may sometimes be asked at borders for an **international health certificate** showing you've had a yellow fever shot.

For security reasons, it's advisable to detail all your important information on one sheet of paper, photocopy it, and distribute a few copies in your luggage, your money-belt, and amongst relatives or friends at home, The sort of things you want to include on this are your travellers' cheque numbers and refund information, travel insurance policy details and 24-hour emergency contact number, passport number, details of relatives or friends to be contacted in an emergency, bank and credit card details, camera and lens serial numbers etc.

Visas

Visas are required by most visitors to Tanzania. At the time of writing, nationals of some Commonwealth countries are exempt from visa requirements, as are nationals of the Scandinavian countries and the Republic of Ireland, but such rulings can change, and it would be advisable for all visitors to check the current situation in advance. If you do require a visa, it *must* be obtained in advance from a Tanzanian Embassy or High Commission. Since early 1996, British nationals require a visa to enter Tanzania, at a cost of £38 (US$50).

All visitors (assuming that they have a visa if required) will have a visitor's pass stamped in their passport when they enter the country. This is issued free and without any fuss when you enter the country. For many years, immigration officials refused to grant a visitor's pass for longer than one month, but on our most recent visit the entry stamp read 'Allowed to stay for three months, employment prohibited', so presumably a three-month period is now standard. If your visitor's pass does expire before three months, it can be extended at any Immigration Office with a minimum of fuss. This is best done in a small town; in Dar es Salaam or Arusha you will face a long queue.

Embassies abroad

There are Tanzanian embassies or high commissions in Angola, Belgium, Britain, Burundi, Canada, China, CIS, Congo, Egypt, Ethiopia, France, Germany, Guinea, India, Japan, Kenya, Mozambique, Namibia, Netherlands, Nigeria, Rwanda, Sudan, Sweden, Uganda, USA, Zambia and Zimbabwe. Below are addresses of those you are most likely to need.

Belgium 363 Avenue Louise, 1050 Brussels; tel: 640 65/640 65-27; direct line: 647 67 49; fax: 646 80 26

Canada 50 Range Road, Ottawa, Ontario KIN 8JA; tel: 613 232 1500/1509; fax: 612 232 5184

Germany Botschaft der Vereinigte Republik von Tansania, Theaterplatz 26, 5300 Bonn, Germany; tel: 0228 358051-4; fax: 0228 358226

Netherlands Prinsessegracht 32, 2514 AP The Hague; tel: 070 365 3800-1; direct line: 070 364 6981; fax: 070 310 6686

UK High Commission of the United Republic of Tanzania, 43 Hertford St, London, England W1Y 8DB; tel: 0171-499 8951; fax: 0171-491 9321

US Embassy of the United Republic of Tanzania, 2139 R Street NW, Washington DC 2000, USA; tel: 202 9396129

Zimbabwe Ujamaa House, 23 Baines Avenue, P O Box 4841, Harare; tel: 4721870; direct line: 4722626; fax: 4724172

Immigration and customs

Once stringently enforced, the official requirements for entering Tanzania are an onward ticket (a ticket out of Tanzania) and sufficient funds (common wisdom is that this is around US$1,000). These days, however, immigration officials seem a lot more relaxed than a few years back; in practice you are most unlikely to be asked about funds provided that you arrive with a return air ticket, and neither ruling is likely to be raised at an overland border. Nevertheless, if you will be arriving with less than US$1,000 on your person, it might be worth carrying a credit card, which will normally be considered to be as good as cash or travellers' cheques.

Assuming that your papers are in order, the only situation in which you are likely to hit problems upon entering Tanzania is with a one-way ticket (though a ticket home from another African country will normally be as good as a return ticket). You obviously won't have an onward ticket if you fly into Tanzania to start extended African travels and only plan to buy a ticket home at a later stage. The smarter you are in appearance, and the more money you have, the less likely it is you'll be refused entry. A credit card will help you to get through, and a visa or visitor's pass for a neighbouring country will back up your claim that you plan to become that country's problem within a reasonable time span. I have met plenty of travellers who flew into Tanzania without an onward ticket, and none had a problem. At the very worst, you may have to buy an air ticket home at the airport before you are allowed to enter the country, in which case you ought to get a ticket for a day as far in advance as the airline and immigration officials will accept, and to check with the airline whether the ticket will be refundable.

GETTING TO TANZANIA
By air

The following airlines fly to Tanzania from Europe or the United Kingdom: Aeroflot, Air Tanzania, British Airways, Gulf Air, KLM, Lufthansa and Swissair. African airlines which fly to Tanzania from elsewhere in Africa include Air Botswana, Air Tanzania, Air Zimbabwe, EgyptAir, Ethiopian Airlines, Kenya Airways, Royal Swazi, South African Airways and Zambia Airways.

There are two international airports on the Tanzanian mainland. The airport at Dar es Salaam is used by the majority of international airlines, and it is the main point of entry for businessmen, but for most tourists Dar is no more than a point of entry, and many hop straight on to flights elsewhere in the country. Kilimanjaro International Airport, which lies midway between Moshi and Arusha, is the more convenient point of entry for tourists, and following recent privatisation is it likely to catch on with more international airlines. For the meantime, however, only a few airlines fly directly to Kilimanjaro from outside the country, most prominently the national carrier Air Tanzania. Quite a number of international flights land at Zanzibar, and many tourists fly into East Africa at Nairobi and transfer from there to Arusha by road or local flight. Once in Tanzania, a good network of domestic flights connects Kilimanjaro, Dar es Salaam and Zanzibar, as well as other less visited towns. You will generally get a better price (and will definitely save yourself a lot of hassle) by booking all your international and domestic flights as a package from home.

Budget travellers looking for flights to East Africa may well find it cheapest to use an airline that takes an indirect route, such as Aeroflot or EgyptAir.

London is the best place to pick up a cheap ticket; many continental travellers buy their tickets there. It is generally cheaper to fly to Nairobi than to Dar es Salaam, and getting from Nairobi to Arusha by shuttle bus is cheap, simple and quick. Be warned, however, that a high proportion of travellers are robbed during their first few days in Nairobi, so it isn't the greatest introduction to the continent. Nairobi is the best place to pick up cheap tickets out of East Africa. For short stays in East Africa, some of the best deals are charter flights to Mombasa (Kenya), a few hours' bus ride from Tanga, or an overnight train ride from Nairobi.

When you fly out of Tanzania, a $20 airport tax must be paid in hard currency. Travellers cheques' are *not* accepted.

Getting a flight that lets you feel as if you've got a good deal is becoming more daunting as local flight specialists fight with global flight consolidators. Put eveybody on the internet and the competition just gets hotter. Below is a list of operators who give good service at a reasonable price. Getting the cheapest price will require several calls and may result in some rather complicated rerouting of the plane.

From the UK

Bridge the World targets the independent traveller. Their offices are at 47 Chalk Farm Road, Camden Town, London, NW1 8AJ; tel: 0171 911 0900; fax: 0171 813 3350; email: sales@bridge-the-world.co.uk; web: www.b-t-w.co.uk.

Flight Centre is an independent flight provider with over 450 outlets worldwide. In the UK head office is at Level 3, Broadway House, Wimbledon, SW19 1RL; tel: 0990 666677; fax: 0181 541 5120. They also have offices in Australia, New Zealand, South Africa and Canada.

Quest Worldwide 4/10 Richmond Road, Kingston-Upon-Thames, Surrey, KT2 5HL; tel: 0181 547 3322; fax: 0181 547 3320. An independent agent that has been in operation for nine years offering competitive prices specialising in long-haul flights.

STA Travel 6 Wrights Lane, London W8 6TA; tel: 0171 361 6262; fax: 0171 937 9570; email: enquiries@statravel.co.uk; web: www.statravel.co.uk. STA has 12 branches in London and 25 or so around the country and at a different university sites. STA also has several branches and associate organisation around the world.

Trailfinders has several offices around the UK. The main office is in London at 194 Kensington High Street, London, W8 7RG; tel: 0171 938 3939; fax: 0171 938 3305; web: www.trailfinders.com. With origins in the discount flight market, Trailfinders now provides a one-stop travel service including visa and passport service, travel clinic and foreign exchange.

Travel Bag provide tailor made flight schedules and holidays for destinations throughout the world. Their main office is at 12 High Street, Alton, Hampshire, GU34 1BN; tel: 01420 541441. The London office is at 52 Regent Street, London, W1R; tel: 0171 287 5535; fax: 0171 287 4522; email: freequote3@travelbag.co.uk; web: www.travelbag-adventures.co.uk.

Travel Mood provide flights and tailor made holidays. 214 Edgware Road, London, W2 1DS; tel: 0171 258 0280; fax: 0171 258 0180.

USIT Campus Travel Head office is at 52 Grosvenor Gardens, London, SW1W 0AG; tel: 0171 730 8111; fax: 0171 730 6893; web: www.usitcampus.co.uk. 40 branches around the country focusing on students and people under 26.

WEXAS is more of a club than a travel agents. Membership is around £40 a year but for frequent fliers the benefits are many. 45–49 Brompton Road, Knightsbridge, London SW3 1DE; tel: 0171 589 3315; fax: 44 171 5898418; email: mship@wexas.com; web: www.wexas.com.

From the USA

Airtech 584 Broadway, Suite 1007, New York, NY 10012; tel: 800 575 TEC or 212 219 7000; email: fly@airtech.com; web: www.airtech.com. Standby seat broker that also deals in consolidator fares, courier flights and a host of other travel related services.
Around the World Travel provides fares for destinations throughout the world. 411 4th Ave, Suite 430, Seattle, WA 98101; tel: 877 327 3638; fax: 206 223 1865; email: travel@netfare.net; web: www.netfare.net.
Council on International Educational Exchange is at 205 East 42nd St, New York, NY 10017-5706; tel: 212 822 2600; fax: 212 822 2699; email: info@ciee.org; web: www.ciee.org. Although Council focus on work exchange trips they also have a large travel department.
Council Travel sells cheap tickets at over 60 offices around the US. The New York office is at 205 East 42nd St, New York, NY 10017-5706; tel: 212 822 2700; web: www.counciltravel.com.
National Centre for Educational Travel has been providing cheap travel services for over 30 years. They are at 438 N Frances St, Madison, WI 53703; tel: 800 747 5551 or 608 256 5551; fax: 301 384 9289; email: ncet@idt.net; web: www2.ios.com/~ncet/.
STA Travel has several branches around the country. Freephone on 800 777 0112. A selection of city branches include; 120 Broadway #108, Santa Monica, Los Angeles, CA 90401; tel: 310 394 5126; fax: 310 394 4041; 10 Downing Street (6th Ave and Bleecker), New York, NY 10014; tel: 212 627 3111; fax: 212 627 3387; 4341 University Way NE, Seattle, WA 98105; tel: 206 633 5000; fax: 206 633 5027.
Worldtek Travel operates a network of rapidly growing travel agencies. For your nearest office contact 111 Water Street, New Haven, CT 06511; tel: 800 243 1723 or 203 777 1483; email: dave.smith@worldtek.com; web: www.worldtek.com.

From Canada

Flight Centre is at 604–1200 West Pender, Vancouver, V6E 2S9; tel: 604 606 9000 or freephone: 188 WORLD31; fax: 604 664 0334.
Travel CUTS is a Canadian student travel organisation with 60 offices throughout Canada. Based in Toronto at 187 College Street, Toronto, M5T 1P7; tel 416 979 2406; fax: 416 979 8167. Call the telephone sales centre toll free on 800 667 2887 for your nearest branch or visit the website at www.travelcuts.com.

From Australia

AusTravel's head office in Australia is at 7 Macquarte Place, Sydney, NSW 2000; tel 2 92 47 48 33; fax: 2 92 51 35 41; email: ausops@oze.mail.com.au. web: www.austravel.com. They also have several offices in Europe and the US.
Flight Centre has over 200 stores in Australia. Head office is at 157 Ann Street, Brisbane, Queensland 4000; freephone: 133 133.
STA Travel is at Shop 10 The Village Centre, 24-30 Springfield Avenue, Kings Cross, Sydney NSW 2011; tel: 2 9368 1111; fax: 2 9368 1609.

From New Zealand

A good starting point for cheap airfares is **Flight Centre** Level 7, 48 Emily Place, Auckland, New Zealand; tel: 0800 FLIGHTS; fax: 9 379 8798.

From South Africa

Flight Centre Shop L3, Eastgate Centre, Bradford Road, Bedfordview, Johannesburg 2008; tel: 11 622 5634; fax: 11 622 5642.
Student Travel Centre is linked to the STA network. The Arcade, 62 Mutual Gardens, Corner of Oxford Road & Tyrwhitt Avenue, Rosebank, Johannesburg 2196; tel: 11 447 5551; fax: 11 447 5775.

Tour operators

Two London travel agents which specialise in Africa include:

Africa Travel Centre 4 Medway Court, 21 Leigh Street, London WC1H 9QX; tel: 0171 387 1211; fax: 0171 383 7512

African Travel Specialists Glen House, Stag Place, London SW1E 5AG; tel: 0171 630 5434; fax: 0171 630 5470

Other UK tour operators which feature Tanzania include:

Abercrombie & Kent Sloane Square House, Holbein Place, London SW1W 8NS; tel: 0171 730 9600; fax: 0171 730 9376

Art of Travel 21 The Bakehouse, 119 Altonburg Gardens, London SW11 1JQ; tel: 0171 738 2038; fax: 0171 738 1893

Bukima 55 Huddlestone Road, London NW2 5DL; tel: 0181 451 2446

Cordial Tours 7 Stokes Drive, Sleaford, Lincs NG34 8BA; tel/fax: 01529 415419

Crusader Travel 57 Church Street, Twickenham, Middlesex TW1 3NR; tel: 0181 892 7606; fax: 0181 744 0574

Explore Worldwide 1 Frederick St, Aldershot, Hants GU11 1LQ; tel: 01252 319448; fax: 01252 343170

Footloose 105 Leeds Rd, Ilkley, West Yorks LS29 8EG; tel: 01943 604030; fax: 01943 604070

Footprint Adventures 5 Malham Drive, Lincoln LN6 0XD; tel: 01522 690852; fax: 01522 501392

Gane & Marshall 98 Crescent Rd, New Barnet, Herts EN4 9NJ; tel: 0181 441 9592; fax: 0181 441 7376

Grenadier Safaris 11–12 Stockwell St, Colchester, Essex CO1 1HN; tel: 01206 549585; fax: 01206 561337

High Places Globe Works, Penistone Rd, Sheffield S6 3AE; tel: 0114 275 7500; fax: 0114 275 3870

Okavango Tours & Safaris Gadd House, Arcadia Av, Finchley, London N3 2TJ; tel: 0181 343 3283; fax: 0181 343 3287

Peak International Tel: 01296 624225

Phoenix Expeditions 52 Roydene Crescent, Leicester LE4 0GL; tel: 01509 881818; fax: 01509 881822

Safari Drive Wessex House, 127 High Street, Hungerford, Berks RG17 7XA; tel: 01488 681611; fax: 01488 685055

Scott Dunn World Tel: 0181 672 1234.

Tim Best Travel Tel: 0171 591 0300; fax: 0171 591 0301

Wildlife Discovery 29 Bell St, Reigate, Surrey RH2 7AD; tel: 01737 223903; fax: 01737 241102

For safari specialists, see pages 121–4.

Overland

All of the established overland routes between Europe and East Africa are difficult at present, though depending on the current political situation (and right now the Eritrea-Ethiopia border area is a problem), it may be possible to get to East Africa via Egypt, northern Sudan, Eritrea and Ethiopia. I've probably met four or five people who've used this route in the last three years, but it's not easy to predict the local political situation in advance, and many people get stuck in the Sudan and either have to turn back or else fly from Khartoum to Ethiopia or Kenya, an expensive option. As for the so-called 'Nile Route', a variant on the above passing through southern Sudan to Uganda, the south of Sudan has been closed to tourists for nigh on a decade.

The final route, via the Sahara and West Africa, was used by several overland truck companies until recently, but it has been shut down for a couple of years, at first due to banditry, more recently after a major bridge collapsed in what was then Zaire, and at the time of writing due to the civil war in what is currently the Democratic Republic of the Congo. This route has always been tough going for independent travellers, whether or not they have a vehicle, and in the present climate of instability I would advise anybody who is considering travelling this way to think seriously about going with an overland truck company. However you plan to travel, it would be advisable to contact a couple of overland truck companies for current advice about safety.

With the end of apartheid, the Cape to Nairobi route has become the backpackers' standard in Africa. Some people start this trip in East Africa, others start in South Africa – there's not a lot in it. The advantage of starting in the south is that you can adapt to African conditions in the more organised environment of South Africa and Zimbabwe before you hit the relative chaos of East Africa; the disadvantage is that you will have to put up with the most trying travel conditions of the trip towards the end, after the novelty of being in Africa has worn off. These days Johannesburg is almost as good as Nairobi for cheap air tickets, so that is not a factor. Either way, my regional guide *East and Southern Africa: The Backpackers Manual*, also published by Bradt, is the only book to cover the full range of backpacking possibilities between Ethiopia and South Africa in one dedicated volume.

There is a proliferation of overland truck companies which run regular trips between southern Africa (normally Johannesburg or Harare) and East Africa. A few of these are:

Acacia Expeditions Ltd, Lower Ground Floor, 23A Craven Terrace, London W2 3QH; tel: 0171 706 4700; fax: 0171 706 4686

Dragoman Camp Green, Kenton Rd, Debenham, Suffolk IP14 6LA; tel: 01728 861133; fax: 01728 861127

Exodus 9 Weir Rd, London SW12 0LT; tel: 0181 675 5550; fax: 0181 673 0779

Kumuku 40 Earls Court Rd, Kensington, London S8 6EJ; tel: 0171 937 8855; fax: 0171 937 6664

Tana Travel 2 Ely St, Stratford-upon-Avon, Warwicks CV37 6LW; tel: 01789 414200; fax: 01789 414420

Truck Africa 6 Hurlingham Studios, Ranelagh Gardens, Fulham, London SW6 3PA; tel: 0171 731 6142

The advantages of travelling on an overland truck are that it will visit remote areas which you would be unlikely to reach otherwise, and that you will see far more than you would by travelling independently for the same period of time. The disadvantages are that you will be in the company of the same 10 to 20 other people for the duration of the trip, and that the truck will cut you off from everyday African life. Most of the people I've spoken to say their main reason for travelling on a truck is safety. It's worth noting, therefore, that this is by-and-large a safe and well-travelled region (something that cannot be said for the overland truck route between Europe and Nairobi via West Africa) and that you will meet plenty of other single travellers. If you feel you would prefer to travel independently, don't let fear swing you in the opposite direction.

Border crossings

Tanzania borders eight countries. A brief outline of frequently used border crossings follows:

To/from Kenya

The most popular crossing is between Nairobi and Arusha via the Namanga border post, and several shuttle bus services run along this route daily in both directions. A reliable option is the Devanu Shuttle, which connects Nairobi to Arusha and Moshi, departing in either direction at 07.30 and 13.30 daily. The trip from Nairobi to Arusha lasts about four hours, and a ticket costs around US$20 one-way. You can book onto the shuttle at most tour operators in any of these towns, or ring 057 4311 in Arusha or 02 222002 in Nairobi.

You can also do the trip between Nairobi and Arusha in stages, by catching a minibus between Nairobi and Namanga (these leave Nairobi from Ronald Ngala Road), crossing the border on foot, and then catching a shared taxi to Arusha. Expect this to take around six hours and cost US$7 total in fares.

Provided your papers are in order, Namanga is a very straightforward border crossing. There is a bank where you can change money during normal banking hours. At other times, you'll have to change money with private individuals – don't change more than you need to as there are several con artists about.

An increasingly popular route between Kenya and Tanzania is from Mombasa to Tanga (three to four hours following recent improvements on the road) or Dar es Salaam. Again, this is straightforward enough, and a couple of buses do the run every day. If you arrive at Tanga after about 13.00, you are strongly advised against taking the bus all the way to Dar es Salaam, as it arrives after dark and you run a high risk of being mugged.

Another route is between Kisumu and Mwanza on Lake Victoria. There are several buses daily along this route, leaving in the early morning and taking around 12 hours.

Several airlines run daily flights between Nairobi and Kilimanjaro International Airport.

To/from Uganda

The best way to cross from Uganda to Tanzania depends on which part of Tanzania you want to visit. The weekly ferry service between Port Bell and Mwanza was suspended after the MV *Bukoba* sank in 1996, but it resumed in early 1999 (see page 252). If that doesn't fit in with your timing, the alternative is to travel by road from Masaka to Bukoba, by ferry from Bukoba to Mwanza and then by train to Dar es Salaam on the coast or Kigoma on Lake Tanganyika. If you are in Uganda and want to get to Arusha or Moshi, it will be quicker, cheaper and more comfortable to travel via Kenya.

The direct route between Masaka and Bukoba passes through the Mutukula border post. If all goes well, you can get from Masaka to Mutukula in a couple of hours. Regular minibuses go as far as Kyotera, where you won't have to wait long to find a pick-up truck going through to Mutukula. If you arrive at Mutukula in the late afternoon and don't think you are going to get as far as Bukoba, you may want to stay at the basic guest house on the Ugandan side of the border and cross into Tanzania the following morning. The road between Mutukula and Bukoba is fairly rough, but a couple of 4x4 vehicles travel up and down it every day with the express purpose of transporting passengers. These take ages to fill up, so it's also worth seeing if you can get a lift with a truck. If you can get a lift as far as Kyaka, there's more transport to Bukoba from there. For details of ferries between Bukoba and Mwanza, see *Chapter 14* (page 252).

Travellers who are heading between Uganda and Arusha via Kenya can travel between Kampala and Nairobi in a day, using any of a number of bus companies. The Akamba Bus is recommended, as is the Lafiq bus. The latter connects with the same company's service from Nairobi to Dar es Salaam via Arusha and Moshi. If you are just passing through Nairobi, remember that it is East Africa's crime capital, and that wandering around with all your luggage on your back is practically asking to be mugged.

To/from Rwanda
The only route between Kigali and Mwanza is by road. This has never been a very popular route, even before Rwanda erupted into genocidal civil war in 1994, and I've not heard of any traveller passing this way since then. For what it's worth, in 1992 you could get public transport between Kigali and the border at Rusumu, where there was a friendly but basic guesthouse on the Tanzanian side. From Rusumu, it was easy to get a truck through to Geita, where there are plenty of guesthouses and also buses through to Mwanza.

To/from Burundi
The straightforward option is the Lake Tanganyika ferry (see *Chapter 9*). The trip can also be done in steps. Minibuses go from Bujumbura to the immigration office at Nyanza Lac and on to the border. At Kagunga, a 20-minute walk past the border, lake taxis run to Gombe Stream and Kalalangabo, 3km from Kigoma. Burundi is another country with a troubled recent history, and if the Lake Tanganyika ferry isn't running there, I would tend to assume it's for a good reason.

To/from the Congo
Cargo boats between Kigoma and Kalemie might sometimes carry passengers, but don't rely on this. Most people used to go via Burundi, but this whole part of central Africa is too dangerous for travel to be recommended.

To/from Zambia
Zambia, the main gateway between East and southern Africa, can be reached by boat or rail. Tazara trains run twice-weekly from Dar es Salaam to Kapiri Mposhi, and are met by a bus to Lusaka. From western Tanzania, the easiest way to get to Zambia is on the Lake Tanganyika ferry (see *Chapter 9*).

To/from Malawi
The turn-off to the Malawi border is 5km from Kyela, on the Mbeya road. From there you can either take a bicycle taxi to the border or wait for a lift. In Malawi, a bus to Karonga arrives at the border at 19.00 and leaves at 06.00. It is forbidden to stay overnight at the border so the bus is of no use to travellers. However, provided that you arrive at the border before late afternoon, you should have no difficulty picking up a ride on a pick-up truck to Karonga.

To/from Mozambique
The only viable border crossing from Tanzania to Mozambique is between Mtwara and Palma. This can be done either by road or by sea, and either way you should be prepared for a bit of adventure. To cross by road, first catch a Land Rover from Mtwara to Mwambo, where you will get your exit stamp, then walk for 5km to the village on the north bank of the Rovumu River, where you will find dugout canoes crossing to Mozambique, then walk another 2km to the immigration office at Namiranga. From here, it's 50km to Palma, and until recently most people had to walk it, or to hang around for a few days in hope of a lucky lift. However, we met a traveller who came this way in mid-1998, and there is now a Land Rover which transports the immigration officials between the border post and Palma

daily and will give travellers a lift for a fee. It leaves the border in the evening at 19.00, and while I don't know at exactly what time it leaves Palma, it would presumably have to be early enough for the officials to be on duty at around 07.00.

To go by sea, take a bus from Mtwara to the nearby fishing village of Msimbati, where you can complete immigration formalities and, depending on the tides and weather, negotiate for space on a dhow heading south (expect to pay around US$6-7 per person). The trip shouldn't take more than ten hours, depending on the weather and where the boat is heading to. If you're lucky, you'll be dropped right at Palma or Mocimboa do Praia, but you may also be dropped on a beach somewhere and have to walk to Palma. If you are heading in the opposite direction, things are much simpler, since you can pick up a dhow at either Palma or Mocimboa do Praia and you'll almost certainly be dropped at Msimbati.

PACKING

There are two simple rules to bear in mind when you decide what to take with you to Tanzania, particularly for those using public transport. Rule one is to bring with you *everything* that you could possibly need and that mightn't be readily available when you need it. Rule two is to carry as little as possible. Somewhat contradictory rules, you might think, and you'd be right – so the key is finding the right balance, something that probably depends on personal experience as much as anything. Worth stressing is that most genuine necessities are surprisingly easy to get hold of in the main centres in Tanzania, and that most of the ingenious gadgets you can buy in camping shops are unlikely to amount to much more than deadweight on the road. If it came to it, you could easily travel in Tanzania with little more than a change of clothes, a few basic toiletries and a medical kit.

Carrying your luggage

Visitors who are unlikely to be carrying their luggage for any significant distance will probably want to pack most of it in a conventional suitcase. Make sure it is tough and durable, and that it seals well, so that its contents will survive bumpy drives to the game reserves. A lock is a good idea, not only for flights, but for when you leave your case in a hotel room – in our experience, any theft from upmarket hotels in Africa is likely to be casual, and a locked suitcase is unlikely to be tampered with. A daypack will be useful when on safari, and you should be able to pack your luggage in such a manner than any breakable goods can be carried separately in the body of the vehicle and on your lap when necessary – anything like a Walkman or camera will suffer heavily from vibrations on rutted roads.

If you are likely to use public transport, then a backpack is the most practical way to carry your luggage. An internal frame is more flexible than an external one. Once again, ensure your pack is durable, that the seams and zips are properly sewn, and that it has several pockets. If you intend doing a lot of hiking, you definitely want a backpack designed for this purpose. On the other hand, if you'll be staying at places where it might be a good idea to shake off the sometimes negative image attached to backpackers, then there would be obvious advantages in using a suitcase that converts into a backpack.

Before I started travelling with piles of camera equipment, my preference over either of the above was for a robust 35cl daypack. The advantages of keeping luggage as light and compact as possible are manifold. For starters, you can rest it on your lap on bus trips, avoiding complications such as extra charges for luggage, arguments about where your bag should be stored, and the slight but real risk of theft if your luggage ends up on the roof. A compact bag also makes for greater mobility, whether you're hiking or looking for a hotel in town. The sacrifice?

Leave behind camping equipment and a sleeping bag. Do this, and it's quite possible to fit everything you truly need into a 35cl day pack, and possibly even a few luxuries – I refuse to travel without binoculars, a bird field guide and at least five novels, and am still able to keep my weight down to around 8kg. Frankly, it puzzles me what the many backpackers who wander around with an enormous pack and absolutely no camping equipment actually carry around with them!

If your luggage won't squeeze into a daypack, a sensible compromise is to carry a large daypack in your rucksack. That way, you can carry a tent and other camping equipment when you need it, but at other times reduce your luggage to fit into a daypack and leave what you're not using in storage.

Travellers carrying a lot of valuable items should look for a pack that can easily be padlocked. A locked bag can, of course, be slashed open, but in Tanzania you are still most likely to encounter casual theft of the sort to which a lock would be real deterrent.

Camping equipment

If you go on a budget safari or do an organised Kilimanjaro climb, camping equipment will be provided by the company you travel with. Taken together with the limited opportunities for camping outside of the safari circuit, this means that for most travellers a tent and sleeping bag will be dead weight in Tanzania. Nevertheless, it is advisable to carry a tent if you plan to travel or hike in remote areas.

If you decide to carry camping equipment, the key is to look for the lightest available gear. It is now possible to buy a lightweight tent weighing little more than 2kg, but make sure that the one you buy is mosquito-proof. Other essentials for camping include a sleeping bag and a roll-mat, which will serve as both insulation and padding. You might want to carry a stove for occasions when no firewood is available, as is the case in many montane national parks where the collection of firewood is forbidden, or for cooking in a tropical storm. If you do carry a stove, it's worth knowing that Camping Gaz cylinders are not readily available in Tanzania. A box of firelighter blocks will get a fire going in the most unpromising conditions. It would also be advisable to carry a pot, plate, cup and cutlery.

Clothes

Assuming that you have the space, you ought to carry at least one change of shirt and underwear for every day you will spend on safari. Organising laundry along the way is a pain in the neck, and the dusty conditions will practically enforce a daily change of clothes. It's a good idea to keep separate one or two shirts for evening use only.

Otherwise, and especially if you are travelling with everything on your back, try to keep your clothes to a minimum, bearing in mind that you can easily and cheaply replace worn items in markets. In my opinion, the minimum you need is one or possibly two pairs of trousers and/or skirts, one pair of shorts, three shirts or T-shirts, one light sweater, maybe a light waterproof wind-breaker during the rainy season, enough socks and underwear to last five to seven days, one solid pair shoes or boots for walking, and one pair of sandals, thongs or other light shoes.

When you select your clothes, remember that jeans are heavy to carry, hot to wear, and slow to dry. Far better to bring light cotton trousers, and if you intend spending a while in montane regions, tracksuit bottoms which will provide extra cover on chilly nights. Skirts are best made of a light natural fabric such as cotton. T-shirts are lighter and less bulky than proper shirts, though the top pocket of a

PHOTOGRAPHY

Tanzania's abundant wildlife, varied scenery and colourfully dressed people are a photographer's dream, and it only takes a small amount of forethought and care to come home with something more appealing than blurred snapshots.

Film

For landscapes and people, low speed 50, 64 and 100 ASA films are ideal. For close-up shots of animals, faster speeds such as 400 ASA will be better, provided that you are working with print film (slide films of 200 ASA or greater tend to produce very grainy results). Print film in the 200 to 400 ASA range is sold at most safari lodges, and in Dar es Salaam, Arusha, Zanzibar and Moshi, but it may be difficult to get hold of elsewhere in the country. If you use slide film or have other specific requirements, bring what you need with you. Slide film is often difficult to get locate in Tanzania, and when you do find it, it's unlikely to have been stored in suitable conditions. Most people tend to go a bit crazy with their camera on safari, so bring plenty of film – five reels for every day you spend on safari is realistic.

Equipment

If you are buying a camera especially for the trip, bear in mind that the simpler the camera is, the less there is to go wrong. This is not so much of a concern on a short holiday, but may be a consideration for a longer and rougher trip, since complex electronic gadgetry is highly sensitive to rain and dust. A solid and reliable camera for long trips in African conditions is the Pentax K1000; a good second-hand one shouldn't cost more than £100 in London. A simple manual focus camera of this sort with a 50 lens (or better 28-70 zoom) will be adequate for photographing landscapes and people. For animal photography, however, a high magnification zoom lens is essential (200 magnification is the minimum that is adequate, 300 or greater is even better). You will have a far higher success rate with an autofocus camera, since animals rarely stay still for long.

Don't forget to bring a couple of spare lens caps and enough batteries.

Dust and heat

In most game reserves, conditions are very dusty, particularly in the dry season, and photographers should make every effort to keep their film and equipment sealed from dust. As far as possible, keep your camera equipment in a sealed bag or covered in a towel, and stow your films in an airtight container or plastic bag. Leave behind any used films in your hotel room, and change film only when the vehicle is stationary. In open-topped vehicles, you should also try to avoid letting camera equipment and film lie in direct sunlight – a small cooler bag is the ideal film container, offering some protection against both heat and dust.

Photographic tips

You will generally get the best results when you photograph in the hour or two of soft light that follows the dawn and precedes sunset. However, this is also when your light readings will be lowest, and as a rule of thumb you are likely to suffer a degree of camera shake (creating a blurred effect) whenever your shutter speed reading is lower than the magnification of your lens – for instance when you need to use a shutter-speed of 150 using a 300 lens. This is an everyday problem when you're in game reserves, and the solution is to lean on a makeshift support such as a beanbag or pillow (or even a couple of T-shirts stuffed into another one), which will generally allow you to shoot at a shutter speed as low as 60. You are also likely to suffer from camera shake when the vehicle's engine is switched on.

It is advisable to shoot *all* photos with the sun directly behind you (side lighting can produce stunning effects in soft light, but it requires careful handling). You'll get more animated wildlife shots by waiting until the sun catches the eye of any animal or person you want to photograph. On safari, try to resist the temptation to take all your photos out of the roof, as this can create unnatural angles, particularly when the animal is close to the vehicle. Far better to shoot through the window, catching the animal square on. There are, of course, exceptions – you'll get a pretty strange angle photographing a giraffe from below, and shots with a lot of scenery might work better taken out of the roof.

Portraits

The question of photographing people is a sticky one, and the first rule at all times is to ask permission and accept gracefully if it is refused, no matter how much it hurts (and if, like Ariadne, photography is the main purpose of your trip, then it can be depressing to miss wonderful photograph after wonderful photograph through the potential subject's refusal to co-operate). It is customary in some parts of Tanzania to pay people take their photograph, and while this may seem contrived, it does make it easier to take good pictures of a willing subject, and in some cases it even provides people with a livelihood. I know what you're thinking, but I've never figured out why tourists who come from societies where is normal for a top photographic model to earn more in a month than most of us do in a lifetime should get so self-righteous about a few Africans scraping a humble living by posing for snaps.

When somebody does agree to let you photograph them, your next question will be how to go about this without every nearby kid leaping into the frame. If you have a point-and-shoot camera, the answer is to take the picture as quickly as you can. On the other hand, if you have a camera that requires a certain amount of fiddling around, then you may have to compromise by first taking a group photo, then trying to clear the frame of extraneous kids, bearing in mind that if they then decide to line up behind you, there's a good chance that the photograph will be spoiled by their shadows. Another thing to bear in mind is that is that people often pose very stiffly when you point a camera at them and relax only when the flash goes off, so it may help to take two shots in quick succession, hoping that the second one will capture a more natural pose. As a rule, you can forget about taking good photos of Africans without fill-in flash, since their skin is very dark by comparison to the bright light.

Sensitivity

Until recently, photographing something outside of a game reserve could land you in trouble. This has relaxed in the last few years, but it remains illegal to photograph military installations or government buildings (bridges, stations etc). If in doubt, ask.

shirt (particularly if it buttons up) is a good place to carry spending money in markets and bus stations, since it's easier to keep an eye on than trouser pockets. One sweater or sweatshirt will be adequate in most parts of the country, though you will need serious alpine gear for Kilimanjaro and to a lesser degree Mount Meru.

Socks and underwear *must* be made from natural fabrics. Bear in mind that re-using sweaty undergarments will encourage fungal infections such as athlete's foot, as well as prickly heat in the groin region. Socks and underpants are light and compact enough that it's worth bringing a week's supply. As for footwear, genuine hiking boots are worth considering only if you're a serious off-road hiker, since they are very heavy whether on your feet or in your pack. A good pair of walking shoes, preferably made of leather and with good ankle support, is a good compromise. It's also useful to carry sandals, thongs or other light shoes.

Another factor in deciding what clothes to bring is the sensibilities of Tanzania's large Muslim population, which finds it offensive for a woman to expose her knees or shoulders. It is difficult to make hard and fast rules about what to wear, but some generalisations may help. Shorts are fine at most beach resorts, in game reserves, and possibly in Dar es Salaam, Zanzibar Town or Arusha where people are used to tourists. Elsewhere, I wouldn't wear shorts. For women, trousers are frowned upon in some quarters but my impression is that they are viewed to be unconventional rather than offensive. The ideal thing to wear is a skirt which covers your knees. A shoulderless T-shirt which exposes your bra – or worse – is unlikely to go down well (you laugh: I met someone dressed like this who couldn't figure out why she was hissed at wherever she went in Tanzania).

Men, too, should be conscious of what they wear. Shorts seem to be acceptable, but few Tanzanian men wear them and it is considered more respectable to wear trousers. Walking around in a public place without a shirt is totally unacceptable.

Many Tanzanians think it is insulting for Westerners to wear scruffy or dirty clothes. Quite accurately, they feel you wouldn't dress like that at home. It is difficult to explain that at home you also wouldn't spend three successive days in crowded buses on dusty roads with a limited amount of clothing crumpled up in a backpack. If you are travelling rough, you are bound to look a mess at times, but it is worth trying to look as spruce as possible.

Other useful items

Most backpackers, even those with no intention of camping, carry a **sleeping bag**. A lightweight sleeping bag will be more than adequate in most parts of Tanzania, better still in this climate would be to carry a sheet sleeping bag, something you can easily make yourself. The one time when you will definitely need an all-weather sleeping bag is on Mount Meru or Kilimanjaro. You might meet travellers who, when they stay in local lodgings, habitually place their own sleeping bag on top of the bedding provided. Nutters, in my opinion, and I'd imagine that a sleeping bag placed on a flea-ridden bed would be unlikely to provide significant protection, rather more likely to become flea-infested itself.

I wouldn't leave home without **binoculars**, which some might say makes *me* the nutter. Seriously though, if you're interested in natural history, it's difficult to imagine anything that will give you such value-for-weight entertainment as a pair of light compact binoculars, which these days needn't be much heavier or bulkier than a pack of cards. Binoculars are essential if you want to get a good look at birds (Africa boasts a remarkably colourful avifauna even if you've no desire to put a name to everything that flaps) or to watch distant mammals in game reserves. For most purposes, 7x21 compact binoculars will be fine, though some might prefer

7x35 traditional binoculars for their larger field of vision. Serious bird-watchers will find a 10x magnification more useful.

Some travellers like to carry their own **padlock**. This would be useful if you have a pack that is lockable, and in remote parts of the country it might be necessary for rooms where no lock is provided. If you are uneasy about security in a particular guesthouse, you may like to use your own lock instead of or in addition to the one provided. Although combination locks are reputedly easier to pick than conventional padlocks, I think you'd be safer with a combination lock in Tanzania, because potential thieves will have far more experience of breaking past locks with keys.

Your **toilet bag** should at the very minimum include soap (secured in a plastic bag or soap holder unless you enjoy a soapy toothbrush!), shampoo, toothbrush and toothpaste. This sort of stuff is easy to replace as you go along, so there's no need to bring family-sized packs. Boys will probably want a **razor**. Girls should carry at least enough **tampons** and/or **sanitary pads** to see them through at least one heavy period, since these items may not always be immediately available. Nobody should forget to bring a **towel**, or to keep handy a roll of **loo paper** which, although widely available at shops and kiosks, cannot always be relied upon to be present where it's most urgently needed.

Other essentials include a **torch**, a **penknife** and a compact **alarm clock** for those early morning starts. If you're interested in what's happening in the world, you might also think about carrying a **short-wave radio**. Some travellers carry **games** – most commonly a pack of cards, less often chess or draughts or travel scrabble. A light plastic **orange-squeezing device** gives you fresh orange juice as an alternative to fizzy drinks and water.

You should carry a small **medical kit**, the contents of which are discussed in the chapter on health, as are **mosquito nets**. If you wear **contact lenses**, bring all the fluids you need, since they are not available in Tanzania. You might also want to bring a pair of glasses to wear on long bus rides, and on safari – many lens wearers suffer badly in dusty conditions. In general, since many people find the intense sun and dry climate irritates their eyes, you might consider reverting to glasses. For those who wear **glasses**, it's worth bringing a spare pair, though in an emergency a new pair can be made up cheaply (around US$10) and quickly in most Tanzanian towns, provided that you have your prescription available.

MONEY
Organising your finances

There are three ways of carrying money: hard currency cash, travellers' cheques, or a credit card. My advice is to bring at least as much as you think you'll need in the combination of cash and travellers' cheques, but if possible to also carry a credit card to draw on in an emergency. I would strongly urge any but the most denominationally chauvinistic of backpackers to bring their cash and travellers' cheques in the form of US dollars, and to learn to think and budget in this currency.

From the point of view of security, it's advisable to bring the bulk of your money in the form of travellers' cheques, which can be refunded if they are lost or stolen. Best to use a widely recognised type of travellers' cheque such as American Express or Thomas Cook, and to keep your proof of purchase discrete from the cheques, as well as noting which cheques you have used, in order to facilitate a swift refund should you require one. Buy your travellers' cheques in a healthy mix of denominations, since you may sometimes need to change a small sum only, for instance when you're about to cross into another country. On the other hand, you don't want an impossibly thick wad of cheques. For a trip to one country, I'd take five US$20 cheques and the remainder of my money in US$100 cheques.

Whatever your bank at home might say, currency regulations and other complications make it practically impossible to break down a large denomination travellers' cheque into smaller ones in most African countries, so don't bring travellers' cheques in denominations larger than US$100.

In addition to travellers' cheques, you should definitely bring a proportion of your money in hard currency cash, say around US$200 to US$300, since you are bound to hit situations where travellers' cheques won't be accepted, and cash gets a better exchange rate than travellers' cheques, especially large denomination bills. This would be not much consolation were all your money to be stolen, so I'd strongly advise against bringing cash only, but would suggest that you save what cash you do bring for situations where it will buy you a real advantage. Note that US dollar bills printed before 1992, particularly larger denominations such as US$100 and US$50, may be refused by banks and foreign exchange (forex) bureaux.

Carry your hard currency and travellers' cheques as well as your passport and other important documentation in a money belt – one that can be hidden beneath your clothing rather than the sort of fashionable externally-worn codpiece which in some circumstances will serve as a beacon rather than protection. Your money belt should be made of cotton or another natural fabric, and everything inside the belt should be wrapped in plastic to protect it against sweat.

Credit cards are widely accepted in at upmarket tourist-oriented shops and facilities in Arusha, Dar es Salaam and Zanzibar, as well as most game lodges and upper range hotels. Otherwise, they are of limited use. You can normally draw up to US$150 daily in local currency against a visa card at any main branch of a large bank, but I wouldn't rely on this except in Dar es Salaam or Arusha. Every time I've travelled in Africa recently I've bumped into at least one person who has strayed a bit too far off the beaten track with only a credit card to support them. I would tend to carry a credit card as a fall-back more than anything, and to be conservative in my assumptions about where I'll be able to draw money against it. No matter how long you are travelling, do make sure that you are set up in such a way that you won't need to have money transferred or drafted across to Tanzania.

An airport departure tax of US$20 is levied on international flights out of Tanzania. Before you pay it, check whether it has already been included in the price of your ticket.

Budget planning

Any budget for a holiday in a country such as Tanzania will depend so greatly on how and where you travel that is almost impossible to give sensible advice in a general travel guide. At one end of the spectrum, a fly-around safari staying at the very best lodges might set you back US$500 per person per day, while at the other end a budget traveller could probably get by on US$10 per person per day in some parts of southern Tanzania.

As a rule, readers who are travelling at the middle to upper end of the price range will have pre-booked most of their trip, which means that they will have good idea of what the holiday will cost them before they set foot in Tanzania. Pre-booked packages do vary in terms of what is included in the price, and you are advised to check the exact conditions in advance, but generally the price quoted will cover everything but drinks, tips and perhaps some meals (safari lodge accommodation is normally on a full-board basis, but city hotels are typically bed and breakfast only, though some packages may include other meals). Another variable, assuming that you are visiting Zanzibar, is whether the package does or doesn't include the cost of a spice tour and other day trips. To give some idea of what 'extras' might entail on a typical package tour, a meal in a top-notch restaurant will cost around US$10–15, a beer in a lodge or upmarket hotel around US$3, a bottle of wine US$15–20, and a soda US$1. Tips are at the discretion of the individual traveller, but you should be looking at around US$10 per day for your safari driver.

For budget travellers, Tanzania can be very cheap, though day-to-day costs are now higher than in countries such as Malawi and Ethiopia, and most recognised tourist activities are relatively expensive. Day-to-day costs vary regionally, and are highest in major tourist centres such as Arusha, Moshi, Dar es Salaam and Zanzibar. Throughout the country, a soft drink will cost you around US$0.50 and a beer slightly over US$1 in a local bar, but twice that in a hotel or restaurant that caters primarily to Westerners. A meal in a local restaurant will costs US$2-3, while a meal in a proper restaurant might cost US$5 to $10. Basic local guesthouses typically cost around US$3-4, though you can expect to pay double this amount in towns which see a lot of tourist traffic. Self-contained rooms in moderate hotels start at around US$10, while you might pay anything up from US$200-650 for a double room in a game lodge. Public transport costs will vary on how far and how regularly you travel, but buses aren't expensive. Taking the above figures into account, I think that budget travellers could get by in most parts of Tanzania on around US$15 per day for one person or US$20 per day for two. Double this amount, and within reason you can eat and stay where you like.

The above calculations don't allow for more expensive one-off activities, such as climbing Mount Kilimanjaro, going on safari, or catching the ferry between Dar and Zanzibar. If you want to keep to a particular budget and plan on undertaking such activities, you would be well advised to treat your day-to-day budget separately from what you are likely to spend on safari. I would set aside at least US$100 for each day you plan to spend on safari (bearing in mind additional costs such as tips and drinks) and perhaps US$150 for each day you plan to spend on Kilimanjaro, again allowing for tips.

ITINERARY PLANNING

Tanzania has a well-defined tourist circuit. It would be no exaggeration to say that as many as 90% of visitors probably divide their time in the country between the two main tourist attractions, which are the game reserves of the northern safari circuit and the island of Zanzibar. If this is what you plan on doing, then any tour operator or safari company in Arusha will be able to put together a package to meet your requirements. A 10–14 day trip is ideal for the Zanzibar-safari combination. You might want to read the section on organising a safari (see *Chapter 7*) before making contact with a tour operator. With Zanzibar, the main decision you need to make in advance is whether you want to be based at a hotel in the old Stone Town, or out on one of the beaches, or a combination of the two. For a short trip to Tanzania, it is advisable to fly between Arusha (the springboard for safaris in northern Tanzania) and Zanzibar. If you are really tight for time, you'll get more out of your safari by flying between lodges. A fly-in safari will also be less tiring than the more normal drive-in safari.

For those with budgetary restrictions, it will probably work out cheaper to make your travel arrangements once you are in Tanzania. It is easier to get a cheap camping safari in Arusha on the spot, and you will be able to stay at cheaper guesthouses and hotels than those favoured by tour operators. The disadvantage of doing this is that you will lose time making arrangements once you are in the country, and will probably need two days to travel overland and by sea from Arusha to Zanzibar. If you plan on arranging things as you go along, I would advise against trying to squeeze a safari and a visit to Zanzibar into a trip of less than 14 days.

After the northern safari circuit and Zanzibar, Tanzania's main tourist attraction is Kilimanjaro, which can be climbed over five or six days. A Kilimanjaro climb is one of those things that you either do or don't want to undertake: for a significant minority of travellers, climbing Kilimanjaro is the main reason for visiting Tanzania, but for the majority it is of little interest. If you want to do a Kili climb, it can be organised in advance through any number of tour operators and safari companies, and there is a lot to be said for arranging the climb through the same operator who organises your safari. As with safaris, it is generally possible to get cheaper prices on the spot. To combine a Kili climb with a few days on safari and a visit to Zanzibar, you would need an absolute minimum of two weeks in the country on an organised package, and even that would be very tight, allowing for no more than two nights on Zanzibar. Bank on at least three weeks in the country if you are travelling independently.

Beyond the above, it is difficult to recommend any particular itinerary. The southern circuit of game reserves is slowly catching on with tourists, most normally combined with a visit to Mafia or Zanzibar Island, but it is not a cheap option. Few would claim that the southern reserves offer a game-viewing spectacle to compare with the Serengeti or Ngorongoro in northern Tanzania, but they are fine reserves by any standard, and the relative exclusivity of tourist facilities in the south means that the reserves have retained more of a wilderness character. Other reserves that are of great interest to fly-in tourists are Gombe Stream, Mahale Mountains and Rubondo Island National Parks, all of which support substantial patches of rainforest habitats and offer the opportunity to see chimpanzees in the wild. Accessibility is a problem with all of the 'chimp reserves' at the time of writing, and short of chartering a direct flight you would need to set aside the best part of a week to visit any of them.

For budget travellers with sufficient time, a visit to the Usambara or Pare Mountains, or to the historical seaports of Tanga, Bagamoyo and Pangani, can easily be appended to the overland trip between Arusha and Zanzibar. With yet more time, and a sense of adventure, the southern and western parts of Tanzania are rich in off-the-beaten-track possibilities, ranging from the Shirazi ruins on Kilwa Kisiwani to the fantastic hiking country around Tukuyu and the memorable steamer ride down Lake Tanganyika. The most sensible advice that I can give to adventurous travellers is to allocate their time generously, or they are likely to spend a disproportionate amount of time on public transport.

To give some idea, if you wanted to visit Rubondo Island overland, you would be looking at a 10 to 14 day round trip from Dar es Salaam, and even Gombe Stream would be a week's round trip. The south coast could be explored comfortably over seven to ten days, the Udzungwa Mountains would be a good four to five day trip, the southern highlands and Lake Nyasa would be good for anything over a week, and the Selous is normally visited on a four to five day safari.

Independent travellers who have a longer period of time could do one of a few loops. You could, for instance, catch a train to Mbeya, spend a few days exploring around Tukuyu, cross to Mtwara via Lake Nyasa and Songea and then work your way up the south coast, a trip that will open your eyes to just how 'untouristy' even a popular tourist destination such as Tanzania can be. Another possibility from Mbeya is to work your way up to Mwanza via Lake Tanganyika taking in some of the western national parks on the way, then catch a bus across the Serengeti to Arusha and return to Dar es Salaam from there. For either of these trips, you would need at least a month.

Travelling in Tanzania

TOURIST INFORMATION AND SERVICES

There are Tanzania Tourist Board (TTB) offices in Dar es Salaam and in Arusha. Both are reasonably helpful and well-informed when it comes to tourist-class hotels and major tourist attractions, but neither is generally able to offer much help when it comes to more remote destinations. The TTB office in Arusha is a good source of information about the various cultural tourism programmes that have been established in northern Tanzania over the past few years, and its list of registered and blacklisted safari companies is a useful resource for travellers who are going on a cheap safari company.

PUBLIC HOLIDAYS

Tourists visiting Tanzania should take note of public holidays, since all banks, forex bureau and government offices will be closed on these days. In addition to Good Friday, Easter Monday, Idd-ul-Fitr, Islamic New Year and the Prophet's Birthday, which fall on different dates every year, the following public holidays are taken in Tanzania:

January 1	New Year's Day
January 12	Zanzibar Revolution Day
February 5	CCM Day
April 26	Union Day (anniversary of union between Tanganyika and Zanzibar)
May 1	International Workers' Day
July 7	Saba Saba Day
August 8	Farmers' Day
December 9	Independence Day
December 25	Christmas Day

MONEY

The unit of currency is the Tanzanian shilling, divided into 100 cents. At the time of writing the exchange rate of roughly US$1 = Tsh 660 is reasonably stable, but like most African currencies the Tanzania shilling has steadily devalued against most hard currencies in recent years. This devaluation was most dramatic in the late 1980s, following a period when the exchange rate had been kept artificially high, resulting in a huge black market economy. In 1986, the exchange rate stood at around US$1 = Tsh 20 and the black market rate at about ten times that. The rate dropped to something like US$1 = Tsh 400 in the early 1990s. By contrast, the Tanzania shilling has devalued by a relatively modest figure of 50% since the first edition of this guide was researched in 1992.

Most upmarket hotels and safari companies quote their rates in US dollars and will demand payment in this or another prominent hard currency. National park fees and port and airport taxes must also be paid in hard currency, and if you don't have the exact amount in US dollar bills or travellers' cheques, you can expect to be given your change in local currency at a laughable exchange rate. In practice, most tourists won't need to pay their park fees directly, as this will be handled by their safari company.

The above exceptions noted, most other things in Tanzania are best paid for in local currency. This includes restaurant bills, goods bought at a market or shop, mid-range and budget accommodation, public transport and most other casual purchases. Throughout this guide, prices are quoted in US dollars at a rate of US$1 = Tsh 667, or, to put it another way, a ratio of US$3 = Tsh 2000. While this may require some adjustments on the part of readers who are unused to thinking in US dollars, it has three obvious advantages over quoting in local currencies. The first of these is that African currencies are notoriously prone to sudden devaluations, which generally result in a corresponding adjustment in local prices over a few months, following the US dollar. The second is that it is far easier to get a feel for prices in a country before your trip when they are quoted in dollars as opposed to an unfamiliar local currency. The third is that the US dollar is the main international currency used in Africa; people travelling between African countries will soon start to think in dollars, and those who are visiting Tanzania in isolation will find life much more straightforward if they bring their cash (and ideally travellers' cheques) in US dollars.

Tanzanian shillings come in Tsh 10,000, 5,000, 1,000, 500, and 200 denomination bills. It is often very difficult to find change for larger denomination bills, so try always to have a fair spread of notes available. Smaller denomination coins are floating around, but they are incredibly bulky and close to valueless in international terms.

Foreign exchange

Foreign currencies can be changed into Tanzanian shillings at any bank or bureau de change (known locally as forex bureaux). Banking hours are from 08.30 to 12.30 on weekdays, and 08.30 to 11.30 on Saturdays. In larger towns, some banks stay open in the afternoon. Most forex bureaux stay open until 15.00 or 16.00.

Tanzania's currency was freed in early 1992, since when a number of forex bureaux have opened, offering far more favourable rates than the banks. There are government-run forex bureaux at the main branch of the National Bank of Commerce in Arusha, Dar es Salaam, Mwanza and Namanga, and privately run forex bureaux in Arusha, Dar es Salaam, Mwanza, Mbeya and Dodoma. You can change money at any time of day at Dar es Salaam airport.

Privately run bureaux give generally the best rates. In Dar es Salaam there can be a variation of up to 10% in the rate offered by various forex bureaux, so it is worth shopping around. Before you change a large amount of money, check the forex bureau has enough high denomination banknotes, or you'll need a briefcase to carry your local currency.

Forex bureaux have killed the black market which previously thrived in Tanzania. Private individuals may give you a slightly better rate, but the official rate is so favourable it seems unfair to exploit this. In Dar es Salaam or Arusha you will be offered exceptionally good rates on the street, but if you are stupid or greedy enough to accept these, you can expect to be ripped off. There are plenty of forged $100 bills floating around Tanzania, and you can assume that anyone who suggests a deal involving a $100 bill is trying to unload a forgery.

At most overland borders there is nowhere to change money legally. You will have to change money with individuals. This is illegal, but as there is no option it is usually fairly open. If you can, get hold of some Tanzanian money in advance (ask travellers coming from Tanzania if they have some to swap). On overland crossings I always carry a small surplus of the currency of the country I am leaving (about US$10 worth), and try to change this into the currency I need. I feel safer swapping African currencies than changing US dollars.

GETTING AROUND
By air
There has been a tremendous improvement in the network of domestic flights within Tanzania in recent years, especially between major tourist centres. In addition to the national carrier, Air Tanzania, several private airlines now run scheduled flights around Tanzania, most prominently Precision Air and Coastal Travels. Between them, these two carriers offer scheduled flights between Dar es Salaam, Zanzibar, Pemba, Mafia, Arusha, Kilimanjaro, Serengeti (Grumeti and Seronera), Lake Manyara, Mwanza, Bukoba, Musoma, Kigoma, Mtwara and Mbeya. There are also regular flights between Arusha and Mombasa and Nairobi in Kenya. For visitors with limited time and sufficient funds, flying is the best way to get around this large country, and any safari operator or tour company will be able to set up flights as required. It should be noted, however, that domestic flights will be prohibitively expensive to travellers with stringent budgetary restrictions. To give some idea, a flight from Arusha to Zanzibar costs US$155 one-way, from Arusha to Mwanza US$145 one-way, and Dar es Salaam to Mbeya US$165 one-way. One flight that is relatively cheap, especially when you consider that the only alternative is a ferry costing around US$30, is from Dar es Salaam to Zanzibar at US$55.

The **Air Tanzania** head office is on Ohio Street in Dar es Salaam; tel: 051 110245 or 118411/2; fax: 051 113114 or 844336; email: commercial@ airtanzania.com. The Arusha office is on Boma Road (tel: 057 3201/2) and they have offices in most cities to which they run international flights.

Precision Air has offices in Arusha, Dar es Salaam and Mwanza – PO Box 1636, Arusha; tel: 057 6903 or 2812; fax: 057 8204; email: precision-ark@ cybernet.co.tz. The agent for Precision Air in Zanzibar is Maha Travel.

Details for Coastal Travels are in the Dar es Salaam chapter under *Tour operators* on page 209.

By rail
There are three main railway lines in Tanzania. The northern line connects Dar es Salaam, Tanga and Moshi. The central line connects Dar es Salaam, Kigoma, Mwanza and Mpanda. The Tazara line connects Dar es Salaam, Mbeya and Kapiri Mposhi (Zambia).

For budget travellers, trains used to be the most reliable and comfortable way of getting around Tanzania, and this remains the case for people travelling between Dar es Salaam and Kigoma or Mwanza in the west of the country. The central line suffered badly in the *El Nino* floods of 1997/8, and all services were suspended for several months, but they have since resumed operating as normal. As a rule, trains along this route are reasonably reliable and prompt, but there has been little maintenance in the last decade and the compartments are very run down with a pervasive smell of sweat and urine.

In northern Tanzania, passenger trains to Tanga were discontinued a few years ago, and services between Dar es Salaam and Moshi have recently gone the same way. I would assume that this is due to the improvement in roads in this part of the country over the 1990s, in which case there is no reason to suppose that these services will be resumed in the foreseeable future.

The Tazara Railway remains the best way of travelling directly between Tanzania and Zanzibar, and it would certainly be my preference were I travelling directly from Dar to Mbeya. It is normally fairly reliable, though when things do go wrong, you could be set for a delay measured in days rather than hours.

Practicalities

There are three classes on all trains. First class consists of two-berth compartments and second class consists of six-berth compartments. Men and women may not share a first or second class compartment unless they book the whole compartment. Third class consists of seated carriages, but there are always more passengers than seats; it's only worth thinking about if you value neither your comfort nor your possessions.

Theft from train windows at night is not unusual. I have heard of someone whose rucksack was taken this way. Close the windows securely when you turn the light off. A block of wood is provided for this purpose; if you cannot find one in your compartment speak to the steward. Don't leave loose objects lying around the compartment; keep your luggage under the bunks. If you leave the compartment take all valuables with you.

All trains have dining cars. Meals are good and reasonably priced. Beers and sodas are normally available. If you travel first class and do not want to leave your cabin empty, the steward can bring meals to you. In second class I would have no hesitation about going to the dining car provided other passengers remain in the compartment. At many stations vendors sell snacks and meals through the window.

It is advisable to book train tickets three days to a week in advance. It is easier to get last-minute bookings on trains heading towards Dar es Salaam than on trains leaving it.

You may read elsewhere that ticket officers sometimes refuse to issue a ticket without a bribe. The story is that you go to the booking office on the morning of departure, and are told there are no tickets. You offer a bribe and are told to come back later, when a ticket magically appears. This has happened to me on a few occasions, but minus the bribe. This is because a number of tickets are automatically held for institutions such as the army, police, and hospitals until a few hours before departure. If they are not taken, they become available to the public. I've not heard or seen anything that supports the bribe story.

Fares

Train fares can be paid in local currency. Approximate sample fares from Dar es Salaam to various destinations (in US dollars) follow:

	1st	2nd
Mbeya	40	25
Kapiri Mposhi	60	40
Kigoma	40	30
Mwanza	40	30

In Dar es Salaam, a 50% discount on the Tazara line is given to anyone with a student card. Sorting this out will take a couple of hours. You must first collect an application form from the Tazara station, then go to the Department of Education on Kivukoni Front where the form will be stamped, and finally return to the station to buy a ticket.

Timetables
Central line

The central line runs from Dar es Salaam to Mwanza and Kigoma, stopping at Morogoro, Dodoma and Tabora. The train splits at Tabora: one half goes to

Mwanza, the other to Kigoma. A third branch from Tabora to Mpanda, run as a separate service, has been discontinued. All trains on the central line were suspended following flood damage to the railway lines in late 1997. The services have recently been resumed, and while I would tend to assume that the timetables given below are still valid, it is possible that they will have changed.

Trains leave Dar es Salaam on Tuesday, Wednesday, Friday and Sunday at 18.00. Trains in the opposite direction leave on Tuesday, Thursday, Friday and Sunday. They leave Mwanza at 19.00 and Kigoma at 16.00. The full journey takes about 40 hours. Tickets can only be booked in advance at Dar es Salaam, Kigoma, Tabora and Mwanza. Elsewhere you will have to get on the train and hope for the best.

There is no direct service between Kigoma and Mwanza. You will have to take a train to Tabora, where you can make an onward booking. Extra carriages are added at Tabora, so most people have no problem getting through.

The train service to Mpanda has been suspended at the time of writing, but may well resume in the near future. Trains used to leave from Tabora on Monday, Wednesday and Friday, and from Mpanda on Tuesday, Thursday and Friday. In both directions, the trains left at 22.45 and took 12 hours.

Tazara line
Two express trains run every week between Dar es Salaam and Kapiri Mposhi (Zambia). These leave from Dar es Salaam on Tuesday and Friday at 17.30, and from Kapiri Mposhi on the same days at 14.16, taking around 36 hours and stopping at Ifakara, Makamako, Mbeya and Tunduma. Three additional slow trains run every week from Dar es Salaam, going as far as Tunduma on the Zambian border. These leave Dar es Salaam on Monday, Wednesday and Saturday at 11.00, stopping at Ifakara and Mbeya and Tunduma. One advantage of the slow trains is that they are scheduled to pass through the Selous Game Reserve during daylight hours, and there is usually plenty of game to be seen.

By boat
There are several useful ocean and lake ferry services in Tanzania. A few boats go daily between Dar es Salaam and Zanzibar, and some continue on to Pemba (see *Chapter 7*). There are ferry services on all three great lakes, run by the Tanzania Railway Corporation. For details see *Chapter 14* (*Lake Victoria*), *15* (*Lake Tanganyika*) and *17* (*Lake Nyasa*).

By bus and *matatu*
Buses form the main mode of transport for independent budget travellers. The bus services in Tanzania used to be among the worst in Africa, with old and poorly maintained vehicles trundling along dramatically potholed roads in a country where spares were practically non-existent. Since the mid-1980s, however, there has been a gradual improvement in Tanzania's major roads and also in the standard of vehicles, and bus services along major routes are reasonably efficient, at least by African standards. There are now reliable express buses connecting Arusha, Moshi, Lushoto, Tanga and Dar es Salaam. Along these routes, you can expect to cover around 60km/hr, including a few breaks for drinks and meals. Bus services along the main south road connecting Dar es Salaam to Morogoro, Iringa and Mbeya are also reasonably quick and reliable, as are services between Mbeya and Kyela, and Dar es Salaam and Dodoma.

For long trips on major routes, it is important to ensure that you use an 'express bus', which should travel directly between towns stopping only at a few prescribed

THEFT ON BUSES

Tanzania buses have a bad reputation for theft, though my experience and that of travellers I've met would suggest that this is probably not so much a general problem as one specific to a few particular routes. Bear the following in mind when you travel by bus:

- The roof is the most risky place to put your luggage, especially on a bus that will travel into the night. Some conductors insist on putting it there (there is often no real option) but if possible try to get it into the body of the bus. If it does not fit on the racks, put it up near the driver.

- Avoid overnight buses. Almost all the theft stories I have heard relate to overnight buses between Arusha and Dodoma or between Dar es Salaam and Mbeya routes.

- Be wary of strangers who offer you food. Instances of travellers being given drugged food and having their possessions taken while they are asleep seem to be on the increase, with long-haul routes the main area of risk. First-hand accounts would suggest that the most likely offenders in this regard are smooth-talking, well-dressed fellow passengers who know how to guilt-trip *wazungu* (Europeans) into acting against their better instincts.

- Be vigilant when the bus is stationary. The snatch-and-grab experts who hang round most bus stations are not above grabbing something through the window. If anyone is hanging around, catch their eye so that they know you are aware of them.

- Don't leave valuables on your lap. It sounds obvious; I once met someone whose money belt was snatched from his lap while he was fiddling in his day pack.

places, rather than stopping wherever and whenever a potential passenger is sighted or an existing passenger wants to disembark. Be warned that so far as most touts are concerned, any bus that will give them commission is an express bus, so you are likely to be pressured into getting in the bus they want you to get in. The best way to counter this is to go to the bus station on the day before you want to travel, and make your enquiries and bookings in advance, when you will be put under less pressure and won't have to worry about keeping an eye on your luggage.

For the nostalgic and masochistic, it is still perfectly possible to capture the flavour of Tanzanian public transport in the 1980s by bussing through more remote areas, where as a generalisation buses are only worth considering where no rail or lake transport exists. Most roads in Tanzania are in very poor shape, the vehicles are old and usually very crowded, and they tend to stop every couple of kilometres to pick up more passengers. A travelling time of around 20km/hr is not unusual, which means that a 250km trip can take around 12 hours. In the southern coastal region, you're pretty much stuck with bus transport, but in the west, you are strongly advised to use trains and ferries. Routes which should be avoided at all costs include the road between Dodoma and Arusha, and the Singida route between Mwanza and Arusha, which can take up to three days.

On some obscure routes there is no formal bus transport. You will generally find such routes are covered by *matatus* or *dala-dalas* – a generic name that seems to cover practically any vehicle that isn't a bus, but is most commonly an overcrowded and overpriced pick-up truck. Wherever you have the choice of using a bus, I would advise against travelling by *matatu*, since the drivers tend to be maniacs, and fatal accidents are commonplace. (Many bus drivers are also rather reckless, but if I were to be involved in an accident on one of the flat roads characteristic of Tanzania, I'd fancy my chances in a bus over a pick-up truck or minibus any day.)

On busy routes, buses leave when they are full. There is no need to book. On long hauls and quiet routes, there is normally a fixed departure time, so it is advisable to book the day before you leave. We were often given wildly inaccurate information about bus schedules. Ask a few people; don't take the word of the first person you speak to. In the main part of the guide I have given the current situation regarding frequency of buses and whether booking is necessary. Things change, however; you should make your own enquiries.

When you check out bus times, be very conscious of the difference between Western time and Swahili time. Many Tanzanians will translate the Swahili time to English without making the six hour conversion – in other words, you'll be told a bus leaves at 11.00 when it actually leaves at 05.00. This fools a high proportion

SOME BUS JOURNEYS IN TANZANIA

This information included in this guideline table of routes, timings and fares has been accumulated over several visits to Tanzania, so may not always be precise, but the dollar prices quoted don't appear to have changed much over the years on journeys I've done several times.

Journey	Vehicle		Km	Duration (hrs)	Fare (US$)
Arusha/Dar es Salaam	bus	647	12–15	10.00	
Arusha/Dar es Salaam	express bus	647	10–12	12.50	
Arusha/Moshi bus	85	1.5–2	1.50		
Tanga/Lushoto minibus	154	3	3.00		
Mwanza/Arusha	bus via Serengeti	692	12–18	75.00*	
Mwanza/Arusha	bus via Singida	855	36+	12.50	
Tanga/Dar es Salaam	express bus	354	4–6	7.50	
Mtwara/Dar es Salaam	bus	555	15–25	6.00	
Dar es Salaam/Morogoro	minibus	196	2–3	3.00	
Dar es Salaam/Iringa	bus	501	12–15	5.00	
Morogoro/Iringa	minibus	305	7	3.50	
Dar es Salaam/Mbeya	bus	851	15–20	8.50	
Dodoma/Iringa bus	251	10+	2.50		
Dodoma/Arusha	bus	687	20+	7.50	
Mbeya/Kyela bus	141	4	2.50		
Mbamba Bay/Mbinga	pick-up truck	61	3+	3.00	
Mbinga/Songea bus	103	3	1.50		
Songea/Njombe	bus	237	5	2.50	
Mbeya/Sumbawanga	bus	322	8+	3.50	
Sumbawanga/Mpanda	lift with truck	235	8+	5.00	
Mpanda/Ikola lift with truck	126	4+	4.00		
Rusumu/Mwanza	lift with truck	400	18+	10.00	

*includes $50.00 in national park fees

of travellers over their first few days in Tanzania. The best way to get around this area of potential misunderstanding is to confirm the time you are quoted in Swahili – for instance ask *'saa moja?'* if you are told a bus leaves at 13.00. See the appendix on *Swahili Time* for more details.

Buses and minibuses are generally very inexpensive. To give some idea, the 647km journey between Dar and Arusha costs around US$12 by express bus, and even less on a standard 'stopping' bus. Overcharging is unusual on short routes and in parts of the country that carry a low volume of tourists. By contrast, it is practically routine for tourists to be overcharged on long-haul buses along the main routes in northeastern Tanzania. Before bussing out of Arusha, Moshi, Tanga or Dar es Salaam, you should try to establish the correct fare in advance. If you don't, I would query the fare as a matter of course (see box *Some bus journeys in Tanzania*)

Hitching

There is little scope for hitching in Tanzania. On routes where there is no public transport you may have to hitch, but generally this will be on the back of a truck and you will have to pay. Hitching is an option on the Arusha-Dar es Salaam-Mbeya road.

Car hire

Self-drive car hire isn't a popular or particularly attractive option in Tanzania, as it is generally more straightforward to visit game reserves on an organised safari.

ACCOMMODATION

Most Tanzanian towns have a variety of moderately priced hotels and cheap guesthouses, and even the smallest village will have somewhere you can stay for a few dollars. There has been a real upsurge in more upmarket accommodation in recent years, and fly-in visitors now have a wide choice of possibilities in most major game reserves and other tourist centres, though the options are limited or non-existent in less popular parts of the country.

I have divided accommodation into four categories: camping, budget, moderate and upper range. These categories are based more on feel than on price, but prices are reasonably consistent. A room in a local guesthouse will generally cost around US$3–4 away from the main tourist centres, and up to US$15 in somewhere such as Arusha, Dar, Moshi or Zanzibar. A room in a moderate hotel might cost anything from US$20 to US$60, and upper-range accommodation can cost anything from US$50 to more than US$600 for a double at the very top of the range.

Remember that the KiSwahili word *hoteli* refers to a restaurant; so if you ask people for a hotel, you will most probably be shown somewhere to eat (see *Swahili* appendix).

Camping

There are surprisingly few campsites in Tanzania, and those that do exist tend to be in national parks, where camping costs US$20 per person. The only area where campers are well catered for is around Moshi and Arusha, where several private sites cater to backpackers and overland trucks. If you ask at moderate hotels in out of the way places, you may sometimes be allowed to camp in their grounds for a small fee.

If you are hiking in areas off the beaten track, a tent will be a distinct asset. You should, however, be discreet; either set up well away from villages or else ask permission from the village headman before you pitch a tent. I've not met many people who have camped rough in Tanzania, but it's hard to imagine there would be a significant risk attached to camping in rural areas, provided you didn't flaunt your presence or leave your tent unguarded for a lengthy period.

Budget

Most budget accommodation in Tanzania consists of small private guesthouses. These are almost exclusively used by locals, and are remarkably uniform in design and price. The typical guesthouse consists of around ten cell-like rooms forming three walls around a central courtyard, with a reception area or restaurant at the front. Toilets are more often than not long-drops. Washing facilities usually amount to a lockable room and a bucket of cold water, though an increasing number of guesthouses do have proper showers, and a few even have hot showers. It is conventional for guesthouse staff to provide a basin of hot water on request.

Tanzanian guesthouses may be basic, and many double as brothels, but the majority are reasonably clean and pleasant, and are good value when compared to similar establishments in some neighbouring countries. You will rarely pay more than US$5 for a room in a Tanzanian guesthouse. I have found that guesthouses run by women or with a strong female presence are generally cleaner and more hospitable than those run by men. There is a strong town-to-town variation in guesthouse quality: in some towns a clean, freshly-painted room with mosquito nets and a fan is standard; in others – Iringa and Bukoba leap to mind – three-quarters of the places we looked at were totally unappealing.

In most medium-sized towns there are a couple of dozen guesthouses, usually clustered around the bus station and often with little to choose between them. In such cases I have avoided making individual recommendations.

There are several church-run guest houses and hostels in Tanzania. These are normally included under budget accommodation.

Moderate

This category covers everything that feels more upmarket than a local guesthouse without really having the facilities you would expect of a genuine tourist-class hotel. It is difficult to generalise, but typically a moderate hotel will have self-contained rooms with running hot or cold showers, and can be paid for in local currency. Most moderate hotels include a continental breakfast in the price of a room, but this rarely amounts to more than dry bread and coffee.

Upper range

These are official tourist hotels, and must be paid for in hard currency. Prices vary wildly, but typically you will be looking at around US$100 for a double room, double that or more for lodge accommodation in national parks or for international standard hotels in the main tourist centres. Room rates invariably include breakfast, and at most game lodges they will also include lunch and dinner. Tourist hotels are concentrated in Dar es Salaam, Zanzibar, Tanga and the Kilimanjaro-Arusha-Serengeti area. There are only a handful in the south and west of the country. Most hotels in this range have a lower rate for Tanzanian residents.

EATING AND DRINKING
Eating

If you are not too fussy and don't mind a lack of variety, you can eat well and cheaply almost anywhere in Tanzania. In most towns numerous local restaurants, called *hotelis*, serve unimaginative but filling meals for around $2. *Hotelis* vary greatly in quality: I have had some very tasty meals in them, but as often as not gristle and sludge would be an appropriate description of what you are served.

Most *hoteli* food is based around a stew eaten with one of four staples: rice, *chapati*, *ugali* or *batoke*. *Ugali* is a stiff maize porridge eaten throughout sub-Saharan Africa. *Batoke* or *matoke* is cooked plantain, served boiled or in a mushy heap. In the Lake Victoria region, *batoke* replaces *ugali* as the staple food. The most common stews are chicken, beef, goat and beans. In coastal towns and around the great lakes, whole fried fish is a welcome change.

Mandaazi, the local equivalent of doughnuts, are tasty when freshly cooked. They are served at *hotelis* and sold at markets. You can eat cheaply at stalls around markets and bus station. Goat kebabs, fried chicken, grilled groundnuts and potato chips are often freshly cooked and sold in these places.

Cheap it may be, but for most travellers *hoteli*-fare soon palls. In most larger towns, there are what could be termed proper restaurants. These are normally within the reach of any budget, and would typically serve a variety of meat, steak and chicken dishes with potato chips or rice, and cost around $5 for a main course. There is considerably more culinary variety in Dar es Salaam and Arusha, where for around $8-10 you can eat very well.

At one time, walking around a Tanzanian market you would see little but onions and bananas. This has improved, and in most towns a reasonable variety of fruits, vegetables, pulses and beans can be bought, depending on the season. The most common fruits are mangoes, oranges, bananas, pineapples, papaya and coconuts. Fresh fruit is dirt cheap in Tanzania.

Note: KiSwahili names for various foods are given in the KiSwahili appendix.

Drinks

The most widely drunk beverage is *chai*, a sweet tea where all ingredients are boiled together in a pot. Along the coast *chai* is often flavoured with spices such as ginger. In some places *chai* is served *ya rangi* or black; in others *mazewa* or milky. Sodas such as Coke, Pepsi, Sprite and Fanta are widely available, and normally cost less than $0.50. In large towns you can often get fresh fruit juice. On the coast and in some parts of the interior, the most refreshing, healthy and inexpensive drink is coconut milk. This is sold by street vendors who will decapitate the young coconut of your choice, which then forms a natural cup from which you can drink the juice. They will then chop the coconut in pieces for you to spoon out the moist flesh.

Tap water in Tanzania is often dodgy, and most travellers try to stick to mineral water, which is available in most tourist centres, coming in 1.5l bottles that cost around US$1. We've been told that in some countries it is common practice to fill mineral water bottles with tap water, but I've not heard of this happening in Tanzania, and wouldn't be concerned about it provided that the bottle is sealed.

The two main alcoholic drinks are beer and *konyagi*. *Konyagi* is a spirit made from sugar cane. It tastes a bit strange on its own, but mixes well and is very cheap. The local Safari lager used to be appalling, but since the national brewery was taken over by South African Breweries a few years ago, there has been a dramatic improvement not only in the quality of Safari, but also in the selection available. Around ten different brands of lager beer are available, of which Castle, Kilimanjaro and Serengeti seem to be the most popular. All beers come in 500ml bottles and cost anything from US$1 at a local bar to US$5 at the most upmarket hotels.

A variety of imported spirits is available in larger towns. South African wines are widely available at lodges and hotels, and they are generally of a high standard and reasonably priced by international standards. I must say that as a South African I do find it hard to bring myself to pay more than US$10 for a bottle of plonk that I know would cost no more than US$2 at home.

SHOPPING

Until a few years ago it was difficult to buy anything much in Tanzania. One of my most vivid memories of Dar es Salaam in 1986 was walking into a general store where a lone shelf of teaspoons was the only stock. Things have improved greatly since then. In Dar es Salaam and most other large towns a fair range of imported goods is available, though prices are often inflated. If you have any very specific needs – unusual medications or slide film for instance – bring them with you.

Toilet roll, soap, toothpaste, pens, batteries and locally-produced food are widely available. *Dukas*, the stalls you see around markets or lining roads, are cheaper than proper shops and are open seven days a week. Even in Dar es Salaam, we were rarely overcharged because we were tourists.

Shopping hours are normally between 08.30 and 16.30, with a lunch break between 13.00 and 14.00.

Curios

A variety of items specifically aimed at tourists is available: Makonde carvings, Tingatinga paintings (see box page 211), batiks, musical instruments, wooden spoons, and various soapstone and malachite knick-knacks. The curio shops near the clock tower in Arusha are the best place to shop for curios. Prices are competitive and the quality is good. Prices in shops are fixed, but you may be able to negotiate a discount. At curio stalls, haggling is necessary. Unless you are good at this, expect to pay more than you would in a shop.

If you have an interest in African music, a good range of tapes is available at stalls in Dar es Salaam city centre. Most are of Congolese groups which are popular in East Africa: Loketa, Kanda Bongoman, Bossi Bossiana and the like.

The colourful *vitenge* (the singular of this is *kitenge*) worn by most Tanzanian women can be picked up cheaply at any market in the country. I've been told Mwanza is a particularly good place to shop for these and other clothes.

MEDIA AND COMMUNICATIONS
Newspapers

The English language *Daily News* is available in Dar es Salaam and other major towns. It doesn't have much international news, but the local news can make interesting reading. The Kenyan *Daily Nation*, available in Dar es Salaam, Arusha and Mwanza, is better.

Stalls in Uhuru Avenue, Dar es Salaam sell *Time* and *Newsweek*, as well as a variety of European, British and American papers. You can sometimes buy foreign newspapers at the bookstall in the New Arusha Hotel in Arusha.

The weekly *East African*, an English language newspaper published in Kenya, gives good regional coverage.

Post

Post from Tanzania is cheap and reasonably reliable. Incoming post arrives surprisingly quickly, and the Poste Restante service in Dar es Salaam is amongst the best in Africa. There is a nominal charge for collecting letters. Mail should be addressed as follows:

Philip Briggs
Poste Restante
Main GPO
Dar es Salaam
Tanzania

Suggest when people write to you they underline your surname, so that the letter doesn't get misfiled. It is advisable to check under both names when you visit the post office.

Phone calls
If you want to make an international phone call or fax, there is a TCC Extelcomms centre in most large towns. The staff are normally helpful and calls are cheap by international standards. Some Extelcomms centres will receive as well as send faxes. Phone calls and faxes to Europe cost around $16 per minute or page.

Internet and email
The internet is catching on in Tanzania, as is email, and there are already internet cafes in Dar es Salaam and Arusha from where you can send email home. The spread of internet use in Africa has been remarkable over the last year or so, and the existence of email represents a real communications revolution on a continent where international lines tend to be unreliable and expensive. I would expect that most Tanzanian towns will have public email and internet facilities within the lifespan of this edition.

Email is by far the cheapest way of communicating with Tanzania from overseas, and it is also the most efficient. With faxes, you will often have to try several times to get through, while post is relatively slow (bank on at least ten days in either direction from Europe), and telephone calls can become seriously costly, especially when the first person you speak to has limited English. I have also found that emails to Tanzania are more often responded to than faxes. Server problems seem to be commonplace, insofar as one in three email messages I receive from Tanzania arrives several days after the date on which it was sent, but most messages seem to get through in the end. However, should you not receive a response within a week or so of emailing somebody in Tanzania, I would be inclined to send the message again.

So far as possible in this edition, I have included email addresses for safari companies, upmarket hotels and any other organisations that readers are likely to want to contact before they arrive in Tanzania. At this point in time, I would guess that around half of the companies you might expect to eventually subscribe to email have actually done so. Any readers who come across a useful email address that isn't listed in this edition are welcome to pass it on to me, as are any organisations that wish to have their email address included in future editions; my address is philari@hixnet.co.za.

INTERACTING WITH TANZANIANS
Tanzania has perhaps the most egalitarian and tolerant mood of any African country that I've visited. As a generalisation, Tanzanians treat visitors with a dignified reserve, something which many Westerners mistake for stand-offishness, but in my opinion is more indicative of a respect both for our culture and their own. Granted, dignified probably won't be the adjective that leaps to mind if your first interaction with Tanzanians comes from the pestilence of touts that hangs around bus stations in Arusha or Moshi, or somewhere similar. But then in most poor countries, you'll find that people who make a living on the fringe of the tourist industry tend be pushy and occasionally confrontational in their dealings – from their perspective, they probably have to be in order to make a living. But I do think that anybody who spends time travelling in Tanzania will recognise the behaviour of touts to be wholly unrepresentative of what is essentially a conservative, unhurried and undemonstrative society.

On the whole, you would have to do something pretty outrageous to commit a serious *faux pas* in Tanzania. But, like any country, Tanzania does have its rules of etiquette, and while allowances will always made for tourists, there is some value in ensuring that they are not made too frequently!

General conduct

Perhaps the most important single point of etiquette to be grasped by visitors is the importance placed on greetings in Tanzanian society. Tanzanians tend to greet each other elaborately, and if you want to make a good impression on somebody who speaks English, whether they be a waiter or a shop assistant (and especially if they work in a government department), you would do well to follow suit, greeting them and asking how they are doing before launching into a direct request. It is also polite (though infuriating) to respond to the ritual of asking what your name is, what country you are from, where you are travelling to etc. When you need to ask somebody directions, it is rude to blunder straight into interrogative mode without first exchanging greetings. With Tanzanians who don't speak English, the greeting *'jambo'* delivered with a smile and a nod of the head will be adequate.

Whenever I visit Tanzania after travelling elsewhere in Africa, I am struck afresh by how readily people greet passing strangers, particularly in rural areas. In Tanzania, this greeting doesn't normally take the form of a shrieked *mzungu* (or whatever local term is used for a white person), or a 'give me money', something that you become accustomed to in some African countries. On the contrary, in Tanzania adults will normally greet tourists with a cheerful *Jambo*, and children with a subdued *Shikamu* (a greeting reserved for elders). I find this to be a very charming quality in Tanzanian society, one that is worth reinforcing by learning a few simple Swahili greetings.

Among Tanzanians, it is considered poor taste to display certain emotions publicly. Affection is one such emotion: it is frowned upon for members of the opposite sex to hold hands publicly, and kissing or embracing would be seriously offensive. Oddly, it is quite normal for friends of the same sex to walk around hand-in-hand, and male travellers who get into a long or intimate discussion with a male Tanzanian should not be surprised if that person clasps them by the hand mid-sentence and retains a firm grip on their hand for several minutes – to a Tanzanian, this is a warm gesture, one that might be particularly appropriate when they want to make a point with which you might disagree. On the subject of intra-gender relations, homosexuality is as good as taboo in Tanzania, to the extent that it would require some pretty overt behaviour for it to occur to anybody to take offence.

It is also considered bad form to show anger publicly. It is more difficult to know where to draw the line here, because many touts positively invite an aggressive response, and I doubt that many people who travel independently in Tanzania will get by without the occasional display of impatience. Frankly, I doubt that many bystanders would take umbrage if you responded to a pushy tout with a display of anger, if only because the tout's behaviour itself goes against the grain of Tanzanian society. By contrast, losing your temper will almost certainly be counterproductive when dealing with obtuse officials, dopey waiters and hotel employees, or uncooperative safari drivers.

Muslim customs

Visitors should be aware of the strong Muslim element in Tanzania, particularly along the coast. In Muslim society, it is insulting to use your left hand to pass or receive something or when shaking hands. If you eat with your fingers, it is also customary to use the right hand only. Even those of us who are naturally right-handed will occasionally need to remind ourselves of this (it may happen, for instance, that you are carrying something in your right hand and so hand money to a shopkeeper with your left) and for those who are left-handed it will require constant effort. In traditional Muslim societies it is offensive for women to expose their knees or shoulders, something that ought to be allowed for, especially on parts of the coast where tourists remain a relative novelty.

Tipping and guides

The question of when and when not to tip can be difficult in a foreign country. In Tanzania, it is customary to tip your guide at the end of a safari and or a Kilimanjaro climb, as well as any cook and porter that accompanies you. A figure of roughly US$5-10 per day is accepted as the benchmark, though it is advisable to check this with your safari company in advance. I see no reason why you shouldn't give a bigger or smaller tip based on the quality of service. Bear in mind, however, that most guides, cooks and porters receive nominal salaries, which means that they are largely dependent on tips for their income. It would be mean not to leave a reasonable tip in any but the most exceptional of circumstances.

In some African countries, it is difficult to travel anywhere without being latched onto by a self-appointed guide, who will often expect a tip over and above any agreed fee. This sort of thing is comparatively unusual in Tanzania, but if you do take on a freelance guide, then it is advisable to clarify in advance that whatever price you agree is final and inclusive of a tip. By contrast, any guide who is given to you by a company should most definitely be tipped, as tips will probably be their main source of income. In Zanzibar and Arusha, a freelance guide may insist upon helping you find a hotel room, in which case they will be given a commission by the hotel, so there is no reason for you to provide an additional tip. In any case, from the guide's point of view, finding you a room is merely the first step in trying to hook you for a safari or a spice tour, or something else that will earn a larger commission.

It is not customary to tip for service in local bars and *hotelis*, though you may sometimes *want* to leave a tip (in fact, given the difficulty of finding change in Tanzania, you may practically be forced into doing this in some circumstances), in which case 5% would be very acceptable and 10% generous. Generally restaurants catering primarily to tourists and wealthy Tanzania residents will automatically add a service charge to the bill, but since most of this service charge is swallowed up by the government, it would be reasonable to reward good service with a genuine tip.

Bargaining

Tourists to Tanzania will sometimes need to bargain over prices, but generally this need exists only in reasonably predictable circumstances, for instance when chartering a private taxi, organising a guide, agreeing a price for a safari or mountain trek, or buying curios and to a lesser extent other market produce. Prices in hotels, restaurants and shops are generally fixed, and overcharging in such places is too unusual for it to be worth challenging a price unless it is blatantly ridiculous.

You may well be overcharged at some point in Tanzania, but it is important to keep this in perspective. After a couple of bad experiences, some travellers start to haggle with everybody from hotel owners to old women selling fruit by the side of the road, often accompanying their negotiations with aggressive accusations of dishonesty. Unfortunately, it is sometimes necessary to fall back on aggressive posturing in order to determine a fair price, but such behaviour is also very unfair on those people who are forthright and honest in their dealings with tourists. It's a question of finding the right balance, or better still looking for other ways of dealing with the problem.

The main instance where bargaining is essential is when buying curios. What should be understood, however, is that the fact a curio seller is open to negotiation does not mean that you were initially being overcharged or ripped off. Curio sellers will generally quote a price knowing full well that you are going to bargain it down (they'd probably be startled if you didn't) and it is not necessary to respond aggressively or in an accusatory manner. It is impossible to say by how much you should bargain the initial price down. Some people say that you should offer half the asking price and be prepared to settle at around two-thirds, but my experience is that curio sellers are far more whimsical than such advice allows for. The sensible approach, if you want to get a feel for prices, is to ask the price of similar items at a few different stalls before you actually contemplate buying anything.

In fruit and vegetable markets and stalls, bargaining is the norm, even between locals, and the most healthy approach to this sort of haggling is to view it as an enjoyable part of the African experience. There will normally be an accepted price band for any particular commodity. To find out what it is, listen to what other people pay and try a few stalls. A ludicrously inflated price will always drop the moment you walk away. When buying fruit and vegetables, a good way to feel out the situation is to ask for a bulk discount or a few extra items thrown in. And bear in mind that when somebody is reluctant to bargain, it may be because they asked a fair price in the first place.

It appears that tourists are routinely overcharged by some conductors on buses connecting Arusha, Moshi, Tanga and Dar es Salaam. One reader who spent three months in northern Tanzania and travelled regularly between towns reckons that overcharging *wazungu* is almost customary on long-haul bus rides in this part of the country, but not on shorter trips, something that concurs with our experience (we have never been quoted the wrong fare on minibuses within Arusha, or when travelling between Arusha and Moshi, yet we've had to argue to get the correct fare on the last three occasions when we travelled between Moshi and Tanga). The best way to avoid being overcharged is to check the correct ticket price in advance with an impartial party, and to book your ticket a day in advance of when you want to travel. Failing that, you will have to judge for yourself whether the price is right, and question it if you have reason to think it isn't. The difficulty here is finding the right balance between standing up for yourself and becoming obnoxious. On our most recent trip to Tanzania, we actually disembarked from a bus in Tanga when the conductor refused to budge on a fare we *knew* to be about double what it should have been, and even that made no difference to his position – fortunately we found another bus heading in the direction we wanted.

A final point to consider on the subject of overcharging and bargaining is that it is the fact of being overcharged that annoys; the amount itself is generally of little consequence in the wider context of a trip to Tanzania. Without for a moment wanting to suggest that travellers should routinely allow themselves to be overcharged, I do feel there are occasions when we should pause to look at the bigger picture. Backpackers in particular tend to forget that, no matter how tight for cash they are, it is was their choice to travel on a minimal budget, and most Tanzanians are much poorer than they will ever be. If you find yourself quibbling over a pittance with an old lady selling a few piles of fruit by the roadside, you might perhaps bear in mind that the notion of a fixed price is a very Western one. When somebody is desperate enough for money, or afraid that their perishable goods might not last another day, it may well be possible to push them down to a lower price than they would normally accept. In such circumstances, I see nothing wrong with erring on the side of generosity.

Women travellers

Women travellers in Tanzania have little to fear on a gender-specific level. Over the years, I've met several women travelling alone in Tanzania, and none had any serious problems in their interactions with locals, aside from the hostility that can be generated by dressing skimpily. Otherwise, an element of flirtation is about the sum of it, perhaps the odd direct proposition, but nothing that cannot be defused by a firm no. And nothing, for that matter, that you wouldn't expect in any Western country, or – probably with a far greater degree of persistence – from many male travellers.

It would be prudent to pay some attention to how you dress in Tanzania, particularly in the more conservative parts of the Swahili coast. In areas where people are used to tourists, they are unlikely to be deeply offended by women travellers wearing shorts or other outfits that might be seen to be provocative, but it still pays to allow for local sensibilities, and under certain circumstances revealing clothes may be perceived to make a statement that's not intended from your side.

More mundanely, tampons are not readily available in smaller towns, though you can easily locate them in Dar es Salaam and Arusha. If you're travelling in out of the way places, it's advisable to carry enough to see you through to the next time you'll be in a large city, bearing in mind that travelling in the tropics can sometimes cause women to have heavier or more regular periods than they would at home. Sanitary pads are available in most towns of any size.

Bearing in mind that Ariadne and I travelled as a couple, and were thus shielded from hassles facing single travellers (male or female), the thoughts and experiences of women travelling alone in Tanzania would be greatly welcomed for the next edition of this guide.

Bribery

Bribery is not much of an issue. There is said to be plenty of corruption in Tanzanian business circles, but it is unlikely to affect tourists. I have never been in a situation where I felt a bribe was being hinted at, nor have I heard of one from another traveller.

Bureaucracy

In the 1980s you often heard stories about travellers clashing with Tanzanian officials. Most incidents were camera-related: it was illegal to take photographs outside tourist areas, largely because of the number of ANC training centres in Tanzania at that time. It may have been paranoid to suspect every backpacker with a camera of being a spy, but as South Africa had used European passport holders disguised as backpackers to bomb an alleged ANC office in Zimbabwe, it was understandable. Things have relaxed greatly since South Africa unbanned the ANC in 1990, and on several trips through Tanzania since then I've experienced nothing more sinister than mild abruptness. In general, Tanzanian officials will go out of their way to accommodate foreigners.

Some travellers behave as if they expect to be allowed to do what they like in African countries, as if they are above the law because they have a white skin and a foreign passport. This attitude is on the decline, but it still persists amongst some budget travellers. So, for the sake of clarity: if, for instance, you climb Kilimanjaro via an illegal route to avoid paying park entrance fees and are arrested, the person who arrests you is not being officious or bureaucratic, he is merely doing his job.

In remote parts of the country you may from time to time be approached by an immigration or police officer who wants to look over your passport. This happened to us a few times and in every instance it was handled in a relaxed, friendly manner. If it happens to you, expect to be asked where you have come from, where you are going, what you are doing in Tanzania etc. Don't read too much into this; it is the typical stuff of KiSwahili small talk. The officer concerned is as likely to be savouring an opportunity to practise his English as he is to have any professional interest in the trivia of your holiday. If you are in a rush, it can be a bit irritating to be cornered like this. There is no point in letting your irritation show. Smile, keep your answers simple, and you will soon be on your way.

CRIME AND SECURITY

Crime exists in Tanzania as it does practically everywhere in the world. There has been a marked increase in crime in Tanzania over recent years, and tourists are inevitably at risk because so far as any criminal is concerned they are far richer than most locals, and are conspicuous by the way they dress and behave, and (with obvious exceptions) because of their skin colour. For all that, Tanzania remains a lower crime risk than many countries, and the social taboo on theft is such that even the most petty of criminals is likely to be beaten to death should they be caught in the act. With a bit of care, you would have to be unlucky to fall victim to serious crime while you are in Tanzania.

Mugging

There is nowhere in Tanzania where mugging is as commonplace as it is in, say, Nairobi or Johannesburg, but there are certainly several parts of the country where walking around alone at night would place you at high risk of being mugged. Mugging is generally an urban problem, with the main areas of risk being Dar es Salaam, Arusha, Tanga and Zanzibar Town, as well as the beach at Pangani, and anywhere in the vicinity of Bagamoyo or Kanduchi Beach. Even in these places, the risk is often localised. In Dar es Salaam, for instance, I have always felt perfectly safe in the area immediately around Maktaba Street, but I would probably catch a taxi if I were crossing from, say, the New Africa Hotel to the Jumbo Inn after dark. The best thing is to ask local advice at your hotel, since the staff there will generally know of any recent incidents in the immediate vicinity.

The best way to ensure that any potential mugging remains an unpleasant incident rather than a complete disaster is to carry as little as you need on your person. If you are mugged in Tanzania, the personal threat is minimal provided that you promptly hand over what is asked for.

Casual theft

The bulk of crime in Tanzania consists of various forms of casual theft, such as bag-snatching or pickpocketing. This sort of thing is not particularly aimed at tourists (and as a consequence not limited to tourist areas), but tourists will be considered fair game. The key to not being pickpocketed is not having anything of value in your pockets; the key to avoiding having things snatched is to avoid having valuables in a place where they are snatchable. Most of the following points will be obvious to experienced travellers, but they are worth making:

- Most casual thieves hang around bus stations and markets. Keep a close watch on your belongings in these places and avoid having loose valuables in your pocket or daypack.

- Keep all your valuables – passport, travellers' cheques etc – in a money belt. One you can hide under your clothes has obvious advantages over one of the currently fashionable codpieces which are worn externally.
- Don't carry your spending money in your money belt. A normal wallet is fine provided it only contains a moderate sum of money. Better still is a wallet you can hang around your neck. If I plan to visit a high risk area such as a busy market, I sometimes wear shorts under my trousers and keep my cash in the shorts pocket. In my opinion, it is difficult for somebody to stick their fingers in the front pocket of a shirt unobserved, for which reason this is normally my favourite pocket for keeping ready cash.
- Distribute your money throughout your luggage. I always keep the bulk of my foreign currency in my money belt, but I like to keep some cash and travellers' cheques hidden in various parts of my pack and daypack.
- Many people prefer to carry their money belt on their person at all times. I think it is far safer to leave it hidden in your hotel room. I'm not saying that it's impossible for a locked hotel room to be broken into, but I've not heard of it happening in Tanzania, whereas I have met countless people who have been pickpocketed, mugged, or had possessions snatched from them. Circumstances do play a part here: in a large city, I would be far happier with my valuables locked away somewhere, whereas in a game lodge the risk of theft from a room has to be greater than that of theft from your person. One factor to consider is that some travellers' cheque companies won't issue refunds on cheques stolen from a hotel room.
- If you have jewellery that is of high personal or financial value, leave it at home.
- If you can afford it, catch a taxi to your hotel when you first arrive in a large town. If you arrive after dark, catch a taxi to your hotel even if you can't afford it.
- Avoid overnight buses. They have a bad reputation for theft. On Zanzibar and on overnight buses I have heard of people being given drugged food and then robbed (see box *Theft on buses*, page 64).
- If you are robbed, think twice before you chase the thief, especially if the stolen items are of no great value. An identified thief is likely to be descended on by a mob and quite possibly beaten to death. I have met a few travellers who found themselves in the bizarre position of having to save someone who had just ripped them off.

Con tricks
Dar es Salaam is not Nairobi as far as con artists are concerned. There are a few dodgy characters who hang around the New Africa Hotel trying to change money, but they are pretty transparent. You may encounter similar characters in Arusha, but you would have to be very gullible to get involved with them.

Documentation
The best insurance against complete disaster is to keep things well-documented. If you carry a photocopy of the main page of your passport, you will be issued a new one more promptly. In addition, keep details of your bank, credit card (if you have one), travel insurance policy and camera equipment (including serial numbers).

Keep copies of your travellers' cheque numbers and *a record of which ones you have cashed*, as well as the international refund assistance telephone number and local agent. If all this information fits on one piece of paper, you can keep photocopies on you and with a friend at home.

You will have to report to the police the theft of any item against which you wish to claim insurance.

Security

Tanzania is a very secure country, with a proud record of internal stability since independence. The bombing of the US embassies in Dar es Salaam and Nairobi had resulted in large-scale cancellations of US tours to Tanzania when we visited in October 1998, this despite a mass of evidence that would provide any rational human with greater cause to give a wide birth to US embassies anywhere in the world than to cancel a holiday in East Africa.

Aside from this, the only part of Tanzania where there is currently a security problem is in the remote tract of Maasailand lying between Lake Natron and the Serengeti. The security situation here is the direct result of the recent incursion of a group of armed Somalis from Kenya, and while it has resulted in several deaths locally, the only effect on tourists to date has been an isolated incident in which a safari vehicle was held up along the road west of Natron. The indications are that this is a short-term problem, and it is unlikely that any responsible safari company would risk taking tourists into this area until it is resolved.

Tanzania shares a western border with the troubled countries of the Congo, Rwanda and Burundi, an area that sees very little tourism. So far as I am aware, the recent civil war in the Congo has had little direct effect on Tanzania, probably because the two countries are divided by Lake Tanganyika. The Rwanda and Burundi border areas have been overrun with refugees at several points over the last few years, a situation that is of some concern to locals, officials and international aid workers, but has had no effect whatsoever on parts of Tanzania that are likely to be visited by tourists.

Health

Dr Jane Wilson-Howarth

PREPARATIONS

Preparations to ensure a healthy trip to Africa require checks on your immunisation status: it is wise to be up to date on tetanus (ten-yearly), polio (ten-yearly), diphtheria (ten-yearly), and for many parts of Africa immunisations against yellow fever, meningococcus, rabies, and hepatitis A are also needed; most travellers should have immunisation against Hepatitis A with Havrix or the new Avaxim; the course of two injections costs about £80, but protects for ten years. Gamma globulin is theoretically an alternative if your trip is a short, spur of the moment, one-off visit; it gives immediate but partial protection for a couple of months and costs around£5. Typhoid immunisation is rather ineffective and it is debatable whether it is necessary for Africa. Immunisation against cholera is no longer required anywhere. Go – if you can – to a travel clinic a couple of months before departure to arrange all these.

Protection from the sun

Give some thought to packing suncream. The incidence of skin cancer is rocketing as Caucasians are travelling more and spending more time exposing themselves to the sun. Keep out of the sun during the middle of the day and, if you must be exposed tothe sun, build up gradually from 20 minutes per day. Be especially careful of sun reflected off water and wear a T-shirt and lots of waterproof SPF15 suncream when swimming; snorkelling often leads to scorched backs of the thighs so wear bermuda shorts. Sun exposure ages the skin and makes people prematurely wrinkly; cover up with long loose clothes and wear a hat when you can. The glare and the dust can be hard on the eyes too, so bring UV-protecting sunglasses and, perhaps, a soothing eyebath.

Malaria prevention

There is no vaccine against malaria, but there are other ways to avoid it; since most of Africa is very high risk for malaria, travellers must plan their malaria protection properly. Seek current advice on the best antimalarials to take. If mefloquine (Lariam) is suggested, start this two-and-a-half weeks (three doses) before departure to check that it suits you; stop it immediately if it seems to cause vivid and unpleasant dreams, mood changes or other changes in the way you feel. Anyone who is pregnant, who has suffered fits in the past, has been treated for depression or psychiatric problems or has a close blood relative who is epileptic should avoid mefloquine. The usual alternative is chloroquine (Nivaquine) two weekly and proguanil (Paludrine) two daily. Otherwise some doctors are suggesting doxycycline; this is unsuitable in pregnancy or for children under 12 years.

Some travellers will opt to carry a course of malaria treatment with them. Travellers to remote parts would probably be wise to carry a course of treatment to

MALARIA IN TANZANIA
Philip Briggs

Along with road accidents, malaria poses the single biggest serious threat to the health of travellers in most parts of tropical Africa, Tanzania included. The Anopheles mosquito which transmits the parasite is most abundant near marshes and still water, where it breeds, and the parasite is most prolific at low altitudes. Parts of Tanzania lying at an altitude of 2,000m or higher (a category that includes the Ngorongoro Crater rim, Mount Kilimanjaro and Meru, and parts of the eastern arc mountains) are regarded to be free of malaria. In mid-altitude locations, malaria is largely but not entirely seasonal, with the highest risk of transmission occurring during the rainy season. Moist and low-lying areas siuch as the Indian Ocean coast and hinterland of Lakes Tanganyika, Victoria and Nyasa are high risk throughout the year, but the danger is greatest during the rainy season. This localised breakdown might influence what foreigners working in Tanzania do about malaria prevention, but all travellers to Tanzania must assume that they will be exposed to malaria and should take precautions throughout their trip (see page 79 for advice on prophylactic drugs and avoiding mosquito bites).

Even those who take their malaria tablets meticulously and do everything possible to avoid mosquito bites may contract a strain of malaria that is resistant to prophylactic drugs. Untreated malaria is likely to be fatal, but even strains resistant to prophylaxis respond well to prompt treatment. Because of this, your immediate priority upon displaying possible malaria symptoms – which might include any combination of a headache, flu-like aches and pains, a rapid rise in temperature, a general sense of disorientation, and possibly even nausea and diarrhoea – is to establish whether you have malaria.

The blood test for malaria takes ten minutes to produce a result and costs about US$1 in Tanzania. A positive result means that you have malaria. A negative result suggests that you don't have malaria, bearing in mind that the parasite doesn't always show up on a test, particularly when the level of infection is mild or is 'cloaked' by partially effective prophylactics. For this reason, even if you test negative, it would be wise to stay within reach of a laboratory until the symptoms clear up, and to test again after a day or two if they don't. It's worth noting that if you have a fever and the malaria test is negative, you may have typhoid, which should also receive immediate treatment. Where typhoid-testing is unavailable, a routine blood test can give a strong indication of this disease.

cure malaria. Experts differ on the costs and benefits of self-treatment, but agree that it leads to over-treatment and to many people taking drugs they do not need; yet treatment may save your life. Discuss your trip with a specialist to determine your particular needs and risks, and be sure you understand when and how to take the cure. If you are somewhere remote in a malarious region you probably have to assume that any high fever for more than a few hours is due to malaria and should seek treatment. Diagnosing malaria is not easy, which is why consulting a doctor is sensible: there are other dangerous causes of fever in Africa which require different treatments. The malaria cure recommended by the British Airways travel clinic in Johannesburg is combination quinine (two x 300mg tablet twice daily for five days) plus doxycycline (100mg twice daily) which is started on day three of treatment. Fansidar seems to be less effective than it used to be, but it and other cures may be suggested by doctors. Whatever the cure you are carrying, it is important to understand it fully.

It is preferable not to attempt self-diagnosis or to start treatment for malaria before you have tested. There are, however, many places in Tanzania where you will be unable to test for malaria, for instance in the game reserves and on most of the popular hiking areas. With malaria, it is normal enough to go from feeling healthy to having a high fever in the space of a few hours (and it is possible to die from falciparum malaria within 24 hours of the first symptoms). In such circumstances, assume that you have malaria and act accordingly – whatever risks are attached to taking an unnecessary cure are outweighed by the dangers of untreated malaria.

It is imperative to treat malaria promptly. The sooner you take a cure, the less likely you are to become critically ill, and the more ill you become the greater the chance you'll have difficult holding down the tablets. There is some division about the best treatment for malaria, but the quinine/doxycycline regime (see below for dosages) is safe and very effective. If these tablets are unavailable, your next best option is probably Fansidar, which is widely available in Tanzania. One cure that you should avoid is Halfan which is dangerous, particularly if you are using Larium as a prophylactic.

In severe cases of malaria, the victim will be unable to hold down medication, at which point they are likely to die unless they are hospitalised immediately and put on a drip. If you or a travelling companion start vomiting after taking your malaria medication, get to a hospital a clinic quickly, ideally a private one. Whatever concerns you might have about African hospitals, they are used to dealing with malaria, and the alternative to hospitalisation is far worse.

Malaria typically takes around two weeks to incubate, but it can take much longer, so you should continue prophylaxis for at least four weeks after returning home. If you display possible malaria symptoms up to a year later, then get to a doctor immediately and ensure that they are aware you have been exposed to malaria.

Every so often I run into travellers who prefer to acquire resistance to malaria rather than take preventative tablets, or who witter on about homeopathic cures for this killer disease. That's their prerogative, but they have no place expounding their ill-informed views to others. Travellers to Africa cannot acquire any effective resistance to malaria, and those who don't make use of prophylactic drugs risk their life in a manner that is both foolish and unnecessary.

The risk of malaria above 1,800m above sea level is low. It is unwise to travel in malarious parts of Africa whilst pregnant or with children: the risk of malaria in many parts is considerable and these travellers are likely to succumb rapidly to the disease.

In addition to antimalarial medicines, it is important to avoid mosquito bites between dusk and dawn. Pack a DEET-based insect repellent, such as Autan, Jungle Jell or Cutters, (roll-ons or stick are the least messy preparations for travelling). You also need either a permethrin-impregnated bednet or a permethrin spray so that you can 'treat' bednets in hotels. Permethrin treatment makes even very tatty nets protective and prevents mosquitoes from biting through the impregnated net when you roll against it; it also deters other biters. Putting on long clothes at dusk means you can reduce the amount of repellent you need to put on your skin, but be aware that malaria mosquitoes hunt at ankle level and will bite through socks, so apply repellent under socks too. Travel clinics usually sell a good range of nets, treatment kits and repellents.

Travel clinics
United Kingdom
MASTA (Medical Advisory Service for Travellers Abroad), London School of Hygiene and Tropical Medicine, Keppel St, London WC1 7HT; tel: 0891 224100. This is a premium line number, charged at 50p per minute. Readers on the Internet may prefer to check their large website: http://dspace.dial.pipex.com/masta/index

British Airways Clinics There are now 30 clinics throughout Britain and three in South Africa. Tel: 01276 685040 (UK) for the address of your nearest one. Apart from providing inoculations and malaria prophylaxis, they sell a variety of health-related travel goods including malaria tablet memory cards, bednets and treatment kits.

Berkeley Travel Clinic 32 Berkeley St, London WIX 5FA (near Green Park tube station); tel: 0171 629 6233.

Fleet Street Travel Clinic 29 Fleet St, London EC4Y 1AA; tel: 0171 353 5678

Nomad Travel Pharmacy and Vaccination Centre 3–4 Wellington Terrace, Turnpike Lane, London N8 0PX; tel: 0181 889 7014.

Trailfinders Immunisation Clinic 194 Kensington High St, London W8 7RG; tel: 0171 938 3999.

Tropical Medicine Bureau This Irish-run organisation has a useful website specific to tropical destinations: http://www.tmb.le

USA
Centers for Disease Control This Atlanta-based organisation is the central source of travel health information in North America, with a touch-tone phone line and fax service. Travelers' Hot Line: (404) 332 4559. Each summer they publish the invaluable Health Information for International Travel, available from the Center for Prevention Services, Division of Quarantine, Atlanta, GA 30333.

Connaught Laboratories PO Box 187, Swiftwater, PA 18370; tel: 800 822 2463. They will send a free list of specialist tropical-medicine physicians in your state.

IAMAT (International Association for Medical Assistance to Travellers) 736 Center St, Lewiston, NY 14092, USA; tel: 716 754 4883.

Also at Gotthardstrasse 17, 6300 Zug, Switzerland.

A non-profit organisation which provide health information and lists of English-speaking doctors abroad.

MEDICAL FACILITIES IN TANZANIA
Philip Briggs

Private clinics, hospitals and pharmacies can be found in most large towns,and doctors generally speak fair to fluent English. Consultation fees and laboratory tests are remarkably inexpensive when compared to most Western countries, so if you do fall sick it would be absurd to let financial considerations dissuade you from seeking medical help. Commonly required medicines such as broad spectrum antibiotics and Flagyl are widely available and cheap throughout the region, as are malaria cures and prophylactics. Fansidar and quinine tablets are best bought in advance – in fact it's advisable to carry all malaria related tablets on you, and only rely on their availability locally if you need to restock your supplies.

If you are on any medication prior to departure, or you have specific needs relating to a known medical condition (for instance if you are allergic to bee stings or you are prone to attacks of asthma), then you are strongly advised to bring any related drugs and devices with you.

Australia
TMVC Tel: 1300 65 88 44; website: www.tmvc.com.au. TMVC has 20 clinics in Australia, New Zealand and Thailand, including:
Brisbane Dr Deborah Mills, Qantas Domestic Building, 6th floor, 247 Adelaide St, Brisbane, QLD 4000; tel: 7 3221 9066; fax: 7 3321 7076
Melbourne Dr Sonny Lau, 393 Little Bourke St, 2nd floor, Melbourne, VIC 3000; tel: 3 9602 5788; fax: 3 9670 8394.
Sydney Dr Mandy Hu, Dymocks Building, 7th floor, 428 George St, Sydney, NSW 2000; tel: 2 221 7133; fax: 2 221 8401.

South Africa
There are four **British Airways travel clinics** in South Africa: *Johannesburg*, tel: (011) 807 3132; *Cape Town*, tel: (021) 419 3172; *Knysna*, tel: (044) 382 6366; *East London*, tel: (0431) 43 2359.

Travel insurance
Don't think about travelling without a comprehensive medical travel insurance policy, one that will fly you home in an emergency. The ISIS policy, available in Britain through STA (tel: 0171 388 2266), is inexpensive and has a good reputation.

Personal first-aid kit
The more I travel the less I take. My minimal kit contains :

- A good drying antiseptic, eg: iodine or potassium permanganate (don't take antiseptic cream)
- A few small dressings (Band-Aids)
- Suncream
- Insect repellent; malaria tablets; impregnated bednet
- Aspirin or paracetamol
- Antifungal cream(eg: Canesten)
- Ciprofloxacin antibiotic, 500mg x 6 (or norfloxacin or nalidixic acid) for severe diarrhoea
- Another broad spectrum antibiotic like amoxycillin (for chest, urine, skin infections, etc.) if going to a remote area
- Antibiotic eye drops– for sore, 'gritty', stuck-together eyes (conjunctivitis)
- A pair of fine pointed tweezers (to remove hairy caterpillar hairs, thorns, splinters, coral, etc)
- Condoms or femidoms
- Maybe a malaria treatment kit and thermometer

MAJOR HAZARDS
People new to exotic travel often worry about tropical diseases, but it is accidents which are most likely to carry you off. Road accidents are very common in many parts of Africa so be aware and do what you can to reduce risks: try to travel during daylight hours and refuse to be driven by a drunk. Listen to local advice about areas where violent crime is rife too.

COMMON MEDICAL PROBLEMS
Travellers' diarrhoea
Travelling in Africa carries a fairly high risk of getting a dose of travellers' diarrhoea; perhaps half of all visitors will suffer and the newer you are to exotic travel, the more likely you will be to suffer. By taking precautions against travellers'

TREATING TRAVELLERS' DIARRHOEA

It is dehydration which makes you feel awful during a bout of diarrhoea and the most important part of treatment is drinking lots of clear fluids. Sachets of oral rehydration salts give the perfect biochemical mix to replace all that is pouring out of your bottom but other recipes taste nicer. Any dilute mixture of sugar and salt in water will do you good: try Coke or orange squash with a three-finger pinch of salt added to each glass (if you are salt-depleted you won't taste the salt). Otherwise make a solution of a four-finger scoop of sugar with a three-finger pinch of salt in a glass of water. Or add eight level teaspoons of sugar (18g) and one level teaspoon of salt (3g) to one litre (five cups) of safe water. A squeeze of lemon or orange juice improves the taste and adds potassium, which is also lost in diarrhoea. Drink two large glasses after every bowel action, and more if you are thirsty. These solutions are still absorbed well if you are vomiting, but you will need to take sips at a time. If you are not eating you need to drink three litres a day plus whatever is pouring into the toilet. If you feel like eating, take a bland, high carbohydrate, diet. Heavy greasy foods will probably give you cramps.

If the diarrhoea is bad, or you are passing blood or slime, or you have a fever, you will probably need antibiotics in addition to fluid replacement. A three-day course of ciprofloxacin 500mg twice daily for three days (or norfloxacin or nalidixic acid) is appropriate treatment for dysentery and bad diarrhoea.

diarrhoea you will also avoid typhoid, cholera, hepatitis, dysentery, worms, etc. Travellers' diarrhoea and the other faecal-oral diseases come from getting other peoples' faeces in your mouth. This most often happens from cooks not washing their hands after a trip to the toilet, but even if the restaurant cook does not understand basic hygiene you will be safe if your food has been properly cooked and arrives piping hot. The maxim to remind you what you can safely eat is:

PEEL IT, BOIL IT, COOK IT OR FORGET IT.

This means that fruit you have washed and peeled yourself, and hot foods, should be safe but raw foods, cold cooked foods, salads, fruit salads which have been prepared by others, ice-cream and ice are all risky. And foods kept lukewarm in hotel buffets are often dangerous. If you are struck, see box below for treatment.

Water sterilisation
It is much rarer to get sick from drinking contaminated water but it happens, so try to drink from safe sources.

Water should have been brought to the boil (even at altitude it only needs to be brought to the boil), or passed through a good bacteriological filter or purified with iodine; chlorine tablets (eg: Puritabs) are also adequate although theoretically less effective and they taste nastier. Mineral water has been found to be contaminated in many developing countries but should be safer than contaminated tap water.

Malaria
Whether or not you are taking malaria tablets, it is important to protect yourself from mosquito bites (see box on page 80 and Malaria prevention, above), so keep your repellent stick or roll-on to hand at all times. Be aware that no prophylactic is 100% protective but those on prophylactics who are unlucky enough to catch

malaria are less likely to get rapidly into serious trouble. It is easy and inexpensive to arrange a malaria blood test. It takes ten minutes and costs around US$1.

Insect bites
It is crucial to avoid mosquito bites between dusk and dawn; as the sun is going down, don long clothes and apply repellent on any exposed flesh. This will protect you from malaria, elephantiasis and a range of nasty insect-borne viruses. Otherwise retire to an air-conditioned room or burn mosquito coils (which are widely available and cheap in Tanzania) or sleep under a fan. Coils and fans reduce rather than eliminate bites. During the day it is wise to wear long, loose (preferably 100% cotton) clothes if you are pushing through scrubby country; this will keep ticks off and also tsetse and day-biting Aedes mosquitoes which may spread dengue and yellow fevers. Tsetse flies hurt when they bite and are attracted to the colour blue; locals will advise on where they are a problem and where they transmit sleeping sickness.

Minute pestilential biting **blackflies** spread river blindness in some parts of Africa between 190N and 170S; the disease is caught close to fast-flowing rivers since flies breed there and the larvae live in rapids. The flies bite during the day but long trousers tucked into socks will help keep them off. Citronella-based natural repellents do not work against them.

Mosquitoes and many other insects are attracted to light. If you are camping, never put a lamp near the opening of your tent, or you will have a swarm of biters waiting to join you when you retire. In hotel rooms, be aware that the longer your light is on, the greater the number of insects will be sharing your accommodation.

Tumbu flies or *putsi* are a problem in areas of East, West and southern Africa where the climate is hot and humid. The adult fly lays her eggs on the soil or on drying laundry and when the eggs come in contact with human flesh (when you put on clothes or lie on a bed) they hatch and bury themselves under the skin. Here they form a crop of 'boils' which each hatches a grub after about eight days, when the inflammation will settle down. In putsi areas either dry your clothes and sheets within a screened house, or dry them in direct sunshine until they are crisp, or iron them.

Jiggers or **sandfleas** are another flesh-feaster. They latch on if you walk barefoot in contaminated places, and set up home under the skin of the foot, usually at the side of a toenail where they cause a painful, boil-like swelling. They need picking out by a local expert; if the distended flea bursts during eviction the wound should be dowsed in spirit, alcohol or kerosene, otherwise more jiggers will infest you.

QUICK TICK REMOVAL
African ticks are not the prolific disease transmitters they are in the Americas, but they may spread Lyme disease, tick-bite fever and a few rarities. Tick-bite fever is a non-serious, flu-like illness, but still worth avoiding. If you get the tick off whole and promptly the chances of disease transmission are reduced to a minimum. Manoeuvre your finger and thumb so that you can pinch the tick's mouthparts, as close to your skin as possible, and slowly and steadily pull away at right angles to your skin. This often hurts. Jerking or twisting will increase the chances of damaging the tick, which in turn increases the chances of disease transmission, as well as leaving the mouthparts behind. Once the tick is off, dowse the little wound with alcohol (local spirit, whisky or similar are excellent) or iodine. An area of spreading redness around the bite site, or a rash or fever coming on a few days or more after the bite, should stimulate a trip to a doctor.

Bilharzia or schistosomiasis
With thanks to Dr Vaughan Southgate of the Natural History Museum, London

Bilharzia or schistosomiasis is a disease which commonly afflicts the rural poor of the tropics who repeatedly acquire more and more of these nasty little worm-lodgers. Infected travellers and expatriates generally suffer fewer problems because symptoms will encourage them to seek prompt treatment and they are also exposed to fewer parasites. However, it is still an unpleasant problem that is worth avoiding.

The parasites digest their way through your skin when you wade, bathe or even shower in infested fresh water. Unfortunately, many African lakes, rivers and irrigation canals carry a risk of bilharzia.

The most risky shores will be close to places where infected people use water, wash clothes, etc. Winds disperse the cercariae, though, so they can be blown some distance, perhaps up to 200m from where they entered the water. Scuba-diving off a boat into deep offshore water, then, should be a low-risk activity, but showering in lake water or paddling along a reedy lake shore near a village is risky.

Although absence of early symptoms does not necessarily mean there is no infection, infected people usually notice symptoms two or more weeks after parasite-penetration. Travellers and expatriates will probably experience a fever and often a wheezy cough; local residents do not usually have symptoms. There is now a very good blood test which, if done six weeks or more after likely exposure, will determine whether you need treatment. Since bilharzia can be a nasty illness, avoidance is better than waiting to be cured and it is wise to avoid bathing in high risk areas.

Avoiding bilharzia

- If you are bathing, swimming, paddling or wading in freshwater which you think may carry a bilharzia risk, try get out of the water within ten minutes.
- Dry off thoroughly with a towel; rub vigorously.
- Avoid bathing or paddling on shores within 200m of villages or places where people use the water a great deal, especially reedy shores or where there is lots of water weed.
- If your bathing water comes from a risky source try to ensure that the water is taken from the lake in the early morning and stored snail-free, otherwise it should be filtered or Dettol or Cresol added.
- Bathing early in the morning is safer than bathing in the last half of the day.
- Covering yourself with DEET insect repellent before swimming will protect you.
- If you think that you have been exposed to bilharzia parasites, arrange a screening blood test (your GP can do this) MORE than six weeks after your last possible contact with suspect water.

Skin infections

Any mosquito bite or small nick in the skin gives an opportunity for bacteria to foil the body's usually excellent defences; it will surprise many travellers how quickly skin infections start in warm humid climates and it is essential to clean and cover even the slightest wound. Creams are not as effective as a good drying antiseptic such as dilute iodine, potassium permanganate (a few crystals in half a cup of water), or crystal (or gentian) violet. One of these should be available in most towns. If the wound starts to throb, or becomes red and the redness starts to spread, or the wound oozes, and especially if you develop a fever, antibiotics will probably be needed: flucloxacillin (250mg four times a day) or cloxacillin (500mg four times a day). For those allergic to penicillin, erythromycin (500mg twice a day) for five days

MARINE DANGERS

Most established tourist beaches in Tanzania can assumed to be safe for swimming. Elsewhere along the coast, it would be wise to ask local advice before plunging in the water, and to err on the side of caution if no sensible advice is forthcoming, since there is always a possibility of being swept away by strong currents or undertows that cannot be detected until you are actually in the water.

Snorkellers and divers should wear something on their feet to avoid treading on coral reefs, and should never touch the reefs with their bare hands - coral itself can give nasty cuts, and there is a danger of touching a venomous creature camoflagued against the reef.. On beaches, never walk barefoot on exposed coral. Even on sandy beaches, people who walk barefoot risk getting coral or urchin spines in your soles or venomous fish spines in your feet.

If you do tread on a venomous fish, soak the foot in hot (but not scalding) water until some time after the pain subsides; this may be for 20-30 minutes in all. Take the foot out of the water to top up otherwise you may scald it. If the pain returns re-immerse the foot. Once the venom has been heat-inactivated, get a doctor to check and remove any bits of fish spine in the wound.

should help. See a doctor if the symptoms do not start to improve in 48 hours.

Fungal infections also get a hold easily in hot moist climates so wear 100% cotton socks and underwear and shower frequently. An itchy rash in the groin or flaking between the toes is likely to be a fungal infection. This needs treatment with an antifungal cream such as Canesten (clotrimazole); if this is not available try Whitfield's ointment (compound benzoic acid ointment) or crystal violet (although this will turn you purple!).

Eye problems

Bacterial conjunctivitis (pink eye) is a common infection in Africa; people who wear contact lenses are most open to this irritating problem. The eyes feel sore and gritty and they will often be stuck together in the mornings. They will need treatment with antibiotic drops or ointment. Lesser eye irritation should settle with bathing in salt water and keeping the eyes shaded. If an insect flies into your eye, extract it with great care, ensuring you do not crush or damage it otherwise you may get a nastily inflamed eye from toxins secreted by the creature.

Prickly heat

A fine pimply rash on the trunk is likely to be heat rash; cool showers, dabbing dry, and talc will help. Treat the problem by slowing down to a relaxed schedule, wearing only loose, baggy 100% cotton clothes and sleeping naked under a fan; if it's bad you may need to check into an air-conditioned hotel room for a while.

Meningitis

This is a particularly nasty disease as it can kill within hours of the first symptoms appearing. Usually it starts as a thumping headache and high fever; there may be a blotchy rash too. Immunisation protects against meningococcus A and C, the common and serious bacterial form in Africa, but not against all of the many kinds of meningitis. Local papers normally report localised outbreaks. A severe headache and fever should make you run to a doctor immediately. There are other causes of headache and fever; one of these is typhoid, which occurs in travellers to Africa. Seek medical help if you are ill for more than a few days.

Safe sex

Travel is a time when we may enjoy sexual adventures, especially when alcohol reduces inhibitions. Remember that the risks of sexually transmitted infection are high, whether you sleep with fellow travellers or locals. About 40% of HIV infections in British heterosexuals are acquired abroad. Use condoms or femidoms; spermicide pessaries help reduce the risk of transmission. If you notice any genital ulcers or discharge get treatment promptly since these increase the risk of acquiring HIV.

Rabies

Small monkeys who are used to being fed by humans may bite and can carry rabies; village dogs must also be assumed to be rabid. Any suspect bites should be scrubbed under running water for five minutes and then flooded with local spirit or dilute iodine. Two post-bite rabies injections are needed even in immunised people, while those who are not immunised need a course of injections. These should be given within a week if the bites are to the face, but if the bites are further from the brain the incubation period is longer and you probably have more time; make sure you get the injections even if you are a very long way from civilisation. The incubation period for rabies can be very long so never say that it is too late to bother. Death from rabies is probably one of the worst ways to go!

Snakes

Snakes rarely attack unless provoked, and bites in travellers are unusual. You are less likely to get bitten if you wear stout shoes and long trousers when in the bush. Most snakes are harmless and even venomous species will dispense venom in only about half of their bites. If bitten, then, you are unlikely to have received venom; keeping this fact in mind may help you to stay calm. Many so-called first-aid techniques do more harm than good: cutting into the wound is harmful; tourniquets are dangerous; suction and electrical inactivation devices do not work. The only treatment is antivenom. In case of a bite which you fear may have been from a venomous snake:

- Try to keep calm - it is likely that no venom has been dispensed.
- Prevent movement of the bitten limb by applying a splint.
- Keep the bitten limb BELOW heart height to slow the spread of any venom.
- If you have a crepe bandage, bind up as much of the bitten limb as you can, but release the bandage every half hour.
- Evacuate to a hospital which has antivenom.

And remember:

NEVER give aspirin; you may offer paracetamol, which is safe.
NEVER cut or suck the wound.
DO NOT apply ice packs.
DO NOT apply potassium permanganate.

If the offending snake can be captured without risk of someone else being bitten, take this to show the doctor – but beware since even a decapitated head is able to bite.

Part Two

The Guide

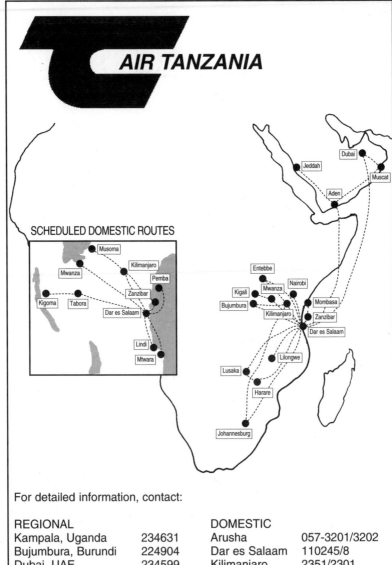

AIR TANZANIA

SCHEDULED DOMESTIC ROUTES

For detailed information, contact:

REGIONAL		DOMESTIC	
Kampala, Uganda	234631	Arusha	057-3201/3202
Bujumbura, Burundi	224904	Dar es Salaam	110245/8
Dubai, UAE	234599	Kilimanjaro	2351/2301
Lusaka, Zambia	228294	Mwanza	2741/40390
Harare, Zimbabwe	752537	Zanzibar	30297/32441
Johannesburg, RSA	6164353	Moshi	55205/6
Lilongwe, Malawi	783636	Mtwara	2036/3147/3417
Mombasa, Kenya	226442		
Muscat, Oman	707222		
Nairobi, Kenya	214783		
Aden, Yemen	241534		

AIR TANZANIA

Arusha

The undisputed safari capital of Tanzania, Arusha is the base from which travellers can visit the country's most renowned game reserves, and it is the busiest tourist centre anywhere on the Tanzanian mainland. Arusha is also an increasingly important gateway into Tanzania, the first town visited by travellers coming from Nairobi in Kenya, and the entry point for an ever-increasing number of fly-in tourists, a trend that is likely to gather further momentum with the recent privatisation of the nearby Kilimanjaro International Airport.

In all probability, your first impression of Arusha will be that practically *everything* revolves around the safari industry. Prolonged exposure to Arusha is unlikely to change your mind on that score. True, this moderately sized town does lie at the heart of the fertile agricultural lands surrounding Mount Meru, but ultimately its economy is ruled by the tourist dollar. Every second vehicle you see in Arusha is a 4x4 sporting a safari company logo. And many of the *matatus* (minibuses) that weave along the streets of Arusha are former safari vehicles. There is something comically incongruous about the sight of your standard crowded Tanzanian *matatu*, but with a bunch of heads sticking out of the open-topped roof as if waiting for an elephant to emerge from the nearest bush.

We've always found Arusha to be a pleasantly relaxed place to hang out, but there is no doubt that it can be daunting on first contact, especially for those who arrive by bus. Competition between the various safari companies is fierce, particularly at the bottom end of the price range, and the 'flycatchers' – the street touts who solicit custom for many budget safari companies – know that their best tactic is to catch backpackers as early as possible. As a consequence, your first few minutes in Arusha bus station are likely to be spent dodging the attention of a dozen yelling touts, all of whom can offer you the cheapest safari and best room in town. Fortunately, once you've run the bus station gauntlet, things do calm down – you can expect to be approached by the occasional flycatcher, but you need only tell them that you've already been on safari and they'll be on their way. I've probably spent some 20 days in Arusha over the years, and can't ever recall hitting a situation that so much as threatened to become unpleasant.

Despite the booming safari industry, Arusha is in appearance something of an African everytown. Founded as a German garrison in 1900, it initially grew to prominence as the service centre for the surrounding farmlands, and even today has a somewhat time-warped urban landscape, with the town centre boasting a high proportion of low-rise buildings dating to the colonial era. In some respects, Arusha encapsulates the conflicting images that greet the modern African traveller; the safari industry may have generated immense wealth, but this also serves to accentuate the vast differences that separate the haves from the have-nots. Here,

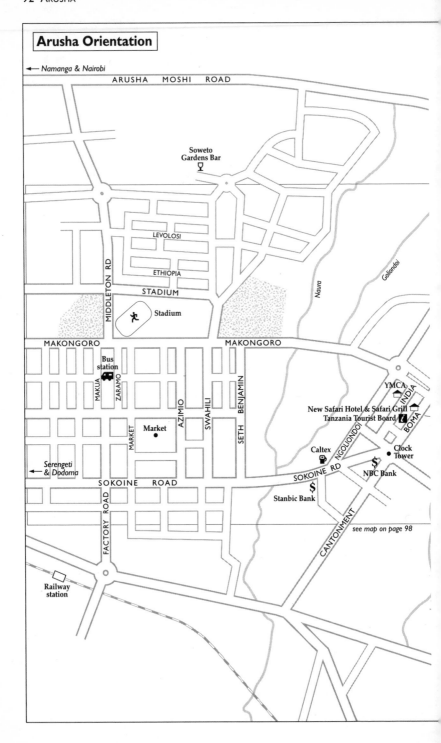

Arusha Orientation

← Namanga & Nairobi

ARUSHA   MOSHI   ROAD

Soweto
Gardens Bar

LEVOLOSI

ETHIOPIA

MIDDLETON RD

STADIUM

Stadium

Naura

Goliondoi

MAKONGORO

MAKONGORO

Bus
station

MAKUA

ZARAMO

AZIMIO

SWAHILI

SETH   BENJAMIN

YMCA

INDIA

New Safari Hotel & Safari Grill
Tanzania Tourist Board

BOMA

Market

Caltex

NGOLIONDOI

Clock
Tower

← Serengeti
& Dodoma

MARKET

SOKOINE   ROAD

NBC Bank

SOKOINE   RD

Stanbic Bank

FACTORY   ROAD

CANTONMENT

see map on page 98

Railway
station

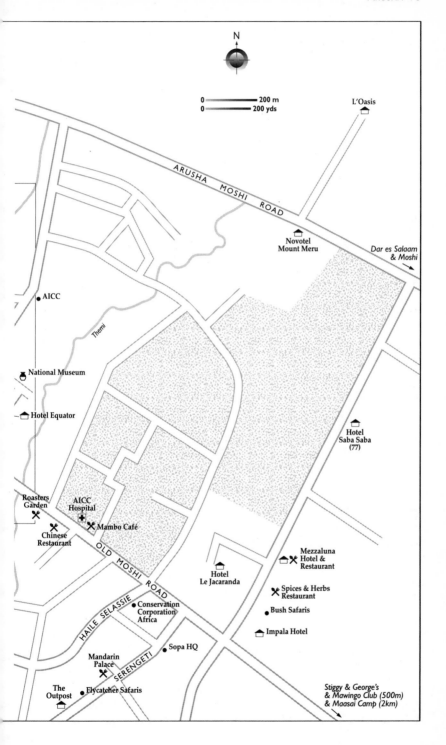

N

0 ——————— 200 m
0 ——————— 200 yds

L'Oasis

ARUSHA MOSHI ROAD

Novotel
Mount Meru

Dar es Salaam
& Moshi

AICC

Themi

National Museum

Hotel Equator

Hotel
Saba Saba
(77)

Roasters
Garden

AICC
Hospital

Mambo Café

Chinese
Restaurant

OLD MOSHI ROAD

Mezzaluna
Hotel &
Restaurant

Hotel
Le Jacaranda

Spices & Herbs
Restaurant

Bush Safaris

Impala Hotel

HAILE SELASSIE

Conservation
Corporation
Africa

Sopa HQ

Mandarin
Palace

SERENGETI

The
Outpost

Flycatcher Safaris

Stiggy & George's
& Mawingo Club (500m)
& Maasai Camp (2km)

too, you'll encounter that spectrum of cultural influences which tends to play havoc with the minds of visitors in search of the real Africa. Which is it, then: the colourfully dressed Maasai and Arusha women who sell traditional beadware on the pavement, the besuited businessmen who scurry in and out of the International Conference Centre, or the swaggering, sunglassed wide-boys who will offer you cheap safaris, change money, cocaine...?

If nothing else, Arusha is an attractively green town, with a skyline dominated by the imposing hulk of Mount Meru, at 4,556m the fifth-highest mountain in Africa. Mount Meru is the dominant geographical feature in Arusha National Park which, despite its proximity to Arusha and manifold points of interest, attracts little more than a trickle of tourism. Also of interest in the immediate vicinity of Arusha is Lake Duluti, an attractive forest-fringed crater lake that lies within easy walking distance of the Moshi Road, and a couple of recently introduced cultural tourism projects that allow travellers the opportunity to visit local villages on the verdant lower slopes of Mount Meru.

The town centre is bisected by the Naura River. The more upmarket part of town lies to the east of the river, and this is where you'll find most of the safari companies, smart hotels, curio shops, banks and official facilities. Major landmarks in this part of town include the Clock Tower and the Arusha International Conference Centre (AICC), home to many safari companies and currently where the UN hearings relating to war crimes in Rwanda are taking place. The more bustling trade area to the west of the river is centred around the market and bus station.

Arusha used to be notorious for having an erratic electricity and water supply, but we experienced no cuts over the several days we spent in Arusha in 1998, so it seems that things have improved. The same cannot be said for the potholed roads, one of the few reminders of the economic doldrums that Arusha found itself in during the tourist industry crisis of the 1980s.

A structural note In previous editions of this guide, Arusha and the northern safari circuit were covered together in one chapter. I have decided to split them for this edition, largely because this ever-expanding combined chapter was becoming long and unwieldly. For readers who pre-book their safari before arriving in Tanzania, this split will simplify things, as all the information pertaining to safari organisation is now contained in one dedicated chapter. The split will make no significant difference to readers who plan on organising their safari once they arrive in Arusha.

GETTING THERE AND AWAY
As tourism to Tanzania increases, so does Arusha play an increasingly pivotal role as the main transport hub for visitors to the country, whether they travel by air or by road.

Air
Kilimanjaro International Airport (KIA) lies roughly halfway along the 120km road connecting Arusha to Moshi. The privatisation of KIA in late 1998 may well encourage more international airlines to land there during the lifespan of this edition. For the time being, however, most Arusha-bound tourists will first land at Dar es Salaam (from where there are daily domestic flights to Arusha) or at Nairobi in Kenya (from where they can either fly to Arusha or else arrange to be transferred by shuttle bus).

In addition to Dar es Salaam and Nairobi, there are scheduled flights between Arusha and Lake Manyara, Ngorongoro, Serengeti, Mwanza, Bukoba, Zanzibar, Pemba, Mafia, Mbeya and Mombasa in Kenya. Some of these flights land at KIA, while others, mostly light aircraft, land at the smaller airport immediately outside Arusha. Most scheduled flights are either with Air Tanzania, whose Arusha office is on Boma Road roughly opposite the post office, or else with Precision Air, whose Arusha office is on the ground floor of the AICC (see page 61 for further contact addresses and sample prices). Most tourists flying around Tanzania will have made their flight arrangements in advance through a tour operator, and this is certainly the recommended way of going about things, but it is generally possible to buy tickets from Arusha to major destinations such as Dar es Salaam and Zanzibar at short notice.

There is a regular shuttle service between the Air Tanzania office in Arusha and KIA, and the staff at the Air Tanzania office will be able to tell you when to be ready to catch it. At around US$5 per head, the shuttle will work out more cheaply than a taxi for one person, but will be more costly than a taxi for three or four people. Note that most upmarket hotels in the Arusha area offer a free transfer service to guests leaving or arriving from KIA.

Rail

There are no passenger services to Arusha, and the train service between nearby Moshi and Dar es Salaam has been suspended for the time being. If this service is resumed, you should be able to make a booking at Arusha's otherwise unused railway station.

Road

A number of companies run express bus services to and from Dar es Salaam. These generally take around eight hours, stopping only at Moshi to pick up further passengers and at Korogwe for a 20 minute lunch break, and tickets cost US$10-12. Most such buses leave early in the morning, so it advisable to make enquiries and a booking the afternoon before you want to leave. Recommended companies include Air Msae, Dar Express and Fresh ya Shamba. The cheaper bus services between Arusha and Dar es Salaam aren't worth bothering with, as they stop at every town and can take anything from 12 to 15 hours to cover the same distance.

A steady stream of minibuses and buses connect Moshi and Arusha. I would avoid using minibuses along this route due to the higher incidence of accidents, but they are generally quicker than buses. This trip usually takes between one and two hours.

The quickest and most efficient road transport between Arusha and Nairobi are the twice-daily shuttle buses run by Devanu. These leave in either direction at 07.30 and 13.30 daily, and take around five hours, depending on how quickly you pass through immigration and customs at Namanga. Tickets cost around US$15 and can be bought from several tour operators in Arusha, or from the booking office on the ground floor of the Ngorongoro Wing of the AICC. It is also possible to get between Nairobi and Arusha in short hops, a cheaper but slower option covered more fully in the section on *Getting to Tanzania* on page 45.

Two bus routes out of Arusha that cannot be recommended are to Dodoma and to Mwanza via Shinyanga, in both cases because the roads are in dreadful condition. Details of travelling between Arusha and Mwanza are included under *Mwanza* in *Chapter 14*.

WHERE TO STAY
Upper range
In Arusha

Mount Meru Novotel PO Box 877, Arusha; tel: 057 2711/2; fax: 057 8221; email: tahifin@habari.yako.co.tz. The only hotel in Arusha to truly approach international standards, the Novotel lies within walking distance of the town centre along the Moshi road. Set in landscaped gardens overlooking the golf course, facilities include a large outdoor swimming pool, two restaurants, and a relatively efficient business centre. Large rooms with en-suite bathrooms, private balconies and satellite television cost US$116/145 single/double, with a 30% discount for Tanzanian residents.

Impala Hotel PO Box 7302; tel: 057 8448/3453; fax: 057 8220/8680; email: impala@cybernet.co.tz. Situated about ten minutes' walk from the town centre, the Impala is rated by many tour operators as the best value in its range in the immediate vicinity of Arusha. The attractively decorated rooms have television, hot showers and a fridge, and cost US$60/72 single/double.

Ilboru Safari Lodge PO Box 8012; tel: 057 7834. Also favoured by tour operators, this lodge lies about 2km from the town centre in leafy suburban grounds below Mount Meru, is a pleasant, peaceful retreat and reasonably priced at US$65/75 single/double.

L'Oasis Lodge PO Box 14280; tel/fax: 057 7089; mobile: 0811 510531. This new hotel charges similar prices to Ilboru, and is equally attractive, set in large green grounds off the Moshi Road, about 500m along a side road signposted from opposite the Mount Meru Novotel.

Towards Usa River

More interesting than any of the upmarket hotels immediately around Arusha is the cluster of accommodation in the Usa River area, about 20km out of town on the Moshi Road, near the turn-off to Arusha National Park.

Mount Meru Game Sanctuary PO Box 659; tel: 057 8106; fax: 057 8273. This place has something of an 'Out of Africa' ambience, consisting of a main stone building and a few semi-detached wooden cabins surrounded by bougainvillaea-draped gardens. The sanctuary includes a large open enclosure in front of the rooms, stocked with a variety of antelope, and also the site of a large papyrus heronry where hundreds of cattle egrets roost at dusk. Behind the main building, a small zoo is home to a few ill or orphaned animals, and there is potentially good birding in the stretch of forest that fringes the Usa River. Despite the artificiality of the surrounds, the sanctuary sets the tone nicely for a safari, particularly if you stay in rooms one and two, where the animals are practically on your doorstep and the evening air reverberates with the incessant squawking from the heronry. Rooms cost US$75/95 single/double b&b. The food is excellent: lunch costs US$12 and three-course dinner US$15.

Mountain Village Lodge PO Box 376; tel: 057 2699; fax: 057 8967; email: ranger-safaris@cybernet.co.tz. Highly regarded by many tour operators, this attractive lodge lies on a coffee farm on the verge of the gorgeous forest-fringed Lake Duluti. On a clear day, the ground boasts views to Mount Meru and Kilimanjaro. The main building is a converted thatched farmhouse dating to the colonial era, and accommodation is in self-contained chalets costing US$62/75 b&b. Other meals cost an extra US$10 each.

Dik Dik Hotel PO Box 1499; tel/fax: 057 8110; email: dikdik@mail.utx.ch. This smart Swiss-owned lodge is set in green grounds with a swimming pool. The restaurant is rated by some as the best in the Arusha area, and the rooms are certainly among the most comfortable we've seen in Tanzania. Rates are US$141/212 single/double b&b or US$160/250 full board.

Ngere Sero Lodge PO Box 425, tel: 057 3629, fax: 057 8690. A small, exclusive retreat, this lodge is set in an old colonial residence on the foot slopes of Mount Meru, with views to Kilimanjaro on a clear day. The grounds are noted for their prolific bird life, and enclose a waterfall and a small lake stocked with trout. Accommodation costs US$100 per person full board.

Tanzanite Hotel PO Box 3063, Arusha; tel: Usa River 169. The closest thing to budget accommodation in this neck of the woods, the Tanzanite is a serviceable hotel offering acceptable rooms for US$50/60 single/double b&b, as well as camping for US$5 per person. Meals cost around US$7.

Moderate

Highly recommended in this range is the **Arusha Resort Centre** (tel: 057 8033), an under-publicised complex with a convenient location on Fire Road about 200m from the Clock Tower. Well-screened double rooms with hot showers cost US$40 b&b, while apartments with en-suite kitchens cost US$40/80 b&b single/double, with a 10% discount for weekly occupation. There is a bar and restaurant attached.

One of the best, cheapest and most conveniently situated hotels in this range is the recently renovated **Pallson's Hotel** (PO Box 773; tel: 057 8602; fax: 057 6411), where clean, pleasant self-contained rooms with hot water and fans cost US$30/40 single/double.

A new recommendation, situated close to the Impala Hotel, is the Italian-owned **Mezzaluna Hotel**, which has clean, comfortable s/c rooms for US$35/45 single/double b&b, and is attached to the excellent Mezzaluna Restaurant. Also quite new, the nearby **Hotel Le Jacaranda** offers reasonable accommodation in what was once a residential property for US$45/50 single/double.

Also in the same part of town, the **Hotel Saba-Saba (77)** (PO Box 1184; tel: 057 3822; fax: 057 8407) claims to be the largest tourist village in East or Central Africa, a title that is not so much meaningless as downright misleading. The hotel consists of several cheerless concrete quadrangles, reminiscent of prison more than any village I've encountered. The rooms are adequate, and sensibly priced at US$30/40, but I feel nothing but pity for any tourist who happens to spend their first night in Africa in such an austere environment.

Back in the city centre, you have the choice of three somewhat utilitarian hotels along Boma Road. The **New Arusha Hotel** (PO Box 88; tel: 057 3241) opposite the Clock Tower is in urgent need of an overhaul and can't really be recommended. Far better, the **New Safari Hotel** (PO Box 303; tel: 057 3261/3115) re-opened in 1998 following extensive renovations, seems pretty good value at US$40/60 s/c single/double. Also recommended, and practically opposite the New Safari, is the **Hotel Equator** (PO Box 3002; tel: 057 8410; fax: 057 8085), which has clean s/c rooms with hot shower for US$40/50 single/double).

Other acceptable moderate hotels in central Arusha include the **Golden Rose Hotel** (PO Box 361, tel: 057 8860 – US$40/50 single/double); the overpriced **Hotel AM88** (PO Box 10045; tel: 057 7873; fax: 057 7168 – US$40/60 single/double) and the **Eland Hotel** (tel: 057 7868/6892 – US$30/40 single/double).

Budget

Quite a wide range of budget accommodation is available in Arusha, ranging from innumerable local guesthouses which offer basic accommodation for around US$5, to a number of cleaner hotels where decent self-contained accommodation costs anything up to US$25 for a double room. For the sake of convenience, the following places are mentioned in roughly descending order of price.

The most expensive place in this range is **The Outpost** (37a Serengeti Street; tel: 057 8405), an Australian-owned backpackers-style hostel in a suburban Arusha garden. It's a nice enough place, but much pricier than such establishments tend to be elsewhere in Africa. As far as I could establish from the receptionist, a bed in a dormitory now costs US$14 per person, while private rooms cost US$24/30 single/double inclusive of a light breakfast. Cheap lunches and dinners are available. To get here from the Clock Tower, follow Uhuru Avenue east out of

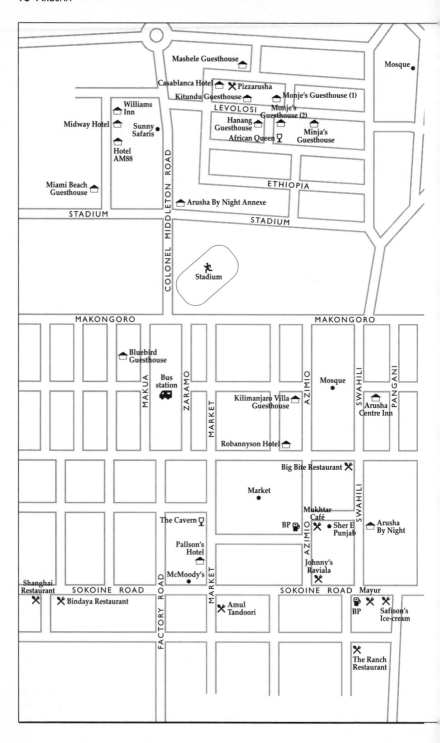

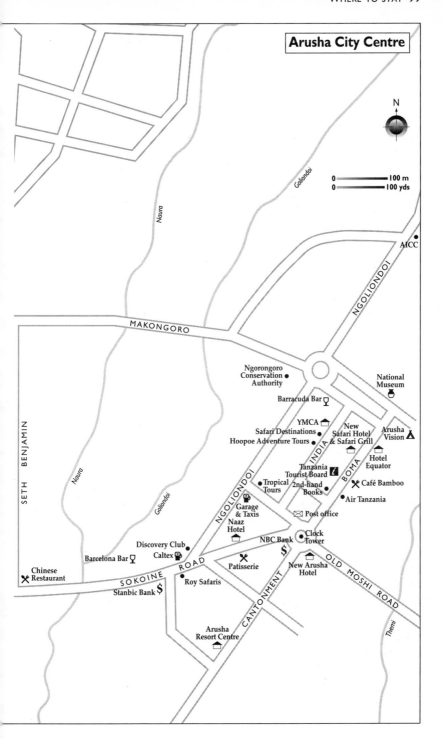

Arusha City Centre

N

0 ——————— 100 m
0 ——————— 100 yds

AICC

MAKONGORO

NGOLIONDOI

Goliondoi

Naura

Ngorongoro
Conservation ●
Authority

National
Museum

Barracuda Bar ⚲

YMCA

Safari Destinations ●
Hoopoe Adventure Tours ●

New
Safari Hotel
& Safari Grill

Arusha
Vision

INDIA

BOMA

Hotel
Equator

Tanzania
Tourist Board *i*

2nd-hand
Books

Café Bamboo

Tropical ●
Tours

● Air Tanzania

SETH BENJAMIN

Naura

Goliondoi

Garage
& Taxis

⊠ Post office

Naaz
Hotel

NGOLIONDOI

Discovery Club ●

Barcelona Bar ⚲

Caltex

NBC Bank

Clock
Tower

Chinese
✕ Restaurant

SOKOINE

ROAD

Patisserie ✕

New Arusha
Hotel

OLD MOSHI ROAD

Stanbic Bank $

● Roy Safaris

CANTONMENT

Themi

Arusha
Resort Centre

town for about 1km, then take the signposted right turn about 500m further, and the house is about 300m down the road to your left.

The **Naaz Hotel** (PO Box 1060; tel: 057 2087) on Sokoine Road, also close to the Clock Tower, has long been popular with travellers. It remains very clean, convenient, quiet and secure, but the rooms are rather variable in standard. The self-contained doubles in the new wing have nets and fans, and feel reasonably priced at US$25, but not the doubles in the old wing, which are rather run-down, use communal showers and cost US$20. There is a good, inexpensive restaurant on the ground floor.

Similar in price and standard is the **Arusha By Night Annexe** near the stadium, which has clean self-contained rooms with hot showers for US$20/25 single/double. Better still, though I've yet to meet a traveller who has stayed there, is the **Arusha Centre Inn**, a multi-storey building close to the market, but it struck me as excellent value for money at US$15/20 for a s/c single/double with hot water, nets and fan.

The **YMCA** used to be quite popular with travellers, but these days it seems very overpriced at US$13/15 single/double for a scruffy room using erratic communal showers. Better value at this sort of price is the recently reconstructed **Robannyson Hotel** opposite the market, where s/c 'singles' with one double bed cost US$7.50, and s/c 'doubles' with two double beds cost US$15. All rooms here have hot running water.

The **Midway Hotel** near the stadium charges US$10 for an ordinary double with nets and fans, or US$15 for an s/c double with nets, fans and a balcony. Practically next door, the **Williams Inn** offers similar accommodation at much the same price. Both of these places are reasonable value without being anything special.

These days, most backpackers head out to the cluster of guesthouses dotted on and around Levolosi Road, a five-minute walk from the bus station passing behind the stadium. All of these places charge around US$4.50/5.00 single/double, and there is plenty of choice.

Our first recommendation in this area is **Monje's Guesthouse**, a quiet, family-run affair which actually consists of three guesthouses on opposite sides of the same road. All three places have clean rooms, friendly staff, hot showers and a vigorously enforced anti-flycatcher policy! Other recommendations in this area are the **Kitundu Guesthouse** (also known as **'K' Guesthouse**), **Minja's Guesthouse** and the **Hanang Guesthouse**, though the last of these places charge double rates to tourists which makes it seem rather overpriced.

If you are heading for the above cluster of lodgings, be warned that the apparent popularity of the **Mashele Guesthouse** is largely because it's the place to which most flycatchers first point travellers. And the reason why the flycatchers do this is because the Mashele is one of the few guesthouses in the area that will let them hassle travellers on the premises – and if having to make friends with half the flycatchers in Arusha isn't reason enough to put you off staying there, then a recent spate of theft from the rooms and barroom brawls between rival flycatchers should be.

Camping

The **Arusha Vision Campsite** (PO Box 12330, tel: 057 2894) lies alongside the river next to the Equator Hotel. The management is very friendly and helpful, and the atmosphere is homely and surprisingly rustic for somewhere only 50m from the town centre. Any qualms about the apparently lax security should be put to rest by a flip through the visitors' book, which is full of raves from travellers who ended up staying a week here. Camping costs US$1.50 per person (you can hire a tent for an extra US$1) and dormitory accommodation costs US$2.50. Food is basic but tasty and there's plenty of it – breakfast costs US$1 and dinner less than US$2. Black tea is free.

Further out of town, about 2km down the Old Moshi Road, **Maasai Camp** is one of the most popular campsites in Tanzania, used mostly by overland trucks but large enough that there's plenty of space for independent travellers. Facilities include an ablution block with hot water, a pool table, volleyball and a lively 24-hour bar. The restaurant is well-known for pizzas, which cost around US$3.50 each. If you're without transport, you can get a taxi here for around US$2, and there are plans to introduce a lift service from the town centre. Camping costs US$3 per person. Tents can be hired for US$3 per night. Self-contained double *banda*s (huts) are under construction at the time of writing, and should be available by the time you read this at around US$25. A safari company called Tropical Trails is based at Maasai Camp; both can be contacted at PO Box 6130, Arusha; tel/fax: 057 8299; email: info@tropicaltrails.com, web: www.tropicaltrails.com.

A similar distance out of town along the main Moshi Road, **Club Afriko** is clearly signposted and readily accessible by public transport. Set in attractive grounds, this low-key site has similar facilities to Maasai Camp, and will probably appeal more to those who prefer to avoid the sort of 'party' atmosphere associated with the sites favoured by overland trucks. Camping costs US$3 per person.

There is a lovely and surprisingly little-used campsite at the **Duluti Club**, on the edge of forest-fringed Lake Duluti, towards Usa River on the Moshi Road. Facilities include an ablution block and a cafeteria serving basic meals and cold drinks. To get there from Arusha, catch any vehicle heading towards Moshi and hop off when you see a large carved wooden giraffe to your left. The turn-off to Duluti Club is signposted to the right opposite this statue; it's about 20 minutes' walk from the main road to the campsite. Camping costs US$3 per person.

You can camp in the grounds of the **Tanzanite Hotel** in Usa River for US$5 per person. There are good facilities for campers and you can eat in the hotel for around US$6-7.

WHERE TO EAT

There are any number of interesting restaurants in Arusha, with a wide number of international cuisines represented and most budgets catered for by a number of places.

Indian restaurants are particularly well represented in the town centre. At the upper end of the price range, the **Shamiara Restaurant** on the second floor of Pallson's Hotel is one of the best, serving huge, very tasty portions for around US$7. The service is *terribly* slow, but the food is worth waiting for. The **Mayur Restaurant** is an Indian vegetarian restaurant serving cheap snacks as well as main meals for around US$7. The **Amul Tandoori Restaurant** is similar in price and standard to the Shamiara, while the excellent **Big Bite Restaurant** is a bit cheaper and serves huge portions. The evening tandoori barbecue at the **Mukhtar Cafe** near the market is also very good and inexpensive. Tasty curries costing around US$3 are available at the nearby **Sher E Punjab Restaurant**, which also doubles as a bar.

There are a couple of good places to eat along the road between the Impala and Saba-Saba Hotels. The **Mezzaluna Restaurant** is generally regarded to serve the best Italian food in Arusha. Pizzas are something of a speciality here, and they cost around US$5. There is an indoor dining room, but weather permitting it's much more pleasant to eat in the spacious thatched garden area. Close by, the **Spices and**

Herbs Restaurant is Arusha's only Ethiopian restaurant. If you're already a fan of sub-Saharan Africa's most distinctive cuisine (a searing, spicy meat or vegetarian stew called *kai wat* served with a flat round sour bread called *injera*) you won't need me to persuade you to give this place a try. Most dishes fall in the US$4-6 range.

A short distance from the Clock Tower along the Old Moshi Road, **Roaster's Garden** is one of the most pleasant garden bars in Arusha; in addition to an endless supply of cold beer, it serves a variety of cheap meals as well as good *nyama choma* (grilled meat). The **Everest Chinese Restaurant** next door is rated the best place of its sort in town, and isn't too expensive at around US$6 for a main course with rice. In the same part of town, the **Mandarin Palace** is another good (and similarly priced) Chinese restaurant, a short distance further from the town centre on Serengeti Road.

Something of an Arusha institution, **Stiggy and George's** lies about 1km from the town centre along the Old Moshi Road, an area you'd only want to visit by night in a taxi. The food here, mostly continental in feel, isn't cheap (around US$8-10 for a main course), and the decor is decidedly lacking in pretension, but Stiggy is an excellent cook and the quality and presentation are up to international standards. Even if you don't want to eat here, the relaxed bar has a pool table and is a pleasant place to hang out.

Back in the town centre, the **Safari Grill** (on the ground floor of the New Safari Hotel) has served reliably filling and relatively inexpensive Western dishes for years, and used to be a favourite with budget travellers, but these days it seems a pretty bland option when you consider what else is on offer. Most main courses cost around US$4–5, and you can also eat at the Rainbow Garden at the back of the hotel. Similar in price, standard and antiquity, the once-popular **Chinese Restaurant** on Sokoine Road serves indifferent Chinese and Western dishes, and again feels like it's past its prime.

A new South African-owned restaurant complex called **The Ranch** is likely to appeal to many travellers. Situated on the corner of Jacaranda Road opposite the Uhuru School, the restaurant here specialises in steak, game meat and pasta, and the complex also includes a fully stocked bar, a rooftop bar, pool tables, and the Colobus Club with resident DJ.

Another recent and welcome addition to Arusha's eateries is the **Patisserie**, on Sokoine Road close to the Clock Tower. In addition to a wonderful range of freshly baked loaves, rolls and pastries, this place serves great light meals, fruit juice and real coffee. A similarly good spot for breakfast, lunch and snacks is the **Cafe Bamboo Restaurant**, which serves good coffee and juice as well as light meals and 'home-cooking' style lunches. On the west side of the market, **Mac's Patisserie** is recommended by a reader for 'almost authentic croissants, juice and cake'.

If it's fast food you're after, **McMoody's** is a sort of Macdonald's clone serving reasonable hamburgers and cheeseburgers for around US$2, and the plastic decor is designed to make fast food junkies feel at home. Rather less successful in its approximation of a Western eating icon is **Chickwings**, several branches of which are dotted around town – unfortunately for devotees of Colonel Sanders, the chicken pieces have a rather odd flavour and are very overpriced. There are more tasty snacks available at **Johnny's Raviala Restaurant**. For good, inexpensive ice-cream cones and sundaes, the place to head for is **Safison's Ice-cream Parlour**, while **YC Dave** on Swahili Street serves good yoghurt and Indian snacks during the day.

Most backpackers who stay in the guesthouses behind the Golden Rose Hotel will find themselves eating at the **Pizzarusha Restaurant** opposite the Mashele Guesthouse. This excellent and unique set-up serves huge tasty meals, ranging from pizzas to curries to steaks, and it is incredibly cheap, with most dishes costing around US$3. The atmosphere is great, too – the building is constructed from traditional materials, and the candle-lit tables look into the kitchen, so you can be sure your food is freshly prepared. A couple of expatriates have complained of tummy problems after eating here, but it was our regular eatery in Arusha, and we worked through the menu without the slightest ill-effect. This is easily the best value restaurant in Arusha, and we recommend it highly.

BARS AND NIGHTSPOTS

There's been a notable increase in nightspots around Arusha in recent years. A popular place with expats, and very central, is the **Discovery Bar**, where you can eat and watch satellite television in the cosy downstairs pub or sip a chilled beer as Arusha passes below you on the upstairs balcony. Sticking in the town centre, there's a good and relatively quiet garden bar at the **New Safari Hotel**. The nearby **Barracuda Bar** (cold beer and good, inexpensive *mishkaki* kebabs and chips) has an altogether more lively, earthy atmosphere, as does the bar attached to the **Chinese Restaurant**, which also sometimes hosts live music. Near to the market, the **Cavern Bar** was pretty quiet when we popped in, but it's about the only place in the town centre with pool tables.

Another good outdoor bar is **Roaster's Garden**, perhaps 200m from the Clock Tower along the Old Moshi Road. Roughly 1km further along this road, **Stiggy and George's** is a popular drinking spot with expats, while the nearby **Mawingo Club** is generally regarded to be Arusha's most lively disco, frequented by locals and expats alike.

There are several decent bars in the same area as the cluster of guesthouses behind the Golden Rose Hotel. The best place to drink in this part of town is **Soweto Gardens**, a relaxed but atmospheric garden bar which normally hosts live bands over the weekends.

USEFUL INFORMATION
Tourist information

The Tanzania Tourist Board (TTB) office on Boma Road is refreshingly helpful and well-informed. It stocks a useful colour road map of Tanzania, which is given free of charge to tourists, though this doesn't stop the booksellers on the streets of Arusha for trying to sell it at silly prices. The TTB has been actively involved in the development of several cultural tourism programmes in northern Tanzania; the Arusha office stocks informative pamphlets about these programmes, and can help out with information on prices and access. If you want to check out a safari company, the TTB office keeps a regularly updated list of all registered safari and trekking companies, as well as those which have been blacklisted. Contact details are PO Box 2348, Arusha; tel: 057 3842/3; fax: 057 8628.

The Netherlands Development Agency (SNV) has been worked with the TTB to help establish the cultural tourism programmes in Ng'iresi, Mulala, Mkuru, Longido, Mto wa Mbu, Usambara, North Pare and South Pare. Although the TTB office can provide pamphlets and information adequate to the needs of most tourists, those with specialised interests are invited to contact SNV directly. The SNV office is in room 643 of the Serengeti Wing of the AICC, PO Box 10455, Arusha; tel/fax: 057 7515; email: tourinfo@habari.co.tz.

Tanzania National Park (TANAPA) has a head office in the Arusha International Conference Centre (AICC). This is the best place to buy booklets on various national parks, as they cost around US$5 here but are sold for three times the price on the streets and at park entrance gates. Contact details are PO Box 3134, Arusha; tel: 057 6091; fax: 057 8216; email: tanapa@habari.co.tz.

The Ngorongoro Conservation Authority head office is on the corner of Goliondoi and Makongoro Roads.

The immigration office on Simeon Road can normally extend visas on the spot.

Safari companies

Arusha is where most visitors embark on a safari to the northern safari circuit, the subject of the next chapter. A selection of reliable safari companies is listed in that chapter on pages 121–4

Safety

Arusha remains a relatively safe town for tourists. The central market vicinity has long been a haven for pickpockets and bag-slashers, so you are advised against walking in the market with valuables or large sums of money. Muggings appear to be on the increase, and they mostly occur at night, so you are advised against walking along quiet roads after dark, and would be prudent to use a taxi when in doubt. Con artists generally take the form of money changers or dodgy safari companies, and I would avoid dealing with either.

Foreign exchange

There are several bureaux de change dotted around Arusha, and it is worth shopping around to find the best rate for US dollars cash. Many bureaux de change won't accept less widely used international currencies or travellers cheques, and in any case we have found that the National Bank of Commerce facing the Clock Tower has offered the best rates for US dollar travellers' cheques on all recent visits. Whatever else you do, don't change money on the streets of Arusha, as you are sure to be ripped off. If you are desperate for local currency, rather ask a shop owner or a safari company to help you out with a small transaction.

Taxis

There are plenty of taxis in Arusha. Good places to pick them up include the market and bus station, the filling station on the junction of Goliondoi Road and the Old Moshi Road, and the open area at the north end of Boma and India Roads. A taxi ride within the town centre should cost roughly US$1.50, though tourists are normally asked a slightly higher price. A taxi ride to somewhere outside the town centre will cost more.

Books, maps and newspapers

The news stand in the foyer of the New Arusha Hotel probably has the largest selection of publications that are likely to be of interest to tourists, for instance travel guides, field guides, maps, current paperback novels, national park booklets and coffee-table books about East Africa. The only other book shop of note is the one on Boma Road next to the Cafe Bamboo Restaurant. A few vendors usually hang around the Clock Tower selling the maps and national park booklets at highly inflated prices. To buy or exchange second-hand novels, there are a couple of stalls dotted around town, the best of which is the stall on the alley which connects Boma and India Roads.

A selection of local newspapers are available on the day of publication, as is the Kenyan *Nation*, which is generally stronger on international news. You won't need to look for these papers as the vendors who sell them will find you quickly enough. The excellent *East African*, a weekly newspaper, is available at several newspaper kiosks, as well as at the news stand in the New Arusha Hotel. The British *Weekly Telegraph* and *International Express* can be bought at the newspaper stands near the

Clock Tower, but do check the price on the cover or you'll probably be overcharged. The American weekly news magazines *Time* and *Newsweek* are also widely sold in Arusha.

Curio shops

Arusha is one of the best places in East Africa to buy Makonde carvings, batiks, Maasai jewellery and other souvenirs. The curio shops are far cheaper than those in Dar es Salaam, and the quality and variety is excellent. Most of the curio shops are clustered between the Clock Tower and India Road. On the outskirts of Arusha, along the road towards the Serengeti and other reserves, the Cultural Heritage Centre stocks one of the best selections of curios you'll come across anywhere in Tanzania, and it can be visited on the way back from a safari, or as a short taxi trip from Arusha.

Post and communications

The main post office is on Boma Road facing the Clock Tower. The telecommunications centre further along Boma Road is a good place to make international phone calls and faxes. The Cybernet Centre at the south end of India Road offers internet access at US$6 per hour and can send email for US$3 per message. There are slightly cheaper email facilities in the business centre next to the Cafe Bamboo Restaurant on Boma Road, and many safari companies will offer cheap or free email services to their clients. The owner of the Pizzarusha Restaurant plans on providing an inexpensive email facility in the near future.

SHORT TRIPS OUT OF ARUSHA

For most tourists, Arusha serves as little more than an enforced stopover en route to the northern safari circuit covered in the following chapter. These aside, the most significant local attraction is the underrated Arusha National Park (covered under a separate heading below), which can be visited as a day or overnight trip out of town, or appended to a longer safari to the other game reserves of northern Tanzania. Of the game reserves covered in the next chapter, only Tarangire and perhaps Lake Manyara are realistic goals for one-day safaris out of Arusha, bearing in mind that both lie a good two-hour drive away, so that the best hours for game viewing and photography will be spent on the road. Either of the above reserves, or for that matter the Ngorongoro Crater, can be visited as overnight trip out of Arusha, an option that might appeal to those without the time or funds to undertake a longer safari.

Otherwise, the possibilities for day trips out of Arusha are more limited than you might expect, with Lake Duluti about the only local place of interest that is readily accessible on public transport. The widely praised SNV-implemented cultural tourism programme at Longido can also be visited on public transport, while similar programmes at the villages of Mulala and Ng'iresi are only accessible though a safari operator. There is another SNV cultural tourism programme based at Mkuru, offering camel rides, hikes and bird walks. Finally, it would be possible to bus to the village of Mto wa Mbu near the gate of Lake Manyara National Park (see page 125), and to embark on some of the outings arranged by the cultural programme there.

Lake Duluti

This attractive forest-fringed crater lake lies little more than 10km from Arusha. The area offers some great bird-watching, with the possibility of clear views of Mount Meru and Kilimanjaro, and it would be a pleasant place to spend a peaceful few days. The lake lies about 2km south of the Arusha-Moshi road, and is fringed by the upmarket Mountain Village Lodge and more rustic Duluti Club campsite (see *Where to stay* above). Both of these places are well signposted and can be reached by foot or in a vehicle.

Mount Meru Foothill Hike

The western slopes of Mount Meru lie outside of Arusha National Park, so there is nothing to prevent keen ramblers from exploring them on foot. The best access point is the dirt road signposted for Club L'Oasis Lodge, which branches from the main Moshi Road opposite the Mount Meru Novotel; a stream next to this junction serves as a carwash. This road continues into the foothills as far as the tree line, passing through bamboo forest on the way. Before you get this far it is possible to divert to a waterfall. About four hours along the road you will reach a plantation of new eucalyptus and pine trees. Here you must scramble down to a stream. If you follow the stream for an hour or so, you arrive at the waterfall. There is a short cut back to the main road, but unless you have a map it is probably more sensible to return the way you came. It may occur to you to attempt to climb Meru from the west in order to save on park fees, but it is illegal to enter the national park without paying fees, and anybody who is caught attempting to do so is liable to be jailed.

Ng'iresi Village

Set on the slopes of Mount Meru some 7km from Arusha town, this cultural tourism programme based in the traditional Wa-Arusha village of Ng'iresi offers many insights into the local culture and agricultural practices. There are also some lovely walks in the surrounding Mount Meru foothills, an area characterised by fast-flowing streams, waterfalls and remnant forest patches. From Ng'iresi, it is possible to walk to Lekimana Hill, from where there are good views over the Maasai Steppe and on a clear day to Kilimanjaro. Another walk takes you to Kivesi Hill, an extinct volcano whose forested slopes support a variety of birds and small mammals.

Three different 'modules' are available at Ng'iresi. The half-day module costs US$16, the full-day module US$21, and the overnight module US$27. All prices include meals prepared by the Juhudu Women's Group and guided activities, while the overnight module also covers the fee for camping in the garden of Mzee Loti. For all modules, a sum of US$4 goes directly towards the improvement of the local primary school. So far as I'm aware, there is no public transport to Ng'iresi, so you must either set up a visit through a safari company or make arrangements with a private vehicle. The TTB office on Boma Road stocks a useful pamphlet about Ng'iresi, and can advise you about current costs and accessibility.

Mulala Village

This is another cultural tourism programme situated in a village on the foot slopes of Mount Meru. Mulala lies at an altitude of 1,450m, some 30km from Arusha, in a fertile agricultural area which produces coffee, bananas and other fruit and vegetables. Several short walks can be undertaken in the surrounding hills, including one to the forested Marisha River, home to a variety of birds and primates, and to Mazungu Lake, where it is said that a *mzungu* was once lured to his death by a demon. Another local place of interest is Mama Anna's dairy, which supplies cheese to several upmarket hotels in Arusha. The tourist programme here is run in conjunction with the Agape Women's Group, which provides most of the guides as well as snacks and camping facilities.

All visitors must pay a village development fee of US$3, while a daily guide fee of US$4.50 is charged per group. Camping costs US$1.50 per person per night, and meals cost around US$4 each.

Mkuru Camel Safari

This cultural tourism programme is based at Mkuru, at the northern base of Mount Meru near a pyramid shaped mountain known as Ol Doinyo Landaree. The main attraction here is organised camelback trips, which range in duration from a short half-day excursion to a week-long camel safari though the surrounding dry plains, which are rich in birds and still support small numbers of game animals. Other options include a bird walk on the plain, or a hike to the top of Ol Doinyo Landaree.

Camel trips cost roughly US$25 per person per night all-inclusive. Visitors must provide their own tent. If you only visit the camel camp, this costs US$5 per person. For walks and hikes, you will pay a village development fee of US$2.50 per person as well as a guide fee of US$6 per group. A cottage is available to tourists at a charge of US$15/18 single/double.

Longido

The cultural tourism project run out of Longido is one of the most accessible in the region for independent travellers, and it is an excellent place to visit for those who want to spend time among the Maasai. The programme co-ordinator is a local Maasai who studied abroad as a sociologist before he was paralysed in a serious accident, and he can tell you anything you want to know about Maasai culture. Three different walking modules are on offer to tourists. The first is a half-day bird walk through the Maasai plains, which also includes a visit to a rural Maasai *boma* (homestead), and a meal cooked by the local women's group. Then there is a full-day tour that follows the same route as the bird walk before climbing to the top of Longido mountain, an ascent of roughly 400m, offering views to Mount Meru and Kilimanjaro on a clear day, as well as over the Maasai plains to Kenya. The two-day module follows the same route as the one day walk, camping overnight in the green Kimokouwa Valley, before visiting a dense rainforest which still harbours a number of buffaloes as well as the usual birds and monkeys. On all modules, you can expect to see a variety of birds (including several colourful finches and barbets), and there is a fair amount of large game left in the area, notably gerenuk, lesser kudu, giraffe, Thomson's gazelle and black-backed jackal. It is worth trying to be in Longido on Wednesday, when there is a busy cattle market.

Longido straddles the main Namanga road roughly 100km from Arusha, so any vehicle heading between Arusha and Namanga can drop you there. There are a couple of guesthouses in the small town, or you can arrange to pitch a tent for US$3 per person. All visitors are charged a daily development fee of US7.50 per day, which will go towards the construction of a much-needed cattle dip. In addition to this, a co-ordination fee of US$7.50 per group per visit must be paid, a daily guide fee of US$6 per group, and a 'present' of around US$3–6 to any *boma* that you visit. Meals are available from the local women's group at USS$4 (lunch or dinner) or US$2.50 (breakfast).

ARUSHA NATIONAL PARK

This small national park not only protects Africa's fifth-highest mountain, but it also boasts clear views to the continent's highest peak, a number of attractive lakes, a spectacular volcanic crater, a habitat diversity encompassing everything from rainforest to lush savannah to alpine moorland, as well as a good variety of large

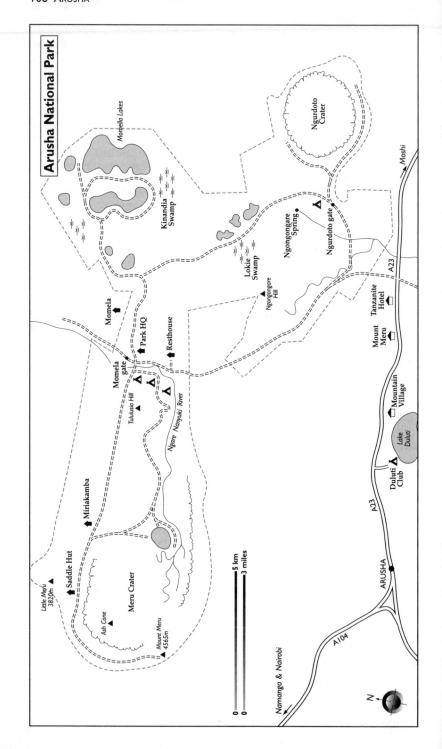

mammals and birds. Situated less than one hour's drive from one of Africa's major safari capitals, you might reasonably expect the 137km² Arusha National Park to be crawling with tourists. Remarkably, however, it is probably the least visited of all national parks in northern Tanzania, making it a wonderful and rewarding off-the-beaten-track excursion for those with an interest in natural history that extends beyond ticking off the so-called 'big five' (see *Chapter 2*).

Arusha National Park's most-publicised drawcard is Mount Meru, the eastern slopes and 4,566m peak of which lie within the park boundaries. Mount Meru is the product of the same volcanic activity that formed the Great Rift Valley 15 to 20 million years ago, and it attained a height similar to that of Kilimanjaro until a massive eruption tore out its eastern wall 250,000 years ago. Meru is regarded as a dormant volcano, since lava flowed from it as recently as 100 years ago, but visitors will be pleased to know that there is no reason to suppose it will do anything dramatic in the foreseeable future. Though low-key by comparison to nearby Kilimanjaro, Mount Meru is regarded by many as perhaps the most rewarding mountain to climb in East Africa, a hike that can be done over three days at half the cost of a Kilimanjaro climb. Details of the hike are given below.

The park still has much to offer non-hikers. The Ngurdoto Crater is in itself worth the entrance fee, a fully intact 3km-wide, 400m-deep volcanic caldera that has often been described as a mini-Ngorongoro. Tourists are not permitted to descend into the crater, but the viewpoints on the forest-fringed rim over the lush crater floor are fantastic. A large herd of buffalo is resident on the crater floor, and with binoculars it is normally possible to pick up other mammals, such as warthog, baboon and various antelope, on the crater floor. Look out, too, for augur buzzard, black eagle and other cliff-associated raptors soaring above the crater. The forests around the crater rim harbour many troops of black-and-white colobus and blue monkey, as well as a good variety of birds including several types of hornbill and the gorgeous Hartlaub's touraco and cinnamon-chested bee-eater.

Another area worth exploring is Momela Lakes to the north of Ngurdoto. This group of shallow alkaline lakes is fed by underground streams, and each has a different mineral content and is slightly different in colour. In the late evening and early morning, it is often possible to stand at one of the viewpoints over the lakes and see Kilimanjaro on the eastern horizon and Mount Meru to the west. The lake area is one of the best places to see water birds in Tanzania: flamingo, pelican, little grebe and a variety of herons, ducks and waders are common. Among the more common mammals around the lakes are hippo. waterbuck and buffalo. You should also come across a few pairs of Kirk's dik-dik, an attractively marked small antelope which seems to be far less skittish here than it is elsewhere in the country.

Other large mammals likely to be seen in Arusha National Park include giraffe, zebra and vervet monkey. Elephant are present according to the official checklist, but several people we spoke to say that they haven't been seen in years, though it is possible a few survive in the forest zone of Mount Meru. The only large predators found in the park are leopard and spotted hyena; we were lucky enough to see both driving between Momela Lodge and the campsite shortly after nightfall. Bird life is varied, with almost 400 species recorded.

From a vehicle, most of the park can be seen in a day. You can walk in the part of the park that lies to the west of the main road accompanied by an armed ranger, whose services cost US$10 per outing. Mount Meru can be climbed in two or three days (see below). The 52-page booklet *Arusha National Park*, available from the National Parks office in Arusha for US$5, contains detailed information on every aspect of the park's ecology and wildlife. An excellent map of Arusha National Park, with a detailed map of the ascent of Mount Meru on the flip, was published in 1997 by Giovanni Tombazzi in collaboration with Hoopoe Adventure Tours. The standard park entrance fee of US$25 per 24-hour period is charged.

The MBT Snake Park at the entrance to Arusha National Park has been recommended for the good collection of reptiles and intelligent guided tour.

Getting there and away

Momela Gate and camp lie roughly 20km from the main Arusha-Moshi road along a signposted turn-off near Usa River. Ngurdoto Gate and campsite lie 8km along this turn-off. The approach road is in fair condition and can be sometimes driven in an ordinary saloon car, though a 4x4 would be essential after rain.

If you do not have a vehicle, the park can be easily be visited as a daytrip or overnight trip out of Arusha. Any safari company can organise this. Most companies can also organise a three-day climb up Meru.

If you want to organise your own climb or spend some time exploring the park on foot you will have to find your own way there. You could hire a taxi in Arusha, but if you are patient you should be able to hitch. Any vehicle heading to Momela Lodge or the village of Ngare Nanyuki will go past the main entrance gate. To get an early start, camp or stay at the Tanzanite Hotel the night before you want to hitch in.

Plenty of locals walk along the main road through the park. It is a long walk from Usa River to Momela Gate, but there's nothing to stop you from doing it.

CLIMBING MOUNT MERU

At 4,566m, Meru is not the highest mountain in Africa; for the achievement-orientated it is no substitute for Kilimanjaro. On the other hand, those who climb both invariably enjoy Meru more. It is not as crowded, considerably less expensive and, although it is steeper and the higher slopes are almost as cold, you are less likely to encounter the health problems associated with Kilimanjaro's altitude.

Meru is just as interesting as Kilimanjaro from a biological point of view and, because comparatively few people climb it, you are more likely to see forest animals. A lot of big game can be seen on the lower slopes. Meru can technically be climbed in two days, but three days is more normal, allowing time to explore Meru Crater and to look at wildlife and plants.

Most people arrange a climb through a safari company in Arusha. The going rate for a three-day hike is around US$200 per person. You can make direct arrangements with park officials at the gate, but won't save much money by doing this. The compulsory armed ranger/guide costs US$20 per day (US$10 park fee and US$10 salary), hut fees are US$20 per night, and there is the usual park entrance fee of US$25 per day. A rescue fee of US$20 per person covers the entire climb. The minimum cost for a three-day climb is therefore US$135 per person plus US$60 divided between the party. Food and transport must be added to this, and porters cost an additional US$5 per day each.

Meru is *very* cold at night, and you will need to bring clothing adequate for Alpine conditions. In the rainy season, mountain boots are necessary. At other times, good walking shoes will probably be adequate. The best months to climb are between October and February.

If you arrange your own climb, check hut availability at the National Park Office in Arusha before you head off to the gate. At present the huts are rarely full, but Meru is growing in popularity, and this could change.

Where to stay
The most convenient place to stay is **Momela Lodge** (PO Box 999, Arusha; tel: 057 6423/6; fax: 057 8264), which lies in the shadow of Mount Meru about 3km past Momela Gate. Dating to the colonial era, this cosy low-key hotel seems a world away from the crowded game lodges of the Serengeti, and its alpine feel is enhanced by the log fires in the bar and lounge. Accommodation in chalets costs US$56/74 s/c single/double b&b or US$80/122 full-board for non-residents. The cost for Tanzania residents works out at around US$16/27 b&b or US$38/70 full-board.

The **National Park Rest House**, 2km from Momela Gate, sleeps up to five people and costs US$20 HC per person per night. You can book it in advance through The Warden, Arusha National Park, PO Box 3134, Arusha, or enquire directly about availability at the gate or the National Parks office in Arusha.

There are four **National Park campsites**: three at the foot of Tululusia Hill, 2km from Momela Gate, and one in the forest near Ngurdoto Gate. All are scenic and near streams, have drop toilets and firewood, and cost US$20 per person. Note, however, that you may not walk between the campsites and the entrance gates without an armed ranger.

ALONG THE DODOMA ROAD
The 420km-long A104 which leads south from Arusha to Dodoma is once of the least travelled in northeastern Tanzania, and those travellers who do decide to bus along it

Day one The trail starts at Momela Gate (1,500m). From there it is a relatively gentle three-hour ascent to Miriakamba Hut (2,600m). On the way you pass through well-developed woodland where there is a good chance of seeing large animals such as giraffe. At an altitude of about 2,000m you enter the forest zone. If you leave Momela early, there will be ample time to explore Meru Crater in the afternoon. The crater is overlooked by the 1,500m cliff rising to Meru Peak. The 3,667m ash cone in the crater is an hour from Miriakamba Hut, and can be climbed.

Day two It is three hours to Saddle Hut (3,600m), a bit steeper than the previous day's walk. You initially pass through forest, where there is a good chance of seeing black-and-white colobus, then at about 3,000m you will enter a moorland zone similar to that on Kilimanjaro. It is not unusual to see Kilimanjaro peeking above the clouds from Saddle Hut. If you feel energetic, you can climb Little Meru (3,820m) in the afternoon. It takes about an hour each way from Saddle Hut.

Day three You will need to rise very early to ascend the 4,566m peak, probably at around 02.00. This ascent takes four to five hours. It is then an eight to nine hour walk back down the mountain to Momela Gate.

Note Some people prefer to climb from Miriakamba Hut to Saddle Hut *and* do the round trip from Saddle Hut to Meru Peak on the second day (eleven hours altogether), leaving only a five-hour walk to Momela on the third. Others climb all the way up to Saddle Hut on the first day (six hours), do the round trip to the peak on the second (eight hours), and return to Momela from the Saddle Hut on the third (five hours).

generally regret the decision. Coming south from Arusha, the A104 is surfaced as far as Kwa Kuchinia, the turn-off to the main entrance gate for Tarangire National Park, but the remaining 300km or so south to Dodoma is in appalling condition, and buses might take anything up to 24 hours to get from one end to the other.

Frankly, the bus trip between Arusha and Dodoma is for masochists only, especially as Dodoma itself is quite possibly the most charmless settlement of its size anywhere in East Africa. It is equally true, however, that there are a couple of spots along the Dodoma road that really *are* worth making an effort to visit. The best-developed of these places is Babati (see map on page 148), which lies no more than 70km south of Kwa Kuchinia along the A104, sparing you the worst of the road, provided that you visit it as a round trip out of Arusha rather than en route between Arusha and Dodoma.

Babati and Mount Hanang

Reaching an elevation of 3,417m, Mount Hanang is the third-highest mountain in Tanzania. It is an extinct volcano, lying to the west of the A104, below the main Rift Valley escarpment. Hanang isn't protected within a national park, which means that it is relatively cheap to climb. The springboard for climbing Hanang is Babati, a small town situated at the junction of the A104 and the B143 to Katesh, the village at the base of the mountain. The mountain affords excellent views over the surrounding Rift Valley, dotted with a number of small volcanic craters, as well as to Lake Balangida at the base of the Rift Valley escarpment.

Another interesting aspect of the Babati and Hanang area is that it is home to a number of ethnic groups who have retained a largely traditional way of life. The Barbaig, for instance, are semi-nomadic pastoralists with cultural affiliations to the Maasai. The Iraqw, by contrast, are a somewhat mysterious group whose claim to have migrated to the area from the Middle East is backed up by the Arabic intonations in their language. Lake Babati, which lies within easy walking distance of Babati town centre, supports a reasonable number of hippos as well as an interesting selection of water birds, and you can organise for a local fisherman to take you onto the water.

So far as I'm aware, there is nothing to prevent travellers from exploring this area independently, though I have yet to hear from anybody who has done so. A few buses daily connect Arusha to Babati, and at least one bus daily runs from Babati to Katesh (at the base of Mount Hanang), taking around three to four hours. There are a several hotels and guesthouses in Babati, and at least one guesthouse is to be found in Katesh. The mountain can be climbed in one day, taking roughly six hours each way, but it would be foolhardy to attempt this hike without a knowledgable local guide.

The more popular alternative to doing it yourself is to arrange your climb through Kahembe's Enterprises, a commendable locally run company which has made great efforts to open up this little-known part of Tanzania to adventurous tourists. Kahembe's arranges a four-day hike using the relatively easy Gendabi route for US$300 per person all-inclusive, and a three-day trip along the steeper Katesh route for US$240 per person. In addition to this, Kahembe offers a wide selection of other local trips, ranging from a three-day Barbaig walking safari, through a couple of seven- and eight-day walking itineraries that visit several local *bomas* as well as incorporating walks on the game-rich verges of Lake Manyara and Tarangire National Parks. They also offer a 16-day 'African rural life adventure' which includes overnight stays with a number of different ethnic groups, as well as an ascent of Mount Hanang, and game walks around Lake Burungi (on the edge on Manyara National Park) and on the eastern shores of Lake Manyara. These trips are not luxurious by any standard, but they are well-organised and informative, and they offer an unforgettable glimpse into a way of life that has vanished in many other parts of Africa.

It is great to see somebody offering trips like this to the increasingly significant proportion of travellers who want to see more of Tanzania than the 'big five', and I've heard only good reports about the packages put together by Kahembe. It is, however, advisable to make advance contact with Kahembe, which you can do by contacting their Arusha agent JM Tours (tel: 057 6773; fax: 057 8801) or by writing directly to Mr Kahembe at PO Box 366, Babati.

Kondoa Rock Paintings

Lying off the main Arusha-Dodoma road to the south of Babati, the rock paintings found in the Kondoa region of Tanzania are the most numerous in East Africa. There are over 100 known sites, the most accessible and interesting of which are reached from the small centre of Kolo. African rock art is overlooked by many tourists, despite the aesthetic value of many paintings, and the questions they raise about the artists, their beliefs and their lifestyle.

The paintings of the Kondoa region are between 200 and 4,000 years old. Rock art weathers quickly in African conditions, which means that many of the older paintings are badly faded, and the tradition may be more ancient than these dates suggest. Most rock paintings are found in caves or rock overhangs, with east- and west-facing sites favoured in the Kondoa region.

Paintings are in a variety of styles and cover a range of subjects. Giraffe and various antelope were favoured subjects and eland seem to have held a special significance. Other paintings depict religious ceremonies. There are also abstract paintings of geometric figures whose significance can only be guessed at. Style changes have been recorded at many sites, with newer paintings superimposed over older ones.

The identity of Kondoa's artists is a mystery. Most southern African rock art is accredited to San hunter-gatherers. San-like people occupied all of East and southern Africa prior to the arrival of Bantu-speakers 2,000 to 3,000 years ago. The Hadza of the Lake Eyasi region and the local Sandawe are thought to be remnant populations of these early hunter-gatherers. Some Sandawe clans claim their forefathers were responsible for the paintings, but there is no tradition relating to them amongst the Hadza. The Wa-Gogo of Dodoma make the improbable claim that the paintings were done by the Portuguese!

Whoever the artists were, their relatively recent disappearance could be linked to the Maasai invasion north of Kondoa 300 years ago, which caused displacement of the local Bantu-speaking people of that area, and may have had a knock-on effect in Kondoa.

Before you visit the paintings, try to get hold of the National Museums of Tanzania Occasional Paper No. 5, a booklet by Fidelis Masao called *The Rock Art of Kondoa and Singada*. I picked up a copy for US$1 at the National Museum in Dar es Salaam.

Getting there and away

Several accessible and highly-rated sites are near the village of Kolo on the Arusha-Dodoma road. The Antiquities Department in Kolo can organise a guide. The paintings are about 10km from the main road. There is no accommodation in Kolo, so a tent would be useful. There are guesthouses in Kondoa and Babati, 25km south and 80km north of Kolo respectively. Some Arusha-based companies will include Kondoa in a safari itinerary by special request, a full-day trip from Tarangire.

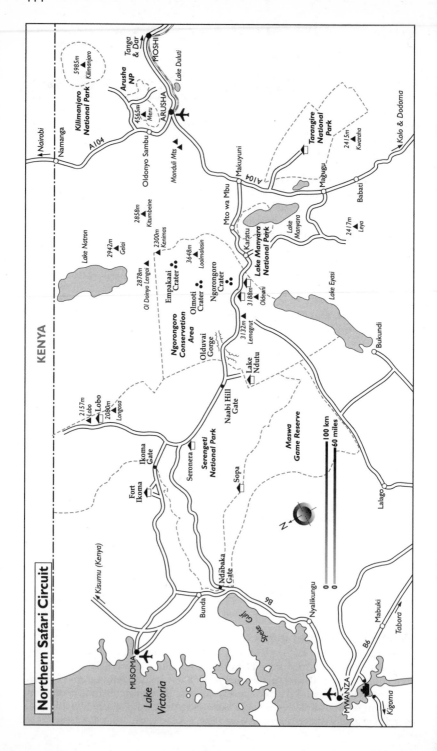

Northern Safari Circuit

The Northern Safari Circuit

The block of game reserves that lies to the west of Arusha will need little introduction to readers. The vast Serengeti National Park and Ngorongoro Crater in particular are possibly the most publicised game reserves in the world. The plains of the Serengeti Plain play host to Africa's greatest wildlife spectacle, the annual migration of more than a million wildebeest and zebra, while also supporting remarkably dense populations of predators such as lion, cheetah, leopard and spotted hyena. En route between Arusha and the Serengeti, the floor of the spectacular Ngorongoro Crater is if anything even more densely packed with large mammals, and the best place in East Africa to see the endangered black rhino. Add to this the less celebrated Lake Manyara National Park, which protects a large shallow lake on the Rift Valley floor, and Tarangire National Park, a vast area of acacia woodland notable for its innumerable ancient baobabs and dense elephant population, and it is no hyperbole to claim that Tanzania's northern safari circuit is quite simply the finest in Africa.

The main reserves in northern Tanzania are covered fully in this chapter, as is the process of organising a safari to these reserves. Although Arusha National Park (covered in the previous chapter) can be appended to your safari, it lies in a different direction from Arusha to the other main game reserves in northern Tanzania, and most people seem to visit it as a self-contained trip out of Arusha. Those who want to climb Mount Meru (in Arusha National Park) or Kilimanjaro (which lies about 100km east of Arusha) will almost certainly want to treat this climb separately from their safari, and might well want to deal directly with a company that specialises in trekking rather than a standard safari company.

Climate

The Ngorongoro Crater rim, lying at an elevation of roughly 2,300m, receives a high rainfall and it tends to be cold at night and misty in the morning. The rest of the region covered in this chapter is warmer, though the crater floor and Serengeti are not especially hot as they lie above the Rift Valley escarpment. Tarangire and Lake Manyara are hot by day, but cool down after dusk. The main rainy seasons, in November and December and from March to May, dictate game-viewing patterns in the region. Game viewing in the Ngorongoro Crater and Lake Manyara is good at any time of year, while Tarangire is best between July and December, and the Serengeti between November and March.

Getting around

Access to the Serengeti, Ngorongoro and Manyara is via the B142, a dirt road which leaves the Dodoma–Arusha road at a village called Makuyuni. The B142 bypasses Lake Manyara at the village of Mto wa Mbu, then snakes up the side of the Rift Valley wall, passes through Karatu, and climbs to Ngorongoro Crater rim. From the crater, the B142 descends to the Serengeti plains, passing through the park headquarters in the Seronera valley before reaching Bunda on the main Musoma-Mwanza road.

It is 80km from Arusha to Makuyuni, 37km from Makuyuni to Mto wa Mbu, 25km from Mto wa Mbu to Karatu, and 18km from Karatu to the village on the crater rim. Seronera lies about halfway along the 300km stretch of road between the crater and Bunda. Tarangire National Park lies just off the main Arusha-Dodoma road, roughly 30km south of the junction with the B142 at Makuyuni.

The only realistic ways of exploring this area are in a private 4x4 or on an organised safari (see *Organising a safari* below). Because of the high entrance fees charged to foreign-registered vehicles, visitors who bring their own vehicle to Tanzania from across the border may still find it works out more cheaply to join an organised safari.

As for public transport, the buses and Land Rovers which run daily along the B142 between Arusha and Mwanza offer a relatively cheap way of seeing something of the Serengeti for those who cannot afford a proper safari, even allowing for the fact that tourists will be required to pay US$50 in park entrance fees over and above the fare. In theory, it is possible to make advance arrangements for one of these buses to drop you off at Seronera, and to pick you up at a later stage, but it's difficult to see any reason why anybody would want to do this. Affordable local buses run daily between Arusha and Karatu, stopping at Mto wa Mbu, but there is no local transport beyond Karatu.

Hitching into most of the reserves covered in this chapter is pretty much out of the question. Relatively few private vehicles pass this way, and most safari companies forbid their drivers to pick up hitchhikers. In any case, people who have paid for a safari, or who are in a private vehicle loaded with supplies, are unlikely to want to carry freeloaders. Even if you were to catch a lift, you may well get stuck in the Serengeti or Ngorongoro and although you will see little game from a campsite or lodge, you will still have to pay park fees.

Further information

Jeanette Hanby and David Bygott have written a series of excellent booklets covering Serengeti National Park, Tarangire National Park and Lake Manyara National Park. These are published by Tanapa and can be bought for US$5 at most book shops in Arusha, as well as at most lodge curio shops. Note, however, that street vendors in Arusha will often ask highly inflated prices for the same booklets. The same authors have written an equally informative and widely available self-published booklet covering the Ngorongoro Conservation Area.

Giovanni Tombazzi's lively, colourful and accurate maps covering (among other places) the Serengeti, Lake Manyara, Tarangire and the Ngorongoro Conservation Area are probably the most user-friendly maps I've seen anywhere in East Africa. Each of these maps shows details of the appropriate conservation area in both the dry and the wet season, and is liberally dotted with illustrations of common trees and other points of interest. Giovanni has also produced a map covering the whole northern safari circuit, useful to those who don't want to splash out on the whole series of more detailed maps. The maps are produced in collaboration with Hoopoe Adventure Tours (see *Safari companies,* pages 121–4 for contact details) who also distribute them in northern Tanzania. As with the booklets mentioned above, these maps are widely available in Arusha and at the national park lodges, but vary in price depending on where you buy them.

Previous page Male lions may spend as much as 23 hours a day sleeping (AZ)

Above Lion, *Panthera leo*, cub in Serengeti National Park (AZ)

Right The cheetah, *Acynonix jubatus*, is the world's fastest land animal, a common predator in open plains such as those of the Serengeti (AZ)

Below A lioness with its zebra kill. Females of the pride do most of the hunting (AZ)

Above left The topi, *Damaliscus lunatus*, is one of the more commonly seen large antelope in the Serengeti National Park (AZ)

Above right Kirk's dikdik, *Madoqua kirki*, easily distinguished from other small antelope by its white eye-circle, Arusha National Park (AZ)

Below Elephant, *Loxodonta africana*, Ngorongoro Crater (AZ)

Above Lilac-breasted roller, *Coracius cordata*, one of the most eye-catching birds of the Serengeti and other lightly wooded habitats (NG)

Above right Superb starling, *Spreo superbus*, often become very tame at game lodges in northern Tanzania (AZ)

Right Hooded vulture, *Necrosyrestes monachus*, waiting at a lion kill, Serengeti National Park (AZ)

Below Lesser flamingoes, *Phoenicopterus minor*, in flight at Lake Magadi in the Ngorongoro Crater (AZ)

ORGANISING A SAFARI

There are two basic approaches to organising a safari. The first is to pre-book a package before you leave for Tanzania; the second is to make your arrangements after you arrive in Tanzania. The first approach is the one taken by most fly-in tourists, and its advantages are self-evident. Pre-booking saves you time once you are in the country, and it ensures that you get the itinerary and lodge bookings you want. The second approach is favoured by most budget travellers, the majority of whom cannot predict in advance exactly when they will be in Arusha. It also has several advantages, most significantly that cheaper rates are generally offered to walk-in clients.

Arusha is the most popular and convenient base from which to organise a safari to Tanzania's northern reserves. Although a small proportion of tourists organise safaris from Moshi, Dar es Salaam and even Mwanza, there are few advantages in doing this. The overwhelming majority of safari companies and the most competitive prices are to be found in Arusha.

With literally hundreds of safari companies operating out of Arusha, competition for custom is fierce, particularly at the bottom end of the price scale where there are several unscrupulous and incompetent companies willing to cut any corner and promise anything in order to keep down costs and attract budget travellers. Given that you are likely to face an onslaught of safari touts from the moment that you arrive in Arusha, with the most dubious companies generally being the most pushy, I feel it is important that you give some advance thought to exactly what you want from a safari. Much of the following advice is aimed primarily at people who organise safaris after they arrive in Tanzania, as it is they who are most likely to be taken in by dodgy companies, but the individual company recommendations and comments regarding itineraries and group sizes will apply equally to people who organise a safari in advance.

The issue for travellers on a limited budget boils down one simple thing: to what degree should you compromise in order to cut costs? There are several ways you can reduce the cost of a safari – by going as part of a group, by using a cheap but possibly unreliable operator, by camping in private campsites rather than in reserves – but every compromise has the potential to spoil your safari. My own view is that if you've gone to the expense of flying to Africa, and the safari is a once-in-a-lifetime experience, it seems a bit shortsighted to cut corners unless it's absolutely unavoidable. But, as a high number of visitors to Tanzania make economically driven decisions which they later regret, it does seem worth laying out in detail the sort of options that exist.

Safari 'types'

There are, in essence, four types of safari package on offer: budget camping safaris, standard lodge-based safaris, upmarket camping safaris, and fly-in safaris. Budget camping safaris are generally designed to keep costs to a minimum, so they will make use of the cheapest camping options, often outside the national parks, and clients are normally expected to set up their own tents. Most backpackers and volunteers working in Tanzania go on budget camping safaris, though even with these there is a gap between the real shoestring operators, who'll skimp on everything, and those operators who offer a sensible compromise between affordability and providing an adequate service.

Most fly-in tourists go on a standard lodge-based safari, which will generally cost around double the price of a similar budget camping safari. For the extra outlay, you get a roof over your head, restaurant food, and a far higher degree of luxury and comfort. If you decide to go on a lodge safari, the probability is that the operator will decide which lodges you stay at. If you have the choice, however, it's worth noting that the TAHI (Tanzania Hotel Investments Ltd) lodges generally have the best natural settings, but the rooms are relatively basic (and correspondingly cheaper than other lodges). These lodges form a government-owned chain which is managed by the French Novotel Group. The Sopa Lodges are far more luxurious and about 30% more expensive, but only the Ngorongoro Sopa Lodge has a setting to compare with its TAHI equivalent. The Serena Lodges are generally the best of the mainstream lodges, and similarly priced to their Sopa counterparts, while the Conservation Corporation Lodges are the absolute tops in terms of both quality and price. In all national parks, there is at least one small lodge or tented camp that doesn't belong to a chain; in many cases these are much cheaper than the chain lodges while offering a less institutionalised 'bush' environment.

Camping isn't necessarily a cost-reducing device. Sleeping under canvas and eating under the stars will unquestionably make you feel more integrated into the bush environment than staying in a lodge, and this is where upmarket camping safaris come into play. At the top end of the range, you can organise safaris using private or so-called 'special' campsites, as well as tented lodges, and these will be as luxurious as any lodge safari, with top-quality food, a full team of staff, large tents, portable showers and the like. The cost of a safari like this will depend on your exact requirements, but it will probably cost at least as much as a similar lodge safari. What you are paying for is exclusivity and a real bush experience.

Regular scheduled flights connect all the main reserves in northern Tanzania, and an increasingly high proportion of safari-goers choose to fly around rather than bump along the long, dusty roads that separate the parks. Flying around will be particularly attractive to those who have bad backs or who tire easily, but it is more expensive and does dilute the sense of magic attached to driving through the vast spaces that characterise this region. Fly-in safaris allow you to see far more wildlife in a shorter space of time, because you don't lose hours on the road.

In all categories of safari, the price you are quoted should include the vehicle and driver/guide, fuel, accommodation or camping equipment and fees, meals and park entrance fees. You are expected to tip the driver and cook. Around US$5 per day per party seems to be par, but you should check this with the company. Drivers and cooks are poorly paid; if they have done a good job, be generous.

Group safaris and private safaris

A factor that all visitors should consider is the size of the group doing the safari. It is almost invariably cheaper to go on safari as part of a group, as the operator can divide most transport costs between a greater number of people. Typically, a group of four people will pay about 30% less per head than a group of two people. This is a considerable saving, but it does have many disadvantages, and I would advise anybody who can afford it to arrange a private safari.

The first problem with forming an impromptu group, or going on an organised group safari, is the obvious one of compatibility. My own experience of going on safari as part of a group has generally been good, but I've also had one horrendous experience with a mother and daughter who did nothing but bicker, moan and ask moronic questions (Is that an African or Indian elephant? How can you tell...?). Had this been a once-in-a-lifetime experience, they would have ruined it.

A group safari will be highly frustrating to those who have a special interest such as birding or serious photography. And, frankly, I think it is unfair to impose this sort of interest on other passengers, who will have little interest in identifying every raptor you drive past, or in waiting for two hours at a lion kill to get the perfect shot. On a private safari, you will almost certainly find the driver to be responsive to your specific needs and interests, and you can use his local knowledge to plan each day to your requirements. For instance, any photographer's top priority will be to be photographing during the first and last two hours of light, not to waste these precious hours on breakfast or sleeping in. On a group safari, the driver simply cannot pander to this sort of individual requirement, nor is it fair to expect him to.

Another consideration regarding group size is that most Land Rovers feel rather cramped with four people in the back, especially when the luggage is in the vehicle, and jostling for head room out of the roof can be a nightmare when four cameras are vying for the best position. If you do decide to go as part of a group, more than four people will get seriously cramped, and will mean some members can't sit next to a window. Some companies are willing to take five or even six people in a Land Rover, but the minuscule saving attached to having more than four people on board really isn't worth it, no matter how tight you are for cash.

A small proportion of companies – generally the large package tour operators – use minibuses as opposed to conventional 4x4s. In my opinion, minibuses have several disadvantages, notably that the larger group size (typically around eight people) creates more of a package tour atmosphere, and that it is difficult for a large group to take proper advantage of the pop-up roofs which are usually found on safari vehicles. In any event, bouncing around rutted roads in a Land Rover is an integral part of the safari experience – it just wouldn't be the same in a minibus.

Finally, there is the question of aesthetics. Without wishing to wax too lyrical, the thrill of being on safari doesn't derive merely from the animals you see. There is an altogether more elusive and holistic quality attached to simply *being* in a place as wild and vast and wonderful as the Serengeti, one that is most easily absorbed in silence, whether you travel on your own or with somebody with whom you feel totally relaxed. Perhaps we are overly sensitive on this point, but it just isn't the same when you have to make small talk to new acquaintances, go through the rote jokes about who should be put out of the vehicle to make the lion move, decide democratically when to move on or stay put, listen to the driver's educational monotones, and generally observe social niceties that seem at odds with the wilderness around you.

Itinerary

Your itinerary will depend on how much time and money you have, and also the time of year. There are endless options, and most safari companies will put together the package you ask for. They know the ground well and can advise you on what is possible, but may tend to assume you will want to cover as many reserves as possible. This is not always the best approach.

A typical five- or six-day safari takes in Ngorongoro, Serengeti, Manyara and Tarangire. A typical three-day trip takes in all these reserves except for the Serengeti. In the dry season (July to October) there is little game in the Serengeti; most safari companies will suggest you spend more time in Tarangire.

The distances between these reserves are considerable and the roads are poor; you will have a more relaxed trip if you visit fewer reserves. On a five-day safari, I would drop either the Serengeti or Tarangire. To visit all four reserves, six days is just about adequate, seven or more days would be better.

I didn't find three days long enough to get a good feel for Tarangire, Manyara *and* Ngorongoro; four days would have been better. The combination of Ngorongoro and Tarangire would make an unhurried three-day safari. If you are limited to two days, you could either visit Tarangire on its own or do a combined trip to Manyara and Ngorongoro. If your budget is really limited, Tarangire can be visited as a day trip from Arusha; it is less than two hours' drive each way.

At the other end of the time scale, there is enough to see and do in the area to warrant a safari of two weeks in duration, or even longer. You could easily spend a few days exploring the Serengeti alone. In a two-week package, you could also visit Lake Natron, the Kondoa-Irangi rock art and/or the northern part of the Ngorongoro Conservation Area.

Safari companies

I cannot overstate the need for caution in your dealings with safari companies, especially if you are shopping around for a cheap price. There are, of course, any number of reputable companies to choose from, but putting together a reliable safari costs money, and at the bottom end of the price scale, reputable companies are overwhelmingly outnumbered by the incompetent and the unethical. To give some idea, less than half the companies currently operating out of Arusha are legally registered, which on its own gives the authorities the right to refuse their vehicles entry to any national park.

Before you panic, I should stress that in Arusha you will generally get what you pay for. If you organise your safari with a registered safari operator asking middle- to upper-range prices, there is no cause for concern, as the problem is pretty much confined to the bottom end of the price scale. It is also the case that the attitude of many budget travellers is largely responsible for allowing this problem to develop. If a significant proportion of travellers will take the cheapest price offered, it is only to be expected that some companies will cut corners in order to undercut their rivals' prices. Likewise, if, after having been warned, you still choose to go on a cheap safari with an unknown quantity, you have little legitimate cause for complaint if the vehicle and service aren't up to scratch. You could even argue that these 'pirate' companies offer a legitimate service – high risk, low cost safaris – and that the only question is whether you want to make use of it.

On a budget camping safari, you will get a better price if you opt to camp at sites outside of the national parks. Tarangire, Manyara and Ngorongoro Crater can all be visited from private campsites, and doing this as opposed to camping within the national parks will cut around US$15 per night from the cost of a safari. The disadvantage of doing it this way is that camping outside the parks will inevitably dilute the safari experience – arguably a false economy unless you're on a very tight budget. You can assume that any cheap safari company will use campsites outside of national parks (except for in the Serengeti, where there is no alternative to the national park campsite), so the onus is on you to specify that this isn't what you want – and to be prepared to pay the extra cost to camp in the parks.

At the time of writing, the lowest price you'll pay for a camping safari is around US$80 per person per day for four people. Superficially, this price may seem extortionate, but when you consider that it covers park entrance fees, camping fees, petrol and car maintenance (both of which are expensive in Tanzania), food, and the services of a cook and driver, it is difficult to see how a company could charge any less and still make a reasonable profit. At the time of writing, Sunny Safaris and Roy Safaris (see below) serve as a reliable benchmark for the lowest price offered by a reputable company. If you are offered a safari for less than this, you can be certain the company will be cutting corners, most commonly by providing a sub-standard vehicle, by keeping petrol costs to a minimum with game drives that last for only one or two hours, or by not paying park fees (and if you think the last of these isn't your problem, then be warned that several regular offenders have recently been turned back from the park gates, end of safari, no refund).

There is little point in naming individual offenders – most companies will change their name if they get any negative press. I've met several people who booked with a 'new' company and, after they had paid, found themselves going on safari with a company they knew to be disreputable. Likewise, I've met many people who asked to look at the vehicle before they paid, and were shown a different vehicle to the one that was used. Once you've paid, any thoughts of a refund belong in the realms of fantasy. To give some idea of the extent of deceit to which some companies will go to attract custom, one blacklisted company recently changed its name to that of another company which gets a rave recommendation in another guide book, and thus duped many travellers into thinking they were using a recommended company. The long and short of it is that you should not take anything at face value.

The situation in Arusha creates a slight dilemma for me. I would ideally like to be able to provide a list of every reputable safari company in Arusha, but there is no practical way of checking them all out myself. Nor is it possible to rely on the experiences of other travellers – even the worst company will get it right some of the time. I've met at least four victims of the most high-profile and unscrupulous cheap company that was operating between 1992 and its closure in 1995 – yet I've also met a good number of satisfied customers who used this company. The best source of information is other safari companies. Within the industry, everybody knows who is and isn't reliable. Ask around, and you'll find the same names keep cropping up with surprising regularity whoever you speak to.

The best advice I can give is to allow yourself a full day or longer to shop around and feel out the situation before you rush into a decision, and to check on any unknown operator with the TTB Office on Boma Road in Arusha. The TTB keeps a regularly updated list of registered companies, as well as a short list of blacklisted companies, and I would tend to assume that *any* company which doesn't appear on the former list is to be avoided. Despite the fact that so many travellers get caught out by dodgy operators, sorting the wheat from the chaff is primarily a question of common sense.

Recommended companies

The list below is by no means definitive, but it provides a good cross-section of the sort of services that are on offer, and except where otherwise noted, it sticks to companies which have maintained high standards over several years. There are, of course, many other good operators in Arusha, but with so many fly-by-night companies around, I prefer to stick to a few select companies in which I have total confidence. This policy may be unfair to other good companies, but my first responsibility is to the readers, and it is vindicated by the simple fact that I've yet to receive one letter of complaint from a reader who used one of the safari operators recommended in the first two editions of this guide.

Although the companies listed below generally specialise in safaris on the northern circuit, most can also set up Kilimanjaro and Meru climbs, fly-in safaris on the southern safari circuit, and excursions to Zanzibar.

Abercrombie and Kent PO Box 427, Arusha; tel: 057 7803; fax: 057 7003. One of the largest safari companies in Arusha, A and K is probably the leading operator when it comes to standardised upmarket minibus packages.
Bushbuck Safaris PO Box 1700, Arusha; tel: 057 7473; fax: 057 8239/2954; email: busbuk@habari.co.tz. This is a reliable and rapidly expanding company, specialising exclusively in lodge-based safaris. Prices and service are relatively upmarket, and it has a large fleet of new 4x4 vehicles and employs well-trained driver-guides. The office is about ten minutes' walk from the town centre next to the Impala Hotel.

Conservation Corporation Africa Private Bag X27, Benmore, South Africa; tel: +27 11 784-7077; fax: +27 11 784-7667; email: reservations@conscorp.co.za. This South African company, lauded throughout southern Africa for its superlative lodges and commitment to genuine eco-tourism, has recently expanded into East Africa. The CCA owns excellent upmarket lodges or tented camps in Ngorongoro, Serengeti and Lake Manyara, as well as on Zanzibar, and it arranges fly-in, drive-in (or mixed) safaris throughout northern Tanzania. The CCA makes no bones about its commitment to high cost, low impact tourism, and its Tanzanian properties are notable for their fine attention to detail, informal and personalised service, well-trained guides and rangers, and general air of exclusivity. If quality lies higher on your priorities than cost, then the CCA is probably the company to contact.

Hoopoe Adventure Tours India Street, PO Box 2047, Arusha; tel: 057 7011; fax: 057 8226; email: hoopoe@aol.com. UK bookings tel: +44 181 4288221; fax: +44 181 4211396; email: hoopoeUK@aol.com. Hoopoe is one of the most highly regarded companies in Arusha, specialising in personalised luxury camping and lodge safaris. I've been on safari with them on three occasions since 1992, and can recommend them without reservation to anybody looking for quality service, reliability, flexibility and reasonable (as opposed to cheap) prices. With Hoopoe, there are no kilometre restrictions, you will camp within national parks, the driver-guides and food are excellent, and portable showers are provided at national park campsites. Their prices for lodge-based safaris are very competitive, and they can arrange safaris using the special campsites in the various parks. Hoopoe has its own tented camps outside Lake Manyara and Tarangire. Following a recent merger with Tropical Tours, Hoopoe is one of the best companies to contact with regard to trekking and walking safaris in Natron, the Ngorongoro Highlands, and the game-rich Maasai plains to the east of the Serengeti.

Let's Go Travel (aka East African Safari and Touring Company) PO Box 12799, Arusha; tel: 057 7111/2814; fax: 057 8997/4199; email: letsgotravel@cybernet.co.tz. This branch of the well-established company of the same name in Nairobi offers prices and services comparable with Hoopoe, and is especially worth contacting if you're basing your East Africa trip out of Nairobi. The office is in the Adventure Centre on Goliondoi Road.

Roy Safaris PO Box 50, Arusha; tel: 057 8010 or 2115; fax: 057 8892; email: roysafaris@intafrica.com; web: http://www.intafrica.com/roysafaris. Founded ten years ago, this dynamic company has established itself as perhaps the leader when it comes to quality budget camping safaris, for which reason it is used by several overland truck companies (who cannot afford to take their foreign registered vehicles into the parks). Budget camping safaris using campsites outside national parks start at US$95 per person per day for four people and US$135 per person per day for two people. Their vehicles are always in excellent condition and the drivers are competent and knowledgeable. Roy also offers semi-luxury camping safaris starting at US$130 per person, and a variety of sensibly-priced lodge safaris. Out of season, they sometimes offer specials on lodge safaris that cost little more than the equivalent budget camping safari. The office is along an alley off Sokoine Road opposite the junction with Goliondoi Road,

Safari Destinations PO Box 2385, Arusha; tel/fax: 057 7940; email: safarides@ raha.com; web: http://www.raha.com/safarides. A subsidiary of Roy Safaris, this company was formed in 1998 to separate their safari and trekking businesses. It therefore specialises in treks on Kilimanjaro and Mount Meru, as well as to lesser known regions such as the Usambara, Lake Eyasi, Lake Natron and the Ngorongoro Highlands. It will be one of the few Arusha companies to organise its own Kili climbs directly rather than work through a Moshi or Marangu-based operator. Their climbs aren't the very cheapest, but nor are they particularly expensive, and you can be sure of getting good food and experienced guides and porters – they also intend to start carrying portable radios on all climbs, which (weather permitting) will allow for contact with the base in emergencies. The office is on India Road next to the YMCA.

Safari Makers PO Box 12902, Arusha; tel/fax: 057 6013; email: safarimakers@ habari.co.tz. This very new company, based on the third floor of the Robannyson Hotel, is included in this list on the basis that it is one of the few registered companies which is prepared to slug it out with the flycatchers and pirate companies for the backpacker trade. Safari Makers do run shoestring safaris, with all the risks that entails, but they also own their vehicles (where most shoestring operators simply hire the cheapest vehicle and driver they can find), and they are reliable in the sense that they will provide a refund or send out a replacement in the event of breakdown. In other words, they're a better bet than most if you are looking for a shoestring safari. Safari Makers is also one of the few companies in Arusha committed to promoting the various cultural programmes established by the SNV, and well worth contacting if you are interested in visiting one of these places

Safaris4you e-mail: safaris4you30@hotmail.com. Safaris4you is the nom-de-plume of Terri Rice, an old Arusha hand and experienced safari operator who recently started freelancing, working through a number of reliable operators depending on the individual requirements of her clients.

Sengo Safaris PO Box 207, Arusha; tel/fax: 057 8424; email: sengo@habari.co.tz. In addition to providing the standard safari options, Sengo organises a number of hikes in northern Tanzania, including a three-day trip to Ol Doinyo Lengai and Natron, three days at Empakaai Crater, a four-day Rift Valley hike, and a six-day hike through the Ngorongoro highlands to Empakaai. All hikes work out at around US$90-120 per person per day. Sengo owns three very reasonably priced rustic camps: Migungu at Lake Manyara, Ikoma in the western Serengeti, and Lake Natron Camp near the lake of the same name. Sengo is a good contact for trip to Lake Natron.

Shah Tours & Travels Ltd PO Box 1821, Moshi, Tanzania; tel: (055) 52370/52998; email: kilimanjaro@eoltz.com; web: www.kilimanjaro-shah.com

Sunny Safaris PO Box 7267, Arusha; tel: 057 7145; fax: 057 8094; email: sunny@ arusha.com. This well-established company offers perhaps the cheapest reliable camping safaris in Arusha. In 1998, they were able to offer camping safaris for as little as US$75-85 per person per day, depending on season and group size. At this price, you won't be camping in national parks, and you might find your driver to be inflexible about doing any excursion that puts extra kilometres on the clock. Otherwise, Sunny offers a thoroughly reliable service, with good vehicles and drivers. They also organise lodge-based safaris at very reasonable rates. Their office is opposite the Golden Rose Hotel.

Thomson Safaris PO Box 6074, Arusha; tel/fax: 057 8551; e-mail: tsafari@aol.com. Catering primarily to the US market, this company offers good lodge-based safaris and, based on the number of their vehicles we saw while we were last on safari, it must be one of the most popular in Arusha. A good contact for Americans who plan on visiting Tanzania.

Tropical Tours PO Box 727, Arusha; tel: 057 8353; fax: 057 8907. This company specialises in walking and mixed walking/driving tours in remote parts of northern Tanzania. Most trips are run in collaboration with local communities. Areas visited include the Monduli Mountains (35km hike over three days through mountain forest and acacia woodland, where there is a good chance of seeing elephants, buffaloes, and various antelope and monkey species); the Longido Mountains (20km hike over three days through pristine montane forest where elephants and buffaloes are still common); northern Maasailand; Mount Meru; and Kilimanjaro (using the less popular routes). They also do attractive semi-safari packages which combine walking and motorised transport in and around the Ngorongoro Crater, Lengai Volcano, and the game-rich plains immediately east of the Lobo part of the Serengeti. If you're looking for something different, this company is highly recommended, and the people who run it are very flexible, knowledgeable and enthusiastic without being pushy. Tropical Tours was bought out by Hoopoe Adventure Tours in late 1998, so if their contact details change, get hold of them through Hoopoe.

Tropical Trails PO Box 6130, Arusha; tel/fax: 057 8299; email: info@ tropicaltrails.com; web: www.tropicaltrails.com. Based at Maasai Camp, this is a genuinely eco-friendly company which arranges standard lodge-based and camping safaris for all budgets, as well as walking excursions on the fringes of the main national parks, and Kili climbs along the Machame and Shira routes. Tropical Trails is especially worth contacting if you have unusual requirements, or you want to get really off the beaten track, and they have some experience in arranging special one-off charity or group events.

Wildersun Safaris PO Box 930; tel: 057 3880; fax: 057 7834. This is a well-established and highly regarded company, concentrating almost exclusively on upmarket lodge-based safaris. The office is on the corner of Goliondoi and Jael Maeda Roads opposite a filling station.

Zara Tanzania Adventures PO Box 1990, Moshi, Kilimanjaro, Tanzania; tel: 055 4240/0808; fax: 055 3105/0233/0011

Miscellaneous warnings

Malaria is present in most parts of the region, with the notable exception of the Ngorongoro Crater rim, and the normal precautions should be taken. Aside from malaria, there are no serious health risks attached to visiting this area: tsetse flies are seasonally abundant in well-wooded areas such as Tarangire and the western Serengeti, and although sleeping sickness is reputedly not a cause for serious concern, they are aggravating enough that it is worth avoiding wearing the blue clothing that attracts them.

Tarangire can be reached via a good tar road, and the drive from Arusha to Lake Manyara involves a 40km stretch of rough road. The roads to the Ngorongoro Crater and Serengeti are very rough, for which reason safari-goers with serious back problems or a low tolerance for bumping around in the back of a vehicle might want to consider flying between the reserves. If one member of a safari party has a particular reason to want to avoid being bumped around, it is worth noting that in most 4x4s, they will be best off in the front passenger seat or the central row of seats – the seats above the rear axle tend to soak up the most punishment.

The combination of dust and glare may create problems for those with sensitive eyes. Sunglasses afford some protection against glare and dust, and if you anticipate problems of this sort, then don't forget to pack some eye drops. Many people who wear contact lenses suffer in these dusty conditions, so it is a good idea to wear glasses on long drives, assuming that you have a pair. Dust and heat can damage sensitive camera equipment and film, so read over the precautions mentioned in the box about photography on page 50.

As is standard practice in many countries, safari drivers earn a commission when their clients buy something from one of the many curio stalls in Mto wa Mbu and elsewhere in the region. There's nothing wrong with this, but it may well mean that your driver is far keener than you to stop at a few stalls in the hope you'll make a purchase. If this isn't what you want, then the onus is on you to make this clear the first time it happens – there's no need to be rude or confrontational, just explain gently that this isn't why you're on safari. Even if you do want to buy curios, don't fall into the obvious trap of assuming that you'll get a better deal buying locally – many of the curios you see in places like Mto wa Mbu probably found their way there from outside, and they will generally be cheaper in Arusha than they will be at roadside stalls which deal exclusively with tourists.

Travellers who are on a budget camping safari and who want to keep down their extra costs should be aware that drinks, though available at all game lodges, tend to be very expensive. A beer at a lodge will typically cost around US$3, as opposed to US$1 in a shop or local bar, and prices of sodas are similarly inflated. It is definitely worth stocking up on mineral water in Arusha (at least one 1.5l bottle per person per day), since this will be a lot more expensive on the road. Once in the reserves, some may feel that it's worth spending the extra money to enjoy the occasional chilled beer or soda at a lodge. Those who don't should ask their driver where they can buy drinks to bring back to the campsite. There are bars aimed at drivers near to all the places where budget safaris camp, and the prices are only slightly higher than in Arusha.

Finally, and at risk of stating the obvious, it is both illegal and foolhardy to get out of your safari vehicle in the presence of any wild animal, and especially buffalo, elephant, hippo and lion.

LAKE MANYARA NATIONAL PARK

Lake Manyara is a shallow, alkaline lake at the base of a cliff-face that is part of the western Rift Valley wall. The northwest of the lake and the land around it are protected in a 330km² national park. In the 1970s, Lake Manyara was famous for its elephants, immortalised by Ian Douglas-Hamilton in his book *Amongst the Elephants*. Poaching has reduced the numbers in recent years; you are unlikely to see a large tusker these days. The park's other claim to fame is its lions, which have a reputation for tree-climbing, behaviour that has also been observed with some regularity in Uganda's Queen Elizabeth National Park.

A visit to Lake Manyara National Park kicks off a high proportion of Tanzanian safaris, and forms an arguably somewhat low-key introduction to a complex of game reserves that's frequently been called the best in the world. From the entrance gate, which lies near a village called Mto wa Mbu, a road winds for several kilometres through a cool, lush, mature fig forest. With appropriate jungle noises supplied by silvery cheeked hornbills, this is the one part of the northern safari circuit which might conjure up images of Tarzan swinging into view. But, unless you're hoping for a rare glimpse of a leopard, the forest isn't really big game territory – you can expect to see baboons and with a bit of luck a few samango monkeys, but otherwise the main point of faunal interest is the diversity of birds and butterflies.

Most safari vehicles emerge from the forest at the hippo pools, where several dozens of hippos can be seen soaking and yawning. This is a lovely spot, with the Rift Valley escarpment rising to the west, and the sparsely vegetated flood plain of Lake Manyara stretching to the distant shore. Giraffes are common in this area – many of them so dark in colour that at a distance they appear almost melanistic. The hippo pools also offer excellent birding, with several varieties of heron, waterfowl and waders usually present, as well as more unusual species such as crowned crane, snipes and pratincoles. Note that following the *El Nino* floods of 1997/8, the hippo pools were totally submerged by the main, as was the flood plain between the fig forest and what is normally the lake shore. This was still the case in September 1998, when we last visited, but it is to be assumed that Lake Manyara will recede to its normal size during the lifespan of this edition.

Generally, the best mammal viewing in this national park is along the road towards Maji Moto Lodge and the hot springs in the south of the park. En route, you pass through tangled acacia woodland with views over the flood plain, where you should see large herds of zebra and wildebeest, the occasional impala and giraffe, and in the marshy area around the springs, plenty of buffaloes. This is also a good road for elephants, the population of which is visibly on the increase since it hit its nadir in the late 1980s.

As for the tree-climbing lions, you'll be lucky to see them in arboreal action – the only lion I've ever seen in Manyara was an impressively maned but mundanely terrestrial male plodding across the flood plain. But, whatever you read elsewhere, this unusual behaviour does still occur in the park (Janet Mears of Bradt

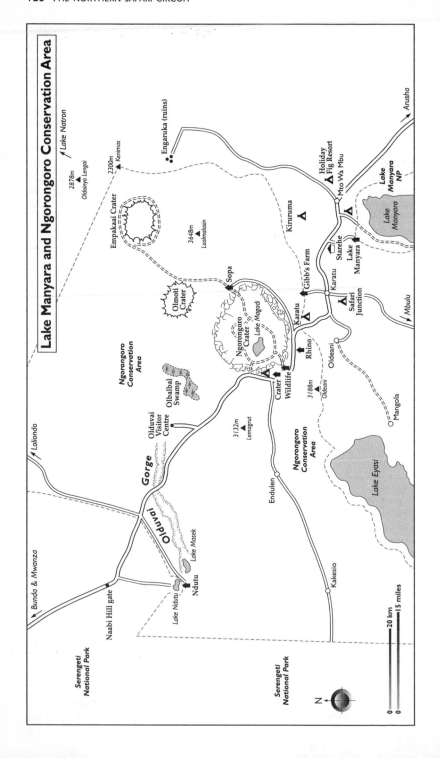

MTO WA MBU

This village close to the Lake Manyara entrance gate sees a large volume of tourist traffic. It is the normal base for budget safaris visiting Lake Manyara, and even if you aren't staying in the village or visiting Lake Manyara, your safari driver will probably stop at the huge curio market in the hope of picking up a commission. Mto wa Mbu (pronounced as one word *mtowambu*) means River of Mosquitoes, and if you do spend the night here, then you'll be in no doubt about how it got its name. Even passing through by day, the curio dealers who will swarm around you the moment you leave your vehicle might draw the obvious analogy.

Mto wa Mbu is a realistic target for backpackers who can't afford a proper safari. Buses connecting Arusha to Karatu all stop at Mto wa Mbu, and there is no shortage of affordable accommodation in the village (see *Where to stay* at Lake Manyara). The nearby Lake Manyara National Park is reasonably accessible to non-motorised travellers, since practically all tourists enter it as a day trip, which means there is no danger of being stranded there overnight. Hitching into the park is forbidden, and most safari vehicles wouldn't stop for hitchers even if it was permitted, so you would be best off asking around in the village about finding a lift or renting a vehicle to take you in for the day.

An equally compelling (and more certain) reason to bus to Mto wa Mbu is the clutch of walking tours that have been set up as part of a cultural tourism programme with the assistance of SNV. One of the most interesting of these walks is the papyrus lake tour, which takes you to the Miwaleni waterfall, as well as to a papyrus lake where Rangi people collect basket- and mat-weaving material, and to the homesteads of Sandawe hunter-gatherers. Other tours take you to Balaa Hill, which boasts excellent views over the village and lake, and to Chagga farms and Maasai *bomas*. The tourism programme is run out of the Red Banana Restaurant in the centre of the village, where you must pay your fees, arrange a guide and (if you like) rent a bicycle. The guide fee works out at US$7.50 per group per day, in addition to which must be paid a village development fee of US$1.50 per person. Bicycle hire costs US$2 per day.

Publications is a first-hand witness), especially during the dry season when lion concentrations are highest. *Acacia tortilis* trees are particularly favoured. Oddly enough, I received a letter from a reader who saw lions in a tree in Tarangire in early 1998, and we ourselves witnessed the same phenomenon recently in the western Serengeti – one suggestion is that this behaviour outside of Manyara is a result of the tsetse fly outbreak that followed the *El Nino* floods of 1997/8.

I've read elsewhere that Lake Manyara is frequently a disappointment to visitors. Certainly, if your expectations are formed by Douglas-Hamilton's book and talk of tree-climbing lions, you're probably in for a slight let down. In my opinion, however, Manyara is a valuable addition to a safari of several days' duration, but I could understand that somebody with limited time might elect to forsake its biological diversity for an additional day on the predator-rich plains of the Serengeti.

Worth noting is that Manyara is a *great* birding reserve – it's perfectly feasible for a casual birder to see 100 species in a day, ranging from the forest-dwelling crowned eagle to a variety of colourful bee-eaters, barbets, kingfishers and rollers. There are, too, the large flocks of flamingos which collect on the shallow alkaline lake – on my most recent visit, their numbers rivalled those on Kenya's famous Lake Nakuru.

The 44-page booklet *Lake Manyara National Park*, published by Tanzania National Parks, gives detailed coverage of the park's flora and fauna. Like all national parks, an entrance fee of US$25 per 24-hour period is charged.

Where to stay and eat

There is only one place to stay within the park boundaries, the recently opened Maji Moto Camp. There is, however, plenty of accommodation bordering the park. Most of the tourist-class lodges are situated on the Rift Valley escarpment overlooking Lake Manyara, while the budget accommodation and campsites are dotted around the small village of Mto wa Mbu outside the main entrance gate.

Upper range

Maji Moto Camp Private Bag X27, Benmore, South Africa; tel: +27 11 784-7077; fax: +27 11 784-7667; e-mail: reservations@conscorp.co.za. Opened in 1997, this Conservation Corporation tented camp is nestled in a grove of acacia trees towards the southern boundary of the park, near to the hot springs from which its name derives. The original camp fell victim to the *El Nino* floods within months of opening, but a new temporary camp has been built on a higher point above the lake. Like other CCA lodges, Maji Moto offers the ultimate in exclusive bush luxury, consisting of ten standing tents with en-suite bathrooms overlooking the lake. Rates are US$325 per person inclusive of meals, drinks, game drives and other excursions.
Lake Manyara Lodge PO Box 877, Arusha; tel: 057 2711/2; fax: 057 8221; email: tahifin@habari.yako.co.tz. The Tahi property is barely recognisable from its shoddy, run-down state of a few years ago. The rooms are still a bit spartan, but they do have mosquito nets and en-suite bathrooms with running hot water. A definite attraction of the lodge is a large swimming pool, but its single best feature remains its peerless position right on the edge of the escarpment. The grounds offer a panoramic view over the forest and lake, with the Rift Valley hills fading to the horizon. With binoculars, you should be able to pick out elephants, giraffes and buffaloes on the Rift Valley floor; closer to home, there is good birding within the lodge grounds. US$135/210/303 single/double/triple full-board.
Lake Manyara Serena Lodge PO Box 2551, Arusha; tel: 057 8175/6304; fax: 057 8282; email: serena@yako.habari.co.tz. Opened in 1996, the Serena lodge lies on the escarpment to the north of the older Tahi lodge. Like other lodges in the Serena chain, it is a very attractive set-up, with ethnic-looking rondavel accommodation, a lush reception area, and communal areas overlooking the lake. Rooms cost US$170/260 single/double full-board.

Moderate

Kirurumu Tented Lodge PO Box 2047, Arusha; tel: 057 7011/7541; fax: 057 8226; email: hoopoe@aol.com. UK bookings tel: +44 181 428-8221; fax: +44 181 421-1396; email: hoopoeUK@aol.com. Owned and managed by Hoopoe Adventure Tours, Kirurumu is perched on the Rift Valley escarpment a short distance north of Lake Manyara, and it offers a grand view across the plains of the Rift Valley. The atmosphere is more rustic than at the lodge, and it will be more attractive to people who prefer to feel close to nature. The food is good and the service friendly and efficient. Accommodation is in luxury double tents, each of which has a private verandah, shower and toilet. Kirurumu offers indisputable value for money at US$65/90 single/double half-board or US$80/120 single/double full-board.
Migunga Forest Camp PO Box 207, Arusha; tel: 057 8424; fax: 057 8272; email: sengo@yako.habari.co.tz. Set in a thick patch of acacia forest below the Rift Valley escarpment near Mto wa Mbu, this is another reasonably-priced rustic camp suitable for those who feel that conventional lodges dilute the safari experience. Reedbuck, bushbuck and buffalo sometimes pass through the camp, while the lesser bushbaby is often seen at night. Roughly 70 bird species have been recorded within the camp. Accommodation is in standing tents with en-suite hot showers, and it costs US$60/100 single/double.

Budget and camping

There's no shortage of affordable lodgings and campsites in Mto wa Mbu, the village that lies on the main road outside the park entrance. Of these places, **Twiga Campsite and Lodge** (PO Box 16, Mto wa Mbu; tel: 0811 510937) is the most popular and attractive. Large s/c double rooms with hot water and nets cost US$20 b&b, or you can pitch a tent in the spacious, neatly cropped campsite for US$5 per person. At the restaurant, a three-course meal costs US$6, while most dishes on the à la carte menu work out at around US$4. There are 'wild video shows' in the lounge every evening.

The older **Holiday Fig Camp** is another popular place with budget safari operators, but the grounds are somewhat cramped and the rooms a touch overpriced. Ordinary doubles cost US$15 and self-contained doubles with fans US$30. Camping costs US$5 per person. Facilities include a restaurant and bar, as well as a swimming pool which I've yet to see in a functional state.

If the above places seem too expensive, the **Jambo Campsite** is a pleasant enough place charging US$3 per person to camp or US$8 for an adequate double room with mosquito netting. The **Camp Vision Lodge** caters primarily to safari drivers, but travellers are welcome and the bright little rooms with nets are excellent value at US$3.

At the top of the escarpment, there are a few lodges in the village at the junction to the Lake Manyara Lodge. These are generally scruffier than the ones in Mto wa Mbu, and they cater mainly to safari drivers, but travellers are welcome. Malaria and mosquitoes are less of a threat at this altitude, and if you happen to be that most optimistic of souls, somebody trying to get around the parks on public transport or by hitching, a room at this junction would enable you to wander up to the lodge for a beer and some long-distance game viewing.

KARATU

This small, dusty town straddling the main road between Manyara and Ngorongoro may not look like much when you pass through coming from Arusha, but it is probably the most populous settlement anywhere along the almost 400km-long B142. Most tourists who are on a lodge-based safari will pass through Karatu in the blink of an eye, but quite a number of camping safaris use the small town as a base for day trips to the nearby Ngorongoro Crater, since camping here is a lot cheaper. Nicknamed 'safari junction', Karatu is also the last place along the B142 which can be reached from Arusha on local bus, a piece of information which sounds a lot more useful than it actually is.

Where to stay

The only upmarket accommodation around Karatu is **Gibb's Farm** (PO Box 2; Karatu; tel: 057 8930; fax: 057 8310), an attractively idiosyncratic set-up which lies 4km from the main road, on a coffee farm bordering a patch of indigenous forest. The colonial-era mood here is a far cry from the relative uniformity that characterises many of the more upmarket lodges in northern Tanzania, and several safari drivers have told me their clients rate it as one of their favourite hotels in Tanzania. Full-board accommodation in s/c bungalows costs US$139/204 single/double.

The spacious **Safari Junction Campsite** is popular with camping safari companies, and it has good facilities including hot showers, a good restaurant, and a bar with occasional live music (we were entertained by two men playing a bongo drum and a *zeze*, the latter being a one-stringed instrument similar to a violin. The site lies 1km out of town and is signposted. Camping costs US$3 per person, while hired tents and log cabins cost US$8/18/24 single/double/triple.

The **Karatu Campsite** lies just off the main road towards Ngorongoro, about 10km from Karatu at Njiapanda. Facilities are good. Camping costs US$5 per person.

There are also a number of cheap local guesthouses and restaurants along the main road through Karatu town.

LAKE EYASI

This little-visited and scenic lake lies on the remote southern border of the Ngorongoro Conservation Area, at the base of the 1,000m-high Eyasi Escarpment on the western Rift Valley wall. There is plenty of wildlife in the area, which is also home to the hunter-gatherer Hadza people. The road to Eyasi branches from the main road between Kidatu and Ngorongoro. There are no tourist facilities, so visitors should be entirely self-sufficient.

NGORONGORO CONSERVATION AREA

This 8,300km² conservation area is named after its central feature, the Ngorongoro Crater, the world's largest intact volcanic caldera, and arguably its most spectacular natural arena. Ngorongoro Crater has often been described as one of the wonders of the world, not only because of its inherent geological magnificence, but also because it serves as a quite extraordinary natural sanctuary for some of Africa's densest populations of large mammals.

The approach road from Karatu to the crater rim is sensational, winding through the densely forested outer slopes to Heroes Point, where most visitors will catch their first breathtaking view over the 260km² crater floor lying 600m below. Even at this distance, it is possible to pick out ant-like formations – thousand-strong herds of wildebeest and buffalo – chomping their way across the crater floor, and with binoculars you might even see a few of the elephants that haunt the fringes of Lerai Forest. And the drive along the crater rim to your lodge will be equally riveting: patches of forest interspersed with sweeping views back across to the Rift Valley, and the possibility of encountering buffalo, zebra, bushbuck and even the occasional leopard.

The Ngorongoro Crater is the main focal point of tourist activity in the crater, and is covered in more detail later in this section. Those who have the time can explore any number of less publicised natural features further afield. Olduvai Gorge, for instance, is the site of some of Africa's most important hominid fossil finds, and can easily be visited en route from the crater rim to the Serengeti. An excellent 84-page booklet, *Ngorongoro Conservation Area*, similar in style to the national park booklets, is readily available in Arusha and has good information on the crater and Olduvai Gorge. It is especially worth buying if you plan to visit some of the off-the-beaten-track parts of the conservation area.

The Ngorongoro Conservation Authority charges an entrance fee of US$25 per person per 24-hour period. This must be paid even if you just pass through the conservation area between Arusha and the Serengeti. An additional crater service fee of US$30 per vehicle is charged upon descending to the crater floor.

The crater rim gets very cold at night, and is often blanketed in mist in the early morning. You will need a jumper or two, and possibly a wind-breaker if you are camping.

Geology and history

The mountains in the Ngorongoro region date from two periods. The Gol Mountains, to your left as you descend from Ngorongoro to the Serengeti, are exposed granite blocks over 500 million years old. Ngorongoro and other free-standing mountains are volcanic in origin, formed during the fracturing process that created the Rift Valley 15 to 20 million years ago. When Ngorongoro peaked in size two to three million years ago, it was a similar height to Kilimanjaro today. There are two other volcanic craters in the area: Olmoti and Empakaai. A volcano just north of the conservation area, Ol Dionyo Lengai (Maasai for Mountain of God), last erupted in 1983.

Evidence found at Olduvai Gorge and Laetoli (discussed more fully later in the chapter) show hominids have occupied the area for at least three million years. It was occupied by hunter-gatherers until a few thousand years ago, when pastoralists moved in. There are, however, still hunter-gatherers living in the Eyasi Basin south of Ngorongoro. These people, called the Hadza, have strong linguistic links with the San of southern Africa.

The fate of the early pastoralists is not known; a succession of immigrants replaced them. The ancestors of the Cushitic-speaking Mbulu arrived 2,000 years ago. The Nilotic-speaking Datoga arrived 300 years ago. A century later the Maasai drove both groups out in a violent conflict; the Datoga to the Eyasi Basin and the Mbulu to the highlands near Manyara. Most place names in the area are Maasai. I have heard several explanations of the name Ngorongoro; the most believable, told to me by a Maasai, is that it is named after a type of Maasai bowl that it resembles.

Europeans settled in the area around the turn of the century. The crater floor was farmed by two German brothers until the outbreak of World War I. One of their old farmhouses is still used by researchers working in the crater, and a few relic sisal plants can be seen in the northeast of the crater. Tourism began in the 1930s when the Ngorongoro Crater Lodge was built on the crater rim. Ngorongoro was part of the original Serengeti National Park proclaimed in 1951, but it was made a separate conservation area in 1956 in order that the Maasai could graze their cattle there. Ngorongoro Crater was made a World Heritage Site in 1978.

Getting there and away

Most tourists visit Ngorongoro as part of a longer safari. However, those who cannot afford to do this could still think about visiting the crater on a shorter one-night self-contained safari out of Arusha.

The Ngorongoro Conservation Authority staff bus between Arusha and the park headquarters used to run twice daily in each direction, stopping at Karatu and Mto wa Mbu. Should it resume, travellers will presumably still be permitted to make use of the service, and to pay normal fares, bearing in mind that the value of arriving at Ngorongoro on a bus is questionable. You could hire a park vehicle to take you into the crater, but unless you are part of a large group this is expensive: US$140 for a full day, plus US$1 per km, plus a US$30 crater fee. Add on park fees and you would be better off organising a safari in Arusha.

Where to stay and eat

There are no accommodation or camping facilities within the crater, and with the exception of Ndutu Lodge on the Serengeti border, all the lodges and the main campsite lie perched on the crater rim.

Upper range

Ngorongoro Crater Lodge Private Bag X27, Benmore, South Africa; tel: +27 11 784-7077; fax: +27 11 784-7667; email: reservations@conscorp.co.za. This top-of-the-range lodge was originally built in 1934 as a private hunting lodge with a commanding view over the crater, and was converted to a hotel shortly after independence in 1961. The property was bought by the Conservation Corporation Africa in 1995, rebuilt from scratch with the

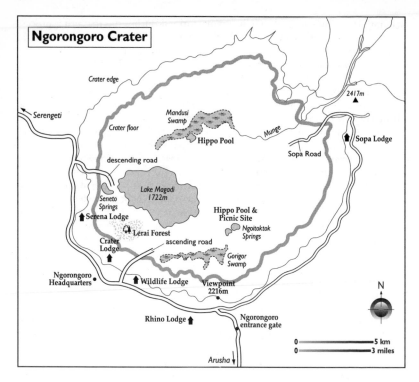

Ngorongoro Crater

stated aim of creating 'the finest safari lodge in Africa', and it re-opened towards the end of 1997. Architecturally, this lodge is literally fantastic. Each individual suite consists of two adjoining round structures, similar to African huts but distorted in an almost Dadaist style, while the large interiors boast a decor as ostentatious as it is eclectic, combining elements of baroque, classical, African, colonial and much more besides in a manner the management describes as 'Maasai meets Versailles'. The entire lodge has been designed in a such a way that the crater is almost constantly in view (even the baths and the toilets have a view!), and the food, service and ambience are all world-class. Whether or not the CCA has succeeded in creating Africa's finest safari lodge is a matter of taste and opinion (the decidedly non-'bush' atmosphere might offend some purists) but it is difficult to fault in terms of ambition and originality, and the fact that it has already been commended in *Conde Naste Traveller*'s prestigious 1998 end-of-year listings says enough. As with other CCA properties, the Crater Lodge charges a straight US$325 per person inclusive of meals, drinks and game drives. Booking details are contained under *Safari companies* on pages 121–4.

Ngorongoro Serena Lodge PO Box 2551, Arusha; tel: 057 8175/6304; fax: 057 8282; email: serena@yako.habari.co.tz. This is probably the pick of the more conventional lodges on the crater rim. It lies along the road to Seronera, on the western crater rim several kilometres past Crater Lodge. Built in a secluded valley with a good view over the crater, the Serena Lodge boasts excellent facilities and good service, and is has been widely praised within the safari industry. Rooms cost US$170/260 single/double full-board.

Ngorongoro Wildlife Lodge PO Box 887, Arusha; tel: 057 2711/2; fax: 057 8221; email: tahifin@habari.yako.co.tz. Like Ngorongoro Crater Lodge, roughly 2km away, this is another relatively old lodge, managed by TAHI. The services have greatly improved in the last few years, particularly the catering. The lodge has a beautiful position on the rim of the crater directly above the yellow fever forest. The rooms are comfortable, with piping hot baths (welcome at this chilly altitude) and windows facing the crater. You can pick out animals on the crater floor using a telescope fixed on the patio. The grounds support a fair range of forest birds, and they're also one of the few places where I've seen tree hyraxes. Nothing flash, but solid value for money at US$135/186/303 single/double/triple full-board.

Ngorongoro Sopa Lodge PO Box 1823, Arusha; tel: 057 6896/6886; fax: 057 8245; email: sopa@africaonline.co.tz. This lies on the eastern crater rim some 20km distant from the park headquarters and the above-mentioned lodges. Accommodation is in large semi-detached rooms resembling stone rondavels from the outside. Each room has two double beds, a heater, a large bathroom with running hot water, a fridge, and a large bay window facing the crater and Ol Mokarot Mountain. There is a swimming pool in front of the bar. The food at the restaurant is excellent. The large, forested grounds are a good place to look for characteristic montane forest birds, with sunbirds (tacazze, golden-winged and eastern double-collared) well represented and a variety of weavers, seedeaters and robins present. Accommodation costs US$155/240 single/double full-board.

Moderate

Run by the Ngorongoro Conservation Authority, **Rhino Lodge** lies a short distance from the conservation headquarters. It isn't the most exciting place to stay, and it has no view worth talking about, but it is certainly the cheapest option at US$55/80 single/double. Making an advance booking is not normally necessary, and the only practical way of going about it would be to drop in at the NCA office in Arusha, or ask a safari company to do this. If this lodge is too expensive for you, your only options will be to camp or to take a room in Karatu.

Budget and camping

The only place where you can pitch a tent on the crater rim is at **Simba Campsite**, about 2km from the park headquarters. This site is hardly great value at US$20 per person (facilities are limited to a cold shower and rubbish pit) but the wonderful view still makes it a preferable option to camping in Karatu, in my opinion at least. The

HIKING IN NGORONGORO CONSERVATION AREA

You are permitted to walk in the conservation area providing you have an authorised guide. Tropical Tours in Arusha and Tropical Trails based at Maasai Camp outside Arusha (see *Organising a safari*) specialise in this kind of thing, but it is possible to make your own arrangements. You could, for instance, hike all the way from Lake Natron to the crater rim, taking in Lengai volcano and other places of interest along the route (see box *North of Ngorongoro Crater* page 136). This would take at least a week and would probably cost around the same as a Kilimanjaro climb. Another area worth exploring on foot is the Lake Eyasi border.

If you want to do something along these lines, contact the Assistant Conservator of Tourism at the Ngorongoro Conservation Authority in Arusha. At present, few people hike in the area so the chances of getting permission are reasonable, but it is very much at the discretion of the NCA and obviously dependent on what resources are available (guides, porters, transportation within the area etc). If you get permission, you will have to organise food yourself. You should also clarify arrangements for a tent, sleeping bag and other equipment. Remember to take warm clothes; parts of the area become cold at night.

only cheap rooms on the crater rim are at the driver's lodge in the village, but tourists are not normally allowed to stay there. Your best bet for a cheap room is in Kidatu. The village near the headquarters has a few basic bars and shops, and there is nothing preventing you from dropping into nearby Wildlife Lodge for a drink or snack.

Exploring the conservation area
Ngorongoro Crater Floor
The opportunity of spending a day on the crater floor is simply not to be missed. There are few places where you can so reliably see such large concentrations of wildlife all year round, and your game viewing (and photography) will only be enhanced by the striking backdrop of the 600m-high crater wall.

There are several notable physical features within the crater. Lerai Forest consists almost entirely of yellow fever trees, a large acacia noted for its jaundiced bark. To the north of this forest, Lake Magadi is a shallow soda lake which covers a variable area depending on season. To the south and east of this, the Gorigor Swamp also varies in extent seasonally, but it generally supports some water. There is a permanent hippo pool at the Ngoitokitok Springs at the western end of the swamp. The northern half of the crater is generally drier, though it is bisected by the Munge River, which is lined by thickets and forms a seasonally substantial area of swamp to the immediate north of Lake Magadi.

THE MAASAI
The area covered in this chapter is the home of the Maasai, a Nilotic-speaking people who arrived in Tanzania from what is now the Sudan about 300 years ago. The Maasai have aroused Western awe and curiosity since the 19th century, when they acquired a reputation amongst slave traders and explorers as fearsome warriors. Caravan routes studiously avoided them, and areas like the Serengeti were amongst the last parts of East Africa ventured into by Europeans.

Maasai remain the most instantly recognisable East African people, though their modern reputation rests as much on their continued proud adherence to a traditional lifestyle as on any of their past exploits. Maasai men drape themselves in red blankets, carry long wooden poles, and have red-ochred hair. The women's actual dress is not dissimilar to the *vitenge* favoured by most Tanzanian women, but they cover themselves in all manner of beaded jewellery.

Maasai are traditionally pastoralists. They believe their god, who resides in Lengai Volcano, made them the rightful owners of all the cattle in the world; a view which, in the past, has made life difficult for neighbouring herders. This arrogance does not merely extend to cattle. They scorned agriculturalist and fish-eating peoples, and were equally disrespectful of Europeans, calling them *Iloredaa enjekat* – Those who confine their farts with clothing. The Maasai now co-exist peacefully with their non-Maasai compatriots, but they show little interest in changing their lifestyle.

The Maasai's main diet is a blend of cow's milk and blood, the latter drained – it is said painlessly – from a strategic nick in the animal's jugular vein. They are reluctant to kill their cattle for meat; the animals are more valuable to them alive. Despite the apparent hardship of their chosen lifestyle, many Maasai are wealthy by any standards. On one safari, our driver pointed out a not unusually large herd of cattle that would fetch the market equivalent of three new Land Rovers.

The open grassland that covers most of the crater floor supports large concentrations of wildebeest and zebra (the population of these species is estimated at 10,000 and 5,000 respectively), and smaller numbers of buffalo, tsessebe, and Thomson's and Grant's gazelle. The vicinity of Lerai Forest is the best area in which to see waterbuck, bushbuck and eland. The forest and adjoining Gorigor Swamp are the main haunt of the crater's elephant population, which typically stands at around 30. All the elephants in the crater are old males, and you stand a good chance of seeing big tuskers of the sort that have been poached away elsewhere in East Africa. Two curious absentees from the crater floor are impala and giraffe, both of which are common in the surrounding plains, Some researchers attribute the absence of giraffe to a lack of suitable browsing fodder, others to their presumed inability to descend the steep crater walls. Quite why there are no impala in the crater is a mystery.

The crater floor reputedly supports the densest predator population in Africa, with around 100 lion and 400 spotted hyena resident. Lion might be encountered just about anywhere, as might hyena, though the latter often seem to rest up on the eastern shore of Lake Magadi during the day. Cheetah are reputedly not resident in the crater, though they are common visitors, most likely to be encountered in the grassland to the north of Lake Magadi. Leopard are resident, particularly in swampy areas, but they are not often seen. Other common predators are the

---

Despite appearances, the Maasai, like us, are living in the 1990s. Large parts of their traditional grazing grounds have been given over to conservation, and in the Serengeti and Tarangire they are no longer allowed to graze their cattle.

In some ways, the Maasai are just another cog in the tourist industry, albeit not always a willing one. Herds of snap-happy tourists leap out of minibuses and Land Rovers to capture their image on film, on the one hand swooning at their noble savagery, on the other shoving a camera at them as though they were just another one of the 'big five'.

Several Maasai homesteads (called bomas) in the vicinity of Tarangire and Ngorongoro are now set up to receive tourist groups, and your safari driver will be able to arrange such a visit. The standard practice is to agree a price for the whole group to enter the boma, and once this has been paid you can pretty much wander around as you please and photograph whoever you like. At well-established 'tourist' bomas, particularly around Ngorongoro, this price might be as much as US$50 per group. It will generally be cheaper in the Tarangire area or around Mto wa Mbu. Although it is officially discouraged, there are still individual Maasai who hang around at places like Ngorongoro waiting for tourists to photograph them.

Whatever the circumstances, it is important to recognise that you must ask permission before photographing any Maasai, and (except where you have already paid a fee to enter the boma) should be prepared to pay for the privilege. Many tourists complain that this custom makes the Maasai 'overcommercialised'. I don't know whether such people believe the Maasai's first priority should be to pander to the aesthetic requirements of tourists, or whether they are just outraged at not getting something for nothing. Either way, we create the demand and the Maasai satisfy it. If you pay to do so, that's just good capitalism, something the West has been keen to encourage in Africa. And if you don't like the idea, then save your film for another subject.

golden and black-backed jackal, the former more frequently encountered as it has more diurnal habits.

The animal that many visitors most want to see in Ngorongoro is the black rhino. The crater is the only place on the northern safari circuit where rhino haven't been poached to local extinction, and most visitors will encounter at least one member of the crater's resident population of roughly 25 animals. The rhinos in the crater evidently spend their nights in Lerai Forest and their days out on the plain, for which reason they are fairly likely to be seen at close quarters when you follow the road fringing the forest in the early morning. We were quite surprised to see that an animal which is normally regarded to be an exclusive browser, and a largely diurnal feeder, should spend most of the day in grassland.

NORTH OF NGORONGORO CRATER

Few tourists venture into the northern part of the Ngorongoro Conservation Area, since it doesn't fit comfortably into the standard three- to five-day safari. There are, however, a few places which would be attractive additions to your itinerary if you had time or wanted to head to less touristed spots. Most experienced safari operators can arrange trips up here, generally taking Lake Natron as their focal point. The roads in the region are poor and may be impassable after rain. If you plan to explore the area, allocate time generously. If you visit this area in your own vehicle, treat it as you would any wilderness trip: carry adequate supplies of food, water, and fuel. You should also have essential spares for your vehicle. If you go with a safari company, avoid those on the lower end of the price scale.

Olmoti Crater This sunken caldera is near to the village of Nainokanoka. A track leads from the village to a ranger's post west of it. The crater can only be reached on foot, so at the ranger's post you will have to organise an armed ranger to guide you. From the ranger's post it is a half-hour walk to the rim. This is a shallow crater, covered in grass, and it offers good grazing for Maasai cattle and a variety of antelope. From the rim you can walk to a pretty waterfall where the Munge River leaves the crater.

Empakaai Crater Almost half the floor of this 6km-wide, 300m-high crater is taken up by a deep soda lake. A road circles the forested rim and another leads to the crater floor. Bushbuck, buffalo and blue monkey are likely to be seen on the rim, which also boasts good views across to Lengai Volcano and, on clear days, Kilimanjaro and Lake Natron. The crater floor is home to a variety of antelope and water birds. With permission from park headquarters, you may camp wild on the crater rim or sleep in a cabin on the southern shore of the lake.

Engaruka Ruins The ruins of a terraced stone city and complex irrigation system, estimated to be over 500 years old, lie on the eastern side of Empakaai. Nobody knows who built the city – there is no tradition of stone building in this part of Africa – but it was almost certainly occupied by the Mbulu people immediately before the Maasai came into the area. There is a road from Mto wa Mbu to Engaruka.

Ol Doinyo Lengai The challenging ascent to the crater of the Maasai Mountain of God, the only active carbonate volcano in the world, passes through some

The crater floor offers some great birding. Lake Magadi normally harbours large flocks of flamingo, giving its edges a pinkish tinge when seen from a distance. The pools at the Mandusi Swamp can be excellent for waterbirds, with all manner of waders, storks, ducks and herons present. The grassland is a good place to see a number of striking ground birds. One very common resident is the kori bustard, reputedly the world's heaviest flying bird, and spectacular if you catch it during a mating dance. Ostrich are also common, along with the gorgeously garish crowned crane, and (in the rainy season) huge flocks of migrant storks. Two of the most striking and visible birds of prey are the augur buzzard, sometimes seen here in its unusual melanistic form, and the foppish long crested eagle.

There are a few hippo pools in the crater, but the one most often visited is Ngoitokitok Springs, a popular picnic spot where lunch is enlivened by a flock of

magnificently arid scenery, and offers spectacular views of the Rift Valley. Lengai last erupted in 1966. Between 1996 and 1998, the crater has been filling with lava, though it has not yet spilt over the edge. The ascent requires a fair degree of fitness, as the track to the top is very steep, climbing in altitude from around 800m to over 3,000m. The ascent normally takes around five hours, with an 05.30 start advised due to the intense heat and lack of shade, and the descent another two hours. Dehydration and sunstroke are a serious threat to hikers who don't take adequate precautions. The mountain lies outside any conservation area, so no park fees are charged for climbing it, but you must pay the guide fee of US$30.

Lake Natron This spectacular soda lake, north of Lengai Volcano, lies at an altitude of 610m in the harsh Kenyan border area below the Rift Valley escarpment. The scenery here has an almost primeval quality, and the concentration of sodium carbonate dissolved in the lake is so high that it is often viscous to the touch. As well as being highly scenic, the lake offers good game viewing and birding. Among the 'specials' of the region are such dry country antelope as gerenuk, lesser kudu and oryx. Natron is the only known breeding ground for East Africa's lesser flamingoes.

The only place to stay in the Natron area is **Natron Lake Camp**, which has a spectacular setting next to a stream below the Rift Valley escarpment, roughly 4km from the southern lake shore. Accommodation in one of the five self-contained huts costs US$50 per person full-board or US$120 per person inclusive of all meals and activities. The camp is owned by Sengo Safaris, PO Box 207, Arusha; tel: 057 8424; fax: 057 8272; email: sengo@ yako.habari.co.tz.

The dusty 122km-drive from Mto wa Mbu to Natron generally takes four hours, and is safe at the time of writing. From Natron, it is possible to proceed to the northern Serengeti, a scenic 194km-drive that takes around eight hours, but this route was not being used in late 1998 due to an outbreak of unrest instigated by Somali exiles from Kenya. At least one police officer and several local Maasai have been killed by the Somali insurgents, and a tourist vehicle was recently attacked in this area, fortunately without any fatalities. There is good reason to hope that this spate of unrest will have been dealt with by the time this book is published, but you are strongly advised to seek the advice of a specialised Natron operator such as Sengo or Tropical Tours before heading this way.

black kites which have become adept at swooping down on tourists and snatching the food from their hands.

Many tourists compare Ngorongoro Crater to a zoo, which is utter nonsense. True, the animals are used to vehicles, but they are habituated, not tame, and they are free to enter and exit the crater as they please. And for all the elitism that is attached to visiting Africa's more remote reserves, I'd much rather spend time in a place such as Ngorongoro, where you can watch the animals behave 'naturally' at close quarters, rather than seeing nothing more interesting than a rump disappearing into the bush. A fairer criticism is that the high tourist traffic robs the crater floor of some of its atmosphere. It is a relatively small area and very open, which means most animal spotting is done by looking for a group of vehicles clustered together in the distance. Personally I feel that the scenery and abundance of animals more than makes up for the mild congestion, but if crowds put you off, then there are other places to visit in the Ngorongoro/Serengeti area. Instead of adding to the crowds then moaning about them, give the crater a miss.

The authorities rigidly forbid tourists from entering the crater before 07.00, and they must be out of the crater before 18.00. This is a frustrating ruling for photographers, since it means that you miss out on the best light of the day, and it has encouraged a situation where most safari drivers suggest that their clients take breakfast before going on a game drive, and carry a picnic lunch. This programme is difficult to avoid if you are on a group safari, but for those on a private safari, it is well worth getting down to the crater as early as permitted – photography aside, this is the one time in the day when you might have the crater to yourself, the one time, in other words, when you can really experience the Ngorongoro Crater of television documentary land. Note that it is forbidden to descend to the base of the crater after 16.00.

The official road down to the crater descends from Malanja Depression to the western shore of Lake Magadi, while the official road up starts near Lerai Forest and reaches the rim on the stretch of road between Wildlife and Crater Lodges. There is a third road into the crater, which starts near the Sopa Lodge, and this can be used either to ascend or to descend. At the time of writing, this situation has been turned around, because the down road was rendered impassable after the heavy rainy season in 1997/8. The 'up-road' thus became the 'down-road', and the Sopa road the only possible 'up-road', a somewhat inconvenient situation for people staying at any lodge other than Sopa, as it entailed a drive of at least one hour back to their lodge. The authorities recently bowed to common sense by allowing vehicles to ascend via the normal 'up-road' after 16.00 (I say common sense because vehicles are not allowed to descend after this time). There is no telling when the official down-road will be repaired and things return to normal.

Olduvai Gorge

The significance of Olduvai Gorge was first recognised by one Professor Katwinkle, an entomologist who stumbled across it in 1911. In 1913, he led an expedition which unearthed a number of animal fossils. The site was abandoned at the start of World War I.

In 1931, Louis Leakey arrived at Olduvai. He thought it an ideal place to uncover traces of early hominids. The gorge cuts through rock beds layered in time sequence from two million years ago to the present and their volcanic origin makes carbon-dating easy. Leakey found ample evidence of human occupation but, without backing, his investigations went slowly. It was only in 1959 that his wife, Mary, uncovered a 1.75 million year old *australopithecus* jawbone. This was the first conclusive evidence that hominids had existed for over a million years and that they had evolved in Africa. After this, the Leakeys received proper funding. They unearthed several more fossils, including *homo habilis*, a direct ancestor of modern man. Leakey died in 1972, but Mary continued working in the area until she retired in 1984. In 1976, at the nearby site of Laetoli, she discovered fossil footprints over three million years old, the most ancient hominid footprints yet discovered.

Birders should definitely divert to the gorge: red-and-yellow barbet, slaty coloured boubou, speckle-fronted weaver and purple grenadier are practically guaranteed to be seen around the museum.

Olduvai Gorge is 3km from the main Ngorongoro-Serengeti road. You may only explore the diggings with a guide, and there is an excellent site museum.

Lake Ndutu

This alkaline lake lies south of the B142 on the Ngorongoro-Serengeti border. When it is full, Maasai use it to water their cattle. In the rainy season it supports large numbers of animals, so Ndutu Lodge (see *Where to stay* above) is a good base for game drives. The acacia woodland around the lake supports different birds to those in surrounding areas. The campsite on the lake shore costs US$40 per person.

SERENGETI NATIONAL PARK

There is little I can say about the Serengeti that hasn't been said already. This is Africa's most famous game reserve, renowned for its dense predator population and annual wildebeest migration, the sort of place that's been hyped so heavily you might reasonably brace yourself for disappointment when you actually get to visit it. But the Serengeti is all it is cracked up to be. The sense of space attached to exploring the vast Serengeti plains is overwhelming, as are the sheer numbers of animals these plains support. The Serengeti is the best game reserve I have visited anywhere in Africa. No competition.

Serengeti National Park covers an area of almost 15,000km², but the Serengeti ecosystem – which includes a number of game reserves bordering the national park as well as Kenya's Maasai Mara Game Reserve – is more than double that size. Most of the national park is open and grassy, broken by isolated granite koppies and patches of acacia woodland. There is little permanent water, so animal migration in the area is strongly linked to rainfall patterns.

The Serengeti was little-known to Europeans until after World War I, when hunters moved in. The national park was created in 1951 and became famous through the work of Professor Bernard Grzimek (pronounced *Jimek*) and his son Michael. At the age of 24, Michael died in an aeroplane crash over the Serengeti. He is buried at Heroes Point on the Ngorongoro Crater rim. Published in the late 1950s, Grzimek's book *Serengeti Shall Not Die* remains worthwhile reading.

Using figures from the 1984/5 census, the Serengeti's most common antelope species are wildebeest (1,300,000), Thomson's gazelle (250,000), impala (70,000) topi (50,000), Grant's gazelle (30,000), kongoni (15,000) and eland (10,000). Other antelope species include Kirk's dik-dik, klipspringer (often seen on koppies) and small numbers of roan, oryx, oribi and waterbuck. After wildebeest, the most populous large mammal is zebra (200,000), and the two are often seen in mixed herds. There are significant numbers of buffalo, giraffe and warthog. Elephant are relatively scarce, and the few remaining black rhinoceros are restricted to the Moru Koppies area. A few primate species are present, of which baboon are the most common and widespread.

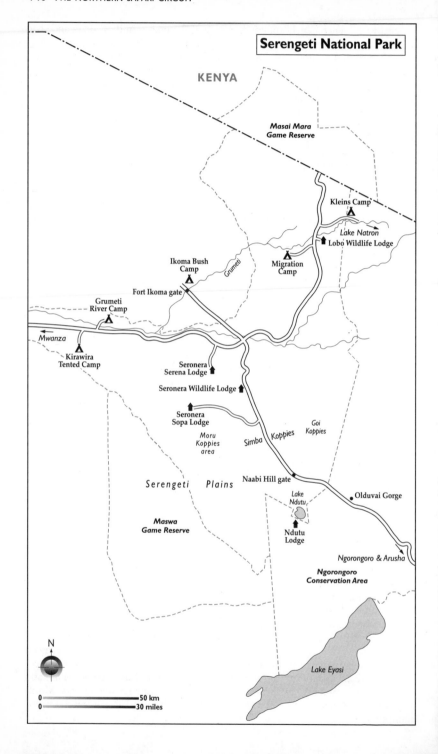

Serengeti National Park

KENYA

Masai Mara
Game Reserve

Kleins Camp

Lake Natron
Lobo Wildlife Lodge

Ikoma Bush
Camp

Grumeti

Migration
Camp

Fort Ikoma gate

Grumeti
River Camp

Mwanza

Kirawira
Tented Camp

Seronera
Serena Lodge

Seronera Wildlife Lodge

Seronera
Sopa Lodge

Moru
Koppies
area

Simba

Koppies

Goi
Koppies

Serengeti   Plains

Naabi Hill gate

Olduvai Gorge

Maswa
Game Reserve

Lake
Ndutu

Ndutu
Lodge

Ngorongoro & Arusha

Ngorongoro
Conservation Area

N

Lake Eyasi

0   50 km
0   30 miles

Ultimately, the success of any safari lies in the number and quality of encounters with big cats. There is something infinitely compelling about these animals, a fascination that seems to affect even the most jaded of safari drivers – many of whom are leopard-obsessive, content to drive up and down the Seronera Valley all day in the search for a tell-tale tail dangling from a tree. And when it comes to big cats, the Serengeti rarely disappoints. Lions are a practical certainty: some 250 to 300 of these animals stalk the plains around Seronera, with the main concentration around Simba Hills north of the Ngorongoro road. It's normal to see two or three prides in the course of one game drive. Sociable, languid and deceptively pussy-cat-like, lions are most often seen lying low in the grass or basking on rocks. The challenge is to see a lion exert itself beyond a half-interested raising of the head when a vehicle stops nearby.

Cheetahs, too, are regularly sighted in the grasslands around Simba Hills, though in direct contrast to their languid cousins, these streamlined, solitary creatures are most normally seen pacing the plains with the air of an agitated greyhound. The Seronera Valley is also home to a healthy population of leopards, which are most often seen lounging in the canopy of the sausage trees and acacias along the Seronera River. Leopards are more easily seen in this area than practically anywhere I've visited in Africa, largely because there are too few trees for them to hide in as successfully as they would in more lush riverine woodland.

Of the other predators which can be seen in the Serengeti, spotted hyenas are very common, perhaps more numerous than lions. Golden jackals and bat-eared foxes appear to be the most abundant canine species on the plains around Seronera, while black-backed jackals are reasonably common in the thicker vegetation towards Lobo. Driving at dusk or dawn, you stand the best chance of seeing nocturnal predators such as civet, serval, genet and African wild cat. The real rarity among canines is the African hunting dog, which may well be extinct in the Serengeti.

Considering its open nature, I was surprised at how rewarding the Serengeti's bird life is. Ostrich are common, as is the kori bustard. A variety of larks, finches and raptors can be seen, but perhaps the most distinctive small bird is the lilac-breasted roller, an exquisitely coloured bird often seen perched on trees alongside the road. In the Seronera area, you can be reasonably certain of seeing three bird species which are thought to be endemic to Tanzania: the beautiful Fischer's lovebird, the grey-rumped spurfowl, and the deceptively babbler-like rufous-tailed weaver.

Maasai, who traditionally occupied the Serengeti plains from the 17th century, are no longer allowed to graze their cattle in the Serengeti. Evidence of their previous occupation of the area can be seen at Moru Koppies, where there are well-preserved Maasai rock paintings.

A 72-page booklet, *Serengeti National Park*, is sold at the National Parks office in Arusha for US$5. Like all the national park booklets, it contains good maps and is an excellent introduction to the local ecosystems.

An entrance fee of US$25 per 24-hour period is charged.

When to visit

Whenever! True, the Serengeti's ungulate populations are seasonal, you need to visit at specific times of year to catch the wildebeest migration, and there is less game in the park during the dry season (July to October). On the other hand, most species (including predators) are resident and territorial, so they do not stray far over the course of any given year. In our experience, the Serengeti in the 'off-season' will still offer game viewing to equal that of any park in Africa, and for some the fact that there will be considerably less tourists around may even be a bonus.

The wildebeest migration

The wildebeest migration follows a fairly predictable pattern, though there are minor variations from year to year. Wildebeest disperse in the southern part of the Serengeti during the rainy season (December to May), calving near the beginning of this period. On game drives around Seronera at this time of year it is not uncommon to see herds of 10,000 animals.

In April or May the animals congregate in preparation for an 800km migration to the western Serengeti and Maasai Mara, which takes place sometime between April and June. During this time, a herd of over a million migrating animals forms a column up to 40km long, one of the most impressive spectacles in the world.

From July to October, the animals spread out into the northern and western Serengeti. The best base is the Lobo area (not really practical for a camping safari). The animals return to the southern plains in November.

Seronera and surrounds

The Seronera area is the most accessible part of the Serengeti for those coming from the direction of Arusha, and it is the site of the main park headquarters as well as a small village, several lodges and camping facilities. The plain, which stretches east from Seronera as far as Ngorongoro, is the 'classic' Serengeti: a vast open expanse studded with rocky koppies and teeming with wild animals, especially between December and May when the wildebeest and zebra are concentrated in the southern Serengeti. Seronera is probably the best base in the park for seeing lion, leopard and cheetah which, combined with its relative proximity to Arusha, means that it also carries the heaviest tourist traffic. It is normally the only part of the park explored by those with limited time.

Where to stay

Seronera Wildlife Lodge PO Box 887, Arusha; tel: 057 2711/2; fax: 057 8221; email: tahifin@habari.yako.co.tz. The most central and popular lodge in the Serengeti, Seronera lies only a couple of kilometres from the synonymous park headquarters. The lodge was built between 1970 and 1974, and it is a fine example of a lodge utilising natural features to create an individual and unmistakably African character. The lodge is built around a granite koppie: the bar, frequented by bats and rock hyraxes, is reached through a narrow corridor between two boulders, while the restaurant is sited in a cavernous space, its natural rock walls decorated with traditional paintings. For some years, the service and facilities at Seronera were significantly inferior to the architecture, and to this day many of the fittings create a slightly tacky 1970s feel. Since being taken over by TAHI, however, there has been a great improvement in service and catering, though it still doesn't match the Sopa or Serena lodges on these scores. Rooms are small but comfortable, with en-suite bathrooms and large windows facing the surrounding bush. The best reason to select this lodge, aside from relative affordability, is simply its brilliant location for game drives, right on the fringe of the wonderful Seronera circuit. Rooms cost US$135/186/303 single/double/triple full-board.

Seronera Serena Lodge PO Box 2551, Arusha; tel: 057 8175/6304; fax: 057 8282; email: serena@yako.habari.co.tz. Situated on a hilltop roughly 20km west of Seronera, this recently opened lodge is probably the most comfortable of the lodges in this part of the Serengeti. Accommodation is in a village-like cluster of Maasai-style double-storey rondavels, built with slate, wood and thatch, creating a pleasing organic feel. The spacious self-contained rooms each have one single and one king-size bed, nets and fans, and hot showers. There is a swimming pool, and the buffet meals are far superior to those in most East African safari lodges. The one negative is that game viewing in the thick scrub around the lodge is poor except for when the migration passes through, and it's a good half-hour drive before you reach the main game-viewing circuit east of Seronera Lodge. Full-board accommodation costs US$170/260 single/double.

Serengeti Sopa Lodge PO Box 1823, Arusha; tel: 057 6896/6886; fax: 057 8245; email: sopa@africaonline.co.tz. This ostentatious lodge lies about 30 minute's drive south of Seronera, on the side of a hill near the Moru Koppies. The rooms here are practically suites: each has two double beds, a small sitting room, a large bathroom complete with bidet, a private balcony and a large window giving a grandstand view over the plains below, perfectly appointed to catch the sunset. The building itself is an idiosyncratic, faintly preposterous construction, with the appearance of an unfinished Greek villa, presumably meant to blend into the rocks. The food is good and facilities include a swimming pool. Game viewing in the surrounding area is generally very good. Prices are similar to the Serena.

Ndutu Lodge PO Box 6084, Arusha; tel: 057 8930; fax: 057 8310. Ndutu is most logically bracketed with the 'Seronera' lodges, since it offers great access to the plains east of Seronera, but technically lies just within the border of the Ngorongoro Conservation Area. It is a low-key and underrated retreat, set in the acacia woodland overlooking Lake Ndutu, and an excellent place to stay if you want to avoid the crowds. Despite lying in

BALLOON SAFARIS

A company called Serengeti Balloon Safaris runs balloon safaris from Seronera at 06.00 daily, departing from the lodge at around 05.30. The package includes transfer to the balloon site, a balloon trip of roughly one hour, and a champagne breakfast set out at a table in the bush. This costs US$300 per person.

A balloon safari is definitely worth the expense if you can afford it. Gliding serenely above the trees as the sun rises allows you to see the expansive plains from a new and quite thrilling angle. It also offers the chance to see secretive species such as bushbuck and reedbuck, and, because you leave so early in the morning, you are likely to spot a few nocturnal predators (we saw hyenas in abundance, civet twice and had a rare glimpse of an African wild cat). That said, any images you have of sweeping above endless herds of wildebeest and zebra may prove a little removed from reality. You'll only see large herds if you're fortunate enough to be in the area during the exact week or two when animals concentrate close to Seronera; for us, the absence of plains animals was a mild disappointment after having spent the day before we got to Seronera driving through thousands upon thousands of wildebeest in the Olduvai area.

The champagne breakfast is set up in the bush, at a different site every day, depending on which way the balloons are blown. It is presented with some flourish: the immaculately uniformed waiters in particular conjure up images of the safaris of old. Our particular mad-hatters' breakfast party was enlivened by the arrival of three male lions, who strolled less than 100m from the table apparently oblivious to the unusual apparition of 24 people eating scrambled eggs and sausages at a starched table cloth in the bush. Presumably, this sort of thing doesn't happen every day, whether you're lion or human.

Balloon safaris can be booked at Seronera on the night before departure, but if you want to be certain of a place it's advisable to book in advance, either through your safari company or directly through Serengeti Balloon Safaris at PO Box 12216, Arusha; tel: 057 8578; fax: 057 8997. The UK office can be contacted at Unit D9, Harleston Industrial Estate, Harleston, Norfolk, IP20 9EB; tel: (01379) 853129; fax: (01379) 853127.

the NCA, Ndutu isn't well positioned for visiting Ngorongoro Crater, but the surrounding plains offer top-notch general game-viewing, particularly during the wet season when they are teeming with wildebeest. Self-contained bungalows costs US$139/204 single/double full-board.

National park campsites
A cluster of seven campsites lies about 5km from Seronera Lodge. Camping costs the usual US$20 per person. Facilities are limited to long-drop toilets and a rubbish pit. You may be able to organise a shower and fill up water containers for a small fee at the lodge. There is a good chance of seeing nocturnal scavengers such as hyena and genet pass through the campsites after dark.

Lobo and surrounds
The wildly beautiful northern Serengeti is characterised by green rolling hills and large granite outcrops covered in lushly foliated trees. The area is particularly worth visiting in September and October, when the wildebeest migration passes through. At other times of the year, game is generally less prolific than in the Seronera area, though Lobo does support the park's main concentrations of elephants, and it is also noted for large prides of lions. For some, the relatively low volume of game will be compensated for by the vast scenery, abundant birds and untrammelled wilderness feel. Out of season, you can drive here for ages without seeing another vehicle.

Where to stay
Lobo Wildlife Lodge PO Box 887, Arusha; tel: 057 2711/2; fax: 057 8221; email: tahifin@habari.yako.co.tz. Another TAHI possession, Lobo Wildlife Lodge was built between 1968 and 1970, at which time the majority of tourism to the Serengeti came directly from Kenya. Lobo has dropped in popularity now that visitors to the Serengeti come through Arusha, which is a shame, because it is an amazing construction. Like Seronera, it's built around a koppie, but the design is even more impressive and imaginative than that of the more southerly lodge, spanning four floors and with a fantastic view over the surrounding plains. Once again, however, the tacky 1970s fittings let the architecture down, and the rooms and food are perfectly acceptable without inviting any superlatives. The surrounding hills can offer some wonderful game viewing (a pride of 20 lions is resident in the immediate vicinity of the lodge), and the grounds are crawling with hyraxes and colourful agama lizards. By game lodge standards, Lobo is pretty good value at US$135/186/303 single/double/triple full-board.

Migration Camp PO Box 1861, Arusha; tel: 0812 400325 or 0811 512065; fax: 057 8669; email: migration.serengeti@cats-net.com. Set in the Ndassiata Hills not far from Lobo, this semi-luxury tented camp opened in June 1995 and changed hands in late 1998. It consists of 13 standing tents built around a koppie overlooking the perennial Grumeti River, in an area supporting large resident populations of lion, leopard, elephant and buffalo. Facilities include a swimming pool, jacuzzi, cocktail bar, library and lounge. An unusual feature of the camp is that short guided game walks can be undertaken along several trails leading out from it. For drive-in visitors, accommodation costs US$155 per person full-board. Fly-in packages inclusive of game drives and walks cost US$275 per person per night full-board.

Kleins Camp Private Bag X27, Benmore, South Africa; tel: +27 11 784-7077; fax: +27 11 784-7667; email: reservations@conscorp.co.za. Recently taken over by the Conservation Corporation Africa, Kleins Camp lies just outside the eastern border of the national park, on a private conservancy leased from the local Maasai. In effect, it functions as an exclusive private game reserve, since camp residents have sole use of this land. Because Kleins Camp lies outside the national park, there are no restrictions prohibiting night drives and guided game walks, both of which add an extra dimension to a safari. The camp has a stunning location on the side of a hill offering panoramic views in all directions, and game viewing in the region is generally good, particularly along the Grumeti River, with a similar range of species as found in the Lobo area. The camp consists of eight self-contained *bandas*, all with hot shower, nets, and a private balcony with a view. Accommodation costs US$325 per person inclusive of all meals, drinks, game drives, game walks and a visit to a Maasai boma. For contact details, see *Safari companies*, page 121–4).

National park campsite
The site outside Lobo Wildlife Lodge is little used by comparison to those at Seronera. It also costs US$20 per person. Facilities are limited to a toilet and rubbish pit. You can pop into the neighbouring lodge for a drink or meal if you like.

The western corridor
The part of the Serengeti which stretches west from Seronera towards Lake Victoria is characterised by dense stands of ghostly grey 'whistling thorn' *acacia drepanolobrium* interspersed with park-like broken woodland. The dominant physical feature of the region is the Grumeti River, its course marked by a thin string of riparian woodland. The crossing of the Grumeti, which usually takes place between May and July, is one of the most dramatic sequences in the annual wildebeest migration, and a positive bonanza for the river's large crocodile population. Tourist traffic in this part of the park is very low: few camping safaris ever come this way, and accommodation is limited to a few small tented camps. The game viewing is superlative between May and July, when the migration passes through, and it is pretty good throughout the year. The broken plains to the south of the Grumeti River between Grumeti River Camp and Kirawira Tented Camp support substantial resident populations of lion, giraffe, wildebeest, zebra and most other typical plains animals, while the riverine forest harbours a few troops of the exquisite black-and-white colobus monkey.

Where to stay
Grumeti River Camp Private Bag X27, Benmore, South Africa; tel: +27 11 784-7077; fax: +27 11 784-7667; email: reservations@conscorp.co.za. Overlooking a small pool near the Grumeti River, this is the archetypal bush camp, for which reason we rate it as our favourite lodge anywhere in the Serengeti. The mood here is pure in-your-face Africa: the pool in front of the bar supports a resident pod of hippos and attracts a steady stream of other large mammals coming to drink, while bird life is prolific both at the water's edge and in the surrounding thickets. At night, the place comes alive with a steady chorus of insects and frogs, and hippos and buffaloes grazing noisily around the tents. This place isn't for the faint-hearted, and you shouldn't even think about walking around at night without an armed escort, as the buffaloes have been known to charge. Facilities include an outdoor *boma*, where evening meals are served (except when it rains), and a small circular swimming pool from where you can watch hippos bathing while you do the same thing. Accommodation consists of ten stylish tents, each of which has a netted king-size bed and en-suite toilet and showers. The atmosphere is very informal, and the service is excellent without ever becoming impersonal. As with other Conservation Corporation properties, accommodation costs US$325 per person, inclusive of all meals, drinks and activities.
Kirawira Tented Camp PO Box 2551, Arusha; tel: 057 8175/6304; fax: 057 8282; email: serena@yako.habari.co.tz. Part of the Serena chain, this is another very upmarket tented camp, set on a small acacia-covered hill offering sweeping views over the western corridor. The Edwardian decor of the communal areas creates something of an 'Out of Africa' feel,

and while the atmosphere is neither as intimate nor as 'bush' as at Grumeti, Kirawira does have a definite charm – and it will probably appeal more to safari-goers who don't find the thought of having hippo and buffalo chomping around their tent a major drawcard. Accommodation consists of 25 standing tents, each of which is set on its own raised platform, and is comfortably decorated with a netted king-size bed and en-suite shower and toilet. There is a large swimming pool, the service is immaculate, and the food is the best we've had in the Serengeti. Accommodation costs US$395/630 single/double inclusive of all meals, drinks and game drives and walks.

Ikoma Bush Camp PO Box 207, Arusha; tel: 057 8424; fax: 057 8272; email: sengo@yako.habari.co.tz. Ikoma Camp lies outside of the national park, roughly 1km from the Ikoma Gate and 40km from Seronera, and it too offers accommodation in simple but comfortable standing tents, at a cost of US$75/130 single/double. Because it lies outside the park boundaries, guided game walks are available.

Kijireshi Tented Camp This little-known camp lies close to Bunda on the western border of the Serengeti. It offers accommodation in furnished tents for US$75 s/c double, and has a bar and restaurant.

TARANGIRE NATIONAL PARK

This national park may be less well-known than others in northern Tanzania, but it is no less rewarding. Like the Serengeti, Tarangire is part of a wider ecosystem within which there is a great deal of migratory movement. During the wet season, most of its animals disperse to the Maasai Steppe, while the wildebeest and zebra move northwest to the Rift Valley floor between Lakes Natron and Manyara.

In direct contrast to the Serengeti, Tarangire comes into its own during the dry season between July and November, when the large herds of game attracted to the permanent waters of the Tarangire River make this reserve every bit as alluring as the Serengeti. In general, Tarangire is more densely vegetated than the Serengeti, covered primarily in acacia and mixed woodland. Near the Tarangire river, however, there is a cover of dense elephant grass broken by the occasional palm tree, and baobab trees are abundant throughout.

Tarangire supports similar large mammals to the Serengeti, but the denser vegetation makes predators such as lion and leopard more difficult to see. It is famous for its elephant, and in the dry season it is no exaggeration to say that you might see 500 elephant in the course of one day. Two localised antelope found in Tarangire are the fringe-eared oryx and gerenuk. According to the 1980 census, the greater Tarangire ecosystem supports 25,000 wildebeest, 30,000 zebra, 6,000 buffalo, 3,000 elephant, 2,700 giraffe, 5,500 eland, 30,000 impala and 2,000 warthog. Tarangire's reputation as the best of the northern reserves for birds is, in my experience, a little overstated. Lake Manyara has a far greater habitat diversity, and there is a considerably greater variety of birds to be seen, at least when compared to the parts of Tarangire which are normally visited by tour vehicles. That said, you should see a good variety of raptors and acacia-associated birds, as well as three bird species endemic to Tanzania: the ashy starling, rufous-tailed weaver and black-collared lovebird.

Most people spend a day in Tarangire and concentrate on the northern circuit. If you have longer, Lake Burungi circuit offers your best chance of seeing black rhinoceros, bushbuck and lesser kudu, the Kitibong Hill area is home to large herds of buffalo, Lamarkau Swamp supports hippo and numerous water birds during the wet season, the southern plains are favoured by cheetah, and Mkungero Pools is the place to look for waterbuck and gerenuk.

A 56-page booklet, *Tarangire National Park*, is available from the National Parks Headquarters in Arusha. A park entrance fee of US$25 per 24-hour period is charged.

Getting there and away

Tarangire lies about 7km off the main Arusha-Dodoma road. Coming from Arusha, this road is tarred as far as the Tarangire turn-off. Most people tag a visit on to the end of a longer safari, but if your time or money is limited, a one- or two-day safari to Tarangire is a viable option.

Where to stay

Tarangire Safari Lodge PO Box 2703, Arusha; tel: 057 4222; fax: 057 7182; email: sss@yako.habari.co.tz. This is the oldest lodge in the park, and it has a prime location on a bluff overlooking the Tarangire River. Game viewing from the verandah can be excellent, with large herds of hippo, giraffe and other animals coming down to the river to drink, and the grounds are a hive of avian activity. There is a swimming pool. Accommodation in standing tents with en-suite toilets is really good value at US$52/65 single/double b&b, and the bungalows are equally well-priced at US$60/75. Lunch costs US$12, dinner US$15, and a limited selection of snacks is available at around US$4 each.

Tarangire Sopa Lodge PO Box 1823, Arusha; tel: 057 6896/6886; fax: 057 8245; email: sopa@africaonline.co.tz. The Sopa lodge matches the customary high standards of this chain, with luxurious rooms and excellent food. My one, rather large, reservation is the indifferent location, alongside a small and normally dry watercourse below a baobab-studded slope – surely a more scenic site could have been chosen? Rooms cost US$165/250 single/double full-board.

Olivers Camp PO Box 425, Arusha; tel/fax: 057 8548. Another fairly new place, Olivers comprises six furnished tents set amongst the Kikoti koppies. The emphasis here is not so much on overnight stays incorporated into a more wide-ranging safari, but on packages of five to seven nights' duration, which allow you to explore the area fully on foot and by vehicle, including a few nights at a mobile wilderness camp and a night drive to seek out nocturnal predators. Accommodation costs US$220/320 single/double full-board.

Naitolia Camp PO Box 12799, Arusha; tel: 057 7111/2814; fax: 057 8997/4199; email: letsgotravel@cybernet.co.tz. This excellent new bush camp is set in 11,000 acres of Maasailand on the northern border of the park. The main camp consists of three attractively furnished canvas, stone and thatch huts, each of which has a king-size bed with walk-in netting and a private balcony, shower and a toilet with a view. Because the camp lies on communal land, guided game walks can be undertaken, with a good chance of spotting giraffe, elephant, zebra and a variety of antelope and birds, and it is possible to be taken to Maasai *bomas* that don't normally receive tourists. Accommodation costs US$225/350 single/double full-board, inclusive of all activities. They also do overnight walking safaris within the community area, using fly-camps, at a cost of US$365/570 single/double per night. There is a separate campsite close to the main camp where campers can pitch their own tents. The lodge management pays a fee of US$20 per client per night to local Masaai communities.

Tamarind Camp PO Box 2047, Arusha; tel: 057 7011/7541; fax: 057 8226; email: hoopoe@aol.com. UK bookings tel: +44 181 428-8221; fax: +44 181 421-1396; email: hoopoeUK@aol.com. Tamarind is a similar set-up to Naitola, situated closer to the national park entrance gate, and owned by Hoopoe Adventure Tours. Accommodation costs a very reasonable US$65/90 single/double half-board, or US$80/120 full-board.

National Park campsites

For those on camping safaris, there are couple of campsites within Tarangire. These are strong on bush atmosphere, but short on facilities, and rather costly at the customary US$20 per person.

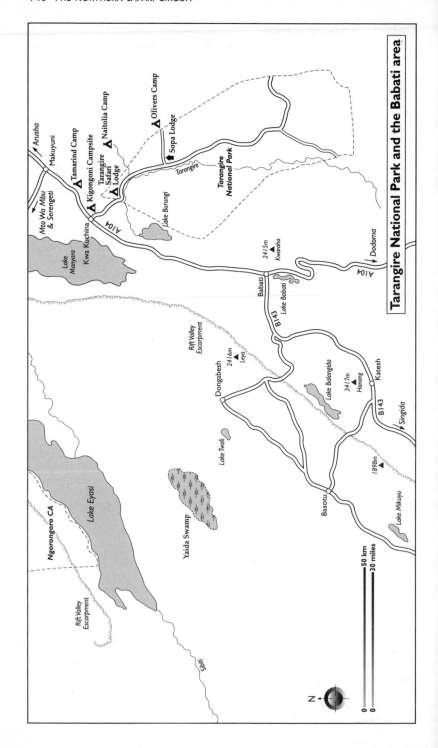

Tarangire National Park and the Babati area

Kigongoni Campsite

This small private camp, which lies a few kilometres outside the park entrance gate, is firmly aimed at budget travellers and used by most budget camping safaris to Tarangire. Camping costs US$3 per person, and rooms are available at US$10 per person. To get to Kigongoni, turn off from the main Arusha-Dodoma road as if heading towards the entrance gate to Tarangire. After about 2km, you'll see the campsite immediately to your left. There is also a small local guesthouse in the village on the junction of the Arusha-Dodoma road and the turn-off to Tarangire. There is no reason why you couldn't catch a Dodoma-bound bus to the turn-off and walk to the camp from there; hitching into the park might not be easy, but at least you don't stand to lose anything in terms of paying park fees while you wait.

Moshi and Kilimanjaro

Kilimanjaro is Africa's highest mountain, and one of the most instantly recognisable landmarks on the continent. It is also the highest mountain anywhere that can be climbed by an ordinary tourist, and thousands of visitors to Tanzania attempt to reach its peak every year. Kilimanjaro straddles the border with Kenya, but because the peaks all lie within Tanzanian territory they can be climbed only from within Tanzania. There are several places on the lower slopes from where the mountain can be ascended, but most people use the Marangu or 'tourist' route which begins at the village of Marangu, largely because this is the cheapest route up the mountain. The less heavily trampled Machame route, starting from the village of the same name, has grown in popularity in recent years, while several other more obscure routes are offered by companies specialising in the mountain. Prospective climbers can arrange their ascent of 'Kili' – as it is popularly called – at one of the hotels in Marangu, or in Arusha town, but the main cluster of trekking companies is to be found in the town of Moshi on the plains to the south of the mountain.

HISTORY

Kilimanjaro's fertile soils have attracted people from all over East Africa for centuries. Ancient stone tools of indeterminate age have been found on the lower slopes, as have the remains of pottery artefacts thought to be at least 2,000 years old. Between 1,000 and 1,500 years ago, Kilimanjaro was the centre of an Iron Age culture spreading out to the coastal belt between Pangani and Mombasa.

Kilimanjaro is now home to the Chagga, a Bantu-speaking group whose ancestors first arrived in the area 500 years ago. The Chagga have no tradition of central leadership. As many as 100 small chieftaincies existed in the mid-19th century. They are efficient agriculturalists, and the lower slopes of Kilimanjaro are covered in their disused dams and irrigation furrows. Because they have always produced a food surplus, the Chagga have a long history of trade with the Maasai and other local groups, and later with Arab caravans.

The first written reference to Kilimanjaro is found in Ptolemy's 4th-century *Geography*. It is also alluded to in an account written by a 12th-century Chinese trader, and by the 16th-century Spanish geographer, Fernandes de Encisco. These allusions fired the curiosity of 19th-century geographers, who outdid each other in publishing wild speculations about the African interior.

In 1848, Johan Rebmann, a German missionary working in the Taita Hills, was told about a very large mountain reputed to be covered in silver and to host evil spirits which would freeze anyone who tried to climb it. It was called Kilimanjaro. When Rebmann visited it, he immediately recognised the silver to be snow. His observations, published in 1849, were derided by European experts who thought it ludicrous to claim there was snow so near the Equator. Only in 1861, when an experienced geologist, Von der Decken, saw and surveyed Kilimanjaro, was its existence and that of its snow-capped peaks accepted. Chagga legend suggests that no local person ever successfully climbed Kilimanjaro before Hans Meyer and Ludwig Purstscheller reached its summit in 1889.

Climate

The higher slopes of Kilimanjaro are cold at all times. Moshi is relatively low-lying and has a climate typical of this part of the African interior, hot by day and cool by night, though it is often more humid than you might expect. Kilimanjaro can be climbed at any time of year, but the hike is more difficult in the rainy months, especially between March and May.

Getting around

Moshi is an important public transport hub, connected by surfaced roads and regular express buses to Dar es Salaam, Tanga and Arusha. If you want to arrange your hike in Marangu, plenty of public transport runs there from Moshi. Most travellers prefer to make all arrangements for the climb in Moshi, and this includes transport to and from the trailhead.

MOSHI

Situated at the heart of a major coffee-growing region, Moshi is an attractive, if intrinsically unremarkable, small town of 140,000 people, salvaged from anonymity by one of the most imposing backdrops imaginable. Moshi lies at the base of Kilimanjaro; at dusk or dawn, when the peaks most often emerge from their customary blanket of cloud, they form a sight as stirring and memorable as any in Africa. Despite the teasing proximity of snow-capped Kilimanjaro, Moshi is not the cool highland settlement you might expect. Instead, lying at an altitude of 810m, Moshi has a surprisingly humid, sticky climate, reminiscent of the coast.

Prior to the arrival of the Germans, Moshi was the capital of the area ruled by Rindi, who came into power in about 1860 and, largely through his diplomatic skills, became one of the most important chiefs in the area. By allying with the Maasai, Rindi extracted large taxes from passing caravans. He made a favourable impression on John Kirk, the British Consul in Zanzibar, and signed a treaty with Carl Peters in 1885. When the first German colonial forces arrived at Kilimanjaro in 1891, Rindi assured them he ruled the whole area. At his insistence, they quelled his major rival, Sina of Kibosha.

Moshi means smoke in Swahili, but the origin of this name is something of a mystery. Some sources suggest that the town was called Moshi because it was the terminus for the steam railway line from Tanga, but my understanding is that the name Moshi predates the arrival of the railway in 1911 by many years. Equally improbable is the suggestion that the reference to smoke is due to the town lying at the base of a volcano – after all, Kilimanjaro hadn't been active for thousands of years when its present Bantu-speaking inhabitants arrived there.

Getting there and away

Moshi can be reached by air, rail or road. The national carrier Air Tanzania flies regularly between Dar es Salaam or Zanzibar and Kilimanjaro Airport (off the main Arusha road), as do several private air companies. If you are flying out of Moshi, the shuttle-bus to the airport leaves from the Air Tanzania office next to the Moshi Hotel; check in advance when it will be leaving.

The bus station in Moshi is one of the most chaotic and aggressive in Tanzania. There are a lot of persistent hustlers here who will try to get you on any bus in order to pick up a commission, so do use your judgement regarding whatever 'express bus' is pointed out to you; overcharging is commonplace. The problem we've found in Moshi is that the self-preservation instinct tends to prevail when you've half a dozen hustlers yelling at you, punching each other, trying to grab your bags, and generally making it advisable to get on *any* bus before things turn ugly. One traveller who spent several weeks in Moshi and travelled to Dar regularly wrote of similar experiences, and said that she was pushed into 'a couple of nightmarish journeys, sitting on a stationary bus for two hours after it was scheduled to leave, then stopping for half an hour at practically every settlement it passed'. This sort of thing isn't such a problem for short trips, for instance to Arusha or Marangu. For long trips out of Moshi, my advice is to go to the bus station and book a seat with a reputable company in advance, so that you don't have to worry about hustlers and your luggage at the same time.

Express buses between Dar es Salaam and Moshi take roughly seven hours, with a 20-minute lunch break in Korogwe. Several express buses leave in either direction every morning; two of the best operators are Air Msae or Dar Express. A ticket should cost around US$10, but you might well be overcharged. A number of other bus companies cover this route, but some take twelve hours or longer to get to Dar. There are also regular buses between Moshi and Tanga.

There is a steady flow of traffic between Arusha and Moshi. The trip takes under two hours by bus. Buses to Arusha, Marangu and other local destinations leave when they fill up, but buses further afield have fixed departure times and should be booked in advance.

Two shuttle buses daily connect Moshi to Nairobi (Kenya) via Arusha. These leave in either direction at 07.30 and 13.30. They are operated by a company called Devanu, whose office is opposite the Moshi Hotel, and they leave Moshi from the Clock Tower circle.

There used to be one train every week between Moshi and Dar es Salaam, but this service has been suspended for a couple of years now.

Where to stay
Upper and mid-range
Keys Hotel PO Box 993, Moshi; tel: 055 52250; fax: 055 50073; email: keys@form-net.com or keys@intafrica.com. Situated in attractive green grounds about 1km from the Clock Tower, the Keys Hotel has offered good value for several years, and it remains the obvious first choice in this range. The self-contained rooms cost US$50 double, with a discount of roughly 50% for Tanzanian residents. Keys is also one of the more reliable places to organise climbs of Kilimanjaro, and while rates are a little higher than at some other places, they do include one night's half-board accommodation at the hotel on either side of the climb. Camping in the grounds costs US$5 per person.

Uhuru Lutheran Hostel PO Box 1320, Moshi; tel: 055 54084; fax: 055 53518. The Lutheran Hostel also offers good mid-range accommodation. There are 60 rooms in the hostel, ranging in price from US$25-35 for a single and US$35-45 for a double (about 30% cheaper for residents). All rooms are self-contained, and have running hot water and private balconies. The food is good. Smoking and drinking are strictly prohibited. The hostel is about 3km out of town on Sekou Toure Road. To get there, walk out of town towards the YMCA and continue straight across the roundabout with the main Arusha road. From the roundabout, it's a direct 1.5km walk, but if you get lost, you can ask for directions to the Police School, which is adjacent to the hostel.

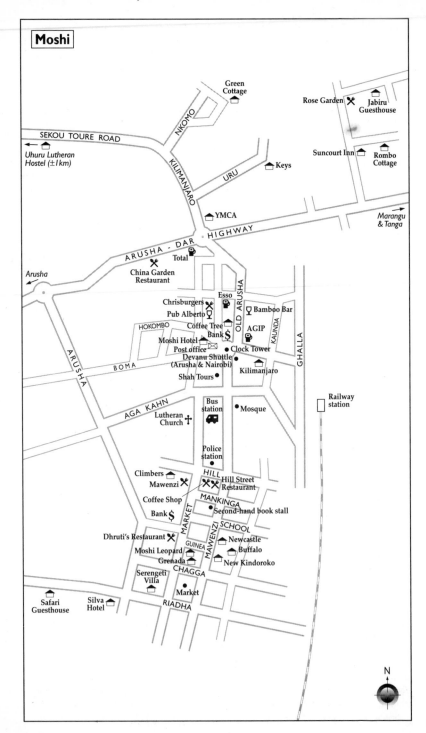

Moshi

Moshi Leopard Hotel PO Box 232, Moshi; tel: 055 50844; fax: 055 51261; email: leopardhotel@eoltz.com. The long-standing shortage of relatively upmarket accommodation in Moshi town centre was remedied in 1997 with the opening of this new hotel on Market Street. It has smart self-contained rooms with balconies for US$30/40 single/double inclusive of continental breakfast.

Moshi Hotel PO Box 1819, tel: 055 55212. This government hotel is also very central, but it really is starting to look very run-down. Still, it seems reasonable value for money at US$10/20 for a single/double using communal showers or US$35 for a self-contained double.

Budget

The main cluster of good budget accommodation lies on and around Mawenzi Road, a couple of blocks south of the bus station. One place here that has maintained high standards and reasonable prices over several years is the **New Kindoroko Hotel** (tel: 54054; fax: 54062) a three-storey building which offers a good selection of different rooms, all with fan and mosquito net. Rooms using communal hot showers cost US$7.50/9.00 single/double, while self-contained rooms with hot showers cost US$9/18 single/double. There is a pleasant courtyard bar, and the restaurant serves good meals for around US$3 and snacks for US$1.50.

A few doors up, the **Hotel Newcastle** (tel: 53203; fax: 51382) is very similar in feel and standard to the New Kindoroka. It's a bit more run-down, perhaps, but seems considerably better value these days at US$8/10 s/c single/double with hot shower, fan and nets. The ground floor restaurant and bar are also good.

On the block behind these two places, the new **Buffalo Hotel** is also very good value, and we met a couple of regular visitors to Moshi who rate it the best place in town. Clean rooms with a fan cost US$7.50/9.00 single/double, using communal hot showers. There is a bar and a good restaurant attached. Closer to the market, the **Grenada Hotel** has reasonable rooms using communal showers at a similar price. The nearby **Silva Hotel** is similar in standard, but more expensive and has cold showers only. Back towards the bus station, off Market Street, the **Climbers Hotel** seems reasonable value at US$7.50 for a s/c double.

There are plenty of cheaper, more basic guesthouses near the market, of which the **Serengeti Villa** is the stand-out. Doubles cost US$4 and self-contained doubles cost US$6. The restaurant here is cheap and there's a friendly bar. Even cheaper are the **Safari Guesthouse** and **New Stand Bar** – both under US$4/room – but they're also rather grotty.

On the other side, the **YMCA** (PO Box 85, tel: (055) 52362) is a perennial favourite with travellers and very secure, and the large swimming pool has had water in it for a few years now. It seems to me a touch overpriced at US$13/15 b&b for a small single/double using communal showers, but plenty of travellers stay there.

The **Coffee Tree Hotel** couldn't be more central. The rooms are very spacious, if a bit run-down, and they have mosquito nets. All in all, it's not bad value at US$4.50 for a double using communal showers and US$6/9 for a self-contained single/double (cold water only). The nearby **Kilimanjaro Hotel** gets dirtier and shabbier with each passing year, but the rooms are certainly affordable at US$3/6 single/double.

There's a cluster of cheap hotels about 1km out of town off the Tanga Road. The **Rombo Cottage Inn** used to be very popular with backpackers, and it remains a friendly, comfortable place, though the recent mushrooming of more central budget hotels means that it doesn't quite attract the traveller custom it once used to. Clean self-contained double rooms cost US$8, and a good restaurant is attached. The **Suncourt Inn** next door has rooms of a similar quality, and is really good value at US$5 for a self-contained double with hot water. Around the corner, the **Jabiru Guest House** is more basic but clean enough and very cheap at US$2/single.

The best place to camp is in the grounds of the **Golden Shower Restaurant**, about 1km from the town centre along the Marangu Road. Camping costs US$3 per person.

Where to eat

Many of the hotels mentioned above have restaurants. The **New Kindoroko**, **Newcastle** and **Buffalo Hotels** are all very good, and reasonably priced at around US$3 for a main dish, as is the **Rombo Cottage Inn**. There are rooftop bars at the Newcastle and New Kindoroka.

For a snack, try **Chrisburgers**, which serves cheap eggburgers and samosas, as well as excellent fruit juice. The attached **Bar Alfredo** is a good place for an evening drink. The **Coffee Shop** on Hill Street is a the best place for breakfast, certainly if you enjoy real coffee, and it also serves a selection of cakes, pies and snacks. The nearby **Hill Street Restaurant** reportedly serves the best chapatis in Tanzania!

One of the best restaurants in Moshi is the Golden Shower, which lies about 1km out of town along the Marangu road. The menu here takes in everything from steaks and fried fish to curry, with most main dishes costing around US$5-6. Walking out here at night would be dodgy, so arrange for a taxi to collect you. The restaurants at the Keys and Leopard Hotels are very good and slightly cheaper. The three-course set meals served at the Moshi Hotel have also been recommended.

The only Chinese restaurant in Moshi is the **China Garden** in the CCM Building on the Arusha–Dar Highway, a few hundred metres from the YMCA. A main course with rice or noodles will set you back around US$5.

For inexpensive Indian food, try **Dhruti's Restaurant** on Market Street opposite the Leopard Hotel, or the **Sikh Club** on Ghalla Street near the Railway Station.

Aleem's Supermarket, on Boma Road to the rear of the post office, has a good range of imported goods and foods. Opposite Aleem's, the **Hot Bread Shop** sells freshly baked bread as well as a selection of cakes and pies.

Useful information

If you are spending some time in Moshi, it's worth getting hold of the *Moshi Guide*, compiled and sold by the people who run the Coffee Shop on Hill Street.

Books There is a good second-hand book stall on Mawenzi Street between the bus station and the Newcastle Hotel.

Foreign exchange There are several forex bureaux in Moshi, including the Clement Bureau de Change near the Clock Tower. There is also a branch of the National Bank opposite the Clock Tower. Although exchange rates in Moshi are fairly good, you will generally get better in Arusha or Dar es Salaam.

Internet and email These services are available at EOLTZ on the Old Moshi Road near the Clock Tower, and at KIT Technology House on Ghalla Street.

Swimming pool The swimming pool at the YMCA is free to hostel residents, but open to visitors for a daily entrance fee of US$5 per person. The Keys Hotel charges a similar price to non-residents who want to swim there, but the pool is smaller and it is further out of town.

Telephone Phonecards can be bought and used at the Tanzania Telecommunications Centre next to the post office on the Clock Tower. This is also the best place to make international phone calls, and to send and receive faxes.

MARANGU

The village of Marangu, which lies about 5km south of the main gate to Kilimanjaro National Park, has something of an alpine feel, surrounded by lush vegetation and bisected by a babbling mountain stream. Once the most popular base for organising Kilimanjaro climbs, Marangu remains a good place to set up climbs with top-quality operators (charging top-of-the-range prices), but these days Moshi is a better and more popular centre from which to arrange a budget climb. Most people who organise climbs in Moshi will do little more than pass through Marangu, as they will be provided with transport as far as the park entrance gate. For those who cannot afford to climb the mountain, Marangu would be a pleasant place to spend a few days taking day walks on the footslopes of Kilmanjaro, were it not for a lack of budget accommodation in the area.

Getting there

Buses between Moshi and Marangu leave in either direction when they are full. Normally, this will be every hour or so, and the trip shouldn't take more than 45 minutes.

Where to stay and eat
Upper range

Kibo Hotel PO Box 102, Moshi; tel/fax: 055 51308. This is a well-established upmarket hotel lying about 1km from the village centre towards the park entrance gate. It has pretty flowering gardens, a relaxed atmosphere, and a good restaurant. The Kilimanjaro climbs organised here are not cheap, but have an impeccable reputation. Self-contained rooms cost US$60/80 single/double.

Marangu Hotel PO Box 40, Moshi; tel: 055 51307; fax: 055 50639; email: marangu@africaonline.co.ke. A comfortable, family-run hotel situated about 5km from Marangu back towards Moshi. Like the Kibo Hotel, the Marangu has an excellent reputation when it comes to organising Kilimanjaro climbs. Self-contained rooms cost US$50 per person b&b.

Capricorn Hotel PO Box 938, Marangu; tel/fax: 055 51309; email: capricorn-ian@form-net.com. This is a newer hotel, situated further up the mountain, roughly 3km before the Kilimanjaro park entrance gate. Accommodation is all self-contained and costs US$55 per person.

Mid-range and budget

The **Babylon Hotel**, 500m and signposted from Marangu Post Office, is the closest thing to a budget hotel in Marangu. On the basis of appearance and facilities, you'd probably describe it as an above-average budget hotel, comparable to somewhere like the Hotel Newcastle in Moshi. The rates, however, place it firmly in the mid-range category, at around US$25/45/60 for a self-contained single/double/triple with hot water. Good, reasonably priced meals are available.

Further up the mountain, the **Kilimanjaro Mountain Lodge** lies just inside the park entrance gate, and charges US$20 per person for a room using communal showers.

Several of the hotels in Marangu allow camping. The Kibo Hotel has the best facilities and charges US$6 per person, while the Babylon Hotel is marginally cheaper at US$5 per person.

MOUNT KILIMANJARO NATIONAL PARK

Reaching an altitude of 5,895m (19,340ft), Kilimanjaro is the highest mountain in Africa, and on the rare occasions when it is not veiled in clouds, the mountain's distinctive silhouette and snow-capped peaks are one of the most breathtaking sights on the continent. There are, of course, higher peaks on other continents, but Kilimanjaro is effectively the world's largest mountain, a free-standing entity rising an incredible 5km above the surrounding plains. It is also the highest mountain anywhere that can be ascended by somebody without specialised mountaineering experience or equipment.

In geological terms, Kilimanjaro is a relatively young mountain. Like most other large mountains near the Rift Valley, it was formed by volcanic activity, first erupting about one million years ago. The 3,962m high Shira peak collapsed around half a million years ago, but the 5,895m high Uhuru Peak on Mount Kibo and 5,149m high Mawenzi peak continued to grow until more recently. Shira plateau formed 360,000 years ago, when the caldera was filled by lava from Kibo after a particularly violent eruption. Kibo is now dormant, and no-one knows when it last displayed any serious volcanic activity. Chagga myths suggesting that there might have been an eruption in the last 500 years do not tally with any geological evidence, so it's possible that they were handed down by previous occupants of the area.

No-one knows for sure where the name Kilimanjaro comes from, or even whether it is Swahili, Maasai or Chagga in origin. *Kilima* is Swahili for little mountain (a joke?); *njaro* is similar to the Chagga word for caravan (the mountain was an important landmark on the northern caravan route), the Maasai word for water (it is the source of most of the region's rivers) and the name of a Swahili demon of cold.

Kilimanjaro National Park, proclaimed in 1977, protects an area of 756km² lying above the 2,700m contour and has been a national park since 1977.

Vegetation and biology

There are five vegetation zones on Kilimanjaro: the cultivated lower slopes, the forest, heath and moorland, alpine, and the barren summit zone. Vegetation is sparse higher up due to lower temperatures and rainfall.

The **lower slopes** of the mountain were probably once forested, but are now mainly covered in cultivation. The volcanic soils make them highly fertile and they support a dense human population. The most biologically interesting aspect of the lower slopes is the abundance of wild flowers, seen between Marangu and the park entrance gate.

The **rainforest zone** of the southern slopes lies between the altitudes of 1,800m and 3,000m. Receiving up to 2,000mm of rainfall annually, this zone displays a high biological diversity, and still supports a fair amount of wildlife. The most frequently seen mammals are the black-and-white colobus and blue monkey, while typical forest antelope include three duiker species and the beautifully marked bushbuck. Leopard, bushpig and porcupine are fairly common but seldom encountered by hikers, while eland, buffalo and elephant are present in small numbers. The forest is home to many varieties of butterfly, and rich in bird life. Most forest birds are difficult to spot, though you should at least hear the raucous silvery-cheeked hornbill and beautiful Hartlaub's touraco.

The semi-alpine **moorland zone**, which lies between 3,000m and 4,000m, is characterised by heath-like vegetation and abundant wild flowers. As you climb into the moorland, two distinctive plants become common. These are *Lobelia deckenii*, which grows to 3m high, and the groundsel *Senecio kilimanjarin*, which grows up to 5m high and can be distinguished by a spike of yellow flowers. This zone supports low animal densities, but a number of large mammals have been recorded. Klipspringer are quite common on rocky outcrops. Hill chat and scarlet-tufted malachite sunbird are two birds whose range is restricted to the moorlands of large East African mountains. Other localised birds are lammergeyer and Alpine swift. Because it is so open, the views from the moorland are stunning.

The **alpine zone** between 4,000 and 5,000m is classified as a semi-desert because it receives an annual rainfall of less than 250mm. The ground often freezes at night, but ground temperatures may soar to above 30°C by day. Few plants survive in these conditions; only 55 species are present, many of them lichens and grasses. Large mammals have been recorded, most commonly eland, but none are resident.

Approaching the summit, the **arctic zone** stats at an altitude of around 5,000m. This area receives virtually no rainfall, and supports little permanent life other than the odd lichen. Two remarkable records concern a frozen leopard discovered here in 1926, and a family of hunting dogs seen in 1962. The most notable natural features at the summit are the inner and outer craters of Kibo, a 120m-deep ash pit, and the Great Northern Glacier, which has retreated markedly since it was first seen by Hans Meyer in 1889.

Climbing Kilimanjaro

As Africa's highest peak and most identifiable landmark, Kilimanjaro offers an irresistible challenge to many tourists. Dozens of visitors to Tanzania set off for Uhuru Peak every day, ranging in age from teenagers to people in their sixties, and those who make it generally regard the achievement to be the highlight of their time in the country. A major part of Kilimanjaro's attraction is that any reasonably fit person stands a fair chance of reaching the top. The ascent requires no special climbing skills or experience; on the contrary, it basically amounts to a long uphill slog over four days, followed by a more rapid descent.

The relative ease of climbing Kilimanjaro should not lull travellers into thinking of the ascent as some sort of prolonged Sunday stroll. It is a seriously tough hike, with potentially fatal penalties for those who are inadequately prepared or who belittle the health risks attached to being at an altitude of above 4,000m. It should also be recognised that there is no such thing as a cheap Kilimanjaro climb. Most reliable operators now charge well in excess of US$500 per person for a five-day climb along the Marangu route; those who cannot afford this sort of sum would be wiser forgetting about the climb than trying to work through a dodgy operator.

Marangu Route

Also known as the 'tourist route', this is the most popular way to the top of Kilimanjaro, largely because it has the best facilities and is cheaper than any other route. It is also probably the safest route, due to the volume of other climbers and good rescue facilities (at least relative to more obscure routes). The main drawback of the Marangu route is that it is heavily trampled by comparison to other routes, and many people have complained that it can feel overcrowded.

Day one: Marangu to Mandara Hut (12km, 5 hours) On an organised climb you will be dropped at the park entrance gate a few kilometres past Marangu. There is a

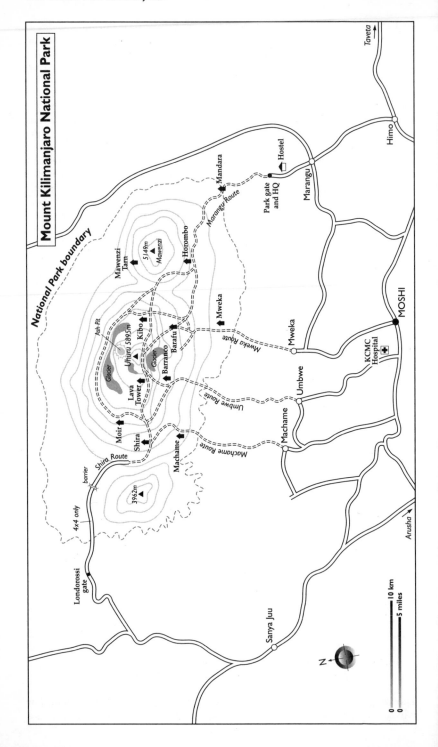

high chance of rain in the afternoon, so it is wise to set off on this four-hour hike as early in the day as you can. Foot traffic is heavy along this stretch, which means that although you pass through thick forest, the shy animals that inhabit the forest are not likely to be seen. If your guide will go that way, use the parallel trail which meets the main trail halfway between the gate and the hut. Mandara Hut (2,700m) is an attractive collection of buildings with room for 200 people.

Day two: Mandara Hut to Horombo Hut (15km, 5 hours) You continue through forest for a short time before reaching the heather and moorland zone, from where there are good views of the peaks and Moshi. The walk takes up to six hours. Horombo Hut (3,720m) sleeps up to 120 people. It is in a valley and surrounded by giant lobelia and groundsel. If you do a six-day hike, you will spend a day at Horombo to acclimatise.

Day three: Horombo Hut to Kibo Hut (15km, 6-7 hours) The vegetation thins out as you enter the desert-like alpine zone, and when you cross the saddle Kibo Peak comes into view. This six- to seven-hour walk should be done slowly: many people start to feel the effects of altitude. Kibo Hut (4,703m) is a stone construction which sleeps up to 120 people. Water must be carried there from a stream above Horombo. You may find it difficult to sleep at this altitude, and as you will have to rise at around 01.00 the next morning, many people feel it is better not to bother trying.

Days four and five: Kibo Hut to the summit to Marangu The best time to climb is during the night, as it is marginally easier to climb the scree slope to Gillman's Point on the crater rim when it is frozen. This 5km ascent typically takes about six hours, so you need to get going between midnight and 01.00 to stand a chance of reaching the summit in time to catch the sunrise. From Gillman's Point it is a further two-hour round trip along the crater's edge to Uhuru Peak, the highest point in Africa. From the summit, it's a roughly seven-hour descent with a break at Kibo Hut to Horombo Hut, where you will spend your last night on the mountain. The final day's descent from Horombo to Marangu generally takes 7–8 hours, so you should arrive in Marangu in the mid-afternoon.

Other routes
Machame route
In recent years, the Machame route has grown greatly in popularity. It is widely regarded to be the most scenic route to the peak, and is relatively gradual, requiring at least six days for the full ascent and descent. The route is named after the village of Machame, from where it is a two-hour walk to the park gate (1,950m). Most companies will provide transport as far as the gate (at least when the road is passable), from where it's a five-to-seven-hour trek through thick forest to Machame Hut (2,890m). There is water near this hut, which sleeps up to 12 people.

The second day of this trail consists of a 9km, six-hour hike through the moorland zone to Shira Hut (3,840m) which is near a stream and can sleep up to eight people. From Shira, a number of options exist: you could spend your third night at Lava Tower Hut (4,630m), four hours from Shira, but the ascent to the summit from there is tricky and only advisable if you are experienced and have good equipment. A less arduous option is to spend your third night at Barranco Hut (3,950m), a tough 12km hike from Shira, then to go on to Barafu Hut (4,600m) on the fourth day, a walk of approximately seven hours. From Barafu, it is normal to begin the steep seven-to-eight-hour ascent to Uhuru Peak at

MOUNTAIN HEALTH

Do not attempt to climb Kilimanjaro unless you are reasonably fit, nor if you have heart or lung problems (although asthma sufferers should be all right). Bear in mind, however, that very fit people are more prone to altitude sickness because they ascend too fast.

Above 3,000m you may not feel hungry, but you should try to eat. Carbohydrates and fruit are recommended, whereas rich or fatty foods are harder to digest. You should drink plenty of liquids, at least three litres of water daily, and will need enough water bottles to carry this. If you dress in layers, you can take off clothes before you sweat too much, thereby reducing water loss.

Few people climb Kilimanjaro without feeling some of the symptoms of altitude sickness: headaches, nausea, fatigue, breathlessness, sleeplessness and swelling of the hands and feet. You can reduce these by allowing yourself time to acclimatise by taking an extra day over the ascent, eating and drinking properly, and trying not to push yourself. If you walk slowly and steadily, you will tire less quickly than if you try to rush each day's walk. Acetazolamide (Diamox) helps speed acclimatisation and many people find it useful; take 250mg for five days, starting two or three days before ascent.

Should symptoms become severe, and especially if they are clearly getting worse, then descend immediately. Even going down a few hundred metres is enough to start recovery. Sleeping high with significant symptoms is dangerous; if in doubt descend to sleep low.

Pulmonary and cerebral oedema are altitude-related problems which can be rapidly fatal if you do not descend. Symptoms of the former include shortness of breath when at rest, coughing up frothy spit or even blood, and undue breathlessness compared to accompanying friends. Symptoms of high altitude cerebral oedema are headaches, poor co-ordination, staggering like a drunk, disorientation, poor judgement and even hallucinations. The danger is that the sufferer usually doesn't realise how sick he/she is and may argue against descending. The only treatment for altitude sickness is descent.

Hypothermia is a lowering of body temperature usually caused by a combination of cold and wet. Mild cases usually manifest themselves as uncontrollable shivering. Put on dry, warm clothes and get into a sleeping bag; this will normally raise your body temperature sufficiently. Severe hypothermia is potentially fatal: symptoms include disorientation, lethargy, mental confusion (including an inappropriate feeling of well-being and warmth!) and coma. In severe cases the rescue team should be summoned.

A US$20 rescue fee is paid by all climbers upon entering the national park. The rescue team ordinarily covers the Marangu route only; if you use another route their services must be organised in advance.

midnight, giving you time to hike back down to Mweka Hut via Barafu in the afternoon, another walk of around eight hours. After spending your fifth night at Mweka Hut (3,100m), you will descend the mountain on the sixth day via the Mweka route, a four-to-five-hour walk.

Note that the huts along this route are practically unusable, though you still get to pay the US$40 'hut fee'. Any reliable operator will provide you with camping equipment and employ enough porters to carry the camp and set it up.

Mweka route

This is the steepest and fastest route to the summit. There are two huts along it: Mweka (3,100m) and Barafu (4,600m). Both are unfurnished uniports which sleep up to 16 people. There is water at Mweka but not at Barafu. This route starts at the Mweka Wildlife College, 12km from Moshi. From there it takes about eight hours to get to Mweka Hut, then a further eight hours to Barafu. You will reach the rim at Stella Point, a six-hour walk from Barafu and one hour from Uhuru Peak. The Mweka Route is not recommended as a way up the mountain, since it is too short for proper acclimatisation, but it is often used to descend the mountain by people climbing along other routes such as Machame.

Shira route

This route crosses the Shira Plateau west of Kibo. You need a 4x4 to do it, as it is 19km from the gate to the trailhead. You can either camp at the trailhead or walk the 4km to Shira Hut. The views from the Shira Plateau are excellent, and there is some game to be seen. If you use this route, spend two nights at Shira in order to acclimatise before you continue. For routes from Shira Hut, see the Machame route.

Umbwe route

This short, steep route is one of the most scenic. It is often used as a descent route. Umbwe route descends from Barranco Hut, and comes out at the village of Umbwe. It is possible to sleep in two caves on the lower slopes along this route.

Arranging a climb

The *only* sensible way to go about climbing Kilimanjaro is through a reliable operator that specialises in Kili climbs. Readers who pre-book a climb through a known tour operator in their own country can be confident that they will be going with a reputable ground operator in Tanzania. Readers who want to make their arrangements after they arrive in Tanzania will find several such companies operating out of Moshi, Arusha and Marangu, and will generally be able to negotiate a better price than if they had pre-booked. A list of respected operators is included in the box overleaf, and while such a list can never be comprehensive, it is reasonable to assume that anybody who can offer you a significantly cheaper package than the more budget-friendly companies on this list is probably not to be trusted.

In 1998, you could safely assume that a five-day Marangu climb with any reliable operator would start an all-inclusive price of around US$550-650 per head for two people. You may be able to negotiate the starting price down slightly, especially for a larger group, but when you are paying this sort of money, it strikes me as sensible to shop around for the best quality of service rather than a fractional saving. A reputable operator will provide good food, experienced guides and porters, and reliable equipment – all of which go a long way to ensuring not only that you reach the top, but also that you come back down alive. You can assume that the cost of any package with a reputable operator will include a registered guide, two porters per person, park fees, food, and transport to and from the gate. It is, however, advisable to check exactly what you are paying for, and (especially for larger parties) to ensure that one porter is also registered as a guide, so that if somebody has to turn back, the rest of the group can still continue their climb. It might also be worth pointing out the potential risk attached to forming an impromptu group with strangers merely to cut 5% or so off the price. If you hike on your own or with people you know well, you can

RECOMMENDED TOUR OPERATORS

Moshi

Most travellers who arrange their climb after they arrive in Tanzania do so in Moshi, where I can recommend four companies without reservation:

Shah Tours Office on Mawenzi Road between the bus station and Clock Tower. PO Box 1821; tel: 055 52370; fax: 055 51449

Keys Hotel See *Where to stay* in Moshi

Trans-Kibo Travels Office in the YMCA. PO Box 558; tel: 055 52017; fax: 055 54219; email: transkibo@habari.co.tz

Zara International Office in the Moshi Hotel. PO Box 1990; tel: 055 54240; fax: 055 53105; email: zara@form-net.com

Marangu

Climbs can be arranged through the Marangu and Kibo Hotels in Marangu. Both of these hotels have been taking people up Kilimanjaro for decades, and they have an impeccable reputation. The standard packages offered by these hotels aren't the cheapest available, but the standard of service and equipment is very high. The Kibo Hotel has the facilities and trained staff to deal with altitude-related emergencies. The 'hard-way' climbs organised by the Marangu Hotel are probably the cheapest reliable deals you'll find, assuming that you are prepared to self-cater. Contact details for both hotels are found under *Where to stay* in Marangu.

Arusha

Most safari companies in Arusha arrange Kilimanjaro climbs, though they will generally work through a ground operator in Moshi or Marangu, which means that they have to charge slightly higher rates. Any of the Arusha-based safari companies listed on pages 121–4 can be recommended, and short-stay visitors who are already going on safari with one of these companies will probably find that the ease and efficiency of arranging a Kilimanjaro climb through that company outweighs the minor additional expenditure.

There are a few companies that arrange their own Kili climbs out of Arusha. **Tropical Tours** has a long track record of organising climbs along the lesser-known routes, and is well worth contacting should you want to do that sort of thing. The similarly named **Tropical Trails**, based at Maasai Camp on the outskirts of Arusha, also has an excellent reputation. Finally, **Safari Destinations** is a new subsidiary of Roy Safaris which will specialise specifically in trekking and climbing on Kilimanjaro, Mount Meru and elsewhere. Details of all these companies are on pages 121–4.

dictate your own pace and there is less danger of personality clashes developing mid-climb.

The standard duration of a climb on the Marangu route is five days. Many people with experience of Kilimanjaro recommend adding a sixth day to this, so that you can acclimatise for a day at Horombo Hut. Others feel that the extra day makes little difference except that it adds around 20% to the cost of the climb. On the basis of anecdotal evidence (admittedly a very limited sample), I've noticed that people who spent six days on the mountain seemed to enjoy the climb more than those who spent five days. However, somebody who owns a climbing company in Arusha and who has kept records for three years has noted only a slightly increased success rate in people who take the extra day, and attributes this to their extra determination to reach the top after having paid more money. The choice is yours.

Of the less popular routes up Kilimanjaro, the one most frequently used by tourists is the Machame Route, with requires a minimum of six days. Most operators will charge at least 25% more for this route, because it requires far more outlay on their part. The huts along the Machame Route are in such poor condition that tents and camping equipment must be provided, along with a coterie of porters to carry and set up the makeshift camp. The same problem exists on all routes except Marangu, so that any off-the-beaten-track climb will be considerably more costly than the standard one. Should you decide to use a route other than Marangu, it is critical that you work through an operator with experience of that route.

The alternative to using a reputable company is to take your chances with a small operator or private individual who approaches you in the street. These guys will offer climbs for around US$100 cheaper than an established operator, but the risks are greater and because they generally have no office, there is little accountability on their side. Many of these guides *are* genuine and reliable, but it's difficult to be certain who you're dealing with unless you have a recommendation from somebody who has used the same person. A crucial point when comparing this situation to the similar one that surrounds arranging a safari out of Arusha is that you're not merely talking about losing a day through breakdown or something like that. With Kilimanjaro, you could literally die on the mountain. I've heard several stories of climbers being supplied with inadequate equipment and food, even of travellers being abandoned by their guide mid-climb. The very least you can do, if you make arrangements of this sort, is to verify that your guide is registered; he should have a small wallet-like document to prove this.

The reason why climbing Kilimanjaro is so expensive boils down to the high park fees. In 1998, these were a daily entrance fee of US$25 per person, plus a rescue fee of US$20 per person per climb, plus a hut fee of US$40 per person per night. In addition to this, a daily entrance fee of US$10 is charged for the guide, along with a rescue fee of US$20. In other words, the fixed costs attached to a five-day Marangu climb work out at more than US$300 per person, to which must be added the cost of transport, food and cooking fuel, and the guide's and porters' salaries. It isn't difficult to figure out why any company offering you a deal significantly below US$550 must be cutting corners somewhere.

Hikers are expected to tip their guides and porters. The company you go with can give you an idea of the going rate is, but around US$5 per day per guide/porter per climbing party is fair.

Other preparations

Two climatic factors must be considered when preparing to climb Kilimanjaro. The obvious one is the cold. Bring plenty of warm clothes, a windproof jacket, a pair of gloves, a balaclava, a warm sleeping bag and an insulation mat. During the rainy season, a rain jacket and rain trousers will come in useful. A less obvious factor is the sun, which is fierce at high altitudes. Bring sunglasses and sun-screen.

Other essentials are water bottles, solid shoes or preferably boots. Most of these items can be hired in Moshi or at the park gate, or from the company you arrange to climb with. I've heard varying reports about the condition of locally-hired items.

A good medical kit is essential, especially if you are climbing with a cheap company. You'll go through plenty of plasters if you acquire a few blisters (assume that you will), and can also expect to want headache tablets.

You might want to buy biscuits, chocolate, sweets, glucose powder and other energy-rich snacks to take with you up the mountain. No companies supply this sort of thing, and although they are sometimes available at the huts, you'll pay through your nose for them.

Maps and further reading

The Walker's Guide and Map to Kilimanjaro by Mark Savage (African Mountain Guides, 32 Sea Mill Crescent, Worthing, UK; tel: 01903 37565) is popular and reliable, with useful practical information printed on the back. It is difficult to locate this map in Arusha, and better to buy one before you visit Tanzania.

Also recommended is Giovanni Tombazzi's *New Map of Kilimanjaro National Park*, published in 1998 in conjunction with Hoopoe Adventure Tours. This map is far more easy to find in Arusha, and it is similarly accurate and detailed. Current climbing tips are printed on the back, along with a low-scale map of the final ascent to Kibo, and day-by-day contour 'graphs' for the Macheme and Marangu routes.

A 60-page national parks handbook, *Kilimanjaro National Park*, has accurate small-scale maps. It is worth buying for its detailed route descriptions and background information, and is available from the National Park office in Arusha for US$5.

Before you leave home – or as a memento when you get back – try to get hold of *Kilimanjaro* by John Reader (Elm Tree Books, London, 1982). Although it is superficially a coffee-table book, it offers a well-written and absorbing overview of the mountain's history and various ecosystems. The photographs are good too.

The Usambara and Pare Mountains

The series of forested mountain ranges that lies to the east of the B1 between Moshi and Tanga offers some of the best and most accessible hiking and rambling possibilities to be had anywhere in northern Tanzania. The main mountain ranges, running from north to south, are the North Pare, South Pare, Western Usambara and Eastern Usambara. The two parts of the Usambara effectively form one geographical entity, divided into eastern and western components largely because of the difficulty of crossing between the two parts of the range. By contrast, the North and South Pare are discrete entities lying to the north and south of the town of Same; they share a name because both ranges are inhabited by the Pare people.

The area covered by this chapter may logically fall into Tanzania's northeastern tourist circuit, but aside from Lushoto in Western Usambara, it doesn't attract a great many travellers. This might change, however, as the mountains are gradually being opened up to small-scale tourism through the combined efforts of the Tanzania Tourist Board (TTB) and a Dutch development organisation called SNV. Over the last year or two, Lushoto has become the site of the most prominent of several tourist programmes initiated by these agencies in northern Tanzania, while similar but less publicised programmes have started operating in the Pare Mountains.

The Usambara and Pare Mountains will be attractive to budget-conscious travellers simply because they allow for a few relatively inexpensive days' break between the wallet-draining tourist centres of Arusha and Zanzibar. Characterised by lush vegetation, some stunning viewpoints, and a refreshingly breezy high-altitude climate, these mountains also offer a great opportunity to limber up your limbs after a few days spent confined in a safari vehicle or sweating it out in the paralysing humidity of the coast. If you have the time, a few days rambling in the Usambara or Pare would serve as good preparation for the infinitely more demanding hike up Kilimanjaro.

Lushoto in the Western Usambara is the established focal point for backpackers in this part of Tanzania, while the Amani Nature Reserve in the Eastern Usambara is a more alluring spot for those with a keen interest in wildlife and birds. Tourist development in the Pare Mountains is comparatively new and low-key, something that will appeal to travellers who want to get right away from any established tourist beat.

Climate

The mountains of northeastern Tanzania have a similar rainfall pattern to most parts of Tanzania, with the short rains falling in November and December and the long rains coming between March and May. Most places of interest in these

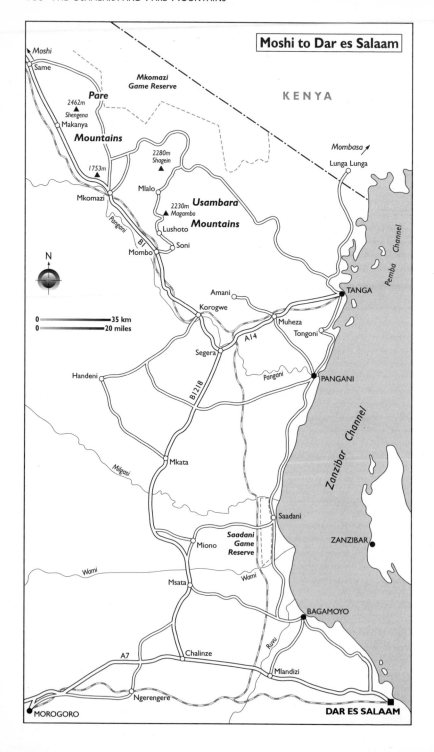

Moshi to Dar es Salaam

mountains lie at an elevation of between 1,500m and 2,000m, so they have a relatively moist and temperate climate, and can be quite chilly at night. By contrast, the lower-lying access towns along the B1 (for instance Korogwe and Same) tend to be hot, dusty and relatively dry.

Getting around

Regular buses run along the surfaced roads connecting Moshi to Tanga and Dar es Salaam. Express buses covering these routes are generally quite fast, typically covering around 80km per hour with stops. Other buses can be very slow, not least because they stop at every town or village.

Regular minibuses connect Lushoto in the Western Usambara to Tanga via Mombo, Korogwe and Muheza. These are a very quick and efficient means of getting around, and they stop to pick up passengers at all the main towns, but they are generally driven with far greater abandon than buses – if you use these minibuses, don't underestimate the risk of being involved in a fatal accident.

There is public transport of sorts connecting the B1 to all the main centres in the various mountain ranges covered in this chapter. Details of individual routes are given under the appropriate heading later in the chapter.

Further information

Most of the places of interest covered in this chapter have been developed for tourism under the TTB and SNV, one result of which is a greater level of organisation than you'll find in other relatively remote parts of Tanzania. There are good tourist information centres in Lushoto, Same, Mbaga and Usangi. Useful pamphlets about the various projects in this area, as well as up-to-date travel information, can be obtained in advance from the helpful TTB office in Arusha. Those with detailed questions or specialised interests can contact the SNV in room 643 of the Serengeti Wing in the Arusha International Cultural Centre; tel/fax: 057 7515; email: tourinfo@habari.co.tz.

THE NORTH PARE

In tourist terms, the North Pare is the least developed of the mountain ranges covered in this chapter, despite lying a mere 50km southeast of Kilimanjaro and Moshi. The main base for exploring the range is the small town of Usangi, which lies roughly 25km from Mwanga on the B1 and is reached via a good dirt road covered by a few buses daily. There is no formal accommodation in Usangi, but you should be able to stay in the three-bedroom resthouse at Lomwe Secondary School for US$3 per person, and if that's full then the teachers are happy to put up visitors for a similar fee (the headmaster of the school is also the co-ordinator of the tourism project). Inexpensive local meals are available by request.

Usangi is an attractive town, ringed by 11 peaks, and particularly lively on the market days of Monday and Thursday. At the secondary school, you can organise a number of excursions to nearby points of interest. A good half-day walk is the Mangatu tour, which takes you through the Mbale Forest to a viewpoint towards nearby Kilimanjaro and Lake Jipe on the Kenya border. The half-day Goma tour visits a set of caves which were dug by the Pare people in the 19th century as a hiding place from the slave raiders. This tour can be extended to a full-day walk which takes in the forested upper slopes of Mount Kindoroka, home to a variety of birds and monkeys. Several other day walks are available to visitors, and it is possible to organise overnight hiking trails. All hikes cost around US$9 per group per day, with an additional village development fee of US$2.50 per day.

SAME

This dusty small town on the B1 south of Moshi is the gateway to Mbaga in the South Pare Mountains, as well as to the Mkomazi Game Reserve on the Kenya border. The most notable feature of Same, aside from the mountainous backdrop, is a strong Maasai presence. You are likely to stop in Same only if you plan on visiting the mountains or Mkomazi, in which case there is a fairly good chance you'll have to spend the night. The tourist centre at the Sasa Kazi Hotel is the best place to ask for current advice about lifts to Mbaga, or about anything else.

The smartest accommodation is at the **Elephant Motel**, which lies no more than 1km from the town centre along the B1 back towards Dar es Salaam, and charges around US$18 for a s/c double. In the town centre, 100m from the bus station, the **Kambeni Guesthouse** is an excellent local lodging, with standard rooms for US$2.50/3.00 and s/c doubles for US$5.50. Also recommended in this range are the **Tumaine Guesthouse** and **Amani Lutheran Centre**. The **Sasa Kazi Hotel** doesn't have rooms but it serves reasonable local meals.

MBAGA AND THE SOUTH PARE

The extensive mountains of the South Pare offer a rich combination of cultural sites and natural attractions, most of which have only recently opened up to visitors following the implementation of a cultural tourism programme in 1998. This project operates out of the Hilltop Tona Lodge in the small town of Mbaga, an attractively well-wooded semi-urban sprawl that follows the main road along the northern slopes of the range. The set-up here is rather low-key by comparison to the Usambara, with a greater emphasis on cultural sightseeing, and we would recommend it to travellers who want to get right away from the beaten tourist track.

A number of activities can be arranged out of Mbaga. One interesting half-day excursion is the walk along the main road towards Gonja to the house of a highly respected traditional healer (who also happens to be a Seventh Day Adventist, so don't bother visiting on Saturdays). Another takes you to the Mghimbi Caves, where the Pare hid from slave raiders in the 1860s, and then to Malameni Rock, where thousands of children were sacrificed to appease evil spirits until the practice was outlawed in the 1930s. For natural history enthusiasts, the day walk to Ronzi Dam through patches of rainforest and montane moorland is recommended, as is the walk to the legendary 'Red Reservoir'. Longer hikes include a three-day hike to the Shengena Forest, which harbours several types of monkey and a wide range of forest birds. Hikers must pay a guide fee of US$6 per group (full-day) or US$3 per group (half-day) as well as a village development fee of US$3 per person per walk. It is possible to explore the roads around the village without a guide, in which case no fees are payable. Another option is a performance of traditional dancing in the evening, which costs around US$8 per group.

In 1902, Mbaga became the site of one of the earliest Lutheran missions in the interior of what was then German East Africa, founded by Jakob Dannholz. The original church built by Dannholz is still in use, an oddly Bavarian apparition in these remote African hills, as is the stone house in which he lived. A more enduring legacy of the man's work, however, is his seminal and sympathetic treatise documenting Pare oral traditions that might otherwise have been forgotten. Written between 1912 and 1918, Dannholz's work was finally translated into English and published in 1989 under the name *Lute: The Curse and the Blessing*. It provides much insight into the cultural sites around Mbaga and can be bought cheaply at most book shops in Same or Moshi.

There is currently no electricity in Mbaga, but it is scheduled to arrive during the lifespan of this edition.

Getting there and away

One bus and a couple of *matatus* daily run along the 35km road connecting Mbaga to Same on the B1. Normally, all transport out of Mbaga leaves before 07.00, and begins the return trip from Same at around 11.00. Depending on demand, one of these vehicles may do a second run backwards and forwards in the afternoon, but this is the exception rather than the rule. There isn't much private transport between Same and Mbaga, so trying to hitch is probably a waste of time. The owner of the Sasa Kazi Hotel in Same doubles as the tourist information officer and he will be able to tell you if he knows of any other vehicles heading up to Mbaga, but realistically, you should probably expect to have to spend the night in Same if you arrive there after 11.00.

With private transport, the direct drive to Mbaga is reasonably straightforward, depending on the current condition of the road. It is also possible to reach Mbaga via a road that skirts the boundary of Mkomazi Game Reserve before passing through the small town of Kisiwani, an old slave trading centre which has retained a distinctly coastal feel, and then ascending the mountains via a spectacular forest-fringed pass. It used to be possible to see a bit of game along this road, but local sources say that they haven't seen much in the last couple of years. The route via Kisiwani covers roughly the same distance as the main road to Mbaga, but it is generally in poorer condition and currently requires a good 4x4.

An obscure onward option from Mbaga takes you to Gonja, which lies about 15km further along the road and is the terminal for buses coming from Same. The Bombo Hospital in Gonja is the largest in the area, and cheap rooms are available at the Vuje Guesthouse.

Where to stay and eat

The **Hilltop Tona Lodge** (PO Box 32, Mbaga; tel: Dar es Salaam 600158) opened in 1998 as part of the South Pare Tourism Programme. Essentially a set of self-contained cottages straddling the main road through the town, the lodge has a wonderful jungle setting and boasts great views over the Mkomazi Plains. There is a natural swimming pool in the river below the lodge. Furnished accommodation starts at around US$4.50 per person depending on the size and quality of the room, or you can camp for around US$1 per tent. The restaurant serves meals in the US$1.50-4.50 bracket. Beer, sodas and mineral water are available.

Cleared **campsites** are to be found in several places in the hills, with the site near Ranzi Dam particularly recommended. Camping costs US$1 and details can be obtained through the Hilltop Tona Lodge.

MKOMAZI GAME RESERVE

Many thanks to Nicholas McWilliam for writing to me with detailed information about this reserve in 1996.

Mkomazi Game Reserve is the southern extension of Kenya's vast Tsavo National Park, covering an area of 3,701km² east of Kilimanjaro and immediately north of the Pare and Usambara mountains. The reserve is practically undeveloped for tourism, and it has been subject to considerable pressure over the last 20 years as the human population around its peripheries has grown in number. Together with Tsavo, Mkomazi forms part of one of East Africa's most important savannah ecosystems, characterised by the semi-arid climatic conditions of the Sahel arc.

In 1992, the Tanzanian government invited the Royal Geographical Society to undertake a detailed ecological study of Mkomazi. Although mammal populations are low, it has been determined that most of the large mammal species found in Tsavo are either resident in Mkomazi or else regularly migrate there from Kenya, including lion, cheetah, elephant, giraffe, buffalo, zebra, impala and Tanzania's most significant gerenuk population. African hunting dogs were recently re-introduced into Mkomazi, as has been a herd of black rhinos from South Africa. Over 400 bird species have been recorded in the reserve, and the recent study noted at least eight species not previously recorded in Tanzania.

Mkomazi does not at present offer game viewing to compare with other reserves in northern Tanzania, and it is certainly not a conventional safari destination. However, this is compensated for by the wild scenery and the near certainty of not seeing another tourist. So far as facilities go, there is a two-bedroom *banda* available at Ibaya Camp on a first-come, first-served basis. Otherwise, there is a basic campsite (little more than cleared areas) about 2km from Zange Gate and another about 20km from Zange overlooking Dindera Dam, a good place to see large mammals. The reserve is best avoided in the rainy season, due to the poor roads, and all visitors should be self-sufficient in water, food and fuel.

Because Mkomazi is not a national park, walking is permitted. The north-eastern portion of the reserve near Zange Gate is very hilly (tough walking but great scenery) and there is a very real chance of encountering large game animals such as lions and buffaloes on foot. The best way to go about organising a walking trip into Mkomazi would be to walk or hitch the 5km from Same to Zange Gate, where you can make arrangements with the warden to hire an armed ranger/guide. To stand a chance of seeing a fair range of large mammals, you would need to spend a couple of days walking in the reserve, so you'd need camping gear and adequate provisions. The owner of the Sasa Kazi Hotel in Same can organise car hire into the reserve.

Entrance to Mkomazi costs US$20 per person per 24-hour period.

MOMBO

This scruffy little town on the Moshi-Dar es Salaam road is the springboard for trips into the Western Usambara. It's a pretty unremarkable place; one traveller comments that 'the best thing about Mombo is the potato samosas you can buy from the street vendors – they really are delicious'. Any bus heading along the B1 can drop you at Mombo, from where a steady stream of minibuses runs up to Lushoto via Soni. It's difficult to imagine that any traveller would actually *want* to spend a night in Mombo, but if for some reason you need to, then the **Midway Inn** and adjacent **Sandali Inn** both have reasonable doubles with net and fan for US$3. The **Midway Express Restaurant**, next to the Midway Inn on the junction of the Lushoto Road, serves acceptable meals for around US$3.

LUSHOTO AND THE WESTERN USAMBARA

Very different in character to the Amani area, the Western Usambara is far more densely populated, and its slopes are relatively cultivated. The mountains around Lushoto, the regional administration centre, are riddled with footpaths and winding roads, open to gentle exploration as well as longer overnight hikes. The area is scenically varied, its steep-sided valleys covered in euphorbia, exotic plantations, small patches of indigenous forest, and cultivated Shambaa homesteads.

Lushoto, the main tourist focus in the mountains, was a town of some note in the German colonial era. Today, it is a strange and slightly anachronistic place. Many buildings on the main street date to the early part of the century, when

Lushoto provided weekend relief for settlers farming the dry, dusty Maasai Steppe below. The still-significant settler community adds to the time-warped feel; we drove in on a Sunday and saw a couple of young girls walking to church in clothes that would not have looked out of place in an Edwardian period drama.

If the main street through Lushoto calls to mind an Alpine village, then the side roads, lined with mud-and-thatch homesteads, are unambiguously African. So, too, is the vibrant market where colourfully-dressed Shambaa women sell their goods. The vegetation around Lushoto reflects these contradictions: papaya trees subvert neat rows of exotic pines and eucalyptus, which in turn are interspersed by patches of lush indigenous forest alive with the raucous squawking of silvery-cheeked hornbill.

Getting there and away
Lushoto lies 33km from Mombo, and the two are connected by a surfaced road which offers splendid views in all directions. Coming from Tanga, the best way to get to Lushoto is to hop on one of the regular minibuses that connect the two via Muheza, Korogwe and Mombo. These take about three hours. Coming from Arusha, Moshi or Dar es Salaam, you will probably need to catch a bus that can drop you at Mombo, and pick up a minibus to Lushoto from there.

THE HISTORICAL BACKGROUND
The Usambara has been occupied by Bantu-speakers for a few thousand years. The people of the mountains, the Shambaa, have a tradition of welcoming refugees from other areas, and until recent times had a loose political system similar to the *ntemi* of western Tanzania. The probable impetus for forging greater unity was the threat posed by the 18th-century Maasai occupation of the plains west of the range.

The first Shambaa leader was Mbegha, the self-styled *Lion King*, who probably originated from the *ntemi* area of western Tanzania. Mbegha united the area peacefully by taking a wife from each major clan, then placing her son in charge of that clan. His army, formed from refugees, seems likely only to have been used in defence. Under the rule of Mbegha's grandson, Kinyashi, the Shambaa became more militarised. Their greatest leader was Kinyashi's son, Kimweri; under his rule the Shambaa controlled much of the area between the Usambara and the coast.

Kimweri's capital at Vuga, near the modern settlement of Soni, was too deep in the mountains to have had much contact with Kilimanjaro-bound caravans. One of Kimweri's sons, Semboja, the chief of Mazinde, on what is now the main Moshi-Dar es Salaam road, came to exert considerable influence over passing traders. By 1867 he had built up a stockpile of arms large enough to enable him to overthrow Kimweri's successor at Vuga. This event split the Shambaa into several splinter groups, and although the leadership was retained by Semboja, he controlled a far smaller area than did his predecessor. The Shambaa figured heavily in the Abushiri Uprising of 1888/9, but after Semboja's son, Mputa, was hanged in 1898, they offered little further resistance to German occupation.

The Usambara was popular with European farmers. Lushoto, originally called Wilhelmstal, was considered a possible capital in the early days of the colony. Evidence of German architectural styles can be seen throughout the region.

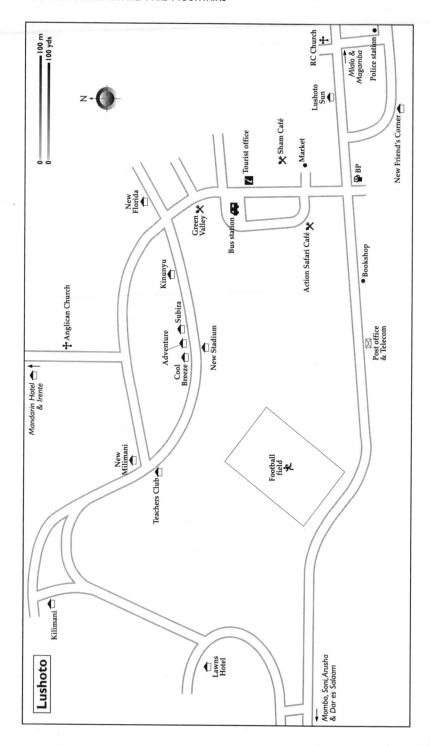

Lushoto

Where to stay

The colonial era **Lawns Hotel** (PO Box 33; tel: Lushoto 5 or 66) is the only vaguely upmarket option in Lushoto. At the time of writing, it might best be described as having a certain faded charm (with the emphasis on the 'faded'), but it does also have the potential to be something rather special when current renovations have been completed. The restaurant serves meals for around US$7, and mountain bike hire and horseback excursions can be arranged through reception. For now, the accommodation at Lawns feels slightly overpriced at around US$13/17 single/double using communal showers and US$23/30 s/c single/double. We felt that travellers who are looking for accommodation in this price range would be better heading out to one of the places in the Magamba Forest (see *Excursions from Lushoto* below).

Dropping in price, the **Lushoto Sun Hotel** has a good central location and very acceptable s/c rooms with hot showers for US$8/12 single/double. The **New Friend's Corner Hotel** around the corner also has self-contained rooms and is a bit cheaper. A similar set-up, the **Mandarin Hotel** is recommended in this range, though its location about 1km from the town centre might arguably count against it.

The **Kilimani Guesthouse** has been popular with travellers for years, and I thought it distinctly overrated when I stayed there a few years ago. However, when we popped past in 1998, it had recently changed ownership and undergone extensive renovations, and looked good value at around US$6/7 single/double.

There is the usual selection of cheap local guesthouses scattered around Lushoto. Of these, the **Teachers Club** looks about the best, despite its misleadingly institutional sounding name, and has clean rooms using communal showers for US$2.20/3.50. There is a string of scruffy places in a similar price bracket along the road between the bus station and the Teachers Club. We stayed at the **Cool Breeze Guesthouse**, which was pretty representative – erratic showers, noisy music, sagging beds and moth-eaten mosquito nets, but perfectly acceptable if these things don't worry you. For current recommendations in this price range, drop in at the tourist office opposite the bus station.

Where to eat

There's a surprising shortage of decent places to eat in Lushoto. Cheap local food and friendly English-speaking staff can be found at the **Action Safari Café** around the corner from the bus station. The nearby **Green Valley Hotel** reputedly serves good, cheap meals, but the cupboard was bare when we were in town – still, it's a great place for a cold beer. The Lushoto Sun Hotel does reasonable chicken and chips for around US$3, or you could splash out on a full dinner at the Lawns Hotel for US$7.

Excursions from Lushoto

A number of day walks and overnight excusions can be undertaken using Lushoto as a base. It is possible to do many of these trips independently, but most travellers organise their outings through the Usambara Mountains Tourism Project (UMTP), whose prominently signposted tourist office faces the bus station. The UMTP can offer sound advice on most aspects of travel in the Western Usambara, and they arrange several different trips with knowledgeable registered guides. All profits are used towards the development of community projects.

Soni

Straddling the surfaced road that connects Mombo to Lushoto, the small town of Soni is of interest primarily for the attractive but less than spectacular Soni Falls.

This waterfall is visible from the main road to Lushoto, but to see it properly you need to stop in the town, from where a short, steep path leads to the rocky base. It is possible to be dropped at Soni en route from Mombo to Lushoto, but since the drive between Soni and Lushoto takes no more than 30 minutes, it is just as easy to visit the waterfall as a day trip from Lushoto, using the regular minibuses that run back and forth to Mombo. If you visit Soni as a day trip, there is no reason to take a guide along. However, the UMTP can organise a number of day walks out of Soni, for instance to the so-called 'Growing Rock' at Mugila, and to the tree nursery at Bangala.

For some, a convincing reason to stop in Soni might simply be that there are a couple of accommodation options which seem far better value for money than anything in Lushoto. Overlooking the waterfall, the **Soni Falls Hotel** was built in the 1930s and has recently been renovated without losing anything of its rustic period feel. Clean, comfortable s/c doubles cost US$14, or you can pitch a tent in the grounds for a small charge. Also recommended is the **Kimalube Hotel**, a friendly, family-run place that lies about 1km back towards Mombo. Double rooms here cost US$5 without breakfast or US$8 with breakfast, and evening meals are available for around US$3. There is running cold water in the showers, and you can ask for hot water to be brought to you in a bucket.

Bambuli
This tiny but beautiful village can be reached from Soni on the back of a pick-up truck. There is one basic local guesthouse in the village, and a better one run by Mary at the hospital, though you may need connections to allowed to stay here. The Saturday market at Bambuli is very colourful, and there are many walking opportunities in the surrounding hills.

Irente viewpoint
An attractive short walk from Lushoto takes you to a stunning viewpoint at the edge of the Usambara overlooking the Maasai Steppe. It is possible to organise a guide to take you there, but once you are out of Lushoto it is easy enough to find your own way. Ask people to direct you to Irente farm. From there it is ten minutes' walk through Irente village to the viewpoint. The round trip takes two to three hours. Look out for the Egyptian vultures which apparently nest on the cliffs below the viewpoint. It is also worth scanning patches of indigenous forest en route for forest birds.

Travellers who want a guide to take them to Irente are advised to organise this through the UMTP, since we've heard of people who went with unofficial guides being robbed on the way. This will cost US$10 per group plus US$2.50 per person.

Magamba Forest
Situated about 15km from Lushoto, this is the most accessible patch of rainforest in the Western Usambara, covering the slopes of Mount Magamba, which at 2,230m is the highest peak in the range. It is of great interest to birdwatchers, with the track to the old sawmill in particular offering a good chance of seeing a wide selection of forest birds, including such highly localised species as the Usambara weaver, Usambara akalat and red-capped forest warbler. A variety of mammals also live in this forest, though only black-and-white colobus and blue monkey are likely to be encountered by the casual visitor. Guided day walks to the forest can be arranged through the UMTP office in Lushoto at a cost of US$10 plus US$2.50 per person.

It is equally possible to visit Magamba under your own steam, staying at one of the two atmospheric lodges in the area or camping in the forest, and walking along various self-guided trails. Built as a colonial residence in 1934, **Grant's Lodge** (tel: 053 42491; fax: 053 43628) is set in an attractive garden and contains four bedrooms and a library with a collection of old books and magazines. Full board accommodation costs US$48 per person. The nearby **Muller's Mountain Lodge** (PO Box 34 Lushoto; tel: 134) is another 1930s residence set in attractive gardens. Rooms cost US$22 per person b&b with lunch or dinner an additional US$8 per head. To reach these lodges in private transport, follow the Mlalo road out of Lushoto for 5km until you reach Magamba, then turn right along a side road for another 5-6km. Using public transport, you can take a bus towards Mlalo as far as Magamba trading centre, but from there you will have to walk the last 5-6km to the lodges. If you are heading to Muller's, you could ask at the BP garage in Lushoto whether the owner is making a trip into town later that day.

There is a **campsite** at the old sawmill in the heart of the forest, with a toilet and running water. Camping costs US$2.50 per day, in addition to which you must pay a daily forest permit of US$4. The best way to get to the campsite is to hire a car in Lushoto; this won't be prohibitively expensive and can be organised through the UMTP.

Mtae

This former German settlement can be reached from Lushoto by bus, along a road with several terrifying hairpin bends. Perched on a ridged peninsula, with a drop of several hundred metres on either side, Mtae offers views to Kenya over the Mkomazi Game Reserve, and on a clear day to Moshi and Kilimanjaro. The nearby 'Butterfly Mountain' can be visited as a day-hike, preferably with a guide, and its forested slopes support a rich bird life as well as many species of colourful butterfly. Buses to Mtae leave Lushoto in the mid-afternoon and take two hours, and return the next morning at 05.30 (if you miss your bus out then you'll be stuck in Mtae for another 24 hours). Rooms at the **Mwivane** and **Kuna Manena Guesthouses** cost around US$2/3 single/double. A café next to the bus stop serves local food and home-made bread, and a few doors down there is a bar selling beer.

Mlalo

This bizarre town sprawls over a large valley situated some 30km from Lushoto by road. It has an insular, almost other-worldly feel, one that made me feel like Indiana Jones entering a misplaced Mediterranean mountain kingdom when I visited it a few years ago. Initially, I was struck by the unusual style of many of the buildings: two-storey mud houses with intricately carved wooden balconies which seem to show both German and Arab influences. The town apparently sprawls for miles, yet even in its nominal centre rural homesteads cling precipitously to steep-sided hillocks. There is no electricity; at night the surrounding hills are lit up by lamps bobbing up and down and flickering like fireflies.

Two buses run daily between Lushoto and Mlalo, leaving Lushoto in the early afternoon and Mlalo at around 07.00. The trip takes around two hours. There are a few guesthouses near the bus stop, of which the **Afilex Hotel** seemed about the best, and also served reasonable meals.

Overnight hikes

The UMTP office in Lushoto can organise a number of guided overnight hikes into the surrounding mountains. The three-day hike through Musambae Forest reputedly offers better birding even than Magamba, and also takes in a visit to an old

German mission. Another possibility is to hike to Mtae, a three- to six-day trip depending on the route you choose. Both hikes cost around US$17 per person per day inclusive of public transport to the trailhead, accommodation and a guide, but hikers are required to pay for their own meals and drinks.

A new and exciting development, likely to come to fruition during the lifespan of this edition, is a guided five-day hiking trail to Amani in the Eastern Usambara. The UMTP office will be able to give full details of this trail once it has opened.

KOROGWE

Probably the largest town along the stretch of the B1 covered in this chapter, Korogwe is an important route focus and the favoured lunch stop of most buses travelling between Dar es Salaam and Moshi or Arusha. Otherwise, it is a less than remarkable place, with only an appealing Usambara backdrop to raise it above dusty small-town anonymity. The improvements in public transport in this part of Tanzania over the last few years make it unlikely that any traveller would end up spending a night in Korogwe these days, but those who explore the Usambara area might well find themselves swapping vehicles here at some point.

Getting there and away

Any bus heading between Moshi and Tanga or Dar es Salaam will be able to drop you in Korogwe, while the regular minibuses that connect Lushoto to Tanga via Mombo and Muheza generally pick up passengers at the bus station that lies just off the main road.

Most express buses between Dar es Salaam and Arusha or Moshi stop at the Korogwe Transit Hotel for a 20-minute lunch break.

Where to stay

The **Korogwe Traveller's Inn**, which lies on the B1 practically opposite the bus station, has adequate s/c doubles for US$8, as well as a bar and restaurant. The newer **Korogwe Transit Hotel** is marginally smarter, and reasonable value at US$14 s/c double, but it is also rather noisy as most of the buses stop here for meals.

There are several cheaper lodgings dotted around town, including the **New Savari Guesthouse** and **Miami Guesthouse**, which lie 100m from the bus station and offer clean double rooms with mosquito nets for around US$3.

Campers will probably want to head for the **Mountain View Resort**, which has cold showers and a bar and restaurant, and lies about 1km from the town centre of the road towards Dar es Salaam.

EASTERN USAMBARA (AMANI NATURE RESERVE)

Proclaimed in 1996, the Amani Nature Reserve in the Eastern Usambara must rank close to being the most underrated reserve anywhere in northern Tanzania, offering the combination of excellent walking, beautiful forest scenery, and a wealth of animal life. Although the nature reserve is a recent creation, Amani was settled by Germany as an agricultural research station in 1902, at which time the surrounding area was set aside to form what is reputedly still the second-largest botanical garden in the world. Lying at an altitude of roughly 900m, Amani remains a biological research station of some note, as well as an important centre for medical research. Most of the buildings date to the German and British colonial eras, giving it the genteel appearance of an English country village transplanted to the African jungle.

The Eastern Usambara is naturally covered in rainforest, though in some places the indigenous vegetation was replaced by tea plantations back in the colonial era, while in others there has been more recent encroachment by subsistence farmers.

Many significant stands of montane forest remain, however, and like all the montane forests of eastern Tanzania, they are characterised by a high level of endemism (the ecology of these forests is discussed in more detail under *Udzungwa National Park* on page 284).

The East Usambara Catchment Forest Project, established in 1991 and funded by FINNIDA, has been charged with implementing a conservation plan to protect the forests of the Eastern Usambara catchment area, the source of fresh water to 200,000 people. The development of Amani for ecotourism, with the emphasis on walking and hiking, has been a high priority of this project. Nine trails have been demarcated at Amani, ranging in length from 3–12km, and leaflets with trail descriptions are available to visitors. The directions in the leaflets are reportedly not 100% accurate, so it might be worth hiking with a trained guide, who will also help you to spot birds and monkeys. Future plans include the rehabilitation of a German stationmaster's house at Kisiwani as an information centre.

In addition to the prescribed walking trails, there is much to be seen along the roads and paths that lie within the research centre and botanical garden. Wandering around the forest-fringed village, you are likely to encounter black-and-white colobus and blue monkey, and may even catch a glimpse of the bizarre giant elephant shrew. Look out, too, for the green-headed oriole, a colourful bird that is restricted to a handful of montane forests between Tanzania and Mozambique, but is common and conspicuous around Amani. Other notable birds found in this part of the Usambara include the Uluguru violet-backed, banded green and Amani sunbirds, long-billed forest warbler, Swynnerton's robin, Fischer's touraco, Nduk eagle owl (a species found only in the Usambara Mountains), Sokoke skops owl and Kretschmer's longbill. The area supports numerous endemic plant species, including nine varieties of African violet (a popular garden flower which originated in the Usambara), and is renowned for colourful butterflies, many of which are also endemic.

You can visit the forest project office in Tanga for further details of developments, or contact them in advance at PO Box 5869, Tanga; tel/fax: 053 43820. An entrance fee of US$5 per person is charged, and guided walks cost US$10 per day.

Getting there and away

The springboard for visits to Amani is the small town of Muheza, which lies about 40km west of Tanga on the main surfaced road to Moshi and Dar es Salaam. All buses between Moshi or Dar es Salaam and Tanga can drop you at Muheza, as can the minibuses that ply back and forth between Tanga and Lushoto. One reader describes Muheza as a 'charming town', for reasons that are lost on me, but it does boast a good half-dozen small guesthouses should you need to spend a night, and Uncle J's Bar is a good place to eat and drink. Muheza is most lively on Thursday and Sunday, the local market days.

Depending on the current condition of the road, there is a daily bus service between Muheza and Amani. In theory, this bus leaves from the market in Muheza at 14.00, but it is unreliable at the best of times and may not run at all after heavy rains, and you're advised to be ready to board an hour in advance if you want a seat. There has reportedly been an increase in private transport between Muheza and Amani in recent years, so that hitching is a distinct possibility – the best place to wait for a lift is in front of the courthouse 1km from the town centre, opposite a sign that reads *Amani Medical Research Centre 32km*.

The drive to Amani is spectacular. Starting at Kisiwani, 7km before Amani, the dirt road climbs through the forest in a succession of tight hairpin bends. In a bus this is nerve-racking, and I was convinced we were the unwitting victims of a pilot scheme, doomed to failure after a maiden attempt. We got there in the end, however, and the bus has been doing this route safely for years.

The bus back to Muheza leaves Amani at 07.00. When we left Amani, we missed the bus, and so we walked the 7km to Kisiwani. The road passes through forest all the way, and we saw plenty of monkeys, butterflies and birds. It is marginally easier to get a lift at Kisiwani than it is at Amani, since the roads to the various tea estates in the area branch off between the two. There is regular transport to Muheza from Bambani, a village about two hours' walk from Kisiwani.

Where to stay and eat

The **Amani Club Resthouse** is a well-maintained stone building dating to the colonial era. The cosy lounge is heated by a log fire in the evenings, and it houses an improbable collection of yellowing books. There is also a newer **IUCN Resthouse** in the village. Both charge around US$15 full board (considerably cheaper for residents and students) and allow camping for US$5 per person.

There is nowhere to eat apart from at the resthouses, though the **Welfare Club** is a pleasant place for a drink and conversation, despite its rather Dickensian title.

Previous page Maasai boy after his initiation ceremony (AZ)

Above Mount Kilimanjaro, the highest free-standing mountain in the world (CH)

Below A small mosque on the outskirts of Arusha (AZ)

Opposite A balloon safari offers a completely different perspective of the vast plains of the Serengeti (AZ)

been warned) a popular disco over weekends. Air-conditioned rooms cost US$50/55/90 double/triple/suite for non-residents and US$32/40/68 for residents, inclusive of a full English breakfast.

Hotel Raskazone Tel/fax: 053 43897. Set on a back road about five minutes' walk from the Mkonge Hotel, this is regarded as the best deal in town by many expatriates. All rooms are s/c with a fridge, telephone, hot shower and nets; those with a fan cost US$20/25 single/double while those with air-conditioning cost US$30/35. All rates are inclusive of a full breakfast, and a discount of around 10% is offered to residents, students and, um, 'back pokers' (it took me a second, too – they mean backpackers). Camping costs US$4 per person.

Motel Panori Tel: 053 46044; fax: 053 47425. Close to the Raskazone and similar in standard, the Motel Panori offers accommodation in two types of room. Those in the old wing are rather run-down and seem poor value at US$24 s/c double, but the rooms in the new wing look very comfortable and seem much better value at US$30 s/c double. The food is arguably the best in Tanga, and most dishes cost around US$6.

Mid-range and budget

The **Marina Hotel** (PO Box 835; tel: 053 44362) has been a reliable mid-range option for many years. Self-contained double rooms with hot running water cost US$12 (with fan) or US$20 (air-conditioned). The newer **Hotel Kola Prieto** is also very smart and comfortable. All rooms are self-contained with hot running water; those with a fan cost US$12/15 single/double and those with air-conditioning cost US$18/23 single/double.

Dropping in price, the **Bandorini Hotel** is well established as the most popular place for budget travellers, and it's been offering excellent value for money for longer than a decade. The owner is a useful source of local travel information, and an excellent cook (for large groups, he does buffets of Indian food which, though not cheap at around US$6 per head, put the food at most upmarket hotels in Tanzania to shame). Rooms cost US$4.50/7.50 single/double with net and fan. The only problem with this place is that it's often fully occupied.

The **Planters Inn** is another well-established travellers' haunt. Dating to the pre-World War I German era, the hotel was reportedly the scene of some extravagant gambling on the part of Tanga's predominantly Greek sisal millionaires during the era of British rule. The building retains a strong period charm with its vast balconies and creaky wooden floors. Unfortunately, it hasn't been maintained with any conviction, and as a result it gets more run-down with each passing year. Nevertheless, the large rooms in the main building are fair value at US$3.00/4.50 single/double with ancient fan. The communal cold showers work spasmodically, otherwise bucket showers are available. Avoid the musty self-contained doubles, which cost US$6 and lie in an outbuilding.

The **Ocean Breeze Hotel**, which opened in September 1998, is arguably the best deal in town, assuming that the prices don't rise and the rooms aren't left to run down, as so often happens in Tanzania. Large clean doubles with net, fan, writing desk, firm double bed and hot-running showers cost US$7.50, and single rooms, under construction when we visited, will cost around US$4.50. The attached restaurant serves indifferent food for around US$2, as well as seriously cold beers and sodas.

A ten-minute walk from the town centre, the **New Era Hotel** has been converted from a private house in a pretty suburban area. Unfortunately, the rooms look like something out of a how-not-to DIY manual; certainly they are nothing to shout about at US$5/10 self-contained single/double. On the plus side, the Englishman and Asian lady who own and manage the hotel generate a friendly atmosphere. You can camp in the grounds for US$3 per person.

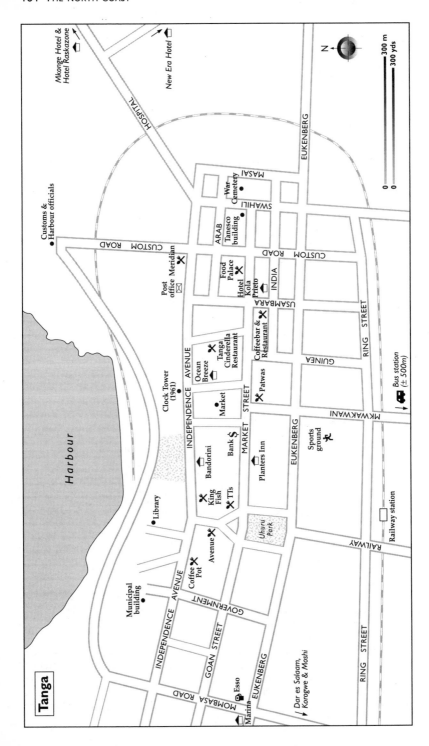

Tanga

For cheap seafront accommodation away from the town centre, about the only option is the **Inn by the Sea** (PO Box 2188, tel: 053 44613). This place could do with a bit of a face lift, but the self-contained double rooms are more than adequate at US$10.50 with a fan or US$15 with air-conditioning. No drink is served, and the food looks rather bland, so you might well find yourself gravitating towards the Mkonge Hotel next door at meal times.

Where to eat

Most of the hotels mentioned above have restaurants of a sort. Only those at the Pandori and Bandorini stand out in any way, the former serving a variety of Western-style dishes, and the latter quite wonderful Indian buffets by advance order only.

If you like Indian food, don't miss out on the **Food Palace**, one of our favourite restaurants anywhere in Tanzania. The kitchen menu is extensive enough to keep you in Tanga for weeks, and there is also an outdoor barbecue in the evenings. Portions are generous, the cooking would comfortably grace a top Indian restaurant in any world city, and the prices are very reasonable – most dishes cost between US$3.50 to US$5 including rice, chips or naan bread. The owner is a devout Muslim, so the restaurant is closed through the month of Ramadan.

The **King Fish Restaurant** seems very popular with locals and travellers alike, though the stench of fried fish that permeates for 100m in every direction struck us as less than enticing. A plate of fish and chips here costs US$2.

The venerable **Patwas Restaurant** has been serving great samosas and fruit juice for more than a decade, and it also offers reasonable Indian meals for around US$3. The owner of this restaurant is a good source of local travel information.

The **Meridian Restaurant** (formerly the Chinese Restaurant) used to be one of the best places to eat in Tanga, but it's now little more than a glorified bar serving a limited selection of local dishes.

Excursions from Tanga
Amboni Caves

These limestone caves 8km north of Tanga are the most extensive in East Africa, reputedly running for several hundred kilometres up the coast. Local people knew about the caves long before Europeans discovered them in 1940; they believe the main cave is inhabited by a fertility god and still leave offerings to this deity. The guide has gathered an admirable collection of anecdotes and tall stories. The forest patch close to the caves offers excellent birding, and it harbours a resident black-and-white colobus troop. For botanists, this is a good place to see the African violet *Santpaulia* in a wild state; it is forbidden to pick or otherwise damage this protected plant.

Amboni lies just off the Tanga-Mombasa road, and any vehicle heading towards Mombasa can drop you off near the entrance. It is also possible to cycle to Amboni – you can hire a bike at the main market square in Tanga. A campsite has recently been opened outside the caves.

Tongoni Ruins

This is the ruin of a Shirazi town which peaked in the 14th and 15th centuries. Even in its heyday Tongoni was probably a minor town, but it was certainly prosperous – the graveyard houses the largest concentration of historical tombs on the East African coast, many of which are threatened by the sea. There is also a ruined mosque at the site. An entrance fee of less than US$1 is charged by the caretaker, who will also show you around the site.

Tongoni is about 20km south of Tanga. To get there catch any bus heading to Pangani and ask to be dropped off at the village of Tongoni, from where it is a ten-minute walk to the ruins. Try to get to Tongoni early in the day, since there will not be much transport back to Tanga later and there is nowhere to stay nearby.

PANGANI

Like Bagamoyo, Pangani is a settlement of great historical note, but one that has largely been bypassed by 20th-century developments. Pangani has probably the most traditionally Swahili character of any of the main ports along the coast north of Dar es Salaam, making it an interesting place to settle into for a few days, with an atmosphere that has much in common with the less accessible ports of the south coast.

The mouth and lower reaches of the Pangani River have played a major role in coastal trade for several centuries, and Pangani itself has been described by one historian as 'the Bagamoyo of the first eighteen centuries of the Christian era'. In fact, the modern town of Pangani, which lies on the north bank of the river mouth, is not particularly ancient, founded as it was by Omani Arabs in around 1820. Throughout the Omani era, Pangani was the main terminus for slave caravans heading to the Lake Victoria region. Although this was a less important caravan route than those to Lakes Nyasa and Tanganyika, Pangani was nevertheless one of the most important 19th-century trading centres on the Tanzanian coast, outranked only by Bagamoyo and Kilwa Kivinje.

For several centuries before the arrival of the Omani, Pangani was situated about 4km upstream from its current position on the river mouth. Known as Muhembo, after a nearby hill, this settlement probably dates to the earliest Shirazi times. The oldest coconut plantation in the area is called El Harth, after an Arab family who arrived in the area in around AD900. Muhembo suffered heavily when it was raided by the Zimba in 1588, and it was practically destroyed by a Portuguese punitive raid in 1635. The probability is that the settlement fell into decline after 1635 and, like many coastal towns, it only recovered under Omani rule.

The most intriguing question about Pangani is whether it was the site of Rhapta, the ancient trading settlement referred to in the *Periplus of the Ancient Sea* and Ptolemy's *Geography*. The case for Pangani as Rhapta is compelling, if largely circumstantial. The *Periplus* places Rhapta four days' sailing south of Lamu and two days south of an island it calls Menuthias. If Menuthias is Pemba, and the landing point used by the ancients was on the north of this island, these directions would fit Pangani. Pointing even more directly to Pangani are the details in Ptolemy's *Geography*, based on the explorations of a Greek merchant called Diogenes, who claimed to have sailed for 25 days up the Rhapta River, where he saw two snow-capped peaks and heard rumours of two large lakes. The Pangani River has its source near Moshi, at the base of snow-capped Kilimanjaro.

No remains of such an ancient settlement have ever been found near Pangani (not entirely surprising if, as Ptolemy implies, the town was at that point some distance upriver from the mouth). Several other possible locations for Rhapta have been suggested, most plausibly the Rufiji mouth, which is so vast that remains of a 2,000-year-old settlement would be very difficult to locate, especially if it were now submerged somewhere in the labyrinthine Rufiji Delta. The Rufiji Mouth is about the right distance south of Mafia Island but, if the directions in the *Periplus* are to be viewed as implacably accurate (which they might well not be), it's much too far south of Mafia. There are also no snow-capped peaks to be seen upriver.

What does seem certain is that the Pangani River has long formed an important route for exploration of the interior, largely because it provides a reliable source of fresh water as far inland as Moshi. It may well have been the main inland trade

route prior to the Portuguese era and quite possibly 2,000 years ago. Ptolemy's information about the African interior, flawed as it may have been, seems too accurate to be dismissed as mere coincidence.

Whatever else, Pangani has an attractive situation. The banks of the Pangani River are heavily forested, and a gorgeous beach stretches to the north of the estuary as far as the eye can see. The town itself is strongly Arabic in feel, and several buildings are said to date back to the slave trade era. Along the waterfront, what appears to have once been a German castle now serves as a sort of 'coconut market', and we picked out at least two Omani mansions in various states of dereliction. There are also several old double-storey buildings with ornate balconies in the small maze of alleys behind the waterfront. The harbour is quite busy, with the main economic impetus apparently coming from traditional fishing. Otherwise Pangani is relaxed and sleepy, and like so many coastal towns, it does not quite seem to belong in the 20th century.

Pangani enjoyed a passing popularity with travellers a few years ago, but on the basis of our most recent visit it seems to have fallen right off the backpacker's map. I'm not sure why this should be. True, if it is prescribed entertainment you are after, then it *is* difficult to think of any compelling reason to visit Pangani. On the other hand, for those travellers to whom travel means something more than careering from one established backpackers' hangout to the next, it is enough perhaps that this strangely time-warped Swahili settlement – like the peaks that captivate mountaineers – should be there at all.

If you do visit Pangani, you might want to ask around about taking a boat up the forested Pangani River, where there is a good chance of seeing a few small mammals, as well as crocodiles and various birds. The Pangani District Council used to charter a ten-seater boat for US$4 per hour, but this no longer seems to be running. However, there are plenty of boats around in the port, so it's simply a matter of finding a willing captain and negotiating a price. There's a good beach in front of the Pangadeco Beach Hotel, but you're advised against taking valuables onto the beach, or from straying too far north from the hotel, as several mugging incidents have been reported.

Getting there and away

A few buses connect Tanga and Pangani daily. In either direction, these leave every two hours or so, and they take roughly two hours. You may also be able to find *matatus* running between Pangani and Muheza, though the only reason you'd be likely to want to do this is if you were heading directly between Pangani and Amani in the Eastern Usambara.

The roads heading south from Pangani to Bagamoyo and the Dar es Salaam highway are little-used. There is no public transport along them. If you want to hitch southwards from Pangani, take the ferry across to the south bank of the river and wait there, but don't expect anything to happen in a rush – if it happens at all!

Where to stay and eat

One of smartest establishments to be found anywhere on the coast of Tanzania, the **Mashado Lodge** (PO Box 14823, Arusha; tel: 057 6585; fax: 057 8020; email: mashado@habari.co.tz) is a fairly recent development perched on a cliff above the south bank of the Pangani River. The resort is primarily designed to cater for game-fishing packages, but other activities can be arranged, for instance excursions to Amani and Saadani Game Reserve. Accommodation starts at US$250pp full board.

At Mkoma Bay, about 2km from Pangani town along the Tanga road, the **Tingatinga Resort** and **Pangani Beach Resort** both have beachfront *banda*

accommodation costing around US$25 s/c double. The Tingatinga Resort can organise various boat and horseback excursions in the area, and both places have a restaurant and bar. We forget to check whether camping is allowed, but neither place is very busy so it's difficult to imagine campers would be turned away. You can make advance enquiries about staying at the Tingatinga Resort at the Tanga Ivory Carvers shop in the Nasaco Building close to the post office in Tanga. These resorts lie no more than 200m from the main road, and any bus heading between Tanga and Pangani can drop you at the turn-off.

So far as we could ascertain, there are only two guesthouses in Pangani town. The better of the two is the **New River View Lodge**, which lies on the main waterfront road perhaps 300m from where the buses stop. This a very clean little place, with running water and electricity when we last stopped by. Rooms with nets cost US$3/6 single/double. The alternative is the **Pangadeco Beach Hotel**, the relatively run-down state of which is arguably compensated for by the excellent beachfront location. This place lies about five minutes' walk from the bus stop. Rooms with nets cost US$3/4 single/double, and the bar has a fridge. A good variety of street food is available along the waterfront road.

SAADANI GAME RESERVE

Saadani is the only East African coastal reserve to harbour large mammals and it is said to be the one place where elephant can still be seen bathing in the Indian Ocean. Saadani protects a wide variety of habitats, including mangrove swamps, coastal thickets and acacia woodland. Animal populations were heavily depleted by poaching in the 1980s, but this is now said to be under control. There is enough game left in the surrounding vicinity for populations to replenish themselves naturally, and the original 300km^2 reserve was recently expanded in area by almost 50% with the government purchase of a well-stocked private game reserve on an adjoining cattle ranch. Resident mammals include leopard, elephant, zebra, greater kudu, Liechtenstein's hartebeest, waterbuck, reedbuck, common duiker, roan antelope, oryx, buffalo, warthog and giraffe, and a small number of lions reputedly still live in the reserve. The bird life is excellent, and the beach is an important nesting site for turtles.

As the nearest game reserve to Dar es Salaam, you might reasonably expect Saadani to be bustling with tourists. In fact, it is one of the least-visited and most underpublicised reserves in Tanzania. In 1992, when researching the first edition of this guide, I met only one person who had visited Saadani, a tour operator from Dar es Salaam, and my own attempts to reach the reserve on public transport proved fruitless both from Pangani and from Bagamoyo. Since then, Saadani has become considerably more accessible, with the clearing of an airstrip and the construction of a tented camp by Tent With a View Safaris, who organise fly-in packages out of Dar es Salaam and Zanzibar. Unfortunately, Saadani remains practically inaccessible to independent travellers – a shame, not least because Saadani would otherwise form part of a most alluring coastal route between Dar es Salaam and Tanga.

The small village of Saadani lies within the reserve on the Pangani-Bagamoyo road. In the early 19th century, Saadani emerged as a major rival to Bagamoyo, but its growth was inhibited by a defensive wall. The wall was built to protect the town's residents from warring Wadoe and Wazigua clans, whose ongoing fighting also dissuaded caravans from passing through the Saadani hinterland. Saadani was briefly considered as a site for the London Missionary Society's first East African mission, but it was passed over in favour of Bagamoyo. If any readers do head out this way, it would be interesting to hear whether there's much to see in the way of

old buildings – in addition to the defensive wall and other Omani period relics, one source claims that the original German customs house in Bagamoyo was 'transported' to Saadani in 1895.

Entrance to the game reserve costs US$20 per person per day.

Getting there and away

Most people who visit Saadani do so as a fly-in package arranged through Tent With a View Safaris (see address below) from Dar es Salaam or Zanzibar.

Coming from Dar es Salaam in a private vehicle, the shortest route on paper is the coastal road via Bagamoyo, but to the best of my knowledge this road has been impassable for the best part of a decade, ever since the government ferry over the Wami River sank. Until such time as the Bagamoyo route becomes viable again, the best route to Saadani is via Chalinze and Miono. Follow the main surfaced road towards Morogoro west out of Dar es Salaam for 105km until you reach the junction town of Chalinze, where you need to turn right as if heading towards Arusha. After 50km, the Arusha road crosses a bridge over the Wami River, and 1.5km further a signpost to your right reads 'Tent With a View Safaris Saadani Game Reserve 58km'. Follow this signposted dirt track through Mandera, Miono (10km) and Mkange (27km), ignoring the signpost to your right for the WWF Forestry Centre (48km) and crossing a railway track (53km) until you reach the reserve entrance gate (58km). From the entrance gate, it's an 8km drive to Saadani village and a further 1km or so to the Tent With a View camp. Parts of this road are *very* rough – it should only be attempted in a good 4x4, and you are advised to ask about the current condition when you book.

Coming from the north, the coastal road from Tanga through Pangani is normally passable, at least in a 4x4 vehicle, but it is also very rough and you are advised to seek local advice before attempting it.

There is certainly no public transport in the coastal road between Dar es Salaam and Saadani, and I've never heard of any between Pangani and Saadani. You can definitely catch a bus from Dar es Salaam to Miono, from where the occasional pick-up truck reputedly continues on to Saadani, but I wouldn't bank on it.

Where to stay

The tented camp run by **Tent With a View Safaris** costs US$85pp per person full-board. Activities run from the camp include driving safaris (US$25pp), dhow safaris (US$25pp) and foot safaris (US$12pp). Contact details are tel: 0811 323318; fax: 051 151106; email: tentview@intafrica.com.

Boldly marked on virtually every map of Tanzania published in the last thirty years, the former government resthouse in Saadani village has spent the last two-thirds of this period quietly attempting to biodegrade. The resthouse was functional in 1992, though even at that time camping in the grounds was probably preferable to taking a room. I have no idea whether the resthouse is still running, but if it is, it will presumably be very cheap.

BAGAMOYO

Situated on a stunning white beach some 70km north of Dar es Salaam, Bagamoyo ranks among the most historically compelling settlements anywhere in East Africa. First settled by traders in the Shirazi era, it peaked in importance in the mid-19th century as a slave trading centre, and remained an important port in the early years of German colonisation. Since then, however, Bagamoyo has waned in significance, a decline testified to by the fact that many of the largest buildings in the modern town date to the Omani and German eras. It

probably offers little consolation to residents of this once-thriving town, but the air of disintegration and stagnation that pervades Bagamoyo does give it an absorbing, museum-like quality.

During the Shirazi era, the main centre of activity on Bagamoyo Beach was Kaole, founded in the 12th century some 5km from modern Bagamoyo. Kaole had strong trade links with Kilwa during the Shirazi era, when it was evidently very wealthy, and it must have enjoyed some prosperity during the Portuguese and Omani periods, which is when most of its decorative graves were erected. It is thought that the modern town of Bagamoyo was founded in the late 18th century as the terminus for the northern slave caravan route. By the mid-19th century approximately 50,000 slaves were shipped from Bagamoyo to Zanzibar annually. Various meanings have been attributed to the name Bagamoyo; *to lose hope* or *where the heart lays down its burden* are two of them. These relate to Bagamoyo being the last place of rest on African soil for captured slaves awaiting shipment.

As the most important mainland port connecting Zanzibar to the caravan routes through the interior, Bagamoyo also became an important springboard for European exploration of Africa. Such Victorian luminaries as Burton, Speke, Grant, Stanley and Livingstone all passed through Bagamoyo at some point in their explorations, and it was their publicising of the horrors of the slave trade that led to the Holy Ghost Fathers establishing a mission at Bagamoyo in 1868. The mission church built at Bagamoyo in 1873 is the oldest in East Africa. It seems fitting that, after his death at Lake Bengweulu in 1873, the preserved body of Livingstone – who called the slave trade 'the open sore of the world' – was carried 1,600km by his porters to the Holy Ghost Mission before being shipped to Zanzibar and England.

The Germans built their headquarters at Bagamoyo in 1888. Stanley arrived there in 1889 after a three-year trip to what was then the Equatoria Province of Egypt (the area north of Lake Albert) and was struck by how it had grown since German occupation. He brought with him the Emin Pasha, the German-born British officer who had defended Equatoria since the fall of Khartoum in 1885. Having survived this, the Emin Pasha – drunk at the time, and notoriously short-sighted – celebrated his safe arrival with a near-fatal fall from the balcony of the officers' mess to the street below. He spent the next six weeks in the mission hospital recovering from head injuries.

Germany eventually deemed Bagamoyo's harbour too shallow for long-term use, and had all but moved their headquarters north to Tanga by 1893. Bagamoyo remained an important regional centre for some years after this (the impressive State House was built in 1897) but its importance has declined steadily since the turn of the century.

Getting there and away

Regular buses to Bagamoyo leave Dar es Salaam from outside Kariakoo Market. The road up is outrageously bad; expect the trip to take four hours. People do visit Bagamoyo as a day trip from Dar es Salaam, but with two long bus trips either side, it is not an attractive prospect. In any case, Bagamoyo deserves an overnight stay.

Hitching between Dar es Salaam and Bagamoyo is relatively easy over weekends, when a number of expatriates go to Bagamoyo. Otherwise, it's probably a complete waste of time.

Where to stay

The last few years has seen the construction of a couple of reasonably upmarket tourist hotels on the beach at Bagamoyo. At the very top of the range is the highly

out. If, like many travellers, you never stray beyond the town centre of quiet, potholed streets lined with German and Asian buildings, Tanga is deceptively sleepy. The hub of Tanga's commercial activity lies away from the centre, in the grid of colourful, crowded streets around the bus station. There is also a well-preserved residential area which sprawls attractively along a wooded peninsula east of the town centre.

Tanga is one of the more modern ports on the coast of Tanzania. Though some sort of fishing settlement must have existed there in Omani times (and before that), it would have been dwarfed in significance by Pangani for most of the 19th century. Tanga's rise to prominence dates from 1892, when it was settled by the Germans after Bagamoyo harbour proved too shallow for their purposes. The first school in German East Africa was built at Tanga in 1893, and a railway line to Moshi was started in the same year. When Dar es Salaam replaced Tanga as the capital, the Germans saw no reason to abandon Tanga as they had Bagamoyo, and its excellent harbour and the rail link to the fertile foothills of Kilimanjaro (completed in 1911) guaranteed its survival. Tanga remains the second-largest port in Tanzania; most of its business comes from sisal exports.

Tanga was the scene of a tragically farcical British raid in the opening stages of World War I. Still seasick after a long voyage from India, 8,000 Asian recruits leapt ashore, got bogged down in the mangroves, stumbled into a swarm of ferocious bees and finally triggered off trip-wires rigged up by the Germans. By the time the raid was aborted, 800 British troops were dead and 500 wounded. In the confusion, 455 rifles, 16 machine guns and 600,000 rounds of ammunition were left on the shore – a major boon to the Germans. This battle forms a pivotal scene in William Boyd's excellent novel *An Ice-cream War*.

Recent years have seen a serious economic decline in Tanga, precipitated by the closure of a number of industries. There has been a corresponding increase in crime, and while the city centre remains reasonably safe, there is a real risk of being mugged if you walk along the road towards the Mkonge Hotel at night, or in the backstreets between the bus and railway stations.

Getting there and away

Regular express buses connect Tanga to Dar es Salaam and Moshi. The trip to Moshi takes around five hours, and the one to Dar es Salaam about six. Several buses daily connect Tanga to Pangani, and a regular stream of minibuses runs between Tanga and Lushoto. Note that the bus station in Tanga lies about ten minutes' walk from the town centre; if you are heavily laden or arrive after dark, you might want to catch a taxi to your hotel.

There are no longer any passenger trains to Tanga. Over the last few years, there have at times been ferry or motorboat services connecting Tanga to the islands of Pemba and Zanzibar, but none lasted very long and nothing appears to be running at the time of writing. It may be possible to catch a fishing dhow between Tanga and Pemba, but this is a dangerous and uncomfortable way of travelling long distances – and it also seems to be illegal for tourists to use dhows.

Where to stay
Upper range
The main cluster of tourist-class accommodation lies in the leafy residential area about 1km out of town along Hospital Road.

Mkonge Hotel PO Box 1544; tel: 053 43440 or 44542; fax: 053 43637; email: bushtrek@tanzanet.com. Part of the Bushtrekker Hotel Group, the Mkonge is ostensibly the most upmarket option in Tanga. Architecturally, it is a rather uninspiring monolith, but it has an attractive location, reasonable facilities, a good bar and restaurant, and (you've

The North Coast

10

The stretch of coast between the Kenya border and Dar es Salaam is not as underdeveloped as the south coast, but it remains surprisingly little-visited by tourists, presumably as a result of having to compete with Zanzibar as the country's main coastal resort area. Like the mountain ranges covered in the previous chapter, the north coast offers little that cannot be seen elsewhere in East Africa, and it can easily be bypassed by those who want to bus directly between Moshi or Arusha and Dar es Salaam. Nevertheless, the north coast is rich in off-the-beaten-track travel possibilities, and it will be highly rewarding to those with the time and initiative to explore them.

The principal town along the north coast is Tanga, a somewhat time-warped port which briefly served as the capital of German East Africa before this role was usurped by Dar es Salaam. Also of interest are the ancient Swahili trading centres of Bagamoyo and Pangani, which lie between Dar es Salaam and Tanga, separated by the remote Saadani Game Reserve.

Climate

This part of Tanzania has a typical coastal climate, hot and humid throughout the year. The short rains fall in November and December and the long rains between March and May. The hottest and most humid period falls between the rains, from mid-December to March. At this time of year, the north coast can be rather oppressive, with daytime temperatures well in excess of 30°C and night-time temperatures rarely falling much below 25°C. By contrast, the period from June to September is much cooler, with temperatures generally dropping below 20°C at night.

Getting around

The surfaced side road to Tanga branches from the B1 between Dar es Salaam and Moshi at Segera. Tanga is connected to both Moshi and Dar es Salaam by regular express buses. There are no longer any passenger train services to Tanga.

This unsurfaced coastal road between Tanga and Dar es Salaam is in poor condition. The stretch between Saadani and Bagamoyo has been impassable for some years, and most other stretches can be navigated in a 4x4 vehicle only. Note that although this chapter works along the coast from south to north, there is no public transport between Bagamoyo and Pangani, so that Bagamoyo is most easily visited as a round trip from Dar es Salaam, and Pangani as a round trip from Tanga.

TANGA

Tanzania's third-largest city and second-busiest port, Tanga is one of my favourite East African towns: relaxed, friendly and atmospheric, and a pleasant place to hang

Top Ruined slave chamber, Zanzibar Island (AZ)

Above Kirk's red colobus, *Procolbus kirkii*, Jozani Forest, Zanzibar (AZ)

Right Woman by a traditional door, Zanzibar Stone Town (AZ)

Dar es Salaam

The largest city in Tanzania, and the country's most
important port, Dar es Salaam may have been stripped of its
status as official capital a few years back, but nobody who
has ever visited the upstart capital of Dodoma will be in
any doubt as to which of these cities is going to remain at
the commercial, social and political heart of Tanzania for the
foreseeable future. Dar es Salaam is the capital of Tanzania in
all but name, a lively, bustling Indian Ocean port which in
modern East Africa is rivalled in maritime significance only by
Mombasa in Kenya.

Dar es Salaam – more often referred to simply as 'Dar' – is not a tourist centre
of any great note. On the contrary, the increasing ease with which one can fly
between Tanzania's main tourist centres means that these days the majority of fly-
in tourists never set foot in Dar. Whether or not this is a good thing is a matter of
opinion: this is one of those cities that draws extreme reactions from travellers, a
real 'love it or hate it' kind of place, and its many detractors would probably regard
any Dar-free itinerary through Tanzania to be a highly desirable state of affairs. But
I must say personally that I like Dar, like it more perhaps than any other major East
African city, since it boasts all the hustle and bustle of somewhere such as Nairobi,
yet has none of that city's underlying aggression or bland architectural modernity.

If nothing else, Dar is imbued with a distinctive sense of place, one derived from
the cultural mix of its people and buildings, not to say a torpid coastal humidity
that permeates every aspect of day-to-day life. Architecturally, the city boasts
elements of German, British, Asian and Arab influences, but it is fundamentally a
Swahili city, and beneath the superficial air of hustle, a laid-back and friendly place.
People are willing to pass away the time with idle chat and will readily help out
strangers, yet tourists are rarely hassled, except in the vicinity of the New Africa
Hotel, where a resident brigade of hissing money-changers froths into action every
time a *mzungu* walks past.

Part of my personal attachment to Dar es Salaam comes from having watched it
undergo a quite remarkable economic renaissance since I first visited Tanzania in
1986. Back then, Dar es Salaam looked decidedly down-at-heel. The streets were
acneous with potholes and the pavements lifeless; shops had long given up the
pretence of having anything to sell; water ran for about an hour on a good day; and
'tourist traffic' was limited to the occasional overland traveller crossing between
eastern and southern Africa. In 1988, when I next passed through Dar, things were
still pretty torpid, but there were definite signs of recovery. By 1992, when I
researched the first edition of this travel guide, Dar had been transformed into a
relatively lively, bustling city, comparable in many ways to Nairobi, and with each
subsequent visit it has become more difficult to recapture the ghost of the weary
urban tip I passed through in 1986. True, many of Dar es Salaam's buildings could

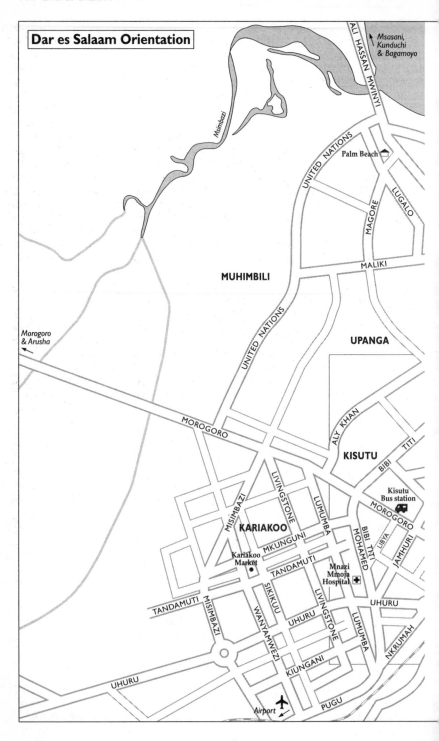

Dar es Salaam Orientation

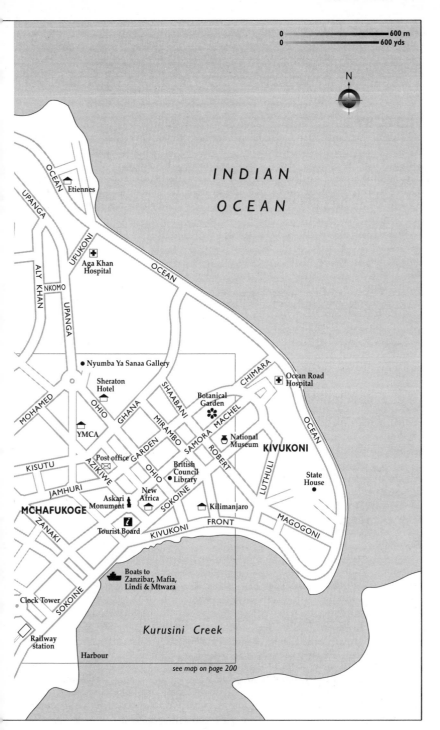

600 m
600 yds

N

INDIAN

OCEAN

OCEAN
Etiennes

UPANGA

ALY KHAN

NKOMO

UFUKONI

Aga Khan
Hospital

UPANGA

OCEAN

● Nyumba Ya Sanaa Gallery

Sheraton
Hotel

MOHAMED

OHIO

GHANA

SHAABANI

MIRAMBO

CHIMARA

Botanical
Garden

SAMORA MACHEL

Ocean Road
Hospital

OCEAN

YMCA

GARDEN

OHIO

National
Museum

ROBERT

KIVUKONI

KISUTU

AZIKIWE

Post office

British
Council
Library

LUTHULI

State
House

JAMHURI

New
Africa

SOKOINE

Askari
Monument

Kilimanjaro

MCHAFUKOGE

ZANAKI

Tourist Board

KIVUKONI

FRONT

MAGOGONI

Boats to
Zanzibar, Mafia,
Lindi & Mtwara

Clock Tower

SOKOINE

Kurusini Creek

Railway
station

Harbour

see map on page 200

do with a scrub and a whitewash, while poverty remains as rife as it does in any large African city. But the overall impression on visiting Dar today is that of a modern, vibrant city: smoothly surfaced streets, pavements spilling over with peddlers and colourful informal markets, well-stocked shops, an increasing number of smart high rise buildings, and water and electricity supplies as reliable as you could hope for.

HISTORY

By coastal standards, Dar es Salaam is a modern town. Until 1862, when Sultan Majid of Zanzibar first visited the area, it was the site of an insignificant fishing village called Mzizima. Majid was so impressed by the natural harbour and surrounding scenery he decided to establish a trading centre. A coral palace called Dar es Salaam (haven of peace) was built in 1866 and a small Arab settlement was established. In 1870, after Majid died, his successor Barghash abandoned all plans for further development.

In 1877 Dar es Salaam was proposed as the starting point for the construction of a road by the anti-slaver Sir William Mackinnon. He hoped the road would encourage legitimate trade between the coast and Lake Nyasa. Known as Mackinnon's Road, the project never took off and was abandoned after 112km had been completed.

Dar es Salaam acquired real significance under German rule. In 1887 a camp was established; four years later the fledgling city was the capital of German East Africa. Between 1893 and 1899 several departments of the colonial government were established there and in 1898 a Roman Catholic Cathedral was built. The construction of the central railway consolidated Dar es Salaam's position; by 1914, when the line was completed, Dar was the country's most significant harbour and trading centre.

Dar es Salaam was captured by a British ship soon after the outbreak of World War I. When German East Africa became Tanganyika, Dar es Salaam remained the capital, and its importance has never been challenged, although the capital is now Dodoma. Dar es Salaam remains the country's economic hub, with a population of around 1.5 million.

GETTING THERE AND AWAY

Dar es Salaam has good local and international transport links. Details of transport to other parts of the country are given throughout this guide, under the relevant town or area, but a brief overview follows:

By air

There are air links between Dar es Salaam and many African and European cities, and domestic flights to most large Tanzanian towns. For further details see the sections on *Flying to Tanzania* in *Chapter 3* and *Air transport* in *Chapter 4*. International and domestic airlines represented in Dar es Salaam are listed under *Airlines* on page 205.

The Dar es Salaam International Airport lies 13km from the city centre, a 20-minute taxi ride which shouldn't cost more than US$10 one-way, though you'll pay a lot more unless you're prepared to bargain. The shuttle bus to the airport, run by Air Tanzania, leaves from in front of the New Africa Hotel every other hour between 08.00 and 16.00, and it returns every other hour between 09.00 and 17.00. The shuttle bus will save you money if you are going out to the airport on your own, but it works out at about the same as a taxi ride for two people, and is more expensive for three. You can get to the airport on a number 67 bus, though I would be hesitant to risk exposing all my valuables in this way, as city buses in Dar es Salaam have something of a reputation for thieves and pickpockets.

By boat

Several boats run between Dar es Salaam and Zanzibar every day, with the more reliable services generally taking around two hours. There are also regular services to Pemba Island, and the *Canadian Spirit* normally travels once weekly to Mtwara on the south coast. All the commercial boat operators have kiosks near the harbour on Sokoine Drive. If you are heading for a place where there is no regular service and have no joy at the harbour, try the Tanzanian Coastal Shipping Line (tel: 26192).

By rail

Trains to northern and western destinations such as Moshi, Mwanza and Kigoma leave from the central railway station on Sokoine Drive. Bookings to these destinations should also be made at this station. Trains to southern destinations such as Ifakara and Mbeya leave from the Tazara Station, 5km from the city centre. The booking office for southbound trains is at Tazara Station. Buses there leave from the Post Office (*Posta*).

Details of all train services are under *By rail* in Chapter 4.

By bus

Some sort of bus service connects Dar es Salaam to virtually every substantial town in Tanzania. There is no central bus station in Dar es Salaam; buses leave from all over the city centre. There is a semblance of a pattern, but it should not be viewed too rigidly.

Buses to Arusha, Moshi and other destinations north of Tanga leave from Kisutu Bus Station, as do most buses to coastal destinations south of Kilwa. This terminal lies on the junction of Morogoro Road and Libya Street, and is often referred to as the Morogoro Road bus station. Most buses to Tanga, Iringa, Mbeya and Songea leave from Mnazi Mmoja on UWT Street. Buses to Bagamoyo, Morogoro and Kilwa and western destinations such as Dodoma and Mwanza generally leave from Kariakoo Terminal, near the synonymous market on Msimbazi Street.

If in doubt, the best place to make enquiries is Kisutu bus station. It is the biggest and the most central bus station, and people seem to have a helpful attitude to travellers.

There is a simple way to navigate through the chaos. Taxi drivers are familiar with the bus system, often speak good English, and, in my experience, are very helpful. Enlisting some knowledgeable support is well worth the price of a taxi-fare (about US$1.50 within the city centre). If you want to leave immediately, a taxi driver is far better equipped than you to cut through the bullshit, find the next bus to leave, and make sure you get a seat.

For long-distance trips, it is worth booking the ticket a day in advance, as this not only guarantees you a seat, but allows you to choose which one you want.

WHERE TO STAY

There are plenty of hotels in the city centre to suit all budgets. It used to be the case that most budget hotels in central Dar would fill up early in the day but, based on our recent visits, it's a lot easier to find a room these days than it was a few years ago. Nevertheless, budget travellers who arrive in Dar late in the afternoon may find it easier to settle for something more expensive and to look for a cheap room on the subsequent morning. Travellers who arrive in Dar after dark stand a high risk of being mugged. Ideally, you should avoid catching a bus that will pull into Dar in the evening, but where there is no choice, then you are strongly advised to look for a room using a taxi.

Although things have improved greatly in recent years, water and electricity cuts are still a real possibility during your stay in Dar es Salaam. If running water is available when you check into your room, I would shower while the going is good.

Upper range

Note that most of the hotels listed below are used primarily by businessmen or by tourists who actually elect to stay near the city centre. There are several more resort-like hotels in this price range situated at beaches some distance further out of Dar. See *Kunduchi* and *Beaches south of Dar* later in this chapter for details.

Dar es Salaam Sheraton Ohio Street, PO Box 791; tel: 051 113525; fax: 051 110725; email: sheratondar@twiga.com. The Sheraton is arguably the top hotel in Dar es Salaam. The attractively decorated rooms have en suite bathrooms, air conditioning, mini-bars and television, and they suffer from none of the shabbiness which characterises most upmarket hotels in Dar es Salaam. The level of service is also a pleasing contrast to the shambling disorganisation you come to expect in many other hotels in the town. There is a 24-hour business centre, and several meeting and business rooms. Other facilities include two restaurants, a shopping arcade, and a gymnasium, sauna and outdoor swimming pool. Ordinary rooms cost US$192/202 s/c single/double exclusive of breakfast, and suites are available ranging in price from US$320 to US$1500.

New Africa Hotel PO Box 9314; tel: 051 117139; fax: 051 116731; e-mail: newafrica@cats-net.com. Recently re-opened following major renovations, the New Africa is the only rival to the Sheraton in the city centre. Built on the site of the legendary Kaiserhof, the first hotel to open in Dar es Salaam at around the turn of the century, the New Africa in its most recent incarnation is a plush and thoroughly modern hotel: all rooms have air-conditioning, satellite television and mini-bar, while services include same-day laundry, international direct dial phone and car rental, and there are two restaurants, a bar and a casino attached. Sad farewells to one casualty of this modernisation, the outdoor bar at the 'old' New Africa, once a popular meeting point with reliably useless service, filling the niche similar to that of the New Stanley in Nairobi. Accommodation at the New Africa costs US$162/192 for a single/double room or US$300 for a double suite.

Sea Cliff Hotel PO Box 3030; tel: 051 600380/7; fax: 051 600476; email: seacliff@tztechno.com; web: www.hotelseacliff.com. A good out-of-town alternative to the above hotels is the recently opened Sea Cliff, which has an attractive seafront setting at the end of Toure Drive on the Msasani Peninsula, a short taxi-ride from the city centre. Facilities include three restaurants and a pastry shop, a swimming pool and gymnasium, and a business centre. Air-conditioned rooms with en-suite showers and satellite television cost between US$150 for a standard double to US$250 for a suite.

Oyster Bay Hotel PO Box 2261; tel: 051 668062/3/4; fax: 051 668631; email: oysterbay-hotel@twiga.com. Another hotel set in seaside suburbia, the Oyster Bay lies about 6km from the city centre on one of the most popular bathing beaches in the Dar area. The restaurant here is very good, and the air-conditioned, sea-facing rooms cost from US$120/150 single/double.

Moderate

Peacock Hotel PO Box 70270; tel: 051 114071; fax: 051 117962; email: mlangila@twiga.com. Arguably the best value in this range, the Peacock Hotel on Bibi Titi Mohammed Street offers self-contained rooms with air-conditioning, hot water, satellite television and fridges at the very reasonable rate of US$60/70 single/double, with a small discount for Tanzanian residents. There is a good restaurant attached.

Starlight Hotel PO Box 3199; tel: 051 137182; fax: 051 119391; email: starlight@cats-net.com. The Starlight Hotel is situated alongside the Peacock, and is similar in standard. It's also very good value at US$40/50 s/c single/double.

Kilimanjaro Hotel PO Box 9574; tel: 051 332099/332100. Once the top hotel in Dar es Salaam, the Kilimanjaro boasts the most attractive location in the city centre, with excellent views over the harbour, but that's about the only thing it has going for it these days. The rooms are looking seriously threadbare, and recent reports from people who have stayed here suggest that both the service and food leave much to be desired. If rumours of an imminent private takeover are to be believed, then perhaps a major refurbishment is on the cards. Rooms cost US$50/60 s/c single/double. The swimming pool is open to non-hotel residents for a fee of roughly US$2.

Embassy Hotel PO Box 3152; tel: 051 117084/6; fax: 051 112634. Of a similar vintage to the Kilimanjaro, and equally run-down, the Embassy charges US$60/70 for a self-contained single/double, or US$40/60 for residents.

Palm Beach Hotel About 20 minutes' walk from the town centre along the Bagamoyo Road, this rambling and rather atmospheric hotel is known as much as anything for its evening barbecues. Rooms are a touch run-down, but air-conditioned, and cost US$35/40 for a self-contained single/double.

Budget
Hostels

Two centrally located places where you should normally have no difficulty finding a room are the **YMCA** (PO Box 767; tel: 051 110833) and **YWCA** (PO Box 2086; tel: 051 122439), which lie a block apart along Maktaba Street. The rooms at the YMCA are small but reasonably clean, and they have nets (but no fans) – fair value at US$13/15 single/double. The YWCA has long been a favourite with couples and single women, and seems slightly better value for money. The rooms are clean, have fans and mosquito nets, and cost US$6 (single), US$9 (double for two women sharing), US$7.50 (compartmentalised double for a couple) and US$15 (self-contained flat). The canteen serves inexpensive if unexciting meals.

Another perennially popular place with a good central location is **Luther House** (PO Box 389; tel: 120734), tucked away in a building behind the main Lutheran Church on the waterfront. It used to be practically impossible to get a room here without booking days in advance, but these days there are normally plenty of vacancies. Little wonder when it's trading on nothing but reputation at US$18/23 for a very tired-looking single/double using communal showers and US$30/37 for a self-contained single/double.

A far better option than any of the above, provided that you don't mind sleeping less centrally, is the excellent **Salvation Army Mgulani Hostel** (tel: 051 851467; email: bamartin@maf.org), which lies 5km out of town on the Kilwa Road. In addition to having a swimming pool and a good restaurant, this place boasts 70 clean self-contained rooms with fans and nets, costing US$6/10/13 single/double/triple.

Near Kisutu bus station

Arguably the best budget hotels in Dar, the **Jambo Inn** (PO Box 5588; tel: 051 114293; fax: 051 113149) lies on Libya Street, a minute's walk from the Morogoro Road bus station, while the nearby **Safari Hotel** (PO Box 21113; tel: 051 119104; fax: 051 116550) is situated at the end of a *cul de sac* off Libya Street. Both of these places are very secure and have been deservedly popular with travellers for as long as I can remember. They offer self-contained rooms with a reliable hot water supply and fans for US$10/16 single/double. Air-conditioned doubles are available at the Safari Hotel

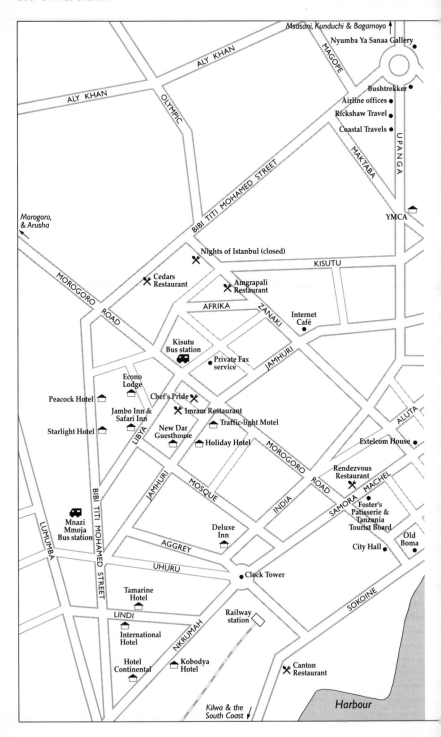

Msasani, Kunduchi & Bagamoyo ↑

Nyumba Ya Sanaa Gallery

ALY KHAN

MAGOPE

ALY KHAN

Bushtrekker ●

OLYMPIC

Airline offices ●

Rickshaw Travel ●

Coastal Travels ●

UPANGA

MAKTABA

BIBI TITI MOHAMED STREET

Morogoro,
& Arusha

YMCA

Nights of Istanbul (closed)

KISUTU

MOROGORO

Cedars
Restaurant

Amgrapali
Restaurant

AFRIKA

ZANAKI

Internet
Café

ROAD

Kisutu
Bus station

● Private Fax
service

JAMHURI

Econo
Lodge

Peacock Hotel

Chef's Pride

Jambo Inn &
Safari Inn

Imrani Restaurant

ALUTA

LIBYA

Traffic-light Motel

Starlight Hotel

New Dar
Guesthouse

Holiday Hotel

Extelcom House ●

JAMHURI

MOROGORO

Rendezvous
Restaurant

MOSQUE

INDIA

ROAD

SAMORA

MACHEL

BIBI TITI MOHAMED STREET

Mnazi
Mmoja
Bus station

Foster's
Patisserie &
Tanzania
Tourist Board

LUMUMBA

Deluxe
Inn

City Hall ●

Old
Boma

AGGREY

UHURU

● Clock Tower

Tamarine
Hotel

SOKOINE

LINDI

Railway
station

International
Hotel

NKRUMAH

Hotel
Continental

Kobodya
Hotel

Canton
Restaurant

Kilwa & the
South Coast ↓

Harbour

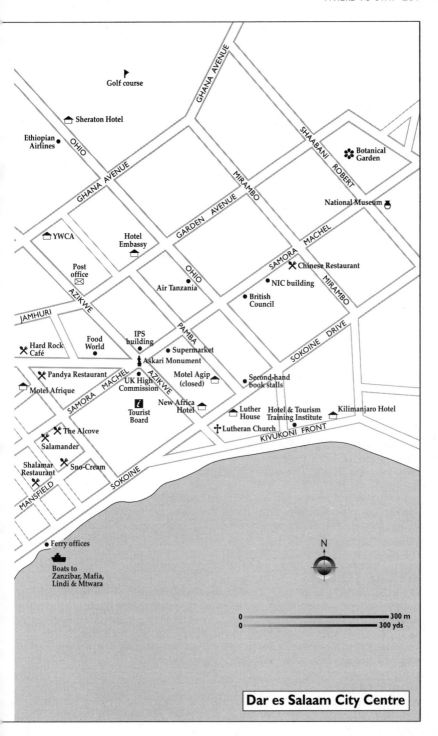

Dar es Salaam City Centre

for US$18 and at the Jambo Inn for US$27. The restaurant on the ground floor of the Jambo Inn serves some of the tastiest and most reasonably priced Indian food you'll find in Tanzania, and a 10% discount on meals is offered to hotel residents.

The **Econo Lodge** (PO Box 8658; tel: 051 116048/9; fax: 051 116053, email: stepin@raha.com) is a much smarter new hotel which spans the gap between the mid-range and budget accommodation. Self-contained rooms with fans cost US$15/23 single/double, while air-conditioned doubles cost US$33. I don't know of any travellers who've stayed here, but on the basis of appearance it is highly recommended.

At the opposite end of the scale, the **New Dar Guesthouse** is a bit of tip, though relatively inexpensive at US$7/8 for a basic single/double with a fan. The **Holiday Hotel** is a similar establishment, where rooms cost around US$8/9 for a single/double. Neither of these hotels feels particularly secure, or has a reliable water supply, and both tend to fill up early in the day.

Around the Clock Tower

The **Hotel Continental** is the least downmarket place to stay in this part of town, which is quite some distance from the main bus station but very close to the railway station. The Continental must once have been quite a smart high-rise hotel, but today it wears an air of neglect which some might conceivably regard as charming, but most will find simply depressing. Still, it isn't bad value at US$15/22 b&b for a self-contained single/double with fan and netting, or US$30 for an air-conditioned double with television and fridge. The chances of this place ever being full are slim, and it's where I'd catch a taxi to were I to arrive in Dar after dark and simply want to find *any* room that isn't ridiculously expensive.

Altogether more cheerful is the **Kobodya Hotel**, which has clean self-contained doubles with hot water, fan and netting for US$10.50. This is probably the best compromise between quality and price available in Dar, for which reason it is often full, but it's certainly worth checking on before you head to any of the other hotels in this area.

Of the rest, the **Tamarine Hotel** is pretty run-down, but it's habitable enough and very reasonably priced at US$4.50/5.50 for a single/double using communal showers and US$7.50 for a self-contained double. Neither the **International Hotel** nor the **Deluxe Inn** are anything special, offering basic doubles with fans for US$9.

Further away from the Clock Tower, the **Motel Afrique** (PO Box 9482, tel: 46557/8) is a conveniently central hotel that slots in somewhere between the budget and mid-range categories. It's reasonably good value at US$7.50 for a single using communal showers and US$21 for a self-contained double with air-conditioning.

WHERE TO EAT

Dar es Salaam has a good range of restaurants to suit all tastes and budgets, and the number of options seems to double every time we return there. Typically, restaurants open for lunch between 12.00 and 15.00 and for dinner between 19.00 and 22.00. Generally food is of a high standard and good value for money. It would be impossible to list every restaurant and *hoteli* in Dar es Salaam, so you might well want to adventure beyond the following recommendations.

Upper range

Most of the large hotels in and around the city centre have at least one restaurant attached. At the very top of the range, and widely regarded to be among the best restaurants in Dar, the **Bandari Grill** on the first floor of the New Africa Hotel serves continental dishes, while the **Saswadee Restaurant** on the ninth floor has an extensive Thai menu. Expect a bill of at least US$15 per head at either of these places. The **Serengeti Restaurant** in the Sheraton prepares sumptuous buffets with a different theme every night; these have been described as the ultimate culinary experience in Dar, but they don't come cheaply at US$32 per head.

The open-air restaurant on the top floor of the Kilimanjaro Hotel has a great view over the harbour, but the food has gone downhill in recent years, and doesn't really justify the price of US$7 for a main course or US$10 for a three-course set menu. The restaurant in the Motel Agip lacks the view of the Kilimanjaro, but it is similar in price and the food is a lot better. The grill on the second floor of the Embassy Hotel serves good steaks and the like in the US$5–6 price range.

The Alcove, a well-established Indian restaurant on Samora Avenue, probably serves the best Indian and Chinese food in the city centre; a main course with rice will cost around US$10. Also recommended in this price range for Indian food is the **Empire Restaurant** above the Empire Cinema on Maktaba Street. Currently being refurbished, the highly rated **Nights of Istanbul** specialises in Indian and Turkish dishes and falls into a similar price bracket. The **Hong Kong Restaurant** around the corner is widely regarded to serve the best Chinese food in the city centre.

The **Hard Rock Café** has an ambience that will be familiar to anybody who has visited one of its namesakes elsewhere in the world. The food is predominantly Western, and nothing too special, but its a good place for a few beers in air-conditioned surrounds (chilled draught is available), the music is varied, and there are pool tables and slot machines upstairs.

There are a great many restaurants of international quality dotted around suburban Dar es Salaam, but these are unlikely to be of interest to the average tourist spending a night in the city. If you want to explore, the obvious place to head for is **The Slipway** (tel: 051 600893 or 600908), an attractively positioned modern shopping complex on Msasani Peninsula. Among the options here are the **Azuma** (Japanese), **Pirates Tavern** (Continental), **Slipway** (pizzas) and **Terrace** (Italian). Also in the Msasani area, the **Dhow Restaurant** in the Hotel Sea Cliff has been described as 'Dar es Salaam's finest eating out experience', while **Smokies Tavern** prepares an excellent rooftop buffet barbecue (meat and seafood) for around US$15 per head, and there is live music on Thursday nights.

One of the most popular out-of-town establishments is the **Europub**, 7km out of town in Kawe off the Old Bagamoyo Road. Set close to the beach, this place does top-quality seafood and Mexican dishes for around US$10, and it also boasts a very lively bar. If you're driving yourself, ring 0811 326969 for directions. Any taxi driver will know where to drop you, but it would be wise to arrange to be collected at a specified time.

Moderate to cheap

The restaurant on the ground floor of the Jambo Inn is arguably the best value for money in the budget range. The extensive menu concentrates on Indian dishes, but it also incorporates a number of Chinese and Western selections. Portions are generous, the food is really tasty, and it's excellent value at around US$3–5 for a main course with rice or naan bread. Food is served throughout the day, and the main menu is supplemented by a tandoor barbecue in the evening. No alcohol is served, but the excellent fresh fruit juice goes some way towards compensating.

Another good Indian place in the same part of town is the **Amgrapoli Restaurant**, which is rather *hoteli*-like in feel, but serves tasty food at very cheap rates. The buffet dinner at the **Pandya Restaurant**, a centrally located Indian vegetarian restaurant, is also great value at around US$4. For inexpensive Chinese food, the **Chinese Restaurant** in the basement of the NIC Building on Samora Avenue has been popular with budget travellers for years, serving a wide range of Chinese dishes in the US$3-5 range. Another firm recommendation is **The Cedars**, a Lebanese restaurant which serves a variety of delicious filled pitta breads for around US$1.50 each.

The centrally located **Salamander Café** has a deserved reputation for serving the best cheap lunches in town. Lunches such as fish and chips and spaghetti bolognaise cost US$3 per serving, and a number of snacks are available throughout the day, though it is closed in the evenings. The air-conditioned snack bar on the ground floor of the Motel Agip serves similar fare at similar prices, and it's open throughout the day. A new place called **Chef's Pride** serves a good selection of snacks and light meals, as well as good fruit juice.

The **Sno-Cream Parlour** is something of a Dar institution, dating back to the days when the city's other ice-cream parlours served nothing but orange juice spiced with flies. These days, the extravagant interior and marvellous sundaes don't have quite the air of surrealism it did back then, but sundaes are still the best in town. Nearby, a newer establishment called **Foster's** serves good coffee and ice-cream, and there is bakery attached.

The best place to buy cheap *mandazi* and other breakfast goodies is outside the post office on Maktaba Avenue.

Bars and nightclubs

There is something of a dearth of decent bars in the centre of Dar, presumably due to the strong Muslim presence, and many hotels and restaurants don't serve alcohol. *The* place for a sensibly priced cold beer used to be the outdoor bar at the New Africa Hotel, which no longer exists. Otherwise, the Hard Rock Café is one of the few genuine drinking holes in the city centre, and the beers aren't as expensive as you might fear. More of a disco than a bar, **Club Bilicanas** is only worth visiting if you intend to settle in for the night, on account of the entrance charge of around US$3 per person. On Kivukoni Front close to the Lutheran Cathedral, the somewhat uninvitingly named **Hotel and Tourism Training Institute** is actually about the earthiest drinking hole in the city centre.

Out of town, among the better places for a drink include Smokies Tavern, Europub and The Slipway, all of which are mentioned in the *Upper range* restaurant listings. You need to hire a taxi or have private transport to reach these places. The **Coco Beach Bar** at Oyster Bay is a good place to while away a day sipping cold beers and eating *mishkaki* kebabs.

TOURIST INFORMATION

The Tanzania Tourist Corporation (TTC) has recently relocated from opposite the New Africa Hotel to a new office on the ground floor of the Matasalamat Building on Samora Avenue. The office is open on weekdays and on Saturday mornings. We found the staff very helpful, but not that knowledgeable when it came to off-the-beaten-track destinations. The address is PO Box 2485, Dar es Salaam; tel: 051 131555 or 120373; fax: 051 116420; email: md@ttb.ud.or.tz.

The bi-monthly **Dar es Salaam Guide**, published by East African Movies Ltd, is a useful source of current information about the city. If you can't locate

AIRLINES

	Address	Tel (051)
Aeroflot	Eminaz Mansion, Samora Avenue	113332
Air France	Peugeot House, cnr Ali Hassan Mwinyi and Bibi Titi	116443
Air India	opp Peugeot House, Bibi Titi St	152642-4
Air Tanzania	ATC Building, Ohio Street	110245-8
Air Zimbabwe	Easy Travel, Hotel Kilimanjaro Lobby	123526
Alliance Air	Raha Towers, cnr Bibi Titi and Maktaba	117044-8
British Airways	Sheraton Hotel, Ohio Street	113820-2
Egypt Air	Matsalamat Building, Samora Avenue	113333
Emirates Air	Haidery Plaza. Ali Mwinyi Road	116100-3
Ethiopian Airlines	TDFL Building, cnr Ohio and Ali Mwinyi	117063-5
Gulf Air	Raha Towers, cnr Bibi Titi and Maktaba	137851-2
Kenya Airways	Peugeot House, cnr Ali Hassan Mwinyi and Bibi Titi	119376-7
KLM	Peugeot House, cnr Ali Hassan Mwinyi and Bibi Titi	113336-7
Swissair	Luther House, Sokoine Drive	118870-2

it elsewhere, a free copy of the magazine should be obtainable from the publisher's office in Mavuno House on Azikiwe Street (tel/fax: 051 111529; email: eam@raha.com) or from the book shop in the foyer of the Sheraton Hotel.

Books

Most bookshops in Dar es Salaam (and in Tanzania for that matter) only stock textbooks, but there are several stalls around the Motel Agip and along Samora Avenue selling second-hand novels and much else besides at very negotiable prices. There are shops or kiosks selling books in the foyers of most tourist class hotels, though the one in the Sheraton tends to be very overpriced. The Novel Idea (tel: 666068) in the Slipway, a shopping mall in the suburb of Msasani, is reputedly the best book shop in town.

The government book shop on Samora Avenue (close to the Askari Monument) mostly stocks textbooks, but it's the best place to buy Swahili dictionaries and phrase books, and will be much cheaper than the street stalls.

The British Council library and reading room has plenty of up-to-date British newspapers and magazines. Membership costs US$2.50 per month. You can sometimes buy recent European and American newspapers at the stalls on Samora Avenue near the Salamander Café.

Cinema and theatre

There are six cinemas in Dar es Salaam. If you are a fan of Indian, kung-fu or gung-ho American war films you will be in your element. Stallone is a massive figure in Tanzania; his face is printed on shopping bags and painted on shops and restaurants. If enthusiastic kids yell 'Rambo' at you don't let it go to your head – they would yell it at Bambi if he happened to be passing.

The only theatre in Dar es Salaam is the *Little Theatre* near Oyster Bay.

The British Council holds weekly film screenings; the programme is posted outside its library.

Communications

The central post office on Azikiwe Street is the place to collect your poste restante, and to buy stamps. There are several kiosks outside the post office selling postcards, envelopes and writing paper.

For international phone calls and faxes, the telecommunications centre is close to the post office, on Simu Street. This is also where you can buy phone cards, which are now more useful than coins when it comes to finding a phone box to use. There are also a few private shops dotted around the city centre offering more efficient international phone and fax facilities at slightly inflated prices. If you're staying in the part of town, there's a good one on Libya St roughly opposite the Kisutu bus terminal.

For internet and email services, visit the Internet Café on Zanaki Street between the junctions with Libya and Jamhuri St. This place offers an hourly internet rate of US$3 or a monthly rate of US$57.50. Sending email costs slightly less than US$1/kb, and international faxes can be sent at US$3 per page. The café's email address is rcl@wilken-dsm.com.

For years, Dar es Salaam had one of the worst telephone exchanges in Africa, and getting through to a number from overseas was a maddening process. The old exchange has recently been replaced, however, and residents now reckon their lines are as reliable as any in East Africa.

Hairdressers

There are unisex salons on the ground floor of the Kilimanjaro Hotel and in the YMCA building.

Maps

The Department of Lands and Surveys building is on Kivukoni Front, about 100m past the Kilimanjaro Hotel. Their map office is not in this building but in a small

EMBASSIES AND DIPLOMATIC MISSIONS

Major embassies and high commissions in Dar es Salaam are listed below. Most are open mornings only and not at all at weekends. Typical hours are 9.00am to 12.30pm, but this varies considerably.

Country	Address	Tel
Algeria	34 Ali Hassan Mwinyi Rd	117619
Belgium	5 Ocean Road, Upanga	112688
Bulgaria	52 Kimweri Rd	113466
Canada	38 Mirambo Close	112831-5
China	2 Kajifcheni Close	667212
Denmark	Ghana Avenue	113887/8
Egypt	24 Garden Ave	113591
Finland	Cnr Mirambo St and Garden Ave	119170
France	Ali Hassan Mwinyi Rd	666021-3
Germany	10th floor, NIC House, Samora Ave	117410/3
Hungary	Plot 204 Chake Chake Rd, Oyster Bay	668573
India	11th Floor, NIC House, Samora Ave	117175/6
Indonesia	299 Ali Hassan Mwinyi Rd	119119
Ireland	Msasani Rd	666211

office tucked away behind a building on the block before it. I had been told buying maps could be a drawn-out process, but I found the staff helpful and the office surprisingly well-stocked. If you plan to hike off the beaten track, 1:50,000 maps of areas such as the Pare, Poroto, Usambara and Udzungwa mountains are available.

The kiosk in the foyer of the New Africa Hotel usually stocks maps of Dar es Salaam and Tanzania; if they don't have what you want, try the TTC office or the bookshop in the Kilimanjaro Hotel.

The recently published *Dar es Salaam City Map and Guide* is accurate, and readily available at most tourist class hotels in the city centre.

Money

Most people change money at one of the numerous forex bureaux which sprang up after the exchange rate was floated a few years ago. Forex bureaux give better rates than banks and are open for longer hours. Rates vary considerably, so shop around before you change large sums. I cannot recommend individual bureaux: the one giving the best rate in town when we first visited Dar es Salaam had dropped almost as low as the bank rate three months later. There are plenty of forex bureaux on Samora Avenue and Zanaki Street.

If you need to change money after the bureaux have closed, you can do so at the airport. It's also possible to do this at any hotel which takes payment in dollars, providing you have a room at that hotel. Do not change money with street dealers. There is no black market worth talking about in Dar es Salaam, but there are plenty of con artists.

Rickshaw Travel is the Tanzanian representative of American Express, and can provide financial services such as emergency cashing of cheques and foreign exchange. Their offices on Ali Hassan Mwinyi Road and in the lobby of the Sheraton Hotel are open from 08.00 to 17.00 on Monday to Saturday. Contact details are PO Box 1889, Dar es Salaam; tel: 051 115110 or 114094; fax: 051

Italy	316 Lugalo Road	115935
Japan	1081 Ali Hassan Mwinyi Rd	115827
Kenya	14th Floor, NIC House, Samora Avenue	112811
Malawi	6th Floor, NIC Life House, Sokoine Drive	113238
Mozambique	25 Garden Avenue	116502
Netherlands	2nd Floor, ATC Building, Ohio Road	118593-7
Norway	Cnr Mirambo St & Garden Ave	118807
Pakistan	149 Malik Road	117630
Poland	63 Ali Kahn Rd	115812
Rwanda	32 Ali Mwinyi Rd	117631
South Africa	Mwaya Rd, Msasani	600484/5
Spain	99B Kinondoni Road	666018/9
Sudan	64 Ali Mwinyi Rd	117641
Sweden	Cnr Mirambo St and Garden Ave	111235
Switzerland	Kinondoni Rd	666008/9
Uganda	7th Floor, Extelcomms House, Samora Ave	117646/7
UK	Hifhadi House, Samora Ave	112953
USA	36 Laibon Road	666010-5
Zambia	cnr Ohio Road and Sokoine Drive	118481/2
Zimbabwe	NIC Life House, Sokoine Drive	116789

113227; email: amex@twiga.com or rickaccts@twiga.com. You can get cash with a credit card at Coastal Travel (see *Tour operators*), though the exchange rate isn't brilliant.

Public transport
The main mode of transport is the *dala-dala*, privately owned minibuses which cover most parts of the city. The most important *dala-dala* is the one outside the new post office on Azikiwe St, but other important stops can be found at the old post office on Sokoine Drive and outside the railway station near the Clock Tower. The route system is confusing for new arrivals which, coupled with the high incidence of theft on both buses and *dala-dalas*, probably makes it rather pointless to try to get to grips with public transport on a short visit to the city. The one exception is if you want to buy a ticket for the Tazara Railway to Zambia, in which case you can hop into a vehicle marked *Vigunguti* at the main post office.

Under no circumstances would I attempt using public transport when I was loaded down with luggage – aside from the crowding, petty theft is a real risk. When you first arrive in town (or at any other time when you are carrying luggage or valuables), use a taxi.

Shopping
Although it has improved greatly in recent years, Dar es Salaam is some way short of being a shopper's paradise. Locally-produced goods are cheapest at stalls such as those lining Maktaba Street. The supermarket on Samora Avenue (see map) is one of many so-called luxury shops, selling a variety of imported foodstuffs and toiletries at inflated prices. I've been told that a supermarket called Supersave, on Kisutu Street, currently offers the best prices on most imported goods. There are several clothes shops and fruit stalls along Zanaki Street. The most colourful place to buy these sort of things is Kariakoo Market (described under *What to Do*). Curio stalls in Dar es Salaam are very expensive when compared to those in Arusha.

The last few years has seen a proliferation of shopping malls constructed in suburban Dar es Salaam. Among the best are the Slipway and Oyster Bay Shopping Centre on the Msasani Peninsula, and the Arcade and Shoppers Paradise on the Old Bagamoyo Road.

Swimming pool
The Missions to Seaman, on Bandari Road near the intersection with Kilwa Road, charges US$3.50 for use of their swimming pool. Good food is available here too.

Taxis
There are taxis all over the place. A good place to find a taxi is in front of the New Africa Hotel, though you are more likely to be overcharged there than elsewhere. The standard price for a ride within the city centre is about US$1.50, though you'll probably be asked slightly more at first.

Tour operators
Most tour operators in Dar es Salaam specialise in visits to the southern reserves. It is more normal to organise northern safaris in Arusha. It is also cheaper, as most tour operators in Dar es Salaam are in the middle to upper range. Some tour companies can do day trips to Bagamoyo. Safaris can usually be arranged through the owners of various camps in the Selous; see *Chapter 16* for details of these.

Because few budget safaris run out of Dar es Salaam, there is no pirate safari industry similar to the one in Arusha, which means that you can be reasonably confident in your dealings with any tour company.

A useful first contact, with an office on Ali Mwinyi Road close to the Sheraton, is **Coastal Travels** (PO Box 3052; tel: 051 117959; fax: 051 118647; email: coastal@twiga.com). This highly regarded company is the main booking agent for many lodges and hotels in southern and central Tanzania, and the islands. It also runs scheduled flights to most major tourist destinations within Tanzania, including Mafia, and arranges personalised safaris throughout Tanzania.

Other well-established tour operators include:

Easy Travel Kilimanjaro Hotel lobby; PO Box 1428; tel: 051 113842
Hippo Tours Kilimanjaro Hotel lobby; PO Box 13842; tel: 0811 320849; email: hippo@twiga.com
Kearsley Travel Indira Gandhi St; PO Box 801; tel: 051 115026-9; fax: 051 115585; email: kearsley@raha.com.
Savannah Tours Sheraton Hotel lobby; PO Box 20517; tel: 051 114339; fax: 051 113736; email: savtour@twiga.com

WHAT TO DO
Dar es Salaam is an interesting city, but not one that offers much in the way of conventional sightseeing. It is worth strolling around the harbour area, and through the backstreets between Maktaba Road and the station. There are several old German buildings in the older part of town near the national museum and botanical gardens.

If you have a couple of days to kill in Dar es Salaam, you might want to spend them at Kunduchi Beach (covered later in this chapter) or Bagamoyo (see *Chapter 10*).

Historical buildings
You can spend a worthwhile couple of hours exploring the several relics of Dar es Salaam's early days which are dotted around the city centre. The oldest surviving building is the **Old Boma** on the corner of Morogoro Road and Sokoine Drive. A plain, rather austere whitewashed monolith, built using coral rubble in the traditional coastal style, the Old Boma is easily recognised by its inscribed Zanzibari door. It was built in 1867 as a hotel to house visitors to the court of Sultan Majid, whose palace stood alongside it, and has since served as the GEAC's first station and the police charge office.

Several late-19th century German buildings have survived into modern times. The **Ocean Road Hospital,** which lies east of the city centre at the end of Samora Avenue, was built in 1897, and is notable for its twin domed towers. The nearby **State House** also dates to a similar time, though it was heavily damaged in World War I, and the modern building, restored in 1922, bears little resemblance to photographs of the original.

The **Lutheran Church** on the corner of Sokoine Drive and Maktaba Road was built in 1898 in a Bavarian style. Following the recent restoration of its exterior, this is a very striking and attractive church, best viewed from the park on Sokoine Drive. A few blocks down on Sokoine Drive, the Gothically influenced **St Joseph's Cathedral** was built between 1897 and 1902. Other buildings dating from the German era include the **City Hall** (on Sokoine Road opposite the Old Boma), several ex-civil servants' residences around the botanical garden, and the buildings housing the Department of Lands and Surveys and Magistrate's Court on Kivukoni Front.

Kariakoo Market

A huge variety of clothes, foodstuffs, spices and traditional medicines can be bought at this lively and colourful covered market which extends on to the surrounding streets in the form of a chaotic miscellany of stalls. The name *Kariakoo* derives from the British Carrier Corps, which was stationed in the area during World War II.

National Museum

This is one of the better museums I have visited in Africa. The section on early hominid development has some of the world's most important fossils. The history displays upstairs have a good selection of exhibits dating back to the era of European exploration and German occupation. If you plan to visit Kilwa Kisiwani, don't miss the display of coins, pottery and other artefacts found during excavations there. Entrance costs US$1.

The area around the museum is notable for its pre-1914 German buildings, recognisable by their red-tiled roofs. The botanical garden, established in 1906 and now pretty run-down, is worth a look, as is the State House, built by the British in 1922. From State House, if you walk back to town along Kivukoni Front, you will be rewarded by good views of the city and harbour. You will also pass the 19th century Lutheran Church, the oldest building in the city.

Nyumba ya Sanaa

This well-known gallery was founded by a nun, and is now housed in an unusually-designed building, erected in 1983 with the help of Norwegian funding. It exhibits arts and crafts made by handicapped people. A variety of carvings, batiks and pottery items can be bought. The standard of craftsmanship is generally regarded to be high. There is a café in the complex.

Oyster Bay

This is the closest swimming beach to the city centre. It is a reasonably attractive spot and very popular at weekends. The Oyster Bay Hotel, which overlooks the beach, is a pleasant place to have a drink. Oyster Bay is difficult to get to using public transport. A taxi from the city centre will cost around US$2.50.

Village Museum and Mwenge Market

The Village Museum consists of life-size replicas of huts built in architectural styles from all over Tanzania. It is open daily from 09.30 to 18.00. There is an entrance fee of US$0.50 as well as a photographic fee of US$1.25 (or US$5.00 for video cameras).

The nearby Mwenge market is a traditional Makonde carving community. It is one of the best places to buy these unique sculptures (see box on page 322). Prices are negotiable.

Both are along the Bagamoyo road, about 10km and 13km from the city centre respectively. To get there, you could board a bus heading towards Bagamoyo and ask to be dropped off. City buses and *matatu*s leave from the post office.

Wildlife Conservation Society

The Wildlife Conservation Society of Tanzania holds monthly talks at their headquarters on Garden Avenue (roughly where the 'a' is on the map).

Kigamboni

A pleasant escape from the city is to take the ferry from Kivukoni to Kigamboni. This leaves throughout the day and charges less than US$1 per person. After disembarking from the ferry, turn left into the road, and after about 2km you will come back to the coast at an attractive beach where there are a couple of bars, and guest houses. Don't walk back to the ferry along the beach, as you will pass through a military area.

KUNDUCHI BEACH

This is Dar es Salaam's major resort beach, situated to the north of the capital, and easily visited either as a day trip or as an alternative to staying in the city. The beach

TINGATINGA PAINTINGS

Visitors to the coast of Tanzania are bound to notice the brightly coloured paintings of fabulous creatures that line the streets of the country's main tourist centres.

These are Tingatinga paintings, unique to Tanzania, and named after their originator Edward Tingatinga. The style arose in Dar es Salaam in the early 1960s, when Tingatinga fused the vibrant and popular work of Congolese immigrants with art traditions indigenous to his Makua homeland in the Mozambique border area (a region well known to aficionados of African art as the home of the Makonde carving). When Tingatinga died in 1972, an accidental victim in a police shoot-out, his commercial success had already spawned a host of imitators, and shortly after that a formal Tingatinga art co-operative was formed with government backing.

In the early days, Tingatinga and his followers produced fairly simple paintings featuring a large, bold and often rather surreal two-dimensional image of one or other African creature on a monotone background. But as the paintings took off commercially, a greater variety of colours came into play, and a trend developed towards the more complex canvases you see today.

Modern Tingatinga paintings typically depict a menagerie of stylised and imaginary birds, fish and mammals against a backdrop of a natural feature such as Kilimanjaro or an abstract panel of dots and whorls. An offshoot style, reputedly initiated by Tingatinga himself, can be seen in the larger, even more detailed canvases that depict a sequence of village or city scenes so busy you could look at them for a hour and still see something fresh.

Tingatinga painters have no pretensions to producing high art. On the contrary, the style has been commercially driven since its inception: even the largest canvases are produced over a matter of days and most painters work limited variations around favourite subjects. It would be missing the point altogether to talk of Tingatinga as traditional African art. With its bold, bright images – tending towards the anthropomorphic, often subtly humorous, always accessible and evocative – Tingatinga might more appropriately be tagged Africa's answer to Pop Art.

Labels aside, souvenir hunters will find Tingatinga paintings to be a lively, original and surprisingly affordable alternative to the identikit wooden animal carvings that are sold throughout East Africa (and, one suspects, left to gather dust in cupboards all over Europe). Take home a Tingatinga panel, and you'll have a quirky but enduring memento of your African trip, something to hang on your wall and derive pleasure from for years to come.

Based on a short article which first appeared in the December 1998 issue of the magazine Discover Africa.

here is attractive and sandy, marred only by concrete piles at regular intervals, reputedly installed to control erosion. It is possible to hire a boat to one of the many small islands dotted along the coast, and most water sports can be arranged.

A short walk from the Kunduchi Beach Hotel, the Kunduchi Ruins are well worth a visit. Little is known about their history, but at least one ruined building, a mosque, dates to the 16th century. The main point of interest, however, is an 18th-century graveyard set amongst a grove of baobab trees. The graves at Kunduchi are notable for being marked by inscribed stone obelisks, a feature not found at any other Swahili graveyard of this period. Pottery collected at the site suggests the town was wealthy and had trade links with China and Britain.

Getting there and away

Kids Transport Service runs a shuttle bus between central Dar and the hotels on Kunduchi Beach. The bus leaves Dar from in front of the New Africa Hotel at 09.00, 14.00 and 17.00 daily, and it leaves from the beaches at around 10.00, 15.00 and 18.00. It stops first at the Kunduchi Beach Hotel, followed by Silversands, Rungwe Oceanic Hotel and the Bahari Beach Hotel. It then returns directly to the city centre.

The trip out takes about an hour. Timings for the return trip are vague. If, for instance, you want to return to Dar es Salaam on the bus which leaves the New Africa at 09.00, it could pass your hotel any time between 09.45 and 10.15.

There are ordinary buses to Kunduchi village, from where you could walk to one of the hotels. This is not recommended, as thefts and mugging are a common occurrence on roads between the hotels.

Where to stay
Upper range
At the top of the range, the **Haven at Kunduchi** (PO Box 23272; tel: 051 650276; fax: 0811 320525) is set in attractive beachfront grounds, and has all the facilities you would expect, including a good restaurant, swimming pool and water sports equipment. Self-contained room with air-conditioning cost US$130/150 single/double full-board.

The attractive **Bahari Beach Hotel** (PO Box 9312; tel: 051 650475-7; fax: 051 650351; email: bushtrek@tanzanet.com) is constructed of coral and thatch in the traditional Swahili style. It has attractive grounds, and facilities include a restaurant, swimming pool, water sports equipment and live music on Sundays. Air-conditioned chalets cost US$90/110 s/c single/double, or US$52/60 for Tanzanian residents. Day visitors are charged a nominal entrance fee.

The **Kunduchi Beach Hotel** (PO Box 9313; tel: 051 138096) is also a very pleasant hotel. All rooms are air-conditioned and sea-facing. There is a restaurant and swimming pool, and boat hire and other water sports can be organised. Rates are slightly cheaper than at the Bahari.

Moderate and camping
The **Rungwe Oceanic Hotel** offers accommodation in comfortable huts, each of which has a fan, mosquito nets and hot water and costs US$25 s/c double. It is a lively place with a bar, a restaurant and a disco, and the adjoining campsite is cheap and popular with overland trucks.

Run by the University of Dar es Salaam, the **Silversands Hotel** (tel: 051 650231; fax: 051 650428; email: silversands@africaonline.co.tz) is a bit run-down but nevertheless pleasant. Facilities include a restaurant and bar, as well as snorkel hire and diving courses. All rooms are self-contained and those with fans cost

US$31/48 single/double while those with air-conditioning cost US$35/54. There is a rather shabby and not very secure looking campsite attached.

BEACH RESORTS SOUTH OF DAR

Two very plush beach resorts lie in blissful isolation along the coast south of Dar es Salaam. About 35km south of the city, **Ras Katuni** (PO Box 1192; tel: 051 128485; fax: 051 112794) lies among the mangroves next to a perfect beach, and the combination of organic building materials and ethnic decor creates a very soothing, relaxed atmosphere. A good selection of water sports is on offer, along with snorkelling and fishing, while the surrounding woodland supports a variety of monkeys and birds. Full-board accommodation costs US$205/270 single/double.

Smarter still is the **Amani Club** (PO Box 1547; tel: 051 600020; fax: 051 602131), which consists of a few air-conditioned self-contained cottages with satellite television and a private verandah. Facilities for fishing, diving and other water sports are available, and there is a swimming pool and tennis court. Full-board accommodation costs US$360/580 single/double inclusive of activities.

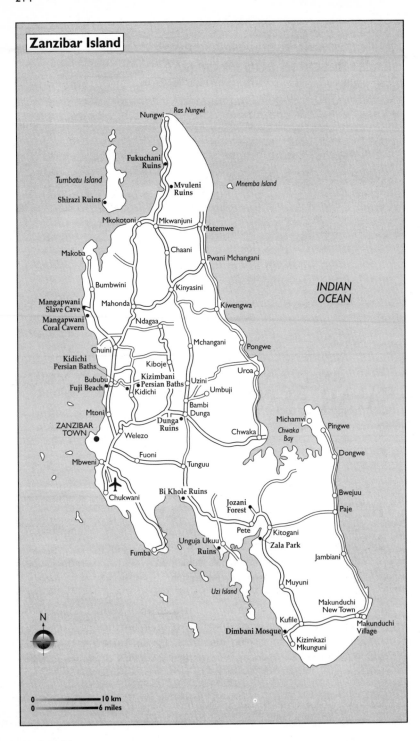

Zanzibar Island

Ras Nungwi
Nungwi

Fukuchani
Ruins

Tumbatu Island

Mvuleni
Ruins

Mnemba Island

Shirazi Ruins

Mkokotoni Mkwanjuni

Matemwe

Makoba

Chaani

Pwani Mchangani

INDIAN
OCEAN

Bumbwini

Kinyasini

Mangapwani
Slave Cave

Mahonda

Kiwengwa

Mangapwani
Coral Cavern

Ndagaa

Chuini

Mchangani

Pongwe

Kidichi
Persian Baths

Kiboje

Uroa

Bububu
Fuji Beach

Kizimbani
Persian Baths
Kidichi

Uzini

Umbuji

Mtoni

Bambi
Dunga

Michamvi

Pingwe

ZANZIBAR
TOWN

Dunga
Ruins

Chwaka

Chwaka
Bay

Welezo

Dongwe

Mbweni

Fuoni

Tunguu

Chukwani

Bi Khole Ruins

Bwejuu

Jozani
Forest

Paje

Pete

Kitogani

Fumba

Unguja Ukuu
Ruins

Zala Park

Jambiani

Uzi Island

Muyuni

Makunduchi
New Town

N

Kufile

Makunduchi
Village

Dimbani Mosque

Kizimkazi
Mkunguni

0 ——— 10 km
0 ——— 6 miles

Zanzibar

by David Else and Philip Briggs

Zanzibar is one of those magical travel names, richly evocative even to the many Westerners who would have no idea where to start looking for it on a global map. Steeped in history, and blessed with a sultry tropical climate and a multitude of idyllic beaches, Zanzibar is also one of those travel destinations that really does live up to expectations. Whether they're after a quick cultural fix or just a palm-lined beach to fall asleep on, everybody agrees that a few days on Zanzibar is the perfect way to round off a dusty safari on the Tanzanian mainland.

A separate state within Tanzania, Zanzibar consists of two large islands, Unguja (Zanzibar Island) and Pemba, plus several smaller islets. Zanzibar Island is about 85km long and between 20km and 30km wide; Pemba is about 75km long and between 15km and 20km wide. Both are flat and low lying, surrounded by coasts of rocky inlets or sandy beaches, with lagoons and mangrove swamps, and coral reefs beyond the shoreline. Farming and fishing are the main occupations on Zanzibar. Most people live in small villages. Cloves are a major export, along with coconut products and other spices. The capital and by far the largest settlement is Zanzibar Town on the west coast.

Zanzibar used to be hard to reach, with a reputation for being expensive and unfriendly. Not any more. The island now positively welcomes tourists, and it offers facilities suitable to all tastes and budgets. For many, the highlight of a stay on Zanzibar is the old Stone Town, with its traditional Swahili atmosphere and wealth of fascinating buildings. For others, it is the sea and the coral reefs, which offer diving, snorkelling and game fishing to compare with anywhere in East Africa. And then there are the clove and coconut plantations that cover the interior of the 'Spice Island', there are the dolphins of Kizimkazi, the colobus monkeys of Jozani and the giant sea turtles of Nungwi... and above all, some will say, those seemingly endless tropical beaches.

Note on authorship The Zanzibar chapter for the first edition of this guide was written by David Else, whose Bradt *Guide to Zanzibar* was and is the only comprehensive guidebook dedicated to the islands. For the third edition of this guide, I have expanded and updated large chunks of the chapter with information based largely on my own visit to the island in October 1998. However, I have not made changes for the sake of it, and have relied on the third edition of David's *Guide to Zanzibar* (published in 1998) for much of the nitty gritty stuff and for detail on Pemba and parts of Zanzibar Island that I didn't get to visit myself.

Climate

Zanzibar has a typical coastal climate, warm to hot all year round and often very humid. It receives more rainfall and is windier than the mainland.

HISTORY

Zanzibar has been trading with ships from Persia, Arabia and India for about 2,000 years. From about the 10th century AD, groups of immigrants from Shiraz (Persia) settled in Zanzibar and mingled with the local Swahili. The Portuguese established a trading station on the site of Zanzibar Town in the early 16th century. At the end of the 17th century they were ousted by Omani Arabs.

In 1840, Sultan Said moved his capital from Muscat to Zanzibar. Many Omani Arabs settled on Zanzibar as rulers and landowners, forming an elite group, while Indian settlers formed a merchant class. The island became an Arab state, an important centre of regional politics, and the focus of a booming slave trade. Britain had interests in Zanzibar throughout the 19th Century; explorers such as Livingstone, Speke and Burton began their expeditions into the African interior from there. In 1890 Zanzibar became a British protectorate.

Zanzibar gained independence from Britain in December 1963. In 1964, the Sultan was overthrown in a revolution. Nearly all Arabs and Indians were expelled. Later the same year, Zanzibar and Tanganyika combined to form the United Republic of Tanzania.

Today, the distinctions between Shirazi or Swahili are often blurred. The islanders fall into three groups: the Hadimu of southern and central Zanzibar, the Tumbatu of Tumbatu Island and northern Zanzibar, and the Pemba of Pemba Island. Many people of mainland origin live on Zanzibar, some the descendants of freed slaves, others more recent immigrants. Many of the Arab, Asian and Goan people expelled in 1964 have since returned.

FURTHER INFORMATION

The only dedicated guide to the islands of Zanzibar and Pemba is David Else's *Guide to Zanzibar* (Bradt Publications, third edition 1998). An extensive range of literature about Zanzibar is stocked at The Gallery on Gizenga Road, Zanzibar Town; email: gallery@swahilicoast.com. The Zanzibar Travel Network can be contacted at info@zanzibar.net; web: http://www.zanzibar.net.

GETTING THERE AND AWAY
By air

An ever-increasing number of airlines offer direct flights between Zanzibar and Dar es Salaam, a 30-minute trip that costs around US$50–60. There are also regular flights to Zanzibar from Kilimanjaro International Airport (between Moshi and Arusha), some of which are direct, taking roughly one hour, while others require a change of plane at Dar and might take three to four hours depending on your connection. The main established airlines covering these routes are Air Tanzania, Precision Air and Coastal Travels, all of which offer a range of other domestic flights (as well as flights to Kenya), so the best choice will depend largely on your other travel plans. Any reliable tour operator will be able to advise you about this.

By boat

A number of hydrofoils and catamarans run between Dar es Salaam and Zanzibar daily, and the booking kiosks for all these boats are clustered together at the ports on Zanzibar and in Dar. New companies seem to come and go with remarkable speed, so there's a lot to be said for asking around before you make any firm arrangements, or by using a tour operator to make your booking (this won't cost much more and saves a lot of hassle). Do be wary of the hustlers who hang around both ports – many are con artists and some are thieves. Tickets must be paid for in hard currency, as must the port tax of US$5.

An efficient boat that's been around for a while is the *Sea Express*, which crosses between Dar and Zanzibar four or five times daily, taking around 70 minutes. Tickets cost US$35, with a port tax of US$5 added, though if you pitch up at the booking kiosk at either port an hour or so before the next crossing, you can normally knock this down to around US$30 inclusive of port tax.

The *Flying Horse* is a slower catamaran which runs once in either direction every day and once at night, taking around three hours for each crossing. The daytime service costs US$30, and probably isn't worth the minor saving over the *Sea Express*, but the night-time service is recommended to those on a tight budget, since it only costs US$15. If you cross by night from Zanzibar to Dar, the boat will arrive at around midnight, but you can sleep on the boat (mattresses are provided) which saves the cost of a night's accommodation.

It is both unsafe and illegal to travel between Zanzibar and the mainland by fishing dhow.

Organised tours

Although a number of local tour operators are listed later in this chapter, it's worth noting that most international companies offering safaris to Tanzania can append a flight to Zanzibar (or a full travel package on the island) to your safari arrangements. Likewise, most safari companies based in Arusha are able to set up excursions to Zanzibar. If you are booking a safari in advance, there is probably a lot to be said for making all your travel arrangements in Tanzania through one company.

Arrival and departure

As Zanzibar is a separate state from mainland Tanzania, *all* visitors are required to complete an immigration card and show their passport and visa upon arrival. Otherwise, entrance formalities are minimal, and you're unlikely to spend longer than a minute being processed. Non-Tanzanians must pay a departure tax of US$20 in hard currency when flying out of Zanzibar Airport on international flights (eg: to Mombasa), and a tax of US$2 for domestic flights.

If you lose your passport while on Zanzibar, you will need to have an Emergency Travel Document issued at the Ministry of the Interior. This will allow you to travel back to the mainland (where nationals of most countries will find diplomatic representation in Dar es Salaam) or directly to your home country.

ZANZIBAR TOWN

Zanzibar's old quarter, usually called the Stone Town, is a fascinating maze of narrow streets and alleyways which lead the visitor past numerous old houses and mosques, ornate palaces, and shops and bazaars. Many buildings in the Stone Town date from the 19th-century slave boom. Houses reflect their builder's wealth: Arab houses have plain outer walls and large front doors leading to an inner courtyard; Indian houses have a more open facade and large balconies decorated with railings and balustrades. Most are still occupied.

A striking feature of many houses is the brass-studded doors and elaborately carved frames. The size of a door and intricacy of its design was an indication of the owner's wealth and status. The use of studs probably originated in Persia or India, where they helped prevent doors being knocked down by war-elephants. In Zanzibar, studs were purely decorative.

The area outside the Stone Town used to be called Ng'ambo (*The Other Side*), and is now called Michenzani (*New City*). Attempts have been made to modernise it: at the centre of Michenzani are some ugly apartment blocks, built by East German engineers as part of an international aid scheme.

Walking is the easiest way to get around Zanzibar Town. Buses, pick-up vans (called *dala-dalas*) and taxis are available. You can also hire bikes and motor-scooters.

Where to stay

It isn't that long ago that even the most robust of budget travellers had difficulty finding acceptable accommodation on Zanzibar, but you'd hardly believe it today. Recent years have seen a positive mushrooming of new hotels in Zanzibar Town, as well as around the island, and there are now numerous options at every level, from basic guesthouses to smart upmarket hotels. As a rule, room rates on Zanzibar are quoted in US dollars, and at the top end of the range the management will probably insist that you pay in hard currency. Our experience was that hotels at the lower end of the price bracket generally accept local currency at an exchange rate similar to those given at forex bureaux.

Most prices include breakfast, though at budget hotels this may amount to little more than a slice of stale bread and a banana. The rates quoted in this guide are high season only, and most upmarket hotels will offer a discount out of season. At the lower end of the price range, rates may be negotiable depending on how busy the hotel is and the intended duration of your stay. It is advisable to make an advance reservation for any upmarket or mid-range hotel, particularly during peak seasons, but this shouldn't be necessary for cheaper lodgings.

Travellers who arrive on Zanzibar by boat can expect to be met by a group of hotel touts. Some are quite aggressive and likely to take you to whichever hotel gives them the largest commission, while others are friendly and will find you a suitable hotel if you tell them what you want. Either way, the service shouldn't cost you anything, since the tout will get a commission from the hotel, and it may save a lot of walking in the confusing alleys of the Stone Town. Given the difficulty of getting past the touts and the general aura of chaos around the ferry port, there is probably a lot to be said for taking the path of least resistance when you first arrive. Should you not like the place you are first directed to, you can always look around yourself once your bags are securely locked away and change hotel the next day.

However you arrive, many of the hotels in the Stone Town cannot be reached by taxi. You are liable to get lost if you strike out on foot without a guide, though we found that people were always very helpful when it came to being pointed in the right direction (bearing mind that the right direction may change every few paces). Most taxi drivers will be prepared to walk you to the hotel of your choice, but they will expect a decent tip.

Upper range

Zanzibar Serena Inn Tel: 054 32277/31015; fax: 054 33019. Bookings can be made at Serena's Arusha office: PO Box 2551, Arusha; tel: 057 8175/6304; fax: 057 8282; email: serena@yako.habari.co.tz. Part of the Serena chain, which also owns lodges in most of the northern game reserves. This hotel, which opened in 1997, is the smartest in the Stone Town, combining international-class accommodation and service with atmospheric Zanzibari decor. The hotel spans two restored buildings on the beachfront, the early 20th-century Extelcomms House and the 19th-century 'Chinese Doctor's residence', the latter where Livingstone slept on one of his many visits to Zanzibar, and later the home of the British consul. In addition to a fine beachfront position, the hotel boasts a swimming pool, bar, restaurant, coffee shop, curio shop and business centre. Large air-conditioned rooms with a sea-facing balcony, mosquito nets, television, and en-suite bathroom cost US\$130/180 single/double b&b. Cheaper midweek rates may sometimes be available through travel agents.

Tembo Hotel PO Box 3974; tel: 054 33005. Around the corner from the Serena, this is another smart hotel set in a restored old residence, combining an excellent beachfront position with ready access to the Stone Town. Facilities include a good restaurant, swimming pool and curio shop. Air-conditioned doubles with en-suite bathrooms cost US$100.

Emerson's House PO Box 4044; tel: 054 32153/30609; fax: 057 33135; email: emerson@africaonline.co.tz. Set in the heart of the Stone Town, in a 19th-century building that originally served as the residence of Sultan Barghash's brother, Emerson's House has been completely restored and furnished in traditional Zanzibari style, leading to it being listed by the British *Sunday Times* as 'one of the great little hotels of the world'. One of the oldest upmarket hotels in Zanzibar, opened about ten years ago, Emerson's doesn't offer bland luxury (the rooms have no air-conditioning, television or fridge) but it *is* highly recommended to those who want to live out their Arabian Nights fantasies while in Zanzibar. Because the hotel has been restored rather than custom-built, each of the rooms is very different in shape and decor, but all have mosquito nets and fans. Rooms cost from US$60 to US$85.

Emerson's and Green PO Box 4044; tel: 054 30171/30609; fax: 054 31038; email: emegre@zanzibar.org. At one time the second-tallest building in the Stone Town, this hotel consists of two adjoining buildings, one of which dates to the early 1800s and the other to the 1870s, when it was the residence of Tharia Topan, the principal financial advisor to Sultan Barghash. In imminent danger of collapse when Emerson (of Emerson's House) and his partner Tom Green bought it in 1994, the building has been faithfully restored and lavishly decorated in period style, and opened as a hotel in 1997. The atmosphere is much like that of the original Emerson's House, though the rooms are larger and more elaborately furnished, with high ceilings, fans, good ventilation through traditional shutters, amazing en-suite bathrooms and netted Arabic four poster beds. The rooftop restaurant offers excellent views over some of the major landmarks in the Stone Town to the harbour, as well as serving some of the best food in town. Double rooms cost US$120.

Mbweni Ruins Hotel PO Box 2542; tel: 054 31832; fax: 054 30536; email: mbweni-ruins@twiga.com. Situated a few kilometres south of town, off the airport road, this exclusive hotel lies in the grounds of the Mbweni Ruins, the remains of a mission school built in the 1870s for freed slaves, and close to St Johns Anglican Church, built in 1882. It is set in attractive, well-maintained grounds overlooking the sea, and the nearby mangroves will be alluring to birders. Facilities include a private beach, swimming pool, nature trail, botanical garden, natural heath centre, airport and town shuttle service, top class restaurant, and boat trips to the nearby islands. Accommodation in air-conditioned rooms with en-suite bathroom costs US$90 per person b&b or US$115 per person full-board.

Fisherman's Resort PO Box 2586; tel: 054 30208; fax: 054 30556. Formerly the Zanzibar Reef Hotel, this large resort-like hotel lies about 7km from the Stone Town and 3km from the airport. The landscaped gardens overlook the sea, and facilities include a restaurant, bar, disco, squash court, sauna, gym, swimming pool, and fishing and water sport equipment. Double rooms with air-conditioning and en-suite bathroom cost US$150 or US$180, depending on whether they are sea-facing.

Mid-range

Built on what is now Kenyatta Road in the early 1800s by Said bin Dhahin, one of the first Omani Arabs to settle on Zanzibar, **Mazson's Hotel** (PO Box 3367; tel: 054 33694; fax: 054 33695) first served as a hotel in the early 20th century before becoming a private residence. Now fully restored, the communal areas are decorated in period style, though the air-conditioned self-contained rooms are rather soulless. Facilities include satellite television and a business centre. Accommodation starts at US$48/64 single/double.

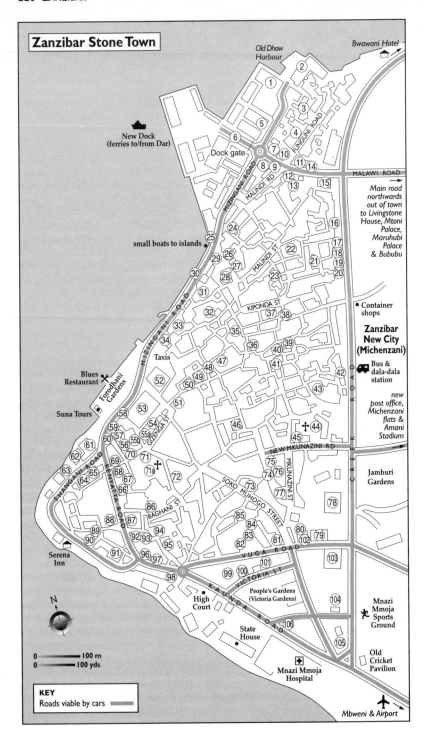

Zanzibar Stone Town

Old Dhow Harbour

Bwawani Hotel

New Dock
(ferries to/from Dar)

Dock gate

MALAWI ROAD

Main road
northwards
out of town
to Livingstone
House, Mtoni
Palace,
Maruhubi
Palace
& Bububu

small boats to islands

MIZINGANI ROAD

MALINDI RD

FUNGUNI ROAD

MALINDI ST

KIPONDA ST

Container
shops

**Zanzibar
New City
(Michenzani)**

Bus &
dala-dala
station

new
post office,
Michenzani
flats &
Amani
Stadium

Taxis

Blues
Restaurant

Forodhani
Gardens

Suna Tours

MIZINGANI ROAD

GIZENGA ST

NEW MKUNAZINI RD

MKUNAZINI ST

CREEK ROAD

Jamhuri
Gardens

S. HANGANI ROAD

KENYATTA ROAD

BAGHANI ST

SOKO MUHOGO STREET

Serena
Inn

VUGA ROAD

VICTORIA ST

People's Gardens
(Victoria Gardens)

Mnazi
Mmoja Sports
Ground

KAUNDA ROAD

High
Court

State
House

Old
Cricket
Pavilion

Mnazi Mmoja
Hospital

N

0 — 100 m
0 — 100 yds

Mbweni & Airport

KEY
Roads viable by cars

KEY

1 Clove Distillery
2 Pagoda Chinese Restaurant
3 Malindi Guesthouse
4 Warere Guesthouse
5 Fish Market
6 Shipping company offices (most in this area)
7 Ciné Afrique
8 Malindi Restaurant
9 DHL office
10 Malindi Guesthouse Annexe
11 Malindi Sports Club (dhow tickets)
12 Passing Show Restaurant
13 ZanAir
14 Petrol station
15 Malindi Police Station
16 Al Jabry Restaurant
17 People's Bank of Zanzibar
18 Zanzibar Tourist Corporation
19 Petrol station
20 Taxi rank
21 Karwan Serai Hotel
22 Narrow Street Hotel
23 Pyramid Guesthouse
24 Old Dispensary
25 Pychi's
26 Gulf Air
27 Ijumaa Mosque
28 Kenya Airways, Oman Air, Mega Speed Liners
29 The Big Tree
30 Sea View Indian Restaurant
31 Old Custom House
32 Kiponda Hotel
33 Palace Museum (People's Palace)
34 1001 Nights
35 Aga Khan Mosque
36 Spice Inn
37 Ithnasheri Mosque
38 Narrow Street Hotel Annexe II
39 House of Spice
40 Hotel International
41 Emerson's House
42 Market
43 Masumo Bookshop
44 Anglican Cathedral/UMCA
45 St Monica's Hotel
46 Hamamni Baths
47 Emerson's and Green Hotel
48 Bottoms Up Bar
49 Clove Hotel
50 Zanzibar Curio Shop
51 Sama Tours
52 House of Wonders
53 Arab Fort
54 The Gallery

55a People's Bank of Zanzibar (main building)
55b People's Bank of Zanzibar (foreign exchange)
56 Coco de Mer Hotel
57 Karibu Inn
58 Orphanage
59 Le Bistrot
60 National Bank of Commerce
61 Old British Consulate
62 Tembo Hotel
63 Starehe Club
64 Fisherman Restaurant
65 Le Pecheur Bar
66 Air Zanzibar
67 Blue Ocean Hotel
68 Post office
69 Luna Mare Restaurant
70 Luis Yoghurt Shop
71 Fahaud Medical Centre
71a St Joseph's Catholic Cathedral
72 Chit Chit Restaurant
73 Equator Tours
74 Green Garden Restaurant
75 Zanzibar Roots Gallery
76 Jambo Guesthouse
77 Flamingo Hotel
78 Haile Selassie School
79 Kiswahili Institute
80 Air Tanzania
81 Fisherman Tours, Maha Tours
82 Florida Guesthouse
83 Culture Music Club
84 Haven Hotel
85 Manch Lodge
86 Chavda Hotel
87 Sunrise Restaurant and Pub
88 Mazson's Hotel
89 Tippu Tip's House
90 Jasfa Tours
91 Africa House Hotel
92 Dhow Palace Hotel
93 Baghani House Hotel
94 Zanzibar Hotel
95 Afya Medical Centre
96 Camlur's Restaurant
97 Maharaja Restaurant
98 Chemah Brothers Tours
99 Two Tables Restaurant
100 Bar Baraza
101 Victoria Guesthouse
102 Majestic Cinema
103 Ben Bella School
104 Peace Memorial Museum Annexe
105 Peace Memorial Museum
106 Zanzibar Milestone

Close by, on an alley leading off the opposite side of Kenyatta Road, the **Baghani House Hotel** (PO Box 609; tel: 054 20165; fax: 054 31816) is a small, friendly place that offers self-contained, air-conditioned rooms in the US$40-70 range. Practically next door to this, the **Dhow Palace Hotel** (PO Box 3974; tel: 054 33012; fax: 054 33008) is similar in price and standard, set in a renovated old house built around a cool central courtyard. The rooms come complete with Persian baths, and lack only sea views. Accommodation starts at US$50/60 single/double.

About 100m further back on Kenyatta Road, close to the old post office, the **Shangani Hotel** (PO Box 4222; tel: 054 33524; fax: 054 33688) offers comfortable air-conditioned double rooms with en-suite bathroom at US$55.

Elsewhere in town, the **Hotel International** (PO Box 3784; tel: 054 33182; fax: 054 30052) near Emerson's House is yet another former residence that has been restored as a hotel. The decor is relatively modern, but very comfortable, and en-suite double rooms with satellite television and air-conditioning start at US$55. The **Kirwan Serai** (PO Box 145, tel/fax: 054 33524 or 33186) is a modern building constructed in traditional Zanzibari style, with tasteful en-suite doubles for US$60.

Budget

Budget accommodation in Zanzibar ranges from a number of modest but comfortable hotels offering double rooms in the US$30–40 range, down to a selection of local guesthouses of the sort you find on the mainland, though relatively pricey at around US$8-10 per person.

One of the best options in the upper end of the budget range is the **Hotel Kiponda**, is a small, quiet hotel which previously served as a Sultan's harem and has been renovated in period style. Consistently popular with travellers, and described by one as a 'budget Emerson's', the Kiponda has plenty of character and a welcoming atmosphere, as well as a convenient location close to the seafront. All in all, good value at US$18/35 single/double.

Similar in price, but lacking the atmosphere, the **Blue Ocean Hotel** (PO Box 4052; tel: 054 33566) off Kenyatta Road charges US$20 per person for functional self-contained rooms. Also lying just off Kenyatta Road, the **Coco de Mer Hotel** (PO Box 2363; tel: 054 30852) is a clean, friendly place where self-contained rooms cost US$25/35 single/double. In the same part of town, roughly opposite the Tembo Hotel, the **Stone Town Inn** (PO Box 3530; tel: 054 33101, fax: 054 33060) has clean rooms using communal showers at US$15 per person, as well as self-contained doubles for US$50. At the other end of the Stone Town, the **Narrow Street Hotel Annex II** (PO Box 3784; tel: 054 33006, fax: 054 30052) is fairly popular with travellers and acceptable value at US$40 for a self-contained room with netting, air-conditioning and Zanzibari-style beds.

A good out-of-town option in this range, situated on the road to the airport, is the new **Island View Hotel** (tel: 054 32666), where clean self-contained doubles with a fan and netting cost US$25. There is no restaurant here at the time of writing, but the owners are helpful about lifts into town during the day and in the evening. This would be a useful option should you arrive in Zanzibar late in the day and not want to muck about looking for a room in the alleys of the Stone Town after dark.

The **Africa House Hotel** (PO Box 216; tel: 054 30708) is a building of some antiquity which served as the English Club from 1888 until the end of the colonial era. At the time of writing, it is very seedy and run-down, certainly not worth the asking rate of around US$30 for a double room, though there is some talk of renovating the place in the mid-term. An added discouragement against staying here is that it seems to serve as the operations centre for most of the island's touts. On the plus side, the sea-facing balcony is a wonderful place for a sundowner.

Dropping in price, most of the lodgings used by backpackers lie in the Malindi area, near the harbour. The **Malindi Guesthouse** (PO Box 609; tel: 054 30165) has been consistently popular with travellers for years and is reasonably priced at US$10 per person. Also recommended is the **Pyramid Guesthouse** (PO Box 254; tel: 054 33000, fax: 054 30045), which lies behind the Ijumaa mosque near the sea-front, and charges US$10 per person for a room using communal showers or US$15 per person for a self-contained room. Another reliable bet is the **Riverman Hotel** (PO Box 1805; tel: 054 33188), which has good facilities and clean rooms with nets and fans for US$10 per person.

St Monica's Hostel near the Anglican Cathedral offers clean, secure accommodation for US$12 per person. Near the People's Gardens, the **Victoria Guesthouse** (tel: 054 32861) and **Garden Lodge** (tel: 054 33298) are both unremarkable but adequately clean places with doubles for around US$16. A newer place that's been recommended by several travellers is the **Haven Hotel** (tel: 054 33454), where clean rooms using communal hot showers cost US$10/16 single/double.

Two of the most popular places with travellers on a strict budget are the **Warere Guesthouse** (tel: 054 31187) and **Flamingo Guesthouse** (tel: 054 32850), both of which charge US$7 per person. The **Bottoms Up Guesthouse** is rather more seedy, and difficult to find in the alleys between the Spice Inn and the House of Wonders, but it is popular with backpackers for its book-swap service, cheap and lively bar. Rooms also cost US$7 per person.

Where to eat

There are now dozens of restaurants catering specifically to tourists, and the following serves as an introduction only.

At the top end of the range, **Emerson's House** has been serving quality food for years, while the rooftop restaurant at Emerson's and Green is generally regarded to live up to its billing as the 'best on the island'. At both places, the fixed menu dinner is a languid affair stretched over the whole evening, and the emphasis is on seafood. Dinner normally costs around US$20 per person, though the price rises to US$25 on evenings when the meal is accompanied by traditional dancing. Space is limited and booking is essential.

There are a few good places to eat on the Stone Town seafront. The newest and trendiest spot in this area is **Blues**, sister to the synonymous restaurant in Cape Town, which serves seafood, pizzas and grills starting at around US$8-10 for a main course. The food at this floating restaurant is as good as any we've had in Tanzania, with the option of eating inside or on the wooden balcony, but the atmosphere lacks for anything that might be called distinctively Zanzibari. Further north along the seafront, **Pychi's** is a great spot for a sundowner, and it serves the best fruit juice in the Stone Town, but the pizzas are pretty uninspiring and small. The nearby **Sea View Indian Restaurant** serves a range of cheap snacks and good fruit juice, as well as a selection of top curries in the US$7-10 range.

Other recommended restaurants and hotels serving main courses in the US$5-10 range include the **Hotel Kiponda** (Zanzibari dishes and sea food), the **Serena Zanzibar Inn** (Continental and sea food), the **Fisherman Restaurant** on Shangani Road (sea food and grills), **Camlur's** on Kenyatta Street (Goan dishes), the **Chit-Chat Restaurant** on Kenyatta Street (Zanzibari and Goan dishes), the **Pagoda Chinese Restaurant** on the north end of the Stone Town (authentic

Chinese food) and **Luna Mare Restaurant** on Gizenga Street (European, Indian and Chinese). There are plenty more to choose from, and the level of competition for custom means that standards are generally reflected by prices.

The **Old Arab Fort** on the seafront puts on displays of traditional dancing at least three times weekly, more often in peak season, accompanied by a reasonable buffet barbecue. Entrance costs US$10 per person, assuming that you want to eat, or US$5 per person to see the dancing only.

The cheapest place to eat in the Stone Town is at **Forodhani Gardens**, opposite the fort, where dozens of vendors serve freshly grilled meat, chicken, fish, calamari, prawns with salad and chips or naan bread. This is far and away the best street food we've come across anywhere in Africa, and you'd have to be seriously hungry or prawn-obsessed not to come back with change from US$3. The stalls in the gardens cater primarily to locals, but plenty of travellers eat here, and many return night after night.

You can eat cheaply in the evening in the Malindi area, near the Ciné Afrique Cinema, where stalls sell cakes, chapatis, samosas and *mandazi*. In the nearby streets several simple and inexpensive eating houses cater mainly for locals, including the **Malindi Restaurant**, **Malkiya Restaurant**, **Al Jabry Restaurant** and the **Passing Show Hotel**.

About the cheapest place for a sit-down meal in the southern end of the Stone Town is the **Dolphin Restaurant** on Kenyatta Road, which serves a wide range of curries and grills for up to US$3 per portion, slightly more if you want to order a tasty side-plate of stir-fried vegetables. The food here is remarkably good at the price, and the service is friendly.

Most tourist restaurants serve beer and many of the larger hotels have separate bars. The roof-top bar at the **Africa House Hotel** is popular at sunset, as is the seafront bar at **Pichy's**. The **Livingstone Bar** in the Baghani House Hotel and **Le Pecheur Bar** next to the Fisherman Restaurant are about the nearest things in Zanzibar to a pub. Both are popular with expatriates, though the latter attracts a fair number of prostitutes and can get dauntingly lively later in the evening. Cheaper beer is available at the seafront **Cave Disco** (near the Tembo Hotel) and the **New Happy Bar** (a few doors down from the Africa House Hotel), since both cater to a predominantly local clientele. The **Garage Club** near the Tembo Hotel is the newest and busiest disco in the Stone Town.

Useful information

The Zanzibar Tourist Corporation head office, in Livingstone House, about 1km from the town centre along the Bububu Road, is the best place to make bookings for the ZTC bungalows on the east coast. For general information, the ZTC office on Creek Road will probably be more clued-up and helpful.

Air companies

The Air Tanzania office is on Vuga Road, near its junction with Creek Road. The Kenya Airways office is at the northern end of Creek Road. Air Zanzibar Ltd (PO Box 1784; tel: 33098) charter flights throughout East Africa. If a plane is flying empty, spare seats are sold to the public. Seats on the newspaper-plane to Dar es Salaam are sold at Masumo Bookshop near the market and cost around US$40.

Books and newspapers

Newspapers from the mainland and Kenya can be bought at Masumo Bookshop behind the market, along with a limited selection of international magazines and paperback novels. Most of the upmarket hotels have curio shops selling guide books, field guides and glossier publications about Zanzibar and East Africa, as does the gallery on Gizenga Street.

Communications
The main post office, which lies outside the Stone Town towards the stadium, is the place to collect poste restante mail addressed to Zanzibar. Other postal transactions can be conducted more conveniently at the old post office on Kenyatta Road. The old post office is also a good place from which to make international phone calls and send faxes, though the private services offered by Zanzibar Global Communications (near the Flamingo Guesthouse) and Next Step Services on Gizenga Street aren't a great deal more expensive and are generally more efficient. Next Step offers e-mail services; the address is step@www.intafrica.com.

Foreign exchange
A number of banks and forex bureaux are dotted around the Stone Town, offering similar exchange rates to those on the mainland. Forex bureaux generally give a marginally higher rates than banks, and they tend to be more efficient, but they may not accept travellers' cheques or relatively obscure currencies. The forex bureau in the International Hotel is efficient and offers good rates, and so far as I'm aware it is the only place in Zanzibar where anybody can change money over the weekend. Avoid changing money at the Commercial Bank of Zanzibar, as it offers very poor rates.

Although most upmarket hotels will accept the major credit cards, drawing money against a credit card is either impossible or expensive. The one exception is Mtoni Marine Centre, the official agent for Visa International, which will allow you to draw funds against a visa card with a minimum of fuss and expense.

Maps
The most accurate and attractive map of the Stone Town is Giovanni Tombazzi's *Map of Zanzibar Stone Town*, which also has a good map of the island on the flip side. Giovanni has lived in the Stone Town for several years, and he spent days pacing the alleys taking distance measurements with a bicycle milometer to ensure the map is more accurate than any of its predecessors. You can buy this map for around US$5 at most upmarket hotels and curio shops.

Survey maps of the island are sold for around US$2 each at the map office in the Commission of Lands and Surveys in the Ministry of Environment building near the old fort and People's Bank of Zanzibar.

Medical facilities
The Zanzibar Medical and Diagnostic Centre (tel: 054 33113, after hours: 33062), which lies off Vuga Road near the Majestic Cinema, is regarded to have the best doctors on the island, and is run to Western standards. For cheap malaria tests, the Fahaud Health Centre near St Joseph's Cathedral has been recommended, and it normally sells various malarial cures.

The main public hospital on Zanzibar Island is at Mnazi Moja, on the south side of the Stone Town. Other private medical centres include Island Private Hospital on Soko Muhogo Street (tel: 054 31837) Afya Medical Hospital near the Zanzibar Hotel (tel: 054 31228) and Mkunazini Hospital near the market (tel: 054 30076).

Swahili lessons
The Taasisi KiSwahili Institute on Vuga Road offers week-long courses for US$80.

Spice Tours and other excursions

The one organised trip that practically all visitors to Zanzibar undertake is a 'spice tour', something that would be logistically difficult to set up independently, and which relies heavily on the local knowledge of a guide. In addition to visiting a few spice plantations, most spice tours include a walk around a cultivated rural homestead, as well as a visit to one of the island's ruins. A traditional Swahili lunch is normally included in the price, which can range from US$10 to US$35 per person.

Several other short excursions can be undertaken out of Zanzibar Town, and while most visitors seem to prefer to do their exploring in the form of an organised day tour, most places of interest on the island *can* be visited independently. Popular excursions from the Stone Town include a boat trip to one or more of the nearby islands, a visit to the dolphins at Kizimkazi, and a trip to Jozani forest to see the endemic Kirk's red colobus. Also easily explored from Zanzibar is the 10km of coastline stretching northwards to the small seaside settlement of Bububu, which boasts a number of interesting ruins, while Fuji Beach at Bububu is the closest public swimming beach to the Stone Town. In fact, the only parts of Zanzibar which are more often visited for a few nights than as a day trip are Nungwi and Mnemba Island in the north, and the several beach resorts that line the east coast of the island.

A number of tour companies operate out of Zanzibar Town, offering the tours mentioned above as well as transfers to the east coast and Nungwi. The better companies can set up bespoke trips to anywhere on the island, as well as make hotel reservations and other travel arrangements. For straightforward day trips and transfers, there is no real need to make bookings before you arrive in Zanzibar, as they can easily be set up at the last minute. If, however, you want to have all your travel arrangements fixed in advance through one company, or you have severe time restrictions, then it would be sensible to make advance contact with one of the companies with good international connections.

While prices vary greatly depending on standard of service, season and group size, the typical cost per person for the most popular outings are US$20 for a Stone Town tour, US$15 for a Prison Island tour, US$35 for a spice tour, US$35 for a trip to Jozani Forest and US$45 for a Kizimkazi dolphin tour. Prices are negotiable, particularly out of season when a group of ten people might be able to fix up a spice tour with a reputable company for as little as US$10 per head, but do be wary of unregistered companies offering sub-standard trips at very low rates.

It's possible to arrange many of the standard tours more cheaply through taxi drivers or independent guides (nicknamed *papaasi* after a type of insect). With spice tours, this may often turn out to be a false economy, in that the guide will lack botanical knowledge and may cut the excursion short, rendering the whole exercise somewhat pointless. One taxi driver who *has* been consistently recommended by travellers over many years is Mr Mitu; his spice tours leave every morning from in front of the Ciné Afrique, though these days they are so popular that you might find yourself joining a fleet of minibuses rather than hopping into Mr Mitu's own vehicle! It makes little difference whether you use *papaasi* to set up trips to the island, because specialist knowledge isn't required, and you can agree in advance how long you want to spend on any given island.

You can assume that any tour operator working through one of the upmarket hotels will be reliable and accountable, bearing in mind that they will deal primarily with a captive big-spending clientele, so their costs may be somewhat inflated. A list of a few recommended and well-established tour companies follows. Most of them offer a pretty similar selection of trips at reasonably uniform prices, and can also make flight, ferry and hotel bookings, so I have only made additional comments where necessary.

Chemah Brothers Tours & Safaris PO Box 1865; tel/fax 054 33385; mobile 0812 750158

Fisherman Tours PO Box 3537; tel: 054 33060; fax: 054 33762; email: fisherman@costech.gn.apc.org. Office on Vuga Road near Air Tanzania. In addition to the normal services, can arrange safari excursions to mainland Tanzania.

Jasfa Tours PO Box 4203; tel: 054 30016. Office near Africa House Hotel. English, French, Spanish and Arabic speaking guides.

Maha Travel Tel: 054 30029, fax: 054 30016. Office on Vuga Road. Agents for Precision Air.

Rainbow Tours PO Box 2173; tel/fax: 054 33469; fax: 054 33701. Office on Gizenga Street. Standard tours plus specialised trips to Jozani, Kizimkazi dolphins and Pemba Island, and game fishing and sailing.

Sama Tours PO Box 2276; tel/fax: 054 33543; email: next@zanzinet.com. UK agent Footloose Adventure Travel; tel: +44 1943 604030; fax: +44 1943 604070. Office on Gizenga Street behind House of Wonders. Spice tours guided by a knowledgeable local naturalist, who knows plant names in several languages. Offer all-inclusive tailor-made tours around the island with guides speaking English, French, German or Italian.

Suna Tours PO Box 2213; tel: 33597. Office in Forodhani Gardens. Agents for several east coast hotels, and good general tours.

Sun 'n' Fun Tours PO Box 666; tel: 054 32132 or 33018; fax: 054 30863. Office in Sea View Indian Restaurant. Good range of trips (including Kizimkazi dolphins) at very reasonable prices. Can arrange car and bicycle hire.

Stone Town walking tour

You can spend many idle hours getting lost in the fascinating labyrinth of narrow streets and alleys of the old Stone Town, and will almost inevitably hit most of the main landmarks within a couple of days of arriving. However, the following roughly circular walking tour through the Stone Town will allow those with limited time to do their sightseeing in a reasonably organised manner (though they are still bound to get lost), and should help those with more time to orientate themselves before they head out to explore the Stone Town without a map or guide book in hand.

The obvious starting point for any exploration of Zanzibar Town is **Forodhani Gardens**, a small patch of greenery lying between Mizingani Road and the main sea wall. Laid out in 1936 to mark the silver jubilee of Sultan Khalifa, the gardens are a popular eating and meeting point in the evening, and the staircase rising from the gardens to the arched bridge to the south offers a good view over the old town.

Three of the most significant buildings in the Stone Town lie alongside each other overlooking the seafront behind the Forodhani Gardens. The **Palace Museum** is the most northerly of these, a large white building with castellated battlements dating from the late 1890s. The palace was the official residence of the Sultan of Zanzibar from 1911 until the 1964 revolution, after which it was renamed the People's Palace. For many years after this, it served as a government office and was closed to the public. Since 1994, however, it has housed an excellent museum, with a variety of displays relating to the early days of the Sultanate, including a room devoted to artefacts belonging to Princess Salme. The graves of all the early Sultans of Zanzibar are in the palace garden.

Next to the Palace Museum, the **House of Wonders** is a square multi-storey building surrounded by tiers of impressive balconies and topped by a clock tower.

It was built as a ceremonial palace in 1883, and was the first building on Zanzibar to have electric lights. Local people called it *Beit el Ajaib*, meaning the House of Wonders. Until recently it was the CCM party headquarters, and it remains closed to the public, though you can see the huge carved doors and two old bronze cannons with Portuguese inscriptions from the outside, and the balcony is covered with curio sellers. The House of Wonders was reputedly scheduled to open as the new National Museum in 1998, but there were no signs of this happening when we visited Zanzibar in October of that year.

Directly facing Forodhani Gardens, the **Old Arab Fort** is probably the oldest extant building in the Stone Town, built by Omani Arabs between 1698 and 1701 over the site of a Portuguese church constructed a century before that, remnants of which can still be seen in the inner wall. A large squarish brown building with castellated battlements, the fort ceased to serve any meaningful military role in the 19th century, since when it has served variously as prison, railway depot and women's tennis club. The interior of the fort is open to visitors, who can climb to the top of the battlements and enter some of the towers. There is a restaurant in the fort, serving cold drinks, and traditional dancing shows take place there on at least three evenings every week.

Heading southwest from the fort, under an arched bridge, the fork to your right is Shangani Road, the site of notable important buildings. Just before following this fork, to your left, the **Upimaji Building** was the home of the German merchant Heinrich Reute (later the husband of Princess Salme) in the 1860s. To the left of the fork is a block of government offices which served as the **British Consulate** from 1841 until 1874, and next to that the **Tembo Hotel**, a restored 19th-century building. As you follow Shangani Road around a curve, you'll come out to a leafy green square, where the **Zanzibar Shipping Corporation Building**, dating to around 1850, stands to your left and the **Zanzibar Serena Inn**, formerly Extelcomms House, to your right.

Perhaps 100m past the Serena Inn, to your left, you'll see the rear of **Tippu Tip's House**, a tall brown building which once served as the residence of Tippu Tip, the influential 19th century slave trader who helped explorers such as Livingstone and Stanley with supplies and route-planning. The building is privately owned and closed to visitors, but if you follow the alley around the rear of the house, you can see its huge carved front door from the street, and the residents will sometimes show visitors around. From here, wander up another 50m past the New Happy Bar, and you'll pass the **Africa House Hotel**, which served as the English Club from 1888 onwards, and is a good place to punctuate your walk with a cold drink on the attractively positioned balcony.

From the Africa House Hotel, a small alley leads on to Kenyatta Road, an important thoroughfare dotted with hotels, shops, restaurants and a number of old buildings with traditional Zanzibari doors. Follow Kenyatta Avenue eastwards for about 300m, passing the somewhat unkempt **Peoples's Gardens**, originally laid out under Sultan Barghash for the use of his harem, until you reach the **Zanzibar Milestone**, an octagonal marble pillar which shows the distance from Zanzibar Town to various settlements on the island and further afield.

Cross the gardens in front of the milestone to the distinctive **Beit el Amani (House of Peace) Memorial Museum**, which houses interesting (though rather poorly organised and labelled) displays relating to the island's archaeology, the slave era, and various palaces, sultans, explorers, missionaries, traditional crafts and coins. In the annexe on the opposite side of the road there is a library and a natural history collection where dodo bones are exhibited. The Zanzibari door at the back of the building is reputedly the oldest in existence. The museum is open from

09.00 to 12.30 and 15.30 to 18.00 every day except Sunday, and there is a small entrance charge.

From the museum, follow Creek Road northwards for about 400m, and to your left you'll easily pick out the imposing **Anglican Cathedral** built by the Universities' Mission in Central Africa (UMCA) over the former slave market between 1873 and 1880. Tradition has it the altar stands on the site of the market's whipping block, and the cellar of the nearby St Monica's Guesthouse is reputed to be the remains of a pit where slaves were kept before being sold. Sultan Barghash, who closed the slave market, is reputed to have asked Bishop Steere, leader of the mission, not to build the cathedral tower higher than the House of Wonders. When the Bishop agreed, the Sultan presented the cathedral with its clock. The foundation of the UMCA was inspired by Livingstone: a window is dedicated to his memory, and the church's crucifix is made from the tree under which his heart was buried in present-day Zambia. Several other missionaries are remembered on plaques around the cathedral wall, as are sailors who were killed fighting the slave trade, and servicemen who died in action in East Africa during World War I. The cathedral is open to visitors for a nominal fee, which also covers entrance to the dungeon below the guesthouse.

A short distance further along Creek Road lies the **covered market**, built at around the turn of the century, and worth a visit even if you don't want to buy anything. It's a vibrant place where you can buy anything from fish and bread to sewing machines and second-hand car spares. Once you've taken a look around the market, follow Creek Road back southwards for 100m or so, passing the cathedral, then turn into the first wide road to your right. This is New Mkunazini Road, and if you follow it until its end, then turn right into Kajificheni Street and right again into Hammani Street, you'll come out at the **Hammani Baths**. This is one of the most elaborate Persian baths on Zanzibar, built for Sultan Barghash, and the caretaker will show you around for a small fee.

Barely 200m from the baths, on Cathedral Street, **Saint Joseph's Catholic Cathedral** is notable for its prominent twin spires, and was built between 1896 and 1898 by French missionaries and local converts. There are now few Catholics on Zanzibar, and the cathedral is infrequently used, but visitors are welcome when the doors are open. The best way to get here from the baths is to retrace your steps along Kajificheni Street, then turn right into the first alley (which boasts several good examples of traditional Zanzibari carved doors) until you reach an open area where several roads and alleys meet – Cathedral Street among them

From the cathedral, continue northwards along Cathedral Street for perhaps 50m, then turn right into Gizenga Street, a good place to check out the work of local Tingatinga artists. Gizenga Street boasts a cluster of curio shops, of which **The Gallery** is widely regarded to be the best, and also stocks a good selection of books and maps about Zanzibar. If you follow Gizenga Street until you see the old Arab Fort to your left, you can conclude your walk by wandering back out to Forodhani Gardens. Alternatively, if you want to keep going, turn right opposite the fort into Harumzi Street, and after continuing straight for about 300m, you'll come to the open square in front of the **Spice Inn**, which is one of the oldest hotels in the Stone Town (and a good place to take a break for a cake or samosa and a fruit juice). A left turn as you enter this square takes you past the Jamat Khan Mosque and on to Jamatini Road, which after about 200m will bring you out at the seafront opposite the **Big Tree**. Known locally as *Mtini*, this well-known landmark was planted in 1911 by Sultan Khalifa and now provides shade for traditional dhow builders.

On Mizingani Road, next to the Big Tree, the **Old Customs House**, a large, relatively plain building dating to the late 19th century, is where Sultan Hamoud

was proclaimed sultan in 1896. Next to this is another large old building, formerly
Le Grand Hotel, which is currently being renovated and likely to re-open under
its original name towards the end of 1999.

From the open area next to the Big Tree, a left turn along Mizingani Road will
take you back to the Arab Fort, passing the above-mentioned buildings. Turn right
into Mizingani Road, however, and after about 100m you'll pass the **Old
Dispensary**, an ornate three-storey building built in the 1890s and recently
restored to its former glory by the Aga Khan. You can continue for a few hundred
metres further, past the port gates, to the **traditional dhow harbour**, though
based on our experience you are unlikely to be allowed inside.

If the above directions seem too complicated, or you want further insight into
the historical buildings of the Stone Town, most tour operators can arrange a
guided city tour for around US$20 (see page 227 for tour operator listings).

ISLANDS CLOSE TO ZANZIBAR TOWN

Several small islands lie between 2km and 6km offshore of Zanzibar, many of them
within view of Zanzibar Town and easily visited from there as a day trip. Boat
transport to Chumbe arranged with an independent guide will cost around US$20,
but you will pay more to go on an organised tour. To cut the individual cost, it is
worth getting a group together.

Changuu (Prison) Island

Changuu was originally owned by a wealthy Arab who used it as a detention centre
for disobedient slaves, and a prison was built there in 1893, but never used. A path
circles the island (about an hour's easy stroll). There is a small beach and a
restaurant, and masks and flippers can be hired for snorkelling. The island is home
to several giant tortoises, probably brought from the Seychelles in the 18th century,
which spend much of their time mating, a long and noisy process which is
apparently successful as the tortoise population is said to be growing. An entrance
fee of US$5 per person must be paid in hard currency.

The **Changuu Island Guesthouse** consists of a group of wooden bungalows
set back from the beach. Accommodation costs US$16/20 single/double, and
should be booked in advance through the one of ZTC offices. Camping is
permitted, and meals are available at the restaurant.

Chapwani (Grave) Island

The site of a Christian cemetery since 1879, Chapwani also has a small swimming
beach and an intermittently functional hotel, details of which can be obtained
through tour operators in Zanzibar Town. Most of the graves on the island belong
to British sailors who were killed fighting Arab slave ships, while others date from
World War I, when the British ship *Pegasus* was sunk in Zanzibar harbour.

Chumbe Island

This coral island and the surrounding reefs have been gazetted as a nature reserve,
most of which is in near pristine condition because the island served as a military
base for many years and visitors were not permitted. Snorkelling here is as good as
anywhere around Zanzibar, with more than 350 reef fishes recorded, as well as
dolphins, turtles and the rare giant coconut crab. On the island, 60 bird species
have been recorded, including breeding pairs of the rare roseate tern, and there are
plans to re-introduce the localised Ader's duiker, which was hunted out in the
1950s. Of historical interest is an ancient Swahili mosque and a British lighthouse
built in 1904. Day trips to the island cost US$50 per person, inclusive of transfers,

guides, snorkelling equipment and lunch, and can only be arranged through reputable tour operators or from the Mbweni Ruins Hotel.

The management encourages overnight stays in the genuinely eco-friendly bungalows, which are self-contained with solar electricity, funnelled roofs designed to collect rain water, and compost toilets. Rates currently start at US$70 per person, but are likely to increase as the island becomes better-known. For further information and reservations, contact Chumbe Island Coral Park, PO Box 3203; tel/fax: 054 31040; radio 156.725ch74.

BUBUBU AND SURROUNDS

The small town of Bububu served as the terminus for a 10km stretch of 36-inch gauge track to connect the north coast to the Arab fort, constructed in 1904 and used until 1928. The springs outside Bububu supply most of Zanzibar Town's fresh water, and the name of the town presumably derives from the bubbling sound that they make. For most tourists, Bububu's main attraction will be Fuji Beach, the closest swimming beach to town, no more than 500m to your left when you disembark from a 'Route B' *dala-dala* at the main crossroad at Bububu.

Of interest in Bububu is a small centuries-old mosque about 200m from the main crossroads, along the road back towards Zanzibar Town. There is a little-known but large double-storey ruin on the beachfront about 500m north from where you arrive at the Fuji Beach. Complete with Arabic frescos, this house must date to the early 19th century, and it could well have been the Bububu residence of Princess Salme in the 1850s, as described in her autobiography.

Between Zanzibar Town and Bububu lie the ruined palaces of Maharubi and Mtoni, and Bububu is the closest substantial settlement to the Persian baths at Kidichi and Kizimbani.

Getting around

Although some of the places mentioned below might be included in your spice tour, it is easy to visit most of them independently, using the combination of 'Route B' *dala-dalas* (which run to Bububu every few minutes from the bus station on Creek Road) and your legs. Another possibility is to hire a motor scooter or bicycle from Sun 'n' Fun Tours, Maharouky Bicycle Hire (between the market and petrol station) or Nasor Aly Mussa's Scooter Service (near the UMCA cathedral).

Where to stay and eat

Most people visit the places listed below as a day-trip out of Zanzibar Town, but it is perfectly possible to explore the area using Bububu as a base. For upmarket authenticity in Bububu (and perhaps anywhere on Zanzibar), you can't beat **Salme's Garden**, a restored 19th-century house set above Fuji Beach and decorated in masterly period style by Emerson of Emerson's House. Set in beautiful grounds, and with a private mosque attached, this house is another candidate for Princess Salme's Bububu residence. It can be rented as a unit or by the room through Nicole (the chef at Emerson's and Green) or through the owners in Italy. Fax: +39 051 234974; email: house.of.wonders@mailbox.dsnet.it.

The **Bububu Beach Guesthouse** provides adequate accommodation one minute's walk from Fuji Beach. Rooms using communal showers cost US$15/16 single/double, while self-contained doubles cost US$25. There is another **anonymous guesthouse** around the corner next to the Cave Bar. The nearby **Cave Bar** serves ice-cold beer in pleasant gardens, while the **Fuji Beach Restaurant** serves OK meals in the US$4–5 range. If you are mobile or don't mind using *dala-dala*s by night, the somewhat misleadingly named **Milan Restaurant** about 4km back towards town serves superb Indian food in the US$5–6 range.

Excursions
Maharubi Palace
This is probably the most impressive ruin on this part of the coast, built in 1882 for the concubines of Sultan Barghash. At one time he kept around 100 women here. The palace was destroyed by fire in 1899, and all that remains are the great pillars which supported the upper storey, and the Persian-style bath-house. You can also see the separate bathrooms for the women, the large bath used by the Sultan, and the original water tanks, now overgrown with lilies. The palace lies about 200m from the Bububu road, roughly 3km from the Stone Town, and it is signposted. A nominal entrance fee of around US$0.30 is charged, and the ticket also allows entrance to most of the other sites in this area. Traditional dhow builders can be seen at work on the beach in front of the palace.

Mtoni Slave Chambers
The ruins of a large slave chamber overlook the beach about 500m north of Maharubi, in the grounds of a Tourism Training College. It is physically possible to walk to the ruins along the beach, though the security people at Maharubi discourage this due to a spate of mugging, so it can only be recommended if you have no valuables on you or are in the company of a trustworthy local. The other option is to go back to the main road and follow this for about 500m until you reach the entrance to the training college.

Mtoni Palace
The ruins of Mtoni Palace lie a short way north of Maharubi, and can be reached along the beach. Mtoni is the oldest palace on Zanzibar, built for Sultan Said in the 1840s. A book written by his daughter Salme describes the palace in the 1850s. At one end of the house was a large bath-house, at the other the quarters where Said lived with his principal wife. Gazelles and peacocks wandered around the large courtyard. Mtoni was abandoned before 1885. Only the main walls and roof remain. It was used as a warehouse in World War I; evidence of this alteration can still be seen. In October 1998, we were told at Maharubi that this palace was closed to tourists, but when we walked there from the main road we were allowed in by the caretaker. Presumably, we were being warned off walking along the beach, so once again you are advised against taking a seaside short cut!

Kidichi and Kizimbani Persian Baths
The Kidichi Baths were built in 1850 for Said's wife, Binte Irich Mirza, the grand-daughter of the Shah of Persia, and are decorated with Persian-style stucco. You can enter the bath-house and see the bathing pool and toilets, but there is mould growing on much of the stucco. The baths lie about 3km east of Bububu; from the main crossroads follow the road heading *inland* (ie turn right coming from Zanzibar Town) and you'll see the baths to your right after a walk of around 30 minutes.

The Kizimbani baths are less attractive and less accessible on foot, lying a further 3km or so inland. The surrounding Kizimbani clove plantation, which is visited by many spice tours, was founded in the early 19th century by Saleh bin Haramil, the Arab trader who imported the first cloves to Zanzibar.

Mangapwani Slave Cave

Near the synonymous village, 10km north of Bububu and 20km north of Zanzibar Town, this large natural cavern and man-made slave cave can easily be visited using a number 2 *dala-dala*. The natural coral cavern has a narrow entrance and a pool of fresh water at its lowest point. The Slave Cave, a square cell cut into the coral, was used to hold slaves after the trade was abolished in 1873. The natural cavern may also have been used to hide slaves, but this is not certain. Coming by *dala-dala*, you'll have to disembark at Mangapwani, where a road forks left towards the coast. About 2km past the village this road ends and a small track branches off to the right. Follow this for 1km to reach the Slave Cave. About halfway between Mangapwani and the track to the Slave Cave, a narrow track to the left leads to the natural cavern.

NUNGWI AND THE FAR NORTH

This large fishing village on the northern end of the island, the centre of Zanzibar's dhow building industry, boasts an attractive beach lined with palm and casuarina trees, while the surrounding waters offer good snorkelling and diving. Nungwi has emerged over the last few years as one of the more popular tourist retreats on Zanzibar, boasting one excellent upmarket hotel as well as a cluster of more low-key guesthouses which might collectively host up to 100 budget travellers on any given day. For many, the main attraction of Nungwi is the scene that centres around these guesthouses, reminiscent of somewhere such as Cape Maclear in Malawi or Twiga Lodge in Kenya, though not so cheap.

A short walk along the beach east of Nungwi brings you to the headland of Ras Nungwi, where there is an old lighthouse (photography forbidden). Next to this, the Mnarani Turtle Sanctuary (entrance US$1) consists of a fenced-off saline natural pool, in which lives a community of perhaps 15 greenback and hawksbill turtles. Further afield, the Fukuchani Ruins lie about 200m of the main road to Zanzibar Town, about 10km south of Nungwi. Also known as the Portuguese House, this well-preserved ruin dates from the 16th century, and while it may have been occupied and even extended by Portuguese settlers, it was almost certainly built in the Shirazi era.

Getting there and away

An erratic handful of *dala-dalas* daily connect Zanzibar Town to Nungwi, but the vast majority of travellers prefer to be transferred by private minibus, which can cost up to US$10 per person depending on group size and your negotiating skills. The ideal would be to get a group together in Zanzibar when you want to head out here, then organise a transfer through a *papaasi*, a taxi driver or a tour company. Unless you have very rigid timings, there is no need to organise your transfer back to Zanzibar Town in advance, since several vehicles can be found waiting around for passengers in Nungwi, especially in the mid-morning.

Where to stay and eat
Upper range

Ras Nungwi Beach Hotel Tel: 054 32512 or 33615; fax: 054 33098; email: rasnungwi@zanzibar.net; web: http://www.zanzibar.net/nungwi/index.htm. This widely praised hotel, built almost entirely with local materials such as fossilised coral limestone, has an organic feel and a beach setting, with an atmosphere that is far less 'packaged' than at most equivalently priced places on the east coast. The emphasis here is very much on diving, snorkelling and water sports, though many visitors are content merely to laze on the idyllic beach, and day trips to most points of interest around the island can be arranged.

The PADI dive centre runs single dives from US$40 per person, as well as discounted packages for those wanting to do several dives, and full five-day courses for US$330. A good selection of water sport and snorkelling equipment can be hired. The restaurant, affiliated to Blues in Zanzibar Town, specialises in seafood and Swahili dishes. All accommodation is en-suite with a ceiling fan, private balcony and netted four-poster bed in the traditional Swahili style. Full-board rates range from US$110/160 single/double in an ordinary room to US$140/220 in a sea-facing chalet, with a substantial low season discount. **Mnarani Beach Cottages** Tel: 054 33440 or 0811 334062. Situated close to the lighthouse on Ras Nungwi, this small cluster of cottages, built in local style, is very good value at US$70 for a double.

Budget

Lying above the beach immediately southwest of Nungwi village, you'll find what is virtually a travellers' village in its own right. The most established guesthouse here is **Amaan Bungalows** (tel: 0811 327747), but there are several more to choose from, of which we felt that the **Baraka Guesthouse** offered the best value for money. Prices are pretty uniform in Nungwi, with ordinary rooms costing around US$10 per person and self-contained rooms US$25-30 for a double. There are several restaurants to choose from. The East Africa Diving and Water Sports Centre organises single dives at US$30 per person, multiple dives at US$25 per person per dive, and full five-day courses for US$300 per person, as well as offering snorkelling and water sport equipment for rent.

A few kilometres south of Nungwi, on the west coast, **Kendwa Rocks** is a relaxed backpackers' haunt where you can pitch a tent for US$4 per person or rent a double bungalow for US$20. Their boat runs up to Nungwi a few times daily to collect passengers; you can ask at the diving centre about the current transfer rate and (vague) timetable.

JOZANI FOREST AND SURROUNDS

The Jozani Forest Reserve protects the last substantial remnant of the indigenous forest which once covered much of central Zanzibar, and it is the most important mammal sanctuary on the island. The main tourist attraction in the forest is Kirk's red colobus, a beautiful and cryptically coloured monkey found only on Zanzibar, and regarded by most authorities to be a distinct species, though it is closely related to the red colobus of West Africa. Although recent estimates place the island's red colobus population as having fallen to as low as 1,000 individuals, the habituated troops at Jozani are easily seen by tourists, and great fun to watch as they more-or-less ignore human observers.

Jozani used to be the main haunt of the Zanzibar leopard, a race that is found nowhere else, but which recent research suggests may well be extinct. The forest is also home to Ader's duiker, a small antelope that effectively may now be a Zanzibar endemic, as it is probably extinct and certainly very rare in Kenya's Sokoke Forest, the only other place where it has ever been recorded. Several other mammal species live in Jozani, and the forest is one of the best birding sites on the island.

The entrance and reception at Jozani Forest lie a short distance from the main road connecting Zanzibar Town to the east coast. Most tour operators can organise day trips to the forest, though it is perfectly possible to visit independently using a number 9 or 10 bus or dala-dala. Also of interest in the Jozani area are Zala Park, a small private zoo lying about 3km past the forest and about 1km off the main east coast road, and the Bi Khole Ruins, the remains of a mid-19th-century homestead lying 6km south of the village of Tunguu to the west of the main east coast road.

THE EAST COAST

The east coast of Zanzibar is where you will find the idyllic tropical beaches you dreamed about during those interminable bus rides on the mainland: clean white sand lined with palms, and lapped by the warm blue water of the Indian Ocean. Some travellers come here for a couple of days, just to relax after seeing the sights of Zanzibar Town, and end up staying for a couple of weeks. Visitors on tighter time restrictions always wish they could stay for longer...

The most popular stretch of coast is in the south, between Bwejuu and Makunduchi. There is plenty of accommodation here, and most hotels have restaurants. You can usually buy fish and vegetables in the villages, but supplies are limited; if you are self-catering, stock up in Zanzibar Town.

Getting there and away

The southern part of the east coast can easily be reached by bus or *dala-dala* – no 6 goes to Chwaka (directly east of Zanzibar Town), no 9 goes to Paje (sometimes continuing to Bwejuu or Jambiani) and no 10 to Makunduchi. Chwaka Bay can be crossed by boat-taxis between Chwaka and Michamvi.

Most travellers prefer to use private transport to the east coast: several tour companies and some independent guides arrange minibuses which cost between US$3 and US$5 per person each way. Unless you specify where you want to stay, minibus drivers prefer to take you to a hotel that gives them commission.

Where to stay and eat

There are numerous hotels and guesthouses dotted along the length of the east coast, and the following north-to-south listings will give a good idea of what is available, without claiming to be comprehensive.

Upper and mid-range

Matemwe Bungalows PO Box 3275; tel: 054 33789; fax: 054 31342. This small, simple but comfortable hotel facing Mnemba Island lies on a low coral cliff above a palm-lined beach. It is a good base for diving and snorkelling, based close to the exceptional Mnemba Atoll. The attached diving school charges US$35 for a single dive and US$350 for a full diving course. Accommodation in en-suite chalets costs US$70 per person.

Shooting Star Cottages PO Box 3076; tel: 054 33386. Situated on Kiwenga Beach, this small, friendly resort is regarded to have one of the best restaurants on the island, and is visited by many people just to eat. There are also six self-contained cottages for rent at US$50 per person full-board, and luxury en-suite double bungalows at US$140 full-board.

Uroa Bay Village Resort Tel: 054 33552; fax: 054 33504. Situated on Uroa Beach, this is regarded to be one of the best upmarket resorts on the island, with a swimming pool and a good range of water sport and sailing and fishing facilities. Full-board accommodation costs US$150 per person.

Tamarind Beach Hotel PO Box 2206; tel/fax: 054 33041/2; mobile: 0811 323566. Also on Uroa Beach, this resort consists of several self-contained villas overlooking the palm-lined seashore. The diving school charges US$35 for a single dive and US$350 for a full course. Accommodation costs US$77/103 single/double b&b, or US$102/173 full-board.

Sunrise Hotel PO Box 3967; fax: 054 30344. This small hotel lies on the southern part of the east coast, about 3km north of Bwejuu village. It is often recommended by travellers, and seems excellent value at around US$70 for a double bungalow with en-suite bathroom. The restaurant is also very good.

Sau Inn PO Box 1656; tel: 054 32215. One of the most highly rated hotels on the southeast coast, the Sau Inn in Jambiani consists of a number of comfortable en-suite rooms and cottages set in pleasant gardens. It's good value at US$40/50 single/double, and the restaurant is excellent.

Budget
Most of the east coast's budget accommodation lies in the villages along the southern part of the coast. The following listing mentions some of the more popular options in each village.

Chwaka
The choice is between the large and frequently empty **Chwaka Bay Beach Hotel**, which charges from US$45 for a double bungalow, and the smaller and more basic **East End Guesthouse**, which charges US$10 per person.

Dongwe
One of the most popular places in the vicinity of this village is the **Twisted Palm**, two open-plan houses with five rooms each, charging US$10 per person bed only or US$25 per person half-board. The **Kilimani Guesthouse** and **Evergreen Resthouse** both charge US$10 per person.

Bwejuu
The popular and constantly expanding **Dere Guesthouse** charges between US$8 and US$10 per person. The restaurant serves good value meals, and snorkelling equipment and bicycles can be hired at very reasonable rates. Double rooms at the smarter **Palm Beach Hotel** cost US$15 per person; beach bungalows US$20 per person. The restaurant serves local meals for between US$3 and US$6 (advance orders are appreciated) and the bar sells beer. Other options include the **Burghani Villa** and **Seven Seas Guesthouse**, both of which charge US$10 per person, while **Jamal's Restaurant** has been recommended for good local food.

Paje
The **Ufukwe** and **Amani Guesthouses** offer clean double rooms for US$8 per person including breakfast. The pleasant **Paradise Beach Bungalows** has better facilities and charges US$10 per person.

Jambiani
Jambiani spreads for several kilometres down the coast. Coming from the north, the first places you'll pass are the **Horizontal Inn** and **Oasis Beach Inn**, both small family-run places where clean rooms cost US$6 per person, including breakfast. Further south, past the health centre and school, good self-contained rooms are available at the **East Coast Visitors Inn** and **Jambiani Beach Hotel** for US$10 per person. The restaurant at the latter hotel serves good local dishes for between US$3 and US$6, and it has a bar. At the southern end of town, the **Shehe Guesthouse** and **Gomani Guesthouse** (the latter perched on low cliff) both offer ordinary accommodation at US$6 per person and self-contained rooms at US$10 per person.

Makunduchi
Makunduchi New Town is at the southern end of the island. Rooms at the **Kigaeni Reef Lodge** cost US$7 per person, including breakfast. You can also camp in the garden for US$3. It has a basic restaurant. Fishing and snorkelling trips can be arranged.

MNEMBA ISLAND LODGE

Private Bag X27, Benmore, South Africa; tel: +27 11 784-7077; fax: +27 11 784-7667; email: reservations@conscorp.co.za.

If you've ever fancied owning your own private tropical island, then a stay at the Mnemba Island Lodge may be the closest you ever get to realising that dream, if only for a few days. The tiny island of Mnemba, which lies a kilometre or so off the northeastern shore of Zanzibar, forms part of the much larger submerged Mnemba Atoll, one of the best diving and snorkelling sites in East Africa. The island itself boasts wide beaches of white coral sand, fine and cool underfoot, backed by patches of tangled coastal bush and a small forest of casuarina trees. The small reefs immediately offshore offer a great introduction to the fishes of the reef for snorkellers, while diving excursions further afield allow you to explore the 40m-deep coral cliffs, a good place to see larger fish including the whale shark, the world's largest fish. The bird checklist for the island, though short, includes several unusual waders and other marine birds.

Accommodation consists of ten large, airy beach chalets, constructed using organic materials. The chalets are very private, separated from the beach and other chalets by thick bush, and each one has a private balcony as well as netting, a fan and an en-suite bathroom. The food is outstanding, and (weather permitting) evening meals are taken at a table on the beach. Accommodation costs US$500 per person per night, inclusive of all meals and drinks, transfers from Zanzibar Town, use of water sport and snorkelling equipment, and dives (including diving courses) with the resident diving instructor.

KIZIMKAZI

The small town of Kizimkazi lies on the southwestern end of the island, and is best known to tourists as *the* place to see humpback and bottlenose dolphins, both of which are resident in the area. Most tourists visit Kizimkazi as an organised day tour out of Zanzibar Town, which costs between US$25 and US$100 all-inclusive per person, depending on group size, season and quality. Sightings cannot be guaranteed, but the chances of seeing dolphins here are very good. It may also be possible sometimes to swim with the dolphins, though you should never encourage your pilot to chase them or try to approach them too closely yourself – with up to 100 people visiting Kizimkazi daily in the high season, there is genuine cause to fear that tourism may be detrimental to the animals. If you do get close enough and you want to try your luck swimming with the dolphins, slip in the water next to the boat, try to excite the dolphins' interest by diving frequently, holding your arms along your body to imitate their streamlined shape, and wait to see whether they join you!

It is possible to visit Kizimkazi independently, in a hired car or using a no 3 bus or *dala-dala*. The only accommodation here is the rather basic **Kizimkazi Beach Villa**, which charges US$8 per person and offers meals in the US$2-5 range. You can usually arrange to hire a boat from the hotel, or to join a group that has come for the day from Zanzibar Town.

If you sleep over at Kizimkazi, it's worth heading out to the Kizimkazi Mosque at the nearby settlement of Dimbani. One of the oldest known mosques in East Africa, Kizimkazi is dated by Kufic inscriptions to AD1107, when Kizimkazi was a large walled city. The Kufic inscriptions, on the niche at the eastern end of the mosque, are in a decorative floriated style similar to some old inscriptions found in Persia. The silver pillars on either side of the niche are decorated with pounded shells from Mafia Island. Two clocks, which show Swahili time, were presented by local dignitaries. To see inside the mosque, now protected by a corrugated iron roof, you must find the caretaker who lives nearby. It is respectful to cover any bare limbs and take off your shoes when you enter.

PEMBA ISLAND
Lying to the northeast of the larger island of Zanzibar, directly east of the mainland port of Tanga, Pemba is visited by few travellers. While tourist facilities on Zanzibar have mushroomed in recent years, Pemba has changed little over the last decade, making it a particularly attractive destination for those who are prepared to put up with relatively basic conditions in order to 'get away from it all'.

Pemba has a more undulating landscape than Zanzibar, and is more densely vegetated with both natural forest and plantation. The main agricultural product is cloves, which Pemba now produces in greater abundance than Zanzibar. There is nothing on the island to compare with Zanzibar's Stone Town, but it does boast a number of attractive beaches, as well as some absorbing ruins dating to the Shirazi era. During holidays, traditional bull fights are sometimes held on Pemba, presumably introduced during the years of Portuguese occupation. Pemba is also a centre for traditional medicine and witchcraft. People seeking cures for spiritual or physical afflictions come from Zanzibar Island and the mainland – even as far away as Uganda and Zaire – to see Pemba's doctors.

The island's largest town is Chake Chake, north of which lies the main port, Wete. Mkoani is a smaller port in the southwest. There are banks and post offices in Chake Chake, Wete and Mkoani, but only the Chake Chake bank can change travellers' cheques. The main hospital is in Chake Chake. There is a ZTC office next to the ZTC Hotel in Chake Chake.

Getting there and away
At the time of writing, Precision Air runs the only scheduled flight between Pemba and Zanzibar (connecting to Arusha and Dar es Salaam). They fly to Pemba every Wednesday and Sunday, but since the service only commenced in late 1998, there is no telling how long it will keep going. Air Tanzania has run scheduled flights between Zanzibar and Pemba in the past, and it may yet resume the service.

Normally, at least one of the boat companies working the Dar es Salaam to Zanzibar route diverts to Pemba a few times every week. The best bet currently is the *Sebidah*, which goes to Pemba from Zanzibar and Dar five times weekly, a six-hour journey that costs US$30. The *Sebidah* connects Pemba to Tanga and Mombasa once a week. However, the situation with boats to Pemba seems to change regularly, so it's advisable to seek current advice in Dar or Zanzibar.

Chake Chake
This is the largest town on Pemba, and several centuries old, but it has never achieved a degree of importance comparable to Zanzibar Town. The busy market area and old port are pleasant to walk around, but sightseeing is pretty much limited to the remains of an Omani Fort near the modern hospital.

The **ZTC Hotel**, a reasonably clean but somewhat run-down angular concrete building, has rooms for US$20/35 single/double and serves reasonable if overpriced meals – the **Machakos Inn** opposite is just as good and a lot cheaper. Two private guesthouses lie about 4km from town, and can be reached by taking a no 34 *dala-dala* towards Wete. The **Venus Lodge** is the first of these, with clean

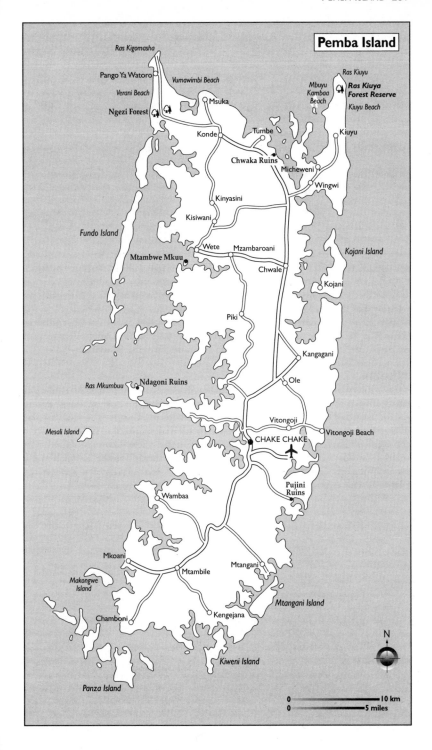

Pemba Island

Ras Kigomasha

Pango Ya Watoro

Vumawimbi Beach

Verani Beach

Ngezi Forest

Msuka

Konde

Tumbe

Chwaka Ruins

Ras Kiuyu

Mbuyu Kambaa Beach

Ras Kiuya Forest Reserve

Kiuyu Beach

Kiuyu

Micheweni

Wingwi

Kinyasini

Kisiwani

Fundo Island

Wete

Mzambaroani

Mtambwe Mkuu

Chwale

Kojani Island

Kojani

Piki

Kangagani

Ras Mkumbuu

Ndagoni Ruins

Ole

Mesali Island

Vitongoji

CHAKE CHAKE

Vitongoji Beach

Pujini Ruins

Wambaa

Mkoani

Makongwe Island

Mtambile

Mtangani

Mtangani Island

Chamboni

Kengejana

Kiweni Island

N

Panza Island

0   10 km

0   5 miles

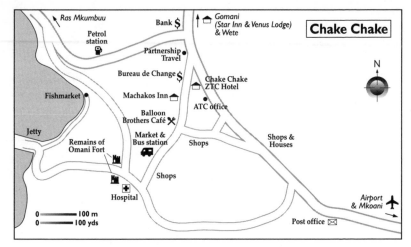

self-contained doubles for US$20. A few hundred metres further, opposite Gombani Stadium, the **Star Inn** has a selection of rooms, ranging in price from US$10 for a basic single to US$30 for a self-contained double. The staff are friendly and the food is good.

For tours, transport bookings and any other travel services, **Partnership Travel** is by far the most switched-on agency in Pemba. Other reliable tour operators are the state-run **ZTC** (next to the hotel) and the **Star Inn**.

Mkoani

This is the smallest of the three main towns on Pemba, but the new boat services connecting it to Zanzibar and elsewhere mean it is also the busiest tourist centre on the island. The **ZTC Hotel** is a similar set-up to the one in Chake Chake, charging identical prices. Far better is the **Jondeni Lodge**, on a hill overlooking the town, where rooms cost US$12/20 single/double. It also serves good food. The main tour operator in Mkoane is **Faizan Tours and Travel**, a reliable and environmentally sensitive bunch who can arrange tours to most places on the island, as well as boat tickets and the like.

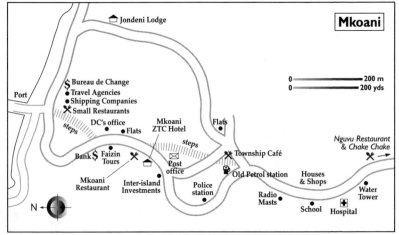

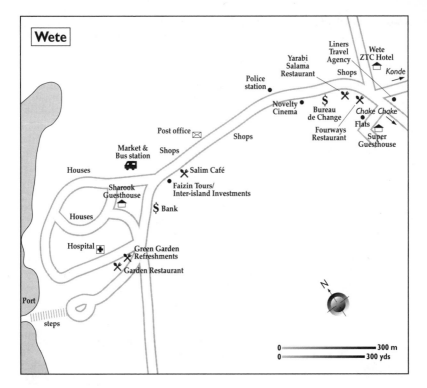

Wete

This town lies on a large inlet on the northwest coast of the island, and it is the best base from which to visit points of interest on northern Pemba. In addition to the overpriced **ZTC Hotel** (same as the one in Chake Chake), accommodation can be found at the **Sharook Guest House**, a simple family-run place near the bus station charging US$8 per person, and at the smarter **Super Guesthouse**, where rooms start at US$15/20 single/double. The Sharook Guesthouse offers a decent range of tours at reasonable prices, and Faizan Tours has a small office on the main street near the market.

Excursions

Chake Chake is linked to Wete by bus and *dala-dala* no 6, and to Mkoani by no 3. These normally run in the morning. You can sometimes hire bicycles through the receptionist at the ZTC Hotel in Chake Chake, or through Faizan Tours in Mkoani. A Mr Nassour, contactable through the ZTC Hotel in Chake Chake, rents out a Suzuki 4x4 and driver for about US$20 per day (petrol is extra). If you want to visit Mesali Island or the Ras Mkumbuu Ruins by boat, he also rents out a motor boat for about US$35 per day (including petrol and captain). Local tour operators are mentioned under the three main towns.

Ras Mkumbuu Ruins These 11th-century ruins on the end of the peninsula west of Chake Chake include the remains of a mosque and several pillar-tombs. The most enjoyable way to reach Ras Mkumbuu is by boat, combined with a visit to Mesali Island.

Mesali Island This small island west of Chake Chake is surrounded by a coral reef. Its idyllic beach is good for swimming, especially if you have a mask and snorkel. The notorious pirate Captain Kidd is reputed to have had a hideout here in the 17th century.

Pujini Ruins This is about 10km southeast of Chake Chake. You can walk there and back in a day, but it is easier to travel by hired bike or car. The ruins are the remains of a 13th-century Swahili town, known locally as Mkame Ndume (milker of men) after a despotic king who forced the inhabitants to carry large stones for the town walls while shuffling on their buttocks. The overgrown remains of the walls and ditches can be seen, as can a walkway which joined the town to the shore, some wide stairways that presumably allowed access to the defensive ramparts, and the site of the town's well.

Ngezi Forest Reserve This small reserve on the north of the island supports an interesting range of vegetation, including the most substantial patch of moist forest on Pemba. It is a good place to seek out the four bird species endemic to Pemba (the Pemba white-eye, green pigeon, scops owl and sunbird) as well as mammals such as the endemic Pemba flying fox, Kirk's red colobus, vervet monkey, blue duiker, marsh mongoose and a feral population of European boars, introduced by the Portuguese and left untouched by their Muslim successors, who don't eat pork. A short nature trail runs through the forest.

Central Tanzania

The vast, dry and predominantly flat badlands that lie at the heart of Tanzania don't feature on many tourist itineraries, and while that much is true of many of the regions covered in this guide, the difference is that it really is difficult to put forward any good reason for exploring central Tanzania. If the bus rides on the south coast aren't quite gruelling enough for your taste, then central Tanzania will certainly hold some appeal. And there must surely be some travellers out there who collect capital cities as others collect passport stamps, in which case a foray into the Tanzanian capital of Dodoma might well be the highlight of your stay in the country. Otherwise, this scenically monotonous region boasts few tourist attractions and even fewer decent roads, and the only realistic reason why a tourist would pass through is because they are using the central railway line, which provides the only reliable transport between the coast, Lake Victoria and Lake Tanganyika.

Oddly, the central region of Tanzania was one of the first to be explored by outsiders. When, between 1905 and 1914, Germany constructed the 1,238km railway line from Dar es Salaam to Kigoma on Lake Tanganyika, they were not trailblazing, but following a centuries-old caravan route that ran through Dodoma and Tabora, reaching the lake shore at Ujiji. The central railway thus follows a route almost identical to the one travelled by Burton and Speke on their quest to find the source of the Nile, as well as the one used by Stanley in his search for Livingstone.

Between Dodoma and Tabora, the railway line passes through what is perhaps the most barren scenery in Tanzania, a seemingly endless drought-prone plain of baked red sand and sparse woodland. The line stops at several small villages, the livelihood of which evidently revolves around selling food to train passengers. The scenery becomes more lush closer to Kigoma, with patches of indigenous forest, swamp and dense *miombo* woodland along the line. Between Tabora and Mwanza the scenery remains arid until the approach to Lake Victoria, where strange granite formations break the monotony.

Getting around

Coming from the coast, the main gateway to the region is Dodoma, which is connected to Dar es Salaam and Morogoro by a good surfaced road and reliable bus services, and to Iringa and Arusha by rough gravel roads and lousy bus services. Heading west from Dodoma, the only sane mode of transport is the central railway line, which connects Dar es Salaam to Kigoma on Lake Tanganyika and Mwanza on Lake Victoria, stopping at Morogoro and Dodoma, and splitting along its northern and western branches at the junction town of Tabora.

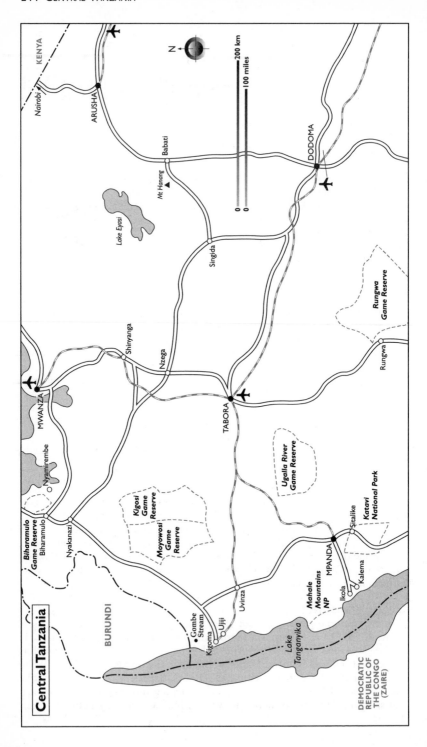

Climate

This dry, dusty part of Tanzania is often very hot, but feels much cooler than the coast because it isn't so humid. In common with most parts of the Tanzanian interior, this region tends to cool down significantly at night. Rainfall patterns are similar to elsewhere in the country, though the level of precipitation is much lower and droughts are a frequent occurrence.

DODOMA

Dodoma is now the official capital of Tanzania, having displaced Dar es Salaam in the early 1990s on the basis that it is more centrally located. Dodoma was an important village on the 19th-century caravan route, and after 1910 when Germany built a railway station there, it served as the local administration centre. Ironically, at one point Germany seriously considered making Dodoma their East African capital, a plan that was shelved during World War I, when the area suffered two famines, claiming over 30,000 lives. Despite this, Dodoma grew steadily between the wars, and its position at the junction of the central railway and the trans-Tanzania road made it one of the country's most important internal crossroads, at least until the road between Iringa and Morogoro was built in the 1950s.

Whatever its past and future claims to importance (and we *are* talking about a town that served as a staging post on the renowned Cape-to-Cairo flights of the 1930s), Dodoma in its present incarnation is unremittingly small-town in atmosphere, and one of the few places in Tanzania where I sensed a slight undercurrent of hostility to *wzungu*. You'd be unlikely to visit Dodoma from choice, and if for some reason you do wash adrift there it probably won't be long before you think about moving on.

Getting there and away

Dodoma is strategically positioned in the centre of Tanzania. As a consequence, many travellers are tempted to cut between other parts of the country through Dodoma, based solely on the information contained on a map. It is emphatically worth stressing that almost any plan which involves bussing through Dodoma should be nipped in the bud – the main roads south to Iringa and north to Arusha are in appalling condition and the latter in particular is among the most gruelling bus trips in Tanzania, taking up to 18 hours. If, however, you insist on trying these routes, buses between Dodoma and Iringa and Dodoma and Arusha leave in either direction in the early morning – you're advised to book a seat an afternoon in advance and to check the exact time of departure bearing in mind you'll almost certainly be quoted Swahili time.

The 350km road between Dar es Salaam and Dodoma is surfaced in its entirety. A fairly steady stream of buses runs between the past and present capitals, generally leaving before midday and taking around seven to eight hours. You can also pick up buses between Dar es Salaam and Dodoma at Morogoro.

Most travellers who pass through Dodoma are on one of the trains crossing between Dar es Salaam and Kigoma or Mwanza. If you feel an overwhelming need to take a more lingering look at Dodoma, or you simply want to cut the two-night train trip by one night, then (coming from the west) there's nothing to stop you from buying a ticket as far as Dodoma, spending the night there and bussing on to Dar es Salaam the next day. Coming in the opposite direction, it's possible to buy a ticket out of Dodoma from the railway station in Dar es Salaam. Westbound trains pass through Dodoma between 08.00 and 10.00 the morning after they leave Dar es Salaam. For further details see *By rail* in *Chapter 4*.

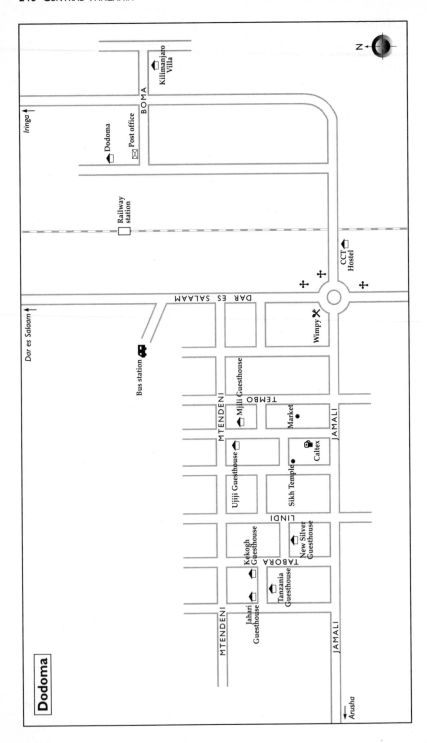

Dodoma

Where to stay and eat

The **Dodoma Hotel** (PO Box 239; tel: 061 22991; fax: 061 24911), formerly run by the TRC but is now in private hands, is an attractively designed building directly opposite the railway station. The rooms are excellent value at $12/15 s/c single/double for Tanzania residents (non-residents must technically pay US$25/30, but we were asked the resident rates when we last stayed here, and so probably will you, unless you draw attention to your non-resident status – tourists aren't exactly something the receptionist encounters on a daily basis). This is also the best place to eat in Dodoma, at least if your culinary demands stretch much beyond *ugali* or rice and slop. The restaurant serves good, sensibly priced meals, for instance steak and chips for $4, as well as a three-course set menu for $7. There is live music in the bar on some nights.

The **Kilimanjaro Villa** is probably the most attractive of the cheaper options, in a leafy suburban property about 500m from the railway station. Large self-contained rooms cost $5/7 and rooms using communal facilities cost US$4/5. Also worth a look is the **CCT Hostel**, a church-run place about 300m from the railway station next to a large domed church, offering a variety of rooms from between US$5 and US$7. This used to be a very clean and reasonably pleasant place to stay, but a recent report suggests it has gone downhill over the last couple of years. Food is available, though alcoholic drinks are banned from the premises.

There are at least ten basic resthouses clustered around the market and bus station. It's difficult to make any specific recommendations – for starters, half of them are likely to be full on any given day – but you should have no problem finding a room for around $2. Most places have nets and communal showers, so I'd tend to pass over a room that doesn't.

The **ice-cream parlour** opposite the Wimpy has been recommended by a reader who visited most major towns in Tanzania as possibly the best in the country. The same reader rates the **NK Disco** as the most kicking spot in the town centre, while another recommends the **Climax Club** on the outskirts of town as a good place to meet expatriates, down a cold beer, eat or swim in the pool.

TABORA

This hot, dusty town is where the railway lines to Kigoma, Mwanza and Mpanda meet. If you travel around western Tanzania, you are likely to spend a day in Tabora at some point, and may even have to spend a night. Tabora is a friendly place, and quite attractive with its shady roads lined with mango and flame trees, but there isn't a great deal more to it than that.

Tabora is the home of the Nyamwezi, Tanzania's second-largest tribe. In the mid-19th century, under the leadership of Mirambo, they controlled the area between Tabora and Lakes Tanganyika, Rukwa and Victoria. The Nyamwezi were actively involved in the slave trade and provided many porters for the central caravan route, and Mirambo, a natural diplomat, kept good relations with Arab traders and European visitors. After Mirambo's death in 1884, however, his successor clashed with the Germans, who captured Tabora in 1893. The large fort overlooking the town dates from this period.

The 19th-century Arab slave-trading post, Kazeh, was a few kilometres from Tabora. Burton and Speke stopped there on their way to becoming the first Europeans to see Lake Tanganyika. In 1872, between his famous meeting with Stanley at Ujiji and his final, fatal expedition to Lake Bengweulu, Livingstone stayed in Kazeh for five months waiting for supplies from the coast. His restored house is now a museum.

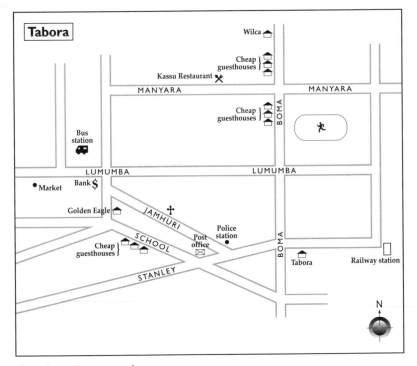

Getting there and away

Tabora is an important railway junction; most people who spend time there do so to make a train connection. Buses run between Tabora and most parts of western Tanzania, but they are not a pleasant option. The twice-weekly bus service between Tabora and Mbeya could be useful to travellers. It takes at least 20 hours.

Where to stay and eat

Formerly called the Railway Hotel, the refurbished **Tabora Hotel** (tel: 062 4566) near the railway station re-opened about two years ago, and it now offers clean s/c double rooms with nets at the very reasonable rate of US$12. The food is good, too. The best option otherwise is probably the **Wilca Hotel** on Boma Road. I don't have current prices but you shouldn't be looking at more than $10 for a self-contained double. The more central **Golden Eagle Hotel** is similar in price and standard. Both hotels serve reasonable meals.

The **Furaha School for the Blind** (Shule ya Furaha) has acceptable doubles for $4. Also recommended is the **Pentecostal Church Hostel** on Lumumba Road. Otherwise, the main cluster of guesthouses is along School Road, and there are also a few, generally more scruffy, rest houses near the bus station and near the Wilca Hotel, with rooms for around $2-3. Most of these places are full most of the time, so at the bottom end of the price range it's not so much a case of which place is the best but of taking a room wherever you find one. The **Vatican** and **Morovian Guest Houses** have been recommended.

Excursions from Tabora

Livingstone's House This museum 6km out of town holds various exhibits relating to Livingstone's stay in Tabora and is worth a look if you have a day to kill.

There are no buses, so you will have to negotiate a price for a round trip by taxi.
Rungwa Game Reserve Rungwa is an extension of the Ruaha ecosystem and
protects similar animals to Ruaha National Park. It is ten hours from Tabora by
bus, and there is no guarantee you will be allowed in. To get there, ask a bus to
Mbeya to drop you at Rungwa village on the park boundary. At the village, speak
to the head ranger for permission to walk in the park and to organise a guide. Bring
a tent and food with you.

SINGIDA AND SHINYANGA

These two towns lie on the main bus route between Arusha and Mwanza, and are
likely to feel like positive urban oases to any travellers mad enough to do this bus
trip, which can take anything from 36 hours to three days. If you somehow find
yourself in Singida, the **Sanai Guesthouse** has been recommended, along with
the **Lutheran Church Hotel** And if you are stranded in Shinyanga, the largest
town along the railway line and road between Tabora and Mwanza, you could try
to **Shinyanga Safari Hotel** or **Mwoleka Hotel**. The countryside around
Shinyanga is characterised by rocky outcrops similar to those found around
Mwanza, but otherwise I'm not aware of any sightseeing in the vicinity of either
town – drop me a line if you make any discoveries.

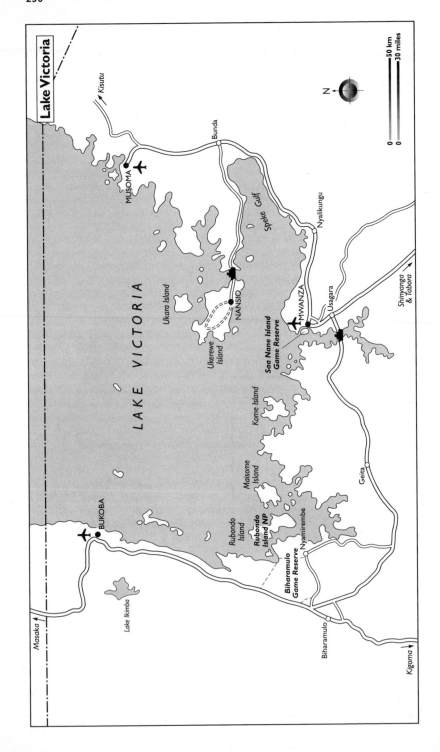

Lake Victoria

The largest lake in Africa and the second-largest freshwater body in the world, Lake Victoria is split between Uganda, Kenya and Tanzania, with the lion's share in Tanzania. The lake lies in an elevated basin between the major forks of the Great Rift Valley. It is shallow by comparison to Lake Tanganyika and Nyasa, only 70m deep on average, and it reputedly has far higher levels of bilharzia. The most important ports on the Tanzanian part of the lake are Mwanza, Musoma and Bukoba.

Most of the people who live around Lake Victoria are fishermen by tradition. The lake's future as a fishery is far from assured. In 1956, Nile perch were introduced to it in order to increase its food yield. These voracious fish have preyed on the cichlid species which naturally occur in the lake. Most Lake Victoria endemics are now extinct or heading that way.

Perch are fished through necessity, but as they are too large to roast on a fire and too fatty to sun-dry, they do not meet local needs. As the number of algae-eating endemics has dropped, the lake's algae level has risen. This is a type of environmental change that perch are known to be sensitive to. Worse still, perch cannibalise their own young when other prey runs out. There is concern that Lake Victoria will become a vast expanse of dead water, leaving a huge gap in the subsistence of lake shore villages and the economy of towns such as Mwanza.

Lake Victoria is visited by few tourists, and it lacks the scenic qualities that make Tanzania's other large lakes so easy to recommend as off-the-beaten-track excursions. The area is mostly of interest to people travelling overland between Tanzania and Uganda, with Mwanza in particular an important route focus and public transport hub.

Getting around

Roads in this part of the country tend to be in poor condition, for which reason most travellers arrive in Mwanza by ferry (see box *Lake Victoria Ferries* page 252) or on the central railway line (see previous chapter). There are also scheduled flights to Mwanza from Dar es Salaam and Arusha, but these are relatively expensive. The only reasonable road in the region is the one connecting Mwanza to Musoma, and this is the only stretch for which buses can be recommended.

Climate

Lying at an altitude of 1133m, Lake Victoria is not quite as hot as the coast or Lakes Tanganyika and Nyasa, but it shares with these areas a sticky tropical climate, with high humidity levels and daytime temperatures generally hovering at around 30°C. The wettest months are November, December, March and April, but

LAKE VICTORIA FERRIES

The Tanzania Railway Corporation (TRC) runs a network of ferries out of Mwanza, and although the international services to Port Bell in Uganda and Kisumu in Kenya were suspended following the tragic sinking of the MV *Bukoba* in 1996, there are still domestic services to Bukoba, Nyamirembe, Kome and Ukerewe Island. Most of the ferries are in unexpectedly good condition, with first- and second-class cabins offering a level of comfort matched in East Africa only by the train between Nairobi and Mombasa in Kenya. The restaurants serve good, inexpensive meals and chilled beers and sodas. First or second class are definitely preferable if you can afford it, because third class tends to be overcrowded and there is a real risk of theft.

Fares and timetables for individual routings follow below. In addition to these fares, a port tax of US$5 must be paid in hard currency upon leaving any Tanzanian port. On international services, should these resume, you may be required to show a vaccination certificate and, if required, a visa for the country you intend to enter.

Mwanza/Port Bell (Uganda) This international service was suspended after the MV *Bukoba* sank in 1996, a tragedy that resulted in hundreds of fatalities, but it was resumed in early 1999. The MV *Victoria* now runs in either direction once weekly, leaving from Mwanza on Sunday afternoon and Port Bell on Monday afternoon. The trip takes 18 hours. Fares are US$55 (own room), US$35 (first class), US$30 (second class sleeping), US$20 (second class sitting) and US$20 (third class). You can take a vehicle on board for US$80.

Mwanza/Kisumu (Kenya) As with ferries to Port Bell, this service has been indefinitely suspended. The ferry used to leave Mwanza at 15.00 on Thursday and Kisumu at 18.00 on Friday, taking 20 hours in either direction. Fares were slightly higher than for the Port Bell ferry.

Mwanza/Bukoba There is one overnight ferry in each direction five days a week, with duties split between MV *Serengeti* and the larger MV *Victoria*. Ferries leave Mwanza at 21.00 or 22.00 every day except Wednesday and Friday, and they leave Bukoba at a similar time every day except Thursday and Saturday. The trip takes around 12 hours. Fares are US$11/7/5 first/second(sitting)/third on MV *Serengeti* and US$14/10/8/5 first/second/second(sitting)/third on MV *Victoria*.

Mwanza/Nyamirembe MV *Clarius* leaves Mwanza at 09.00 on Wednesday and arrives in Nyamirembe at around 18.00 the same day. The return trip leaves Nyamirembe at 07.00 Thursday and arrives in Mwanza at 18.00 the same day. The fare is US$12 first class, US$6 second class sitting or US$4 third class.

Mwanza/Nkome MV *Clarius* leaves Mwanza at 08.00 on Wednesday and Saturday and arrives at Kome Island at 18.00. In the opposite direction, the boat leaves Kome at 08.00 Thursday and Sunday and arrives at Mwanza at 18.00. The fare is US$4 second class sitting and US$3 third class. Ferries stop at Mchangani and Lugata on Kome Island, and at Lushamba and Itabagumba.

Mwanza/Nansio (Ukerewe Island) There is one ferry daily in each direction. The trip takes about three hours and costs US$4 second class sitting or US$3 third class. The boat normally leaves Mwanza at 09.00 and Nansio at 13.30, but the schedule may vary slightly so check it in advance.

average monthly rainfall figures of 100mm or greater are recorded through the period November to May.

MWANZA

According to the 1988 census Mwanza is the second-largest town in Tanzania. It is a relaxed place which, after years of stagnation, seems to have picked up in economic terms far more quickly than most Tanzanian towns. Mwanza has a reasonably cosmopolitan flavour; it has a large Indian population, good links with Kenya and Uganda, and is a focus for overland travellers and expats. Scenically, Mwanza is notable for the bizarre granite outcrops which surround it, the best-known of which is the precariously perched Bismark Rock at the harbour entrance.

Getting there and away

Relatively few fly-in tourists to Tanzania visit Mwanza, since it is far removed from the main tourist centres of the northern and coastal districts. The town is, however, a major transport hub for people travelling more widely in East Africa, boasting rail connections to the coast and to Lake Tanganyika, and direct ferry services across Lake Victoria to Kenya and Uganda.

Trains between Mwanza and Dar es Salaam on the coast run four days a week in each direction, stopping at Tabora where you can disembark to connect with rail services to Kigoma on Lake Tanganyika. Details of ferry services on Lake Victoria are included in the box *Lake Victoria Ferries* opposite.

Buses connect Mwanza to several other parts of the country, but the only routes where these services are quick and reliable are along the eastern shore of the lake, to Musoma and Kisumu in Kenya. Roads which follow the lake shore west of Mwanza are in poor condition as far as Bukoba, so if you're heading this way you are advised to catch the ferry to Bukoba and use road transport from there. I would advise strongly against catching buses headed towards Kigoma, Tabora, Dodoma or Dar es Salaam, as the roads are in terrible condition, and the trip is normally measured in days rather than hours.

The best source of current information about flights out of Mwanza is the **Fourways Travel Service** around the corner from the Pamda Hostel. You can also book tickets here.

Where to stay
Upper range

The **Hotel Tilapia** (PO Box 82 or 190, Mwanza; tel: 068 42109/50517; fax: 50141) is Mwanza's one truly upmarket hotel: a relatively new private development on the Lake Victoria shore near the jetty for Saa Nane Island. Large, comfortable, air-conditioned rooms are very reasonably priced at US$60/double or US$90/suite ($42 and US$60 respectively for residents), and facilities include a swimming pool, a well-regarded restaurant, and an attractive wooden bar and patio overlooking the lake and Saa Nane.

In the town centre, the government-owned **New Mwanza Hotel** (PO Box 25; tel: 068 3202) was undergoing renovations in 1998, but should re-open before the end of 1999. It is conveniently located, and used to be pretty good value at US$40 for an air-conditioned double, though it is difficult to say whether this will still be the case when it re-opens.

Moderate

The **Lake Hotel** (PO Box 910; tel: 068 42030), conveniently situated between the railway station and town centre, is an excellent hotel in this range. The large, nicely

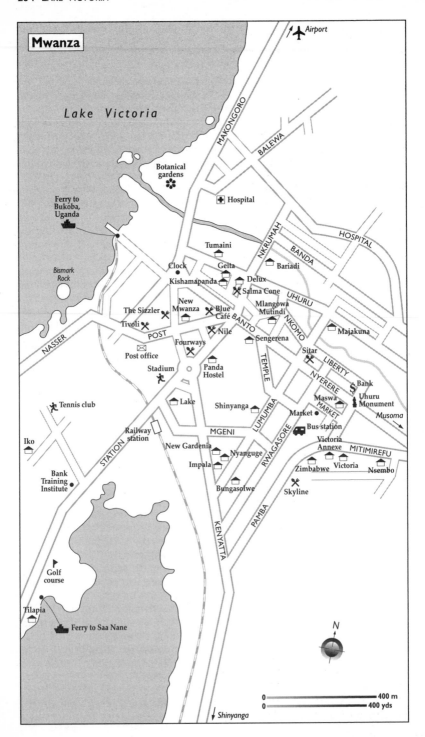

Mwanza

CROSSING BETWEEN MWANZA AND ARUSHA

A fair number of travellers arrive in Mwanza wanting to cross directly to Arusha. This is a problematic route, and there is no quick and cheap way of doing it. If time is a greater factor than money, the best thing to do is to go directly across the Serengeti. At least three buses do this trip every week, as do a number of private Land Rovers which carry passengers – ask about a seat in advance at the bus station in Mwanza or Arusha. The problem with this route is that you cross two conservation areas, which means paying US$50 in park entrance fees over and above the bus fare. This is a waste of money if you already plan to go on safari. On the other hand, for those who can't afford to do a safari proper, it actually makes for a cheap way of seeing the Serengeti – the road passes right through the heart of the reserve and game viewing will be excellent for the six months of the year when animals are concentrated in the southern part of the Serengeti ecosystem. Land Rover drivers (but not bus drivers) are reportedly happy to stop for the occasional photograph!

The cheap and nasty way of getting between Mwanza and Arusha is to use one of the buses which cross south of the Serengeti through Singida and Shinyanga. This is a hellish ride, taking at least 36 hours and sometimes as long as three days, and passing through a dry, unattractive part of the country where stops are most likely to be dictated by breakdowns and flat tyres. Looking on the bright side, there is nothing much along the way to spend your money on – just take plenty of food and water with you.

Otherwise, you're pretty much restricted to heading towards Dar es Salaam by train and bussing to Arusha from there (you could, of course, catch a train as far as Dodoma and then bus through to Arusha, but this involves another unappetising bus trip). This could be a sensible option under some circumstances (basically if you want to visit Dar es Salaam or Zanzibar en route to Arusha), but otherwise it seems rather pointless, as it probably means four days travelling and you'll end up spending as much money as you would have spent crossing the Serengeti in a day.

A final, rather convoluted option would be to cross via Kenya: buses to Kisumu take ten hours, then you could bus or take the overnight train to Nairobi, and finally a minibus through to Namanga border post. This route is only worth considering if it doesn't require additional visa expenses (which will depend on your nationality), but by using the train to Nairobi you could conceivably get through in less then 36 hours.

furnished and well maintained rooms wouldn't look out of place in a government hotel, and they are all self-contained with a sporadic hot water supply, and mosquito nets. Rooms cost around US$10/12 single/double, including a poor breakfast. The restaurant has apparently closed for good, but the outdoor bar remains one of the better drinking holes in Mwanza.

The **Delux Hotel** is another sensibly priced place, a little run down when compared to the Lake Hotel, but correspondingly cheaper at US$8/10 self-contained single/double. At one time it used to be difficult to find a vacant room after midday, but this no longer seems to be the case. There is a good restaurant, two bars, and a disco attached, the latter generating a level of noise that may become annoying if you've no intention of joining in.

The **Iko Hotel** (PO Box 2469; tel: (068) 40900) is a pleasant and friendly place on a rocky hill overlooking the lake near the golf course and Hotel Tilapia. Although the hotel is only three years old, the rooms already show signs of wear, but they remain fair value at US$20 for a comfortable s/c double or US$40 for a suite. There is a restaurant serving meals for around US$4, as well as a bar. The surrounding suburban lanes make for attractive rambling and birding.

The **Tema Hotel**, 5km out of town on the Shinyanga Road, has acceptable self-contained doubles for US$14.

Budget

There is no shortage of affordable accommodation in Mwanza, with perhaps 20 guesthouses dotted around the city centre. On the whole, the scruffiest places are those closet to the bus station, and it's worth the walk to stay elsewhere.

One place that currently stands out is the **Panda Hostel** managed by the Tema Hotels Group, who also do all the catering on trains and ferries in Tanzania. The rooms recently received an overdue coat of paint, and they seem very good value at US$4/6 self-contained single/double with mosquito net, while the communal showers no longer leave anything to be desired. There's a restaurant on the ground floor (if you've already eaten on a train or ferry, you know what to expect) and a rooftop bar where you can get cold beers and sodas.

Another very reliable option is the **Kishamapanda Guest House**, opposite the Delux, which has bright rooms for US$4/5 single/double and self-contained doubles for US$6. As with the Delux, it used to be practically impossible to find a vacant room here, but this seems no longer to be a problem.

Near the bus station, the **Victoria Hotel** is looking ever more run down, but the rooms are adequately clean and have mosquito nets and fans (the latter not working when I last checked). They seem fair value at US$4/5 single/double, but are not nearly as good as the large self-contained rooms costing US$6/8 in the adjoining **Victoria Hotel Annexe**.

In 1992, the then newly built **Nsembo Hotel** had some superficial pretensions to superiority, though it was already showing signs of rapid wear and tear, and the toilets were overrun with cockroaches. Come 1998, the hotel is looking very tired, the staff remain as unfriendly as ever, but the rooms seem worth a try at US$6 for a self-contained double.

Most of the other places marked on the map are standard guesthouses with rooms in the US$3-5 range. The best of a fairly ordinary bunch are probably the **Zimbabwe**, **Tumaini**, **Nsembo**, **Nyanguge** and **Shinyanga Guesthouses**.

Where to eat

The **Sizzler Restaurant**, opposite the New Mwanza Hotel, is one of the newest restaurants in the town centre, and in my estimation perhaps the best value for money. It serves a variety of Indian dishes for around US$5, supplemented by a few Western and Chinese items. In the evenings, an outdoor barbecue does *mishkaki*, chicken tikka and fresh chapatis and roti bread. The restaurant used to close Thursdays but is now open daily for lunch and dinner.

Two more good restaurants have opened in the vicinity of the New Mwanza over the last year year or so. The **Szechwan Mahal** is arguably the top restaurant in town, serving a variety of Chinese and Indian dishes for around US$10 per head. The **Kuleana Pizzeria** serves first-class pizzas for around US$3–6.

Of the older places, the **Sitar Restaurant** remains fairly popular with travellers, though last time I ate there I thought the food looked and tasted as if it had been cooked in Brylcream. What feedback I've heard since tends to confirm this is still the case. For sheer value for money, you won't beat the restaurant on the ground floor of the **Delux Hotel**, where massive portions of a variety of Asian and African dishes cost between US$2 and US$3. I've had a recent report that the restaurant here looks rather seedy – but then it always has looked rather seedy, and still managed to produce a great feed!

Similar in price, but not nearly as good, the **Tivoli Restaurant**, **Fourways Restaurant**, and the restaurant on the ground floor of the **Panda Hostel** are all worth a try if you're in town long enough to want a change of scene.

Salma Cone serves great ice-cream sundaes and fresh popcorn at reasonable prices, while fresh brown bread can be bought at the pizzeria near the New Mwanza Hotel.

Excursions from Mwanza
Saa Nane Island
This small, rocky island in Lake Victoria has been set aside as a game reserve and zoo. On both accounts it is a bit of a washout; re-introduced buck wander around aimlessly and several listless predators are confined in small cages, as is a decidedly pissed-off looking chimpanzee.

All this detracts from the island's real attraction, the small animals which inhabit it naturally. It is crawling with lizards such as the gaudily coloured rock agama. We also saw a few water monitors, the largest African lizard, crash gracelessly through the undergrowth. Bird life is profuse. Fish eagle, pied kingfisher and white-bellied cormorant are common near the lake shore. Twitchers will have little difficulty spotting such localised species as swamp flycatcher, yellow-throated leaflove, grey kestrel and slender-billed weaver. Rock hyrax are the most visible mammal.

The motorboat to Saa Nane leaves from a jetty 15 minutes' walk from Mwanza town centre. It departs at 11.00, 13.00 and 15.00 and 1700, and returns an hour later. You can spend as long as you like on the island for an admission fee of US$1. At present, you may not stay overnight.

Sukoma Museum
Tanzania's largest tribe, the Sukoma, live in and around Mwanza. The Sukoma Museum, 20km out of town, displays exhibits relating to their lifestyle. Try to visit it on a Saturday, when the Sukoma Snake Dance is performed in tandem with a live python. If you visit the museum on weekdays it may well be deserted. You can camp for US$2 per person, but facilities are limited to running water and one toilet.

The Sukoma Museum is a short walk from Kissesa on the Mwanza-Musoma road. Any bus to Musoma can drop you off there.

Ukerewe Island
Ukerewe Island is two to three hours from Mwanza by ferry; see *Lake Victoria Ferries* box for details. The island's largest town, Nansio, is also the ferry terminal. The round trip to Nansio is a good way to see some of Africa's largest lake. In addition to the ferries, occasional vehicles connect Nansio to Bunda on the main Mwanza–Musoma road.

Nansio is a scruffy little town. You will have an hour to wander around while you wait to re-embark the ferry, which is more than adequate. The island itself is very pretty, however, and the sandy beaches west of Nansio are said to be bilharzia-free. If you have a couple of days spare in the Mwanza area, you could do worse than spend them exploring Ukerewe using Nansio as a base.

The **Gullu Beach Hotel** (PO Box 308, Nansio; tel: 068 50764; fax: 068 41726) lies on the lake shore about 500m from Nansio Port. A variety of rooms is available: singles, doubles and triples using communal showers cost US$5/7/10 for residents and US$8/13/17 for non-residents, while self-contained doubles cost US$10 for residents and US$16 for non-residents. All rooms have mosquito nets and rates include breakfast. Camping costs US$3pp resident or US$6pp non-resident. There is a restaurant and bar. Fishing boat hire costs US$150 per day.

If this is too expensive, there are several local guesthouses in Nansio, of which the **Panda Hostel** and **Island Inn** are about the best. The Island Inn has a restaurant.

Kome and Maisome Islands
Adventurous travellers may be intrigued by these two large islands in Lake Victoria, both of which can be reached by ferry from Mwanza. According to maps, both islands have substantial areas of forest; it seems likely they will harbour similar animal species to those which occur naturally on Rubondo Island National Park. It's less likely there will be any formal accommodation; assume you'll need a tent. A survey map might also be handy. Depending on who you speak to, the staff at the ferry office in Mwanza can be very helpful with information about places where ferries stop.

Ferries from Mwanza to Nyamirembe/Nkome stop at both islands on Monday, Wednesday and Thursday; ferries returning to Mwanza stop at both islands on Tuesday, Thursday and Friday (see *Lake Victoria Ferries* for details).

BUNDA
Bunda, the largest town on the Mwanza-Musoma road, is a route focus of sorts. It is where Arusha-based safari companies drop off passengers heading to Mwanza, and the best place to catch a pick-up to Ukerewe Island.

The scenic road between Mwanza and Bunda is in good condition. It passes first through dry, flat country dotted with small koppies and Sukoma homesteads and offers regular glimpses of Lake Victoria. Before reaching Bunda it skirts the Serengeti; at the right time of year there is some wildlife to be seen.

Bunda is no more than moderately intriguing. More substantial than maps suggest, it has a scenic position at the foot of a range of steep granite hills. If you have the inclination to climb one of these, you would have a superb vantage point over Lake Victoria and the Serengeti plains.

There are several guesthouses and *hotelis* in Bunda. Rooms cost less than US$2.

MUSOMA
Musoma lies on a pretty part of the Lake Victoria shore, but apart from strolling around town or lazing at the Silver Sands Inn, it offers little to travellers. People coming from Kisumu (Kenya) used to stop in Musoma to pick up a ferry to Mwanza, but since the Musoma-Mwanza road was re-surfaced the ferry service has been discontinued, and Musoma sees few tourists.

Where to stay and eat
The colonial-style **Railway Hotel** lies on the lake shore about 3km from the town centre. In the town centre, on Kahawa Street, the **Orange Tree Hotel** is clean, has a bar and restaurant, and is a bit cheaper at around US$5 for a single or US$9/11 for a s/c single/double. The best budget hotel is **Silver Sands Inn**, overlooking the lake 1km from the town centre. Meals are served on request and soft drinks are available. The **Mennonite Centre** is clean, friendly and popular with travellers, but it is often full. The basic **Butata Lodge** is cheap, clean and friendly, and the rooms have mosquito nets.

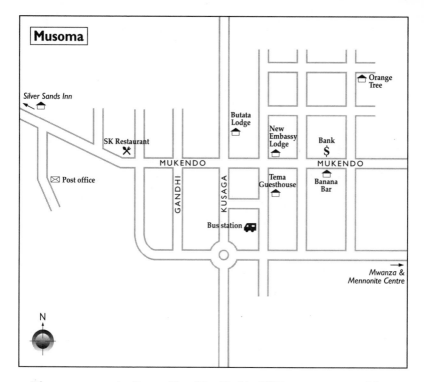

The restaurant at the Orange Tree Hotel is fair. **SK Restaurant** serves Western and Indian meals. Several bars and *hotelis* line Mukendo Road; the **Banana Bar** and **Embassy Lodge** look reasonable.

RUBONDO ISLAND NATIONAL PARK

This remote national park, which protects the 240km² Rubondo Island, was until recently very difficult to visit. This has all changed following the recent opening of an upmarket tourist lodge on the island and the possible introduction of scheduled flights in the near future, and Rubondo must now rank as one of Tanzania's most alluring destinations for those with enough money and an interest in forest animals. An attractive aspect of the island is that all game viewing is done on foot or by boat.

The predominant vegetation type is rainforest, but there are also patches of grassland and papyrus swamp. Several large mammal species are present. Sitatunga, bushbuck, vervet monkey, otter, hippopotamus and various duikers are indigenous to the island, while elephant, chimpanzee and giraffe have been introduced. Rubondo is rich in forest- and water-associated birds, with almost 400 species recorded. Fishing is good, as testified by the record catch of an 108kg Nile perch.

An entrance fee of US$15 per 24-hour period must be paid in hard currency.

Getting there and away

At present, the simplest way to get to Rubondo is to catch a scheduled flight from Dar es Salaam or Arusha to Mwanza, then to charter a flight from Mwanza, which will cost between US$360 and US$540 depending on the size of the aircraft. An air charter is best organised through through Flycatcher Safaris, the Arusha-based owner of Rubondo Island Camp (see overleaf). The management of the camp are currently negotiating for scheduled flights to be introduced between the Serengeti and Rubondo, but there is no telling when such a service will materialise.

For those driving themselves to Rubondo, the best place to head for is Nkome Port on the mainland, which can be reached from Mwanza via Geita. The stretch of road between Geita and Nkome may be impassable in the rainy season and it requires a good 4WD at the best of times. At the ranger post at Nkome, you can arrange a boat transfer to the island through Flycatcher Safaris, which will cost around US$150–250 per group, depending on the size of boat required.

Using public transport to reach Rubondo, the place to head for is Muganza on the mainland. Muganza is connected to Mwanza by a daily bus, but this is a long, cramped ride. A more attractive option, at least in one direction, would be to catch the weekly ferry from Mwanza to Nyamirembe Port (see *Lake Victoria Ferries* for details), from where it's about 20km by road to Muganza – transport is light so you may have to walk some or all of this stretch. Once in Muganza, the Lutheran Mission Hospital can radio through to the park rangers to arrange for a boat to collect you. This will probably cost around US$30 each way, to which must be added another small fee for a vehicle to take you to the campsite once you arrive at the island. It is possible to charter a boat to Rubondo directly from Nyamirembe, but this can cost as much as US$120 each way.

If you use the ferry in both directions, you will have to spend a week in the vicinity of Rubondo. There are guesthouses in Nyamirembe, so you could spend a couple of nights there to save on park fees. Exploring the roads around Nyamirembe could well pay dividends. The port borders Biharamulo Game Reserve, a stretch of brachystegia woodland which provides sanctuary to 30 large mammal species including elephant, zebra, buffalo, hippopotamus, roan antelope and common reedbuck.

Where to stay

The recently opened **Rubondo Island Camp** consists of ten luxury self-contained *bandas*, each of which has a private verandah facing the lake. The camp lies in a patch of forest, and the swimming pool is built in a natural rock outcrop. Full-board rates are US$180/320 single/double in high seasons and US$120/200 in low seasons. Boat and foot excursions can be arranged at the camp, as can fishing expeditions. The camp is managed by and can be booked through Flycatcher Safaris, PO Box 591 Arusha; tel: 057 6963; fax: 057 8261; email: flycat@arusha. com or flycat@swissonline.ch. It is possible to make direct contact with the camp at tel: 00871 761 467 690 or email: rubondo@hf.habari.co.tz.

The cheaper alternative is the attractively positioned national park campsite, where you can pitch a tent for US$10 per person or rent a simple '*mabati banda*' at a cost of US$20 per person. People staying at the national park site should bring all food and drink with them from Mwanza.

BUKOBA

This quiet, attractive port, reputedly foounded by the Emin Pasha in 1890, is situated in an area of lush green hills rolling down to the Lake Victoria shore. Bukoba is the centre of a thriving coffee industry, but otherwise it has a distinct air of decline. There are a number of impressive Indian-style buildings in the town centre, but most are in poor condition. In better condition is the large church built by Bishop Hirth between 1893 and 1904. There is little in the way of sightseeing in Bukoba, but it is an agreeable place, and the marshy area between the town and the lake supports a surprisingly large variety of waterbirds.

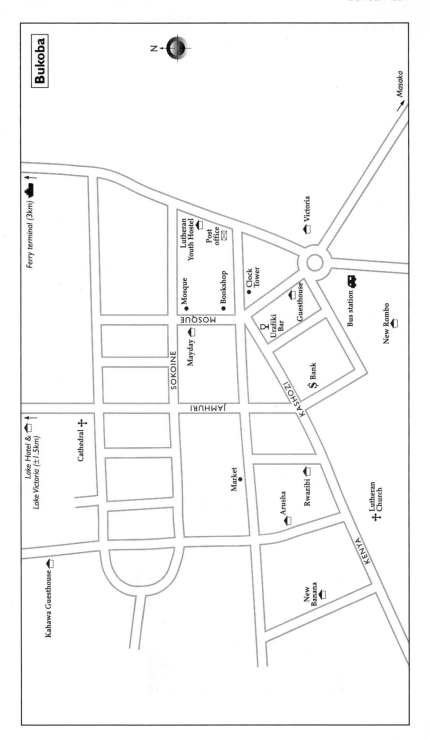

Getting there and away

Travellers who visit Bukoba generally do so on their way to or from Uganda. Details of this route are in *Chapter 3*. Details of ferries between Bukoba and Mwanza are given under *Lake Victoria Ferries* (see box on page 252). Occasional buses connect Bukoba to Mwanza and Kigoma. Personally, I think you would be crazy to contemplate using them.

Precision Air flies between Mwanza and Bukoba. Tickets can be bought at the airstrip near the Lake Hotel.

Where to stay

In the town centre, the most upmarket accommodation – or so they say – is to be found at the **New Banana Hotel**, which has dingy self-contained doubles without running water for US$10. Altogether more alluring are the meals, notably the excellent whole tilapia and chips for US$2. Much better value than the New Banana is the **Rwazibi Hotel**, which has oddly shaped but comfortable and brightly painted self-contained doubles for US$8 and suites for US$12.

On the lake shore, out towards the ferry jetty, the **Lake Hotel** has a faded colonial charm and a scenic position, though the rooms are nothing special at US$12/16 s/c single/double. You can camp in the grounds for US$3pp. The nearby **Coffee Tree Hotel** is similar in price, but lacks character.

The indisputable pick of the cheaper accommodation is the **Lutheran Youth Hostel**, where clean, secure four-bed dormitories and double rooms cost less than US$2 per person. Excellent value for money. The nearby **Catholic Youth Centre** has self-contained rooms for US$7/8 single/double, and good business facilities including a fax machine, computer and secretarial services. If you prefer not to stay in an institution, the **Kahawa Guest House** is the best of the more basic places, followed by the **Mayday Hotel** and then a string of rather dismal also-rans.

Lake Tanganyika and the Southwest

Following the contours of the Rift Valley along the border between Tanzania and the Congo, Lake Tanganyika is something of a statistician's dream, measuring 675km from north to south, an average of 50km wide, and reaching a depth of up to 1,435m. Tanganyika holds a volume of water seven times greater than that of Lake Victoria (the largest lake on the continent), and it is the longest freshwater body in the world, as well as the second-deepest after Lake Baikal in Russia. It is also a very beautiful lake, hemmed in by the verdant hills on either side of the Rift Valley, and boasting the clearest water you are likely to see.

Formed roughly 20 million years ago, Lake Tanganyika is regarded to be an inland sea, overflowing into its sole outlet, the Lukuga River, only in years of exceptionally high rainfall. Due to its great age and isolation from any similar habitat, Lake Tanganyika forms one of the most biologically rich aquatic habitats in the world, supporting more than 500 fish species of which the majority are endemic cichlids. The most important fish economically is the *dagaa*, a tiny plankton-eater which lives in large shoals and is sun-dried on the lake shore for sale throughout western Tanzania.

The only substantial town on the Tanzanian part of the lake shore is Kigoma, founded under German rule as the railhead from the coast, only a few kilometres away from the 19th-century Arab settlement at Ujiji. An important slave trading post, Ujiji is also where Burton and Speke first reached the lake shore in 1858, and where the historic meeting between Livingstone and Stanley took place in 1872. The two national parks that fringe the lake shore, Gombe Stream and Mahale Mountains, support a mosaic of different vegetation types, but are of most interest to tourists for their populations of rainforest-dwelling chimpanzees. Some distance east of the lake, the little-known Katavi National Park protects an expanse of dry bush and similar wildlife species to more accessible southern reserves such as Ruaha. Very few fly-in tourists ever get close to Lake Tanganyika, but the area does attract an erratic trickle of backpackers, for whom the weekly lake ferry service ranks as one of East Africa's most compelling public transport rides.

Climate

Lake Tanganyika lies at the relatively low altitude of 730m, and the climate along the lake shore is correspondingly hot and sticky. Much of the lake hinterland is similarly hot and low-lying, though the higher reaches of the Mahale Mountains are relatively cool.

Getting around

Within Tanzania, the main means of access to Lake Tanganyika is the central railway line connecting Dar es Salaam on the coast to Kigoma. The central line can

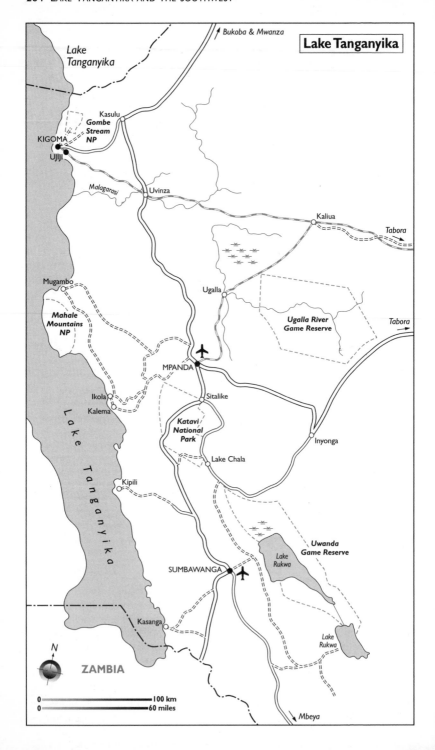

MV LIEMBA

Originally called the *Graf van Goetzen*, the MV *Liemba* was railed to Kigoma by the Germans and assembled there during World War I, but even before it had embarked on its maiden voyage, the Germans sank it to prevent it from falling into British hands. The boat was salvaged and re-named in 1924 and has steamed up and down the lake almost continually since then. The oft-repeated story that *Liemba* was used in the filming of *The African Queen* is, to the best of my knowledge, a myth.

In theory, the *Liemba* does a round trip every week between Kigoma, Bujumbura and Mpulungu, stopping at several small ports on the lake shore south of Kigoma. It departs from Kigoma at 16.00 Wednesday and arrives in Mpulungu at 10.00 Friday. It then turns back at 16.00 Friday and arrives in Kigoma at 10.00 Sunday. It leaves Kigoma at 16.00 Sunday and arrives in Bujumbura at 10.00 Monday. The return trip from Bujumbura departs at 16.00 Monday and arrives back in Kigoma at 10.00 Tuesday. Due to sanctions against Burundi, the Bujumbura leg of this voyage hasn't been running for some time, but rumour is that it will resume with the imminent lifting of these sanctions. A second boat, MV *Umoja*, operates on the lake within Tanzania. When only one boat is running, as is often the case, this boat will do the Bujumbura-Mpulungu run and the domestic service will be suspended.

Tickets bought in Tanzania can be paid for in local currency. Kigoma to Mpulungu costs US$22.50 first class and US$18.25 second class. Both classes consist of four-bunk cabins. Tickets bought in Zambia or Burundi must be paid for in US dollars and cost double what they would in Tanzania. Both boats have a restaurant. Meals cost US$1.25. A bar serves beer and sodas.

The ferry stops at lake-shore villages such as Mugambo, Ikola, Kalema and Kasanga. If you don't want to go into Zambia, Kasanga is the place to get off. There is a basic guesthouse and road transport from Kasanga to Sumbawanga and on to Mbeya. The ferry arrives at Kasanga in the early morning, so there is plenty of time to find a lift.

There is nowhere for ships to dock at these villages. When the ferry arrives it is greeted by a floating market selling dried fish and other foodstuffs, while passengers are ferried to and from the shore on rickety fishing boats. Viewed from the upper decks this is richly comic; if you are embarking or disembarking it is a nightmare. The hold seethes with passengers climbing over each other to get in and out; the ticket officer frantically tries to identify and extract a fare from the newcomers; at the exit, the smaller boats ram each other trying to get the best position.

If you have the inclination to explore Lake Tanganyika slowly, small boats do run between minor ports, but I cannot vouch for their regularity or reliability. Most settlements along the lake shore have no formal accommodation, so you are advised to carry a tent.

also be used to get between Kigoma and Mwanza (on Lake Victoria), changing trains at Tabora. Full details of the central line are included in *Chapter 13*.

The only other way to travel between the coast and the lake is by plane. Air Tanzania runs scheduled flights between Dar es Salaam and Kigoma on Monday, Wednesday and Friday, and there are also flights connecting Kigoma to Mwanza and Nairobi, but cancellations are commonplace, so it may be that your only option is to charter a flight.

There are no direct road links between Kigoma and the coast, and although it is normally possible to bus between Kigoma and Mwanza, this is an arduous trip and not recommended to any but the most staunch of travellers. There is a limited amount of road transport along the road which runs parallel to the lake, via Mpanda, Katavi National Park and Mpanda to Sumbawanga, but this too is no joyride, and I haven't heard of or heard from a traveller who has attempted this route since I did it myself in 1992.

The most attractive mode of transport in this part of Tanzania is the legendary *MV Liemba*, which sails weekly between Kigoma and Mpulungu in Zambia, and is likely to resume a service to Bujumbura in Burundi in the near future. See box *MV Liemba* for details.

KIGOMA

This is the largest town on Lake Tanganyika, founded in 1915 when the central railway line reached the lake, and it remains the most significant transport hub in this part of Tanzania. Despite its relatively remote setting, Kigoma has a surprisingly cosmopolitan mood, and at times it is crawling with backpackers, African businessmen and overland trucks, all waiting for a transport connection. The town itself is small and easy-going, snaking uphill from the lake shore along a long avenue lined with mango trees, and the surrounding hills are very scenic without offering a great deal in the way of prescribed tourist attractions other than the 'Kaiser House' built in the German colonial era. Most people who make it as far as Kigoma will view the day trip to nearby Ujiji as close to mandatory, and Kigoma does serve as the base for visits to the habituated chimpanzees of Gombe Stream and Mahale Mountains National Parks.

Getting there and away

The only realistic ways to get to Kigoma are by air, rail or water. The railway is covered in *Chapter 13* and the ferry in the box MV *Liemba* on page 265. You could come to Kigoma by road from Mwanza, but you would measure the journey in days. Air Tanzania flies from Dar es Salaam to Kigoma three times weekly, on Monday, Wednesday and Friday.

Where to stay

The most upmarket place to stay around Kigoma is the new **Kigoma Hilltop Hotel** (PO Box 1160, Kigoma; tel: 0695 4435; fax: 0695 4434; email: kht@raha.com), which is perched dramatically above a cliff overlooking the lake roughly 2km from the town centre. Facilities include a swimming pool, two restaurants, water sports equipment, fishing, snorkelling, various indoor games. a gymnasium, secretarial services, a generator and a private beach. Accommodation is in self-contained, air-conditioned chalets with satellite television and fridge. Standard rooms cost around US$35/50 single/double, and suites range in price from US$90 to US$130.

Two mid-range hotels lie on the outskirts of Kigoma, less than ten minutes' walk from the ferry jetty and railway station. The newer **Aqua Hotel** has comfortable rooms and good facilities, while the **Railway Hotel** (aka Lake Tanganyika Beach Resort and Hotel) is marginally cheaper and more cosy.

Two hotels in the town centre are geared to budget travellers. The friendly **Lake View Hotel** has clean, comfortable rooms with mosquito nets for US$2/3 single/double. The similarly-priced **Kigoma Hotel** is scruffier, but just as friendly. There are several guesthouses on the main road towards Ujiji, but they're mostly rather uninviting.

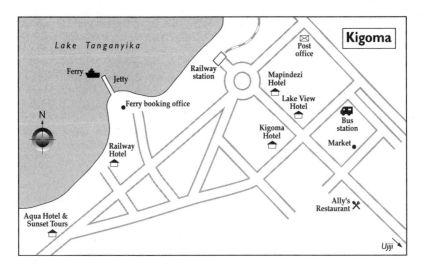

Where to eat

There are restaurants at the three large hotels. Otherwise, **Ally's** serves a wide variety of inexpensive meals, as well as snacks, fresh bread and pastries. The Lake View and Kigoma Hotels have fair restaurants. A new recommendation, **Stanley's Restaurant**, is situated opposite the Lake View Hotel and serves reasonably priced Western dishes

Excursions from Kigoma
Ujiji

Most people who pass through Kigoma make a trip to Ujiji, 10km away. Said to be one of Africa's oldest market villages – whatever that means – Ujiji was a 19th-century Arab trading post, and still shows Swahili influences you wouldn't normally associate with this part of the country. Ujiji is where Burton and Speke first set foot on the Lake Tanganyika shore. Livingstone lived here for several months in 1872, and it is where Stanley uttered the immortal phrase: 'Doctor Livingstone, I presume?'. There are plaques in Ujiji commemorating both of these events, and there's also a museum dedicated to Livingstone, though the latter amounts to little more than a collection of absurdly-captioned paintings of Livingstone.

The monument to Livingstone and Stanley stands under a mango tree, and it bears a plaque which was originally set in a large obelisk; the present stone setting was built shortly after World War II. In fact, there was an earlier monument to Livingstone and Stanley, erected by Belgium after the end of World War I, which consisted of a bland, whitewashed concrete slab covering the base of the original mango tree under which the meeting is said to have taken place. Unfortunately, this concrete eyesore caused the roots of the original tree to decay: photographs taken in 1921 and 1930 show that over the course of a decade a flourishing and thickly foliated tree had been reduced to a bare stump with only a few scraggly branches remaining. In August of 1930, the tree was finally felled, but not before the District Officer of Kigoma, Captain Grant, had the foresight to graft a new tree from the original. It is this grafted tree which now hangs over the monument, where a brass plaque donated by the Royal Geographical Society reads 'Under the mango tree which then stood here Stanley met Livingstone 10th November 1872'.

All of which is rather poignant until you discover that Stanley's journal suggests the meeting took place near the old market, several hundred metres from the modern monument, and that the tree shown in the 1921 photograph was too young to have offered any significant cover in Livingstone's day. The probability is that when locals were quizzed by their German colonisers about where the famous meeting took place, they simply invented a plausible site – a scenario that will be familiar to anybody who has regularly asked for directions in Africa. What *is* beyond doubt, incidentally, is that the meeting actually took place in Ujiji – I've heard that a similar plaque can be found somewhere in Burundi, but I've never come across any serious historical suggestion that Stanley and Livingstone met anywhere other than Ujiji.

For all its historical associations, Ujiji today is something of a backwater, and people who visit expecting to find a thriving market town are invariably disappointed. In most respects, Ujiji could be any one of dozens of fishing villages on the lake shore – and once you've dutifully snapped a picture of yourself and a pal shaking hands in front of the Livingstone plaque, the most interesting aspect of the town is being able to watch the local fishermen and boat builders ply their trades.

There is regular road transport between Ujiji and Kigoma. Should you want to overnight in Ujiji, there is a basic guesthouse.

Kitwe Point Sanctuary

This 300-acre sanctuary, on the lake shore 5km south of Kigoma, was recently deeded to the Jane Goodall Institute by the government after plans to develop it as a educational wildlife zoo faltered. In addition to a few zebra, wildebeest and vervet monkey, the sanctuary is home to three orphaned chimpanzees who were confiscated by the Tanzania authorities in 1994. It lies in an area of regenerating forest, next to the lake, and would presumably also be of interest to birders. Visitors are welcome to visit the sanctuary at feeding time (16.00) daily except for on Wednesdays, Sundays, and the first Monday of any given month. *Matatus* from Kigoma to the village of Katonga terminate about 20m from the sanctuary entrance.

Gombe Stream National Park

Gombe Stream is renowned for its chimpanzees and the research done into their behaviour by primatologist Jane Goodall. Gombe was gazetted as a game reserve in 1943 and made a national park in 1968. Goodall arrived there in 1960 sponsored by Louis Leakey, who felt her lack of scientific training would allow her to observe chimpanzee behaviour without preconceptions. After initial difficulties trying to locate them, Goodall overcame the chimps' shyness through the combination of a banana-feeding machine and sheer persistence.

Since the late 1960s Goodall's work has achieved both popular and scientific recognition. Her painstaking studies of individual chimps and the day-to-day social behaviour of troops have been supplemented by a series of observations confronting conventional scientific wisdom. Observations which initially caused controversy – tool-making, inter-troop warfare and even cannibalism – have since been confirmed and accepted. Much of Goodall's work is described in her books *In the Shadow of Man* and *Through a Window*. The study of Gombe's chimpanzees is now the longest-running study of an individual wild animal population in the world.

In addition to roughly 100 chimpanzees, Gombe Stream supports a significant baboon population, the subject of research since 1967. Other common primates are vervet, blue, red-tailed and red colobus monkeys. Most other mammals found there are secretive or nocturnal, so they are seldom seen by visitors. Over 200 bird species have been recorded.

To see the chimpanzees you will need to go on a guided walk. They are most frequently observed at a feeding station near the main camp. If they are not there, you will have to go deeper into the forest. The only part of the park where you may walk unguided is along the lake shore. The forest reaches down to the beach, so you should see plenty of birds, butterflies and primates in this area, especially towards dusk when many nocturnal animals come to drink at the lake.

Because they are genetically similar to humans, chimpanzees are susceptible to the same diseases. If you are unwell, do not visit the park. Even a common cold has the potential to kill a chimpanzee who may not have your immunity.

Gombe Stream used to be quite popular with backpackers travelling through western Tanzania, but park fees have been increased several times in recent years to keep down the volume of visitors. At present the entrance fee is US$100 per 24-hour period for visitors and US$40 for expatriates, and a further US$20 is charged to stay overnight. Fees must be paid in hard currency.

A 72-page booklet, *Gombe Stream National Park*, is the most comprehensive in the series published by Tanzania National Parks. It's an essential purchase if you plan to visit the park, and includes checklists and detailed coverage of chimpanzee behaviour. It may be difficult to buy a copy outside of Arusha.

Getting there and away
Gombe Stream lies 16km from Kigoma, and independent travellers have the option of reaching the park by lake-taxi. These are uncovered and can become uncomfortably hot in the sun, so if you have an umbrella, take it along. Lake-taxis leave from a village 3km from Kigoma at roughly 11.00. They take four hours to get to Gombe, and cost US$2. From Kigoma, you can hire a taxi to take you to the village from which the lake-taxis leave. Lake-taxis returning to Kigoma pass Gombe Stream at around 05.45.

The Kigoma Hilltop Hotel (see address under *Where to stay* in Kigoma) organises package excursions to Gombe, a 25-minute trip each way on their recently imported motorboats. Their packages range from three to eight days in duration (with the first and/or last night being spent at their hotel in Kigoma) and vary greatly in price depending on duration and number of passengers. To give an idea, a three-day trip (which includes one night in the park) would cost US$600 for one person, US$550 per person for two people, and US$400 per person for five people, while a five-day package (including two nights in the park) would cost US$900, US$800 and US$575 per person for one, two and five people. These rates include national park fees, guide fees, all meals, boat transfers, collection from the airport, accommodation in Kigoma and in the national park *banda*s. The rates do not include flights (or other transport) to Kigoma from elsewhere in the country. The hotel also organises combined packages to Gomba and Mahale, lasting from six to eight days in total and costing from US$1,500/1,650 per person for two people for six/eight days to US$850/1075 per person for six people for six/eight days.

The Aqua Hotel also organises trips to Gombe on a private boat. An all-inclusive four-day package works out at around US$600 per person sharing. Their combined eight-day package taking in both Gombe and Mahale costs around US$1,250 per person. Both packages include park fees, food, transport and accommodation or camping.

Where to stay
The camp is not far from the lake shore. Accommodation in *banda*s costs US$20 per person per night. There is a communal kitchen, but be warned that the camp is plagued by a baboon troop which is likely to attack anybody who carries food

openly between their *banda* and the kitchen. It is also possible to pitch a tent on the lake shore, but this costs the same as staying in a *banda*. If you do camp, don't leave any food in your tent, or the baboons are likely to knock it down. All food must be brought from Kigoma, and the baboon situation makes it advisable not to bring any fruit.

Mahale Mountains National Park

Gazetted in 1985, Mahale Mountains National Park protect a 1,613km² knuckle of land that juts into Lake Tanganyika 150km south of Kigoma. Part of the Rift Valley escarpment, the range runs in a roughly north-south direction and consists of at least eight peaks topping 2,000m in altitude. Mahale was first documented in VL Cameron's *Across Africa*, published in 1877, but aside from sporadic visits to the lower slopes by the White Fathers based at Kalema between 1911 and 1916, the area was practically unknown to the outside world as recently as 1935, when Dollman exhibited a chimpanzee skull found at Mahale to the Linnean society of London. This highest peak in the range, the 2,462m Nkungwe, was first conquered by a European in 1940, and it was only in 1958 that a team of Oxford scientists started serious scientific exploration of the area. Though not as well publicised as their peers at Gombe Stream, the chimps of Mahale have been the subject of ongoing research by Japanese scientists since 1961, a year before Jane Goodall arrived at Gombe.

The lake shore west of the mountains is very scenic. The western foothills receive an annual rainfall of 2,000mm, and are covered in lush lowland forest. The drier eastern slopes are covered in *miombo* woodland. At altitudes above 2,000m there is both bamboo and montane forest. For tourists, the main attraction of Mahale Mountains is that it protects Tanzania's largest chimpanzee population: an estimated 700-1,000 chimps are resident within the park boundaries and a similar number inhabit forest reserves on the fringes of the national park. Several troops are habituated, and they can be visited by tourists. Other lowland forest species found at Mahale are similar to those found at Gombe, including red colobus, and with the addition of typical west African species such as brush-tailed porcupine and giant forest squirrel. An endemic race of the Angola black-and-white colobus monkey is found in the park's montane forests. The eastern slopes of Mahale support woodland species: elephant, lion, roan antelope, buffalo and giraffe. These often stray into the forest; lions have killed several chimps, and African hunting dogs have been seen on the beach.

Chimps are less readily seen than at Gombe Stream, but most people feel that Mahale's scenery and wilderness atmosphere make up for this, and the chimps are still very approachable by comparison to those in neighbouring Uganda. All game viewing is on foot, but you may not walk without a guide. Guides can be organised when you arrive at the headquarters at Kasiha. If you want to hike into the mountains or to climb Nkungwe peak, arrangements should be made in advance.

An entrance fee of US$50 per 24-hour period for tourists and US$20 for expatriates must be paid in hard currency. It is not recommended that you visit the park during the rainy season (November to April). Much of the information in the National Parks booklet *Gombe Stream National Park* will be useful to visitors to Mahale.

Getting there and away

One of the attractions of Mahale is its remoteness. It can only be reached by plane or boat. Any tour operator in Arusha or Dar es Salaam will be able to organise a chartered plane to Kigoma or to the airstrip in Mahale. It is possible to charter a boat from Kigoma to Mahale; the Kigoma Hilltop Hotel in Kigoma can arrange visits from five to eight days in duration, as can the Aqua Hotel. To give an idea of price, a five-day package will cost US$1,100 per person for two people, and US$645 per person for five, while an eight-day visit will cost US$1,450 per person for two people and US$950 per person for five. The Kigoma Hilltop Hotel also does combined Gombe and Mahale packages (see under *Gombe Stream National Park*)

Greystoke Safaris owns Ottoman Camp, the only permanent tented lodge in Mahale, and can arrange full fly-in packages from Arusha, Dar es Salaam, Mwanza or Mfuwe in Zambia. See *Where to stay* for contact details.

The only way for budget travellers to get to and from Mahale is on the Lake Tanganyika ferry. This stops at Mugambo, the village 15km north of the park boundary, seven hours after it leaves Kigoma. On the return trip, the ferry stops at Mugambo at 04.00 and arrives at Kigoma seven hours later. From Mugambo, most people hire a private boat to the headquarters at Kasiha. We did, however, receive a letter from someone who walked the 15km to the boundary. He says you are unlikely to get lost as the mountains are in front of you the whole way and the path is flat. You will pass through several villages, where you must exchange greetings with the village headman, who can usually be found at the school. Unfortunately, he did not say what he did once he got to the boundary. It is another 15km from there to Kasiha.

Where to stay
The privately-run **Ottoman Camp** is the only luxury tented camp in the park, set on a soft sand beach on the shores of Lake Tanganyika. Consisting of only six double tents, it has an exclusive remote character. In addition to chimp-tracking, visitors can snorkel in the lake from the camp's 15m sailing dhow, the only one of its sort in this part of Tanzania. Accommodation costs around US$400 per person per night, inclusive of all meals and activities. You can direct your bookings and enquiries to **Greystoke Safaris**, PO Box 150, Usa River; tel: 0811 511443; fax: 057 8060, email: greystoke@luxurious.com.

The national park campsite and resthouse at Kasiha cost US$20 per person per night. Bring all the food you need from Kigoma.

SOUTHWEST TANZANIA
This section follows the little-used B8, which connects northwest Tanzania to the southern town of Mbeya via Katavi National Park and the towns of Mpanda and Sumbawanga. It is one of the most obscure routes anywhere in Tanzania, so much so that I've not heard of any traveller heading this way since I did so in 1992 while researching the first edition of this book. This information in this section is largely unchanged from what was included in the first edition, but there is no reason to suppose that it will have changed greatly in the interim. And should any bold readers decide to head this way, I really would appreciate it if they scribbled down a few notes for the next edition as they went along...

Mpanda and Kalema
The small town of Mpanda is the terminus of the southern branch of the central railway line. It's less than remarkable, but I found it to be very friendly and helpful place, presumably because so few tourists pass through.

On the lake shore west of Mpanda, Kalema is a far more interesting little place, and worth exploring if you travel to Mpanda by lake ferry. Kalema was an important staging post between Mpala (in Zaire) and Tabora during the slaving era. In 1879, it was occupied by Belgians with slaving interests, and then in 1885 it was settled by the White Fathers, who built a church and mission. When I visited

Kalema in 1992, I was struck by the incongruity of the mission building, which I remember as having a whitewashed, rather Mediterranean appearance. What I didn't realise was that I was looking at one of the oldest buildings in the Tanzanian interior, dating to 1893, and fortified with ramparts and gun slits, which helped to ward off frequent attacks by the Wabende in the early years of the mission. The White Fathers' church, built in 1890, was certainly still standing at the end of World War II. I imagine that it's still there today.

Surprisingly, the Kalema Mission is the best part of 1km inland from the jetty. The story is that when the White Fathers landed in Kalema, the level of Lake Tanganyika was marginally higher than it is today and so the hill under which the mission was built would then have been right on the shore. This drop in water level is most probably explained by the blockage of rocks and silt in the lake's main outlet, the Lukuga River in Zaire, something that was noted by Stanley when he passed through the area.

Getting there and away

The obvious way to get to Mpanda used to be on one of the thrice-weekly trains that connected it to Tabora. My understanding is that this service was suspended after the *El Nino* floods of 1997/8, and I have no idea when or indeed whether it will ever be resumed. The railway station in Dar es Salaam, Kigoma or Tabora would be your best source of current information. The occasional truck uses the road connecting Kigoma and Mpanda, but it will be a rough ride.

A more interesting way to reach Mpanda is via Ikola or Kalema on the Lake Tanganyika shore. The Lake Tanganyika ferry passes both villages in the mid-morning of the day after it sails out of Kigoma towards Mpulungu. There is no regular transport on to Mpanda and nowhere to stay in either Ikola or Kalema, so you are advised to carry a tent. Except after rain when the road becomes impassable, a truck runs between Ikola and Mpanda most days, a five-hour trip.

Where to stay

The **City Guest House** on the Sumbawanga road is convenient, clean, cheap and friendly, and it has a restaurant and bar. Most truckies use this guesthouse, so it's a good place to ask around for lifts to Katavi. The **Stima Guest House** in the town centre is more basic but fine. There are other guesthouses around the market.

Katavi National Park

In *Ivory Knights*, Nicholas Gordon describes Katavi as 'isolated and unloved, and in need of support'. He does not exaggerate – when we arrived in November 1992 we were only the 18th party of tourists to visit it in over two years, and the first to arrive without a vehicle. Katavi may be Tanzania's most obscure national park, but it offers excellent game viewing and has a real wilderness atmosphere. It is also surprisingly easy to visit independently.

The dominant vegetation type is *miombo* woodland, broken by the grassy Katavi flood plain and palm-fringed Lake Chala in the south. Most large African mammals are present, including significant populations of elephant (over 4,000), hippopotamus and buffalo, predators such as lion, leopard and spotted hyena, and herbivores such as sable and roan antelope, zebra, giraffe, eland and waterbuck. Over 400 bird species have been recorded.

If you arrive without your own vehicle, a park vehicle can run you from the entrance gate to a cement hut overlooking Katavi flood plain. Game viewing from the hut is fantastic: we saw more than 100 hippo grazing one evening, and herds of 200 buffalo and 50 elephant. There is a good chance of spotting predators as they cross the plain. If you take an armed ranger to stay with you, you can walk on to the plain – an invigorating experience.

There is a fair road network in Katavi. If you have a vehicle, the Lake Chala region is rewarding. A detailed map is pinned up in the ranger's office. Plenty of game can be seen from the Mpanda–Sumbawanga road which bisects the park. No fee is charged for just passing through.

An entrance fee of US$15 per 24 hours must be paid in hard currency, as must a camping fee of US$20 per person or a hut fee of US$30 per person. A park vehicle costs US$0.50 per km (about US$20 to the flood plain and back) and an armed ranger US$10 per day. A two-night stay should thus work out at around US$100 per person all inclusive.

Katavi National Park was doubled in size in December 1997, and it is rumoured that it will be extended further towards Lake Rukwa in 1999, which will make it the second-largest national park in Tanzania.

Getting there and away
There may be the odd bus between Mpanda and Sumbawanga, but in 1992 I had to rely on paid lifts with trucks. A good place to ask about a lift is the City Guest House or Agip garage in Mpanda. The entrance gate to Katavi lies just off the main road, 1km south of Sitalike village. Sitalike is 35km from Mpanda and 200km from Sumbawanga.

Heading south from Katavi may involve a long wait at Sitalike. By the time you get there from the hut at Katavi, most traffic to Sumbawanga will have already come past. There is nowhere to stay at Sitalike, so if nothing comes towards mid-afternoon try to get back to Mpanda. If you got stuck, you could probably camp at the entrance gate and try again the next morning.

If you are heading to Katavi in your own vehicle, make sure you have enough petrol. There is nowhere to fill up between Mpanda and Sumbawanga.

For fly-in packages to to Katavi and/or Mahale, contact Greystoke Safaris, the owners of Katavi Camp (see *Where to stay* for contact details).

Where to stay
Katavi Camp is an exclusive tented bush camp overlooking the Chala flood plain, where large numbers of animals congregate. Consisting of only four double tents, accommodation costs around US$400 per person, inclusive of meals and activities. The management arranges fly-camp safaris into the new park extension, towards Lake Rukwa and the Rungwa River, as well as game walks and drives in open-topped Land Rovers. The camp is owned by Greystoke Safaris, who arrange fly-in packages to Katavi and nearby Mahale Mountain National Park. Contact details are PO Box 150, Usa River; tel: 0811 511443; fax: 057 8060; email: greystoke@luxurious.com.

The only other accommodation in the park is an unfurnished two-room concrete hut overlooking Katavi flood plain 15km from the entrance gate. The hut is rudimentary, but it has a stunning situation, and there is excellent game viewing from the balcony. Bring your own sleeping bag. Firewood is available, but drinking water must be brought from a spring near the entrance gate. The rangers will fill up a jerry-can on request. Bring all provisions from Mpanda or Sumbawanga.

You may camp at a number of places in the park. The best site is at Lake Chala. Campsites are basic, with firewood but no drinking water.

Uwanda Game Reserve/Lake Rukwa
Uwanda lies 20km southeast of Katavi. Together, they make for one of the most alluring wilderness destinations in East Africa. Uwanda's dominant feature is Lake

Rukwa, a shallow alkaline lake with an extensive flood plain which attracts large ungulate herds after the November rains.

Rukwa is subject to seasonal fluctuations. Often it is split into two expanses of open water separated by a marsh. Mammals found are similar to those in Katavi, but one antelope species, the localised puku, is rarely seen anywhere but Uwanda. Rukwa is notable for albino giraffes, unusually-striped zebra, and a high crocodile density. Over 400 bird species have been recorded.

It is only feasible to visit Uwanda in your own vehicle. You must carry adequate spares, fuel, food, water, and camping equipment. Roads are rough and may become impassable after rain. The safest time to visit is between March and October, but there is more game in the wet months. Rukwa can be approached from either Mbeya, Sumbawanga or Katavi.

Sumbawanga

Due to its name, which sounds like the chorus in a Hollywood musical about Africa, I approached Sumbawanga with some curiosity. Sadly, it turned out to be a dusty, unlovable place. You will probably only want to spend a night before you move on.

For the seriously adventurous, the Mbizi Mountains between Sumbawanga and Lake Rukwa might be of interest. The little I know about this range whets my appetite, but we didn't have time to explore. According to a ranger at Katavi, you can get from Sumbawanga to the village of Kijiji on the back of a pick-up truck and from there walk to another village called Mpondo, where there are spectacular views over Lake Rukwa. The implication was that this could be done as a day trip, but I wouldn't bank on it. Maps of the area suggest a road continues on to Rukwa, passing through patches of forest on the way. My feeling is that if you have the appropriate maps and equipment the area could be well worth exploring on foot, but I would suggest you get permission from the district headquarters in Sumbawanga before you attempt it.

Getting there and away

There is a fair amount of traffic from Mpanda, but what you get is pot luck. Fate dealt us a truck filled a metre deep with timber, which exaggerated the roughness of the road – as did the absence of suspension. Be very, very kind to fate the day before you head out this way.

There are several buses every morning between Sumbawanga and Mbeya. In both directions they leave at 07.00. Book a seat in advance. It is an eight-hour trip on a fair road which passes through Tunduma.

If you are heading to Kasanga on Lake Tanganyika, there are a couple of buses a week. If you ask at the market before midday, you should find a pick-up truck heading that way.

Where to stay and eat

The only proper hotel is the **Upenda View Inn**, a pleasant place with newly-furnished rooms, a good restaurant and a bar and garden. When we visited, the staff were irritatingly dopey, but this could easily change.

There is no shortage of guesthouses, and most look perfectly adequate. The **Zanzibar Guest House** behind the bus station has acceptable rooms for US$2/2.50 single/double.

The food at the Upenda View is good and not prohibitively expensive, but there are plenty of cheaper *hotelis* around if you prefer.

The Tanzam Highway and Southern Safari Circuit

The Tanzam Highway, so-named because it links Tanzania to Zambia, is the main road through southern Tanzania. It forks southwards from the main Dar es Salaam-Arusha road at Chalinze, some 100km west of Dar, before passing through (or by) Morogoro, Mikumi, Iringa and Mbeya, reaching the Zambian border at Tunduma. The road distance between Dar and Tunduma is roughly 1000km. This chapter picks the road up at Chalinze and follows it southwards to Iringa.

The region's most significant physical features are the Uluguru Mountains near Morogoro and the Udzungwa Mountains near Mikumi. It is passed through by Tanzania's largest river, the Rufiji, and its main tributary, the Great Ruaha. The stretch of road from Iringa to Morogoro is very scenic, first following the Ruaha River through the baobab-clad foothills of the Udzungwa Mountains, then passing through Mikumi National Park.

The Tanzam Highway offers access to southern Tanzania's most alluring conservation areas. This southern safari circuit is far less developed for tourism than its northern equivalent, and what facilities and safari packages do exist are generally tailored towards the upper end of the market. By comparison to the northern reserves, only a tiny proportion of visitors to Tanzania explore any of the southern reserves, and those who do tend to visit one specific reserve rather than following a circuit through several. In terms of game viewing, these southern reserves don't really compare to the Serengeti and Ngorongoro – what could? – but they are still very well-stocked and have a somewhat more untrammelled character. It is probably fair to say that, was this cluster of reserves not in the same country as the Serengeti, then it might well be more widely recognised as one of the finest in Africa.

The most popular safari destination in southern Tanzania is probably the Selous, the largest game reserve in Africa (and possibly in the world), covering a vast area of *miombo* woodland lying between the Tanzam Highway and the south coast. Of the others, many people with long experience in Africa rate the Ruaha National Park, which lies to the west of the highway near Iringa, as one of their favourite reserves anywhere on the continent. Also very rich in big game, Mikumi National Park is bisected by the Tanzam Highway, which makes it of great interest to those travellers who bus or drive between Iringa and Morogoro. The more recently proclaimed Udzungwa Mountains National Park, which lies south of Mikumi towards Ifakara, doesn't offer a conventional safari experience, but it is of great interest to hikers and birders.

While the region covered in this chapter boasts some excellent game viewing for those who are in a position to set up organised safaris, it has relatively little to offer independent budget travellers. The only glaring exception to this generalisation is

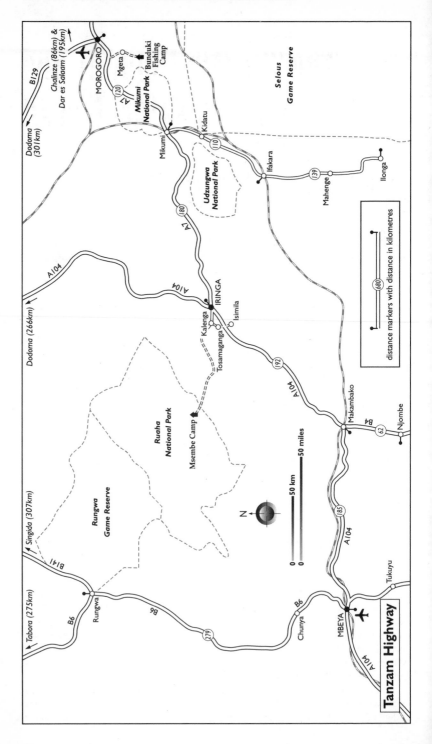

Tanzam Highway

the Mikumi, Udzungwa and Ifakara area, which offers much to backpackers with an energetic, explorative temperament. Both Iringa and Morogoro are lively and substantial towns with inherently attractive settings, making them good stopovers along the long road between Dar and Mbeya, but neither could be described as a compelling travel destination. Morogoro might one day serve as a base for hikes into the Uluguru, but there are no indications as yet that any significant tourist development will take place on this mountain range. Iringa, by contrast, is a good base for day trips to two spots that are as fascinating and accessible as they are underpublicised, the Isimila Stone-Age Site and Kalenga Museum.

Climate

Much of the area covered in this chapter is low-lying, hot and dry. The towns running along the eastern base of the Udzungwa Mountains have a relatively moist climate, and can be swelteringly hot and humid during the rains. The higher slopes of the Udzungwa and Uluguru Mountains are more temperate, as is the town of Iringa, where you might even find yourself putting on a light jumper in the evening. The rainfall pattern is typical of Tanzania, with the bulk of the rain falling between November and March. Aside from the main mountain ranges, this part of Tanzania is characterised by low rainfall figures.

Getting around

There is plenty of transport along the Tanzam Highway. The road is tarred and reasonably well-maintained, though it is quite heavily potholed in a few areas. In addition to direct buses between Dar es Salaam and Mbeya, which take up to 20 hours, there are also local bus services connecting the various towns along the way. Hitching is a possibility along this road, though the only time I have tried it, outside Iringa, I waited two hours without any luck before being picked up a bus!

The Tazara Railway runs roughly parallel to the Tanzam Highway for most of its length. Coming from the south, the railway and road run alongside each other between Mbeya and the junction town of Makambako, before the railway line forks to the east, passing through Ifakara and the northwestern corner of the Selous Game Reserve en route to Dar es Salaam.

There is not a great deal of transport running along the side roads off the Tanzam Highway, though at least one bus daily connects Morogoro and Mikumi to Kidatu, the springboard for visits to Udzungwa National Park. A variety of light vehicles serve as *matatu* transport between Kidatu and Ifakara, and the latter town is connected to Dar es Salaam and Mbeya by the Tazara Railway.

The only realistic way to visit the main game reserves on the southern circuit is on an organised safari. In contrast to the northern safari circuit, the reserves in southern Tanzania are most normally visited as part of a fly-in package, though it is equally possible to arrange a road safari to any of them. Several companies in Dar es Salaam arrange safaris along the southern circuit, as do most of the Arusha-based safari companies listed on pages 121–4 in *Chapter 7, The Northern Safari Circuit*.

CHALINZE

Just over 100km west of Dar es Salaam, Chalinze is one of the most important junction towns in Tanzania, where the Tanzam and Northern Highways split. If you are travelling between the north and south of the country, and want to bypass Dar es Salaam, you will find a vehicle heading in your direction at Chalinze.

Its strategic position aside, Chalinze is enlivened only by the numerous vendors and stalls which sell food and curios to passing bus passengers. There are a couple of basic guesthouses.

MOROGORO

Morogoro is a likeable town, spacious, well-maintained and dominated scenically by the Uluguru Mountains which tower attractively 2,000m above it. Morogoro is the centre of a major agricultural region and its fruit market is known countrywide. There are few tourist attractions around Morogoro, but its healthy, lively feel – three hotels had live music playing on one occasion when I visited – makes it worth a minor diversion.

Getting there and away

Buses between Dar es Salaam and Morogoro leave every hour or so and take about three hours. There is regular transport from Morogoro to Iringa and Dodoma. A bus leaves Morogoro for Kidatu at around 14.00 daily.

Where to stay
Upper range

The **Morogoro Hotel** (PO Box 1144, tel: 056 3270; fax: 051 117376; email: bushtrek@tanzanet.com), part of the Bushtrekker chain, lies on the slopes of the Uluguru roughly 2km out of town. It has pleasant grounds and the usual facilities, but hasn't seen much maintenance in recent years. Rooms cost US$60/65 s/c single/double.

A newer and better option is the **Kola Hill Hotel** (PO Box 1755; tel: 056 3707; fax: 056 4394), which lies in the Uluguru foothills about 3km from the town centre along the old Dar es Salaam road. Here, a self-contained double room with a fan and running hot water costs US$22, while one with air-conditioning costs US$32. All rooms are slightly cheaper for Tanzania residents. Meals are available.

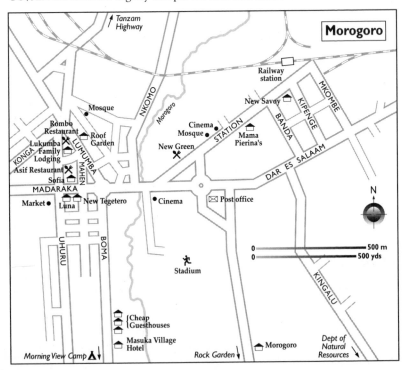

Moderate

Out towards the railway station, **Mama Pierina**'s is a pleasant place to stay, and popular with expats. Bright, clean double rooms with fans, nets and hot showers cost US$8/11 single/double. There's a good restaurant attached. Nearby, the **New Savoy Hotel** (formerly the plain old Savoy) does little to live up to its recent name extension: the rooms are frightfully run-down, there's no running water, and the service is, well, a little on the hesitant side. Still, some respect is due for the sheer gall of asking US$15 for a room.

About ten minutes' walk from the town centre along Boma Road, the **Masuka Village Hotel** (PO Box 930; tel: 056 4774/4430) lies in flowering gardens at the base of the Uluguru Mountains. It's an attractive retreat, and surprisingly inexpensive at US$11 for a self-contained double with nets and hot showers – worth the walk out.

In the town centre, the **New Tegetero Hotel** seems exceptional value: large clean doubles with hot water, nets and fans for US$9. By contrast, the **Sofia Hotel** and **Roof Garden Hotel** both feel a touch overpriced at US$16 and US$11 respectively for an unexceptional self-contained double.

Budget

There are a few basic guesthouses dotted around town. The main cluster, along Boma Road towards the Musuka Village Hotel, are mostly rather scruffy and overpriced. Far better is the **Lukumba Family Lodging** in the town centre and – arguably the best value in town – the **Luna Hotel**, which has spacious self-contained doubles with fan and net for US$6.

Where to eat

Mama Pierina is universally acclaimed as the best restaurant in Morogoro. A diverse menu includes pizzas, curries and steaks for between US$5 and US$8 per main course. The veranda is a pleasant place for a cold beer. Also worth trying is the **New Green Restaurant**, which serves good Indian and Portuguese dishes at reasonable prices.

Excursions from Morogoro
Rock Garden Resort

This untended botanical garden on the lower slopes of the Uluguru Mountain lies about 1km past the Morogoro Hotel, and is worth the walk up, particularly if you are interested in birds or plants.

Uluguru Mountains

This range lies directly east of Morogoro. It rises to 2,646m. Like most eastern Tanzanian mountains, it contains extensive areas of forest. The Uluguru are less accessible than the Usambara or Udzungwa, but there is no reason why a determined hiker should be put off. Maps are available from the Department of Lands and Surveys in Dar es Salaam.

A possible base for hiking into the Uluguru is the disused **Morning View Camp** near a patch of natural forest halfway up the mountain. Though originally a research centre for Sokoine University, permission to camp there must now be obtained from the Department of Natural Resources, 2km out of town on Kingalu Road. Check the water situation before heading out. To get to Morning View, head out on Boma Road past Masuka Village Hotel for about 8km. You might get a lift some of the way, but don't bank on it.

Another possibility in the Uluguru area is the abandoned **Bunduki Fishing Camp** south of Morogoro. This ceased to function in the 1970s and the buildings are no longer habitable, but it remains a beautiful spot, on a river below an attractive waterfall enclosed by rainforest, and it would be of particular interest to birders. If you are self-sufficient and have the appropriate equipment, you could almost certainly camp at Bunduki (I recently spoke to somebody who did this in 1993). To get there, follow the Iringa road south of Morogoro for 20km until you reach Masomba College, then turn left towards Mgeta. Bunduki is reportedly about 10km past Mgeta. There is at least one bus daily to Mgeta.

SELOUS GAME RESERVE

Roughly 45,000km^2 in extent, the Selous is Africa's single largest game reserve, three times larger than the Serengeti, more than twice the size of South Africa's Kruger National Park, and roughly 50% bigger than Belgium or Swaziland! It also supports enormous numbers of animals: roughly 30,000 elephant, 200,000 buffalo, 80,000 wildebeest and significant populations of almost every other species of African mammal, including the rare African hunting dog and black rhinoceros. The Selous, in short, is the ultimate African wilderness, and its very name exudes an air of mystique among lovers of the African bush.

Most safari operators in Dar es Salaam run safaris to the Selous, but before you rush off and book one, be aware that there is a degree of hype attached to the above description. Firstly, if you discount manmade borders, there are several parts of Africa (the Serengeti is one) where a cluster of separately managed reserves forms a contiguous ecosystem comparable in size to the Selous. Secondly, the reserve is divided into two unequal sections by the Rufiji River, and the nine-tenths of the remote tract of African bush described above that lies to the south of the river is practically inaccessible unless you have your own 4x4 and are thoroughly self-reliant, or are prepared to pay a fortune to make individual arrangements with a tour operator.

In reality, the Selous most people see is the relatively small part of the reserve that lies to the north of the Rufiji, and while there is definitely less tourist traffic here than in the northern reserves, the area is far more developed for tourism than the phrase 'only five small camps in a 45,000km^2 wilderness' might lead you to expect. The area is not as scenic as the northern reserves, nor are you likely to see as many animals or as much variety as you would in, for instance, the Serengeti. When we were there all the camps seemed intent on showing their visitors a particular pride of lions which had been resident in one area for a week. Spot-the-lion-along-with-three-other-vehicles is a game you can play in any large African reserve, but in theory is the type of thing people go to Selous to avoid.

That's not to say Selous isn't worth visiting, just that you might want to temper your expectations. Perhaps the best features of the reserve are the walking and boat safaris offered by all the camps. The muddy Rufiji River teems with hippo and massive crocodiles, and these can be approached very closely in a boat. The bird and animal life along the banks of the Rufiji is stunning, with a variety of antelope likely to be seen, as well as large herds of buffalo and elephant. Of the birds, the African skimmer is often seen on the sand banks exposed during the dry season, fish eagles perch on the *borassus* palms which line the river, and waders, herons, kingfishers and weavers are all well-represented.

Game walks, led by armed rangers, provide an opportunity to look at small mammals and birds which you might overlook on game drives. There is a real sense of excitement attached to wandering around in the bush in a small group, knowing that at any moment you might encounter a lion or elephant. Game drives can also be excellent, though the thick *brachystegia* woodland makes animal spotting more of a challenge than in most of the northern reserves. Most game drives centre

THE SELOUS: SOME HISTORY

Because of tsetse fly, much of the area that is now the Selous has never been densely populated. People who lived in the area suffered badly at the hands of the slave caravans in the 19th century. Better-populated areas such as the Mutumbi Hills were virtually cleared of human habitation by the famine induced by the Germans after the Maji-Maji uprising.

The Selous is named after Frederick Courteney Selous, an English elephant hunter, explorer, naturalist and writer (his best-known book is *A Hunter's Wanderings in Africa*). Selous spent most of his life in East and southern Africa; amongst his many exploits, he was a white hunter for Theodore Roosevelt and the trailblazer for the troop of settlers sent by Cecil Rhodes to take over the area that became Rhodesia (now Zimbabwe). In World War I, Selous volunteered for service and was made a captain in the 25th Royal Fusiliers. He died in battle in 1917 at the age of 64, of wounds inflicted while advancing on a German encampment on the Beho river. His grave is on the north of the river near Selous Safari Camp.

The part of the reserve north of the Rufiji was proclaimed in 1905. Kaiser Wilhelm gave part of it to his wife as a present, which earned it the nickname of *Shamba la Bibi* (The Woman's Field). Selous received its current name in 1922 and reached its present size and shape in the 1940s, when the government moved the remaining tribes out of the area to combat a sleeping sickness epidemic. It has been declared a World Heritage Site, one of three in Tanzania.

around the series of small lakes that lies between the main camps, and animals likely to be seen in this area include lion, elephant, impala, greater kudu, eland, giraffe, zebra, wildebeest and buffalo.

Not only does the Rufiji divide the reserve from a tourist's viewpoint, but it acts as a natural barrier between the ranges of two wildebeest subspecies (eastern white-bearded wildebeest north of the river and Nyasa wildebeest to the south). The Rufiji also forms the southern limit of the range of the Maasai giraffe, though this is in part due to the absence of acacia trees south of the river.

Roads within the Selous become impassable after heavy rain. As a consequence the camps close towards the end of the wet season, in April, and re-open in July. An entrance fee of US$15 per person per day is charged.

You'll hear a few different pronunciations of Selous; to the best of my knowledge *Selloo* is correct.

Getting there

Most safari companies in Dar and all the camps listed under *Where to stay* offer a variety of fly-in an drive-down packages. Because of the distances involved, four days would be the minimum realistic length for a drive-down safari. The price of a safari will vary greatly depending on which camp you stay at, your length of stay, how you travel to the reserve, and the size of your group. There is, however, no budget camping safari industry dedicated to the Selous, and most packages will be at least as expensive as a top-of-the-range lodge safari of similar duration in northern Tanzania.

Those who are driving themselves to the Selous can either follow the unsurfaced road along the south coast through Kibiti to approach the reserve along its eastern border, or else follow the surfaced Tanzam Highway west from

Dar to Morogoro, from where a 130km long road leads southwards to the norther border. At the time of writing, the coastal route takes at least twelve hours, while the drive between Morogoro and the Selous takes around eight hours. The Morogoro route obviously makes more sense for those who are visiting other reserves from the Tanzam Highway. Otherwise, you should seek the advice of whichever camp you are heading to, as the better route will vary according to the location of your camp, and the current state of the different roads, and you will need precise directions.

You can get to the Selous by train, but must make advance arrangements with the camp you plan to visit. Take the Tazara rail and disembark at either Fuga Halt or Kisaki, depending on the camp's instructions. Rail is the most practical way of getting to Selous Safari Camp or Stiegler's Gorge cheaply.

Where to stay
All the camps in the Selous fit firmly into the upper end of the price range, with rates comparable to the better lodges in the Serengeti. The rates quoted below are all full-board, and include activities such as game drives, guided walks and river trips.

Beho Beho Camp PO Box 2261, Dar es Salaam, tel: 051 668062/3/4; fax: 051 668631, email: oysterbay-hotel@twiga.com. Situated on a hill overlooking the plains around the lakes, accommodation here is in self-contained cabins. It is possible to swim in the nearby hot springs. US$375/600.

Mbuyini Tented Camp PO Box 1192, Dar es Salaam, tel: 051 128485; fax: 051 112794. This relatively new and very popular camp is set in the riparian forest lining the Rufiji River, close to Selous's grave. US$290 per person sharing.

Mbuyu Tented Camp PO Box 2341, Dar es Salaam, tel: 0812 781971; fax: 051 116413, email: aircon@twiga.com, website: http://www.watanetwork.kenpubs.co.uk. This camp is built around a large baobab tree. Accommodation is in luxury self-contained tents on the banks of the Rufiji, near the lakes. Plenty of animals can be seen from the bar overlooking the river. US$315/550 single/double.

Rufiji River Camp PO Box 13824, Dar es Salaam, tel: 0811 320849, fax: 051 75165, email: hippo@twiga.com. This is the oldest camp in the Selous, built on a bank overlooking the Rufiji. Accommodation is in standing tents with communal toilets. US$228 per person sharing.

Sand River Camp PO Box 1344, Dar es Salaam. This is the newest camp in the Selous, and one of the smartest, overlooking a stretch of the Rufiji that's teeming with hippos and attracts plenty of other game. US$365 per person sharing.

MIKUMI
The small town of Mikumi straddles the Tanzam Highway at the southern border of Mikumi National Park. It has grown rapidly in the last few years, partly because it is the main service town to the adjacent national park, partly because of its importance as a stopover along the Tanzam Highway. Mikumi is also of significance to travellers aiming for Udzungwa National Park, since it lies at the junction with the B127 to Ifakara.

The recent opening of the **Genesis Motel** (PO Box 40, Mikumi; tel: Mikumi 40) means that there is now some decent and affordable accommodation in Mikumi town. A self-contained double at this motel costs US$14, inclusive of a full English breakfast, and the restaurant has a varied menu. There are also several guesthouses in the town, and you can get a reasonable meal at the *hoteli* with the covered veranda at the junction with the B127.

MIKUMI NATIONAL PARK

Mikumi is Tanzania's third-largest national park, covering 3,230km². It is relatively flat, but flanked by the Uluguru and Udzungwa mountains to the north and south respectively. Mikumi was gazetted in 1964, when the large herds which gathered on the Mkata flood plain were threatened by hunters after the area was opened up by the construction of the Morogoro-Iringa road. It was extended to share a border with the Selous in 1975.

Mikumi's main vegetation type is open grassland interspersed with patches of miombo and acacia woodland and the odd solitary baobab. The area becomes marshy after rain. A wide variety of mammal species is present; amongst the more commonly seen are elephant, buffalo, wildebeest, impala, warthog, zebra and giraffe. There are significant populations of three antelope species which are rare in the northern Tanzanian reserves: greater kudu, roan and sable antelope. Predators include lion, leopard, African hunting dog, and black-backed jackal.

A park entrance fee of US$20 per person per 24-hour period must be paid in hard currency. A 44-page booklet, *Mikumi National Park*, available at the National Park headquarters in Arusha for US$2.50, contains a wealth of background information, a good map, and details of the animals and birds found in the park.

Getting there and away

Mikumi is bisected by the Tanzam Highway. It can be reached in an ordinary saloon car, but a 4x4 is needed to drive within the park. You should see plenty of game from a bus passing through the reserve; on one trip I counted ten mammal species, including a herd of 20-odd eland and four herds of elephant.

Safaris to Mikumi run from Dar es Salaam, four hours away by road. A two-day, one-night trip is normal, though a visit could be combined with a longer road safari to the Selous or Ruaha.

I have never heard of a traveller doing so, but it would be much cheaper (and presumably quite straightforward) to organise a day trip into the national park out of Mikumi town. The Genesis Motel should be able to put you in touch with the owner of a suitable vehicle. Mikumi may not be the most fashionable reserve in Tanzania, but it is perhaps the only one that offers the combination of large numbers of plains animals and quick access from a reasonably substantial town located on a major thoroughfare.

Where to stay

Mikumi is a popular weekend trip for residents of Dar es Salaam. It is advisable to book over weekends and public holidays.

Upper range

Mikumi Wildlife Camp Oyster Bay Hotel; tel: 051 668062; fax: 051 668631; email: oysterbay-hotel@twiga.com. This relatively inexpensive safari camp offers accommodation in ten self-contained *banda*s for US$120/140. It also has a few five-bed dormitories, costing from US$70 for one person to US$125 for five people. Meals cost US$20 each.

Mikumi Wildlife Lodge PO Box 14 Mikumi; tel: Mikumi 27. Similarly priced accommodation is available at this government-run lodge, which lies 3km from the main road on a ridge above a waterhole. It has a swimming pool, a restaurant and bar, and a gift shop. Accommodation costs US$50 per person, with a 25% discount available to Tanzanian residents and a 50% discount to all visitors between Easter Monday and the end of June. Lunch and dinner cost around US$11 each.

Budget and camping

The three campsites near the main gate cost US$20 per person. They have long-drop toilets and firewood, but water is not available. Special campsites cost US$40 per person. The cheapest option is to lodge in Mikumi town, and drive into the park from there.

UDZUNGWA NATIONAL PARK

Tanzania's newest national park opened to the public in October 1992. Covering an area of 1,900km², it protects the remote Udzungwa Mountains and an extensive montane forest community. Altitudes within the national park range from around 250m to over 2,500m. Facilities remain limited, but with publicity Udzungwa seems likely to become a major draw for hikers and nature lovers.

There are many similarities between the forests of west Africa, Madagascar and the eastern Tanzanian mountains. Madagascar was once part of the African mainland, so these forests may once have been linked physically. The dispersal of seeds during cyclones may also be a factor. Madagascar split from the mainland about 165 million years ago and the eastern Tanzanian forests have been isolated from those in West Africa for over five million years. Forests such as those of the Udzungwa and Usambara are separated by large distances and thus have a high level of endemism. More than 25% of Udzungwa's plant species are not present elsewhere.

Two types of monkey, the Uhehe (or Gordon's) red colobus and the Sanje crested mangabey, the latter discovered as recently as 1979, are restricted to the Udzungwa Mountains, though scientific opinion differs as to whether they should be classified as subspecies of more widespread species or as full species in their own right. What is most remarkable about both of these Udzungwa endemics is their geographical isolation. Aside from one other population on the Tana River in Kenya, crested mangabeys are largely restricted to the Congo and northwestern Uganda. No red colobus occur elsewhere in the mountains of eastern Tanzania, though they are found on Zanzibar Island and in the Lake Tanganyika region. In addition to the endemic monkeys, the forests of the Udzungwa harbour blue, red-tailed, and black-and-white colobus monkey. And since Udzungwa is part of the Mikumi-Selous ecosystem, it also supports small numbers of several large game species, including lion, elephant, leopard, buffalo and sable antelope.

Udzungwa is particularly alluring to birdwatchers. A good range of forest birds is present, including several very rare or localised species. At least four bird species are thought to be endemic to the Udzungwa Mountains: rufous-winged sunbird, Iringa akalat, Lagdens's bush shrike and Udzungwa partridge. The forests of Udzungwa are still relatively unexplored in scientific terms, and most of these species were first described in the last decade or two. Of particular interest is the Udzungwa partridge, which was first discovered in 1991 and has since been placed in an entirely new genus more closely related to the hill partridges of Asia than any African birds. In addition to the above, three bird species are regarded to be endemic to the Kibasira Swamp near Ifakara.

An entrance fee of US$15 per person per 24-hour period must be paid in hard currency.

Getting there and away

The access road to Udzungwa National Park is the B127, which connects Mikumi town on the Tanzam Highway to Ifakara town on the Tazara railway, a distance of roughly 100km. The park can be approached either by road or by rail, and if you are visiting as a round trip out of Dar es Salaam, then the ideal would be to come by rail and return by road. This is because the slow train from Dar to Ifakara passes through the Selous Game Reserve in daylight. Returning by road, you will pass through Mikumi National Park.

Coming by road from Mikumi town, your first goal will be Kidatu, a small town straddling the B127 roughly 20km to the north of the entrance gate to the Udzungwa National Park. At least one daily bus runs between Morogoro and Kidatu, leaving Mikumi at 14.00 and arriving in Kidatu at nightfall. There is also a bus service between Dar es Salaam and Ifakara, which leaves Dar at 08.00 and arrives in Ifakara roughly eight hours later, stopping en route at Mikumi, Kidatu and Mangula.

The alternative to using one of these direct services is to catch any bus heading along the Tanzam Highway, ask to be dropped in Mikumi town, and make your way to Kidatu from there. The odd private vehicle runs between Mikumi and Kidatu, and at worst you can always pick up the bus when it passes through Mikumi at around 16.00. If you have to spend a night in Kidatu, there is plenty of accommodation (see *Where to stay* below).

The entrance gate to Udzungwa lies no more than 100m from the B127, at the village of Mangula, roughly halfway between Kidatu and Ifakara. Several crowded pick-up trucks run daily between Kidatu and Ifakara, and they can drop you at Mangula.

All trains on the Tazara line stop at Ifakara (see *By rail* in *Chapter 4*). They are scheduled to arrive there in the evening, so you should plan on a night at one of Ifakara's basic guesthouses.

Where to stay

There is no accommodation in the park. If you have a tent you might be allowed to camp at the entrance gate, but there are no facilities and it will cost US$20 per person. Far better to stay in Mangula, a few hundred metres from the entrance gate, where there are a couple of good hotels.

Until recently the only option in Mangula, the **Twiga Guesthouse** lies a mere 200m from the entrance gate and offers clean s/c doubles for around US$10. The canteen serves cheap, filling meals, the bar has a fridge, and the grounds look across to the mountains. The new and smarter **Udzungwa Mountain View Hotel** (PO Box 99, Mangula; tel/fax: 065 3357) is under the same ownership as the Genesis Hotel in Mikumi. Self-contained doubles here cost US$15 including a full English breakfast, and there is also a campsite attached. The restaurant has a varied menu, with most dishes costing around US$7, and the hotel can organise day trips and hikes into the adjacent national park.

There is also plenty of accommodation in **Kidatu**, a hot, mosquito-ridden town dominated by the Udzungwa's craggy peaks. Surrounded by sugar plantations, and the site of a major hydro-electric plant on the Great Ruaha River, Kidatu is considerably larger and busier than most maps suggest, and travellers using the bus from Morogoro may have to spend a night here before proceeding to Mangula the next day. The **Mkanga Guesthouse** and **Stop Over Lodge** offer adequate but basic rooms for around US$4. The slightly more expensive **Maryland Lodge**, 200m from the main road, has spotless rooms with mosquito nets and fans. A limited range of meals is served and there is a beer garden with a fridge.

There are a few basic guesthouses in **Ifakara**, the major transport hub in this remote part of Tanzania. The **Nshanga Guesthouse** has recently been recommended.

Excursions from Mangula
In the national park

There are now a few short walking trails which start at the entrance gate. The shortest, a half-hour unguided round trip, leads to a small forest-fringed waterfall in the forest. You should see plenty of monkeys along this trail, including the red colobus, and if you sit quietly at the waterfall in the early morning or evening, you might see monkeys come to drink at the pool below it.

The guided walk to the Sanje Waterfall deeper in the reserve is a round trip of at least four hours' duration, and it will take longer if you stop to look at birds and monkeys. This walk offers excellent forest birding, and you can be practically sure of seeing the endemic red colobus as well as black-and-white colobus. Unfortunately, the endemic mangabey and birds are somewhat more elusive, and you would be fortunate to catch a glimpse of any of them. The Sanje Waterfall itself drops more than 150m over a sheer ledge.

Several longer walks are available. There is a seven-hour round trip to the nearest peak, and an overnight hike to the 2,111m Mwanihana peak. Anybody who is serious about trying to see the endemic birds should do one of these walks on to the higher slopes. Guides and porters are available, but you should bring all food etc with you.

The roads around Mangula make for pleasant walking, and you'll see plenty of birds from them, though not monkeys.

Kibasira Swamp… and Mahenge

If you've come this far, and you're seriously into birds or fancy a bit of adventure, the little-known Kilombero River near Ifakara would be well worth the slight effort required to reach it. The most accessible point along the river is the Kibasira Swamp, which is crossed by a ferry on the Mahenge road about 5km from Ifakara. There is a limited amount of public transport along this road, but a better option might be to hire a bicycle from one of the stands near the market in Ifakara – the road out is reasonably flat and this would give you the autonomy to come and go as you please.

The Kibasira Swamp made ornithological headlines in the mid-1980s when the local doctor observed there a previously undescribed species of weaver (subsequently named the Kilombero weaver and illustrated in the Van Perlo field guide). Since then, two further new bird species (both members of the genus *cisticola*) were found to occur in the swamp. These are currently awaiting formal description, but have tentatively been dubbed the melodious and Kilombero cisticola. All three of these birds are thought to be endemic to this large swamp, and can be seen with relative ease from around the ferry jetty.

Even if obscure birds hold little interest, the Kibasira Swamp is worth visiting. The scenery is very atmospheric, and quite a bit of wildlife moves through this thinly-populated area, flanked to the east by the Selous Game Reserve and to the west by the Udzungwa Mountains. You can arrange with a local fisherman to take a canoe out onto the river, which still supports substantial numbers of crocodile and hippo, as well as a wide variety of water-associated birds.

If the swamp doesn't sate your appetite for exploration, a limited amount of public transport connects Ifakara to the town of Mahenge, 80km further south near the base of the Mbarika Mountains. The site of an important German fort in the colonial era, Mahenge is just about as far off any beaten tourist track as it gets in Tanzania, and it could offer some interesting walking and possibly game-viewing possibilities. There is at least one place to stay in Mahenge, the **Original Pogoro Guesthouse**. And if you do head down this way, let me know how it went!

IRINGA

It would be misleading to describe Iringa as exciting, but the town is an interesting and agreeable place to spend a couple of days in transit between Dar es Salaam and Mbeya. Situated on a hill offering great views over the Ruaha Valley, this compact town has an atmospheric old German quarter near the market, while Majumba Street, the main trading road, is very colourful and lively. The market itself is an excellent place to buy locally woven rugs and baskets.

The Iringa area is the home of the Hehe, a relatively modern grouping which was forged in the 1850s by a chief called Munyigumba, and consolidated under the militant leadership of Munyigamba's son and successor Mkwawa, whose legendary status was recognised by foe and follower alike. Mkwawa was a cunning military tactician who expanded his territory to include large parts of the caravan route between Tabora and the coast. The name *Hehe* is believed to derive from the battle-cry he initiated, a loud *hee-hee*.

When colonialism was imposed on the Tanzanian interior, Mkwawa refused to acknowledge the German administration and blocked their trade caravans from passing through his territory. In 1891 Emil Zalewski and 1,000 German troops were dispatched to quell the Hehe. After a few skirmishes, Mkwawa ambushed Zalewski, killing half his men and making off with over 300 rifles and all their ammunition. Over the next three years Mkwawa set about fortifying his capital at Kalenga. Iringa, incidentally, is a European corruption of the Hehe word *lilinga*, which means fort.

In October 1894, Kalenga was attacked and demolished by the Germans, who stood a battery of cannons along the ridge of a hill which overlooks it. Amongst other blows, a direct hit was scored on the arsenal holding the gunpowder Mkwawa had borrowed in 1891. Mkwawa went on the run; for the next four years he fought the Germans using guerrilla tactics. When faced with capture in 1898, he shot himself through the skull rather than be taken alive. His skull, originally taken to Germany, was returned to Tanzania in 1954 and now rests in the Mkwawa Museum in Kalenga.

Kalenga makes for an interesting day trip out of Iringa, as does the Isimila Stone-Age Site with its bizarre rock formations. Iringa is the also the springboard for visits to Ruaha National Park.

Getting there and away

You can get to Iringa easily from anywhere on the Tanzam Highway. Getting away from Iringa is less simple. The apparent busyness of Iringa bus station is deceptive; few buses actually start their journey there and although plenty will be going in your direction it may be difficult to find a seat. It is advisable to book a seat in advance. Iringa is about nine hours from Dar es Salaam by bus.

Seats for Dodoma-bound buses should also be booked in advance. The road is terrible; the trip takes up to 12 hours.

Where to stay

The closest thing in Iringa to a tourist-class hotel is the new **MR Hotel** (PO Box 431, Iringa; tel: 064 2006; fax: 064 2661), which is centrally located on Mkwawa Road, and has clean self-contained double rooms with a television for around US$40. Less central, but also very acceptable, the **Isimila Hotel** (PO Box 452, Iringa; tel: 064 2605; fax: 065 2868) has small but clean rooms with hot running water for US$9/12 s/c single/double. The nearby **Iringa Hotel** (PO Box 48; tel: 064 2039), formerly run by the TRC, is very run-down by comparison, but it has a nice atmosphere and is pretty good value at US$12 for a s/c double. Similar in standard, the **Baptist Conference Centre** comes highly recommended, charging

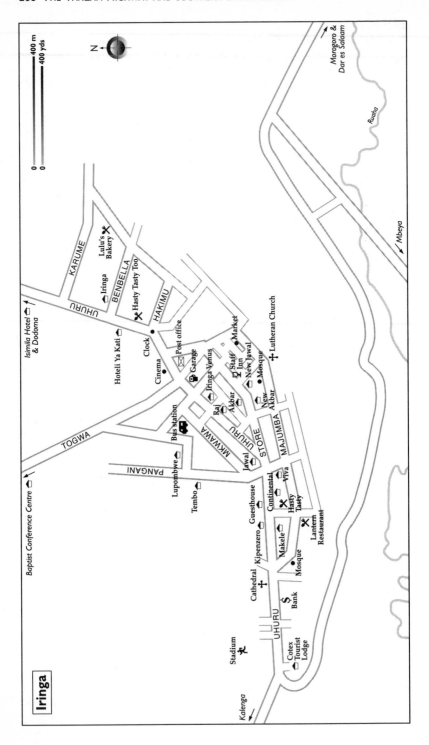

around US$15 for a double room, but since it lies about 3km out of town (on Togwa Road) it is probably only of interest to those with private transport.

For cheaper accommodation, the **Lutheran Centre Guest House** remains a reliable bet, with basic but clean rooms for US$4. A newer recommendation is the **Mount View Hotel** (PO Box 658; tel: 064 2697/2503), where singles cost US$4.50 and s/c doubles cost US$7.50. Otherwise, there are dozens of basic guesthouses dotted around the town centre, charging a fairly uniform US$3-5 for a room. Among the better places when I was last in Iringa were the **Lupombwe**, **Tembo**, **Iringa Venus** and **New Akbar** guesthouses.

Where to eat
There is a good choice of restaurants in Iringa. For lunch, **Hasty Tasty** and **Hasty Tasty Too** serve a variety of tasty and inexpensive stews, juices, and Indian snacks. The **Raj Hotel**, Iringa's top restaurant, has a varied menu and is open long hours. Main courses cost about US$3. The Iringa Hotel serves three-course set menus for US$2.50. Its bar is well-stocked and cheap; a sociable place to linger for the evening.

The **Lantern Restaurant** has great views over Majumba Street and across to the hills surrounding Iringa. The menu lacks surprises but the food is good. After you eat, you can relax and enjoy the view at the attached bar. Main courses cost US$2.

Excursions from Iringa
Kalenga
This small village on the banks of the Ruaha was the site of Mkwawa's fortified capital before it was destroyed by German cannon fire in 1894. A small museum houses Mkwawa's bullet-shattered skull and several of his artefacts. The well-informed and enthusiastic caretaker speaks good English and will happily take you around the village.

To the untrained eye Kalenga is an unremarkable African village, but the caretaker can point out several remnants of Mkwawa's capital: the remains of fortified walls, the mound used by the chief to address his people, and the foundations of his home. He will also point out the ridge from where the Germans unleashed the barrage of cannonfire which destroyed the capital. This hill has since become known as Tosamaganga (throwing stones), and is now the site of a quaint 1930s Italian mission.

Pick-up trucks to Tosamaganga and Kalenga leave Iringa every hour or so. They wait for passengers at the end of the surfaced road 200m past Samora Stadium. At Kalenga you will be dropped off next to the market; it is a five-minute meander through the village from there to the museum. Keep asking for directions. If your Swahili is limited, asking for Mkwawa will get you further than asking for a museum.

Isimila Stone-Age Site
In a dry river bed 22km south of Iringa lies one of East Africa's richest stone-age sites. Its significance was recognised in 1951 by a schoolboy who collected two rucksacks full of stone implements, amongst them a 40cm-long, 4kg hand axe. Isimila was first excavated by Professor Howell of Chicago University in 1957.

Isimila was inhabited by stone-age people of the Late Acheulian culture about 60,000 years ago, at which time it was a shallow lake. A small museum houses a number of their tools, including cleavers and hand axes. You can also see fossilised bones and teeth of the extinct *hippopotamus gorgops*. In another gulley, ten minutes' walk away, a group of striking 10m-high sandstone pillars, carved by a river which dried up years ago, look like the set for a Lilliputian western.

The turn-off to Isimila is signposted on the Tanzam Highway south of Iringa, a few metres past the 20km marker – any bus heading that way can drop you there. It is a 20-minute walk from the road to the site. On the way you pass through a small group of huts where the caretaker lives. Ask for him on your way past.

You can negotiate with a taxi driver to do a round trip to Isimila. This cost us about US$15. The caretaker at the site speaks little-to-no English – if your Swahili is limited an English-speaking taxi driver will be a definite asset.

Mufindi

This highland area to the south of Iringa, known for its tea production, has recently become accessible to tourists with the opening of the **Mufindi Highland Lodge** on a farm owned by Foxtreks (the same people who own Ruaha River Lodge). Lying at an altitude of above 2,000m, the lodge consists of eight self-contained log cabins set on a hill overlooking two dams, and charges US$55 per person full-board. There is excellent walking in the surrounding rainforest, which harbours similar species to those found in Udzungwa National Park, as well as some good drives and mountain biking opportunities. The lodge lies some 50km to east of the Tanzam Highway, and can be reached from Iringa by following the highway southwards, then turning left at Mafinga. Booking details are the same as for Ruaha River Lodge (see *Ruaha National Park* below).

RUAHA NATIONAL PARK

Ruaha is Tanzania's second-largest national park, covering an area of 12,950km², though there is some talk that it will relinquish this status following proposed extensions to Katavi National Park. The greater Ruaha ecosystem, which includes the contiguous Rungwa and Kizigo Game Reserves, covers roughly 26,000km² in extent, and it is regarded to be one of the wildest areas anywhere in Tanzania. Only the small area around the Great Ruaha River has been developed for tourism, and even this sees relatively few visitors, though there are plans to extend the internal road system from the present 400km to 1,500km.

The fauna and flora of Ruaha is transitional between southern and eastern African. A wide variety of habitats is protected within the park, including evergreen forest and swamp, but the dominant vegetation type is *brachystegia* (or *miombo*) woodland, followed by broken acacia grassland, dotted with baobab trees. The roads following the Ruaha River are the best for game viewing.

Ruaha lies at the southerly extent of the range of several large mammal species, including lesser kudu, Grant's gazelle and striped hyena. It is probably the last accessible part of East Africa where the African hunting dog survives in significant numbers, and it harbours a number of mammals which are rare or absent in northern Tanzania, for instance roan and sable antelope and greater kudu. The elephant population is the largest of any Tanzanian national park, and despite heavy losses due to poaching, some 12,000 elephants live within the greater Ruaha ecosystem. Other common mammals include buffalo (over 30,000 in 1990), zebra (over 20,000), giraffe and warthog. Impala are the most numerous antelope, and waterbuck, eland, and bushbuck are also likely to be seen. Big cats are present in large numbers, and although the heavy cover means that you will see lions less frequently than in the Serengeti, it is an excellent place for leopard. Over 400 bird species have been recorded.

A 64-page booklet, *Ruaha National Park*, is available from the National Park headquarters in Arusha and sometimes from the entrance gate of Ruaha. It contains maps, animal descriptions and checklists, and details of where to look for localised species.

Ruaha is best visited between July and November, when animals concentrate around the river. Internal roads may be impassable during the rainy season (December to May).

An entrance fee of US$15 per 24-hour period must be paid in hard currency.

Getting there and away

The park headquarters at Msembe are 120km from Iringa along a road that is suitable for 4x4 vehicles only. Any safari company in Dar es Salaam can organise a driving safari to Ruaha, bearing in mind that you will use up the best part of two days just getting there and back.

The better option is to fly from Dar es Salaam. There are three scheduled flights from Dar es Salaam and Zanzibar weekly, operating on Monday, Thursday and Saturday, and costing US$300 per person return. Any safari company will be able to put together a fly-in package as you require. Ruaha River Lodge (see below) offers an all-inclusive fly-in package for US$240/400 single/double per night, as well as fly-in walking safaris from US$290 per person.

Another option is to fly to Iringa from Dar or Arusha via Moshi, and make your way to the park by road. The flights to Iringa run on Tuesday and Thusday and cost US$105 from Dar or US$150 from Arusha. From Iringa, it is a 2-3 hour drive to Ruaha, and 4x4 vehicles can be hired by advance arrangement through Foxtreks at US$180 per vehicle for the trip.

Backpackers may be able to arrange a camping safari to Ruaha out of Iringa at a price comparable to that of a camping safari in the northern reserves. Only one company in Iringa offers 4x4 hire: Iringa Safari Tours (PO Box 107, tel: 064 2718/2291). Their office is on Uhuru Avenue between Benbella Street and Karume Road; the owner can also be contacted at the Iringa Hotel. The price will depend on how long you want the vehicle for, but expect to pay around US$250 for up to four people for three days. This covers vehicle hire, a driver and fuel. Park entrance fees, food and accommodation costs must be added to this.

Hitching to Ruaha is for incurable optimists only.

Where to stay

Ruaha River Lodge Bookings through Foxtreks, PO Box 10270, Dar es Salaam; tel/fax: 0811 327706; email: fox@twiga.com. This highly regarded and comfortable private camp is situated on a koppie above a set of rapids on the Ruaha River. Game viewing is excellent from the camp, with hippos resident on the river and many other animals coming down to drink. Accommodation is in *banda*s or fixed tents. There is a restaurant and bar. Full-board accommodation for drive-in customers costs US$140/200 single/double in addition to which must be paid US$35 per person per game drive. A full fly-in package arranged through Foxtreks costs US$240/400 single/double inclusive of all meals, game drives, park fees and airport transfer but exclusive of the cost of the flight.

Msembe Camp This basic camp is near the headquarters and the river. There are nine double *banda*s and two family *banda*s. All are self-contained, with bedding, firewood and water provided. There is a basic campsite with pit toilets but no water. Campsites and *banda*s cost US$20 per person.

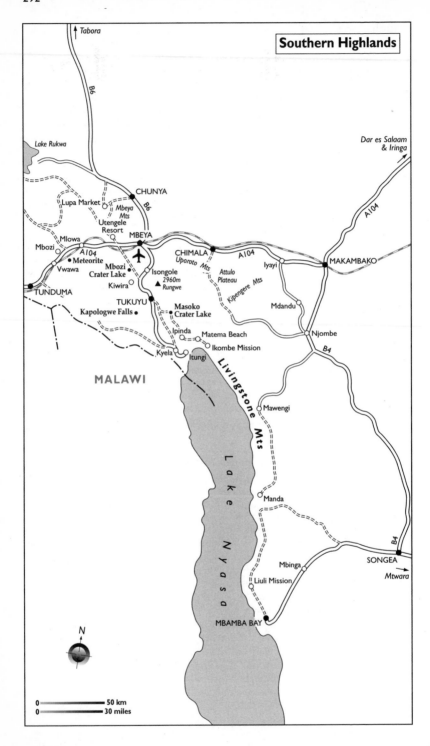

The Southern Highlands and Lake Nyasa

Bounded by the Tanzam Highway to the west, Songea to the east, Makambako to the north, and Zambia and Malawi to the south, the part of southern Tanzania covered in this chapter is exceptionally pretty and reasonably easy to get around, a combination which should make it particularly attractive to budget travellers. Yet, oddly enough, practically the only tourist traffic passing through this area consists of backpackers who are dashing between Dar es Salaam and Malawi. So fixed is this pattern that when I last took a bus past the turn-off to the Malawi border near Kyela, I was virtually forced off the bus – nobody there believed that any tourist would want to continue to the Tanzanian part of Lake Nyasa!

The principal town is in this part of Tanzania is Mbeya, an important route focus for overlanders, since it is where travellers heading to Malawi will disembark from their bus or train to divert eastwards off the Tanzam Highway. Other major towns in the region include Tukuyu, Songea, Njombe and Kyela. The most significant physical feature in this part of Tanzania is Lake Nyasa (the name used locally for the Tanzanian portion of Lake Malawi). A number of mountain ranges form the Rift Valley escarpment on either side of the lake: the Poroto and Kipengere lie to the north and east of Lake Nyasa, while the Livingstone Mountains rise dramatically to the immediate west.

Climate

With altitudes ranging from below 500m to over 2,500m, this region has a varied climate. Lake Nyasa (478m) is hot and humid, but the rest of the region is temperate, and in the highlands you'll need some reasonably warm clothing at night. The area around Tukuyu has the highest rainfall of anywhere in Tanzania, so it is best visited during the dry season between May and October.

Getting around

Mbeya, the main gateway to the region, can be approached by rail or road from Dar es Salaam or by road from western Tanzania. See *Mbeya* for details. Songea, the main route focus on the eastern side of the lake, can be approached from Makambako on the Tanzam Highway, from Mbamba Bay on the lake shore, or from Mtwara on the south coast.

Within the region there is plenty of transport along the Mbeya–Kyela road, the Songea–Makambako road and the Tanzam Highway. Two ferries a week run between Itungi and Mbamba Bay on Lake Nyasa. Transport on side roads is less erratic than in most parts of the country, but it can still be pretty rough going.

MBEYA

Mbeya was established in 1927 to service the Lupa goldfields near Chunya, which closed in the 1950s. Surrounded by rich agricultural lands and boasting a strategic position along the Tanzam Highway and Tazara Railway, Mbeya has continued to prosper. It is an appealing town, with a skyline dominated by the impressive – and climbable – Mbeya Range. It also has an unusually Westernised, bustling feel and shows few of the signs of neglect that characterise many other Tanzanian towns. Mbeya is mainly used by travellers as a stop-off point on the way to Zambia or Malawi, but it is a good base for exploring the southern highlands.

Getting there and away

Most people travel between Mbeya and Dar es Salaam by rail. There are five trains a week on the Tazara line (see *By rail* in *Chapter 4* for details). There are regular buses between Dar es Salaam and Mbeya, an 893km trip which takes around 20 hours. Overnight buses on this route have a bad reputation for theft; it is advisable to split the trip at, for instance, Iringa.

From Arusha or Moshi, the most direct route to Mbeya is via Dodoma, but the roads connecting Arusha, Dodoma and Iringa are so bad that it will be quicker and more comfortable to travel via Chalinze/Dar es Salaam.

From western Tanzania, the most comfortable option would be to get to Dar es Salaam by train and proceed to Mbeya from there. A more adventurous route goes via Mpanda and Sumbawanga; see *Chapter 15*. At least two buses every week run along the little-used road connecting Tabora to Mbeya, passing through one of the most remote parts of Tanzania. This trip will take at least 20 hours.

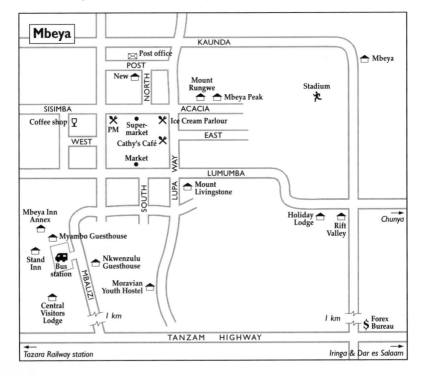

Buses to local destinations such as Kyela, Tukuyu, Njombe and Tunduma leave regularly on a fill-up-and-go basis. Buses to more distant destinations should be booked in advance.

Where to stay

There are three tourist-class hotels in Mbeya. The **Mount Livingstone Hotel** (PO Box 1401; tel: 065 3331/4; fax: 065 4190) is definitely the smartest of these places, with rooms costing US$40/60 s/c single/double, and a 50% residents' discount. The **Rift Valley Hotel** (tel: 065 4429) and **Mbeya Peak Hotel** (tel: 065 3473) both charge around US$18/24 s/c single/double. All these places have nets and hot water, and there are good restaurants attached.

For cheaper accommodation, the government-owned **Mbeya Hotel** is a bit faded, but it's reasonable value at around US$10/14 s/c single/double with nets and cold showers. Much better value is the clean **Holiday Lodge** (tel: 065 2821/3375), where large double rooms with nets cost around US$5. Similar in price, but more institutional in character, the **Moravian Youth Hostel** lies a couple of minutes' walk out of town along Jacaranda Road, and offers clean, secure accommodation which has long been popular with travellers.

There are dozens of basic guesthouses dotted around the bus station area. One of the more appealing is the **Central Visitors Lodge** (tel: 065 2507), a conspicuous brown-and-blue double-storey building behind the bus station. Also worth a look are the **Mbeya Inn Annexe**, **Nkwenzulu**, **Myambo** and **Stand Guesthouses**, all of which have rooms in the US$3–5 range.

Where to eat

The restaurant at the Holiday Lodge is the outstanding place to eat in the budget range, serving good, cheap stews with chips or rice. For a proper restaurant meal, the Mount Livingstone Hotel is highly recommended, both for the quality of the food and for its varied menu, and the restaurant in the Rift Valley Hotel is also pretty good. **Eddy's** on Sisimba Road has also been recommended.

The restaurant at the **Utegele Country Resort** (see *Mbeya Range*), open daily except Monday, is highly regarded. Meals cost around US$5.

Useful information
Tazara railway station
This is a few kilometres from Mbeya on the Tanzam Highway towards Zambia. The booking office is at the station. Your best bet is either to get a taxi or take a bus towards the Zambian border and ask to be dropped off.

Shopping
Mbeya is the place in which to stock up if you are planning a few days' hiking or camping in the surrounding area. The supermarkets on Market Square sell a fair variety of imported goods. Fruit and vegetables are best bought at the market. Plenty of small *dukas* (stalls or small shops) surround the market. For ice-creams and packaged food items, try **Ramji's Supermarket** in the THB Building near the post office – it's also a good place to pick up recent international newspapers and magazines.

Excursions
Chunya
This intriguing small town, 70km north of Mbeya, was the centre of the 1920s/1930s gold rush. Mining stopped in the 1950s when it ceased to be

profitable. Chunya then enjoyed a short-lived tobacco boom before degenerating into something approaching a ghost town. Many of the grander buildings are now boarded up and there is a general air of faded prosperity. You can still see local prospectors panning the river which runs through the town. There is talk of working the gold again using modern methods.

A few pick-up trucks, leaving from near the Mbeya Peak Hotel, ply the scenic road from Mbeya to Chunya every day. You can normally get to Chunya and back in a day, but there are a couple of guesthouses if you want to stay the night, or are forced to.

World's End Viewpoint, just off the Chunya road 21km from Mbeya, offers excellent views across the Rift Valley escarpment to the Usunga Flats.

If you have your own vehicle, it is possible to continue past Chunya to Lake Rukwa (see *Chapter 15*).

Mbeya Range

The mountains which tower over Mbeya are of less biological interest than the more extensive ranges covered later in the chapter, but there are good views over the Rukwa region from the peaks and wild flowers are abundant in the wet season. The most accessible peak, Kaluwe (2,656m), can be climbed in a few hours from Mbeya by following a path which starts behind the hospital.

The highest point in the range is Mbeya peak (2,834m). This is most easily climbed from Luiji, a village about 20km from Mbeya town. The climb takes six hours and is steep in parts, so it should only be attempted if you are reasonably fit. To get to Luiji, ask any bus heading south from Mbeya to drop you at the turn-off near Mbalizi. It is 9km from Mbalizi to Luiji. I am not aware of any public transport, so expect to walk.

The only accommodation in Luiji is at Utegele Country Resort, built on a coffee farm ($20 s/c double). A cheaper campsite should be operating at the resort by the time you read this.

If you want to do a longer hike in the area, you can cross from Mbeya Peak to Pungulume (2,230m) at the western extreme of the range. Utegele Country Resort can give you details.

Mbozi meteorite

This 15-ton meteorite, discovered in 1942, is believed to be the third-largest in the world. It lies 10km off the Tanzam Highway southwest of Mbeya. The turn-off is signposted, but the meteorite is difficult to reach without private transport.

TUKUYU

Tukuyu is a shapeless small town salvaged from anonymity by having one of the most appealing settings in Tanzania. It is ringed by the Poroto Mountains and lies at the base of Mount Rungwe, a dormant volcano which at approximately 2,960m is the second-highest point in the southern highlands. Tukuyu is the obvious base for exploring the Poroto, a range dotted with waterfalls, crater lakes, and patches of forest – all capped by stirring views to Lake Nyasa more than 1,000m below.

The area between Tukuyu and Nyasa is home to the Nyakyusa people, whose neatly painted homes were described by the explorer Joseph Thomson as 'perfect arcadia'. It is a fertile region, with rich volcanic soils and an annual rainfall of over 1,500mm. The dirt roads that criss-cross the area are lined with small subsistence farms growing bananas, mangos, tea and coffee.

Tukuyu was founded as a German administration centre in the late 19th century, and originally called Nieu Langenburg. The old Langenburg, on Lake Nyasa near Ikombe, was abandoned due to the high incidence of malaria and is now a mission.

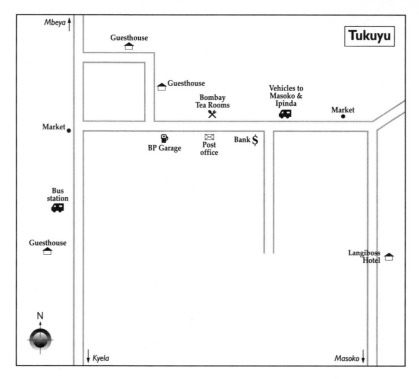

If you plan on hiking, the area is best between May and October. At other times there is rain most afternoons. Tukuyu is cold at night.

Getting there and away
Tukuyu is on the tarred Mbeya-Kyela road. Regular buses run in both directions on a fill-up-and-go basis.

Where to stay and eat
The **Langiboss Hotel** (tel: 0658 2080) is all a traveller could wish for. The rooms are clean and comfortable, the manager speaks English and is well-informed about local attractions, and there is even a hot shower. The hotel lies 1km out of town and has a marvellous view of Mount Rungwe. There is a bar and restaurant (meals must be ordered in advance). If you are hiking, you can leave excess gear at the hotel. US$1.50/2.00 single/double. If it is full there are plenty of scruffy guesthouses dotted around the town.

There is a campsite on the grounds of the **Pentecostal Holiness Association Mission**, the turn-off to which is signposted 10km from Tukuyu on the Mbeya road. The priest in charge is helpful and knows the surrounding area well. It is a half-hour walk from the turn-off to the mission.

Excursions
This area is ideal for casual rambling. Wander along any of its winding dirt roads and you will be rewarded with lovely views and scenery, varied bird life and vegetation, and regular glimpses into rural African life. Even on by-roads there is a fair amount of traffic (expect to pay for lifts, though), so exploring the area over a few days from one base is possible.

The following are some of the more accessible spots, most of which are easily visited as a day trip from Tukuyu. With time, initiative and 1:50,000 maps, you can explore further. A 1969 publication called *Welcome to Mbeya* has plenty of useful walking information, but you'll have some difficulty locating a copy.

Ngozi Crater Lake

The most spectacular crater lake in the Poroto Mountains is over 2km long and circled by 200m-high cliffs. To get to the rim you walk up the forested southeastern slopes, rich in plant and bird life. Ngozi is attributed with magical powers locally. A faded signpost marks the turn-off to Ngozi a few kilometres from Isongole village. From there a driveable dirt track continues for 5km before it reaches the footpath to the rim. From Isongole, the trip takes two to three hours each way on foot. It is advisable to organise a guide; the path is not always clear, particularly during the rainy season.

Kiwira Natural Bridge

A natural rock bridge, formed 400 years ago by water-cooled lava from Mount Rungwe, spans the Kiwira River further along the same road as the Pentecostal Holiness Association Mission (see *Where to stay*). To walk there from the mission takes a couple of hours. Trucks run most days from the main road to an army base near the bridge, and may give tourists a lift. Ask for details at the mission.

Mount Rungwe

If you are reasonably fit, Rungwe can be climbed and descended in about ten hours. Alternatively, if you have a tent and are adequately prepared, you could spend a couple of days exploring the slopes. The most popular route starts at Isongole, bypasses Shiwaga Crater, then takes you through extensive patches of forest. A 1:50,000 map of Rungwe is available from the Department of Lands and Surveys in Dar es Salaam.

Masoko Crater Lake

This attractive crater lake is one of the easiest beauty spots to visit in the Tukuyu area. It also has some interesting historical associations: the solid stone building on the rim of the crater was constructed in around 1912 to house the German Fifth Field Garrison, and it was the base from which Germany fought British troops in the neighbouring Nyasaland Protectorate. The stone building housed British troops between the wars, and it now serves as a courthouse.

Masoko, like most crater lakes, has attracted several legends. It is rumoured that towards the end of World War I, the Germans dumped a fortune in gold bars, money and military vehicles into the lake to avoid their falling into British hands – believable enough when you consider the same thing happened to the *Liemba* on Lake Tanganyika, but almost impossible to verify if there is any truth in the story that the lake is over 3km deep. Difficult to say whether there's anything to be read into the fact that the occasional German coin is washed up on the shore of the lake. Locals claim that swimming in the lake is tantamount to suicide, and there are also stories that the courthouse is haunted.

Masoko lies roughly 15km from Tukuyu along the Ipinda/Matema road. A fair amount of traffic heads this way – predominantly overcrowded pick-up trucks. You may prefer to walk out: it's gently downhill most of the way, and very pretty with intimate, cultivated slopes occasionally giving way to magnificent vistas to Lake Nyasa. With an early start, you'll have no problem getting a lift back.

Kapologwe Falls

The main attraction of this waterfall is that you can wade through the river to a large cave behind it. Without a vehicle, it's a bit far from the main road to make for a viable day trip (12–15km each way). The turn-off is 10km from Tukuyu on the Kyela road.

HIKING FROM IZYONJE TO MATEMA BEACH

Gerhard Buttner is the first person I've heard from who has hiked across the Kitulo Plateau, and he sent me a letter describing the trip in February 1998. The following is an edited extract:

'We settled on a north-to-south route connecting some spots described in Welcome to Mbeya. Starting at Izyonje near Lake Ngozi, we hiked via the Kitulo Plateau (where the Kitulo Government Farm rents out an entire three-bed guesthouse for US$3) through Mtorwi, Makete and Bulongwa to Matema Beach on the shores of Lake Nyasa.

'Hardly any English is spoken in these mountains. The area has some scenic spots, but many are highly populated farming settlements and finding isolated camping spots was not easy. People couldn't quite understand what we wanted in this area, but they were never unfriendly in spite of a rumour that we had come to plant bombs in the forest! Local people walk across parts of these mountains, but the last people before us to attempt crossing the whole area were two Germans who never completed their journey in the 1980s because they nearly landed in jail as suspected South African spies. A few times, villagers joined us for a few hours to show us the way, without ever asking for a guiding fee. We communicated with their few words of English and our limited Swahili You will need your own food, but ugali, potatoes and some tomatoes and onions can occasionally be traded.

'The most spectacular part of the walk was the endless drop down to Matema Beach. Villagers walk this path once a week on market day, as a greater variety of products is available on the plains around Matema.'

Unfortunately, Gerhard doesn't mention how many days it took them to hike this route. He does say that knowing the Swahili words listed in the language section of this guide without having to look them up is the minimum you'll need to get by. He also notes that what several maps show as the 'Kipengere Mountains' are referred to by locals as the Livingstone Mountains, and that the name Kipengere is used locally to refer to the inhabited plains.

As something of an aside to the above, I remember that when I was researching the first edition of this guide, Hilary Bradt passed me a letter written a few years earlier by a couple of hikers who had aborted their trip after having spent a day or two convincing the police not to lock them up as spies. This was almost certainly the German couple Gerhard heard about, so it really does sound as if Gerhard might have been the first mzungu to cross this way in a decade! If you decide to follow in his footsteps, do write and let me know how it went.

Kitulo Plateau

The Poroto Mountains extend westwards into the Kipengere Range almost as far as Njombe, creating an extensive highland area with a number of possible access points. The Kitulo Plateau, which connects the two ranges, boasts the highest peak in the southern highlands, Mount Mtorwi (2,961m), as well as the 2,929m Chaluhangi Dome. The plateau is noted for the wild flowers which blanket it after the November rains, and the pastoral Nji people who inhabit it. If you have a vehicle, the approach from Chimala on the Tanzam Highway climbs a succession of dizzying hairpin bends and is said to be very dramatic. There is little in the way of public transport in the region, so access could be a problem for backpackers.

The Department of Lands and Surveys in Dar es Salaam stocks 1:50,000 maps of the region. It would be foolish to think of hiking without them. If you need to locate the maps once you are in the area, then you should be able to find them at the engineering shop in the Stadium in Mbeya. You should carry appropriate equipment and be largely self-sufficient in terms of food. See the box *Hiking from Izyonje to Matema Beach* for a recent account of a hiking trip across the Kitulo Plateau.

LAKE NYASA

Lake Nyasa is the Tanzanian portion of Lake Malawi (as explained on page xii, calling it Lake Malawi will not get you very far in Tanzania). Whatever you call it, it is without a doubt the most scenic of Africa's three great lakes, and although most travellers visit the Malawian part, the Tanzanian portion is equally attractive. Lake Nyasa contains 30% of the world's cichlid species. These colourful fish can easily be observed in the lake's clear water.

Lake Nyasa has a bad reputation for cerebral malaria. Take your pills and continue to take them for four weeks after you leave the area. If you show any signs of malaria, get to a doctor quickly.

Getting there and away

The gateway to Nyasa is Kyela, 10km from Itungi Port on the lake shore. Regular buses between Mbeya and Kyela take about four hours and stop at Tukuyu. The 1,000m descent from Tukuyu to Kyela is breathtaking; make sure you get a window seat. The contrast between the pleasantly cool highlands around Tukuyu and the cloying heat of the lake shore may come as something of a shock.

Ferries on Lake Nyasa

Few travellers are aware of the ferry service between Itungi Port and Mbamba Bay, the best way to see the northern part of Nyasa. The scenery is dominated by the Livingstone Mountains which rise sharply on the east shore. The ferry stops at several fishing villages where the locals approach in dugouts, selling fish, fruit and other goods to passengers.

The ferry to Mbamba Bay runs twice a week. It leaves Itungi at 07.00 on Monday and Thursday and arrives at Mbamba Bay at around midnight the same day, after stopping at Lupingu, Manda, Lundu, Nindai and Liuli. After arriving at Mbamba Bay, the Monday ferry turns around more-or-less immediately, to arrive back at Itungi at 17.00 the next day. The Thursday ferry continues travelling onto Nkhata Bay in Malawi, arriving some time on Friday, before starting the return voyage to Itungi. These times are *very* approximate.

A third ferry leaves Itungi at 07.00 on Wednesday and arrives back on Thursday afternoon. This stops at most lakeside villages, including Matema, but doesn't go as far as Mbamba Bay. It is about an hour from Itungi to Matema, so you could use the ferry to get there and back if the timing was suitable.

In theory MV *Songea* does the Monday and Friday run and the smaller MV *Iringa* does the Wednesday run. We went on a Friday and MV *Iringa* was used, so this may not always be the case. Lake Malawi can get very choppy, and the smaller boat is not much fun in rough weather. MV *Songea* is said to be much smoother.

Note that the Malawian MV *Ilala* normally crosses between Nkhata Bay and Mbamba Bay and back once weekly. In theory, it leaves Nkhata Bay at 01.00 on Tuesday morning, arrives at Mbamba Bay three to four hours later, and then starts the return trip at 07.30. In practice, the MV *Ilala* is just about always six to twelve hours behind schedule, and when it falls too far behind, the crossing to Mbamba Bay is omitted from its weekly voyage.

There is no accommodation in Itungi. You will have to spend the night in Kyela and get a vehicle to Itungi at around 05.30 on the morning of departure. Vehicles leave from in front of the TRC office, 1km out of town. There is a booking office at the TRC building, but as the ticket officer travels with the ferry it serves no practical function. You can buy a ticket at Itungi while you wait for the ferry to be loaded up.

There is one class, and it is not overcrowded. Tickets cost US$4. Meals are available on board, as are sodas and beers.

Kyela

Kyela is not my favourite town. It is sweaty and scruffy, and has more than its fair share of people who feel an uncontrollable need to yell *Mzungu!* at any passing European. The town centre is a small grid of roads around a central market. The TRC office is 1km from the market in the same direction as Itungi.

Where to stay and eat

There are loads of indifferent guesthouses in Kyela. Rooms cost under US$2. If you are catching the ferry, try either the **nameless lodge opposite the TRC office** or the **New Vatican City Lodge** 300m towards town. In the town centre, the **nameless guesthouse opposite the Ram Hotel** is acceptable. So is the **Kyombo Guest House** on the main road 200m towards Tukuyu. **Mkoko's Restaurant**, behind the market, has a shady veranda and a fridge stocked with beer and sodas.

Matema Beach

This beach on the northern tip of Lake Nyasa is rated the best anywhere on the lake. With the Livingstone Mountains rising sharply to the east and the Poroto Range on the western horizon, it is difficult to imagine a more visually attractive setting. Matema is the kind of place you could settle into for a while: swimming in the warm bilharzia-free water, taking short walks, chatting to the locals – or just waiting for the sun to set behind the Poroto.

Getting there and away

There is a daily bus between Mbeya and Matema, passing through Tukuyu, Kyela and Ipinda, but since it arrives at Matema after dark and leaves at 05.00, it's not that convenient.

It is easier to get to Matema using light vehicles, If you can't find a pick-up truck running directly between Kyela and Matema, you should find one from Kyela to Ipinda, a large village 27km from Matema. There is also the odd pick-up truck running between Tukuyu and Ipinda via Masoko Crater Lake. The daily bus aside, there is normally some private transport between Ipinda and Matema, especially on Saturdays, and most vehicles will stop to pick up passengers for a small fee. There is a basic but adequate guesthouse in Ipinda, behind the bank ($1/2 single/double). I have heard that you can walk between Ipinda and Matema along a river which comes out at Lake Nyasa 3km west of the mission, but I've no idea how long this would take.

The day before you plan to leave Matema, ask the mission if any of their vehicles are heading to Ipinda the next morning.

The ferry which leaves Itungi at 07.00 Wednesday arrives at Matema an hour later. It also stops at Matema on Thursday afternoon on its way back to Itungi. Ferries to Mbamba Bay *do not* stop at Matema.

Where to stay
The **Lutheran Mission Resort** on the shore has spotless *banda*s with comfortable beds and mosquito nets. A kiosk sells cold sodas and coffee/tea, and a canteen serves enormous buffet-style meals. These must be ordered in advance and cost US$2.50 per head. The home-made bread served at breakfast is wonderful. Double *banda*s cost US$10, *banda*s sleeping four cost US$20. You can camp for around US$5 per tent.

Excursions
In the stifling heat of the lake shore even the shortest stroll feels like a major excursion. The time to explore is the early morning. One warning: if you head further afield, ask before you swim. There are no crocodiles at Matema, but they are common on nearby parts of the shore, where they kill villagers with a frequency that suggests caution is advisable.

There are a few local spots worth looking at. The best-known is Matema Pottery Market, held every Saturday at the village 1km east of the resort. The pots are crafted by the Kisi who live on the northwestern lake shore and are sold as far afield as Dar es Salaam. On weekdays, you could try to arrange for a fisherman to row you to the peninsula where the pottery is made.

About 500m past the village, the shore becomes rockier. This is a good place to see colourful cichlids. Crocodile are common at the river mouth 3km west of Matema and hippo have been seen a short way upriver.

Liuli
This is the last-but-one stop on the southbound ferry trip, an attractive natural harbour protected by a rocky peninsula, topped by the sphinx-like formation from which derived the village's German name, Sphinxhafen. Liuli is the site of the largest mission in this part of Tanzania, and the burial place of William Johnson, the Anglican missionary who co-founded the Likoma mission on an island in the Malawian part of the lake. Johnson is one of the most fondly remembered of all the missionaries who worked in the Lake Nyasa area; for 46 years he preached from a boat all around the lake shore, despite being practically blind and well into his seventies when he died in 1928. Johnson's grave was for several decades a pilgrimage site for Malawian Christians.

Liuli's greatest claim to posterity is as the site of the first naval encounter of World War I, an incident which was described by *The Times* in London as 'Naval Victory on Lake Nyasa' and by a participant, Mr G M Sanderson, as "pure comedy".

Shortly after war was declared, the British Commissioner of Nyasaland dispatched the protectorate's only ship, the *Gwendolyn,* to destroy its German counterpart, the *Hermann Von Wessman*. The *Gwendolyn*'s captain, Commander Rhoades, was informed at Nkhata Bay that the *Wessman* was docked for repairs at

Liuli. He arrived at Liuli in the cover of dawn with a somewhat nervous crew: their only gunner was a Scots storeman who had trained several years previously as a seaman-gunner and who freely admitted that he remembered little of his training. After several misfires, caused by a combination of dud ammunition and rusty aiming, a shell finally connected with the German boat.

'Immediately afterwards,' wrote Sanderson several years later, 'a small white dinghy put off from shore, in which was a European clad in a singlet and a pair of shorts pulling furiously for the *Gwen*. Rhoades ordered "Cease fire" and blessed silence fell. It was his drinking pal [Captain Berndt], the skipper of the *Wessman*, with whom every meeting was a drinking party. The dinghy came alongside and its furious occupant leaped to his feet and, shaking both fists above his head, exclaimed "Gott for dam, Rrroades, vos you drunk?". The news that the war had arrived had not yet reached him. When Rhoades informed him that he was a prisoner, one could see his anger turn to horror as he realised his fatal mistake.'

Good enough reason to pause when the boat stops at Liuli, though it's an open question whether you'd think about disembarking. Liuli lies on a lovely stretch of shore; the German mission and Johnson's grave are still there; and, who knows, with a bit of imagination you might even be able to conjure up the image of a semi-naked and infuriated Captain Berndt gesticulating from his dinghy.

More pragmatically, there's nowhere to stay, and when you want to move on you'll be reliant on the occasional mission vehicle heading to Mbamba Bay, or more likely the next ferry. Of course, if you have a tent and you don't mind a couple of days' wait for transport out, this might just add up to a most attractive off-the-beaten-track option – food, at least, shouldn't be a problem on the shore of this most fish-rich of lakes.

Mbamba Bay

The southernmost town on the Tanzanian part of Lake Nyasa lies on a pretty coconut-lined beac. The port boasts numerous good vantage points to watch the sunset, and there is the chance to on a boat trip on the lake. A few years back, accommodation was limited to one very basic guesthouse, but there are now several possibilities, partly as a result of the recent resumption of international ferry services to Nkhata Bay in Malawi. The only upmarket accommodation in the area is the **Chinula Beach Resort** (PO Box 2983 Mbeya; tel: 065 4481), which lies on a pristine 4km stretch of sandy beach about 8km north of Mbamba Bay. There are good snorkelling facilities at Chinula, and the manager will meet you in Mbamba Bay by prior arrangement. Most local guesthouses have no electricity and a sporadic water supply. The **Neema Beach Guest Garden Hotel Bar and Pharmacy** (PO Box 14 Mbamba Bay) is reasonable: s/c rooms cost US$7/8 single/double, there is a bar, dining room and patio, and solar-charged lanterns are provided when the generator is down. The **Nyasa View Lodge** is rather run-down by comparison, and several other guesthouses offer basic rooms with a mosquito net for around US$1.50.

The MV *Ilala* leaves Mbamba Bay for Nkhata Bay at 14.00 every Tuesday.

Mbinga

From Mbamba Bay, a 60km dirt road winds its way up the valley wall through well-developed *miombo* woodland to a grassy plateau and Mbinga. This is a thrilling route, the road clinging to the mountainside and offering dramatic views back to the lake.

There used to be an erratic bus service between Mbamba Bay and Mbinga, but this doesn't seem to operate anymore. A few 4WD vehicles cover the road daily, however, leaving when they are full and taking about three hours in good weather. When I did the trip in 1992, in light rain, it took closer to seven hours. Most of this time I spent trudging through mud while the driver tried to free his vehicle; the rest of it I clung terrified and dripping to the sides of the overloaded vehicle while it skidded uncertainly around the precipitous road. Recent reports suggest the road hasn't improved any since 1992, and I imagine it would be impassable after heavy rain.

Mbinga is an oasis. You can get hot tea there. Had I arrived in a more rational state, I would probably call it a typically dull small African town, but... Whatever else, once you hit Mbinga there is plenty of transport along a well-maintained dirt road to Songea. There is even a 'Special Video Bus' to Dar es Salaam three days a week. There are a few basic guesthouses and *hotelis* dotted around Mbinga's bus station, while the **Mbicu Hotel** offers s/c rooms with satellite television and air-conditioning, as well as a restaurant and coffee bar.

SONGEA

Songea is a large, lively town at the junction of the road to Mbamba Bay and the road connecting the Tanzam Highway to the south coast. If you arrive in Songea from the south coast or Lake Nyasa, its busy market, well-stocked supermarkets and general state of good repair are a welcome re-connection with the modern world. Until the ivory moratorium in 1989, Songea was a major centre for poachers smuggling ivory out of the Selous. This may well account for the town's comparative prosperity.

Getting there and away

A recently built tar road connects Songea to Njombe and the Tanzam Highway. Regular buses run along it. Buses to Njombe and Mbeya go when they are full; buses to Dar es Salaam should be booked in advance.

For details of crossing between Songea and the south coast via Tunduru, see box *Travelling from Mtwara to Songea*, page 320.

Where to stay

The closest thing in Songea to an upmarket hotel is the **New Africa Hotel**, which has s/c double rooms for around US$20, and a good restaurant and bar. Dropping

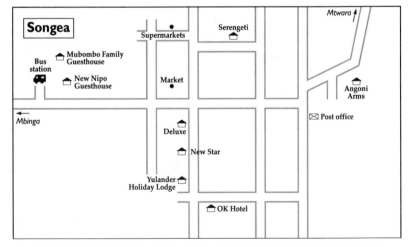

in price, the **Hotel Angoni Arms** on the Tunduru road is a bit run-down, but likeably idiosyncratic and fair value at around US$10 for a double. Back in the town centre, the **OK Hotel 92** has been good value for years: it currently charges around US$7 for a double, and has a lively bar and good restaurant. On the opposite side of the same road, the quieter but similarly priced **Yulander Holiday Lodge** is also worth a try

As usual there are plenty of guesthouses at the bus station and in the town centre, typically charging around US$2 for a room. A recent recommendation is the **Mkomi Guesthouse**, on the main road near the bus station. The **Deluxe Guesthouse**, a two-storey hotel in the town centre, has acceptable rooms with mosquito nets, but it's bit run-down. Around the corner, the **New Star Guesthouse** is also clean and friendly, and the rooms have mosquito nets.'

NJOMBE

There is not much of interest in this quiet, pleasantly situated small town. If you have a spare afternoon it could be a pretty area in which to do some walking. There is an attractive waterfall on the Ruhudji River, next to the main road 2km north of the town centre. Njombe is cold at night.

Getting there and away

Njombe lies 237km from Songea (the distance is marked incorrectly on some maps) along a good tar road, and the bus ride between them takes less than five hours. There are regular buses in all directions from Njombe. In fact, for such a sleepy-looking town, it has one of the most chaotic bus stations I have seen. Watch your belongings.

Where to stay

The two-storey **Milimani Motel** (tel: 0631 2408), 250m from the bus station towards Songea, has a good bar and restaurant. Rooms are inexpensive, clean, comfortable and spacious, and the showers are hot. The **Lutheran Centre Hostel** offers beds in clean, recently furnished dormitories for less than US$1 per person and it has a canteen. It is 50m and signposted from the main road, just before the Milimani. Of several guesthouses around the bus station, the best is the **Shamba Guesthouse**.

MAKAMBAKO

This important junction town is a good place to hitch a lift from in any direction. If you get stuck there is a Lutheran Hostel, and also a couple of private lodges.

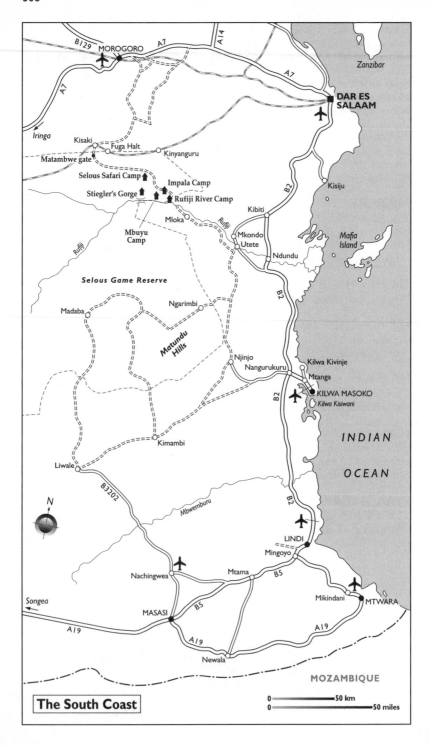

The South Coast

The Coast South of Dar es Salaam

The 500km coastline stretching from Dar es Salaam southwards to the Ruvuma River on the Mozambique border has a remote character, and it is rarely visited by outsiders. The only towns of any size along the south coast are Kilwa Masoko, Lindi and Mtwara, and the combination of poor roads and long distances has rendered these places as among the most isolated towns of their size in East Africa. From a traveller's perspective, the area offers little to those who value their creature comforts: only in Mtwara is there anything resembling a tourist hotel, few people anywhere speak even the most rudimentary English, there are no organised tourist attractions, and public transport tends to be overcrowded, uncomfortable, and painfully slow.

Despite all this, the south coast is a fascinating, thought-provoking and often enchanting area, endlessly rewarding to those with a sense of adventure and curiosity. The older towns are profoundly Swahili in character, and the crumbling German and Arab buildings that line their roads generate a time-warped atmosphere, like something out of a Graham Greene novel. The people, too, retain a gracious, slow pace of life, one into which it is easy to slip, provided that you dress and behave in accordance with the conservative Muslim culture that dominates the region. Scenically, the south coast is all you might expect: stunning palm-lined beaches, thick mangrove swamps, and (as you head away from the beaches) baobab-studded acacia scrub. And, while there is an element of travel for its own sake attached to exploring this region, it does boast one genuine travel highlight in the form of the ruined city of Kilwa, far and away the most impressive and significant of the medieval Swahili ruins that line the Indian Ocean coast of Africa.

The south coast's isolation can easily be romanticised, but there is a depressing reality behind the picturesque images. I was struck by the number of beggars, cripples and blind people in the towns, the malnourished children in roadside villages and the total lack of industry. This situation should be partly remedied if and when long-standing plans to extend the Mtwara-Lindi tar road to Dar es Salaam ever come to fruition.

This chapter includes coverage of the Makonde Plateau, the area immediately inland of Lindi and Mtwara, renowned for its carving and painting traditions. The major towns on the plateau are Masasi and Newala.

Climate

Like the rest of the Tanzanian coast, this region is hot and humid at all times. The ideal time to visit is in the drier, cooler months between April and October.

Getting around

During the dry season there are daily buses between Dar es Salaam and all the large towns covered in this chapter, but the road is often impassable during the rains. Buses to Lindi and Mtwara leave Dar es Salaam from Morogoro Road bus station. Buses to Kilwa leave from in front of Kariakoo Market. There are good local services on the tar roads connecting Lindi, Mtwara and Masasi. The south coast can be reached by road from the southern highlands; see box *Travelling from Mtwara to Songea* on page 320.

The ideal way to explore the south coast would be to take a boat from Dar es Salaam to Mtwara and then work your way back overland. For years, the only boat to cover this route was the *Canadian Spirit*, which always ran to a rather whimsical schedule and ceased operating altogether in 1998. In early 1999, a new boat called the MV *Safari* started a weekly run between Dar es Salaam and Mtwara, leaving Dar es Salaam at 12.00 every Wednesday and from Mtwara at 10.00 on Friday. The voyage takes roughly 24 hours and a first-class fare costs around US$15 one-way, to which must be added a US$5 port tax, the latter payable in hard currency.

KILWA AND SURROUNDS

There are three settlements called Kilwa. The oldest, Kilwa Kisiwani – Kilwa on the island – lies on a small island 2km offshore. It is the site of the most impressive ruins on the East African coast, those of the medieval city of Kilwa – the *Quiloa* of Milton's *Paradise Lost* and once thought to be the site of King Solomon's mythical mines.

The other settlements are both on the mainland. Kilwa Kivinje (Kilwa of the Casuarina Trees) was a major 19th-century slave trading centre, only rivalled in importance on the mainland by Bagamoyo. Kilwa Masoko (Kilwa of the Market) is a more modern town, and is now the regional headquarters.

Although the Kilwa area is primarily of historical interest, the surrounding coast is lovely. The seas around Kilwa have the world's densest dugong population. Dugong are large, bizarre-looking marine mammals, believed to have been the origin of the mermaid myth. Common as they are, you would be lucky to see one.

History

It is a reflection of the widespread ignorance regarding Africa's past that while tourists flock to Tanzania's game reserves only a handful pass through Kilwa every year. Even more disturbing is the fact we were told by a number of people in Kilwa (including the caretaker) that the Husuni Kubwa – the island's most impressive building and the apex of Swahili architectural aspirations – was Portuguese-built. With the above in mind, the following history is as detailed as space and the known facts will allow.

As with all African history, many details of Kilwa's past are open to conjecture. There have been extensive archaeological diggings on the site and some contemporary descriptions have survived. The primary historical source is the *Kilwa Chronicle*, written in 1520 under the supervision of the then-exiled Sultan of Kilwa. Two versions of this exist, one dating from 1565 and the other from the 19th century. Discrepancies exist, but the broad history of Kilwa is well-understood.

Kilwa was occupied by precursors of the Swahili in the 9th century. In about 1150 the island was bought by a trader called Ali bin Al-Hasan, generally regarded to be the founder of the Shirazi Dynasty which dominated coastal trade until the Portuguese invasion. His importance can be gauged by the fact that coins bearing his name – probably minted long after his death – have been found as far afield as Pemba and Mafia Islands.

Although Kilwa's importance grew under Al-Hasan and his successors, its eventual dominance of the gold trade is linked to the arrival of Abu-al-Mawahib, a trader from Sofala in modern-day Mozambique, and is most plausibly explained by a simple accident of geography. Gold arrived at the coast from the interior at Sofala, but until the mid-13th century it was sold to the Arabs at Mogadishu, in modern-day Somalia. The normal explanation for this is that Arab vessels could not reach Sofala within the annual monsoon cycle, and that the gold was transported up the coast by a succession of local middlemen.

As the volume of coastal trade increased, improvements in Arab navigation and ship design allowed them to penetrate steadily further south. Sofala would have been beyond their reach whatever they did – winds south of Kilwa are notoriously fickle – but it seems likely to have suited Sofala's traders to cut out the middlemen by bringing the centre of trade closer to home. In this scenario, Kilwa would have been the ideal compromise – by the mid-13th century it was evidently within reach of Arab vessels, yet it was near enough to Sofala for traders there to control the trade from top to bottom.

The source of Kilwa's gold, shrouded in mystery for centuries, gave rise to such myths as the Queen of Sheba and King Solomon's Mines. It is now thought that the gold was mined in the Zimbabwean interior and arrived at Sofala via the Zambezi valley. There are strong parallels between the timing of the rise and fall of Kilwa and that of Great Zimbabwe. Furthermore, a coin minted at Kilwa was found at Great Zimbabwe in 1971. There are, however, no cultural parallels between the cities or their architecture. Assuming they were linked, it is uncertain what the mechanisms of trade were. No evidence suggests coastal traders ever visited Great Zimbabwe.

Kilwa prospered throughout the golden age of Swahili (1250–1450). It was the dominant town on the coast, considered by the medieval traveller, Ibn Battuta, who visited it in 1331, to be 'one of the most beautiful and well-constructed cities in the world'. It had a population exceeding 10,000, the first coin mint in sub-Saharan Africa, and an extensive system of wells which is still in use today. The Friday Mosque and Husuni Kubwa, the most impressive buildings on the island, if not the entire coast, date to this period. In addition to gold, Kilwa exported ivory and ebony, and it imported such fineries as eastern cloth and Chinese porcelain.

Kilwa's wealthy traders lived in houses of coral and had small private mosques. Ordinary townsmen lived in mud-and-wattle huts. Even though some Arab traders settled on Kilwa, the vast majority of its occupants were local Swahili. The island was too small to be self-sufficient in food, so had extensive agricultural interests on the mainland.

In 1498, the Portuguese explorer, Vasco da Gama, rounded the Cape and sailed up the east coast on his way to establishing trade links with India. He described Kilwa in detail, but as he never visited the city, his oft-quoted report is probably pure fabrication. In fact, though it was still a trading centre of note, Kilwa was well past its peak by this time. For reasons that are unclear, Mombasa dominated coastal trade from about 1450 onwards. Da Gama met with a hostile reception in Mombasa; perhaps the Sultan there exaggerated Kilwa's strength in order to frighten the Portuguese away from the coast.

Da Gama's description of Kilwa might explain why it was so heavily targeted when the Portuguese took over the coast in 1505. Three-quarters of its residents were either killed or forced to flee. A Portuguese fort was built, the gold trade moved to Mozambique and the Sultan exiled to the mainland. By 1512 the town was virtually abandoned; even the Portuguese had moved on. In 1589, those residents who had remained were attacked and eaten by a tribe called the Zimba. The city was left to crumble.

The island came briefly to life in the late 18th century, after the Omani captured the coast from the Portuguese. Omani Arabs occupied Kilwa for a period, which is when they built the large fort which is visible from the mainland. They seem to have relocated to the mainland town of Kilwa Kivinje in the early 19th century.

Kilwa Kivinje became the centre of the southern slave trade. By the mid-19th century it was a very wealthy town, with up to 20,000 slaves passing through annually. In 1873, the Sultan of Zanzibar outlawed the slave trade. It survived at Kilwa longer than anywhere else, but had been stopped entirely by the end of the 1870s. Many of Kilwa's slave traders established rubber plantations and business continued to prosper. In 1886, Kilwa Kivinje become a German administrative centre.

Kilwa Kivinje remained a town of regional importance during the first half of this century, but since the end of World War II it has gradually been reduced to backwater status. The more modern town of Kilwa Masoko is now the regional headquarters.

Getting there and away
A good tar road connects Kilwa Masoko to Nangurukuru on the main Dar es Salaam–Mtwara road. Vehicles from Nangurukuru to Kilwa Masoko run every hour or so and take 20 minutes. Nangurukuru has a guesthouse, should you get stuck there.

The daily Nacet bus between Dar es Salaam and Kilwa Masoko leaves at some time between 05.00 and 06.00 in either direction. The Dar es Salaam terminus for these buses is near the Malapa Hotel on Mnazi Mmoja, and it is strongly advised that you make enquiries and book a ticket a day or two before you want to travel. It might also be wise to arrange for a taxi to collect you at your hotel on the morning you want to leave, as you don't really want to wander in this part of Dar es Salaam in the dark. The alternative would be to catch a bus to Mtwara or Lindi (these leave from the Morogoro Road bus station), get off at Nangurukuru, and make your way to Kilwa from there. The problem with this, however, is that you may well end up spending the night at Ndundu on the Rufiji River – ghastly, according to those who've had the experience. The road between Dar es Salaam and Kilwa is very rough, and the journey takes about 12 hours on a good day.

I have not been able to find direct buses to Kilwa from any other towns on the south coast. You can, however, hop on or off any bus running between Dar es Salaam and Lindi at Nangurukuru.

The *Canadian Spirit* never stopped at Kilwa so far as I'm aware, and there is no reason to think that any new boat service between Dar and Mtwara will stop here either.

Kilwa Masoko
Kilwa Masoko is the best-equipped base for exploring the Kilwa area, though it is of less inherent interest than its two more antiquated namesakes. Few tourists make it to Kilwa, but the atmosphere is very welcoming, and anybody who speaks English is likely to accost you for a chat. The nominal town centre consists of a small grid of dirt roads emanating from a central market, and it lies about 1km inland of the harbour, to which it is connected by a tar road. All the accommodation is in the town centre near the market, while most government buildings and banks are found along the main tar road towards the harbour.

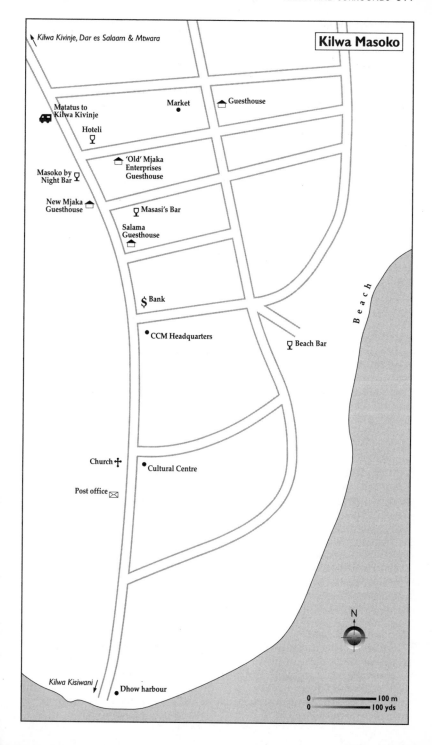

Kilwa Masoko

Kilwa Kivinje, Dar es Salaam & Mtwara

Market

Guesthouse

Matatus to
Kilwa Kivinje

Hoteli

'Old' Mjaka
Enterprises
Guesthouse

Masoko by
Night Bar

New Mjaka
Guesthouse

Masasi's Bar

Salama
Guesthouse

Bank

CCM Headquarters

Beach Bar

Beach

Church

Cultural Centre

Post office

N

Kilwa Kisiwani

Dhow harbour

0 ——— 100 m
0 ——— 100 yds

Aside from being a useful base, Kilwa Masoko does boast an attractively sandy baobab-lined beach, a short distance east of the harbour. To get there from the town centre, walk down the main tar road for about 300m, then turn left at the CCM buildings (just past the bank near a statue of a running man), from where it's about 100m to the beach.

Where to stay and eat

A relatively new place which has received several recommendations is the **Masoko Hilton Hotel**, which charges around US$7.50 for a self-contained double with fan and net. Another dependable option, the **New Mjaka Guesthouse** offers clean self-contained double rooms with a fan and net at a similar price. If these places are too expensive, then the 'old' **Mjaka Enterprises Guesthouse** is friendly and clean, and the single rooms with net and fan are good value at around US$2. The **Salama Guest House** is similar to this and has double rooms. There is an anonymous guesthouse behind the market, scruffier but popular with bus drivers, making it a good place to stay if you want to be woken for the 05.00 bus to Dar es Salaam.

Kilwa Kisiwani

The modern settlement of Kilwa Kisiwani is little more than a mud and thatch village, unremarkable in itself, but surrounded by some of the most compelling ruins in East Africa. The island is separated from the mainland by a 2km channel; the only way to reach it is in one of the small fishing dhows moored in Kilwa Masoko's harbour.

Permission to visit the island must be obtained from the **Kilwa Cultural Centre**, which lies in the local government headquarters in Kilwa Masoko, on the main tar road roughly opposite the post office. There is no charge for this (other than a nominal harbour tax), and the procedure is straightforward enough, though you will need to fill in a few forms and must bring your passport. If possible, I would get the formalities dealt with on the day before you plan to go to the island.

The Cultural Centre can organise a fishing dhow to take you to the island. The price is negotiable and depends on how long you plan to spend there. Expect to pay around US$10 per party for a half-day return trip. A fisherman called Juma Meli, a resident of the island, recommended by one reader as a "real gent", asks reasonable rates and has a well-maintained dhow. If you want to spend a night on the island, the Cultural Centre has restored a **small cottage** for the use of tourists. The Cultural Centre is opposite the post office, on the main tar road halfway between the town centre and the harbour.

There is a caretaker/guide on Kilwa Kisiwani. Although he is helpful, he speaks little English, has a minor obsession with medieval toilets (perhaps it's the only English word he knows) and is less than fully conversant with the island's history. He will expect a tip.

Before you visit Kilwa, don't miss the excellent display in the National Museum in Dar es Salaam.

Around the island

The Gereza is the partially collapsed quadrangular building which draws the eye as you sail across to the island. Gereza is a Swahili word meaning prison; it in turn is derived from a Portuguese word meaning church. The Gereza on Kilwa, however, is a fort. It was built by Omani Arabs in about 1800 and incorporates the walls of a smaller Portuguese fort built in 1505. It has thick coral walls and an impressive arched door.

Walking uphill from the Gereza, you pass first through the small modern village before coming to the main ruins. There are a number of interesting buildings here; an ornate Domed Mosque and the so-called Great House stand out. West of these is the triangular Mukatini Palace, parts of which are very well-preserved. The palace was built in the 15th century after the Husuni Kubwa fell into disuse (see below), and is enclosed by a crumbling 18th-century wall built by the Omani. Also of interest are the remains of the ancient well system, still used by the villagers today.

The most impressive building in the main ruins is the Great Mosque, also known as the Friday Mosque. This multi-domed building is the largest mosque of its period on the coast, and was built during the 14th-century gold boom as an extension of an earlier 11th century mosque. Most of its magnificent arches and domes are still intact, but many of the outbuildings are crumbling. In the 14th century the Great Mosque would have been the focal point of community life in Kilwa, where Friday prayers were held. A few hundred metres south of the mosque, a graveyard houses the tombs of many of Kilwa's sultans.

The most remarkable building on Kilwa lies about 1km east of the main ruins, on a low cliff overlooking the sea. Known locally as the Husuni Kubwa, this building was described by the eminent archaeologist Neville Chittick, who carried out excavations on the island from 1958 onwards, as "the only attempt to go beyond the merely practical and approach the grand" in pre-colonial Africa.

The word *Husuni* derives from an Arab word meaning fort, but there is no evidence to suggest the building ever was one. The name was probably acquired centuries after the building fell into disuse. The Husuni Kubwa was the Sultan of Kilwa's palace, used as both a dwelling place and a store house. The name *Husuni* has been attached to it by virtue of a nearby smaller, square building, the Husuni Ndogo, which superficially resembles a fort (*kubwa* and *ndogo* are KiSwahili for large and small). The purpose of the Husuni Ndogo is something of a mystery – there is no comparable building elsewhere in East Africa – but it may have been a fortified market place.

The Husuni Kubwa was built by Al-Hasan ibn Talut, the first ruler of the Abu-al-Mawahib dynasty, in the early 14th century, and was probably lived in for three generations. In some aspects – its geometrical design, for instance – it is a typical Swahili building, but its scale and complexity are unprecedented and many of its features are unique. The building includes domestic quarters, an audience court, a staircase leading down the cliff to the sea, large ornamental balconies and a swimming pool. The Husuni Kubwa is in poor condition, but the main features are clearly discernable.

Songo Mnara

Further ruins dating to the Shirazi era can be found on Songo Mnara Island, an easy day trip from Kilwa Masoko. There is supposedly a daily passenger boat between Kilwa Masoko and Songo Mnara via Pande, but it doesn't always run. You can also arrange private transport in a local fishing dhow, and once again a good person to speak to is Juma Meli. The ruins on Songo Mnara don't match those on Kilwa Kisiwani, but it makes for an enjoyable day out, and a good reason to stay on an extra day at Kilwa before braving the public transport again.

Kilwa Kivinje

This small, run-down town is a living memorial to its more prosperous past. The overall impression is of a once-important town gradually returning to its fishing village roots – much of the main street consists of boarded-up shops, while mud huts have been built using the walls of old Omani fortifications. I knew little about Kilwa Kivinje when I arrived there, but was able to piece together much of its history just by walking around.

The town came to prominence as an Omani slave-trading centre in the early 19th century. The crumbling remains of Omani dwellings and fortifications are dotted all around, and while none is habitable, many are in good enough condition to allow you to imagine what they must have looked like 150 years ago. There is an interesting mosque and, to the east of the town, an old Muslim graveyard.

The whitewashed German Boma overlooks the waterfront. It is the town's largest building, used as an administrative centre into the 1950s, but it serves no apparent purpose now. A cannon, presumably dating to World War I, stands on the common (complete with park benches) between the Boma and a stone sea-wall. Behind the Boma a small monument commemorates two Germans who died in 1888.

Along the main street lie glimpses of Kilwa Kivinje in the 1940s and 1950s: double-storey buildings with ornate balconies, small homes with Zanzibar-style doors, and shops still carrying steel advertising boards which must date to the 1950s. The main covered market, still in use today, is said to have been built by the Germans.

As well as being historical, Kilwa Kivinje is a pretty town. It lies on an attractive stretch of coast surrounded by mangroves, and has a peaceful Muslim atmosphere. I could think of worse places to settle into for a few days. The **Savoy Guest House**, on the beachfront near the German Boma, may not live up to its name, but it is clean and cheap: double rooms with fans and mosquito nets cost US$2. A couple of *hotelis* near the market serve cheap, basic meals.

LINDI
updated for the third edition by Len Coleman
This compact port on the west bank of the Lukuledi Estuary is the capital of the vast but thinly populated Lindi region, which at 66,000km² is about the same size as the Republic of Ireland. Lindi was founded by Omani Arabs in the late 18th century: in the 19th century it was part of the Sultanate of Zanzibar and for many decades it served as an important stop on the slave caravan route between Lake Nyasa and Kilwa Kivinje.

It is not immediately obvious today that Lindi was once an important Swahili trading centre. The chimney-like stone tower opposite the NBC Club is a relic of Omani rule, when it is said to have been used to hold prisoners, and the clock-tower on the roundabout at the town centre was built under the rule of the Sultan of Zanzibar. Otherwise, unlike Zanzibar or even Kilwa Kivinje, Lindi has a modern layout of interlocking gridiron streets, and buildings rarely exceed two storeys in height.

There is every indication that Lindi was once a prosperous port. With one eye closed, you can even imagine that the main beach served as a resort of sorts, possibly used by farmers living upcountry. Today, however, the beachfront benches are all broken, and they probably go months at a stretch without being perched on by a tourist. In the town centre, numerous posh colonial-era buildings are ruined or heading that way, while the derelict German Boma (marked on a 1970 map as the Area Commissioner's Residence) houses nothing but trees. A cyclone which hit the town in the 1950s may go some way to explaining this general state of disrepair, but the deeper cause of Lindi's decline has been the development of Mtwara as the main port and city for this part of Tanzania.

Whatever its history – and even that seems to have been lost or forgotten – Lindi is now something of a backwater. It is a pleasant and interesting place to visit, but ultimately a depressing reminder of what much of Tanzania was like in the mid-

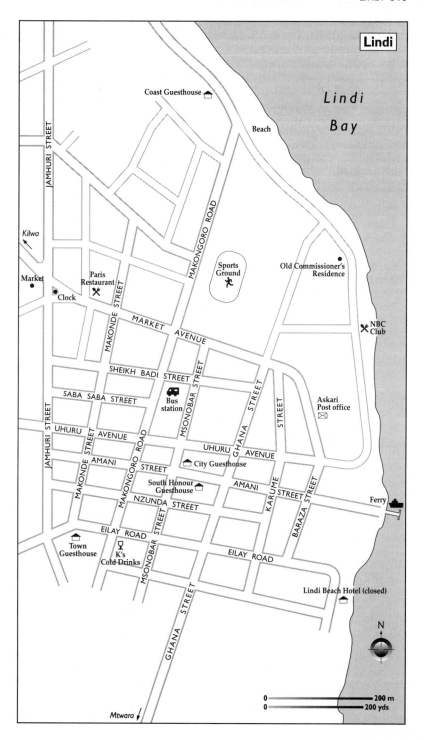

1980s. The only part of town which seems to escape the general air of torpor is the busy bus station, which – when the electricity is working – rings late into the night with the chimes of Congolese guitars and the pumping bass of reggae. Here the town's unemployed youth and orphaned children hang around all day, breaking into unselfconscious dances, while vendors scrape a living selling fried chicken and dried fish, melting sweets and single cigarettes to passing bus passengers. Another modern landmark, and a sporadic host to large crowds, is the football stadium on Makongoro Street – somewhat improbably, Lindi's football team is in the Tanzanian First Division.

A number of excellent beaches is scattered around Lindi Bay. The largest, on the northern edge of town, is white and sandy with hardly any rocks; a few small wooden fishing boats lie on the shore and children play football throughout the day. On the west side of the bay are several more secluded beaches – including Ras Bora, Mitema (the biggest and best) and Mitwero.

From Lindi, regular motorised ferries cross the Likuledi estuary, taking about five minutes, and leaving from the jetty next to the defunct Beach Hotel. The ferries land at Kitunda, a small village where the people spend their time drinking local beer and farming their *shambas*. There is little to do in Kitunda, but there is a fantastic view if you walk a little way up the hill. A half-hour walk up the coast from Kitunda takes you to a quiet and thickly vegetated beach. The Lukuledi estuary can be explored more thoroughly by hiring a local boat at a negotiable price – crocodiles can reportedly be seen 10–12km upstream. It is also possible to hire a boat in the bay, to do some snorkelling or to visit the large colony of fruit bats resident on Kisiwa Cha Popo (Island of Bats).

GOOD INTENTIONS

In the first edition of *Guide to Tanzania*, I commented that Mtwara sprawled in a manner suggesting that somebody once intended greater things for it. And indeed they did, as became clear recently when I came across P H Johnston's gushing article about Mtwara Bay in an issue of the Tanganyika Notes and Records dating to the late 1940s.

Prior to World War II, Mtwara was a village of little note when compared to the nearby, more historical settlement of Mikindani. Its one pre-war claim to posterity was that it was used as a location for the original silent version of *The Blue Lagoon*. (According to Johnston, another film crew arrived in 1928 – is there *anybody* out there who can elaborate on his assertion that 'strange but unfounded tales reached the home press as a result of this incursion into Mtwara'?).

In February 1947, Mtwara was chosen by the British administration as the port to be used by the infamous Groundnut Scheme of 1946–51. The idea behind this scheme was to turn southern Tanzania into a major groundnut producer; Britain pumped some 30 million pounds into creating the appropriate infrastructure before realising that the land was unsuitable and received insufficient rainfall to grow groundnuts. Not only was the scheme an expensive failure, but by coercing local farmers into replacing subsistence crops with groundnuts, its administrators caused more suffering than they ever alleviated. And an entirely new port was built at Mtwara, 'to meet not only the needs of the groundnut project but also such further requirements as future development beyond the groundnut areas might call for'. If you've visited Mtwara, this isn't even funny, just grimly ironic.

In 1992, I met a Dutchman who was working for the fishery department at

Getting there and away

There are buses between Dar es Salaam and Lindi most days. They leave Dar es Salaam at the Morogoro Road bus station and should be booked in advance. This is a long trip, with an enforced overnight stop on the Rufiji, so it would be far more sensible to bus to Kilwa, spend a few days there, and then head on to Lindi, picking up a bus from Nangurukuru.

Lindi is connected to Mtwara and Masasi by good tar roads. A few buses run daily to and from Mtwara, leaving when they are full. There are no direct buses between Lindi and Masasi; buses to Masasi leave from Mtwara and bypass Lindi at Mingoyo.

A small, very crowded bus does a daily run between Lindi and Newala. It leaves Newala at 05.00, gets to Lindi at midday, and then turns back.

Where to stay

There is nothing in the way of flash accommodation in Lindi, but travellers have the choice of numerous cheap and decent guesthouses. It is worth paying the extra for a place with mosquito-proofing or nets, because there is a lot of standing water around and insect activity. The **Nankolowa Guesthouse** is particularly recommended for its excellent menu, well-furnished rooms and friendly staff – ordinary rooms cost US$6 and self-contained rooms with a fan US$9. Of the rest, the **South Honour** and **Town Guesthouses** are friendly and offer clean rooms with mosquito nets and fans for less than US$5.

The **Lindi Beach Hotel** has a lovely position, but when I last looked in it would have been of interest only to masochists and entomologists. According to

Mwanza on Lake Victoria. He had been baffled as to why so much of the fish exported from the lake was being sent to Mtwara. On a brief visit to this most remote of Tanzanian ports, situated on a stretch of coast abundantly rich in fish, he established that there was no deep-sea fishing equipment available to the residents of Mtwara. Just a large, modern and utterly useless port.

The surprising thing about Johnston's article, given that colonials are generally portrayed as a bunch of exploitative taskmasters, is its genuine idealism. Paternalistic it might be, culture-bound it most definitely is, but the tone is more than anything one of giddy optimism. The groundnut project is 'a great decision ... one that will be, beyond doubt, the turning point in the history of at least one small part of Africa and its people... one that will advance the area and its people and provide opportunities of such progress in so short a time that none would ever have dreamed possible'. He even goes so far as to talk of Mtwara as a 'future Mombasa'.

It is easy enough to sneer when you have hindsight on your side. To give Johnston his due, his otherwise elegiac piece of prose ends soberly enough: 'Let it be hoped,' he asks, 'that our planners will really plan soundly', a prophetic plea that might as well have been written 20 years ago – or for that matter yesterday.

Fifty years after the Groundnut Scheme was first mooted, I spent an evening with a Danish Aid worker who, after two months observing conditions in an African village, made the chilling observation that the West ought to implement a scheme which would 'teach African women how to bring up children properly'. She, and all the other culture-bound meddlers who would save Africa from itself, would do well to read Johnston's article, and then to visit Mtwara: a sprawling memorial to good intentions gone awry.

Christopher Jerram, who lived in Lindi in the 1950s, the Beach Hotel has always been a bit of a tip (in his day it was nicknamed the Dysentery Arms) and the latest report is that the roof has collapsed and the hotel is no longer operational. All things considered, travellers who want a beachfront room would be better off heading for the **Coast Guesthouse** – it's a bit scruffy and the rooms lack mosquito nets, but it's cheap, pleasant and has the beach on its doorstep.

Where to eat

The food at the **Nankalowa Guesthouse** is recommended, but you must place an order over breakfast. Otherwise, two of the best places to eat and drink are the **NBC Club** and the **Seaview Hotel**. Another recent recommendation is the **Malaika Restaurant**.There are also a few *hotelis* around the market, and vendors sell snacks all day at the bus station.

A local speciality is large prawns (up to 20cm long excluding antennae), which are caught mainly in the rainy season. Prawns aren't generally consumed locally or served at restaurants in Lindi, but you can order direct from the fish market near the Beach Hotel. They are of excellent quality, and the price is good (around US$2–3 per kg). The best time to buy is in the late afternoon before 16.30. It shouldn't be a problem to arrange for somebody to cook them for you.

MINGOYO

This village is on the junction of the roads to Lindi, Mtwara and Masasi. If you are heading from Lindi to Masasi, you must head to Mingoyo to pick up a vehicle. Mingoyo apparently thrives on its position. The vendors here offer an array of roadside snacks second to none: fried and stewed chicken, fish, prawns, meat kebabs, cakes and fruit. There didn't appear to be any accommodation in Mingoyo when I was last in the area.

MTWARA

This is probably the largest town on the south coast, and an important springboard for travellers crossing over the Ruvuma River into neighbouring Mozambique (see *Getting to Tanzania,* page 43). Large it may be, Mtwara is also a somewhat dispersed settlement. The small town centre lies about 1km inland, and is surrounded by open fields. The harbour is 1.5km northeast of this, the market and bus station are about 1km to the south, the beach is about 2km to the north, and there appears to be a small industrial area to the east of the harbour.

If Mtwara is less than scintillating, the surrounding coast offers some consolation. A good swimming beach is within easy reach of the town, near the (now abandoned) Beach Hotel. Local expats raved about the beach on the sandbar protecting the harbour entrance, but you need a boat to get there. Otherwise, much of the coastline immediately around Mtwara consists of coral flats; interesting for the rock pools that form on them and the wading birds that visit.

A canoe ferry runs regularly between Mtwara (leaving from behind the Catholic Church) to an attractive beach on the opposite side of the harbour.

Getting there and way

During the dry season, buses between Dar es Salaam and Mtwara leave daily from the Morogoro Road bus station and should be booked in advance. This trip takes between 24 and 36 hours, normally with an overnight stop at the Rufiji River, so I would strongly recommend that you break it up with stops either at Lindi or Kilwa – better still at both places!

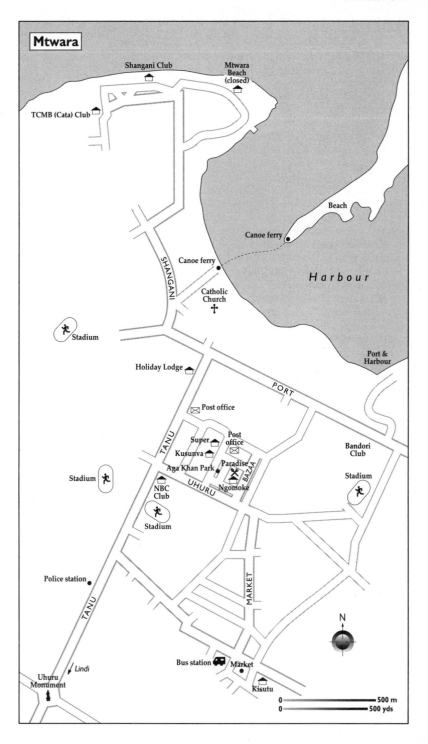

Mtwara

TRAVELLING FROM MTWARA TO SONGEA

This box has been edited from notes made by Joe Williamson and Mike Wilks, who travelled from Mtwara to Mbamba Bay and back again in early 1999.

The wild, scenic route between the south coast and Lake Nyasa is one of the most remote and least travelled in Tanzania. It is a trip that will take at least three days, longer if you want to break it up with a day's rest, and the road is mostly in poor condition. After the El Nino rains of 1997/8, the stretch between Songea and Tunduma was for some time covered by 4WD vehicles only, but there are still cheap buses on some stretches.

The journey is broken into three legs: Mtwara to Masasi (200km), Masasi to Tunduru (200km) and Tunduru to Songea (273km). The road degrades from Masasi onwards, but each leg can usually be done in a single day, though travel times depend greatly on the weather and availability of transport. Overall, 4WD vehicles are the fastest option on the roads west of Masasi, especially in the rainy season, but they may not be as comfortable as buses, are often double the price of a bus or lorry, and don't have fixed departure times. In this part of the country, you should try to establish the departure time and agree on a price as far in advance as possible, but even then you might wait for a few hours until there is a full load.

You may be able to do two legs in a day but this will mean leaving very early. It is best to get to the departure area between 04.30 and 06.00 to have guaranteed transport. It also helps to catch the first available vehicle while there are people waiting to go otherwise you may wait up to a day until there is a full vehicle ready to leave. The travelling times quoted are for dry season although it did start raining before our return trip so the return journey times were longer. Be prepared for travel times to double in the wet season.

Leg one: Mtwara/Mikindani to Masasi

Transport starts in Mtwara but we caught it in Mikindani and stopped in Ndanda instead of continuing to Masasi. The journey takes up to four hours by bus on mostly tarmac or good-quality roads with frequent stops and costs about US$3 between Mtwara and Masasi. The main stops en route are at Mnasi Moja (where the road forks to Lindi) and Ndanda. At most villages, the children offer a variety of fresh food and a selection of packaged food. In addition to food there are often odds and ends ranging from door locks to trainers on offer at the larger bus stands, such as Ndanda.

The first buses leave from the Indian section and then the main roundabout in Mtwara at about 05.30 and depart roughly every half hour until mid-afternoon. In Mikindani the buses stop by the Old Prison. The Ndanda bus stop is a major lay-by near the hospital. A reasonable guesthouse can be found in Ndanda. For details of accommodation in Masasi, see *Masasi* page 323.

The *Canadian Spirit* used to sail between Dar es Salaam and Mtwara weekly, and the route is likely to be taken over by another boat in the near future. See *Getting around* at the beginning of the chapter for details.

There are several buses daily between Mtwara and Masasi, and Mtwara and Lindi. These leave when they are full, and take a few hours only.

For details of crossing from Mtwara in Mozambique, see *To/from Mozambique*, on page 48.

Leg two: Masasi to Tunduru

This 200km trip takes upwards of eight hours by lorry. We left from Masasi at 12.30 and travelled in a lorry with no shade and 20–30 people for company. Make sure you have a padded bag to sit on or use a grain sack if they are carrying them. There was one major stop for food and sodas. Elsewhere we stopped long enough only for people to get on and off at most of the villages. We had to pay in dollars (US$20) but the going rate is around US$6 per person in local currency. Coming in the opposite direction, there is a bus which leaves Tunduru at 04.30 most days, but it takes a long time and we found that Land Rovers were best for the return trip.

Tunduru is an old mining town, but for travellers it serves as little more than a place to stop over for the night. Focused along one main street, the town is quite prosperous, but something of a backwater. Tunduru did enjoy a brief period of notoriety between 1985 and 1988 when, according to Nicholas Gordon's Ivory Knights, it was plagued by man-eating lions. Almost 50 people were killed, including the game warden sent to sort out the problem, and a further 28 wounded. The offending cats have since been shot.

We stayed in the Naweka Guesthouse which was adequate, with running water in the early morning and electricity in the evenings. The cost is about US$3 per night for a single room and US$4.50 for a self-contained room with a fan but no nets. The Yakiti Guesthouse is more basic, charging around US$2 for a single with a mosquito net. The Sunrise Guesthouse had self-contained rooms but no mosquito nets and cost US$4.50. Restaurants include the Greenland Bar and Al Jazira Hotel.

Leg three: Tunduru to Songea

This should ideally be covered in a Land Rover, as the road is much worse than the stretch between Masasi and Tunduru. The trip takes at least seven hours, passing through many uninhabited areas which become rather tedious scenically. The cost is about US$9 for lorries and US$12 for Land Rovers. Namtumbo is a good place on the way for refreshment.

Arriving in Songea, we were besieged by offers of trips to various places, and felt the bus stand square reflected the bustling and prosperous feel of the town. Songea is possibly smaller than Mtwara but more centred and seems to have a better range of goods available, partly because the climate allows for a more regular and varied supply of fruit and vegetables. For changing money, there is the NBC (weekdays 08.30–15.00 and Saturday 08.30–12.00) as well as a CRDB bank. For accommodation, see *Songea* page 304.

The obvious onward options from Songea are either to visit Mbamba Bay on the shore of Lake Nyasa, or else to head up to Njombe along the road to the Tanzam Highway.

Where to stay and eat

The most upmarket option is the **Makonde Beach Resort** (aka Litingi's), where a self-contained double with television costs US$24. The resort is clearly signposted a few kilometres out of town along the Mikindani road. The rocky beach is good for swimming at high tide and the view is attractive.

There are a few places to stay along the beach at Shangani, 3km from the bus station. The venerable **CATA Club** (run by the Cashew Authority of Tanzania) offers double rooms for about US$7.50. The **Mtepwezi Guesthouse** and **Tingatinga Inn** are also recommended, and the latter has a reputation for good prawns. The nearby **Shangani Club**, closed at the time of writing, should re-open soon, while the **Mtwara Beach Hotel** has been derelict for years.

In town, comfortable accommodation can be found at the **Lutheran Mission**, which charges around US$10 for a room and lies on the left as you approach the first roundabout coming from Mikindani. There are several cheaper guesthouses in and around the town centre, charging around US$3/5 for a single/double room. The **Ngomoke** and **Nandope Guesthouses** have been recommended, as has the **Jagaju Holiday Lodge** on the road towards Shangani Beach. The guesthouses around the bus station are mostly very basic: exceptions include the **Kapilima Guesthouse**, where a self-contained double costs US$8, and the slightly cheaper **Chindima** and **Kisutu Guesthouse**. Most of these guesthouses have nets and fans.

The local eateries in Mtwara are concentrated around the bus station; they are all similar in same price, and serve chip omelettes and goat kebabs. The **Finn Club** (daily membership US$1) has satellite TV, table tennis and the best variety of food on offer in Mtwara. For a night out, the **Bandari Club** near the harbour usually has a live band.

AROUND MTWARA
Mikindani

This small village lies only 10km north of Mtwara, but it is far older than its larger neighbour and has considerably more character. Little more than a fishing village today, Mikindani was founded roughly 1,000 years ago by Shirazi traders, since when it has variously been occupied by the Portuguese, Omani Arabs, Germans and British. Mikindani is where Livingstone set off for his last expedition into the interior, an event commemorated by the predictable plaque. The alleys of the old quarter boast a few dilapidated Zanzibar-style buildings, as well as ruins dating back to the slave-trading era (including the former slave market) and a number of German colonial buildings. The disused fort on the seafront was built in the 16th century by the Portuguese and was later renovated by Omani Arabs, who used it as a slave prison. The fort was occupied by Germany until it was bombarded by the British Navy in World War I.

For years neglected by travellers, Mikindani has recently been the focus of some exciting tourist developments which are likely to come to fruition during the course of 1999. The old German Boma, originally built in 1895, is currently being restored and will soon open as a guesthouse, restaurant, and the base from which to develop low-key eco-tourism in Mikindani. This will tie in with developing the underused overland route to Mozambique for backpackers, and generally creating a greater awareness of the travel possibilities along this historical and beautiful stretch of coast.

The developments at Mikindani have been initiated and overseen by a British charity called Trade Aid in Tanzania, who have used Gap students from the UK to develop the project, with the eventual aim of creating a sustainable ecotourist structure that will be used to fund various community projects as well as providing employment and educational opportunities to locals. If you want to find out more about the project and check on the latest developments, or you can offer assistance in the form of equipment, cash or expertise, contact details in the UK are tel: 01425 65 7774, fax: 01425 65 6684, email: tradeaid@netcomuk.co.uk.

Mikindani is highly accessible, straddling the main road between Mtwara and Lindi. All buses heading north from Mtwara stop at Mikindani, so it can easily be visited as a day trip from Mtwara. Better, however, would be to spend a couple of nights in the area. In addition to the accommodation in the Boma, which should be open by July 1999 and will cost around US$50 per room, the charity has opened a hostel aimed at budget travellers and charging around US$5 per person per night. Another option is the small Litingi Hotel, which lies on an attractive stretch of coast along the Mtwara road 2km from Mikindani.

Msimbati

The beach at Msimbati, about one hour from Mtwara by bus, has been known to travellers for some time as the best place to pick up dhow transport to Mozambique. But it is also a very beautiful spot in its own right, totally unspoilt and lined with broad palm trees. The beach shelves steeply, so swimming is good even at low tide, and the offshore reefs provide great snorkelling and diving.

MAKONDE

Among the most renowned sculptors in Africa, the Makonde of southern Tanzania probably came to the area from what is now northern Mozambique several centuries ago, and oral tradition suggests that they have been practising their craft for at least 300 years. In its purest form, the intricate ebony carvings of the Makonde relate to their cult of womanhood; they are traditionally carried by the (male) carver as a good luck charm. This custom started when the first carver, who according to folklore was a person but not yet a man, carved a piece of wood into the shape of a woman and left it outside his home overnight. Overnight, the carving was transformed into a real woman. Twice the woman conceived, but both times the child died after three days. Each time, the pair moved higher onto the plateau, believing this would bring them luck. The third child lived and became the first true Makonde.

Typically, Makonde carvings consist of one or more people in a highly stylised and distorted form. Traditional carvings often depict a female figure surrounded by children. But, like any dynamic art form, Makonde is responsive to external influences and subject to changes in fashion; in recent years, carvings have become increasingly abstract and have incorporated wider moral and social themes. Recent innovations include *Ujamaa* sculptures, which relate to Tanzania's collective social policy, and *Sheteni*, grotesque but evocative figures modelled on Makonde ancestral spirits. Makonde carvings have become highly collectable in the West and are regarded as amongst the best and most imaginative produced anywhere in Africa.

Many of the carvings you see elsewhere in Tanzania come from the Makonde Plateau (many, too, are carved by Makonde who have settled in Arusha or Dar es Salaam), but you will need contacts to see any on the plateau itself. Most are bought by dealers for distribution in the more touristy parts of the country. In fact, the only carvings we saw in Mtwara were made not of ebony, but of ordinary wood covered in black boot polish. If you can buy directly from the carvers, however, you will get a far better price than you would in Arusha or Dar es Salaam. By cutting out the middleman, the carver will also get a fair price.

Another intriguing aspect of traditional Makonde culture is *sindimba* dancing, performed by men and women together using stilts and masks, but in the ordinary course of things, you are unlikely to come across this.

A *banda* complex is currently under construction at Msimbati and scheduled for completion in late 1999. The *banda*s will be self-contained, with fans and nets, and should cost around US$25. In addition to a beachfront bar and restaurant, snorkelling and sailing equipment will be available for hire. The Trade Aid people at Mikindani are the best source of current information about these developments.

THE MAKONDE PLATEAU

The Makonde Plateau lies immediately inland of Mtwara and Lindi. It is the home of East Africa's most renowned craftsmen, the Makonde carvers (see box opposite). The two main towns on the plateau are Newala and Masasi. The road to Newala is interesting, climbing the plateau through dense miombo woodland and passing numerous Makonde villages. These villages are immaculately neat and orderly, and apparently rarely visited by tourists – every time the bus stopped a crowd of curious children gathered around us and stared in amazement. There is a strong missionary presence in the area. Most schools and hospitals are run by missions. Some missions insist on importing Western luxury goods for local distribution. As a consequence, all sorts of unlikely items are offered for sale at the roadside, ranging from lace petticoats to name-brand chocolates and toiletries.

The most attractive way to explore the Makonde Plateau is as a circuit from Mtwara, Mikondani or Lindi, stopping at Masasi and Newala.

Masasi
Updated for the third edition by Dan Cherry
The principal town on the Makonde Plateau, Masasi is the end of the tar road for travellers heading cross-country towards Songea and Lake Nyasa, and it will feel like something of a return to comfort for travellers coming from that part of Tanzania. Masasi is an unexpectedly modern and bustling small town – people on the coast joke that it is '*kama Ulaya*' (like Europe), which might be stretching a point, but does reflect its sense of prosperity relative to somewhere like Lindi or Mikindani. A number of the Tanzania's leading lights originate from Masasi, including the current President, Benjamin Mkape, who still has a house in the town.

The Masasi Hills, which surround the town, consists of several striking granite outcrops, reminiscent of the famous koppies found in Zimbabwe. Reaching altitudes of up to 951m, these hills are very beautiful, and have been awarded legal protection. Climbing the hills is easily within most people's grasp, and the views from the top are worth the effort. Snakes and leopards still inhabit the hills, but vervet monkeys are a more common (and friendly) sight and there are worn tracks up most of the hillsides.

Getting there and away
Buses between Mtwara and Masasi leave roughly hourly throughout the day, stopping at Mikindani and Mingoyo. The tar road is in a good state of repair, but the 200km trip takes from five to seven hours due to frequent stops. A ticket currently costs around US$3.

There is a bus every other day in each direction between Masasi and Dar es Salaam. This leaves from in front of the Masasi Hotel, not from the regular bus station. Seats should be booked in advance at the Masasi Hotel.

A daily bus runs between Newala and Masasi, leaving Newala some time between 05.00 and 06.00 and arriving at Masasi at around 11.00. The bus then returns to Newala.

For details of the cross-country route between Masasi and the Lake Nyasa region, see box *Travelling from Mtwara to Songea,* page 320.

Where to stay and eat

There are plenty of basic guesthouses to choose from. A step up from these, clean and spacious rooms with fans and mosquito nets are available at the **Masasi Hotel** and **Panama Guesthouse** for around US$3/4 single/double room. Better quality still is the **Saidi Guesthouse**, where rooms with en-suite bathrooms and television cost around US$10/13 single/double.

Most of the guesthouses serve basic food, and there are many cheap eating places around the main squares. The **Top Spot Restaurant** near the Masasi Hotel serves cheap meals and cold beers and sodas in a garden.

Newala

Updated for the third edition by Nick Andrews

This isolated, friendly town on the Makonde Plateau near the Mozambique border lacks any major landmarks or sense of history, but it is worth a visit just for the view across the Ruvuma River to Mozambique. If you've spent a while on the coast, the bracing climate – Newala is one of the coldest places in southern Tanzania, prone to chilly breezes and damp mists – should also prove to be rather refreshing. The town itself is rather nondescript, with squat concrete houses in the centre of town changing to mud huts with thatch roofs as you head further out.

There are some stunning viewpoints along the ridges around Newala, offering a panoramic view to the Ruvuma River and Mozambique. The favourite local spots are from the German Castle which dominates the Ruvuma River viewpoint, and the Shimu ya Mungu ('Hole of God'), a vast steep-sided drop over the Ruvuma Valley to the mountains beyond. More ambitiously, you could cycle to the Ruvuma River as a day trip (bikes can easily be hired so long as you leave a deposit) following the central road through town downhill. It is also possible to visit the old *boma*, and (assuming that you speak Swahili) to organise a short tour with the head of police, whose office occupies the ground floor. This will cost about US$1.50. At the cinema in the market, you can watch badly filmed videos with dodgy colours and a worse sound track for next to nothing.

Visitors should bring their passports and legal immigration documents to Newala, since the immigration officer is very keen and checks all the guesthouses daily.

The large mission hospital next to the market would be useful in an emergency.

Getting there and away

Reaching Newala from Mtwara is simple. Direct buses leave every twice an hour from the main bus stand in Mtwara throughout the day from around 06.00, using the poorly maintained dirt route, a six- to seven-hour journey which costs around US$3 per ticket. Another option is to go via Masasi, first catching a bus from Mtwara to Masasi, then changing bus for Newala. The trip from Masasi to Newala takes two hours or so along a reasonably well-maintained road and costs around US$2.

From Newala itself, four to five buses leave for Masasi every morning between 06.00 and midday. This trip is worth doing for the views during the first half hour out of Newala, where the road folloed a dramatic ridge.

Where to stay and eat

There are more than 15 guesthouses in Newala, most of which lie around the market and bus station and offer accommodation of a similar standard – a simple room with communal toilet facilities and bucket-showers for around US$2–3. Two places stand out, **Plateau Lodge** and **Country Lodge**, both of which have ordinary and self-contained rooms in the US$8–15 range. The County Lodge can be found on the road to Masasi, and the Plateau Lodge is well signposted from the market, up towards 'Shimu ya Mungu', and the old German *boma* on the very top of the hill.

There are many places to eat, mostly in the market area. Meals on offer include the normal fish, rice, *ugali*, as well as the local favourite *chipsi mayai* (chip omelette), all for under US$2 each. Several notches above this is the food at the Country Lodge – a prawn salad, fresh fish and rice cooked to your preference for as little as US$5 – though a few hours' advance warning is required to eat here. The market sells speciality fruit such as *embe dodo* (large mangoes) and delicious custard apples.

Lukwika-Lumesule Game Reserve

Covering an area of about 600km², this little-known reserve is bordered by the Ruvuma River, and lies roughly 100km south of Masasi. It reputedly still supports populations of lion, elephant, leopard, hippo and crocodile, as well as various antelope species. Basic *bandas* and camping facilities are available. The people who run the Trade Aid centre in Mikindani are currently looking into possibilties with this reserve, and should be able to provide travellers with current information about access and costs. They may also possibly start running safaris to the reserve from Mikindani.

Mafia

by Christine Osborne

While Zanzibar has become a popular tourist resort, Mafia Island lying only 160km south, remains virtually unknown. Poor communications with the mainland and a rather unfortunate name have not served Mafia well, but a steady trickle of visitors are unanimous in singing its praise. Mafia is one of the safest places in the Indian Ocean and there are no hustlers to spoil a holiday.

Historians believe that the name *Maf'a* – or Mafia as it is known – derives from *Ma'afir,* a Himyaritic tribe from ancient Yemen who dominated the coast of what was known as Azania from Kilwa to the Rufiji River around 1000BC. The word may also come from the Arabic *morfiyeh* meaning group – in this case a group of islands.

The Mafia Archipelago is scattered over the Indian Ocean 21km off the Rufiji River Delta in central Tanzania. The largest of a score of islands, atolls and tidal sandbars, Mafia itself is approximately 50km long by 15km across, and is surrounded by a barrier reef teeming with marine life of which 822km² has been gazetted a marine park by the World Wide Fund for Nature. To date 400 species of fish and five different types of turtles have been recorded in the zone around Chole Bay.

Natural vegetation on Mafia ranges from tidal mangrove thickets and scrubby coastal moorlands to palm-wooded grassland and lowland rainforest. Baobabs are prominent along with the native *Albinza*. A patch of coastal high forest, the Chunguruma Forest is a dense tree canopy interlaced with lianas and having an abundant floor covering of ferns.

A large reed-lined lake in central Mafia is probably an old lagoon which was cut off from the ocean thousands of years ago. Here live half a dozen hippo which were washed out to sea during flooding in the Rufiji River system. Other island fauna includes a colony of flying foxes, several species of bushbabies, a type of pygmy shrew and a monitor lizard known as *kenge*. Monkeys and squirrels were introduced for the pot by the Portuguese.

An official bird list kept by Kinasi Lodge records sightings of more than 120 different species, including five different types of sunbird, living in and around the hotel gardens. There are also thought to be at least five endemic species of þutterfly on the island.

While Mafia makes an ideal holiday for people interested in nature and outdoor activities, its big attraction for many visitors is that it remains locked in a time warp of the early 20th century.

The population of the archipelago, currently estimated to be around 40,000, lives in rustic fishing communities and farming villages dotted all over Mafia and the smaller in-shore islands. The majority are Muslim but there are many Christians. Voodoo also manifests itself in ritual dances linked to the lunar cycle.

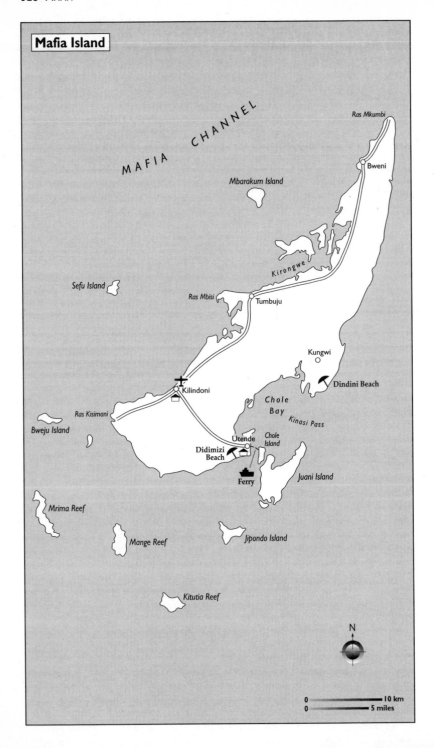

Mafia Island

While traditionally reserved, the islanders are tolerant of visitors provided they dress discreetly and behave in a manner becoming local customs. Mafia women wear the colourful patterned *kanga* of the Swahili coast, and on weekends and religious holidays men exchange Western dress for the long, white *kanzu*. Older folk who remember the British can speak some English, but to make yourself understood it is best to learn a little Swahili.

History

Little seems to have been written about the islands but, as they lie on the ancient shipping lanes, it seems certain that they must have played an active role in local history. There is a reference to Mafia in the *Periplus of the Ancient Sea* written around AD50, while the fabled *Menthuia,* mentioned by the ancients could just as easily have been Mafia as either Zanzibar or Pemba.

Ptolemy's *Geography,* a standard source of information until the 16th century, mentions 'a low island... to the east of a cape with a river...' He also writes of sewn boats and hollowed-out tree canoes which are still widely used on Mafia today.

Definite knowledge of the archipelago begins in the late 10th century when a merchant family from Shiraz in Persia settled on the mainland in Kilwa. One of the sons, Bashat, is thought to have established a settlement at Kua on Juani Island and possibly also at Ras Kisimani on Mafia in the early 11th century.

By the 14th century Kilwa had become a prosperous port which inevitably drew the attention of the Portuguese as they ventured east. On his first voyage to Mombasa, Vasco da Gama reported sighting Mafia off his starboard bow on April 4 1498. Annexing the coast in 1515, the Portuguese subsequently marked in *Morfiyeh* on their navigation charts.

After Kilwa was sacked by tribes from Central Africa in 1588, Zanzibar became the main Indian Ocean entrepot. Further defeat, this time inflicted by the Sultan of Oman in Mombasa in 1698, saw Portugal lose its grip on its Azania strongholds, including Mafia until finally the Yaarubi Dynasty gained control of the coastline extending from Lamu to Kilwa.

In 1829 when the old Shirazi town of Kua was destroyed by cannibals from Madagascar, the Sultan moved his local seat to Chole, taking with him a large slave labour force. In 1890 after paying Oman four million deutschmarks for part of the coast which included Mafia, Germany sent a local administrator who also settled on Chole and constructed some buildings whose ruins can still be seen.

In January 1915, Mafia was captured by British forces for use as a base for an assault against the German cruiser *Konigsberg* which, having evaded capture in the Rufiji Delta, was finally sunk on August 11. A 6c German *Tanganyika Territory* stamp overprinted *Mafia* by the British and listed at £9,000 in *Stanley Gibbons* catalogue makes philatelists one of the few groups of people aware of the existence of Mafia.

Climate

The Mafia Archipelago experiences a tropical climate tempered by ocean breezes. Rainfall averaging 2,000mm a year occurs mainly between April and May, although November can also be wet. February and March are hot and humid, while a strong southerly wind, the *kusi,* blows during July. The best holiday period is from June until mid-October, when the islands enjoy blue skies with temperatures kept pleasant by light coastal breezes.

MAFIA ISLAND
Getting there and away

Getting to Mafia used to be a difficult exercise without a confirmed reservation at Kinasi Lodge on Mafia Island which has an aircraft to transfer guests. In late 1998, the domestic airline Precision Air began a thrice-weekly service to the island from Dar es Salaam via Zanzibar for $100 return by 19-seater aircraft.

Going to Mafia by sea remains difficult, as the coastal shipping service provided by the *Canadian Spirit* has ceased (see *Getting around* in *Chapter 18*). Intrepid travellers might consider catching a dhow from Dar es Salaam: the sailing time is 10–12 hours or longer, and a single fare costs 5,000 shillings or less, depending on your ability to bargain.

Kinasi Lodge transfers clients from Dar es Salaam and the Selous Game Park (for $70 per person one-way) and from Zanzibar ($100 per person one-way). The flight by Cessna takes about 45 minutes from Dar es Salaam – add an hour if you come via the Selous on a spectacular flight tracing the Rufiji River Delta. Zanzibar to Mafia is one hour's flight.

Mafia's small airport is a short walk from the main town of Kilindoni, but it is a 15km drive to where the hotels are located at Utende. The airport has a comfortable waiting room and basic toilets but there are no other facilities. Visitors holding a hotel reservation will be met at the airport. Individual travellers should ask for a Land Rover taxi which costs $15 to Utende. There is a $3 airport departure tax.

Travel around Mafia

The island infrastructure is basic. Hardly any villages are connected to mains water or electricity and at the time of writing there are no tarmac roads. The road to Utende is rough in places, but the main west coast road from Kilindoni to Bweni has been re-graded. Elsewhere roads are sandy tracks or paths.

At present there is no public transport on Mafia, which holds only 35 vehicles, mainly Land Rover pick-ups and 4x4s belonging to the hotels, UNICEF and to the Hellas fish processing factory. Hitch-hiking is an accepted means of getting about, but usually means a long wait. Islanders also use *jahazis*, widely referred to in English as dhows, to commute between Kilindoni and outlying villages on Mafia, and for inter-island travel. Bicycles can be rented by arrangement with the Hotel Lizu in Kilindoni.

Where to stay

Mafia cannot accommodate more than 100 or so visitors at a time and the fact that it is not overrun with tourists is part of its charm. There is currently one basic establishment and three tourist hotels, all on the main island.

The **Pole Pole Bungalow Resort** (Bookings fax: 255-51 116239; email archipelago@tanzania. org) is an eco-tourist concept at Utende with nine bungalows built of basic natural materials. Two large bungalows have en-suite bathrooms. Beachfront *bandas* are more simple and there is basic accommodation for divers. *Pole Pole* (which means 'take it easy' in Swahili) costs $120–180 per person full-board. Italian-managed, it offers snorkelling, boat-trips and fishing.

The **Mafia Island Lodge** (Bookings: PO Box 2, Mafia; tel: 76) is a package-type hotel built by the government in 1971 and now run by TTH. Accommodation in separate blocks consists of 40 small but comfortable double rooms with air conditioning and en-suite bathrooms. On a palm-lined beach facing Chole Island, the hotel offers swimming, sailing and fishing. It has a large, gloomy bar and restaurant. Rooms cost $210 double, full-board.

Kinasi Lodge (Bookings: fax: 255-51 843495; email: kinasi@intafrica.com or via Africa Archipelago, tel: 0181-780 5838; email-worldarc@compuserve.com) is the ultimate Indian Ocean hideaway. It is owned by Peter Byrne an agricultural economist born on Manus Island in the western Pacific. It is named after Kinasi

Pass, the indigo pass in the outer reef which surrounds Mafia like a picture frame. Fourteen well-furnished bungalows with *makuti* roofs (made of palm leaves) are set in a coconut plantation overlooking Chole Bay. Large, comfortable beds are enveloped in vast mosquito nets and there is constant hot water. A winning feature is the colonial-style wooden verandah with armchairs and a hammock.

Catering is based on seafood with local fruits such as mangoes, paw-paws and passionfruit and fresh vegetables flown in from the mainland.

The $130 cost per day to stay at Kinasi includes full board and daily laundry service. Activities include swimming in the lagoon or hotel pool, snorkelling, fishing and diving (see box on page 332), sailing in a Laser (small sailing boat) or traditional *ngalawa* and excursions to other islands. The lodge has constructed a two-hour nature walk for bird-watching along the coastal flats which are rich in waders. Bul-buls, wood doves, sunbirds and tinkerbirds (similar to woodpeckers) are common brush species. Mountain bikes are available for exploring local villages. Closed during the wet season April-May.

The **Lizu Hotel** (Bookings c/o Post Office, Mafia or tel: 96) is the only comfortable place to stay in Kilindoni. It has basic double rooms with fan and shared washing facilities for $10.50, and one room with en-suite bathroom. A simple bar-restaurant at the rear of the hotel sells beers for $1 shillings and Scotch whisky by the bottle ($18). Simple rice and seafood meals are available. Used by local traders, the hotel is a minute's walk from the market and ten minutes to the dhow landing.

Kilindoni

All arrivals on Mafia pass through Kilindoni, the main town as well as the island airport and sea port. New by East African standards, it was established by the Germans in 1913 on discovering that Chole Island lacked a deep-water anchorage. While Kilindoni has none of the Arab architecture of the Stone Town on Zanzibar, its coralstone and lime mortar shop-houses with quaint signs and rusting corrugated iron roofs exude an ambience of old Indian Ocean days.

What to see

Peaceful rather than bustling, the **market** is the centre of local life. Tomatoes, chillies, potatoes, onions, limes, dried prawns, bananas, cassava and whatever the trader can get his hands on are arranged in little piles. Stalls sell fish, spices, pottery, *kangas* and second-hand clothes. A **café** at the back is the only place in Kilindoni where a starving tourist might conceivably eat a plate of sardines and maize meal soup. There are more stores on the road descending to the dhow landing. The **Market General Supply Store** and the **Peace and Love** sell soft drinks.

A **bank** and a **post office** are located on the airport road. The National Microfinance Bank is open 08.30-15.00 and 08.30-12.30 on Saturdays.

Stamps are sold at the post office, but your letter may take months to leave Mafia. Kinasi Lodge will mail your post in Dar es Salaam.

Off the **main square**, Utende Road has a rather gross monument presented by the fish factory. On the left is a grey weatherbeaten **mosque** and further along the Roman Catholic church. Beyond a final shop-house selling dried fish are rice fields and finally coconut plantations near Utende.

The **dhow landing** in Kilindoni usually has 15-20 *jahazis* moored on the beach. Whether unloading fish or mending their nets, the fishermen object strongly to being photographed, as do the people frying cassava chips and cooking octopus on small stoves under the trees. A café next to the fish factory sells soft drinks.

Excursions from Kilindoni

Bweni village is approximately 47km north of Kilindoni. The drive up the west coast of Mafia takes about two hours direct or all day if you want to include swimming and a picnic. Bring everything you are likely to need from your hotel.

About 8km from Kilindoni is a picturesque swamp covered in mauve lotus. Small tilapias and catfish dart among the reeds. Further on, the old agricultural village of **Kirongwe** counts a score of houses, three stores and a market selling the usual dried octopus, bananas and coconuts. Beyond here the countryside is intensively cultivated with beans, pigeon pea and cassava. Sykes and vervet monkeys raiding the crops flee at the sound of any vehicle.

The north of Mafia is markedly different to the southern, wetter part which is dominated by vast coconut plantations. After **Jimbo**, the landscape suddenly becomes grassland plateau with outcrops of *mia'a* or palm, and baobabs similar to the mainland coastal plain. Birdlife is plentiful with bee-eaters and lilac crested rollers flashing amongst the trees and large flocks of guinea fowl scuttering off the road. While only about 30m above sea level, it is noticeably cooler than on the coast.

Bweni village, built behind a glistening white sand beach, seems a likely spot for future tourism development. Its traditional Swahili-style houses of coralstone and lime plaster are dotted among slender coconut palms. Someone will slash the top off a young coconut for you to try *madafu*, its sweet, fresh juice. Bweni women are experts at weaving striped prayer mats from the palms on the plateau.

Ras Mkumbi is a 3km drive on a good stretch of road from Bweni to the lighthouse at **Ras Mkumbi**. Built on coral rag on the northern tip of Mafia, the red and white structure is kept locked but the key is obtainable from a keeper in the village. It is worth climbing the 15m up to the top for a spectacular view of the Mafia Channel lying between the archipelago and the mainland. The stretch of deep blue water is reputed to offer some of the best big game-fishing in East Africa.

Kisimani Mafia, Ras Kisimani or **Kisimani Mafia** (KiSwahili for 'the place of the well') lies at the opposite end of the island 30 minutes' drive from Kilindoni. The town was an important centre during the Shirazi domination of Kilwa between the 12th and 14th centuries. Legend says the hands of the Sultan's chief mason were cut off after he built the palace, so that he could never repeat the task. The story goes on to claim that this was why a few months later Kisimani was inundated by the sea.

There is little left of Kisimani now, but you can see the famous well down on the beach. Wandering about, you might find a few coins and pottery shards. The shady coconut palms are a nice spot for a picnic, but bring everything you want to eat or drink. A fare to Kisimani can be negotiated with one of the Land Rover pick-ups near the market place.

Utende is the small village at the end of the road from Kilindoni. Its inhabitants are mainly Makonde tribespeople from the mainland who keep their fishing boats in Chole Bay. One or two shop-houses sell strings of dried octopus and fish. Like everywhere else on Mafia, it is quite safe to explore, being only ten minutes' walk from any of the hotels.

Other excursions

Other interesting villages on Mafia are inaccessible by road and, like the off-shore islands, may only be visited by boat. Given advance warning, Kinasi Lodge can arrange an excursion with overnight camping. The islands of Chole, Juani and Jipondo off the coast at Utende are easily visited from the main island.

Baracuni Island, lying 12km northwest of Mafia, can be visited by arrangement. Uninhabited and said to be very beautiful, it is used by fishing dhows.

The village of Mchangani is the goal for an interesting excursion winding for nearly 3km up a creek on the north side of Chole Bay. Sykes monkeys can be seen in the mangrove forests and fish eagles are commonly observed. The village of Mchangani lies on the east bank of the creek. Depart only on a high tide.

Dindini Beach is likewise only accessible at high tide. It faces the ocean from Mafia Island just north of Chole Bay. Behind the beach is a large sea-fed rock pool which contains marine life. There are also low sand dunes and interesting vegetation on the coral rag.

Didimizi Beach is the lovely beach seen from Chole Bay, around 4km from Kinasi Lodge. You could arrange for a vehicle going to Kilindoni to drop you at the turn-off and walk back. Take refreshments.

CHOLE ISLAND
Chole is the lush, tropical island lying to the west of Kinasi Pass. With the adjacent islands of Juani and Jipondo, it forms a barrier between Mafia and the open ocean. The shallow reef in front is rich in soft corals, sea anemones and sponges, sloping to 15m, it is a good spot to practice drift diving. The bay itself is ideal for sailing and wind surfing.

Getting there and away
Kinasi Lodge and the Pole Pole Bungalow Resort on Mafia Island operate boat-trips to Chole, or you can visit it independently from Mafia. A dhow dubbed the 'Chole taxi' leaves the Mafia Lodge beach fairly regularly throughout the day – last sailing at 16.00 – a crossing of 10-15 minutes depending on the wind and tide, for a cost of $0.30 one-way.

Practicalities
If you plan to stay more than a few hours on the island it is advisable to bring a picnic and refreshments from your hotel. There is no transport and nothing that yet passes as either a restaurant or a hotel on Chole, which is pronounced *Choley*.

What to see
Behind the landing site on Chole are several huge pink frangipani trees which were probably planted by the Germans. The large ruin which must have enjoyed a wonderful view over Chole Bay was the house of the German administrator. A path behind the new market leading to the village brings you to a prison, whose broken cells are invaded by tangled tree roots. Farther along and also in ruins is a Hindu temple.

Hanging upside down in a nearby baobab is a colony of fruit bats of the same family as the Comoros Islands' lesser flying fox (*Pteropus seychellenis comorensis*). Each evening the bats fly across Chole Bay to feed on the cashew nut and mango trees of Mafia. Like the Comoros bats they dip over the surface of the water – an action which scientists believe may be an attempt to rid themselves of parasites. A more enchanting local explanation claims 'they are washing before evening prayers'.

Beyond the flying fox colony is Chole Village, where the American Emerson from Zanzibar is constructing a tree-house camp. The tree-houses with a view of the mangroves will eventually cost $120 full-board. Here you can buy a pamphlet with an explanation of traditional life for $1.50.

The Chole people cultivate smallholdings of cassava, beans, mangoes, paw-paw, citrus and passionfruit. Encouraged by Kinasi Lodge, the latter has flourished and is now exported to Mafia. Most of the menfolk fish. Winding past traditional houses, the path brings you to a beach where fishermen can be seen mending nets, or making sails and coconut coir ropes.

Chole's school and small hospital were built on foreign aid. A young Zanzibari woman is training local women how to market their weaving while her husband is teaching some of the younger men *Tingatinga* art.

JUANI ISLAND

The boat trip from Mafia to Juani takes about ten minutes longer than it does to Chole, but the island can only be approached at high tide. The landing, in a small bay sheltered by dense mangroves, is covered in thousands of opened oyster-shells. Seafood is the staple diet on Juani, but unlike Chole, Juani has no well water, and locals practice rain-dependent cultivation.

POPULAR DIVES

Kinasi Wall This sheltered bank reef sloping from 8–21m and extending for approximately 800m is a great place to see many species of corals and a variety of shoaling and reef fish, including wrasse and large groupers. Also turtles, the hawkesbill being the most commonly encountered.

Chole Wall Joining Kinasi Wall is another long bank of coral sloping to 15m, which offers good visibility and a rich tapestry of corals with clouds of brilliant fish. It forms an excellent introduction for beginners as well as a great night dive.

The Pinnacle A 12m spire of ancient coral rock pokes out of the water inside of Kinasi Pass. There is a thrilling dive down to the base 24m deep, with a variety of large local residents including a huge cod, a moray eel and giant batfish

Kinasi Pass After descending the pinnacle, divers usually head out into the pass for an awesome drift-dive among shoals of juvenile and adult reef fish, parrotfish, groupers, tunny, barracuda and big pelagics including sharks, which come in with the current. Dutch tourists who had dived in many exotic locations described it as 'fantastic'.

The Dindini North Wall and **Forbes Bay** Part of the barrier reef on the southeastern coast of Mafia, these are two of many thrilling dives outside the bay. Grouper, sharks, guitarfish and enormous tuna are seen off the Dindini Wall, which lies close to the drop-off where the edge of the continental shelf plunges to more than 300m. Forbes Bay presents a spectacular coral wall frequented by a great diversity of fish, including many large rays. The boat trip to the site, 10km north of Kinasi Pass, is a thrilling excursion past jagged cliffs, with the chance of taking giant trevally and other gamefish on a trolling rig.

What to see

Beneath three big baobabs near the landing, your shoes crunch on a buried civilisation. Bits of blue and white pottery from Shirazi suggesting trade links with China are embedded in the dirt.

In the past, people from the mainland came to Juani to bathe in a seawater cave reputed to have curative properties for rheumatism. It is a long, difficult walk across to the ocean side, where there are also said to be three turtle-nesting beaches.

The Kua Channel slices a tiny chunk off Juani as it opens into Chole Bay. It makes a superb picnic excursion with bird-watching and swimming. A friendly grouper lives in one of the rock pools at the southern end.

The ruined city of **Kua** is found on the west coast of Juani. A trail hacked out of the undergrowth leads up to the ruins of what was the old Shirazi capital of Mafia. The large building shedding masonry you first come to on your left was the king's palace. Locals revere it as a 'spirit place' leaving offerings such as bits of glass.

An old caretaker of the palace expects and deserves a small gratuity. The ruins in front of his hut are the foundations of the house where local legend says the Kua people took revenge against their enemies from Ras Kisimani.

The path then passes other ruined edifices, including two mosques which date from the 14th century, and a series of tombs. You can also see ruins of a double-storey house with basement quarters for the slaves from Kilwa. Altogether the ruins stretch over a 35-acre site

JIPONDO ISLAND

Jipondo is a long, low-lying island another 20 minutes' sail from Juani. It too has little fresh water, so the inhabitants perform their ablutions in the sea. Coming ashore, a white mosque is one of the first things you see. The big *jahazi* at the entrance was built 15 years ago, but it has never been launched and is subsequently something of a museum piece.

Jipondo people are well known boat-builders who use only traditional tools. Even the nails are hand-made and the holes are plugged with local kapok and shark's fat. Local women play a prominent role in trading as well as fishing. They also sail boats, which is unusual in African society, and are more affable and confident than women elsewhere.

Another unusual aspect of Jipondo is that cultivation is carried out at one end of the island while the people live in an urban community at the other. The village, which consists of traditional Swahili-style houses with *makuti* roofs, is laid out in a grid pattern. As on Chole and Juani, there is no transport other than boats which shelter on the western side of the narrow neck of the island.

On holidays Jipondo children hold sailing races in toy *ngalawas* with sails made out of plastic bags. The island has one school but no other social services, and only a basic shop. Local cattle are given water each evening from one or two private wells. Otherwise the island depends on rain which is trapped in a primitive concrete catchment area.

DIVING OFF MAFIA

Underwater Mafia is a paradise for divers and snorkellers, with a staggering variety of hard and soft corals and an immense variety of tropical fish. Kinasi Lodge specialises in diving holidays and offers every conceivable type of dive site – reefs and bommies, channels, walls, caves, drift, ocean and night dives. All these are accessible in a day, while diving safaris catering for 12 people can be arranged to destinations further afield such as Ras Mkumbi, Forbes Bay southeast of Mafia, and the spectacular reef complex around the Songo Songo Islands. This island group lies about 80km south of Mafia and about 50km north of Kilwa.

Kinasi operates **Blue World Diving and Watersports** under a qualified PADI instructor. Four-day open water courses requiring only a minimum of experience cost from $350; speciality courses such as night and drift dives cost from $150. The hotel has an excellent dive shop with underwater cameras for hire and sale (bring your own film). The Pole Pole Resort also offers dive excursions from $40 per person.

Almost all Mafia's best diving is in depths of less than 30m. The Marine Park off Chole Bay has most examples of coral including giant table corals, delicate seafans, whip corals and huge stands of blue and pink-tipped staghorn coral. As well as the spectacular variety of reef fish are turtles and large predatory fish such as grouper, napoleon and barracuda. Manta rays and several species of shark are encountered in Kinasi Pass.

FISHING OFF MAFIA

Mafia is one of the world's great fishing grounds. I had heard this since my childhood, but although mad about fishing, it was many years before I found myself fighting a giant trevally in the Kinasi Pass.

That there are big fish around Mafia is certain. There are even huge fish off Mafia, but at the time of writing few facilities for catching the legendary pelagics (fish of the open ocean). You will catch kingfish, barracuda, dorado and trevally, and the reef fishing is second to none, but marlin, sailfish and wahoo – prey of most serious international fishermen – are a rare sight when the boat returns.

Of the local fishing grounds, Mafia itself, the deep channel off Ras Mkumbi and the inshore waters of the Rufiji Delta offer some of the best opportunities in East Africa. In 1950, the author Sir Arthur Conan Doyle set an all-Africa record for a dorado of 34.2kg, which still stands, and judging from the size of the fish you see while blue-water diving, Mafia has the potential to break many other world records. A dog-toothed tuna landed when I was there weighed 55kg.

The main game-fishing season extends from August to March, but reef and channel fishing on both light and heavy tackle as well as fly-fishing in the saltwater creeks is good at any time. July to November is the main season for dog-toothed and yellowfin tuna, bonito, kingfish, wahoo, trevally, cobia and rainbow runners following the bait fish. December to March is the billfish run.

Other species such as the five-fingered jack and the horse mackerels *karambisi* and *kolikoli* are caught at all times using fish bait or spoons. The wahoo found on the seaward side of most reefs, will strip off 50–60m in the first burst while kingfish can take 90m or more in the initial run. Six-inch feathered jigs, spoons and the *Rapala magnum* are popular lures, while a fresh bonito – if you can land one – makes excellent bait for the bigger pelagics.

A member of the International Game Fishing Association, Kinasi Lodge has basic weighing facilities. Their boat takes four rods with tackle supplied, but keen fishermen might prefer to bring their own equipment. It is also possible to rent a traditional outrigger for inshore casting. A very limited number of fishing lines, hooks and sinkers are sold in Kilindoni Market.

There is an annual Mafia Island fishing competition staged in February by Kinasi Lodge.

Appendix 1

LANGUAGE

Swahili, the official language of Tanzania, is a Bantu language which developed on the East African coast about 1,000 years ago and has since adopted several words from Arabic, Portuguese, Indian, German and English. It spread into the Tanzanian interior along with the 19th-century slave caravans and is now the *lingua franca* in Tanzania and Kenya, and is also spoken in parts of Uganda, Malawi, Rwanda, Burundi, Congo, Zambia and Mozambique.

Even if you are sticking to tourist areas, it is polite and can be useful to know a bit of Swahili. In Dar es Salaam, Zanzibar, Arusha, Moshi and the northern game reserves, you can get by with English well enough. If you travel in other parts of the country, you will need to understand some Swahili.

There are numerous Swahili-English dictionaries on the market, as well as phrasebooks and grammars. A useful dictionary for travellers is Baba Malaika's *Friendly Modern Swahili-English Dictionary* (MSO Training Centre for Development Co-operation, PO Box 254, Arusha, second edition 1994), which costs around US$25. Better still, though probably too heavyweight for most travellers, is the *TUKI English-Swahili Dictionary* (University of Dar es Salaam, 1996; ISBN 9976 91129 7), which costs around US$16. Peter Wilson's *Simplified Swahili* (Longman) used to be regarded as the best book for teaching yourself Swahili, but it has probably been superseded by Joan Russell's *Teach Yourself Swahili* (Hodder and Stoughton, 1996; ISBN 0340 62094 3), which comes complete with a cassette and costs around US$15. Of the phrasebooks, the Lonely Planet or Rough Guide's *Swahili* are both good. It is best to buy a Swahili book before you arrive in Tanzania as they are difficult to get hold of once you are there.

For short-stay visitors, all these books have practical limitations. Wading through a phrasebook to find the expression you want can take ages, while trying to piece together a sentence from a dictionary is virtually impossible. In addition, most books available are in Kenyan Swahili, which often differs greatly from the purer version spoken in Tanzania.

The following introduction is not a substitute for a dictionary or phrasebook. It is not so much an introduction to Swahili as an introduction to communicating with Swahili-speakers. Before researching this guide, my East African travels had mainly been in Kenya, Uganda and parts of Tanzania where English is relatively widely spoken. We learnt the hard way how little English is spoken in most of Tanzania. I hope this section will help anyone in a similar position to get around a great deal more easily than we did at first.

Pronunciation

Vowel sounds are pronounced as follows:

a   like the a in *father*
e   like the e in *wet*

i like the ee in *free*, but less drawn-out
o somewhere between the o in *no* and the word *awe*
u similar to the oo in *food*

The double vowel in words like *choo* or *saa* is pronounced like the single vowel, but drawn out for longer. Consonants are in general pronounced as they are in English. *L* and *r* are often interchangeable, so that *Kalema* is just as often spelt or pronounced *Karema*. The same is true of *b* and *v*.

You will be better understood if you speak slowly and thus avoid the common English-speaking habit of clipping vowel sounds – listen to how Swahili-speakers pronounce their vowels. In most Swahili words there is a slight emphasis on the second last syllable.

Basic grammar

Swahili is a simple language in so far as most words are built from a root word using prefixes. To go into all of the prefixes here would probably confuse people new to Swahili – and it would certainly stretch my knowledge of the language. They are covered in depth in most Swahili grammars and dictionaries. The following are some of the most important:

Pronouns

ni	me		*wa*	they
u	you		*a*	he or she
tu	us			

Tenses

na	present
ta	future
li	past
ku	infinitive

Tenses (negative)

si	present
sita	future
siku	past
haku	negative, infinitive

From a root word such as *taka* (want) you might build the following phrases:

Unataka soda	You want a soda
Tutataka soda	We will want a soda
Alitaka soda	He/she wanted a soda

In practice, *ni* and *tu* are often dropped from simple statements. It would be more normal to say *nataka soda* than *ninataka soda*.

In many situations there is no interrogative mode in Swahili; the difference between a question and a statement lies in the intonation.

Greetings

There are several common greetings in Swahili. Although allowances are made for tourists, it is rude to start talking to someone without first using one or other formal greeting. The first greeting you will hear is *Jambo*. This is reserved for tourists, and a perfectly adequate greeting, but it is never used between Tanzanians (the more correct *Hujambo*, to which the reply is *Sijambo*, is used in some areas).

The most widely-used greeting is *Habari?*, which more-or-less means *What news?*. The normal reply is *Nzuri* (good). *Habari* is rarely used by Tanzanians on its own; you might well be asked *Habari ya safari?*, *Habari yako?* or *Habari gani?* (very loosely, *How is your journey?*, *How are you?* and *How are things?* respectively). *Nzuri* is the polite reply to any such request.

A more fashionable greeting among younger people is *Mambo*, especially on the coast and in large towns. Few tourists recognise this greeting; reply *Safi* or *Poa* and you've made a friend.

In Tanzanian society it is polite to greet elders with the expression *Shikamu*. To the best of my knowledge this means *I hold your feet*. In many parts of rural Tanzania, children will greet you in this way, often with their heads bowed and so quietly it sounds like *Sh..oo*. Don't misinterpret this by European standards (or other parts of Africa where *Mzungu give me shilling* is the phrase most likely to be offered up by children); most Tanzanian children are far too polite to swear at you. The polite answer is *Marahaba* (I'm delighted).

Another word often used in greeting in *Salama*, which means peace. When you enter a shop or hotel reception, you will often be greeted by a friendly *Karibu*, which means *Welcome*. *Asante sana* (thank you very much) seems an appropriate response.

If you want to enter someone's house, shout *Hodi!*. It basically means *Can I come in?* but would be used in the same situation as *Anyone home?* would in English. The normal response will be *Karibu* or *Hodi*.

It is respectful to address an old man as *Mzee*. *Bwana*, which means *Mister*, might be used as a polite form of address to a male who is equal or senior to you in age or rank, but who is not a *Mzee*. Older women can be addressed as *Mama*.

The following phrases will come in handy for small talk:

Where have you just come from?	*(U)natoka wapi?*
I have come from Moshi	*(Ni)natoka Moshi*
Where are you going?	*(U)nakwenda wapi?*
We are going to Arusha	*(Tu)nakwenda Arusha*
What is your name?	*Jina lako nani?*
My name is Philip	*Jina langu ni Philip*
Do you speak English?	*Unasema KiIngereze?*
I speak a little Swahili	*Ninasema KiSwahili kidigo*
Sleep peacefully	*Lala salama*
Bye for now	*Kwaheri sasa*
Have a safe journey	*Safari njema*
Come again (welcome again)	*Karibu tena*
I don't understand	*Sielewi*
Say that again	*Sema tena*

Numbers

1	*moja*		30	*thelathini*
2	*mbili*		40	*arobaini*
3	*tatu*		50	*hamsini*
4	*nne*		60	*sitini*
5	*tano*		70	*sabini*
6	*sita*		80	*themanini*
7	*saba*		90	*tisini*
8	*nane*		100	*mia (moja)*
9	*tisa*		150	*mia moja na hamsini*
10	*kumi*		155	*mia moja hamsini na tano*
11	*kumi na moja*		200	*mia mbili*
20	*ishirini*		1,000	*elfu (moja)* or *mia kumi*

Swahili time

Many travellers to Tanzania fail to come to grips with Swahili time. It is essential to be aware of it, especially if you are catching buses in remote areas. The Swahili clock starts at the equivalent of 06.00, so that *saa moja asubuhi* (hour one in the morning) is 07.00, *saa mbili jioni* (hour two in the evening) is 20.00 etc. To ask the time in Swahili, say *Saa ngapi?*.

Always check whether times are standard or Swahili. If you are told a bus leaves at nine, ask whether the person means *saa tatu* or *saa tisa*. Some English-speakers will convert to standard time, others won't. This does not apply so much where people are used to tourists, but it's advisable to get in the habit of checking.

Day-to-day queries

The following covers such activities as shopping, finding a room etc. It's worth remembering most Swahili words for modern objects, or things for which there would not have been a pre-colonial word, are often similar to the English. Examples are *resiti* (receipt), *gari* (car), *polisi* (police), *posta* (post office) and – my favourite – *stesheni masta* (station master). In desperation, it's always worth trying the English word with an *ee* sound on the end.

Shopping

The normal way of asking for something is *Ipo* or *Zipo?*, which roughly means *Is there?*, so if you want a cold drink you would ask *Soda baridi zipo?* The response will normally be *Ipo* or *Kuna* (there is) or *Hamna* or *Hakuna* (there isn't). Once you've established the shop has what you want, you might say *Nataka koka mbili* (I want two cokes). To check the price, ask *Shillingi ngape?* It may be simpler to ask for a brand name: *Omo* (washing powder) or *Blue Band* (margarine), for instance.

Accommodation

The Swahili for guesthouse is *nyumba ya wageni*. In my experience *gesti* works as well, if not better. If you are looking for something a bit more upmarket, bear in mind *hoteli* means restaurant. We found self-contained (*self-contendi*) to be a good key-word in communicating this need. To find out whether there is a vacant room, ask *Nafasi zipo?*

Getting around

The following expressions are useful for getting around:

Where is there a guesthouse?	*Ipo wapi gesti?*
Is there a bus to Moshi?	*Ipo basi kwenda Moshi?*
When does the bus depart?	*Basi itaondoka saa ngapi?*
When will the vehicle arrive?	*Gari litafika saa ngapi?*
How far is it?	*Bale gani?*
I want to pay now	*Ninataka kulipa sasa*

Foodstuffs

avocado	*parachichi*	food	*chakula*
bananas	*ndizi*	fruit(s)	*(ma)tunda*
bananas (cooked)	*matoke/batoke*	goat	*(nyama ya) mbuzi*
beef	*(Nyama ya) ngombe*	mango(es)	*(ma)embe*
bread (loaf)	*mkate*	maize porridge	
bread (slice)	*tosti*	(thin, eaten at	
coconuts	*nazi*	breakfast)	*uji*
coffee	*kahawa*	maize porridge	
chicken	*kuku*	(thick, eaten as	
egg(s)	*(ma)yai*	staplewith	
fish	*samaki*	relish)	*ugali*

meat	*nyama*
milk	*maziwa*
onions	*vitungu*
orange(s)	*(ma)chungwa*
pawpaw	*papai*
pineapple	*nanasi*
potatoes	*viazi*
rice (cooked plain)	*wali*
rice (uncooked)	*mchele*

rice	*pilau*
salt	*chumvi*
sauce	*mchuzi/supu*
sugar	*sukari*
tea	*chai*
(black/milky)	*(ya rangi/maziwa)*
vegetable	*mboga*
water	*maji*

Days of the week

Monday	*Jumatatu*
Tuesday	*Jumanne*
Wednesday	*Jumatano*
Thursday	*Alhamisi*

Friday	*Ijumaa*
Saturday	*Jumamosi*
Sunday	*Jumapili*

Useful words and phrases

afternoon	*alasiri*
again	*tena*
and	*na*
ask (I am asking for…)	*omba (ninaomba…)*
big	*kubwa*
boat	*meli*
brother	*kaka*
bus	*basi*
bar (or any vehicle)	*gari*
child (children)	*mtoto (watoto)*
cold	*baridi*
come here	*njoo*
excuse me	*samahani*
European(s)	*mzungu (wazungu)*
evening	*jioni*
far away	*mbale kubwa*
friend	*rafiki*
good	*mzuri*
(very good)	*(mzuri sana)*
goodbye	*kwaheri*
here	*hapa*
hot	*moto*
later	*bado*
like	*penda*
(I would like…)	*(ninapenda…)*
many	*sana*
me	*mimi*
money	*pesa/shillingi*
more	*ingine/tena*
morning	*asubuhi*
nearby	*karibu/mbale kidogo*
night	*usiku*

no	*hapana*
no problem	*hakuna matata*
now	*sasa*
only	*tu*
OK or fine	*sawa*
passenger	*abiria*
pay	*kulipa*
please	*tafadhali*
person (people)	*mtu (watu)*
road/street	*barabara/mtaa*
shop	*duka*
sister	*dada*
sleep	*kulala*
slowly	*polepole*
small	*kidogo*
soon	*bado kidogo*
sorry	*polepole*
station	*stesheni*
stop	*simama*
straight or direct	*moja kwa moja*
thank you	*asante*
(very much)	*(sana)*
there is	*iko/kuna*
there is not	*hamna/hakuna*
thief (thieves)	*mwizi (wawizi)*
time	*saa*
today	*leo*
toilet	*choo*
tomorrow	*kesho*
want	*taka*
(I want…)	*(ninataka…)*
where	*(iko) wapi*
yes	*ndiyo*
yesterday	*jana*
you	*wewe*

Useful conjunctions include *ya* (of) and *kwa* (to or by). Many expressions are created using these; for instance *stesheni ya basi* is a bus station and *barabara kwa Mbale* is the road to Mbale.

African English
Although many Ugandans speak a little English, not all speak it fluently. Africans who speak English tend to structure their sentences in a similar way to how they would in their own language: they speak English with Bantu grammar.

For a traveller, knowing how to communicate in African English is just as important as speaking a bit of Swahili, if not more so. It is noticeable that travellers who speak English as a second language often communicate with Africans more easily than first language English-speakers.

The following ground rules should prove useful when you speak English to Africans:

- Unasema KiEngereze? (Do you speak English?). This small but important question may seem obvious. It isn't.
- Greet in Swahili then ask in English. It is advisable to go through the Swahili greetings (even Jambo will do) before you plough ahead and ask a question. Firstly, it is rude to do otherwise; secondly, most Westerners feel uncomfortable asking a stranger a straight question. If you have already greeted the person, you'll feel less need to preface a question with phrases like I'm terribly sorry and Would you mind telling me which will confuse someone who speaks limited English.
- Speak slowly and clearly. There is no need, as some travellers do, to speak as if you are talking to a three-year-old, just speak naturally.
- Phrase questions simply and with Swahili inflections. This bus goes to Mbale? is better than Could you tell me whether this bus is going to Mbale?; You have a room? is better than is there a vacant room?. If you are not understood, don't keep repeating the same question; find a different way of phrasing it.
- Listen to how people talk to you, and not only for their inflections. Some English words are in wide use; others are not. For instance lodging is more likely to be understood than accommodation.
- Make sure the person you are talking to understands you. Try to avoid asking questions that can be answered with a yes or no. People may well agree with you simply to be polite.
- Keep calm. No-one is at their best when they arrive at a crowded bus station after an all-day bus ride; it is easy to be short tempered when someone cannot understand you. Be patient and polite; it's you who doesn't speak the language.
- It can be useful to know that the Ugandan phrase for urinating is 'short call'. Useful, because often you will be caught short somewhere with no toilet, and if you ask for a toilet will simply be told there is none. By contrast, if you tell somebody you need a 'short call', you'll be pointed to wherever locals take theirs!

Appendix 2

FURTHER READING
History and biography
A limited number of single volume histories covering East Africa and/or Tanzania are in print, but most are rather textbook-like in tone, I've yet to come across one that is likely to hold much appeal to the casual reader. About the best bet is Iliffe's *Modern History of Tanganyika* (Cambridge, 1979). For a more general perspective, Oliver and Fage's *Short History of Africa* (Penguin, sixth edition, 1988) is rated as providing the best concise overview of African history, but it's too curt, dry, wide-ranging and dated to make for a satisfying read.

If I were to recommend one historical volume to a visitor to Tanzania, it would have to be Richard Hall's *Empires of the Monsoon: A History of the Indian Ocean and its Invaders* (Harper Collins, 1996). This highly focused and reasonably concise book will convey a strong historical perspective to the general reader, as a result of the author's storytelling touch and his largely successful attempt to place the last 1,000 years of east and southern African history in an international framework.

Considerably more bulky, and working an even broader canvas, John Reader's *Africa: A Biography of the Continent* (Penguin, 1997) has met with universal praise as perhaps the most readable and accurate attempt yet to capture the sweep of African history for the general reader. I must confess I haven't yet got around to looking at this book in detail, but based on reviews and the author's other work, I have no hesitation in recommending it to interested readers.

Several books document specific periods and/or regions in African history. Good coverage of the coastal Swahili, who facilitated the medieval trade between the goldfields of Zimbabwe and the Arab World, is provided in J. de Vere Allen's *Swahili Origins* (James Currey, 1992). Among the better popular works on the early era of European exploration are Hibbert's *Africa Explored: Europeans in the Dark Continent* (Penguin, 1982) and those well-known classics of the genre history as adventure yarn Alan Moorehead's *The White Nile* and *The Blue Nile*, first published in 1960 and 1962 respectively and still available in Penguin paperback. An excellent biography pertaining to this era is Tim Jeal's *Livingstone* (Heinemann, 1973, recently reprinted). For an erudite, compelling and panoramic account of the decade that turned Africa on its head, Thomas Packenham's gripping 600-page tome *The Scramble for Africa* was aptly described by one reviewer as '*Heart of Darkness* with the lights switched on'. For a glimpse into the colonial era itself, just about everybody who sets foot in East Africa ends up reading Karen Blixen's autobiographical *Out of Africa* (Penguin, 1937).

Field guides and natural history
If you have difficulty finding African natural history books at your local bookshop and you're not flying directly to South Africa (where you can pick them up easily) get hold of the Natural History Book Service, 2 Wills Road, Totnes, Devon TQ9

SXN; tel: 01803 865913 or Russel Friedman Books in South Africa; tel: 011 702-2300/1; fax: 011 702 1403).

Mammals

The standard mammal field guides for years, largely through lack of competition, have been Dorst and Dandelot's *Field Guide to the Larger Mammals of Africa* (Collins) and Haltennorth's *Field Guide to the Mammals of Africa (including Madagascar)* (Collins). These remain the most easily located books in the UK, but both suffer from a ponderous style, outdated distribution and taxonomical information, and mediocre drawings.

Fortunately, the recent democratisation of South Africa has also led to this country's publishers of wildlife books spreading their coverage to countries further north, with excellent results. Chris and Tilde Stuart's *Field Guide to the Larger Mammals of Africa* (Struik, 1997) is ideal for space-conscious travellers who are serious about putting a name to all the large mammals they see. Better for most backpackers is the same authors' *Southern, Eastern and Central African Mammals: A Photographic Guide* (Struik, 1993), which is about 60% lighter but still gives adequate detail for 152 mammal species. The Stuarts have also written the coffee-table format *Africa's Vanishing Wildlife* (Southern Book Publishers, 1996), an outstanding book of its sort and highly recommended as advance reading or a souvenir.

Another excellent mammal field guide, probably the best if your interest extends to bats and other small mammals, is Jonathan Kingdon's *Field Guide to African Mammals* (Academic Press, 1997). Not a field guide in the conventional sense so much as a guide to mammalian behaviour, Richard Estes' *The Safari Companion* (published in the UK by Green Books, in the USA by Chelsea Green and in South Africa by Russel Friedman Books) is well-organised and informative but impractically bulky for the purposes of most backpackers.

Birds

Ber Van Perlo's *Illustrated Checklist to the Birds of Eastern Africa* (Collins, 1995) is the best compact identification manual for East Africa (don't confuse it with John Williams' obsolete *Field Guide to the Birds of East Africa*, also by Collins), describing and illustrating all 1,488 bird species recorded in Eritrea, Ethiopia, Kenya, Uganda and Tanzania with distribution maps.

In a different league altogether, Zimmerman, Turner, Pearson, Willet and Pratt's *Birds of Kenya and Northern Tanzania* (Russel Friedman Books, 1996) is a contender for the best single-volume field guide available to any African country or region. This is certainly the guide that I would recommend to any serious birder sticking to northern Tanzania (it provides complete coverage for the northern safari circuit, the Usambara and Pare Mountains, and Pemba Island, and although it stops short of Dar es Salaam and Zanzibar, this wouldn't be a major limitation). Unfortunately, it's too bulky, heavy and expensive to be of interest to any but the most bird-obsessed of backpackers, and the gaps in coverage would start to show in reserves to the south of Dar or in the Lake Victoria and Lake Tanganyika region.

Other field guides

Struik Publishers in South Africa produce top-quality field guides to everything from trees to fish, reptiles and amphibians, but it's probably the case that such books are too esoteric to find their way into even a tiny proportion of backpacks. Readers with specific interests should contact one of the addresses above for recommendations.

Wildlife studies

Those with an interest in ape behaviour would do well to read Jane Goodall's books about chimpanzee behaviour, *In the Shadow of Man* (Collins, 1971) and *Through a Window* (Wiedenfield and Nicholson, 1990), based on her acclaimed research in Tanzania's Gombe Stream National Park. Also available is Nishida's *Chimpanzees of Mahale* (University of Tokyo, 1990), based on the similarly long-standing research project in Mahale Mountains National Park.

Bernhard Grzimik's renowned book *Serengeti Shall Not Die* (Collins, 1959) remains a classic evocation of the magic of the Serengeti, and its original publication was instrumental in making this reserve better known to the outside world. Ian Douglas-Hamilton's *Amongst the Elephants* (Penguin, 1978) did much the same for publicising Lake Manyara National Park, though the vast herds of elephants it describes have since been greatly reduced by poaching.

National Parks

A series of excellent booklets has been published in association with Tanapa, covering most of the national parks in Tanzania. These are widely available in Arusha, and will cost US$5 at a reputable book shop and considerably more when bought from a street vendor.

Travel literature
Travel guides

To the best of my knowledge, this Bradt guide is the only practical travel guide dedicated solely to Tanzania. There are, however, a couple of good travel guides in print aimed more at package tourists and perhaps souvenir buyers; Camerapix's *Spectrum Guide to Tanzania* and Struik's *Travellers Guide to Tanzania* are recommended. The locally published *Tourist Guide to Tanzania* by Gratian Luhikula is strong on background information, particularly cultural aspects, but the practical information is limited and dated. Bradt also publishes a dedicated *Guide to Zanzibar*, the most useful book for those who are travelling to the islands in isolation of the mainland.

For people combining a visit to Tanzania with one of other of its neighbours, a limited number of dedicated guides are available to most countries bordering Tanzania. For practical information, your best bet for Uganda, Mozambique, Malawi or Zambia is the appropriate Bradt guide (we're not being partisan, there are no other practical guides dedicated individually to these countries), while of several travel guides to Kenya I would wholeheartedly recommend Richard Trillo's *Kenya: The Rough Guide*. Camerapix publishes glossier *Spectrum Guides* to Kenya, Uganda and Zambia.

A number of compendium guides are available to various regions in eastern and southern Africa. Lonely Planet's *East Africa* is strong on Kenya and parts of northern Tanzania, somewhat weaker on Uganda and the rest of Tanzania, and provides the best coverage available to Rwanda, Burundi and eastern Congo. A Lonely Planet guide that will be useful to serious hikers is *Trekking in East Africa*, which covers most popular trekking areas between Ethiopia and Malawi. Footprint's *East Africa Handbook* covers similar ground, but with greater detail on less popular areas, and additional chapters on Ethiopia, Eritrea and Somalia. For backpackers planning an overland trip through eastern and southern Africa, the only single-volume guide dedicated to this region as a unit is Bradt's *East and Southern Africa: The Backpacker's Manual*, which covers practically every possible route and accessible attraction from northern Ethiopia south to Cape Town.

Two reasonably modern travelogues that touch on Tanzania are Dervla

Murphy's *The Ukimwi Road* (John Murray, 1993) and Shiva Naipaul's *North of South* (Penguin).

Coffee-table books

The best book of this sort to cover Tanzania as a whole is *Journey through Tanzania*, photographed by the late Mohamid Amin and Duncan Willets, and published by the Kenyan company Camerapix. Also recommended are M. Iwago's superb *Serengeti* (Thames and Hudson, 1987) and John Reader's *Kilimanjaro*. For Zanzibar, Javed Jafferji's atmospheric photos are highlighted in *Images of Zanzibar*, while *Zanzibar – Romance of the Ages* makes extensive use of archive photographs dating to before the turn of the century. Both were published by HSP Publications in 1996, and are readily available on the island.

Travel magazines

The TTB produces a quarterly magazine called *Tantravel*, which normally includes a few interesting articles as well as plenty of ads, and can normally be picked up at Air Tanzania and tourist board offices. Even better is the quarterly magazine *Kakakuona: African Wildlife*, which is produced by the Tanzania Wildlife Protection Fund, and frequently includes several good articles. For details of subscriptions, fax: 051 863496.

For readers with a broad interest in Africa, the stable of award-winning magazines published by Black Eagle Publications in South Africa is highly recommended, both for the content and the coffee-table standard reproduction. Their three magazines *Africa – Environment and Wildlife*, *Africa – Birds and Birding* and *Discover Africa* concentrate respectively on the continent's wildlife and game reserves, its bird life, and more general tourism possibilities. Subscription details: tel: +27 21 686 9001; fax: +27 21 686 4500; email: wildmags@iafrica.com; web: http://www.discover-africa.com.

Another excellent magazine, dedicated to tourism throughout Africa, is *Travel Africa*. Subscription details: tel/fax: +44 1865 434220; email: subs@travelafricamag.com; web: http//:www.travelafricamag.com.

Two more South African magazines devoted to African travel are *Out There* (adventure tourism) and *Getaway* (general tourism). Both of these magazines tend to devote the bulk of their coverage to southern Africa, though the December 1998 issue of *Getaway* was dedicated entirely to Tanzania (subscriptions and back issues tel: +27 21 531 0404.

Health

Self-prescribing has its hazards so if you are going anywhere very remote consider taking a health book. For adults there is *Bugs, Bites & Bowels: the Cadogan Guide to Healthy Travel* by Jane Wilson-Howarth (1999); if travelling with the family look at *Your Child's Health Abroad: A manual for travelling parents* by Jane Wilson-Howarth and Matthew Ellis, published by Bradt Publications in 1998.

Maps

A number of maps covering East Africa is available. The best is the Austrian-published Freytag-Berndt 1:2,000,000 map. The best map of Tanzania that I've seen is the BP 1:1,250,000 map that I bought in Dar es Salaam in 1992, but this seems to be long out of print. For most tourists, the map of Tanzania produced by the TTB and given away free at their offices in Arusha or Dar will be adequate.

A series of excellent maps by Giovanni Tombazzi covers most of the northern reserves, as well as Kilimanjaro, Mount Meru and Zanzibar. Colourful, lively and accurate, these maps are widely available throughout northern Tanzania, or they can be ordered directly from the co-publisher Hoopoe Adventure Tours (for contact details, see *Safari companies* page 122).

Town plans and 1:50,000 maps covering most parts of the country can be bought from the Department of Land and Surveys map sales office on Kivukoni Front in Dar es Salaam.

Fiction

Surprisingly few novels have been written by Tanzanians or about Tanzania (even a friend who has studied African literature failed to come up with one indigenous Tanzanian novelist). An excellent novel set in World War I Tanzania is William Boyd's *An Ice-cream War*, while the same author's *Brazzaville Beach*, though not overtly set in Tanzania, devotes attention to aspects of chimpanzee behaviour first noted at Gombe Stream.

A Tanzanian of Asian extraction now living in Canada, M G Vassanji, is the author of at least one novel set in Tanzania and the Kenyan border area, the prize-winning *Book of Secrets* (Macmillan, 1994). This is an atmospheric tale, with much interesting period detail, revolving around a diary written by a British administrator in pre-war Kenya and discovered in a flat in Dar es Salaam in the 1980s. Vassanji is also the author of *Uhuru Street*, a collection of short stories set in Dar es Salaam.

Novels set elsewhere in Africa, but which may be of interest to visitors to Tanzania, include the following:

Brink, A *An Act of Terror* or *A Dry White Season*
Cartwright, J *Maasai Dreaming*
Conrad, J *Heart of Darkness*
Dagarembga, T *Nervous Conditions*
Godimer, N *July's People*
Lambkin, D *The Hanging Tree*
Lessing, D *The Grass is Singing, Children of Violence* (5 volumes)
Mazrui, A *The Trial of Christopher Okigbo*
Mungoshi, C *Coming of the Dry Season*
Mwangi, M *Going down River Road*
Naipaul, VS *A Bend in the River*
Okri, B *The Famished Road*
Theroux, P *Jungle Lovers*
Thiong'o, N *Petals of Blood* or *A Grain of Wheat*
van der Post, L *A Story like the Wind*

Bradt Publications
Travel Guides

October 1998

Dear Readers,

Collectively, the readership of this travel guide will experience a great many more aspects of Tanzania than any one person can hope to, and they will be able try out a far wider selection of hotels, campsites, safari companies and restaurants. I would therefore like to extend an eager invitation to each and every one of you to write to me about your trip.

Even the smallest snippet of information will be welcome. Should you, for instance, let me know about one good new hotel in Arusha, not only will you help me to do my job, but you will also perform a valuable service to that hotel and to travellers who pass that way in future. While every contribution is of value, it would be especially gratifying to hear from readers who explore lesser-known parts of the country, as well as from volunteers and other readers who spend long enough in one particular town or region to gain an intimate knowledge of its local attractions and facilities.

So, whether you want to make my day with a blow-by-blow account of your travels, or to spoil it by pointing out why I'm wrong about simply everything, your time and effort in writing will be greatly appreciated. Every letter will make for a better fourth edition, which in turn will enhance the travels of those who follow in your footsteps.

Every correspondent will be acknowledged in the next edition, so do print your name clearly!

Happy travels,

Philip Briggs

c/o Bradt Publications
41 Nortoft Road, Chalfont St Peter, Bucks SL9 0LA
England
Tel/fax: +44 1494 873478
email: philari@hixnet.co.za

MEASUREMENTS AND CONVERSIONS

To convert	Multiply by
Inches to centimetres	2.54
Centimetres to inches	0.3937
Feet to metres	0.3048
Metres to feet	3.281
Yards to metres	0.9144
Metres to yards	1.094
Miles to kilometres	1.609
Kilometres to miles	0.6214
Acres to hectares	0.4047
Hectares to acres	2.471
Imperial gallons to litres	4.546
Litres to imperial gallons	0.22
US gallons to litres	3.785
Litres to US gallons	0.264
Ounces to grams	28.35
Grams to ounces	0.03527
Pounds to grams	453.6
Grams to pounds	0.002205
Pounds to kilograms	0.4536
Kilograms to pounds	2.205
British tons to kilograms	1016.0
Kilograms to British tons	0.0009812
US tons to kilograms	907.0
Kilograms to US tons	0.000907

5 imperial gallons are equal to 6 US gallons
A British ton is 2,240 lbs. A US ton is 2,000 lbs.

Temperature conversion table

The bold figures in the central columns can be read as either centigrade or fahrenheit.

Centigrade		Fahrenheit	Centigrade		Fahrenheit
−18	**0**	32	10	**50**	122
−15	**5**	41	13	**55**	131
−12	**10**	50	16	**60**	140
−9	**15**	59	18	**65**	149
−7	**20**	68	21	**70**	158
−4	**25**	77	24	**75**	167
−1	**30**	86	27	**80**	176
2	**35**	95	32	**90**	194
4	**40**	104	38	**100**	212
7	**45**	113	40	**104**	

OTHER BRADT GUIDES TO AFRICA AND THE INDIAN OCEAN

Cape Verde Islands   Aisling Irwin, Colum Wilson
240pp, 8pp colour, 27 maps, £11.95, 1 898323 73 9, 1st edition
East and Southern Africa: The Backpacker's Manual   Philip Briggs
544pp, 150 maps, £13.50, 1 898323 60 7, 1st edition
Eritrea   Edward Paice
192pp, 12pp colour, 16 maps, £10.95, 1 898323 41 0, 2nd edition
Ethiopia   Philip Briggs
368pp, 8pp colour, 57 maps, £11.95, 1 898323 66 6, 2nd edition
Ghana   Philip Briggs
272pp, 8pp colour, 37 maps, £11.95, 1 898323 69 0, 1st edition
Madagascar   Hilary Bradt
368pp, 16pp colour, 43 maps, £12.95, 1 898323 97 6, 6th edition
Madagascar Wildlife: A Visitor's Guide   Hilary Bradt, Derek Schuurman, Nick Garbutt
144pp, full colour, £14.95, 1 898323 40 2, 6th edition
Malawi   Philip Briggs
256pp, 8pp colour, 33 maps, £11.95, 1 898323 84 4, 2nd edition
Maldives   Royston Ellis
272pp, 16pp colour, 8 maps, £11.95, 1 898323 23 2, 1st edition
Mauritius, Rodrigues and Réunion   Royston Ellis, Derek Schuurman
304pp, 8pp colour, 14 maps, £12.95, 1 898323 87 9, 4th edition
Mozambique   Philip Briggs
240pp, 8pp colour, 39 maps, £11.95, 1 898323 45 3, 1st edition
Namibia   Chris McIntyre
488pp, 16pp colour, 57 maps, £12.95, 1 898323 64 X, 1st edition
South Africa   Philip Briggs
320pp, 8pp colour, 30 maps, £11.95, 1 898323 52 6, 3rd edition
Southern Africa by Rail   Paul Ash
288pp, 8pp colour, 35 maps, £11.95, 1 898323 72 0, 1st edition
Uganda   Philip Briggs
320pp, 8pp colour, 34 maps, £11.95, 1 898323 79 8, 3rd edition
Zambia   Chris McIntyre
336pp, 8pp colour, 32 maps, £12.95, 1 898323 99 2, 2nd edition
Zanzibar   David Else
240pp, 8pp colour, 13 maps, £11.95, 1 898323 65 8, 3rd edition

Send for a catalogue from:
Bradt Publications,
41 Nortoft Road, Chalfont St Peter, Bucks SL9 0LA, England
Tel/fax: 01494 873478
Email: bradtpublications@compuserve.com
Web: www.bradt-travelguides.com

Index

*Page references in **bold** indicate main entries; those in italics indicate maps.*

To help us prepare a Bradt guide for your next trip, please complete this card and return it to us. If you include your name and address, your card will be entered into a quarterly draw to receive the Bradt guide of your choice.

Which other Bradt guides have you used?

Which non-Bradt guidebooks have you used?

Where was your last trip overseas?

Where are you planning your next trip?

Where would you plan your dream trip?

Which magazines/newspapers do you read regularly?

Would you like to receive our catalogue and details of competitions and special offers? Yes/No

Name . . . . Age   16-25   26-45   46-60   60+

Address . . . .

. . . . Postcode . . . .

Bradt Travel Guides/TZ/3/99

41 Nortoft Road

Chalfont St Peter

Bucks SL9 0LA

ENGLAND